The Collected Works of Spi

Eerſte Deel

Der

ZEDEKUNST.

VAN GOD.

Bepalingen.

I. BY [a] oorzaak van zich zelf verſta ik het geen, welks [b] wezentheit [c] wezentlijkheit [d] inſluit; of het geen, welks natuur niet anders, dan [e] wezentlijk, bevat kan worden.

a *Cauſa ſui.* b *Eſſentia.* c *Exiſtentia.* d *Involvere.* e *Exiſtens.*

II. Dat ding, 't welk door een ander van de zelfde natuur [f] bepaalt kan worden, word in zijn [g] geſlacht [h] eindig gezegt. Tot een voorbeelt; het [i] lighaam word eindig gezegt; om dat wy altijt een ander, dat groter is, bevatten. Dus word ook een [k] denking door een andere bepaalt. Maar 't lighaam word door geen denking, noch de denking door enig lighaam bepaalt.

f *Terminare.* g *Genus.* h *Finita.* i *Corpus.* k *Cogitatio.*

III. By [l] zelfſtandigheit verſta ik 't geen, dat in zich is, en door zich bevat word: dat is, welks [m] bevatting niet de bevatting van een anderding, van 't welk het [n] gevormt moet worden, behoeft.

l *Subſtantia.* m *Conceptus.* n *Formare.*

IV. By [o] toeëigening verſta ik 't geen, dat het [p] verſtant wegens de [q] zelfſtandigheit, als haar [r] wezentheit [ſ] ſtellende, [t] bevat.

o *Attributum.* p *Intellectus.* q *Subſtantia.* r *Eſſentia.* ſ *Conſtituens.* t *Concipere.*

V. By [u] wijze verſta ik [w] d'aandoeningen der [x] zelfſtandigheit, of dit, 't welk in iets anders is, daar door het ook bevat word.

u *Modus.* w *Affectiones.* x *Subſtantia.*

VI. By God verſta ik een [y] wezend, [z] volſtrektelijk [a] oneïndig: dat is, een [b] zelfſtandigheit, die uit [c] oneïndige toeëigeningen [d] beſtaat, van de welken yder een eeuwige oneïndige [e] wezentheit uitdrukt.

y *Ens.* z *Abſolutè.* a *Infinitum.* b *Subſtantia.* c *Attributa infinita.* d *Conſtare.* e *Eſſentia.*

THE
Collected Works
OF
SPINOZA

VOLUME I

Edited and Translated by
Edwin Curley

PRINCETON UNIVERSITY PRESS
PRINCETON, NEW JERSEY

Copyright © 1985 by Princeton University Press
Published by Princeton University Press, 41 William Street,
Princeton, New Jersey 08540
In the United Kingdom: Princeton University
Press, Guildford, Surrey

All Rights Reserved

Library of Congress Cataloging in Publication Data will be
found on the last printed page of this book

ISBN 0-691-07222-1

This book has been composed in Linotron Janson type

Clothbound editions of Princeton University Press books
are printed on acid-free paper, and binding materials are chosen
for strength and durability. Paperbacks, although satisfactory
for personal collections, are not usually suitable
for library rebinding

Printed in the United States of America by Princeton
University Press, Princeton, New Jersey

ALL OUR knowledge of Scripture must be sought from Scripture itself alone. . . . The universal rule for interpreting Scripture is that we must attribute nothing to Scripture as its teaching which we have not seen most clearly on the basis of an historical inquiry. The kind of historical inquiry I mean must . . . I. take account of the nature and properties of the language in which the books of Scripture were written . . . II. collect the doctrines of each book and so organize them that we can readily find all those that bear on the same topic; and next, note all those which are ambiguous or obscure or which seem contradictory . . . finally, III. tell the circumstances and fate of all the prophetic books of which we have any record: the life, dispositions and intentions of the author of each book, who he was, when and on what occasion he wrote, to whom and in what language; how the book was first received, into whose hands it fell, how many different readings there are of the text, who first accepted it as sacred, and finally how all the books now agreed to be sacred were united into one.

—*Theological-Political Treatise*, vii (III/99-101)

Contents

CONTENTS

Glossary-Index

General Preface

THIS IS the first installment of what is intended to be a two-volume edition of the complete works of Spinoza, with new translations. The project is one I have been working on, intermittently, for some fourteen years now. My aim in undertaking it has not been primarily to provide English readers with translations better than the existing ones, though I would hope, of course, to have done that. My goal, however, has been more to make available a truly satisfactory edition, in translation, of Spinoza's work. Let me enumerate the features I regard as required in a satisfactory edition.

1. That it should provide good translations is only the most obvious, though no doubt the most important, requirement. No one should underestimate the difficulty of meeting it. By a good translation I understand one which is accurate wherever it is a question of simple accuracy, shows good judgment where the situation calls for something more than accuracy, maintains as much consistency as possible in the treatment of technical terms, leaves interpretation to the commentators, so far as this is possible,[1] and, finally, is as clear and readable as fidelity to the text will allow. Anyone may be excused for thinking it enough just to provide good translations. Often we have had to settle for rather less.

2. Still, we have a right to expect more of a truly satisfactory edition. One further requirement is that its translations should be based on a good critical edition of the original texts. Of the works presented in this volume, only two, Descartes' "Principles of Philosophy" and the Metaphysical Thoughts, were published during Spinoza's lifetime. The Ethics, the Treatise on the Intellect, and most of the letters were first published in the Opera posthuma (OP) shortly after Spinoza's death in 1677. The Short Treatise was discovered only in the nineteenth century, in what is generally presumed to be a Dutch translation of a lost Latin original. Inevitably these works raise many textual problems.

The first editor to produce a genuinely critical edition of the original texts was Gebhardt, whose four-volume edition of Spinoza's Opera appeared in 1925.[2] One reason Gebhardt's work was a landmark in

---

[1] I have tried, in general, to avoid tendentious translations, leaving it to the Glossary-Index to make most of the necessary explanations. Sometimes, however, a translator can hardly avoid taking a stand on disputed issues (e.g., in E ID4). Where it has seemed to me that important questions of interpretation might depend on the translation adopted, I have tried to indicate this in the notes.

[2] Spinoza Opera, ed. C. Gebhardt, 4 vols. (Heidelberg: Carl Winter, 1925). In view of

Spinoza scholarship is that before him no editor had systematically compared the Latin text of works like the *Ethics* and the *Treatise on the Intellect* with the contemporary Dutch translations which appeared in the other posthumous edition of 1677, *De Nagelate Schriften van B.D.S.* (NS). Since the translator[3] of the NS appears to have been working, in part at least, from a manuscript copy, rather than from the printed text of the OP, a comparison of the two versions often helps to establish the text in doubtful cases. To see the importance of this, one need only consider how many references the geometric method forces Spinoza to make to previous axioms, definitions, propositions, etc., and how easy it is for mistakes in such references to go undetected in proofreading. But a close study of the NS translations can be useful in many ways.[4]

One of the principal initial reasons for undertaking this project was to provide translations based on the Gebhardt edition. When I began, Spinoza's masterwork, the *Ethics*, had never been translated into English from Gebhardt's text, though other, lesser works had been. Ex-

---

Spinoza's role in the development of contemporary standards of historical scholarship, it is ironic that this task was so long neglected.

[3] Or translators. Gebhardt assumed that there was just one translator, Glazemaker, and that he began his work well before Spinoza's death (see Gebhardt II/315). The NS translations are generally careful and were already in the press five months after Spinoza's death (21 February 1677). But as Joachim (2, 3) pointed out, the evidence for ascribing the translations to Glazemaker is not very strong. And Thijssen-Schoute (1, 10) suggested (on the strength of Letter 28) that others may have collaborated. If two or more translators did collaborate on the work, then we need not postulate that they started work long before Spinoza's death, though probably portions of the NS translations of the *Ethics* date from the mid-1660s.

I think the treatment of technical terms in the NS confirms the hypothesis of more than one translator. Interesting in this connection is the treatment of *mens* and *anima*. As Giancotti Boscherini points out (1, 131), the Dutch translator of the *Ethics* almost invariably uses *ziel* for both *mens* and *anima*. In the other works he "has abandoned such uniformity" and uses, predominantly, *geest* for *mens* and *ziel* for *anima* (which, as Giancotti Boscherini notes, is Glazemaker's regular policy in his translation of Descartes' *Regulae*). To me this would suggest that different translators were at work on different parts of the NS and that Glazemaker was probably not the translator of the *Ethics*. A recent and very thorough examination of this issue by Akkerman (2, 77-214) concludes that Balling probably translated E I-II and that Glazemaker was the translator of E III-V.

[4] A good example is E IP28S (II/70/1-15). See particularly editorial note 59. I must add, however, that I think Gebhardt sometimes regards an appeal to the NS as more decisive than it really is. Cf. E IP29D (II/70/26) and editorial note 63.

It is, of course, often difficult to know what to make of a variation. Even in the case of *Descartes' Principles* and the *Metaphysical Thoughts*, where the translations appeared during Spinoza's lifetime and with his approval (cf. Letter 21), a variation may reflect a revision in which we should see Spinoza's hand (cf. I/257), an exercise in free translation (Akkerman 2, 106-107, gives numerous examples), or a mistake (cf. I/270/18-20). In the case of the *Treatise on the Intellect* and the *Ethics* we cannot be sure that the translations had his approval.

isting translations were based on inferior nineteenth-century editions. And though Wolf's excellent translation of the *Short Treatise* had been based on a careful study of the original manuscripts, there was no doubt that his work had been superseded by Gebhardt's.

During the time I have been working on this project, much has happened. We do now have an English translation of the *Ethics* based on the Gebhardt text.[5] But while Gebhardt's remains the best available complete edition of the texts, it has, in its turn, been superseded, to some extent at least, by a number of recent scholarly works. Of the developments relevant to this volume, the most notable are that: 1) in 1977 the Wereldbibliotheek published, as the first installment in a new Dutch edition of the complete works, an edition of the correspondence, undertaken by Professors Akkerman, Hubbeling, and Westerbrink (AHW); although this edition presents all the letters in Dutch, the editors have taken great pains to get an exact text, and their work must be treated as the equivalent of a new critical edition; 2) in 1982, the third installment of the Wereldbibliotheek series contained a new critical edition, by Professor Mignini (Mignini 1), of that most troublesome of all Spinozistic texts, the *Short Treatise*; Mignini's conclusions, as presented in the apparatus of his edition and in two long articles (Mignini 2, 3), will no doubt be controversial, but there can also be no doubt that he has shed a very different light on this work; and finally 3), Professor Akkerman is preparing a new critical edition of the *Ethics*, which will contain the many emendations of the text suggested by the extensive critique of Gebhardt's editorial work which he published in 1980 (Akkerman 2); it is clear that Akkerman has greatly illuminated the text of the *Ethics* and that his new edition will be a significant improvement on Gebhardt's. Further details of the advances made by recent textual research will be found in the prefaces to the works concerned and in the notes.

3. After the quality of the translation and of the text translated, perhaps the next most important requirement in a satisfactory edition is that it should be as comprehensive as possible. There is no doubt that the *Ethics* is the definitive expression of Spinoza's mature thought in metaphysics, epistemology, psychology, and ethics. But its elliptical style makes it an often cryptic text, which imposes great demands on the reader. Ideally, it should be read in the context of the whole of the Spinozistic corpus. Even if we do not apply to Spinoza's own work all of his principles for the interpretation of Scripture,[6] it re-

---

[5] By Samuel Shirley, published by Hackett Publishing Co., 1982.

[6] Cf. the *Theological-Political Treatise*, vii (III/99-101). No doubt Spinoza thought these rules applied only to works which, like Scripture, are inherently obscure, not to works

mains true that the other Spinozistic texts constitute our most important data for the interpretation of the *Ethics*. A satisfactory edition would not omit any that might be of use to the perplexed, so that they might readily find all those passages that bear on the same topic.

4. A corollary of this is that it is, if not a requirement, at least extremely desirable that all the translations be by the same hand. If we are to compare discussions of the same topic in different works (or in different passages of the same work), then it is essential that technical terms be treated consistently, an unlikely result if different translators are at work. The problem of comparison is compounded by the fact that the works are sometimes in different languages in the original.

Consider, for example, the term *admiratio* in the *Ethics*. This has been variously rendered by "astonishment" (White) and "wonder" (Elwes). The translator of the *Ethics* in the *Nagelate Schriften* used *verwondering*, a term which also occurs in the *Short Treatise*, where Wolf rendered it by "surprise." None of the three English translations is unreasonable, but their variety obscures the fact that a discussion of *verwondering* in the *Short Treatise* is concerned with the same topic as a discussion of *admiratio* in the *Ethics*.

The Dutch *gebeurlijk* (= *contingens*) provides another example. This comes out as "accidental" in Wolf, whereas its Latin equivalent is translated by "contingent" in Elwes and White. A good student, of course, will probably guess that what Spinoza says about the accidental in one work bears on what he says about the contingent in another. But a better student will worry that perhaps some subtle distinction is intended. And he may also be puzzled by the fact that Spinoza seems sometimes to imply that there are accidents and sometimes to deny it; his puzzlement might be relieved if he checked the original, where he would discover that Wolf uses "accidental" for *toevallig* in the one context, and for *gebeurlijk* in the other. But he also might not know what to make of that information. The complexities of the Glossary-Index are intended to give the reader some appreciation of the Latin and Dutch realities which lie behind the English appearances.

5. If the Spinozistic corpus is to be seen in its proper perspective, it is also desirable, if not essential, that the works be arranged in chronological order. Spinoza's writings span a period of some twenty years. It is inevitable that over the course of that length of time Spinoza would change his mind about *something*. I think in fact that he

---

which, like Euclid's geometry, are inherently intelligible (III/111). No doubt, also, he would have classed his own work with Euclid's. But three hundred years of Spinoza scholarship have amply demonstrated that he was too optimistic about the intelligibility of his work.

changed his views about quite a number of things, and that a chronological arrangement should help to bring that out.[7] Spinoza scholars have often sought to unfold "the latent processes of thought" that lay "behind the geometrical method." If we are not satisfied with literary romances masquerading as scientific history, we may find some value in examining the works that actually did lead up to the *Ethics*.

To some extent my arrangement of the texts is arbitrary. The decision which will probably be most surprising to nonspecialists seems to me eminently defensible. The *Ethics* was first published after Spinoza's death in 1677. The *Theological-Political Treatise* was first published in 1670. But we know from the correspondence that a substantial manuscript of the *Ethics* was in existence by the middle of 1665. We do not know how much revision that manuscript may have undergone in the next twelve years before it was published, but it seems best to treat the *Ethics* as coming before the *Theological-Political Treatise* and to see a shift in Spinoza's interests in the late 1660s.[8]

More controversial among specialists, no doubt, will be my decision to present the *Treatise on the Emendation of the Intellect* before the *Short Treatise*, which until very recently has invariably been thought to be Spinoza's earliest work. Now, however, Mignini has challenged that assumption, arguing with considerable force that the *Treatise on the Intellect* is earlier, not only in its date of composition, but also in the stage of development it represents. I am inclined to agree with that judgment, at least as regards the date of composition. To me the correspondence makes it clear that the *Treatise on the Intellect* must have been written before September 1661, and that Spinoza was still working on a manuscript of the *Short Treatise*, which he then had thoughts of publishing, early in 1662.

6. Finally, it seems to me that a satisfactory edition of Spinoza's works ought to contain a good deal more in the way of scholarly aid than English readers are accustomed to find in editions of modern philosophers. Students of modern philosophy must generally settle for much less help than students of ancient philosophy are used to.[9] At a minimum a satisfactory edition should have: a thorough index;[10] pref-

---

[7] My model here is Alquié's superb edition of Descartes' works.

[8] See the prefaces to the *Ethics* and to Letters 17-28 and the discussions in Freudenthal 5, 1:147ff. and Giancotti Boscherini 2, I, xx-xxii.

[9] Though things are changing for the better. We might note here the new translation of Leibniz's *New Essays* by Bennett and Remnant (Cambridge), the new edition of Locke's *Essay* by Nidditch (Oxford), and the translations of Leibniz's *Discourse on Metaphysics*, *Correspondence with Arnauld*, and *Correspondence with Clarke*, published by Manchester University Press.

[10] Pollock, in introducing the index to his *Spinoza*, aptly cites the following lovely remark, attributed by Henry Wheatley to John Baynes: "The man who publishes a

aces to each work indicating something of that work's history and special problems; notes that call attention to the more significant variant readings, ambiguities, obscurities, apparent contradictions, and debates among the commentators; and some systematic way of warning the reader about terms that may be difficult to render into English.[11] To make it easier for readers to consult the original and to trace references in secondary sources, it should adopt a standard pagination based on the Gebhardt edition.

Such is the kind of edition I have aimed at producing. Whether I have succeeded is for others to judge. But I should like to forestall two possible criticisms. First, it has not been my intention to produce a translation and commentary. Desirable as that might be, it seemed to me that it was more important, at this stage in the history of Spinoza studies, to present as much of the primary text as possible, as well as possible, and that I could not produce as comprehensive an edition as I would like to if I attempted to note *every* passage that is ambiguous, obscure, or apparently contradictory. If I am to produce a comprehensive edition in which all the work is by the same hand, I must try to complete it in my lifetime, and there is no way of knowing how long that may be. My notes also do not attempt much cross-referencing. The index should make notes of that kind largely superfluous. Second, I recognize that it would have been very desirable to have the original texts on the facing pages. Perhaps someday it will be possible to produce an edition using these translations (or some of them) and having that feature. But for now it seems more important to make the translations available in as inexpensive a format as possible.

Let me close by commenting on certain formal features of the translation and on certain peculiarities of the Latin language, which is most often the language of the texts translated in this volume. I have generally tried to be faithful to the capitalization of the Gebhardt edition, which reflects that of the original editions. I do this, not because I think the use of the capitals in those editions has any philosophical significance, but simply out of deference to those scholars who do attach significance to matters of capitalization. I incline to the view that the use of capitals in works like the *Opera posthuma* probably reflects the tastes of Spinoza's printers rather than his own considered preferences. Certainly the autographs of Spinoza's letters suggest that. But it seemed to me that it would do no harm to accommodate the views of those with whom I differ on this point.

---

book without an index ought to be damned ten miles beyond Hell, where the Devil could not get for stinging nettles."

[11] For more on this theme, see the Glossary-Index.

As for punctuation and paragraphing, on the other hand, I have taken considerable liberties, breaking up long sentences and long paragraphs whenever it seemed to me that to do so would make Spinoza's argument clearer. This necessarily involves a certain element of interpretation, but it seemed to me that the potential gain in intelligibility justified the risk. I have also interpolated occasional section numbers, phrases, and terms, in square brackets and without explanation, where they seemed helpful. Square brackets are also used, with an explanation, to indicate textual variations and doubtful passages. This happens quite frequently with footnotes in the *Short Treatise*. I have used italics to indicate those occasions when "or" represents *sive* or *seu*. Generally,[12] *sive* and *seu* mark an equivalance, rather than an alternative. Lettered notes are Spinoza's; numbered notes are mine.

This is perhaps the proper place to warn readers who have no Latin at all about certain features of that language. There are no articles, definite or indefinite, in classical Latin.[13] So whenever the translation of a Latin passage has either a definite or an indefinite article, the reader should be aware that this involves an element of interpretation on the part of the translator. Sometimes, of course, it will be quite clear which should be used. Sometimes it will not matter philosophically. But sometimes it both matters and is not clear. The NS are of some help here, to the extent that one thinks it likely that Spinoza carefully reviewed those translations. But I am not sure how much weight to attach to their usage.

A related matter concerns the use of personal pronouns. It is sometimes observed that the use of personal pronouns is less common in Latin than in English, since the subject of the verb is often implicit in the verb ending. And often when personal pronouns are used, the masculine and neuter forms are the same. So unless a translator is prepared to violate the conventions of English, his translation is much more likely than the Latin original to convey the impression that God is being thought of as a person (and a male person at that). This would

[12] But not, I think, invariably. Cf., for example, II/57/13,79/23. Sometimes Spinoza uses *aut* or *vel* where we would expect *sive*. Cf. II/51/23, 52/8,146/2

[13] In medieval Latin, however, *ille* came to be used as a definite article and there appear to be some traces of that usage in Spinoza. Cf. II/89/4. Analogously, it seems to me that *aliqui* is sometimes best rendered by the indefinite article, e.g. at II/50/25, 28, 30, 31, 34 and II/83/31. In the latter case, this may have some philosophic significance, since that passage provides us with a gloss on one of the central propositions of Part I of the *Ethics* (P16).

Spinoza's Latin has sometimes been stigmatized as that of the late medieval scholastics. No doubt much of the technical vocabulary is borrowed from the scholastics. But the reader will find a juster appreciation of Spinoza's Latin in Akkerman 2, 1-35.

certainly be a mistaken impression, but I know no good way to remove it.

IT REMAINS only for me to acknowledge my indebtedness to the many persons and institutions who have helped to bring this project to its present stage. First, I must thank the Institute of Advanced Studies of the Australian National University in Canberra, where the bulk of the work was done, under virtually ideal conditions. I am equally indebted to Professor John Passmore, who was the head of the Philosophy Department during most of my years in Australia, who encouraged this project, commented critically on a draft translation of the *Ethics*, and provided me with a model of historical scholarship which has sustained my spirits through many hours of hard work. I should like to dedicate this edition to him, and only hope that he will be pleased with the finished product.

Many others have been extremely kind and helpful in many ways: Hermann de Dijn (who read a draft translation of the *Short Treatise* with great care), Jonathan Bennett (who provided me over the years with innumerable excellent suggestions about my translation of the *Ethics*), Paul Eisenberg (who shared with me a copy of his own meticulous translation of the *Treatise on the Intellect* and commented helpfully on the whole project), Frederick Copleston (who gave me some very useful comments on the *Metaphysical Thoughts*), Fokke Akkerman (who communicated to me the emendations to be incorporated in his forthcoming critical edition of the *Ethics*), G. van Suchtelen and F. Mignini (who made available to me a prepublication copy of the new critical edition of the *Short Treatise*), Marie Boas Hall and Thomas Falco (who answered queries that I had about the correspondence between Spinoza and Oldenburg), and Stephen Voss, Margaret Wilson, Alan Donagan, and Genevieve Lloyd (all of whom made constructive suggestions of one kind or another about certain aspects of the translation).

Of previous translators and editors whose works I have consulted, I am indebted most, of course, to Gebhardt, but also to Abraham Wolf, for his translations of the *Short Treatise* and the *Correspondence*; to Charles Appuhn, Roland Caillois, Madeleine Francès, and Robert Misrahi, for their excellent French translations of the works; to Fokke Akkerman, H. G. Hubbeling, and A. G. Westerbrink, whose recent Dutch edition of the correspondence is a major contribution to Spinoza studies. I have also found Professor Giancotti Boscherini's *Spinoza Lexicon* a tremendously valuable tool.

I should also like to thank Sandy Thatcher of the Princeton University Press, for his initial interest in this project and his patient prodding over the years; Jean Norman, for her research assistance; and Isabel Sheaffe, Anna van der Vliet, and Audrey Thiel, for their secretarial assistance.

In spite of all the help I have received, and my own best efforts to avoid error, I am sure that mistakes must remain. As Spinoza himself remarks, *nullus liber unquam sine mendis repertus est.* (III/149) I would ask readers who detect anything that needs correction—typographical or translation errors, omissions from the index or from other scholarly aids—to send me notice of it, c/o the Princeton University Press.

Short Titles and Abbreviations

PAGE references to Gebhardt's edition *Spinoza Opera* (4 vols. [Heidelberg: Carl Winter, 1925]), will be made in the following form: I/611 = volume I, page 611. Frequently I will use the Gebhardt pagination, including line numbers, to refer to passages in Spinoza's text, thus II/37/5-9 = volume II, pages 37, lines 5-9. These volume, page, and line numbers are given in the margins of the translation to make it easier to consult the original and to trace references in secondary sources.

I also adopt the following system of short titles and abbreviations, for use whenever it seems preferable not to use the Gebhardt volume, page, and line numbers:

KV = *Short Treatise on God, Man and His Well-Being* = *Short Treatise*

TdIE = *Treatise on the Emendation of the Intellect* = *Treatise on the Intellect*

Ep. = *Letters*

PP = *Parts I and II of Descartes' "Principles of Philosophy"* = *Descartes' Principles*

CM = *Appendix Containing Metaphysical Thoughts* = *Metaphysical Thoughts*

E = *Ethics*

OP = *Opera Posthuma*

NS = *Nagelate Schriften*

A = axiom

D = (immediately following a roman numeral) = definition

D = (immediately following an arabic numeral) = demonstration

P = proposition

C = corollary

S = scholium

Exp = explanation

So PP ID5 = *Descartes' Principles*, Part I, Definition 5. E IP8S2 = *Ethics*, Part I, proposition 8, scholium 2. KV II, xxv, 1 refers to Part II, chapter xxv, section 1 of the *Short Treatise*. "TdIE, 101" refers to section 101 of the *Treatise on the Intellect*. It should be understood that the division of the *Short Treatise* and the *Treatise on the Intellect* into sections is the work of later editors (Sigwart and Bruder, respectively).

ABBREVIATIONS

As for works other than Spinoza's, I generally refer to the Adam and Tannery edition of Descartes' works as AT, to Descartes' *Principles of Philosophy* as the *Principles*, and to the Latin translation of his *Passions of the Soul* as PA. Secondary sources are identified by the author's name, a number if there is more than one work by the same author in the reference list, a volume number, if necessary, and the page number. The reference list may be found at the back of the book.

Earliest Works

Treatise on the Emendation of the Intellect

EDITORIAL PREFACE

THE *Treatise on the Emendation of the Intellect* (TdIE), a short, difficult, but fascinating discourse on method, was first published in Spinoza's *Opera posthuma* in 1677. But as the editors of that collection tell us in their preface, both its style and its content show it to be one of Spinoza's earliest works. If the reference in Letter 6 to a "whole short work" (*integrum opusculum*) is indeed to this treatise, as scholars have generally assumed,[1] then a draft of it must have existed at least by early in 1662, and quite likely Spinoza wrote it before that.[2]

Various forward references in Spinoza's notes to this treatise indicate that at some stage of his work on it Spinoza conceived it as introductory to another work, to be called (perhaps) *Philosophy*, a work which would have discussed in a systematic way topics in philosophical theology (II/29, n. z), philosophy of mind (II/15, n. o), epistemology (II/14, nn. k and l), ethics (II/6, n. a; II/7, n. b; II/8, n. c), and perhaps much else (cf. II/9, n. d). Some of the references suggest a work more like the *Short Treatise* than the *Ethics*,[3] and Gebhardt argued that the "short work" referred to in Letter 6 was a two-part work, with the TdIE as a methodological prolegomenon to the more systematic KV. According to Gebhardt (I/407), the Latin original of the KV was already in existence when Spinoza began writing the TdIE around the time of Letter 6. But if what I have suggested above is correct (see n. 2), then Gebhardt must be wrong at least about the date of composition of the TdIE. Mignini would argue that Gebhardt is wrong also in thinking that the TdIE was an integral part of the short work

[1] Spinoza describes his *opusculum* as being devoted to the question "how things began to be and by what connection they depend on the first cause . . . and also on the emendation of the intellect." This strongly suggests that our TdIE was part of the *opusculum*. But Mignini has cast doubt on this. See the annotation at IV/36/13.

[2] I would be inclined to say earlier than Letter 2 at least, i.e., before September 1661, for reasons suggested in the annotation at II/9/12. Cf. Mignini 2, 106. If, as Mignini thinks, the TdIE is earlier than the KV, and if, as he also thinks, the first draft of the KV was written around the middle of 1660 (see Mignini 1, 239), then the TdIE would have been written a good deal earlier than the spring of 1662.

[3] Notably II/29, n. z. On the other hand, some of the things promised in the forward references do not appear in our version of the KV any more than they do in E, e.g., the extended discussion of wealth foreshadowed in II/6, n. a.

3

Spinoza refers to in Letter 6. Emphasizing the incompleteness of our text of the TdIE, he contends that it could not have been correctly described in Letter 6 as *having been composed* and that it is earlier than the KV, not merely in date of composition, but also in the stage of the development of Spinoza's thought that it represents.[4] If Mignini's arguments for the priority of the TdIE are not conclusive, he has, I think, at least established that there is no reason to regard the KV as the earlier work.[5] So at this stage the position would seem to be that, if the TdIE is not in fact earlier that the KV, it was probably written at about the same time as the KV and as an introduction to it.

In its importance for the study of the development of Spinoza's thought, the *Treatise on the Intellect* invites comparison with Descartes' *Regulae*. Both are early, unfinished works that show the direction of their author's thought at a formative stage, that indicate the problems concerning him and the solutions he was inclined toward. Both discuss certain important themes more fully than does any work their author later published. But both works also need to be read with the consciousness that the lines of thought presented in them may not have proved ultimately to be satisfactory to the author.

For example, some have argued that in this treatise Spinoza has not fully emancipated himself from Descartes on the distinction between will and intellect,[6] and it seems clear that he does tend to confuse mind and intellect.[7] I would argue that the discussion of the four kinds of knowledge is not clearly thought out.[8] And Joachim has suggested that

[4] Mignini contends that the teaching of the KV is closer to that of E than is the teaching of the TdIE in regard to the following topics: the nature of the intellect and the doctrine of method, the theory of the kinds of knowledge, the nature of fictions, the will, final causation and perfection. This is not the place for a discussion of his arguments, but I will observe that my own attempt to study the development of Spinoza's thought about truth (Curley 9), an attempt made before I was aware of Mignini's work, would have proceeded more smoothly had I adopted his chronology.

[5] This, essentially, is the judgment of M. Matheron, in a recent review of Mignini's work (*Bulletin de l'Association des Amis de Spinoza*, no. 10, 1983): "Si les arguments positifs avancés par Mignini, bien qu'ils donnent beaucoup à penser, ne sont *peut-être* tout à fait convaincants (personellement j'avoue hésiter encore sur ce point), ses arguments négatifs, en revanche, sont décisifs: nous admettions tous comme allant de soi, parce qu'on nous l'avait enseigné, que le C.T.[i.e., KV] était antérieur au TRE [i.e., TdIE], et Mignini *démontre* qu'il n'y avait à cela *absolument aucune raison!*"

[6] See Joachim 2, 59, and cf. Mignini 2, 140. Joachim construes this as a survival of Cartesian doctrines advocated in the KV. Mignini, it seems, regards it as evidence of the priority of the TdIE to the KV. I myself am not satisfied with the evidence that Spinoza adopts the Cartesian distinction between will and intellect either in the TdIE or in the KV. For example, it seems to me that § 78 of the TdIE effectively anticipates Spinoza's critique of the Cartesian doctrine of suspense of judgment in E IIP49S. And I take it that KV II, xiv, also criticizes the Cartesian distinction, though on different grounds.

[7] See the annotation at II/9/12.   [8] See Curley 2; cf. Joachim 2, 24-33.

the whole work may have been intended only to present a popular, imprecise exposition of Spinoza's thought on these topics.[9]

The most important question, perhaps, is whether the whole concept of method, as Spinoza here presents it, is not incoherent, and so doomed to failure.[10] On the one hand, the truth is supposed to require no sign, and having a true idea is supposed to be sufficient to remove doubt (§ 36); on the other, the method is supposed, among other things, to teach us what a true idea is, and how to distinguish it from other perceptions (§ 37).

But whatever reservations we may have about the doctrine of this work, it is clear that *in the main* it continued to satisfy Spinoza for some years. A letter to Bouwmeester in 1666 (Letter 37) repeats some of the *Treatise*'s main themes—that the intellect, unlike the body, is not subject to chance, external causes, but has the power of forming clear and distinct ideas; that it is necessary above all to distinguish between the intellect and the imagination (this being identified with distinguishing between true ideas and all the rest, the false, fictitious and doubtful). And an interchange with Tschirnhaus in 1675 (Letters 59 and 60) indicates that Spinoza had communicated something similar to him informally, and had given Tschirnhaus some reason to expect that before long he would publish his treatise on method.

Naturally, then, there have been a variety of suggestions as to why the *Treatise* never was published in Spinoza's lifetime. The editors of the *Opera posthuma* remark that the importance of the topic, the deep contemplations and extensive knowledge it required, made Spinoza's progress with it very slow. Appuhn suggests that Spinoza broke off the composition because he could not see any satisfactory solution to the problems raised at the end (§§ 102-103, 106-110), and that he did not return to finish it because he came to think it more important to concentrate on his other works on moral and political philosophy (the *Ethics*, the *Theological-Political Treatise*, and the *Political Treatise*). Koyré, on the other hand, tends to emphasize the difficulty raised in § 46 (see the note to II/18/1-2). Ironically, Joachim's excellent commentary on this work itself remained unfinished at his death because he was unable to resolve to his satisfaction the problem of how Spinoza meant to conclude the *Treatise*.

If the character of this work as unfinished, highly problematic, and only posthumously published invites comparison with Descartes' *Regulae*, the apparently autobiographical character of the opening sec-

---

[9] Cf. Joachim 2, 89-90.
[10] So Joachim argues at any rate. Cf. Joachim 2, 102-111.

tions equally invites comparison with the *Discourse on Method*. The tone of the two works is quite different, of course. The dissatisfaction Descartes presents as leading him to philosophy is with the uncertainty of the learning that had been imparted to him as a student. Spinoza's dissatisfaction is with the insufficiency of the ends men commonly pursue.

Of course scholars have doubted whether these opening passages should be taken as strictly autobiographical (just as they have doubted the accuracy of Descartes' account of his life in the *Discourse*). As Koyré remarks (Koyré 2, xix), the theme *de vero bono et de contemptu mundi* is as old as the world itself. Various Stoic authors (e.g., Marcus Aurelius and Seneca) have been cited. And Elbogen calls attention to the work of a medieval Jewish author, Shem Tov Falaquera, whose *Ha-Mevak-kesh* similarly offers knowledge as the path to salvation. However that may be, it remains, as Koyré also remarks, highly significant that Spinoza should begin a treatise on method by reflecting on the true good.

The paragraph numbers in brackets are those introduced by Bruder and are included for ease in making and following references. Lettered footnotes are Spinoza's, numbered footnotes are mine. I have adopted the lettering of Gebhardt's edition, though (even allowing for differences in the Latin alphabet) it is not entirely consecutive.

NOTICE TO THE READER[1]

THIS *Treatise on the Emendation of the Intellect* etc., which we give you here, kind reader, in its unfinished [NS: and defective] state, was written by the author many years ago now. He always intended to finish it. But hindered by other occupations, and finally snatched away by death, he was unable to bring it to the desired conclusion. But since it contains many excellent and useful things, which—we have no doubt—will be of great benefit to anyone sincerely seeking the truth, we did not wish to deprive you of them. And so that you would be aware of, and find less difficult to excuse, the many things that are still obscure, rough, and unpolished, we wished to warn you of them. Farewell.

[1] By the editors of the *Opera posthuma*.

II/5

5

Treatise on the Emendation of the Intellect and on the way by which it is best directed toward the true knowledge of things[2]

[1] AFTER experience had taught me that all the things which regularly occur in ordinary life are empty and futile, and I saw that all the things which were the cause or object of my fear had nothing of good or bad in themselves, except insofar as [my] mind was moved by them, I resolved at last to try to find out whether there was anything which would be the true good, capable of communicating itself, and which alone would affect the mind, all others being rejected—whether there was something which, once found and acquired, would continuously give me the greatest joy, to eternity.

[2] I say that *I resolved at last*—for at first glance it seemed ill-advised to be willing to lose something certain for something then uncertain. I saw, of course, the advantages that honor and wealth bring, and that I would be forced to abstain from seeking them, if I wished to devote myself seriously to something new and different; and if by chance the greatest happiness lay in them, I saw that I should have to do without it. But if it did not lie in them, and I devoted my energies only to acquiring them, then I would equally go without it.

[3] So I wondered whether perhaps it would be possible to reach my new goal—or at least the certainty of attaining it—without changing the conduct and plan of life which I shared with other men. Often I tried this, but in vain. For most things which present themselves in life, and which, to judge from their actions, men think to be the highest good, may be reduced to these three: wealth, honor, and sensual

10

15

20

25

II/6

---

[2] The translation of this title is disputed. The Latin for the main title is *Tractatus de Intellectus Emendatione*, the Dutch *Handeling van de Verbetering van't Verstant*. Joachim (2, 1) argued that no English term could reproduce the *exact* implications of the Latin, but recommended "Purification of the Intellect" as rightly suggesting a project of restoring the intellect to its "natural perfection, by eliminating from it . . . ideas which are not *its own* but have come to it from an external source." DeDeugd's criticism of Joachim (1, 50-57), while rightly pointing out that the Dutch version cannot plausibly bear that meaning, gives insufficient weight to § 16. Eisenberg (3) argues that no term can reproduce the exact implications of the Latin, since Spinoza's phrase has no *exact* implications. At the time of writing this work Spinoza inconsistently conceived of the intellect both as inherently pure and as needing purification. He did not clearly distinguish between the mind, which cannot be entirely freed of external influences, and the intellect, which has no need to be. No translation will solve such difficulties.

The subtitle in the NS reads: "and at the same time of the means of making it perfect."

pleasure.³ The mind is so distracted by these three that it cannot give the slightest thought to any other good.

[4] For as far as sensual pleasure is concerned, the mind is so caught up in it, as if at peace in a [true] good, that it is quite prevented from thinking of anything else. But after the enjoyment of sensual pleasure is past, the greatest sadness follows. If this does not completely engross, still it thoroughly confuses and dulls the mind.

The mind is also distracted not a little by the pursuit of honors and wealth, particularly when the latterᵃ is sought only for its own sake, because it is assumed to be the highest good. [5] But the mind is far more distracted by honor. For this is always assumed to be good through itself and the ultimate end toward which everything is directed.

Nor do honor and wealth have, as sensual pleasure does, repentance as a natural consequence. The more each of these is possessed, the more joy is increased, and hence the more we are spurred on to increase them. But if our hopes should chance to be frustrated, we experience the greatest sadness. And finally, honor has this great disadvantage: to pursue it, we must direct our lives according to other men's powers of understanding—fleeing what they commonly flee and seeking what they commonly seek.

[6] Since I saw that all of these things stood in the way of my working toward this new goal, indeed were so opposed to it that one or the other must be given up, I was forced to ask what would be more useful to me. For as I say, I seemed to be willing to lose the certain good for the uncertain one. But after I had considered the matter a little, I first found that, if I devoted myself to this new plan of life, and gave up the old, I would be giving up a good by its nature uncertain (as we can clearly infer from what has been said) for one uncertain not by its nature (for I was seeking a permanent good) but only in respect to its attainment.

[7] By persistent meditation, however, I came to the conclusion that, if only I could resolve, wholeheartedly,⁴ [to change my plan of life], I

ᵃ I could explain this more fully and distinctly, by distinguishing wealth that is sought for its own sake, or for the sake of honor, or for the sake of sensual pleasure or for the sake of health and the advancement of the arts and sciences. But I reserve this for its own place; such an exact investigation is not appropriate here.

³ The choice of this particular trinity is probably influenced by Aristotle. Cf. the *Nicomachean Ethics* I, 4, and the *Short Treatise* II, v, 6.

⁴ "*Modò possem penitùs deliberare.*" *Deliberare* can mean '*to deliberate*' and most translators have given us something like "If only I could reflect thoroughly [on the matter]." But *deliberare* can also mean 'to decide as a consequence of deliberation' and I follow Koyré in thinking that to be the meaning here. When Spinoza comments on this phrase in § 10 it seems clear that he thinks of his difficulty as more volitional than intellectual. Cf. E IVP14.

would be giving up certain evils for a certain good. For I saw that I was in the greatest danger, and that I was forced to seek a remedy with all my strength, however uncertain it might be—like a man suffering from a fatal illness, who, foreseeing certain death unless he employs a remedy, is forced to seek it, however uncertain, with all his strength. For all his hope lies there. But all those things men ordinarily strive for, not only provide no remedy to preserve our being, but in fact hinder that preservation, often cause the destruction of those who possess them,[b] and always cause the destruction of those who are possessed by them.[5]

[8] There are a great many examples of people who have suffered persecution to the death on account of their wealth, or have exposed themselves to so many dangers to acquire wealth that they have at last paid the penalty for their folly with their life. Nor are there fewer examples of people who, to attain or defend honor, have suffered most miserably. And there are innumerable examples of people who have hastened their death through too much sensual pleasure.

[9] Furthermore, these evils seemed to have arisen from the fact that all happiness or unhappiness was placed in the quality of the object to which we cling with love. For strife will never arise on account of what is not loved, nor will there be sadness if it perishes, nor envy if it is possessed by another, nor fear, nor hatred—in a word, no disturbances of the mind. Indeed, all these happen only in the love of those things that can perish, as all the things we have just spoken of can do.

[10] But love toward the eternal and infinite thing feeds the mind with a joy entirely exempt from sadness.[6] This is greatly to be desired, and to be sought with all our strength.

[b] These things are to be demonstrated more accurately.

[5] The NS has: "often cause the destruction of those who possess them (if one may speak thus), and always of those who are possessed by wealth." It seems likely that the parenthesis is an addition by the translator and bears on the notion of being possessed by wealth.

[6] OP: "Sed amor erga rem aeternam, & infinitam solâ laetitiâ pascit animum, ipsaque omnis tristitiae est expers"; NS: "Maar de liefde tot d'eeuwige en oneindige zaak voed de geest [margin: mens] met blÿschap alleen, en is van alle droefheit uitgesloten." The translation of this important passage is disputed. Joachim (2, 18, n.4) notes that various translators have rendered it as if it were the love that was exempt from sadness (which makes the Latin ungrammatical, but is what the Dutch implies). He, however, sees here a foreshadowing of the doctrine that God is exempt from sadness. (I.e., *ipsa* refers not to *amor*, but the eternal and infinite thing.) This is possible, both grammatically and philosophically, but Joachim surely goes too far when he contends that this interpretation is necessary to explain why love for God feeds the mind with unmixed joy. Appuhn, Koyré, and Caillois all take *ipsa* to refer to *laetitia*, an alternative Joachim does not discuss, and to my mind the one most likely.

But not without reason did I use these words *if only I could resolve in earnest*.[7] For though I perceived these things [NS: this evil] so clearly in my mind, I still could not, on that account, put aside all greed, desire for sensual pleasure and love of esteem.

[11] I saw this, however: that so long as the mind was turned toward these thoughts, it was turned away from those things, and was thinking seriously about the new goal. That was a great comfort to me. For I saw that those evils would not refuse to yield to remedies. And although in the beginning these intervals were rare, and lasted a very short time, nevertheless, after the true good became more and more known to me, the intervals became more frequent and longer—especially after I saw that the acquisition of money, sensual pleasure, and esteem are only obstacles so long as they are sought for their own sakes, and not as means to other things. But if they are sought as means, then they will have a limit, and will not be obstacles at all. On the contrary, they will be of great use in attaining the end on account of which they are sought, as we shall show in its place.

[12] Here I shall only say briefly what I understand by the true good, and at the same time, what the highest good is. To understand this properly, it must be noted that good and bad are said of things only in a certain respect, so that one and the same thing can be called both good and bad according to different respects. The same applies to perfect and imperfect. For nothing, considered in its own nature, will be called perfect or imperfect, especially after we have recognized that everything that happens happens according to the eternal order, and according to certain laws of Nature.

[13] But since human weakness does not grasp that order by its own thought, and meanwhile man conceives a human nature much stronger and more enduring[8] than his own, and at the same time sees that nothing prevents his acquiring such a nature, he is spurred to seek means that will lead him to such a perfection. Whatever can be a means to his attaining it is called a true good; but the highest good is to arrive—together with other individuals if possible—at the enjoyment of such a nature. What that nature is we shall show in its proper

---

[7] "*Modò possem seriò deliberare.*" In referring back to II/6/21 Spinoza does not in fact quote himself exactly.

[8] Wendel and Cassirer thought it necessary to emend this passage so that it would read: "man conceives a nature much stronger than his own human nature." But I find Gebhardt's arguments against this conclusive (II/322-323). The text as it stands is supported by the NS and paralleled by passages both in the *Short Treatise* (II,4; I/60/21ff.) and the *Ethics* (IV, Pref., II/208). Koyré (2, 98-99) is right to remark that the passage is a difficult one on any reading, but his comments do not seem to me to stress sufficiently the necessity both of man's conceiving such a stronger nature and of his striving to attain it.

place: that it is the knowledge[c] of the union that the mind has with the whole of Nature.[9]

[14] This, then, is the end I aim at: to acquire such a nature, and to strive that many acquire it with me. That is, it is part of my happiness to take pains that many others may understand as I understand, so that their intellect and desire agree entirely with my intellect and desire. To do this it is necessary,[d] *first* to understand as much of Nature as suffices for acquiring such a nature; *next*, to form a society of the kind that is desirable, so that as many as possible may attain it as easily and surely as possible.

[15] *Third*, attention must be paid to Moral Philosophy and to Instruction concerning the Education of children. Because Health is no small means to achieving this end, *fourthly*, the whole of Medicine must be worked out. And because many difficult things are rendered easy by ingenuity, and we can gain much time and convenience in this life, *fifthly*, Mechanics is in no way to be despised.

[16] But before anything else we must devise a way of healing the intellect, and purifying it, as much as we can in the beginning, so that it understands things successfully, without error and as well as possible.[10] Everyone will now be able to see that I wish to direct all the sciences toward one end[e] and goal, viz. that we should achieve, as we have said, the highest human perfection. So anything in the sciences which does nothing to advance us toward our goal must be rejected as useless—in a word, all our activities and thoughts are to be directed to this end.

[17] But while we pursue this end, and devote ourselves to bringing

[c] These things will be explained more fully in their place.

[d] Note that here I take the trouble only to enumerate the sciences necessary for our purpose, without attending to their order.

[e] In the sciences there is only one end, toward which they must all be directed.

[9] If this is taken, as it may be, to mean "knowledge that man is a part of nature, and subject to its universal laws," then the doctrine is very Stoic. Cf. Marcus Aurelius, *Meditations*, VII, 9-13; X,6. But the passage is also one which, more than any other perhaps, encourages the interpretation of Spinoza as a mystic.

[10] That the intellect requires purification (*expurgatio*) is a Baconian doctrine. Cf. the *Novum Organum* (Bacon, I, 139 = IV, 27). For healing (*medendi*) the NS has simply "improving" (verbeteren). Eisenberg (3, 175) argues that passages like this one are symptomatic of a tendency to confuse the intellect with the mind "at least during much of the time that he wrote the treatise." And since, in Letter 2 (IV/8-9), Spinoza is quite critical of Bacon for not distinguishing the intellect from the mind, and for supposing that the intellect is deceived by its own nature, it seems likely that, by the time of writing that letter (September 1661), Spinoza would have regarded passages like this as unsatisfactory. Note that in that letter Spinoza criticizes Bacon for comparing the intellect to an uneven mirror (cf. Bacon, I, 164). A similar comparison occurs in the purification of the intellect passage cited above, except that there it is the mind that is compared to an uneven mirror. See also Mignini 2, 106.

the intellect back[11] to the right path, it is necessary to live. So we are forced, before we do anything else, to assume certain rules of living as good:

1. To speak according to the power of understanding of ordinary people, and do whatever does not interfere with our attaining our purpose. For we can gain a considerable advantage, if we yield as much to their understanding as we can. In this way, they will give a favorable hearing to the truth.

2. To enjoy pleasures just so far as suffices for safeguarding our health.

3. Finally, to seek money, or anything else, just so far as suffices for sustaining life and health, and conforming to those customs of the community that do not conflict with our aim.

[18] Having laid down these rules, I come now to what must be done first, before all else: emending[12] the intellect and rendering it capable of understanding things in the way the attainment of our end requires. To do this, the order we naturally have requires me to survey here all the modes of perceiving which I have had up to now for affirming or denying something without doubt, so that I may choose the best of all, and at the same time begin to know my powers and the nature that I desire to perfect.

[19] If I consider them accurately, I can reduce them all to four[13] main kinds:

1. There is the Perception we have from report or from some conventional sign.[14]

2. There is the Perception we have from random experience,[15] that is, from experience that is not determined by the intellect.

---

[11] Latin: *"intellectum . . . redigamus."* NS: *"het verstant . . . te brengen."* But the language of purification in the preceding paragraph seems to justify the suggestion of returning to an original state of rectitude.

[12] NS: *"zuiveren,"* purify.

[13] NS: *"three"*; but it goes on to enumerate four kinds, as the OP does. Gebhardt thought this might naturally be explained on the assumption that in an earlier draft of the *Treatise* Spinoza had divided the kinds of 'knowledge' into three (as in the *Short Treatise* and the *Ethics*) rather than four. He also took it as evidence that the Dutch translation was made, not from the text of the *Opera posthuma*, but from an independent, earlier manuscript, in which revisions were not consistently carried out. For counterargument see Mignini 2, 126-127.

[14] On the translation here, and on the classification generally, see Joachim 2, 24-33, and Curley 2, 25-59.

[15] As Joachim notes, this passage echoes one in Bacon, *Novum Organum* I, 100 (Bacon, I,203 [= IV, 95]). He also calls attention to aphorisms 25, 70, and 105. Perhaps Bacon's influence is also to be seen in Descartes' *Regulae*, AT X, 427.

But it has this name only because it comes to us by chance, and we have no other experiment that opposes it. So it remains with us unshaken.

3. There is the Perception that we have when the essence of a thing is inferred from another thing, but not adequately. This happens, either ᶠwhen we infer the cause from some effect, or when something is inferred from some universal, which some property always accompanies.[17]

4. Finally, there is the Perception we have when a thing is perceived through its essence alone, or through knowledge of its proximate cause.

[20] I shall illustrate all of these with examples. I know only from report my date of birth, and who my parents were, and similar things, which I have never doubted. By random experience I know that I shall die, for I affirm this because I have seen others like me die, even though they had not all lived the same length of time and did not all

ᶠ When this happens, we understand nothing about the cause except what we consider in the effect. This is sufficiently evident from the fact that then the cause is explained only in very general terms, e.g., *Therefore there is something, Therefore there is some power,* etc. Or also from the fact that the terms express the cause negatively, *Therefore it is not this, or that, etc.* In the second case something clearly conceived is attributed to the cause on account of the effect, as we shall show in an example; but nothing is attributed to it except *propria*, not the essence of a particular thing.[16]

[16] OP: "In secundo casu aliquid causae tribuitur propter effectum, quod clarè concipitur, ut in exemplo ostendimus; verùm nihil praeter propria, non verò rei essentia particularis." This note has more than its share of difficulties. (1) What does *in secundo casu* refer to? Eisenberg suggests that it *could* be translated "in a (more) favorable case," adding a third case to the two already mentioned in the note, but neither he nor I thinks it very likely. Or it could be translated as I have it and refer to the case described in the immediately preceding sentence. But this does not make much sense of the note. Or it could refer to the second case mentioned in the text, in spite of the fact that the note as a whole is attached to the first disjunct. I opt for the third alternative. (2) What is the antecedent of *quod clare concipitur?* Eisenberg thinks it is obviously *effectus*, in spite of the gender difficulties. I follow Joachim in taking it to be *aliquid.* (3) What does *particularis* modify? Most translators have favored *essentia.* I follow the NS (along with Joachim and Eisenberg) in making it modify *rei*, though grammar is neutral on the question. See also the note on *proprium* in the English-Latin-Dutch section of the Glossary-Index.

[17] OP: "vel cùm concluditur ab aliquo universali, quod semper aliqua proprietas comitatur"; the NS in effect supplies *causa* as the subject of *concluditur*: "when one infers the cause from some universal which is always accompanied by some property." Elwes takes the *quod* clause as subject: "when it is inferred from some general proposition that some property is always present." Koyré has: "when one draws a conclusion from the fact that a universal is always accompanied by a certain property." Interpreting Spinoza's note f as I do, I would say that the something which is inferred is a clearly conceived property of a cause, though this is inconsistent with the general description of this kind of knowledge at II/10/16. I am not much moved by the latter consideration, since the second example given in § 21 is also inconsistent with the general description. See the discussions in Joachim 2, 30-32, and Curley 2, 40-49.

die of the same illness. Again, I also know by random experience that oil is capable of feeding fire, and that water is capable of putting it out. I know also that the dog is a barking animal, and man a rational one. And in this way I know almost all the things that are useful in life.

[21] But we infer [one thing][18] from another in this way: after we clearly perceive that we feel such a body, and no other, then, I say, we infer clearly that the soul is united[g] to the body, which union is the cause of such a sensation; but we cannot understand absolutely from this what[h] that sensation and union are. Or after we have come to know the nature of vision, and that it has the property that we see one and the same thing as smaller when we look at it from a great distance than when we look at it from close up, we infer that the sun is larger than it appears to be, and other things of the same kind.[20]

[22] Finally, a thing is perceived through its essence alone when, from the fact that I know something, I know what it is to know something, or from the fact that I know the essence of the soul, I know that it is united to the body. By the same kind of knowledge, we know that two and three are five, and that if two lines are parallel to a third line, they are also parallel to each other, etc. But the things I have so far been able to know by this kind of knowledge have been very few.

[23] That you may understand all these things better, I shall use only one example. Suppose there are three numbers. Someone is seeking a fourth, which is to the third as the second is to the first. Here merchants will usually say that they know what to do to find the fourth number, because they have not yet forgotten that procedure

---

g We see clearly from this example what I have just noted. For we understand nothing through that union except the sensation itself, that is, the effect,[19] from which we inferred the cause, concerning which we understand nothing.

h Although such a conclusion is certain, it is still not sufficiently safe, unless we take the greatest care. For those who do not take such care will immediately fall into errors. When things are conceived so abstractly, and not through their true essence, they are immediately confused by the imagination. What in itself is one, men imagine to be many. For to the things they conceive abstractly, separately, and confusedly, they give names which they use to signify other more familiar things. Hence they imagine these things in the same way as they are accustomed to imagine the things to which the names were first given.

18 I follow Appuhn, Koyré et al., in supplying "one thing" here; parallelism with II/10/16 would require the "essence of a thing," but the strict accuracy of that description is put in some doubt both by the second example Spinoza gives and by his note to II/10/17.

19 OP: *effectus*, which is ungrammatical, given seventeenth-century conventions about the use of accents. Gebhardt emends to: *effectûs*, "of the effect." But most translators have preferred to emend to *effectum*, which is supported by the NS, and which I take to be correct.

20 Cf. § 78.

25 which they simply heard from their teachers, without any demonstration.

II/12 Others will construct a universal axiom from an experience with simple numbers, where the fourth number is evident through itself—as in the numbers 2, 4, 3, and 6. Here they find by trial that if the second is multiplied by the third, and the product then divided by the first, the result is 6. Since they see that this produces the same number
5 which they knew to be the proportional number without this procedure, they infer that the procedure is always a good way to find the fourth number in the proportion.

[24] But Mathematicians know, by the force of the demonstration of Proposition 19 in Book VII of Euclid, which [21] numbers are proportional to one another, from the nature of proportion, and its property, viz. that the product of the first and fourth numbers is equal to
10 the product of the second and third. Nevertheless, they do not see the adequate proportionality of the given numbers. And if they do, they see it not by the force of that Proposition, but intuitively, [NS: or] without going through any procedure.

[25] To choose the best mode of perceiving from these, we are required to enumerate briefly the means necessary to attain our end:
15

1.[22] To know exactly our nature, which we desire to perfect, and at the same time,

2. [To know] as much of the nature of things as is necessary,
(a) to infer rightly from it the differences, agreements and
20 oppositions of things,
(b) to conceive rightly what they can undergo and what they cannot,
(c) to compare [the nature of things] with the nature and power of man.

This done, the highest perfection man can reach will easily manifest itself.
25 [26] Having considered these requirements, let us see which mode of perceiving we ought to choose.

As for the first, it is evident in itself that from report—apart from the fact that it is a very uncertain thing—we do not perceive any essence of a thing, as is clear from our example. And since the exist-
30 ence of any singular thing[23] is not known unless its essence is known

[21] OP: "*quales*," 'what kind of;' but NS: *welke*. Cf. Joachim 2, 31, n. 2.
[22] Here I adopt Joachim's emendation of the numbering and punctuation. Joachim 2, 34, n 2.
[23] OP: "*singularis existentia alicujus rei.*" As at II/10/34, this is ambiguous. Here the NS take *singularis* to modify *existentia*, but wrongly, I think.

15

(as we shall see afterwards), we can clearly infer from this that all the certainty we have from report is to be excluded from the sciences. For no one will ever be able to be affected by simple report, unless his own intellect has gone before.

II/13   [27] As for the second,[i] again, no one should be said to have the idea of that[24] proportion which he is seeking. Apart from the fact that it is a very uncertain thing, and without end, in this way no one will ever perceive anything in natural things except accidents. But these
5   are never understood clearly unless their essences are known first. So that also is to be excluded.

     [28] Concerning the third, on the other hand, we can, in a sense, say that we have an idea of the thing, and that we can also make inferences without danger of error. But still, it will not through itself
10   be the means of our reaching our perfection.

     [29] Only the fourth mode comprehends the adequate essence of the thing and is without danger of error. For that reason, it is what we must chiefly use. So we shall take care to explain how it is to be used, that we may understand unknown things by this kind of knowledge
15   and do so as directly as possible; [30] [NS: i.e.] after we know what Knowledge is necessary for us, we must teach the Way and Method by which we may achieve this kind of knowledge of the things that are to be known.

     To do this, the first thing we must consider is that there is no infinite regress here. That is, to find the best Method of seeking the
20   truth, there is no need of another Method to seek the Method of seeking the truth, or of a third Method to seek the second, and so on, to infinity. For in that way we would never arrive at knowledge of the truth, or indeed at any knowledge.

     Matters here stand as they do with corporeal tools,[25] where someone
25   might argue in the same way. For to forge iron a hammer is needed; and to have a hammer, it must be made; for this another hammer, and other tools are needed; and to have these tools too, other tools will be needed, and so on to infinity; in this way someone might try, in vain, to prove that men have no power of forging iron.

---

     [i] Here I shall discuss experience somewhat more fully, and examine the Method of proceeding of the Empiricists and of the new Philosophers [NS: . . . the Empiricists, who want to do everything through experience . . .].

     [24] OP: "*illius*," NS: "*enige*." Perhaps we should read: *ullius*, 'any'.

     [25] The comparison which follows may have been suggested by any of various passages in Bacon [e.g., I, 126 (= IV, 14); I, 152 (= IV, 40); I, 157 (= IV, 47)]. But as Joachim notes (2, 53), Spinoza makes a rather different use of the comparison. Similar remarks apply to a passage in Descartes' *Regulae* (AT X, 397). Neither Bacon nor Descartes uses the analogy to counter a threatened regress.

30   [31] But just as men, in the beginning, were able to make the easiest things with the tools they were born with (however laboriously and imperfectly), and once these had been made, made other, more difficult things with less labor and more perfectly, and so, proceeding
II/14 gradually from the simplest works to tools, and from tools to other works and tools, reached the point where they accomplished so many and so difficult things with little labor, in the same way the intellect, by its inborn power,[k] makes intellectual tools for itself, by which it
5   acquires other powers for other intellectual works,[l] and from these works still other tools, or the power of searching further, and so proceeds by stages, until it reaches the pinnacle of wisdom.

      [32] It will be easy to see that this is the situation of the intellect, provided we understand what the Method of seeking the truth is, and
10   what those inborn tools are, which it requires only[26] to make other tools from them, so as to advance further. To show this, I proceed as follows.

      [33] A[27] true idea[m] (for we have a true idea) is something different from its object. For a circle is one thing and an idea of the circle
15   another—the idea of the circle is not something which has a circumference and a center, as the circle does. Nor is an idea of the body the body itself. And since it is something different from its object, it will also be something intelligible through itself; that is, the idea, as far as its formal essence is concerned, can be the object of another objective essence, and this other objective essence in turn will also be, consid-
20   ered in itself, something real and intelligible, and so on, indefinitely.

      [34] Peter, for example, is something real; but a true idea of Peter[28] is an objective essence of Peter, and something real in itself, and altogether different from Peter himself. So since an idea of Peter is something real, having its own particular essence, it will also be some-

---

[k] By inborn power I understand what is not caused in us by external causes. I shall explain this afterwards in my Philosophy.

[l] Here they are called works. In my Philosophy, I shall explain what they are.

[m] Note that here we shall take care to show not only what we have just said, but also that we have so far proceeded rightly, and at the same time other things that it is quite necessary to know.

[26] Spinoza does seem to mean that these inborn tools are needed only provisionally, until better ones can be made with them, though as Joachim remarks (2, 54, n. 1) this is obscure. Other translators (e.g., Appuhn, Koyré) take Spinoza to mean that these inborn tools are all the intellect requires to make more advanced ones.

[27] NS: "The true idea." But I take it that this must be a generalizing use of the definite article, since no basis has been laid for reference to any particular true idea (or for any assumption that, ultimately, there is only one true idea).

[28] Joachim (2, 54, n. 2, 80, n. 1) contends that by a "true idea of Peter" Spinoza here means the true idea which someone else may have of Peter. The example Spinoza gives at the end of this paragraph seems to confirm this.

17

thing intelligible, i.e., the object of a second idea, which will have in itself, objectively, whatever the idea of Peter has formally; and in turn, the idea which is [the idea] of the idea of Peter has again its essence, which can also be the object of another idea, and so on indefinitely. Everyone can experience this, when he sees that he knows what Peter is, and also knows that he knows, and again, knows that he knows that he knows, etc.

From this it is evident that to understand the essence of Peter, it is not necessary to understand an idea of Peter, much less an idea of an idea of Peter. This is the same as if I said that, in order for me to know, it is not necessary to know that I know, much less necessary to know that I know that I know—no more than it is necessary to understand the essence of a circle in order to understand the essence of a triangle.[n] Indeed, in these ideas the opposite is the case. For to know that I know, I must first know.

[35] From this it is clear that certainty is nothing but the objective essence itself, i.e., the mode by which we are aware of the formal essence[29] is certainty itself. And from this, again, it is clear that, for the certainty of the truth, no other sign is needed than having a true idea. For as we have shown, in order for me to know, it is not necessary to know that I know. From which, once more, it is clear that no one can know what the highest certainty is unless he has an adequate idea or objective essence of some thing. For certainty and an objective essence are the same thing.

[36] Since truth, therefore, requires no sign, but it suffices, in order to remove all doubt, to have the objective essences of things, or, what is the same, ideas, it follows that the true Method is not to seek a sign of truth after the acquisition of ideas, but the true Method is the way that truth itself, or the objective essences of things, or the ideas (all those signify the same) should be sought[o] in the proper order.

[37] Again, the Method must speak about Reasoning, or[30] about the intellection; i.e., Method is not the reasoning itself by which we understand the causes of things; much less the understanding of the causes of things, it is understanding what a true idea is by distinguishing it

---

[n] Note that here we are not asking how the first objective essence is inborn in us. For that pertains to the investigation of nature, where we explain these things more fully, and at the same time show that apart from the idea there is neither affirmation, nor negation, nor any will.

[o] In my Philosophy, I shall explain what seeking is in the soul.

[29] OP: "*modus, quo sentimus essentiam formalem.*" It is unclear whether *modus* should be taken as a technical term here.

[30] Perhaps, as Joachim suggests (2, 162, n. 4), we should read *et* for *aut* here: "Reasoning and intellection."

18

25   from the rest of the perceptions; by investigating its nature, so that from that we may come to know our power of understanding and so restrain the mind that it understands, according to that standard, everything that is to be understood; and finally by teaching and constructing certain rules as aids, so that the mind does not weary itself in useless things.

30   [38] From this it may be inferred that Method is nothing but a
II/16 reflexive knowledge, or an idea of an idea; and because there is no idea of an idea, unless there is first an idea, there will be no Method unless there is first an idea. So that Method will be good which shows how the mind is to be directed according the standard of a given true idea.[31]

5   Next, since the relation between the two ideas is the same as the relation between the formal essences of those ideas, it follows that the reflexive knowledge of the idea of the most perfect Being will be more excellent than the reflexive knowledge of any other ideas. That is, the most perfect Method will be the one that shows how the mind is to be directed according to the standard of the given idea of the most
10 perfect Being.

   [39] From this you will easily understand how the mind, as it understands more things, at the same time acquires other tools, with which it proceeds to understand more easily. For, as may be inferred from what has been said, before all else there must be a true idea in us, as an inborn tool; once this true idea is understood, we understand
15 the difference between that kind of perception and all the rest. Understanding that difference constitutes one part of the Method.

   And since it is clear through itself that the mind understands itself the better, the more it understands of Nature, it is evident, from that that this part of the Method will be more perfect as the mind understands more things, and will be most perfect when the mind attends
20 to, *or* reflects on, knowledge of the most perfect Being.

   [40] Next, the more the mind knows, the better it understands its own powers and the order of Nature. The better the mind understands its own powers, the more easily it can direct itself and propose rules to itself; the better it understands the order of Nature, the more

---

[31] OP: "*datae verae ideae*"; NS: " *'t gestelde ware denkbeelt.*" Koyré argues that the term *datae* in this kind of expression is best suppressed, since it does not imply what it is likely to suggest, viz. that the true idea is given to us. All that is implied is that there is a true idea. Gueroult (1, 1:30, n. 42) argues against this that the qualification implies that the true idea is an actual eternal essence in the infinite or finite intellect, and hence produced by God, not by the intellect. Man finds the Idea "en lui sans lui." Although uncertain of the correctness of Gueroult's interpretation, I find it impossible to follow Koyré's policy, which seems to lead to serious difficulty in contexts like § 43.

easily it can restrain itself from useless pursuits. In these things, as we have said, the whole of the Method consists.

[41] Moreover, the idea is objectively in the same way as its object is really. So if there were something in Nature that did not interact with other things, and if there were an objective essence of that thing which would have to agree completely with its formal essence, then that objective essence would not interact[p] with other ideas, i.e., we could not infer anything about it.[32] And conversely, those things that do interact with other things (as everything that exists in Nature does) will be understood, and their objective essences will also have the same interaction, i.e., other ideas will be deduced from them, and these again will interact with other ideas, and so the tools for proceeding further will increase, which is what we were trying to demonstrate.

[42] Next, from what we have just said, that an idea must agree completely with its formal essence, it is evident that for our mind to reproduce completely the likeness of Nature,[33] it must bring all of its ideas forth from that idea which represents the source and origin of the whole of Nature, so that that idea is also the source of the other ideas.

[43] Here, perhaps, someone will be surprised that, having said that a good Method is one which shows how the mind is to be directed according to the standard of a given true idea, we should prove this by reasoning. For that seems to show that this is not known through itself. So it may be asked whether our reasoning is good? If our reasoning is good, we must begin from a given [true?] idea; and since to begin from a given [true?] idea requires a demonstration, we must

[p] To interact with other things is to produce, or be produced by, other things.

[32] The NS version of this sentence runs: "If there were something in nature that did not interact with other things, then its objective essence, which would have to agree completely with the formal essence, would also not interact with other ideas, i.e., we would not be able to understand or infer anything about it." I have translated the Latin (as emended by Gebhardt to correct a grammatical mistake); Gebhardt thinks it obvious that the conditionalization of the reference to the objective essence is a change made by Spinoza after the Dutch translation was done. But I share Joachim's feeling (2, 100, n. 2) that the Dutch makes better sense. Gebhardt also adds a phrase in l. 31 from the Dutch, so that the conclusion of the sentence might be translated: "we could neither understand nor infer. . . ." But it is very unlikely that this indicates an earlier and fuller about the translation of this clause. Joachim (2, 100) offers: "that our mind may reflect use two Dutch verbs to render one Latin one."

[33] OP: "*ut mens nostra omninò referat Naturae exemplar.*" It is difficult to be confident about the translation of this clause. Joachim (2, 100) offers: "that our mind may reflect ideally in all respects its real Original—i.e., may reflect the formal essence of Nature in its totality and in all its parts," drawing on § 91 for the gloss. As Joachim points out later (215, n. 1) this passage is prima facie incompatible with his interpretation of Spinoza's conception of truth.

again prove our reasoning, and then once more prove that other reasoning, and so on to infinity.

[44] To this I reply that if, by some fate, someone had proceeded
in this way in investigating Nature, i.e., by acquiring other ideas in
the proper order, according to the standard of the given true idea, he
would never have doubted[q] the truth he possessed (for as we have
shown, the truth makes itself manifest) and also everything would
have flowed to him of its own accord.[34]

But because this never or rarely happens, I have been forced to lay
things down in this way, so that what we cannot acquire by fate, we
may still acquire by a deliberate plan, and at the same time so that it
would be evident that to prove the truth and good reasoning, we require no tools except the truth itself and good reasoning. For I have
proved, and still strive to prove, good reasoning by good reasoning.
[45] Moreover, in this way men become accustomed to their own internal meditations.

But the reason why Nature is rarely investigated in the proper order, is, first, that men have prejudices whose causes we shall explain
afterwards in our Philosophy. And then, the task requires a considerable capacity for making accurate distinctions (as we shall show later)
and much effort. Finally, there is the condition of human affairs, which
are quite changeable, as we have already shown. There are still other
reasons, which we shall not go into.

II/18   [46] If, by chance, someone should ask why I did [not][35] immedi-

___

[q] As we also do not here doubt the truth we possess.

[34] I believe § 104 provides a helpful gloss on this passage.

[35] There is no negation in either the OP or the NS, but most editors have felt the
need to supply one. If one is supplied, then it seems we must also assume a gap in the
text after "I reply to him." Koyré understands the text in this fashion, and conjectures
that Spinoza eventually came to regard the objection as well-founded, so that he con-
centrated on the *Ethics* and put the *Treatise* to one side (cf. his note to this passage, and
the *Avant-propos*).

Gebhardt at one stage thought likewise, but by the time he produced his edition of
the *Works* had come to the conclusion that the text must be defended, not emended (II/
326-327). He takes Spinoza to be replying not to an objection to his procedure here,
but to an objection to his procedure in his projected *Philosophy*. Eisenberg (1, 45-49, n.
82) joins Gebhardt in defending the text.

I prefer Koyré's reading. I cannot deal fully here with the arguments offered by
Gebhardt and Eisenberg, but I will make the following observations: (1) the text of the
OP is supported by the NS, but if the conjectured omissions were in Spinoza's ms.,
this confirmation does not amount to much; quite possibly the ms. contained a passage
which Spinoza struck out and never replaced; (2) I do not see why the emendation
would make § 46 a mere duplication of II/17/8-34; (3) if Spinoza were switching suddenly from a defense of his procedure in the *TdIE* to a defense of his procedure in his
Philosophy, I would expect a more explicit indication of it; (4) Eisenberg construes *osten-
derim* in II/18/2 as a future perfect (indicative): "If anyone should seek [perhaps] to know
why I shall have shown the truths of Nature in that order at once, before everything.

ately, before anything else, display the truths of Nature in that order—for does not the truth make itself manifest?—I reply to him [. . .]
and at the same time I warn him not to try to reject these things as
false because of Paradoxes that occur here and there; he should first
deign to consider the order in which we prove them, and then he will
become certain that we have reached the truth; and this was the reason
why I have put these things first.

[47] But perhaps, afterwards, some Skeptic would still doubt both
the first truth itself and everything we shall deduce according to the
standard of the first truth. If so, then either he will speak contrary to
his own conciousness, or we shall confess that there are men whose
minds also are completely blinded, either from birth, or from prejudices, i.e., because of some external chance. For they are not even
aware of themselves. If they affirm or doubt something, they do not
know that they affirm or doubt. They say that they know nothing,
and that they do not even know that they know nothing. And even
this they do not say absolutely. For they are afraid to confess that
they exist, so long as they know nothing. In the end, they must be
speechless, lest by chance they assume something that might smell of
truth.

[48] Finally, there is no speaking of the sciences with them. (For as
far as the needs of life and society are concerned, necessity forces them
to suppose that they exist, and to seek their own advantage, and in
taking oaths, to affirm and deny many things.) For, if someone proves
something to them, they do not know whether the argument is a proof
or not. If they deny, grant, or oppose, they do not know that they
deny, grant, or oppose. So they must be regarded as automata, completely lacking a mind.

[49] Let us now return to our subject. First [§§ 1-17], we have treated
the end toward which we strive to direct all our thoughts; second [§§
18-29], we learned which is the best perception, by whose aid we can
reach our perfection; third [§§ 30-48], we learned which is the first
path our mind must enter on to begin well—which is to proceed in
its investigation according to certain laws, taking as a standard a given
true idea.

If this is to be done properly, the Method must, first [§§ 50-90],
show how to distinguish a true idea from all other perceptions, and to
restrain the mind from those other perceptions; second [§§ 91-98],

---

. . . But both morphology and syntax require us to construe it as present perfect subjunctive. And the concluding line of the paragraph (in which Eisenberg construes *prae-
miserim* as present perfect subjunctive) makes it clear that Spinoza intends to defend
what he has already done.

35
II/19

teach rules so that we may perceive things unknown according to such a standard; third [§ 99–?], establish an order, so that we do not become weary with trifles. When we came to know this Method [§ 38], we saw, fourth, that it will be most perfect when we have the idea of the most perfect Being. So in the beginning we must take the greatest care that we arrive at knowledge of such a Being as quickly as possible.

5

[50] Let us begin, therefore, from the first part of the Method, which is, as we have said, to distinguish and separate true ideas from all other perceptions, and to restrain the mind from confusing false, fictitious, and doubtful ideas with true ones. It is my intention to explain this fully here, so as to engage my Readers in the thought of a thing so necessary, and also because there are many who doubt even true ideas, from not attending to the distinction between a true perception and all others. So they are like men who, when they were awake, used not to doubt that they were awake, but who, after they once thought in a dream that they were certainly awake (as often happens), and later found that to be false, doubted even of their waking states. This happens because they have never distinguished between the dream[36] and the waking state.

10

15

[51] In the meantime, I warn the reader that I shall not discuss the essence of each perception, and explain it by its proximate[37] cause, because that pertains to Philosophy, but shall discuss only what the Method demands, i.e., what false, fictitious and doubtful ideas are concerned with, and how we shall be freed from each of them. Let the first inquiry, therefore, be about the fictitious idea.

20

[52] Since every perception is either of a thing considered as existing, or of an essence alone, and since fictions occur more frequently concerning things considered as existing, I shall speak first of them— i.e., where existence alone is feigned, and the thing which is feigned in such an act is understood, *or* assumed to be understood. E.g., I feign that Peter, whom I know, is going home, that he is coming to visit me, and the like.[r] Here I ask, what does such an idea concern? I see that it concerns only possible, and not necessary or impossible things.

25

30

[53] I call a thing impossible whose nature[38] implies that it would

[r] See further what we shall note concerning hypotheses that we clearly understand; but the fiction consists in our saying that such as these exist in the heavenly bodies.

[36] OP: "*somnum*," but NS: "*dromen*." So probably we should read: *somnium*.

[37] NS: "*eerste/prima*." So perhaps Spinoza originally wrote: "first cause."

[38] Gebhardt adds the phrase "in existing" from the NS, but I agree with Joachim (2, 116, n. 2) that this is at least unnecessary, if not wrong. Similarly Gebhardt's addition at II/19/1 seems wrong given that Spinoza goes on (both in the OP and in the NS) to enumerate a fourth task of the method. His text would be translated: "Third [NS: and finally]. . . ."

II/20 be contradictory for it to exist; necessary whose nature implies that it would be contradictory for it not to exist; and possible whose exist-ence,[39] by its very nature, does not imply a contradiction—either for it to exist or for it not to exist—but whose necessity or impossibility of existence depends on causes unknown to us, so long as we feign its

5 existence. So if its necessity or impossibility, which depends on ex-ternal causes, were known to us, we would have been able to feign nothing concerning it.

[54] From this it follows that, if there is a God, or something om-niscient, he can feign nothing at all.[40] For as far as We are concerned, after I know that I exist,[s] I cannot feign either that I exist or that I do

10 not exist; nor can I feign an elephant which passes through the eye of a needle; nor, after I know the nature of God, can I feign either that he exists or that he does not exist.[t] The same must be understood of the Chimera, whose nature implies that it would be contradictory for it to exist. From this what I have said is evident: that the fiction of which we are speaking here does not occur concerning eternal truths.[u]

15 I shall also show immediately that no fiction is concerned with eternal truths.

[55] But before proceeding further, I must note here in passing that

[s] Because the thing makes itself evident, provided it is understood, we require only an example, without other proof. The same is true of its contradictory—it need only be examined for its falsity to be clear. This will be plain immediately, when we speak of fictions concerning essence.

[t] Note. Although many say that they doubt whether God exists, nevertheless they have nothing but the name, or they feign something which they call God; this does not agree with the nature of God, as I shall show later in the proper place.

[u] By an eternal truth I mean one, which, if it is affirmative, will never be able to be negative. Thus it is a first and eternal truth *that God is*; but *that Adam thinks* is not an eternal truth. *That there is no Chimera* is an eternal truth; but not *that Adam does not think*.

[39] Joachim (ibid.) suggests reading *essentia*, though the OP's *existentia* is supported by the NS. If it were not for the immediately following phrase (*ipsâ suâ naturâ*), I would think this almost certainly correct. I have translated the Latin as it stands, but (with Eisenberg) I feel certain that what Spinoza *means* is that the essence of the thing by itself does not entail either that the thing cannot, or that it must, exist.

[40] The text of the OP would be translated: "From this it follows that, if there is a God, or something omniscient, we (*nos*) can feign nothing at all. Since this makes very little sense, earlier editors and translators often supplied a phrase to fill it out: "we can feign nothing at all about it." Gebhardt's text, which I have translated, reads *eum* for *nos*, following the NS. Slightly preferable, perhaps, would be van Vloten and Land's *hoc* (= this being) for *nos*. Textual emendation is a dangerous game, but if anything in this area is certain, we can be sure that the text of the OP is corrupt. For a full discus-sion see Gebhardt (II/328-330) or Eisenberg 2, 56-60. Eisenberg gives a clear explanation of the thought: since hypotheses concern only the possible (i.e., things whose existence or nonexistence depends on causes unknown to us), a being to whom nothing was unknown would not be able to regard anything as merely possible, hence would not be able to form hypotheses about anything.

24

the same difference that exists between the essence of one thing and the essence of another also exists between the actuality or existence of the one thing and the actuality or existence of the other. So if we wished to conceive the existence of Adam, for example, through existence in general, it would be the same as if, to conceive his essence, we attended to the nature of being, so that in the end we defined him by saying that Adam is a being. Therefore, the more generally existence is conceived, the more confusedly also it is conceived, and the more easily it can be ascribed fictitiously to anything. Conversely, the more particularly it is conceived, then the more clearly it is understood, and the more difficult it is for us, [even] when we do not attend to the order of Nature, to ascribe it fictitiously to anything other than the thing itself.[41] This is worth noting.

[56] Now we must consider those things that are commonly said to be feigned, although we understood clearly that the thing is not really as we feign it. E.g., although I know that the earth is round, nothing prevents me from saying to someone that the earth is a hemisphere and like half an orange on a plate, or that the sun moves around the earth, and the like. If we attend to these things, we shall see nothing that is not compatible with what we have already said, provided we note first that we have sometimes been able to err, and now are conscious of our errors; and then, we can feign, or at least allow, that other men are in the same error, or can fall into it, as we did previously.

We can feign this, I say, so long as we see no impossibility and no necessity. Therefore, when I say to someone that the earth is not round, etc., I am doing nothing but recalling the error which I, perhaps, made, or into which I could have fallen, and afterwards feigning, or allowing, that he to whom I say this is still in the same error, or can fall into it. As I have said, I feign this so long as I see no impossibility and no necessity. For if I had understood this, I could

---

[41] The clause "when (*ubi*) we do not attend to the order of Nature" is puzzling enough to have prompted attempts at emendation. Gebhardt is probably right to reject Elbogen's suggestion that it has simply been misplaced, but might have considered more seriously Stern's suggestion that we should read *etsi* for *ubi*: "*even if* we do not attend . . ." It would not take a great deal of carelessness in the writing or the reading for a handwritten *etsi* to be taken for an *ubi* and *etsi* would not require a subjunctive (*pace* Gebhardt). Koyré (2, 106) has a plausible gloss: for Spinoza there are as many modes and degrees of existence as there are modes and degrees of essence; the existence of a man is different from that of an animal or an inanimate object; even when we do not attend to the order of nature (which is a necessary, but not sufficient condition of all feigning), we cannot attribute to a man an animal's mode of existence unless we think in general terms.

have feigned nothing at all, and it would have had to be said only that I had done something.[42]

[57] It remains now to note also those things that are supposed in Problems. This sometimes happens even concerning impossible things. E.g., when we say "Let us suppose that this burning candle is not now burning, or let us suppose that it is burning in some imaginary space, *or* where there are no bodies." Things like this are sometimes supposed, although this last is clearly understood to be impossible.[43] But when this happens, nothing at all is feigned. For in the first case I have done nothing but recall to memory[x] another candle that was not burning (or I have conceived this candle without the flame), and what I think about that candle, I understand concerning this one, so long as I do not attend to the flame.

In the second case, nothing is done except to abstract the thoughts from the surrounding bodies so that the mind directs itself toward the sole contemplation of the candle, considered in itself alone, so that afterwards it infers that the candle has no cause for its destruction. So if there were no surrounding bodies, this candle, and its flame, would remain immutable, or the like. Here, then, there is no fiction, but[y] true and sheer assertions.[44]

[58] Let us pass now to fictions that concern either essences alone or essences together with some actuality *or* existence. The most important consideration regarding them is that the less the mind understands and the more things it perceives, the greater its power of feign-

---

[x] Afterwards, when we speak of fiction that concerns essences, it will be clear that the fiction never makes, or presents to the mind, anything new, but that only things which are in the brain or the imagination are recalled to memory, and that the mind attends confusedly to all of them at once. Speech and a tree, for example, are recalled to memory, and since the mind attends confusedly, without distinction, it allows that the tree speaks. The same is understood concerning existence, especially, as we have said, when it is conceived so generally, as being. Then it is easily applied to all things which occur in the mind together. This is very much worth noting.

[y] The same must also be understood concerning the hypotheses that are made to explain certain motions, which agree with the phenomena of the heavens; except that when people apply them to the celestial motions, they infer the nature of the heavens from them. But that nature can be different, especially since many other causes can be conceived to explain such motions.

[42] Koyré suggests glossing "done something" by "uttered some words."

[43] Joachim (2, 120 n.) suggests that Spinoza has in mind Descartes' *Principles* IV, 95-101, though it is not clear that Descartes is there involved in either of the suppositions Spinoza here discusses.

[44] I have translated the text of the OP ("*verae ac merae assertiones*") as it stands, but in spite of the support of the NS and Joachim's defense (2, 121, n. 2), I question whether *verae* ('true') is correct. Appuhn has: "assertions pure and simple," which seems more in keeping with parallel passages (II/21/20-21, 21/27-28, 22/20-21).

ing is; and the more things it understands, the more that power is diminished.

For example, as we have seen above, we cannot feign, so long as we are thinking, that we are thinking and are not thinking; in the same way, after we know the nature of body, we cannot feign an infinite fly, or after we know the nature of the soul,[z] we cannot feign that it is square, though there is nothing that cannot be put into words.

But as we have said, the less men know Nature, the more easily they can feign many things, such as, that trees speak, that men are changed in a moment into stones and into springs, that nothing becomes something, that even Gods are changed into beasts and into men, and infinitely many other things of that kind.[45]

[59] Someone, perhaps, will think that fiction is limited by fiction, but not by intellection.[46] That is, after I have feigned something, and willed by a certain freedom to assent that it exists in nature in this way, this has the consequence that I cannot afterwards think it in any other way. For example, after I have feigned (to speak as they do) that body has such a nature, and willed, from my freedom, to be convinced that it really exists in this way, I can no longer feign an infinite fly; and after I have feigned the essence of the soul, I can no longer feign that it is square.

[60] But this needs to be examined. First, either they deny or they grant that we can understand something. If they grant it, then necessarily what they say about fiction will also have to be said about intellection. But if they deny it, let us—who know that we know something—see what they say.

Evidently, they say that the soul can sense and perceive in many ways, not itself, nor the things that exist, but only those things that are neither in itself nor anywhere; that is, the soul can, by its own force alone, create sensations or ideas, which are not of things; so they consider it, to some extent, as like God.[47]

[z] It often happens that a man recalls this term *soul* to his memory, and at the same time forms some corporeal image. But since these two things are represented together, he easily allows that he imagines and feigns a corporeal soul: because he does not distinguish the name from the thing itself. Here I ask my readers not to hasten to refute this, which, as I hope, they will not do, provided that they attend as accurately as possible to the examples, and at the same time, to the things that follow.

[45] Elbogen points out that most of Spinoza's examples come from Ovid's *Metamorphoses*. But note that there seem to be references also to the Judaeo-Christian doctrine of creation and the Christian doctrine of the incarnation. Cf. Parkinson, 101-102, and E IP8S2, II/49/35.

[46] Koyré sees an allusion both to theologians who hold a voluntarist theory of belief and to Hobbes' *De Corpore* I, iii, 8.

[47] Wolfson (1, 2:110-111) thought that this passage was undoubtedly directed against

Next, they say that we, or our soul, has such a freedom that it compels us, or itself, indeed its own freedom. For after it has feigned something, and offered its assent to it, it cannot think or feign it in any other way, and is also compelled by that fiction so that even other things are thought in such a way as not to conflict with the first fiction. As they are here forced to admit the absurdities which I review here, because of their own fiction, we shall not bother to refute them with any demonstrations.

[61] Rather, leaving them to their madness, we shall take care to draw from the words we have exchanged with them something true and to our purpose, viz.:ª when the mind attends to a fictitious thing which is false by its very nature, so that it considers it carefully, and understands it, and deduces from it in good order the things to be deduced, it will easily bring its falsity to light. And if the fictitious thing is true by its nature, then when the mind attends to it, so that it understands it, and begins to deduce from it in good order the things that follow from it, it will proceed successfully, without any interruption—just as we have seen that, from the false fiction just mentioned, the intellect immediately applies itself to show its absurdity, and the other things deduced from that.

[62] So we ought not to fear in any way that we are feigning something, if only we perceive the thing clearly and distinctly. For if by chance we should say that men are changed in a moment into beasts, that is said very generally, so that there is in the mind no concept, i.e., idea, *or* connection of subject and predicate. For if there were any concept, the mind would see together the means and causes, how and why such a thing was done. And one does not attend to the nature of the subject and of the predicate.

Descartes, citing *The Passions of the Soul* III, 152. He might, with equal justice, have cited the Fourth Meditation's claim that it is principally our free will that justifies our thinking of ourselves as made in God's image (AT VII, 57). De Deugd (90-91) countered that Descartes nevertheless does not ascribe to man a power to create ideas *ex nihilo* (which is what is in question here in § 60). Still, I do not think that would be a terribly implausible reading of certain passages in the Third Meditation (AT VII, 43-44). Descartes may be the target.

ª Although I seem to infer this from experience, and someone may say that this is nothing, because a demonstration is lacking, he may have one, if he wishes; since there can be nothing in nature that is contrary to its laws, but since all things happen according to certain laws of nature, so that they produce their certain effects, by certain laws, in an unbreakable connection, it follows from this that when the soul conceives a thing truly, it proceeds to form the same effects objectively. See below, where I speak of the false idea. [In the OP this note is attached to the last sentence in § 60. Gebhardt places it here, following the NS. De Deugd has defended the placement of the OP (88, n. 1). But Eisenberg (2, 69) argues persuasively that the note is intended, not to disprove the view discussed in § 60, but to support the view presented in § 61.]

28

[63] Next, provided the first idea is not fictitious, and all the other ideas are deduced from it, the haste to feign things will gradually disappear. And since a fictitious idea cannot be clear and distinct, but only confused, and since all confusion results from the fact that the mind knows only in part a thing that is a whole, or composed of many things, and does not distinguish the known from the unknown (and besides, attends at once, without making any distinction, to the many things that are contained in each thing), from this it follows, first, that if an idea is of some most simple thing, it can only be clear and distinct. For that thing will have to become known, not in part, but either as a whole or not at all.[48]

[64] Secondly, it follows that if, in thought, we divide a thing that is composed of many things into all its most simple parts, and attend to each of these separately, all confusion will disappear.

Thirdly, it follows that a fiction cannot be simple, but that it is made from the composition of different confused ideas, which are different things and actions existing in nature; or rather, from attending at once,[b] without assent, to such different ideas. For if it were simple, it would be clear and distinct, and consequently true. And if it were made from the composition of distinct ideas, their composition would also be clear and distinct, and therefore true. For example, once we know the nature of the circle, and also the nature of the square, we cannot then compound these two and make a square circle, or a square soul, and the like.

[65] Let us sum up again briefly, and see why we do not need to fear that the fiction will in any way be confused with true ideas. For as for the first [fiction][49] of which we spoke before, viz. where the thing is clearly conceived, we saw that if that thing that is clearly conceived (and also its existence) is, through itself, an eternal truth, we can feign nothing concerning such a thing. But if the existence of the thing conceived is not an eternal truth, we need only to take care to

---

[b] Note that the fiction, considered in itself, does not differ much from the dream, except that the causes which appear to the waking by the aid of the senses, and from which they infer that those presentations are not presented at that time by things outside them, do not appear in dreams. But error, as will be evident immediately, is dreaming while awake. And if it is very obvious, it is called madness.

[48] This sentence occurs only in the OP, which may indicate either an oversight on the part of the translator (as Leopold thought) or a later addition (as Gebhardt thought). This paragraph and the following are very strongly reminiscent of Descartes' teaching in the *Regulae*, Rules 10 and 12, AT X, 399, 418, and 420. But even here there is nothing Spinoza could have derived only from Descartes. As Koyré points out, a similar doctrine is taught by St. Thomas, *Summa theologiae*, Ia. 17, 3.

[49] OP: "*primam*," NS: "*het eerste denkbeelt*" (= *ideam*). But parallelism with l. 12 requires: *fictionem*.

compare the existence of the thing with its essence, and at the same time attend to the order of Nature.

As for the second fiction, we said that it consists in attending at once, without assent, to different confused ideas, which are of different things and actions existing in Nature. We saw also that a most simple thing cannot be feigned, but [only] understood, and also that a composite thing can be understood, provided that we attend to the most simple parts of which it is composed. Indeed we also cannot feign from them any actions that are not true; for at the same time we will be forced to consider how and why such a thing happened.

[66] With these matters thus understood, let us pass now to the investigation of the false idea so that we may see what it is concerned with, and how we can take care not to fall into false perceptions. Neither of these will be difficult for us now, after our investigation of the fictitious idea. For between fictitious and false ideas there is no other difference except that the latter suppose assent; i.e. (as we have already noted), while the presentations appear to him [who has the false idea], there appear no causes from which he can infer (as he who is feigning can) that they do not arise from things outside him. And this is hardly anything but dreaming with open eyes, *or* while we are awake. Therefore the false idea is concerned with, or (to put it better) is related to the existence of a thing whose essence is known, *or* to an essence, in the same way as a fictitious idea.

[67] [The false idea] that is related to existence is emended in the same way as the fiction. For if the nature of the thing known presupposes necessary existence, it is impossible for us to be deceived concerning the existence of that thing. But if the existence of the thing is not an eternal truth (as its essence is), so that[50] its necessity or impossibility of existing depends on external causes, then take everything in the same way as we said when we were speaking of fictions. For it may be emended in the same way.

[68] As for the other kind of false idea, which is related to essences, or also to actions, such perceptions must always be confused, composed of different confused perceptions of things existing in nature— as when men are persuaded that there are divinities in the woods, in images, in animals, etc.; or that there are bodies from whose composition alone the intellect is made; or that corpses reason, walk, and speak; or that God is deceived, and the like. But ideas that are clear and distinct can never be false. For the ideas of things that are con-

[50] OP: "*sed quòd necessitas.*" Joachim (2, 153, n. 2) suggests emending by deleting *sed*. That still leaves a somewhat awkward construction. What Spinoza *means*, I think, is that the second clause is a consequence of the first, not a separate condition.

ceived clearly and distinctly, are either most simple, or composed of most simple ideas, i.e., deduced from most simple ideas. But that a most simple idea cannot be false, anyone can see—provided that he knows what the true is, *or* the intellect, and at the same time, what the false is.

[69] As for what constitutes the form of the true, it is certain that a true thought is distinguished from a false one not only by an extrinsic, but chiefly by an intrinsic denomination. For if some architect conceives a building in an orderly fashion, then although such a building never existed, and even never will exist, still the thought of it is true, and the thought is the same, whether the building exists or not.[51] On the other hand, if someone says, for example, that Peter exists, and nevertheless does not know that Peter exists, that thought, in respect to him is false, or, if you prefer, is not true, even though Peter really exists. Nor is this statement, Peter exists, true, except in respect to him who knows certainly that Peter exists.

[70] From this it follows that there is something real in ideas, through which the true are distinguished from the false. This will now have to be investigated, so that we may have the best standard of truth (for we have said that we must determine our thoughts from the given standard of a true idea, and that method is reflexive knowledge), and may know the properties of the intellect. Nor must we say that this difference arises from the fact that the true thought is knowing things through their first causes.[52] In this, indeed, it differs greatly from the false, as I have explained it above. For that Thought is also called true which involves objectively the essence of some principle that does not have a cause, and is known through itself and in itself.

[71] So the form of the true thought[53] must be placed in the same thought itself without relation to other things, nor does it recognize the object as its cause, but must depend on the very power and nature of the intellect. For if we should suppose that the intellect had perceived some new being, which has never existed (as some conceive God's intellect, before he created things—for that perception, of course,

---

[51] As Joachim notes (2, 91-98), there are two passages in Descartes that Spinoza may have in mind here, one in the Fifth Meditation and one in the Second Replies (AT VII, 64, 103-104). Spinoza's examples are awkward for those interpreters who emphasize other passages in which Spinoza apparently adopts a correspondence theory of truth (e.g., myself, in Curley 3, 52-56, 122-126, 134-137, 142). But the examples are awkward in any case, since apparently incompatible with the general proposition they are supposed to illustrate, which is not so awkward. For further discussion see Curley 9.

[52] Koyré is probably right to see an allusion to Hobbes here. Cf. *De Corpore* I, i, 8.

[53] OP: "*cogitationis*," NS: "*kennis/cognitio*." Gebhardt thinks the OP represents Spinoza's correction of a mistake he made in the ms. from which the NS translation was done.

could not have arisen from any object), and that from such a perception it deduced others legitimately, all those thoughts would be true,
and determined by no external object, but would depend only on the
power and nature of the intellect. So what constitutes the form of the
10   true thought must be sought in the same thought itself, and must be
deduced from the nature of the intellect.

[72] To investigate this, therefore, let us consider some true idea, of
which we know most certainly that its object depends on our power
of thinking, and that it has no object in nature. For it is clear from
what has already been said that we shall be able more easily to inves-
15   tigate what we wish to in such an idea. E.g., to form the concept of
a sphere, I feign a cause at will, say that a semicircle is rotated around
a center, and that the sphere is, as it were, produced by this rotation.
This idea, of course, is true, and even though we may know that no
sphere in nature was ever produced in this way, nevertheless, this
perception is true, and a very easy way of forming the concept of a
sphere.

20   Now it must be noted that this perception affirms that the semicircle is rotated, which affirmation would be false if it were not joined
to the concept of a sphere, or to a cause determining such a motion,
or absolutely, if this affirmation were isolated. For then the mind would
only tend to affirm of the semicircle nothing but motion, which neither is contained in the concept of the semicircle nor arises from the
25   concept of the cause determining the motion. So falsity consists only
in this: that something is affirmed of a thing that is not contained in
the concept we have formed of the thing, as motion or rest of the
semicircle.

From this it follows that simple thoughts cannot but be true; for
example, the simple idea of a semicircle, or of motion, or of quantity,
30   etc. Whatever they contain of affirmation matches their concept, and
does not extend itself beyond [the concept]. So we may form simple
ideas at will, without fear of error.

[73] It only remains, then, to ask by what power our mind can form
these [simple ideas] and how far this power extends. For once this is
35   discovered, we shall easily see the highest knowledge we can reach. It
II/28   is certain that this power does not extend to infinity. For when we
affirm of a thing something not contained in the concept we form of
it, that indicates a defect of our perception, *or* that we have thoughts,
5   *or* ideas, which are, as it were, mutilated and maimed. For we saw
that the motion of a semicircle is false when it is in the mind in isolation, but true if it is joined to the concept of a sphere, or to the

concept of some cause determining such a motion. But if it is—as it
seems at first[54]—of the nature of a thinking being to form true, *or
adequate*, thoughts, it is certain that inadequate ideas arise in us only
from the fact that we are a part of a thinking being, of which some
thoughts wholly constitute our mind, while others do so only in part.

[74] But we still need to consider something which was not worth
the trouble of noting concerning fictions, and which gives rise to the
greatest deception—viz. when it happens that certain things that appear in the imagination are also in the intellect, i.e., that they are
conceived clearly and distinctly. For then, so long as the distinct is
not distinguished from the confused, certainty, i.e., a true idea, is
mixed up with what is not distinct.

For example, some of the Stoics heard, perhaps, the word *soul*, and
also that the soul is immortal, which they only imagined confusedly;
they also both imagined and at the same time understood that the most
subtle bodies penetrate all others, and are not penetrated by any. Since
they imagined all these things at once—while remaining certain of this
axiom—they immediately became certain that the mind was those most
subtle bodies[55] and that those most subtle bodies were not divided,
etc.

[75] But we are freed from this also, as long as we strive to consider
all our perceptions according to the standard of a given true idea,
being on guard, as we said in the beginning, against those we have
from report or from random experience. Moreover, such a deception
arises from the fact that they conceive things too abstractly. For it is
sufficiently clear through itself that I cannot apply what I conceive in
its true object to something else. Finally, it arises also from the fact
that they do not understand the first elements of the whole of Nature;
so proceeding without order, and confusing Nature with abstractions
(although they are true axioms), they confuse themselves and overturn
the order of Nature. But we shall not need to fear any such deception,
if we proceed as far as we can in a manner that is not abstract, and
begin as soon as possible from the first elements, i.e., from the source
and origin of Nature.[56]

[54] OP: "*uti primâ fronte videtur.*" Most translators (including the NS) have taken this
to be presented as no more than a plausible hypothesis. But Joachim suggests (2, 91)
that it is presented as a self-evident principle: "as is apparent at first glance." Cf. § 106.

[55] Joachim (2, 159, n. 1) suggests following the NS, which reads: ". . . that was such
a most subtle body. . . ."

[56] Gueroult (1, 1:169 n.) identifies the "first elements of the whole of Nature," which
constitute the source and origin of Nature, with the attributes that constitute God or
substance. I agree (Curley 3, 42) and infer that God is not to be identified with the
whole of Nature, but only with *Natura naturans*.

[76]⁵⁷ But as for knowledge of the origin of Nature, we need not have any fear of confusing it with abstractions. For when things are conceived abstractly (as all universals are), they always have a wider extension in our intellect than their particulars can really have in nature. And then, since there are many things in nature whose difference is so slight that it almost escapes the intellect, it can easily happen, if they are conceived abstractly, that they are confused. But since, as we shall see later, the origin of Nature can neither be conceived abstractly, *or* universally, nor be extended more widely in the intellect than it really is, and since it has no likeness to changeable things, we need fear no confusion concerning its idea, provided that we have the standard of truth (which we have already shown). For it is a unique and infiniteᶻ being, beyond which there is no being.ᵃ

[77] So far we have been speaking of the false idea. It remains now to investigate the doubtful idea—i.e., to ask what are the things that can lead us into doubt, and at the same time, how doubt is removed. I am speaking of true doubt in the mind, and not of what we commonly see happen, when someone says in words that he doubts, although his mind does not doubt. For it is not the business of the Method to emend that. That belongs rather to the investigation of stubbornness, and its emendation.

[78] There is no doubt in the soul, therefore, through the thing itself concerning which one doubts. That is, if there should be only one idea in the soul, then, whether it is true or false, there will be neither doubt nor certainty, but only a sensation of a certain sort. For in itself [this idea] is nothing but a sensation of a certain sort.

But doubt will arise through another idea which is not so clear and distinct that we can infer from it something certain about the thing concerning which there is doubt. That is, the idea that puts us in doubt is not clear and distinct. For example, if someone has never been led, either by experience or by anything else, to think about the deceptiveness of the senses, he will never doubt whether the sun is larger or smaller than it appears to be. So Country People are generally surprised when they hear that the sun is much larger than the earth. But in thinking about the deceptiveness of the senses, doubt

---

ᶻ These are not attributes of God that show his essence, as I shall show in [my] Philosophy. [Since this topic is one taken up in the *Short Treatise* (KV I, ii-vii), but not in the *Ethics*, this note is evidence that the work referred to in the TdIE as "my Philosophy" was more like the *Short Treatise* than the *Ethics*.]

ᵃ This has already been demonstrated above. For if such a being did not exist, it could never be produced; and therefore the mind would be able to understand more things than Nature could bring about—which we have shown above to be false.

⁵⁷ Koyré refers us here to E IIP38 and Hobbes, *De Corpore* I, vi, 4-13.

34

arises. I.e., [the person] knows that his senses have sometimes deceived him, but he knows this only confusedly; for he does not know how the senses deceive.[58] And if someone, after doubting, acquires a true knowledge of the senses and of how, by their means, things at a distance are presented, then the doubt is again removed.

[79] From this it follows that, only so long as we have no clear and distinct idea of God, can we call true ideas in doubt by supposing that perhaps some deceiving God exists, who misleads us even in the things most certain. I.e., if we attend to the knowledge we have concerning the origin of all things and do not discover—by the same knowledge we have when, attending to the nature of the triangle, we discover that its three angles equal two right angles—anything that teaches us that he is not a deceiver [NS:, then the doubt remains]. But if we have the kind of knowledge of God that we have of the triangle, then all doubt is removed. And just as we can arrive at such a knowledge of the triangle, even though we may not know certainly whether some supreme deceiver misleads us, so we can arrive at such a knowledge of God, even though we may not know whether there is some supreme deceiver. Provided we have that knowledge, it will suffice, as I have said, to remove every doubt that we can have concerning clear and distinct ideas.

[80] Further, if someone proceeds rightly, by investigating [first] those things which ought to be investigated first, with no interruption in the connection of things, and knows how to define problems precisely,[59] before striving for knowledge of them, he will never have anything but the most certain ideas—i.e., clear and distinct ideas. For doubt is nothing but the suspension of the mind concerning some affirmation or negation, which it would affirm or deny if something did not occur to it, the ignorance of which must render its knowledge of the thing imperfect. From this it is [to be] inferred that doubt always arises from the fact that things are investigated without order.

[81] These are the matters I promised to discuss in this first part of the Method. But to omit nothing that can lead to knowledge of the intellect and its powers, I shall say a few words about memory and forgetting. The most important consideration is that memory is strengthened both with the aid of the intellect and also without its aid. For regarding the first, the more intelligible a thing is, the more easily

---

[58] In the OP this sentence is printed as a footnote annexed to the Latin phrase here represented by "But in thinking. . . ." Gebhardt (following a suggestion of Leopold's) adopts the reading of the NS, which brings it into the text. Joachim (2, 182 n.) thinks this a mistake.

[59] OP: "*quomodò quaestiones sint determinandae.*" I adopt Joachim's paraphrase (2, 183).

it is retained; and conversely, the less intelligible, the more easily forgotten. E.g., if I give someone a large number of disconnected words, he will retain them with much more difficulty than if I give him the same words in the form of a story.

[82] It is also strengthened without the aid the intellect, by the force with which the imagination, or what they call the common sense, is affected by some singular corporeal thing. I say *singular*, for the imagination is affected only by singular things. If someone, e.g., has read only one Comedy,[60] he will retain it best so long as he does not read several others of that kind, for then it will flourish in isolation in the imagination. But if there are several of the same kind, we imagine them all together and they are easily confused. I say also *corporeal*, for the imagination is affected only by bodies. Therefore since the memory is strengthened both by the intellect and also without the intellect, we may infer that it is something different from the intellect, and that concerning the intellect considered in itself there is neither memory nor forgetting.

[83] What, then, will memory be? Nothing but a sensation of impressions on the brain, together with the thought of a determinate duration[d] of the sensation, which recollection also shows. For there the soul thinks of that sensation, but not under a continuous duration. And so the idea of that sensation is not the duration itself of the sensation, i.e., the memory itself. But whether the ideas themselves undergo some corruption, we shall see in [my] Philosophy.

If this seems quite absurd to anyone, it will suffice for our purpose if he thinks that the more singular a thing is, the more easily it may be retained, as the example of the Comedy just mentioned makes clear. Further, the more intelligible a thing is, the more easily it too is retained. So we cannot but retain a thing that is most singular if only it is also intelligible.

[84] In this way, then, we have distinguished between a true idea and other perceptions, and shown that the fictitious, the false, and the

---

[d] But if the duration is indeterminate, the memory of the thing is imperfect, as each of us also seems to have learned from nature. For often, to believe someone better in what he says, we ask when and where it happened. Although the ideas themselves also have their own duration in the mind, nevertheless, since we have become accustomed to determine duration with the aid of some measure of motion, which is also done with the aid of the imagination, we still observe no memory that belongs to the pure mind.[61]

[60] OP: "*Fabulam amatoriam*," NS: "*tooneelspel van liefde*." Literally, love story or romantic play. But the marginal note in the NS suggests that Spinoza may originally have written *Comoedia*. The change (if there was one) was presumably made only for stylistic reasons and was not made consistently (cf. l. 29).

[61] OP: "*sit purae mentis*," NS: "*gantschelijk tot de ziel behoort*" (= belongs entirely to the mind).

other ideas have their origin in the imagination, i.e., in certain sensations that are fortuitous, and (as it were) disconnected; since they do not arise from the very power of the mind, but from external causes, as the body (whether waking or dreaming) receives various motions.

But if you wish, take imagination any way you like here, provided it is something different from the intellect, and in which the soul has the nature of something acted on. For it is all the same, however you take it, after we know that it is something random, by which the soul is acted on, and at the same time know how we are freed from it with the help of the intellect. So let no one be surprised that here, where I have not yet proved that there is a body, and other necessary things, I speak of the imagination, the body and its constitution. For as I have said, it does not matter what I take it to be, after I know that it is something random, etc.[62]

[85] We have shown that a true idea is simple, or composed of simple ideas; that it shows how and why something is, or has been done; and that its objective effects proceed in the soul according to the formal nature of its object. This is the same as what the ancients said, i.e., that true knowledge proceeds from cause to effect—except that so far as I know they never conceived the soul (as we do here) as acting according to certain laws, like a spiritual automaton.

[86] From this we have acquired as much knowledge of our intellect as was possible in the beginning, and such a standard of the true idea that now we do not fear confusing true ideas with false or fictitious ones. Nor will we wonder why we understand certain things that do not fall in any way under the imagination, why there are some things in the imagination which are completely opposed to the intellect, and finally why there are others that agree with the intellect; for we know that those activities by which imaginations are produced happen according to other laws, wholly different from the laws of the intellect, and that in imagination the soul only has the nature of something acted on.

[87] From this it is also established how easily they can fall into great errors, who have not accurately distinguished between imagination and intellection. Such errors as: that extension must be in a place, that it must be finite, that its parts must be really distinguished from one another, that it is the first and only foundation of all things, that it occupies more space at one time than at another, and many

---

[62] The NS at this point gives (instead of "etc.") a version of the lines occurring above 12-14. But they add that the imagination is not only *random*, but also *unconscious*, and that the soul is *entirely* acted on.

other things of the same kind, all of which are completely opposed to the truth, as we shall show in the proper place.

[88] Next, since words are part of the imagination, i.e., since we feign many concepts, in accordance with the random composition of words in the memory from some disposition of the body, it is not to be doubted that words, as much as the imagination, can be the cause of many and great errors, unless we are very wary of them.

[89] Moreover, they are established according to the pleasure and power of understanding of ordinary people, so that they are only signs of things as they are in the imagination, but not as they are in the intellect. This is clear from the fact that the names given to things that are only in the intellect, and not in the imagination, are often negative (for example, infinite, incorporeal, etc.), and also from the fact that they express negatively many things that are really affirmative, and conversely (for example, uncreated, independent, infinite, immortal). Because the contraries of these are much more easily imagined, they occurred first to the earliest men, and they used positive names. We affirm and deny many things because the nature of words—not the nature of things—allows us to affirm them. And in our ignorance of this, we easily take something false to be true.

[90] We avoid, moreover, another great cause of confusion which prevents the intellect from reflecting on itself—viz. when we do not distinguish between imagination and intellection, we think that the things we more easily imagine are clearer to us, and think we understand what we imagine. Hence, what should be put later we put first, and so the true order of making progress is overturned, and no conclusion is arrived at legitimately.

[91][e] To arrive finally at the second part of this Method, I shall set forth first our aim in this Method, and then the means to attain it. The aim, then, is to have clear and distinct ideas, i.e., such as have been made from the pure mind, and not from fortuitous motions of the body. And then, so that all ideas may be led back to one, we shall strive to connect and order them so that our mind, as far as possible, reproduces objectively the formal character of nature, both as to the whole and as to the parts.

[92] As for the first, our ultimate end requires (as we have already said) that the thing be conceived either through its essence alone or through its proximate cause. If the thing is in itself, *or*, as is commonly

---

[e] The principal Rule of this part (as follows from the first part) is to review all the ideas we discover in us from the pure intellect, so that they are distinguished from those we imagine. This will have to be elicited from the properties of each, i.e., of the imagination and the intellection.

said, is the cause of itself, then it must be understood through its essence alone; but if it is not in itself, but requires a cause to exist, then it must be understood through its proximate cause. For really, knowledge[f] of the effect is nothing but acquiring a more perfect knowledge of its cause.

15 [93] Therefore, so long as we are dealing with the Investigation of things, we must never infer anything from abstractions, and we shall take very great care not to mix up the things that are only in the intellect with those that are real. But the best conclusion will have to be drawn from some particular affirmative essence, *or*, from a true and 20 legitimate definition. For from universal axioms alone the intellect cannot descend to singulars, since axioms extend to infinity, and do not determine the intellect to the contemplation of one singular thing rather than another.

[94] So the right way of discovery is to form thoughts from some given definition. This will proceed the more successfully and easily, 25 the better we have defined a thing. So the chief point of this second part of the Method is concerned solely with this: knowing the conditions of a good definition, and then, the way of finding good definitions. First, therefore, I shall deal with the conditions of definition.

[95] To be called perfect, a definition will have to explain the inmost 30 essence of the thing, and to take care not to use certain *propria* in its place. So as not to seem bent on uncovering the errors of others, I shall use only the example of an abstract thing to explain this. For it II/35 is the same however it is defined. If a circle, for example, is defined as a figure in which the lines drawn from the center to the circumference are equal, no one fails to see that such a definition does not at all explain the essence of the circle, but only a property of it. And though, as I have said, this does not matter much concerning figures and other 5 beings of reason, it matters a great deal concerning Physical and real beings, because the properties of things are not understood so long as their essences are not known. If we neglect them, we shall necessarily overturn the connection of the intellect, which ought to reproduce the connection of Nature, and we shall completely miss our goal.

10 [96] These are the requirements which must be satisfied in Definition, if we are to be free of this fault:

1. If the thing is created, the definition, as we have said, will have to include the proximate cause. E.g., according to this law,

---

[f] Note that it is evident from this that we cannot [NS: legitimately or properly] understand anything of Nature without at the same time rendering our knowledge of the first cause, *or* God, more ample.

39

a circle would have to be defined as follows: it is the figure that is described by any line of which one end is fixed and the other movable. This definition clearly includes the proximate cause.[63]

2. We require a concept, *or* definition, of the thing such that when it is considered alone, without any others conjoined, all the thing's properties can be deduced from it (as may be seen in this definition of the circle). For from it we clearly infer that all the lines drawn from the center to the circumference are equal.

That this is a necessary requirement of a definition is so plain through itself to the attentive that it does not seem worth taking time to demonstrate it, nor to show also, from this second requirement, that every definition must be affirmative.

I mean intellectual affirmation—it matters little whether the definition is verbally affirmative; because of the poverty of language it will sometimes, perhaps, [only] be able to be expressed negatively, although it is understood affirmatively.

[97] These are the requirments for the definition of an uncreated thing:

1. That it should exclude every cause, i.e., that the object should require nothing else except its own being for its explanation.[64]

2. That, given the definition of this thing, there should remain no room for the Question—does it exist?

3. That (as far as the mind is concerned) it should have no substantives that could be changed into adjectives, i.e., that it should not be explained through any abstractions.

4. Finally (though it is not very necessary to note this) it is required that all its properties be inferred[65] from its definition.

All these things are evident to those who attend to them accurately.

[98] I have also said that the best conclusion will have to be drawn from a particular affirmative essence. For the more particular an idea

---

[63] Cf. Hobbes, *De Corpore* I, i, 5, and his *Examinatio et emendatio mathematicae hodiernae,* second dialogue. See also Cassirer 2:98ff.

[64] According to Gueroult (1, 1:172-173), Spinoza later modified this requirement and came to regard his definition of God (E ID6) as a genetic, causal definition. It would still be true that God requires nothing else except his own being (i.e., the elements of his being, the attributes) for his explanation. But it would not be correct to say that a definition in terms of those elements excludes every cause. Whereas the notion of being *causa sui* is here treated as if equivalent to being without a cause, later it will be treated more positively. The key passage is in Letter 60 (IV/270-271).

[65] OP: "*concludantur,*" NS: "*verklaart worden*" (literally: 'be explained').

is, the more distinct, and therefore the clearer it is. So we ought to seek knowledge of particulars as much as possible.

[99] As for order, to unite and order all our perceptions, it is required, and reason demands,[66] that we ask, as soon as possible, whether there is a certain being, and at the same time, what sort of being it is, which is the cause of all things, so that its objective essence may also be the cause of all our ideas, and then our mind will (as we have said)[67] reproduce Nature as much as possible. For it will have Nature's essence, order, and unity objectively.

From this we can see that above all it is necessary for us always to deduce all our ideas from Physical things, *or* from the real beings, proceeding, as far as possible, according to the series of causes, from one real being to another real being, in such a way that we do not pass over to abstractions and universals, neither inferring something real from them, nor inferring them from something real. For to do either interferes with the true progress of the intellect.

[100] But note that by the series of causes and of real beings I do not here understand the series of singular, changeable things, but only the series of fixed and eternal things. For it would be impossible for human weakness to grasp the series of singular, changeable things, not only because there are innumerably many of them, but also because of the infinite circumstances in one and the same thing, any of which can be the cause of its existence or nonexistence. For their existence has no connection with their essence, *or* (as we have already said) is not an eternal truth.

[101] But there is also no need for us to understand their series. The essences of singular, changeable things are not to be drawn from their series, *or* order of existing, since it offers us nothing but extrinsic denominations, relations, or at most, circumstances, all of which are far from the inmost essence of things. That essence is to be sought only from the fixed and eternal things, and at the same time from the laws inscribed in these things, as in their true codes, according to which all singular things come to be, and are ordered. Indeed these singular, changeable things depend so intimately, and (so to speak) essentially, on the fixed things that they can neither be nor be conceived without them. So although these fixed and eternal things are singular, nevertheless, because of their presence everywhere, and most extensive power, they will be to us like universals, *or* genera of the definitions of singular, changeable things, and the proximate causes of all things.

[66] Accepting Leopold's emendation of the text. Cf. Joachim 2, 214 n.
[67] Cf. §§ 42, 91, and 95.

10   [102] But since this is so, there seems to be a considerable difficulty in our being able to arrive at knowledge of these singular things. For to conceive them all at once is a task far beyond the powers of the human intellect. But to understand one before the other, the order must be sought, as we have said, not from their series of existing, nor
15   even from the eternal things. For there, by nature, all these things are at once. So other aids will have to be sought beyond those we use to understand the eternal things and their laws.

    Nevertheless, this is not the place to treat them, nor is it necessary until after we have acquired a sufficient knowledge of the eternal things
20   and their infallible laws, and the nature of our senses has become known to us. [103] Before we equip ourselves for knowledge of singular things, there will be time to treat those aids, all of which serve to help us know how to use our senses and to make, according to certain laws, and in order, the experiments that will suffice to deter-
25   mine the thing we are seeking, so that at last we may infer from them according to what laws of eternal things it was made, and its inmost nature may become known to us, as I shall show in its place.[68]

    Here, to return to our theme, I shall only try to treat those things that seem necessary for us to be able to arrive at knowledge of eternal things, and for us to form their definitions according to the conditions
30   laid down above. [104] To do this, we must recall what we said above:[69] when the mind attends to a thought—to weigh it, and deduce from it, in good order, the things legitimately to be deduced from it—if it is false, the mind will uncover the falsity; but if it is true, the mind will
35   continue successfully, without any interruption, to deduce true things
II/38   from it. This, I say, is required for our purpose. For our thoughts cannot be determined from any other foundation.[70] [105] If, therefore, we wish to investigate the first thing of all, there must be some foundation that directs our thoughts to it.

5   Next, because Method is reflexive knowledge itself, this foundation, which must direct our thoughts, can be nothing other than knowledge

---

[68] Various scholars (Leopold, Appuhn, Joachim) have seen in this sentence a digression, probably added by Spinoza as a marginal note. Gebhardt, following both the OP and the NS, retains it in the text, rightly, I think.

[69] I take the reference to be to § 61, as Gebhardt apparently does at II/337. But at II/338 he apparently takes it to be to § 70, as part of his case for his emendation of II/38/1-2.

[70] OP: "Nam ex nullo fundamento cogitationes nostrae terminari queunt." Elwes' translation of that text is as reasonable as any: "For our thoughts may be brought to a close by the absence of a foundation." Gebhardt (following the NS) emends to: "Nam ex nullo alio fundamento cogitationes nostrae determinari queunt," which is what I have translated. But Appuhn's conjecture is also plausible: "Nam ex nullo fundamento cogitationes nostrae determinari nequeunt" (= "for without a foundation our thoughts cannot be determined"). For a fuller discussion see Eisenberg 1, 103-105, or Gebhardt II/337-339. Cf. Aristotle, NE, 1098 b1-12.

of what constitutes the form of truth, and knowledge of the intellect, and its properties and powers. For once we have acquired this [knowledge], we shall have the foundation from which we shall deduce our thoughts and the way by which the intellect, according to its capacity, will be able to reach the knowledge of eternal things, with due regard, of course, to its own powers.

[106] But if forming true ideas pertains to the nature of thought, as shown in the first part, here we must investigate what we understand by the powers of the intellect. Since the chief part of our Method is to understand as well as possible the powers of the intellect, and its nature, we are necessarily forced, by what I have taught in this second part of the Method, to deduce these from the very definition of thought and intellect.

[107] But so far we have had no rules for discovering definitions. And because we cannot give them unless the nature, *or* definition, of the intellect, and its power are known, it follows that either the definition of the intellect must be clear through itself, or else we can understand nothing. It is not, however, absolutely clear through itself; but because its properties (like all the things we have from intellect) cannot be perceived clearly and distinctly unless their nature is known, if we attend to the properties of the intellect that we understand clearly and distinctly, its definition will become known through itself. We shall, therefore, enumerate the properties of the intellect here, and consider them, and begin to deal with out innate tools.g

[108] The properties of the intellect which I have chiefly noted, and understand clearly, are these:

1. That it involves certainty, i.e., that the intellect knows that things are formally as they are contained objectively in itself.

2. That it perceives certain things, *or* forms certain ideas, absolutely, and forms certain ideas from others. For it forms the idea of quantity absolutely, without attending to other thoughts, but it forms the ideas of motion only by attending to the idea of quantity.

3. Those that it forms absolutely express infinity, but determinate ideas it forms from others. For if it perceives the idea of a quantity through a cause, then it determines [that idea] through [the idea] of a quantity,[71] as when it perceives that a body arises from the motion of some plane, a plane from the motion of a line, and

---

g Cf. above [II/13-14ff.].

[71] The text is evidently corrupt here. Gebhardt emends along lines suggested by the NS. I believe his version of the text makes sense if understood as I have translated it. For an alternative version and full discussion, see Eisenberg 1, 107-109.

finally, a line from the motion of a point. These perceptions do not help to understand the quantity, but only to determine it. This is evident from the fact that we conceive them as arising from the motion, although the motion is not perceived unless the quantity is perceived, and also because we can continue the motion to form a line to infinity, which we could not do at all, if we did not have the idea of infinite quantity.

4. It forms positive ideas before negative ones.

5. It perceives things not so much under duration as under a certain species of eternity, and in an infinite number—or rather, to perceive things, it attends neither to number nor to duration; but when it imagines things, it perceives them under a certain number, determinate duration and quantity.

6. The clear and distinct ideas that we form seem to follow so from the necessity of our nature alone that they seem to depend absolutely on our power alone. But with confused ideas it is quite the contrary—they are often formed against our will.

7. The mind can determine in many ways the ideas of things that the intellect forms from others—as, for example, to determine the plane of an ellipse, it feigns that a pen attached to a cord is moved around two centers, or conceives infinitely many points always having the same definite relation to some given straight line, or a cone cut by some oblique plane, so that the angle of inclination is greater than the angle of the cone's vertex, or in infinite other ways.

8. The more ideas express of the perfection of some object, the more perfect they are. For we do not admire the architect who has designed a chapel so much as one who has designed a notable temple.

[109] I shall not linger over the other things that are referred to thought, such as love, joy, etc. For they contribute nothing to our present purpose, nor can they be conceived unless the intellect is perceived. For if perception is altogether taken away, then all these are taken away.

[110] False and fictitious ideas have nothing positive (as we have shown abundantly) through which they are called false or fictitious, but they are considered as such only from a defect of our knowledge. So false and fictitious ideas, as such, can teach us nothing concerning the essence of thought. It is rather to be sought from the positive

10   properties just surveyed, i.e., we must now establish something common from which these properties necessarily follow, *or* such that when
it is given, they are necessarily given, and when it is taken away, they
are taken away.

The rest is lacking.

Short Treatise on God, Man, and His Well-Being

EDITORIAL PREFACE

In 1704, Gottlieb Stolle, later to become professor of political science at Jena, visited Holland. His travel diary contains the following account of an interview with Jan Rieuwertsz the Younger, the son of Spinoza's friend and publisher:

> After this he brought out another manuscript, which his father had also transcribed, but in this case, from Spinoza's own hand. This was the *Ethics*, i.e., a Dutch *Ethics*, as Spinoza originally composed it. This *Ethics* was organized quite differently from the printed one. For whereas in the latter everything is worked out by the more difficult mathematical method, in this everything was divided into chapters and argued in a continuous succession (without the artificial proof of each point), as in the *Theological-Political Treatise*.
>
> Rieuwertsz assured me also that the printed *Ethics* was much better worked out than this manuscript, but he acknowledged that it contained various things not in the printed version. In particular he pointed out a chapter on the Devil, which was Chapter XXI, and which is not in the printed *Ethics*. In this Spinoza treated the question "Whether the Devil exists?" and began by examining the definition that the Devil is a spirit contrary to the divine essence, and having its essence through itself. In this sense he seemed to deny the Devil's existence.
>
> According to Rieuwertsz, some friends of Spinoza had copied this manuscript, but it had never been printed, because there was already in print a fine edition of the more orderly Latin version, whereas the work which had been overlooked was written far too freely.[1]

This is our first definite[2] indication of the existence of the *Short Treatise*, a work that had to wait for another century and a half before the rediscovery of two manuscript versions permitted its publication.

The work which thus made its entry into the Spinozistic corpus is a scholar's delight, but it is hard to believe that anyone as familiar with its problems as Wolf could ever have recommended it as suited

---

[1] Freudenthal 1, 227ff. Some of the details of Stolle's account, however, seem incorrect. The chapter on the Devil is XXV in our manuscript. More important, Stolle's claim that the work was originally written in Dutch is contradicted by the subtitle.

[2] Though Letter 6 (IV/36/10-25) is almost certainly referring to this work. And L. Meyer apparently referred to it in his *Philosophia Sacrae Scripturae Interpres* (1666).

to be an introduction to Spinoza's philosophy. True, it contains expositions of many central themes of Spinoza's thought in a shorter and less demanding form than does the *Ethics*. But the work bristles with difficulties.[3]

First of all, it is clear that neither of the manuscripts that form the basis for modern editions is Spinoza's own manuscript. At best they are copies of lost manuscripts, and each of them seems to contain a number of copyist's errors. Quite possibly our best manuscript is only a copy of a copy (cf. Mignini 1, 235), though it is probably not far from the original.

Secondly, it is also clear that these manuscripts are copies of a work Spinoza himself never fully prepared for publication, a work in progress which was intended in the first instance only for private circulation among friends interested in studying Spinoza's philosophy.[4] So, for example, there are inconsistencies, repetitions, and expressions of uncertainty about whether particular topics would be treated later, some of which surely would have been emended if Spinoza had given the work a final revision for publication.

Again, written in the margins of the older, and probably more authentic of the manuscripts, are many notes, whose authorship and relation to the text are often obscure. Some must certainly come from Spinoza himself; others must certainly not; but the origin of many others is a matter of speculation,[5] and there is the further possibility that some reader's notes have, in the process of copying, inadvertently been brought into the text. In addition, some of the longer notes may be intended to replace sections of the text, and some passages of the text may be superseded versions which have inadvertently been re-

[3] The classic article on this topic is Freudenthal 2, which exercised considerable influence on Gebhardt and other subsequent editors and translators. It should be noted, however, that the most recent editor, Mignini, reacts strongly against many of Freudenthal's and Gebhardt's conclusions. The general tendency of his work is to affirm the integrity of the manuscript.

[4] As drafts of the *Ethics* and the geometric exposition of Descartes' *"Principles"* were circulated. Cf. Letters 8 and 13. Letter 6 (IV/36), however, indicates that at that stage Spinoza was contemplating publication of the *Short Treatise*.

[5] Gebhardt brackets the notes he prints but does not regard as Spinoza's. I have normally indicated this by a bracketed comment following the note. Sometimes I find Gebhardt too ready to bracket notes and where it has seemed to me that there was reason to retain the note, I have indicated this. Many of the notes in Part II are mere marginal summaries of the central point in the text (in the manner of the marginal notes Meyer added to the *Metaphysical Thoughts*). Gebhardt relegates all of these to his textual commentary. The new critical edition by Mignini, however, prints them with the text. Since Mignini's edition became available to me only at a very late stage of my work on this translation, I have not tried, as he does, to reproduce in print the exact arrangement of the manuscript. But I have tried, in my notes, to give an account of any marginalia that might have any importance.

tained. Some editors ascribe these hypothetical retentions, some apparent illogicalities in the ordering of materials, and even the chapter divisions, to the editorial work of a zealous, but not very acute, disciple.

As if these were not difficulties enough, there is doubt whether Spinoza wrote this work in Dutch or in Latin. Stolle's travel diary describes it as written in Dutch. But the subtitle says it was originally written in Latin, for Spinoza's pupils, and then translated into Dutch, for a wider audience. The first of these witnesses is not entirely reliable, but the authority of the second is unclear.

Gebhardt, in company with nearly every other scholar who has considered the question, regarded the work as a translation of a lost Latin original, principally on the ground that there are many apparent mistakes in the text which can best be explained as translation errors. But recently his arguments have been challenged by Boehm, who has established at least that Gebhardt's conclusion is less certain than he took it to be. It is extremely difficult, of course, to demonstrate that any particular passage is corrupt, and doubly difficult to demonstrate that the error can only be set right by assuming a Latin original that has been mistranslated (though this is what Gebhardt sometimes claims). Nevertheless, I think Gebhardt is probably right to postulate a lost Latin original, even if his arguments for this hypothesis are unsatisfactory.[6]

If we do assume that our work is a copy of a translation of a lost original, we add to the possible sources of textual error, and increase the uncertainty of an already uncertain text. But this question is primarily of interest to the textual critic. However it is decided, the translator must think of the technical terms as if they were translations of Latin terms. At the time when the *Short Treatise* was written, Latin was still the main language of philosophical discussion. Most of Spinoza's other works, like most of Descartes' and Hobbes', were first written in Latin and then translated into the vernacular. The vernacular languages were like Latin itself before Cicero. They lacked a well-

---

[6] Boehm considers the eleven passages that Gebhardt cites at I/428 and finds only one of them even partly convincing. Without going into details of specific passages, I would suggest that Gebhardt's list omits some of the strongest cases. For example, I think the use of *geloof* at I/54/10-11, where one would expect *waan*, is better evidence for Gebhardt's thesis than the cases he cites. In Curley 1, I argue that other inconsistencies in the use of technical terminology indicate that two different translators may have had a hand in producing different strata in our manuscript. Some of Boehm's arguments are *ad hominen*, directed against Gebhardt's theory that the *Treatise* was first dictated in Dutch, then reworked in Latin, and then translated back into Dutch. Someone who thinks the manuscript a translation, however, need not adopt that theory of its composition, as Mignini's work illustrates.

established philosophical vocabulary. Glazemaker's useful practice of indicating the Latin terms in the margins of his Dutch translations of Descartes and Spinoza was a step toward the creation of such a vocabulary. But the process was incomplete when the *Short Treatise* was translated, and the treatment of technical terms there is not as firm as in other contemporary Dutch translations of Spinoza's works.

A further difficulty that hampers the study of the *Short Treatise* is the uncertainty about the relationship between the two manuscripts. It is clear that one of them (called "codex A" by Schaarschmidt) dates from the seventeenth century, is older than the other (called "codex B" by Schaarschmidt), and was at least a partial source for the later manuscript. It is also clear, however, that "codex B" sometimes has a better reading than "codex A." The question is whether the transcriber of "codex B," an eighteenth-century Dutch doctor named Monnikhoff, had access to another source, which enabled him to correct some of the defects of "A."

The first editor to consider this issue, Schaarschmidt, did not think highly of Monnikhoff's corrections and took them to have no value for the establishment of the text. Sigwart thought better of them and inferred that Monnikhoff also had access to another, hypothetical manuscript, called "C." Wolf shared this view and consequently incorporated a great deal of information about "codex B" in his translation. Gebhardt's position is that while many of Monnikhoff's corrections are justified, others are not, and that Monnikhoff relied only on his own good judgment in making them. So what was formerly called "codex A" Gebhardt refers to simply as "the manuscript" and what was formerly called "codex B" he treats as an attempt at a critical edition, deserving the respect due any intelligent exercise in textual criticism, but not possessing any special authority. Mignini has accepted this view (Mignini 1, 226) and my translation, like that in the Pléiade edition, assumes that it is correct.

Finally, to put an end to the listing of problems, it is generally thought that the work contains various strata, dating from different periods. The notes, for example, were probably written later than the main text. It seems to have been Spinoza's habit to go back over works he had previously written and to make marginal notes, amplifying, correcting, and flagging topics for further discussion. Similarly, the appendices seem to be a later addition. The dialogues have sometimes been thought to be earlier than the main text, and theories of Spinoza's development have been constructed on that assumption,[7] though the

---

[7] On this, see Freudenthal 2. The references to other parts of the *Treatise* and the

more usual view now would be that both dialogues are later than the main body of the text.

At this stage there appear to be two main theories of the composition of this work. According to Gebhardt (I/424-431), Spinoza originally dictated a work on these topics in Dutch to friends in Amsterdam prior to his departure for Rijnsburg; then in Rijnsburg he revised portions of the manuscript in Latin in the form of separate treatises, of which the present TdIE is the only one to survive both in Latin and in Dutch; these treatises Spinoza sent to Amsterdam, where they were immediately translated into Dutch (by Pieter Balling) for the benefit of those members of the Spinoza circle who could not read Latin (principally, Jarig Jelles); in response to questions from the friends in Amsterdam, Spinoza added notes, appendices, and dialogues; finally, Jelles put this disorganized material into order for his private use, and added various notes and observations of his own.

Mignini, however, has a very different account of the manuscript. According to his theory (Mignini 1, 230-240), Spinoza's friends asked him (either while he was still in Amsterdam, or on his departure for Rijnsburg) to write a concise exposition of his most important ideas on metaphysics and ethics; Spinoza wrote the treatise in Latin, about the middle of 1660, exclusively for the friends and not for immediate publication; his friends asked for a Dutch translation and suggested that the work be published; Spinoza corrected the Latin text and added notes and dialogues in response to the objections of his friends; someone translated the work into Dutch with a view to publication, and someone (possibly the translator) added marginal notes and cross-references; toward the end of 1661 (Mignini's date for Letter 6), Spinoza made revisions on a Dutch copy of the work, adding still more notes, marginalia, and cross-references, and reworking some parts of the text; then, toward the end of 1661 or early in 1662, Spinoza abandoned the project of publishing the *Short Treatise* and decided to rework this material into an entirely different, geometric form; he added to the Dutch manuscript two mysterious sequences of numbers,[8] indicating what materials he wished to retain and in what order, and then began to

---

dialogues' connection with one another seem good evidence of this, though Gueroult apparently regards both dialogues as earlier than the main text (Gueroult 1, 472). In Curley 1, I argue that at least the second dialogue and certain sections of II, xxvi, are later than the main body of the text.

[8] Mignini's edition was the first to reproduce these sequences of numbers in the text itself. It is clear that they are not footnote numbers. To distinguish them from footnotes, they are set in italics in this edition. Mignini has argued at some length (Mignini 3) that these numbers represent Spinoza's own thoughts about the reordering of his material, a transitional phase, intermediate between the order of the *Short Treatise* and the order of the *Ethics*. The first series stops abruptly in I, i, presumably because the

write the *Ethics*; finally, someone made a copy of Spinoza's Dutch copy of the manuscript, translating any Latin additions or correcting their style if they were written in Dutch. Our manuscript A would stem from this copy.

Clearly, if Mignini's theory is correct, our manuscript would be a considerably more trustworthy account of Spinoza's thought at that stage of his development than it would be on Gebhardt's theory. Equally clearly, it is going to be very difficult to decide which is correct, or at least nearer the truth. This is not the place for that kind of investigation, but perhaps it will be helpful to at least mention the principal sources of data bearing on these theories. They are: 1) the subtitle of the work (11/7-11); 2) the conclusion of the main text (112/20-113/6); 3) a marginal note attached to the conclusion; 4) passages in the letters which either inform us about the KV or provide us with analogies from the histories of Spinoza's other works (Letters 6, 8, 12a, 13, and 15); 5) so-called "doublet" passages (e.g., 85/3-19, 55/16-29); 6) expressions of uncertainty about the contents of the work (43/33-34, 60/33-34, 78/11); and 7) the sequences of superscript numbers (*passim*). Perhaps it is not too much to hope that future investigations will clarify our understanding of the history of this work.

In the face of all these difficulties, it is not surprising that some scholars have doubted the value of studying this work.[9] But this is an overreaction. First of all, as Rieuwertsz recognized, this work does contain discussions of topics not treated in the *Ethics*, or not treated so fully there, some of them of considerably greater interest to the modern reader than the chapter on the devil. For example, the discussions of definition (I, vi), of God's causality of the finite (Second Dialogue), and of the distinction between *natura naturans* and *natura naturata* (I, viii, ix) are all valuable supplements to the exceedingly brief treatment these topics get elsewhere.

Secondly, even where Spinoza's discussion of a topic is sketchy or

---

copyist would not take the trouble to reproduce features of the manuscript that meant nothing to him. The second series, which runs, with some lacunae, throughout KV II, is better preserved. If Mignini's ingenious hypothesis about these numbers is correct, the consequences are very important. Not only would we be able to feel greater confidence in the integrity of our manuscript, since Spinoza himself would have seen something closely approximating our manuscript but also we would have an insight into the development of Spinoza's thought between the *Short Treatise* and the *Ethics* and a further tool for the establishment of the text (cf. Mignini on KV I, i, 1, and on II, xix, 12). In such matters proof is out of the question, but it seems fair to say that no one else has advanced any plausible alternative explanation of the number sequences.

[9] Cf. Francès in Pléiade, 3: "Sauf entre les mains de commentateurs spécialisés de ce philosophe ou de critiques de textes méfiants par profession, la confrontation de cette copie suspecte au reste de l'oeuvre de Spinoza offre beaucoup plus d'inconvénients que d'avantages."

immature compared with later treatments (e.g., in the analysis of the emotions), it remains extremely interesting to see the stages he went through in arriving at the mature doctrine. The literary form of the *Ethics* has been a stumbling block to Spinoza's readers from the beginning, partly, perhaps, because that work is so very well worked out. We would like to have some grasp of the processes of thought that lay "behind the geometrical method." To achieve that grasp, we must examine the earlier works that did in fact lead up to the *Ethics*.[10]

A further advantage which has been claimed for the *Short Treatise* is that it may help us to understand better Spinoza's position in relation to Christianity, which in turn is useful for the proper interpretation of the *Theological-Political Treatise*. Appuhn has even argued (Appuhn 1, 27) that though it contains many propositions incompatible with Christian dogma, the *Short Treatise* is nevertheless much more open to a Christian reading than is the *Ethics*. Appuhn does not contend that Spinoza was ever a Christian in any formal sense, only that at a certain stage of his life certain Christian ideas and sentiments "penetrated his soul." But even this may go too far. At any rate, the Pléiade editors argue, in their preface and notes, that the use of traditional religious language here is designed to gradually lead susceptible minds away from anthropomorphic conceptions.

Finally a word about the Outline. This was first discovered by Boehmer in 1851, bound with a copy of Colerus' biography of Spinoza. That copy also contained a marginal note, apropos of Colerus' discussion of Spinoza's unpublished works (Colerus does not mention the *Short Treatise*):

Among some lovers of philosophy there exists a manuscript treatise by Spinoza; though not composed in the geometric manner, as his printed *Ethics* is, nevertheless it contains the same thoughts and topics. From its style and arrangement it is easy to see that it is of the author's earliest works. After this rough draft of his thought, in the course of time he composed his *Ethics*. And though in the later work the same topics are presented more extensively and in a more polished way, in geometric order, nevertheless because such a mathematical order is quite uncommon in metaphysical matters, and few people are practiced in them, many find the *Ethics* more obscure than this treatise. Only in the beginning of its Appendix is a small portion of the treatise composed in geometric order. [I/412]

Discovery of the outline was instrumental in leading to the discovery of the first manuscript of the *Short Treatise*. But its primary interest

---

[10] As Gueroult frequently does in the appendices to Gueroult 1, on such topics as: the definitions of substance and attribute (I, app. 2), God's essence (I, app. 6), the proofs of God's existence (I, app. 8), determinism (I, app. 16), the physics of bodies (II, app. 7), and the different kinds of knowledge (II, app. 16).

today lies in the possibility (argued for by Freudenthal) that its author may have had access to a better manuscript than any we possess. This suspicion is raised particularly by its account of the first chapter of Part I, though it should be noted that Gebhardt and Mignini reject Freudenthal's conjecture (see the note at I/15/7).

The section numbers are not in the original, but are due to Sigwart, and are included for convenience in making references (and following references in secondary sources). I, iii, 2 = Part I, chapter iii, section 2.

I/3

A SHORT OUTLINE OF BENEDICT
DE SPINOZA'S *TREATISE ON GOD, MAN, AND HIS*
WELL-BEING CONSISTING OF TWO PARTS,
FOLLOWED BY AN APPENDIX[1]

THE FIRST Part of this Treatise is divided into ten Chapters.

In the 1st Chapter, the Author shows that he has an idea of God; according to this idea he defines God as a being consisting of infinite Attributes, of which each is infinitely perfect in its kind. From this he then infers that existence belongs to [God's] essence, or that God necessarily exists.

But in order to discover further what perfections in particular are contained in the Divine nature and essence, he passes in the 2nd Chapter to a consideration of the nature of substance. He tries to prove that substance is necessarily infinite; consequently that there cannot exist more than one substance;[2] that one cannot be produced by another, but that whatever is belongs to that one Substance (which he calls God); that thus Thinking and Extended nature are two of its infinite Attributes, each of which is supremely perfect and infinite in its kind; that therefore (as he explains more fully later), all singular finite and limited things, such as Human Souls and Bodies, etc., must be conceived as modes of these attributes, through which these Attributes (and thereby, Substance, or God) are expressed in infinite ways.

---

[1] The author of this outline has usually been thought to be the Amsterdam philosopher, Willem Deurhoff (1650-1717). Some, however, attribute it to Monnikhoff. Cf. Gebhardt I/436.

[2] In B (i.e., in Monnikhoff's version of this outline, which he prefaced to his manuscript of the *Short Treatise*): "that there can only exist one of the same nature." Cf. I/20/4.

All of this is explained more fully in Dialogues.[3]

30   In the 3rd Chapter he deduces what sort of cause God is of things, viz. that he is an immanent cause, etc. But in order to make known what (in his opinion) God's essential Attributes are, he passes to:

I/4   The 4th Chapter, where he maintains that God is a necessary cause of all things, and that it was as impossible for them to have had a nature different from that already posited or to have been produced by God in another form or order, as it would be for God to have another nature or essence than that which belongs to his actual and infinite existence. And the aforementioned production, or posited necessity of things to exist and act, is here called God's first 'Attribute.'

In Chapter 5 the author considers, as a second 'Attribute' of God, a striving, by which (so he maintains) the whole of nature, and consequently each thing in particular, has tended to preserve its state and being. This striving, insofar as it concerns the totality of things, is called God's general providence; but insofar as it belongs to each individual, in itself, without regard to the other parts of Nature, it is called God's particular providence.

In Chapter 6 a third 'Attribute' of God is considered: his Predestination, or predetermination, which extends to the whole of nature, and to each thing in particular, and excludes all contingency. This doctrine is based mainly on Chapter 4. For once one has granted his fundamental principle that the Universe (which he calls God) is necessary, both as to its essence and its existence, and that everything there is belongs to it, it follows unavoidably from this false principle that nothing contingent can occur in the universe.[4] After this, to clear away difficulties raised against him, he sets out his thoughts concerning the true causes of evil, sin, confusion, etc. With this he concludes his study of God's essential 'Attributes,' and proceeds to Chapter 7, where he enumerates certain 'Attributes' of God which he regards as only relational, not *propria*, or also, indeed, as Denominations of his essential Attributes. He also takes this opportunity to examine and rebut briefly the opinions of the Peripatetics concerning the nature of the definition of God and the proof of his existence.

I/5   But in order that the reader may conceive clearly the difference there is (in the Author's opinion) between *natura Naturans* and *natura Naturata*, he expands on this briefly in the 8th and 9th Chapters.

Then in Chapter 10 (as in Chapter 6), he shows that after men have formed certain universal ideas, and reduced things to them, and com-

---

[3] Freudenthal (followed by Wolf) asserted that the Dialogues were not mentioned in the Outline, which might cast doubt on their authenticity. But as Gebhardt points out, that is incorrect.

[4] Whoever the author of this outline was, he was clearly not a Spinozist.

pared [things] with [these ideas], they form from this concepts of good and evil, and call things good insofar as they agree with this universal idea, but evil insofar as they differ from it, and have no agreement with it. So good and evil are nothing but beings of reason, or modes of thinking.

This concludes the first Part of this Treatise.

In the second the Author explains his thoughts about Man's existence, how man is subjected to and slave of the Passions; then how far the use of his reason extends; and finally, by what means he may be brought to his Salvation and perfect Freedom.

After having spoken briefly in the Preface of this Part about Man's nature, he goes on to treat:

In the 1st Chapter, of the particular kinds of knowledge or perception, and how they are produced in Man in four ways,

1. By report, some story or other sign.
2. By bare experience.
3. By good and pure reasoning, or true Belief.
4. By internal enjoyment and clear intuition of the thing itself.

All of this is clarified and explained by an example taken from the Rule of Three.

In order that the Effects of these four kinds of knowledge may be clearly and distinctly perceived, their definitions are given in the 2nd Chapter, and after that the effects of each are taken separately. As effects of the first and second kinds of knowledge, he notes the Passions which are contrary to good reason; of the third kind, good desires; and of the fourth, genuine love, with all its consequences.

First, then, in the 3rd Chapter, are treated the Passions originating from the first and second kinds of knowledge, i.e., from Opinion: such as Wonder, Love, Hate and Desire.

After that, in the 4th Chapter, he shows the utility for man of the third kind of knowledge, by teaching him how he has to live according to the true guidance of reason, and so arouses him to embrace what alone is worthy of love; which teaches him also to distinguish carefully the Passions which arise from Opinion, and indicates which he should follow, and which avoid. To apply this use of reason more particularly, our Author treats

In the 5th Chapter, of Love.

In the 6th, of Hate and Aversion.

In the 7th, of Desire, Joy, and Sadness.

In the 8th, of Esteem and Disdain; of Humility and Legitimate Self-esteem; of Pride and Self-depreciation.

In the 9th, of Hope and Fear; of Confidence and Despair; of Vac-

illation, Strength of Character, Daring and Emulation; of Cowardice
and Dismay; and finally, of Jealousy.

In the 10th, of Remorse and Repentance.

In the 11th, of Mockery and Ridicule.

In the 12th, of Love of Esteem, Shame and Shamelessness.

In the 13th, of Favor; Gratitude, and Ingratitude.

And finally, in the 14th, of Longing.

Having finished with what, in his judgment, required to be noted
regarding the Passions, he passes to:

The 15th Chapter, where the last effect of true Belief, or the third
kind of knowledge, is introduced, as the means by which the true is
separated from the false, and becomes known to us.

Having discovered what, in his opinion, Good and Evil, Truth and
Falsehood are, and also what the well-being of a perfect Man consists
in, Spinoza then considers it necessary to inquire as to whether we
arrive at such a well-being freely or by necessity.

In this connection, he shows in the 16th Chapter what the Will is,
maintaining there that it is not at all free, but that we are in every
respect determined by external causes to will, to affirm or deny this
or that.

But in order that the Will should not be confused with Desire, he
indicates in the 17th Chapter the difference between them. He thinks
that, like Intellect and Will, desire also is not free, but that each and
every desire, like this or that volition, is determined by external causes.

And to entice the Reader to embrace all the preceding, in the 18th
Chapter he elaborates on all the advantages which in his judgment are
implied in this.

But in the 19th and 20th Chapters, our author inquires whether by
that Belief, or the third kind of knowledge, Man can be brought to
the enjoyment of the greatest Good and the highest Blessedness, and
freed of the Passions, insofar as they are evil.

As far as the last is concerned, he inquires how the soul is united
with the Body and receives from it various affections; these, conceived
under the form of good or evil, are regarded as the cause of all the
various Passions. And since, according to the 1st Chapter of this Part,
the Opinions by which those affections of the Body are thought good
or evil (thus giving rise to the Passions) are founded either on the first
kind of knowledge (on report or some other external sign) or on the
second kind of knowledge (on some experience of ours), he persuades
himself in the 21st Chapter of this conclusion: since what we find in
ourselves has more power over us than what comes from outside, reason can be the cause of the destruction of those Opinions which we
acquire only through the first kind of knowledge, because reason does

I/8 not come to us from outside, as those opinions do; but it does not have
the same power over those which we acquire by the second kind of
knowledge, since what we enjoy in ourselves cannot be overcome,
even through something more powerful, if it is outside us and we only
contemplate it through reason.

5 Since, then, reason, or the third kind of knowledge, has no power
to bring us to our well-being or to overcome the Passions which proceed from the second kind of knowledge, Spinoza proceeds in the
22nd Chapter to discover what the true means for this may be. Since
10 God is the greatest good the Soul can know and possess, he concludes
that if we once acquire a union with him, or knowledge and love of
him, as close as our union with the Body, not one arising from reasoned conclusions, but one consisting of an internal enjoyment of and
immediate union with God's essence, then by this fourth kind of
15 knowledge we shall have attained our greatest Salvation and Happiness. Therefore, this fourth kind of knowledge is not only necessary,
but also the only means. And because in this way the most excellent
effect and an immutable constancy arise in those who enjoy it, he calls
20 it Rebirth.

Since, in his opinion, the human Soul is the idea, in the thinking
25 being, of a certain thing, and the soul is united to the thing by this
idea, he concludes from that in the 23rd Chapter that its constancy or
change must be estimated according to the thing of which it is the
idea. Consequently, if the Soul exists only in union with a thing which
30 is temporal and subject to change (as the Body is), it must necessarily
be acted on and perish with it. On the other hand, if it undergoes
union with a thing whose nature is eternal and immutable, it will be
exempt from all Passion, and will share immortality.

But in order to omit nothing worth noting regarding this, our Au-
I/9 thor inquires in the 24th Chapter whether Man's Love for God is
reciprocated, i.e., if man's love has the result that God loves Man.
Rejecting this, he explains what, according to his previous Teaching,
5 Divine and Human Laws are. Then he rebuts the opinions of those
who maintain that God manifests himself and makes himself known
to Man through something other than his own essence, such as a finite
and limited thing, or by some external sign, whether by words or by
Miracles.

10 And since in his opinion the duration of a thing depends on its own
perfection, or on its union with something else of a more perfect nature, he denies that there is a Devil, because he judges that something
which lacks every perfection or union with perfection (as he defines
15 the Devil) can have neither essence nor existence.

Then, having put the Devil to one side, and having deduced the

57

passions from the sole consideration of human nature, and indicated the means by which they are restrained and the supreme Salvation of the human race is attained, our Author proceeds to note in the 26th Chapter the nature of Man's true Freedom, which arises from the fourth kind of knowledge. For this purpose he introduces the following Propositions:

1. The more essence a thing has, the more it has of action, and the less of Passion.

2. That all Passion proceeds not from an internal, but from an external cause.

3. That whatever is not produced by an external cause also has nothing in common with it.

4. That the effect of an immanent cause cannot change or perish so long as the cause endures.

5. That the freest cause of all, and that which he thinks agrees best with God, is the immanent.

From these Propositions, he deduces the following:

1. That God's essence has an infinite action and involves a denial of any Passion. Hence whatever is united with it thereby participates in that action and is free of all Passion and corruption.

2. That the true intellect cannot perish.

3. That all the effects of the true intellect, which are united with it, are the most excellent of all, and are necessarily eternal with their cause.

4. That all our external effects are the more perfect the more they can be united with us.

From all this he concludes then that human freedom consists in a firm existence which our intellect possesses through immediate union with God, so that neither it[5] nor its effects can be subjected to any external cause, or be destroyed or changed by it. Hence it must persevere with an eternal and constant duration.

And with this Spinoza finishes the Second and last Part of his Work.

However, he had added a kind of Appendix after this, containing nothing but a short sketch of the things contained in the preceding.

---

[5] The manuscript, has *zij*, which Meijer and Appuhn gloss as "the human soul." If the reference is to "the (true) intellect," as the context would lead us to expect, grammar would require *het*. Nevertheless, that would be a more accurate account of II, xxvi.

The first part of this, on the nature of Substance, is arranged in the Geometrical manner, agreeing essentially with his printed *Ethics* up to IP8. And finally, in the second half of this Appendix, he inquires what the human soul is, and what its union with the Body consists in.

Furthermore, Spinoza has provided the whole Work with notes intended to elaborate and Clarify many passages.

25

I/11

Short Treatise on God, Man,
and His Well-Being[1]

PREVIOUSLY written in Latin by B.D.S. for the use of his pupils, who wished to devote themselves to the practice of *ethics* and *true philosophy*, and now translated into Dutch for the use of lovers of *truth* and *virtue*, so that those who boast so much on this subject, and press their dirt and filth on the simple as if it were ambergris, may one day have their mouths shut for them, and may stop blaming what they still do not understand: *God, themselves, and how to help people have regard for one another's well-being*: and to cure those who are sick of mind, through the spirit of gentleness and forbearance, following the example of the *Lord Christ*, our best *teacher*.[2]

I/13

TABLE OF THE CHAPTERS CONTAINED IN
THE TWO FOLLOWING BOOKS, VIZ.

THE FIRST, treating of God, and what pertains to him, having the following chapters:[3]

---

[1] Meijer suggests that the "short" (*korte*) of the title translated *contractus* rather than *brevis*, and so had reference to the somewhat summary style of exposition, not to the length of the work.

The term translated by "well-being" is *welstand*. The Pléiade editors (Pléiade, 1361) suggest that this translates *beatitudo*; in his Latin translation of the outline, Meijer renders it by *salus* (an interpretation supported by the NS at E VP36CS). If either is correct there are religious overtones not captured by "well-being." I retain Wolf's translation mainly because I am reluctant to alter the title of a work when it has become well-entrenched.

[2] This long subtitle was evidently not written by Spinoza himself. The Pléiade editors (Pléiade, 1362) remark that the tone suggests a follower of one of the Protestant sects flourishing in Holland at that time—possibly Jarig Jelles, for whom the translation of the *Short Treatise* may have been done.

[3] Note that the two dialogues following Chapter II are not mentioned in the Table of the Chapters.

[4] The title here given to the second book is not the same as that given at the beginning of Book II. Note also that the appendices and the Preface to Book II are not mentioned.

The First Part
Of God and What Pertains to Him¹

CHAPTER I

THAT GOD IS

[1]² [. . .] Regarding the first question, viz. whether there is a God? we say that this can first be proven a priori, as follows:

1. ¹Whatever we clearly and distinctly understand to belong to the natureᵃ of a thing, we can truly affirm of that thing:

²But we can understand clearly and distinctly that existence belongs to God's nature. Therefore, [we can truly affirm existence of God.]

[2] Alternatively, it can also be proven as follows:

2. The ³essences of things are from all eternity and will remain immutable to all eternity.

God's existence is [his] essence. Therefore, [God's existence is from all eternity and will remain immutable to all eternity.]

[3] [God's existence can be proven] a posteriori as follows:

⁴If man has an Idea of God, then Godᵇ must exist formally.

---

¹ The manuscript gives no title for this part of the work, though there is one for the second part. Gebhardt supplies a title from the Table of Contents.

² The abrupt beginning of this chapter has suggested to some scholars that some material might have been lost. Also suspicious is the absence of a definition of God. Freudenthal conjectured that the chapter may originally have begun: "Man has in him an idea of God as a being consisting of infinite attributes, of which each is infinitely perfect in its kind. We shall first [in Chapter I] show that such a being exists, and then [in Chapter II] show what he is. . . ." This is based partly on the summary of Chapter I in the Outline, which Freudenthal conjectured to rest on a lost, more complete manuscript. Although Gebhardt had accepted this conjecture in his translation of the *Short Treatise* (1922), in his edition (1925) he rejected it on the ground that the summary in the Outline contains nothing that could not have been reconstructed from passages in the existing manuscript. Mignini defends the integrity of the text at length.

I incline to the view that the ms. Spinoza circulated among his friends probably did not begin with a definition of God, that Spinoza had not yet appreciated the need to begin an a priori proof of God's existence with a true definition of God (cf. I/249/22) and that n. b in this chapter may owe its existence to someone's having objected to the absence of a definition of God. In this connection, I think the absence of definitions in the first appendix is significant.

ᵃ Understand the definite nature, by which the thing is what it is, and which cannot in any way be taken from it without destroying it, as it belongs to the essence of a mountain to have a valley, or the essence of a mountain is that it has a valley. This is truly eternal and immutable, and must always be in the concept of a mountain, even if it does not exist, and never did.

ᵇ From the subsequent definition (in Chapter II) of God as having infinite attributes, we can prove his existence as follows: whatever we clearly and distinctly see to belong to the nature of a thing, we can also truly affirm of the thing; but to the nature of a

I/16   ⁵But man has an Idea of God. Therefore.

[4] The first [premise] we prove as follows:

If there is an Idea of God, the cause of [this Idea] must exist formally and contain in itself whatever the Idea has objectively. But there
5   is an Idea of God. Therefore.

[5] To prove the first premise of this argument, we lay down the
following principles:

1. That the things knowable are infinite.

2. That a finite intellect cannot comprehend the infinite.

10   3. That a finite intellect can understand nothing through itself
unless it is determined by something external. For just as it has
no power to understand everything at once, so it also has no
power to begin by understanding this before that, or that before
this. Not being able to do either the first or the second, it can do
15   nothing.

[6] The first (or major) [premise of the argument in § 4] is proven
as follows:

If man's [capacity of forming] fiction[s] were the sole cause of his

---

being that has infinite attributes, an 'attribute' belongs, which is Being. Therefore.³

If someone now replies that this may indeed be affirmed of the Idea, but not of the
thing itself, that is false. For the Idea [of this being and] of the attribute belonging to it
I/16   does not exist materially. So what is affirmed [of the Idea], is affirmed neither of the
30   thing nor of what belongs to it, so that there is a great difference between the Idea and
the Object: therefore, what is affirmed of the thing is not affirmed of the Idea, and vice
versa.⁴

³ Meijer incorporated this and the following two notes into the text immediately after
section 2. In favor of this arrangement it may be said (1) that n. b at least seems
misplaced in the manuscript as it stands, since it bears on the a priori arguments more
than it does on the a posteriori argument, (2) that notes b, c, and d make a good deal of
sense if they are read as forming one continuous discussion, and (3) that this arrangement makes more intelligible the account of the chapter given in the Outline, which
mentions this argument, but not the others. Like Freudenthal, Meijer thought the author of the Outline may have had access to a better manuscript than we have.

Gebhardt rejected Meijer's arrangement on the ground that the second note presupposes the a posteriori arguments and must follow it. But though the second note does
refer to the a posteriori argument, it is independent of it. And the question whether
my idea of God is something I have feigned or invented arises just as crucially in the
ontological argument as it does in the a posteriori argument. (Cf. AT VII, 64, 115-120.)

I suspect that these notes represent material that would have been incorporated in
the text in connection with the a priori arguments (or possibly replacing them) in a
subsequent revision.

⁴ The text of the paragraph just ended looks defective as it stands in the manuscript,
though Mignini thinks it can be defended. Gebhardt has a long discussion of various
proposed emendations. The bracketed additions reflect my acceptance of suggestions
made by Appuhn and Freudenthal.

Idea, then it would be impossible for him to perceive anything. But he can perceive something. Therefore.

20   [7] The first [premise of the argument of § 6] is proven by the first principle, viz. *that the things knowable are infinite.* For according to the second principle, <u>man cannot understand everything, since the human intellect is finite</u>; and being [by hypothesis] determined by no external things to understand this before that, or that before this, it would be 25   impossible for him (according to the third principle) to be able to understand anything.

     [8] ᶜFrom all of this the second point is proved, viz. that the cause

I/16   ᶜ Furthermore, it is also false to say that this idea is a fiction, for it is impossible to have it unless [its object] exists. This is shown below,⁵ to which we add the following:
35   It is indeed true that when an Idea has first come to us from the thing itself, and we
I/17   have made it universal by abstraction, our mind⁶ can also then feign many particular things of this Idea, to which we can also ascribe many other properties abstracted from
5   other things. But it is impossible to do this unless we first know the thing itself of which they are abstractions.

     But if it is once granted that this Idea is a fiction, then all the other Ideasᵈ we have
10   must no less be fictions. If this is so, how is it that we find so great a difference between them? For we find some whose existence is impossible, such as all the monstrous animals one composes of two natures, like a beast that would be both bird and horse, and other things of that kind. It is impossible for them to have a place in Nature, which we find to be differently constituted.

15   ᵈ That other Ideas exist is, indeed, possible, but not necessary. But whether they exist or not, their essence is always necessary like the Idea of a triangle, or that of the soul's love without the body,⁷ etc., so that even if I thought at first that I had feigned them, afterwards I would still be forced to say that they are and would be no less the same, even if neither I nor any other man had ever thought of them. That is why they
20   are not feigned by me, and also must have a subject outside me, which is not me, a subject without which they cannot be.

     In addition to these, there is still a third idea, which is unique. This brings with it a necessary being, and not, like the preceding ones, only the possibility of existence. For though the essence of the others is indeed necessary, their existence is not. But of this both the existence and the essence are necessary, and without its existence, its essence is not.⁸
25   So I see now that the truth, essence or existence of any thing does not depend on me. For as has been shown in connection with the second kind of Ideas, they are what they are without me, whether according to their essence alone or according to their essence and existence together. I find this to be true also—indeed much more so—of this third, unique idea: not only does it not depend on me, but on the contrary he alone
30   must be the subject of what I affirm of him, so that if he did not exist, I would not be able to affirm anything at all of him, though I can do this of other things, even if they do not exist. [I find] also that he must be the subject of all other things.

     From what has now been said, it is clear that the Idea of infinite attributes in the
35   perfect being is no fiction. But we shall still add the following: After the preceding

     ⁵ Gebhardt takes the reference to be to sections 5-8.

     ⁶ Ms: *verstand.* But I doubt that this can represent *intellectus* here.

     ⁷ Appuhn sees in this an allusion to the purely intellectual love described in Descartes' letter to Chanut, 1 Feb. 1647.

     ⁸ The Dutch here is too compressed to be readily intelligible. I follow Gebhardt's conjecture as to its meaning.

I/17 of man's Idea is not his capacity for forming fictions, but some external cause which compels him to understand one thing before another, and

I/18 is nothing other than that the things exist formally, and are nearer to him than others, whose objective essence is in his intellect. So if man has an Idea of God, it is clear that God must exist formally (but not eminently, since there is nothing more real or more excellent above or

5 outside him).[9]

[9] That man has an Idea of God is clear, because he understands his 'attributes,'[e] which he could not produce because he is imperfect. But that he understands these attributes is clear from his knowing that

10 the infinite cannot be composed of a number of finite parts, that there cannot be two infinites, but Only One, that it is perfect and immutable. This last he knows because he knows that no thing through itself seeks its own destruction,[f] and that it cannot change into some-

15 thing better, since it is perfect, which it would not be if it changed— and also that such a being cannot be acted on by something coming from outside, since it is omnipotent.

[10] From all of this, then, it follows clearly that one can prove God's existence both a priori and a posteriori. Indeed, the a priori

---

reflections on Nature we have not yet been able to find in it more than two attributes that belong to this all-perfect being. And these give us nothing by which we can satisfy ourselves that these would be the only ones of which this perfect being would consist.

40 On the contrary, we find in ourselves something which openly indicates to us not only that there are more, but also that there are infinite perfect attributes which must pertain to this perfect being before it can be called perfect.

And where does this Idea of perfection come from? It cannot come from these two, for two gives only two, not infinitely many. From where, then? Certainly not from me,

45 for then I would have had to be able to give what I did not have. From where else, then, than from the infinite attributes themselves, which tell us that they are, though they so far do not tell us what they are. For only of two do we know what they are.

I/18 [e] His 'attributes': it is better [to say] "because he understands what is proper to God,"

30 because those things are not God's attributes. God is, indeed, not *God* without them, but he is not God through them, because they indicate nothing substantive, but are only like *Adjectives*, which require *Substantives* in order to be explained. [Gebhardt brackets this note because he suspects it of being an interpolation.]

[f] The cause of these changes would have to be either outside it or in it. Not outside

35 it, for no substance which, like this one, is in itself depends on anything outside it; so it can undergo no change from outside. Also not in it, for no thing, much less this one, wills its own destruction. All destruction comes from something outside. [Gebhardt brackets this note as doubtful, on the ground that it merely restates more clearly what is said in the text.]

[9] Wolf finds the clause I have placed in parentheses "both irrelevant and inaccurate," and suspects it of being a reader's interpolation. But he also makes a plausible suggestion as to what may be intended, viz. that nothing could contain more reality formally than is contained objectively in the idea of God. Gebhardt takes the clause in this sense, and conjectures a mistranslation of the Latin.

20 proof is better. But, [it will be objected,][10] the things one proves in
this way, one must prove through their external causes, which is an
evident imperfection in them, since they cannot make themselves known
through themselves, but only through external causes. But God, the
first cause of all things, and also the cause of himself, makes himself
25 known through himself. So what Thomas Aquinas says[11]—that God
could not be proved a priori, because he supposedly has no cause—is
not of much importance.

I/19

Chapter II
What God is

[1] Now that we have demonstrated that God is, it is time to show
5 what he is.[1] He is, we say, a being[a] of which all, or infinite, attributes
are predicated, each of which is infinitely perfect in its own kind.

[2] In order to express this opinion of ours clearly, we shall first set
out the following four things:

I/19

10 [a] The reason for this is that since Nothing can have no attributes, the All must have
all attributes; and just as Nothing has no attributes because it is nothing, Something
has attributes because it is something. So the more it is Something, the more attributes
15 it must have. Consequently, God, being most perfect, infinite, and the Something-that-
is-all, must also have infinite, perfect, and all attributes.

[10] The interpretation of this passage has been disputed. Wolf, Sigwart, and Appuhn
took the phrase here translated "in this way" to be a reference to the a posteriori way,
and the passage to defend Spinoza's preference for a priori proofs over a posteriori ones.
Meijer, Dunin-Borkowski, and Gebhardt (rightly, I think) take the phrase to refer to
the a priori way, and the passage to expound an objection Spinoza is about to reply to.
Mignini objects that this cannot be done without emending I/47/16, a step Gebhardt
was unwilling to take. Mignini prefers to insert a "not" in l. 20, reading: "For the things
one does not prove in this way. . . ." But his interpretation assumes that an a posteriori
proof is a proof through external causes. That is hard to reconcile with Spinoza's usual
(e.g., in KV I, i, 3; E IP10S; but see KV II, xxiv, 12) contention that God's existence
can be proven a posteriori. The a posteriori proof Spinoza has offered in this chapter
would be a posteriori in the sense common in the seventeenth century (cf. the Glossary
on "a priori"), but not in Mignini's sense. I think we must recognize that I/47/16 is a
corrupt text, even if we have no straightforward emendation to suggest for it.
[11] The reference is apparently to *Summa theologiae* Ia,2,2. The annotation in Aquinas
1, 2:10-11, is helpful.
[1] Meijer thought it contrary to seventeenth-century ways of thinking to prove God's
existence before investigating his nature, citing Descartes' *First Replies*: "According to
the laws of the true logic, one must never ask of a thing *whether it exists* unless one first
knows *what it is*." (AT VII, 107-108). On this ground he thought the first two chapters
"in this form" could not have come from Spinoza. But even Descartes did not consistently follow the 'laws of the true logic.' Both in the analytic *Meditations* and in the
synthetic *Principles* the question of my existence is raised before the question of my
nature.

1. That[b] there is no limited substance,[4] but that every substance must be infinitely perfect in its kind, viz. that in God's infinite intellect no substance can be more perfect than that which already exists in Nature.

2. That there are not two equal substances.

3. That one substance cannot produce another.

4. That in God's infinite intellect there is no substance which does not exist formally in Nature.

[3] As for the first, viz. *that there is no limited substance*, etc., if anyone should wish to maintain the contrary, then we would ask him the following: is this substance then limited through itself, i.e., has it limited itself thus and did it not want to make itself more unlimited?

[b] If we can prove that there can be no limited substance, then every substance belonging to the divine being must be unlimited.[2] We do this as follows:

1. Either it must have limited itself, or another must have limited it. It did not limit itself, for being unlimited, it would have had to change its whole essence. It is also not limited by another, for that other would have to be either limited or unlimited. Not the former; therefore, the latter. So the other is God. God, then, would have to have limited it either because he lacked the power, or because he lacked the will. But the first is contrary to his omnipotence, and the second is contrary to his goodness.

2. That there cannot be a limited substance is [also] clear from this, that such a substance would necessarily have to have something which it had from Nothing. But this is impossible. For from where does it have that in which it differs from God? Never from God, for God has nothing imperfect or limited, etc. So from where, if not from Nothing? Therefore, there is no substance except an unlimited one.

From this it follows that there are not two equal unlimited substances.[3] For if there were, there would necessarily be a limitation.

And from this it follows in turn that one substance cannot produce another. As follows: the cause which would produce this substance must have the same attribute as the one produced, and also, either as much perfection, or more, or less. Not the first, for then there would be two equal substances. Not the second, for then there would be a limited substance. Not the third, for Something does not come from Nothing.

An alternative proof: if a limited substance came from an unlimited one, then the unlimited one would also be limited, etc. Therefore, one substance cannot produce another.

And from this it follows in turn that every substance must exist formally. For if it does not exist, there is no possibility of its being able to come to be.

[2] Even in the *Ethics*, after he has proven that there is only one substance, Spinoza will still speak of the attributes as substances constituting the divine nature. Cf. II/57/13-14, 22-23.

[3] Gueroult (1, 1:474-475) protests against the translation of *gelijk* by "like." The practice of the translators of the *Ethics* seems to be against Gueroult's claims about seventeenth-century Dutch usage (since *gelijk* is used for both *aequus* and *similis*), but I agree that the context here requires "equal."

[4] *Bepaalde zelfstandigheid*. Wolf has *finite substance* (similarly, Appuhn, Pléiade, Gueroult). Certainly this is correct in spirit (cf. I/26/5-6). But if the Latin were *finita*, we would expect *eindig*.

or is it limited through its cause, which either could not, or would not give it more?

15   [4] The first is not true, because it is impossible that a substance should have willed to limit itself, especially a substance which has existed through itself. I say, then, that it is limited through its cause, which is necessarily God.

    [5] Now if it is limited through its cause, that must be either because
20   its cause could not or would not give more. That he could not have given more would be contrary to his omnipotence. That ᶜhe could
I/21   have, but would not, smacks of envy, which is not in any way in God, who is all goodness and fullness.[7]

    [6] The second, that there are not two equal substances, we prove because every substance is perfect in its kind. For if there were two
5   equal substances, they would necessarily have to limit one another, and consequently, would not be infinite, as we have previously proven.

    [7] Concerning the third, the one substance cannot produce another,
10   if someone wishes to maintain the contrary, we ask whether the cause which would have to produce this substance has the same attributes as the one produced or not?

    [8] Not the latter, for Something cannot come from Nothing. Therefore, the former. And then we ask again whether, in that attribute[8]
15   which would be the cause of what is produced, there is as much perfection as in what is produced, or more, or less? We say there cannot be less, for the reasons already given. We also say there cannot be more, because then these two would be limited, which is contrary to

I/20
25   ᶜ To say here that the nature of the thing required this [limitation], and therefore it could not be otherwise, is to say nothing.[5] For the nature of the thing cannot require anything unless it exists. If you say that one can nevertheless see what belongs to the nature of a thing that does not exist, that is true *as regards existence*, but not at all *as regards essence*.

    In this lies the difference between *creating* and *generating*: *creating*, then, is bringing a thing about *as regards essence and existence together*; but in *generating* a thing comes about
30   *as regards existence only*.[6] Therefore, there is no creating in Nature, but only generating.

    So if God creates, he creates the nature of the thing together with the thing. And so he would be envious if (being able but not willing) he had created the thing in such a way that it would not agree with its cause *in essence and existence*.

35   But what we here call *creating* cannot really be said to have ever happened, and we mention it only to show what we can say about it, once we make the distinction between *creating* and *generating*.

    [5] Possibly Spinoza has in mind Descartes' Fourth Meditation (AT VII, 60), but the line of thought does not begin with Descartes. Cf. *Summa theologiae* Ia, 25,6.

    [6] Cf. *Summa theologiae* Ia,45,1.

    [7] On this theme, see Lovejoy.

    [8] So the manuscript reads. The inclination to emend to *substance* persists (Meijer, Appuhn, Pléiade), but I agree with Gebhardt and Mignini that the text is defensible.

what we have just proven. So there would have to be as much. Then there would be two equal substances, which is clearly contrary to our preceding proof.

[9] Furthermore, what is created has not in any way proceeded from Nothing, but must necessarily have been created by him who exists. But that something should have proceeded from him and that afterwards he should still have it no less than before—this we cannot conceive with our intellect.

[10] Finally, if we wish to seek the cause of that substance which is the principle of the things which proceed from its attribute, then we shall have to seek in turn the cause of that cause, and then again, the cause of that cause, and *so on to infinity*; so if we must stop somewhere (as we must), we must stop with this unique substance.

[11] Fourth, that no substance or attributes exist in God's infinite intellect which do not exist formally in Nature, we can prove as follows:

1. From God's infinite power, because there can be no cause in him by which he could have been moved to create one thing sooner or more than another.

2. From the simplicity of his will.

3. Because he cannot omit doing any good, as we shall prove later.

4. Because it is impossible that what does not exist now could come to be, since one substance cannot produce another. What is more, if that happened, there would be infinitely many more substances not existing than existing; and that is absurd.[9]

[12] From all of these it follows that of Nature all in all is predicated, and that thus Nature consists of infinite attributes, of which each is perfect in its kind. This agrees perfectly with the definition one gives of God.

[13][10] Some want to argue against what we have just said—that no

---

[9] The text here is in doubt and has frequently been suspected of being a reader's interpolation. Wolf offers: ". . . there would be more infinite substances not in existence than there are in existence . . . ," but finds neither that nor the version I prefer very intelligible. Gebhardt explains that the absurdity claimed consists in this: that on the hypothesis some substances would be merely possible, not actual, whereas existence belongs to the essence of substance. One difficulty with Gebhardt's explanation is that it is not easy to see the relevance of there being *more* nonexistent substances than existent ones.

[10] The series of objections and replies which occupies sections 13-16 has often been thought to be a later addition. As for their content, cf. E IP17C2S.

thing is in God's infinite intellect unless it exists formally in Nature—
in the following way: if God has created everything, then he cannot
create more. But that he should not be able to create more would be
contrary to his omnipotence. Therefore.

[14] Regarding the first point, we grant that God cannot create more.
As for the second, we say that we acknowledge that if God could not
create everything that is creatable, that would be contrary to his omnipotence; but it is not in any way contrary to it if he cannot create
what is contradictory in itself (as it is to say that he has created everything and could still create more).

And certainly it is a much greater perfection in God, that he has
created everything that was in his infinite intellect, than it would be
if he had not created it, and (as they say) never could have.

[15] But why say so much about this? Don't they themselves argue[d]
as follows (or shouldn't they?): if God is omniscient, then he cannot
know more; but that God cannot know more is contrary to his perfection. Therefore.

But if God has everything in his intellect, and through his infinite
perfection cannot know more, why can we not say that he has also
produced everything he had in his intellect, and brought it about that
it is, or will be, formally in Nature?

[16] Because we know, then, that everything is equally in God's
infinite intellect, and that there is no cause for his creating this sooner
or rather than that, and that he could have produced everything in a
moment, let us see if we cannot use against them the same weapons
they take up against us: if God can never create so much that he could
not create still more, then he can never create what he can create; but
that he cannot create what he can create, is self-contradictory. Therefore.

[17] The reasons why we have said that all these attributes which
are in Nature are only one, single being, and by no means different
ones (though we can clearly and distinctly understand the one without
the other), are as follows:

1. Because we have already found previously that there must be
an infinite and perfect being, by which nothing else can be understood but a being of which all in all must be predicated. For of a
being which has some essence, [some] attributes must be predicated, and the more essence one ascribes to it, the more attributes

[d] That is: when we make them argue from their belief that God is omniscient, then
they cannot argue otherwise. [Gebhardt brackets this note as certainly not from Spinoza, on the ground that it only repeats what is said in the text.]

one must also ascribe to it. So if a being is infinite, its attributes must also be infinite, and that is precisely what we call a perfect being.

2. Because of the unity which we see everywhere in Nature; if ^ethere were different beings in Nature, the one could not possibly unite with the other.

3. Because, as we have already seen,[11] one substance cannot produce another, and if a substance does not exist, it is impossible for it to begin to exist. We see, however,^f that in no substance (which we nonetheless know to exist in Nature) is there, so long as it is conceived separately, any necessity of existing. Since no existence pertains to its particular essence, it must necessarily follow that Nature, which comes from no cause, and which we nevertheless know to exist, must necessarily be a perfect being, to which existence belongs.[12]

[18] From all that we have said so far it is clear that we maintain that extension is an attribute of God. Nevertheless, this does not seem possible at all in a perfect being. For since extension is divisible, the perfect being would consist of parts. But this cannot be attributed to God, because he is a simple being. Moreover, when extension is divided, it is acted on; and that too cannot in any way be the case in God (who is not susceptible of being acted on, and cannot be acted

^e I.e., if there were different substances which were not related to one single being, then their union would be impossible, because we see clearly that they have absolutely nothing in common with one another—like thought and extension, of which we nevertheless consist.

^f I.e., if no substance can be other than real, and nevertheless no existence follows from its essence if it is conceived separately, it follows that it is not something singular, but must be something that is an attribute of another, viz. the one, unique, universal being.

Or thus: every substance is real, and the existence of a substance, conceived in itself, does not follow from its essence. So no real substance can be conceived in itself; instead it must belong to something else. I.e., when our intellect understands substantial thought and extension, we understand them only in their essence, and not in their existence, i.e. [we do not understand] that their existence necessarily belongs to their essence. But when we prove that they are attributes of God, we thereby prove a priori that they exist, and a posteriori (in relation to extension alone) [that it exists] from the modes that must have it as their subject.

[11] Wolf remarks that this is not shown in the *Treatise* as we have it, and infers that something is missing. Dunin-Borkowski points out that the reference might be to I/19/33-43. Gebhardt, who regards that note as a later addition, suggests instead I/21/26-32. More plausibly, the reference may be to I/22/5-9.

[12] Probably we should read: "to whose essence existence belongs." Unless we assume a copyist's error, the conclusion seems redundant, and the similarity of *Wezenheid* and *Wezenlijkheid* makes such an error only too easy.

on by any other being, since he is the first efficient cause of everything).

[19] To this we reply:

1. That part and whole are not true or actual beings, but only
beings of reason; consequently in Nature[g] there are neither whole
nor parts.

2. A thing composed of different parts must be such that each
singular part can be conceived and understood without the others.
For example, in a clock that is composed of many different wheels,
cords, etc., I say that each wheel, cord, etc., can be conceived
and understood separately, without needing [the understanding
of] the whole as a whole. Similarly with water, which consists of
straight, oblong particles.[13] Each part of it can be conceived and
understood, and can exist, without the whole.

But since extension is a substance, one cannot say of it that it
has parts, since it cannot become smaller or larger, and no parts
of it could be understood separately. For in its nature it must be
infinite.

That it must be without parts also follows from this: if it did
consist of parts, it would not be infinite through its nature, as we
have said it is. But it is impossible that parts could be conceived
in an infinite Nature, for all parts are, by their nature, finite.

[20] To this we may add that if extension consisted of distinct parts,
then it would be intelligible that some of its parts might be destroyed
even though it remained and was not destroyed by the destruction of

[g] In Nature, i.e., in substantial extension. For if this were divided, its nature and
being would be destroyed at once, since it consists only in infinite extension, or what
is the same, being a whole. But, you will say, is there no part in extension prior to all
its modes? None, I reply.

But, you say, if there is motion in matter, it must be in a part of matter, not in the
whole, since the whole is infinite. For in what direction would it be moved, since there
is nothing outside it? Then in a part.

I reply: there is no motion by itself, but only motion and rest together; and this is,
and must be, in the whole; for there is no part in extension.

If you still say that there are parts in extension, then I ask: when you divide the
whole extension, can you also, according to the nature of all parts, cut off from the
others the part you cut off with your intellect? Assuming that you can, I ask what there
is between the part cut off and the rest?

You must say: either a vacuum, or another body, or something of extension itself.
There is no fourth alternative. Not the first, for there is no vacuum, something positive,
but not a body. Not the second, for then there would be modes where there can be
none, since extension as extension is without and prior to all modes. The third then.
And so there is no part, but only extension as a whole.

[13] Cf. Descartes, *Les météores*, chap. 1, AT VI, 233.

some of its parts. This is clearly a contradiction in something which
is infinite through its own nature, and can never be, or be understood
to be, limited or finite.

[21] Furthermore, concerning the parts in Nature, we say (as we
said before) that division never occurs in the substance, but always
and only in the modes of the substance. So if I want to divide water,
I divide only the mode of the substance, not the substance itself; the
substance[14] is always the same, [though] now [it is the substance] of
water, now [the substance] of something else.

[22] Division, then, or being acted on, always happens in the mode,
as when we say that a man perishes, or is destroyed, that is only
understood of the man insofar as he is a composite being and mode of
substance, and not the substance itself on which he depends.

[23] Moreover, we have already said,[15] and will say again, that outside God, there is nothing, and that he is an immanent cause. But
being acted on, when the agent and the one acted on are different, is
a palpable imperfection. For the one acted on must necessarily depend
on what, outside him, has produced this state of being acted on. In
God, who is perfect, this cannot happen.

[24] Further, one can never say of such an agent, which acts in
himself, that he has the imperfection of being acted on, because he is
not acted on by another; similarly, the intellect, as the Philosophers
also say, is a cause of its concepts. But since it is an immanent cause,
who would dare say that it is imperfect when it is acted on by itself?

[25] Finally, substance, because it is the principle of all its modes,
can with much greater right be called an agent, rather than one acted
on. With this, we consider that we have answered all the objections
satisfactorily.

[26] The further objection may be made, however, that there must
necessarily be a first cause which makes this body move; for when it
is at rest, it cannot possibly move itself. And since it is clear that there
is motion and rest in Nature, these must, they think, come from an
external cause.

[27] But it is easy for us to answer this. For we grant that if body
were a thing existing through itself, and had no other property than
length, breadth, and depth, then if it really were at rest, there would
be no cause in it for it to begin to move itself. But we have posited
above that *Nature is a being of which all attributes are predicated.* This

---

[14] The ms. reads *Modes.* I follow Mignini, who prefers Monnikhoff's emendation.

[15] In the *Treatise* as we have it, this has not been said already, though it will be said
in the First Dialogue. This has prompted the conjecture that the dialogue was originally
placed earlier.

being so, nothing can be lacking to it to produce everything there is
to produce.

[28] So far, then, we have spoken of what God is; now we shall say
only a word about his attributes: those which are known to us consist
of only two, viz. thought and extension, for we are speaking here only
of attributes which one could call God's proper attributes, through
which we come to know him in himself, and not as acting outside
himself.

[29] Everything which men ascribe to God besides these two attributes, must, if it does otherwise belong to him, either be an extrinsic
denomination, such as existing through himself, being eternal, one,
immutable, etc., or be in respect to his actions, such as that he is a
cause, a predeterminer, and ruler of all things. These are all *propria* of
God, but they do not give us any knowledge of what he is.

[30] However, we shall say later, in the following chapters, how
these 'attributes' can have a place in God. But to make this better
understood and explain it further, we thought it good to add the following discourses, consisting of a:

DIALOGUE[1]

BETWEEN THE INTELLECT,[2] LOVE,

REASON, AND LUST[3]

[1] *Love*: I see, Brother, that my being and perfection depend entirely
on your perfection; and since the perfection of the object you have
conceived is your perfection, and mine in turn proceeds from yours,
tell me, I beg you, whether you have conceived a supremely perfect
being, which cannot be limited by anything else, and in which I too
am contained.

[2] *Intellect*: For my part, I consider Nature only as completely infinite and supremely perfect. If you doubt this, ask Reason. He will
tell you this.

---

[1] Avenarius (1) argued that this dialogue antedated the rest of the *Short Treatise* and
represented a very early stage of Spinoza's thought in which he was primarily under
the influence of Bruno. (Sigwart 1 and 2 give a number of parallel passages in Bruno,
but they are not restricted to this dialogue.) The present consensus (following Freudenthal) seems to be that both dialogues are later than the main body of the work, whose
doctrines they presuppose.

[2] *Verstand*. None of the Latin terms which *verstand* usually translates seem quite right,
since in the dialogue it is contrasted with reason in the way intuitive knowledge typically is.

[3] *Begeerlijkheid*. A term not used elsewhere in contemporary Dutch translations of
Spinoza. Meijer warns against confusing it with *begeerte* and suggests the Dutch term
lust, or "love in the lower sense," as a gloss.

15   [3] *Reason*: I find the truth about this indubitable: for if we want to limit Nature, we will have to limit it, absurdly, with a Nothing. We avoid this absurdity by maintaining that it—i.e., infinite Nature, in
20   which everything is contained—is an eternal Unity, Infinite, omnipotent;[4] the negation of these we call Nothing.

    [4] *Lust*: It will be marvelous, indeed, if this should turn out to be consistent: that Unity agrees with the Diversity I see everywhere in Nature: For how could this be?
25   I see that intellectual substance has nothing in common with extended substance and that the one limits the other[5] [5] and if, in addition to these two substances, you want to posit still a third, which is perfect in everything, then you will involve yourself in manifest contradictions. For if this third substance is posited, apart from the
30   first two, it will lack all the attributes which pertain to these two. And this is impossible in a whole, outside which no thing is.[6]

I/29   [6] Furthermore, if this being is omnipotent and perfect, it will be such because it has produced itself, and not because something else has produced it. Nevertheless, it would be even more omnipotent if it could produce both itself and something else.

5   [7] Finally, if you call it omniscient, it must know itself, and at the same time, you must understand that the knowledge of oneself alone is less than the knowledge of oneself together with the knowledge of other substances.

    All these are manifest contradictions. That is why I would have
10   advised Love to content herself with what I show her, and not to look for other things.[7]

---

[4] The manuscript here is extremely confused, with marginal insertions whose authority and proper placement are unclear. I have followed a suggestion of Freudenthal's. Gebhardt favors an emendation which would be translated: "For if we want to limit Nature we will have to limit it, absurdly, with a Nothing, conceived as having the following attributes: it is one, eternal, existing through itself, infinite. We avoid this absurdity by maintaining that it—that is, infinite Nature and everything contained in it—is an eternal unity, infinite, omnipotent, etc." Gebhardt regards as decisive a passage in the *Metaphysical Thoughts* (I/268/22-24) which condemns believers in a creation *ex nihilo* for imagining nothing as something real.

[5] Freudenthal, followed by Wolf and Appuhn, introduced a negation here: "The one does not limit the other." Certainly it is good Spinozistic doctrine that a thing can only be limited by another of the same kind (cf. E ID2, Epp.3,4). Gebhardt argues that there is no reason to credit Lust with this Spinozistic view, and Mignini seems to agree. But I take it that the first thing Lust claims to see here (that intellectual substance and extended substance have nothing in common) is also good Spinozistic doctrine (cf. E IP2). Since Lust seems to be trying to deduce unwelcome conclusions from Spinozistic assumptions, I find the emendation plausible.

[6] Some have wanted to reject this sentence as an interpolation. Gebhardt defends it.

[7] Because Reason makes no reply to the objections of sections 6 and 7, Freudenthal and Wolf thought them an interpolation. Gebhardt argues that since the dialogues are only supplementary to the main text, Spinoza may have considered what is said else-

[8] *Love*: O dishonorable one! What have you shown me except that from which my immediate destruction would result? For if I had ever united myself with what you have shown me, straightaway I would have been pursued by two of the human race's main enemies—Hate and Repentance—and often also by Forgetfulness. So again I turn to Reason, that he may continue, and shut the mouths of these enemies.

[9] *Reason*: O Lust! I tell you that what you say you see—that there are distinct substances—is false. For I see clearly that there is only one, which exists through itself, and is a support of all the other attributes.[8]

And if you want to call the corporeal and the intellectual substances in respect to the modes which depend on them, you must equally call them modes too, in relation to the substance on which they depend. For you do not conceive them as existing through themselves. In the same way that you call willing, sensing, understanding, loving, etc., different modes of what you call a thinking substance (all of which you lead back to one, making one of them all), so I also infer, by your own proof, that infinite extension and thought, together with other infinite attributes (or as you would say, substances) are nothing but modes of that unique, eternal, infinite Being, existing through itself; and of all of these we make (as we have said) One Unique being or Unity, outside which one cannot imagine anything.

[10] *Lust*: In this way of speaking that you have, I think I see a very great confusion. For you seem to want the whole to be something outside of or without its parts, which is indeed absurd. For the Philosophers all say unanimously that *the whole is a second notion, which is no thing in Nature, outside human thought*.

[11] Moreover, as I gather from your example, you confuse the whole with the cause; for as I say, *the whole consists of and exists through its parts*; that is why you imagine the thinking power as a thing on which the intellect, love, etc., depend. And you cannot call it a *whole*, but a cause of the effects you have just named.

[12] *Reason*: I certainly see how you call all your friends together against me. So what you have not been able to do with your false reasoning you try to do now with ambiguous words—the usual practice of those who oppose the truth. But you will not succeed in getting Love on your side in that way.

---

where (presumably at I/22/14ff.) a sufficient refutation. But even so, it is puzzling that the objections should be included without any indication of their having been answered elsewhere. Possibly something is lost or misplaced.

[8] The Pléiade editors (Pléiade, 1368) call attention to the oddity of this expression and conjecture a mistranslation from the Latin original or a copyist's omission.

You say, then, that since the cause is a producer of its effects, it must be outside them. You say this because you know only of the transitive and not of the immanent cause, which does not in any way produce something outside itself. For example, the intellect is the cause of its concepts; that is why I called the intellect a cause (insofar as, or in the respect that its concepts depend on it);[9] and on the other hand, I call it a whole, because it consists of its concepts. Similarly, God is, in relation to his effects or creatures, no other than an immanent cause, and also a whole, because of the second consideration.

I/31

Second Dialogue

Relating Partly to the Preceding, Partly to the Second Part to Come, between Erasmus and Theophilus

[1] *Erasmus*: I have heard you say, Theophilus, that God is a cause of all things, and moreover, that he can be no other cause than an *immanent* one. If, then, he is an *immanent cause* of all things, how could you call him a remote cause? For that is impossible in an immanent cause.

[2] *Theophilus*: When I said[1] that God is a remote cause, I said that only in respect to those things [which do not depend on him immediately and not those things] which God has produced immediately (without any circumstances, by his existence alone). But I have not at all called him a remote cause absolutely. You could also have inferred this clearly from my words. For I also said that we can, *in some way*, call him a remote cause.[2]

---

[9] Here (with Gebhardt, Wolf et al.) I follow Monnikhoff rather than the manuscript, in which the parenthesis would read: "insofar as, or in the respect that, it depends on its concepts." Mignini defends this more difficult reading by arguing that as the intellect is the cause of its concepts (cf. I, ii, 24) so the concepts must be considered a cause of the intellect, insofar as they constitute it (appealing to II, xv, 5). Perhaps so, but in that case Spinoza offers no reason in this passage for calling the intellect a cause.

[1] This has not yet been said, but (assuming that *verder* here and *laatste* there both represent *remota*) will be said at I/36/18-19. This is one thing which gives plausibility to Meijer's proposal to place the Second Dialogue after Chapter III. Against that separation from the First Dialogue is the apparent continuity between them. Moreover, many subsequent references are to passages coming much later than Chapter III. The bracketed addition follows a suggestion made by Van Vloten and Land, and persuasively defended by Mignini.

[2] My italics. Gebhardt correctly has *verder* in ll. 8, 10, and 14, but wrongly emends to *eerder* in l. 16. That makes the qualification pointless. Note that Francès, who accepts Gebhardt's emendation, omits the qualification both here and in the passage to which Spinoza is apparently referring. The variations in Dutch wording (*verder* for *laatste*, *in eenigen manieren* for *eenigzins*) seem to confirm the hypothesis that the Second Dialogue

[3] *Erasmus*: Now I understand sufficiently what you want to tell me; but I note also that you said[3] that the effect of an internal cause remains united with its cause in such a way that it makes a whole with it. If that is so, then I think God cannot be an immanent cause. For if he and what he has produced make together a whole, then you ascribe more essence to God at one time than at another. Please, relieve me of this doubt.

[4] *Theophilus*: If you want to escape this confusion, Erasmus, pay close attention to what I am about to tell you. The essence of a thing does not increase through its union with another thing, with which it makes a whole. On the contrary, the first thing remains unchanged.

[5] I shall give you an example, so that you will understand me better. A sculptor has made various figures of wood, in the likeness of parts of a human body. He takes one of these, which has the shape of a human breast, adds it to another, which has the shape of a human head, and makes of these two a whole which represents the upper part of a human body. Will you say now, on that account, that the essence of the head has increased, because it has been united to the breast? That would be a mistake, for it is the same as it was before.

[6] To make this even clearer, I shall give you another example, viz. an idea I have of a triangle and another, arising from the extension of one of the angles. The angle formed by this extension is necessarily equal to the two opposite internal angles, etc. I say that these [ideas] have produced a new idea, viz. that the three angles of the triangle are equal to two right angles. This idea is so united to the first, that it can neither be nor be conceived without it.

[7] [And of all the ideas which anyone has, we make a whole, or (what is the same) a being of reason, which we call the intellect.][4]

You see now that although this new idea is united to the preceding one, no change takes place on that account in the essence of the preceding one. On the contrary, it remains without the least change. You

---

was translated by a different hand than the bulk of the *Short Treatise*. Cf. Curley 1, 333-334. Mignini also reads *verder* in l.16.

[3] Cf. I/110/32-111/2, and I/30/30-31. The fact that Spinoza also maintains that whole and part are beings of reason and do not exist in Nature (e.g., at I/24/19ff) has caused some perplexity. Freudenthal 2, 7-9, suggested that the latter doctrine was not meant to entail that the concepts were entirely without foundation in reality, that in saying that finite things formed a whole with God, Spinoza meant to express their dependence on him as immanent cause.

[4] Gebhardt retains this sentence in the text, as a third example, though others (Van Vloten and Land, Appuhn) have thought it an interpolation. Here I think Gebhardt is wrong; the rest of section 7 seems to continue the second example.

25   can also see this in each idea which in itself produces love. This love does not in any way increase the essence of the idea.

[8] But why pile up examples? For you yourself can see this clearly in the matter we are speaking of. I have said[5] distinctly that all the attributes, which depend on no other cause, and to define which no

30   genus is necessary, belong to God's essence. And because created things do not have the power to form an attribute, they do not increase God's essence, no matter how closely they are united to him.

[9] To this we may add that the whole is only a being of reason and

I/33   differs from the universal only in these respects: that the universal is made of various disunited individuals, whereas the whole is made of various united individuals, and that the universal includes only parts of the same kind, whereas the whole includes parts of the same kind and of another kind.[6]

5   [10] *Erasmus*: As far as that question is concerned, you have satisfied me. But you have also said[7] that the effect of an internal cause cannot perish so long as its cause endures. I see, indeed, that this is certainly true. But since it is, how can God be an internal cause of all things, since many things perish?

10   According to your previous distinction,[8] you will say that God is properly a cause of those effects he has produced immediately, through his attributes alone, without any further circumstances, and that these therefore cannot perish so long as their cause endures; but [you will

15   add] that you do not call God an internal cause of those effects whose existence does not depend immediately on him, but which have come to be from some other thing (except insofar as their causes neither do nor can act without God or outside him); and these, then, can perish, since they have not been produced by God immediately.

20   [11] But this does not satisfy me. For I see that you conclude[9] that

---

[5] The reference is apparently to I/46/34ff.

[6] Busse wanted to take this section away from Theophilus and put in in the mouth of Erasmus, as an objection Spinoza's spokesman must answer (placing it earlier). His ground was the apparent contradiction between saying that God and his effects form a whole and that the whole is only a being of reason, which does not exist in reality. Freudenthal pointed out other places where the two halves of this contradiction are asserted, so it cannot be removed so easily. Cf. I/31/20.

[7] At I/110/22-27.

[8] Possibly I/31/10-14 rather than I/35/29-I/36/3. This distinction will recur in an important and difficult passage in the *Ethics*, II/70/2-15. For discussion of some of the issues involved see Curley (1) and (3), chap. 2.

[9] At I/111/12-20. It is interesting to see that the immortality of the intellect is recognized as problematic in Spinoza's philosophy from the very beginning. But it is seen as raising problems relating to God's causality, not the parallelism of the attributes.

the human intellect is immortal, because it is an effect that God has produced in himself. Now it is impossible that more was needed, to produce such an intellect, than God's attributes alone. For to be a being of such an eminent perfection it must have been created from eternity, like all other things which depend immediately on God. And if I am not mistaken, I have heard you say this yourself. How will you slip out of this without leaving difficulties behind?

[12] *Theophilus*: It is true, Erasmus, that those things which have been created by him immediately (those which for their existence required nothing but God's attributes) have been created from eternity. But it should be noted that even if it is necessary for the existence of a thing that a particular modification be present and [so] something outside God's attributes, that still does prevent God from being able to produce [such] a thing immediately. For of the things required to make things exist, some are required to produce the thing, and others for it to be able to be produced.

For example, if I want to have light in a certain room, I light [a candle] and this, through itself, lights the room—or I open a window [shutter], and though opening it does not itself make light, still it brings it about that the light can come into the room. Similarly, for the motion of a body, another body is required, which must already have that motion which passes from it to the first body.

But to produce an idea of God in us, no other particular thing is required which has what is produced in us; all that is necessary is that there be in Nature a body such that its idea represents God immediately.[10] This too you could have inferred from my words. For I have said[11] that God is known only through himself and not through something else.

[13] But I tell you this: so long as we do not have such a clear idea of God that it so unites us to him as not to let us love anything outside him, we cannot say that we are truly united with God, and so depend immediately on him.

If you still have anything to ask me, leave it for another time. Right now I am required elsewhere. Farewell.

[14] *Erasmus*: For the moment I have nothing. But I shall think about what you have just told me until the next time we meet. I commend you to God.

---

[10] Appuhn offers the following gloss: "The existence of the body is not the determining cause of the idea of God, but a condition which must be satisfied for this idea, existing from all eternity in the intellect, to become conscious of itself."

[11] Cf. I/101/3ff.

Chapter III

[How God is a Cause of All Things][1]

[1] We shall now begin to treat of those 'attributes' we have called Propria.[a] And first, how God is a cause of all things.

We have already said before that one substance cannot produce another, and that God is a being of which all attributes are predicated. From this it clearly follows that all other things cannot in any way exist or be understood without or outside him. So we have every reason to say that God is a cause of all things.

[2] Since it is customary[2] to divide the efficient cause into eight parts, let us now investigate how, and in what way God is a cause?

1. We say that God is an emanative or productive cause of his actions, and in respect to the action's occurring, an active or efficient cause. We treat this as one thing, because they involve each other.

2. He is an immanent and not a transitive cause, since he does everything in himself, and not outside himself (because outside him there is nothing).

3. God is a free cause, not a natural one, as we shall show very clearly when we treat the question whether God can omit doing what he does? At that point we shall explain what true freedom consists in.

4. God is a cause through himself, and not an accidental cause. This will be more evident after our discussion of predestination.

5. God is a principal cause of the effects he has created immediately, such as motion in matter, etc., where there can be no place

---

[a] The following are called *Propria* because they are nothing but *Adjectives* which cannot be understood without their *Substantives*. I.e., without them God would indeed not be God; but still, he is not God through them, for they do not make known anything substantial, and it is only through what is substantial that God exists.

[1] The manuscript has no title at this point. Gebhardt supplies "Of God's Immanent Actions" from the running heads of subsequent pages of the manuscript. Mignini argues persuasively that these are without authority and supplies "That God is a Cause of All Things" from the Table of Contents, on the assumption that that represents the original title. I have been guided by the second sentence, which seems to describe more accurately the actual contents of the chapter.

[2] This division of causes is to be found in Burgersdijk's *Logic* and, with a slight variation in the order, in Heereboord's *Meletemata*. On these philosophers and their relation to Spinoza see the Editorial Preface to *Descartes' Principles*. For comment on Burgersdijk's classification of causes, see Wolf 2, 190-195; Wolfson 1, 1:303-304; and Gueroult 1, 1:224-257.

for the subsidiary cause, which is confined to particular things (as when God makes the sea dry by a strong wind,[3] and similarly in all particular things in Nature).

The subsidiary initiating cause is not applicable to God, because there is nothing outside him that could constrain him. The predisposing cause, on the other hand, is his perfection itself, through which he is both a cause of himself, and consequently of all other things.

6. God alone is the first, or initiating, cause, as is clear from our preceding proof.

7. God is also a general cause, but only in the respect that he produces different things. Otherwise, such a thing can never be said of him. For he does not need anyone to produce effects.

8. God is the proximate cause of those things that are infinite and immutable, and which we say that he has created immediately; but he is, in a sense, the remote cause of all particular things.

Chapter IV

Of God's necessary Actions

[1] We deny that God could omit doing what he does, and we shall prove this also when we treat of predestination, where we shall show that all things depend necessarily on their causes.

[2] But this is also proven through God's perfection, for it is true beyond any doubt that God can make everything just as perfectly as it is conceived in his Idea. And just as the things he understands he cannot understand more perfectly than he does understand them, in the same way he has made them so perfect, that they cannot proceed more perfectly from him.

Moreover, when we conclude that God could not have omitted doing what he has done, we derive this from his perfection, because in God it would be an imperfection to be able to omit what he does, without, however, assuming in God a subsidiary initiating cause, which would have moved him to act, for then he would not be God.

[3] But now the dispute arises again as to whether God can omit doing everything that is in his Idea and that consequently he can produce perfectly? and whether such an omission is a perfection in him?

---

[3] The reference is to Exodus 14:21, an example which will recur in the *Metaphysical Thoughts* (I/265/14) and the *Theological-Political Treatise* (III/90/20ff).

We say that since everything that happens is done by God, it must be predetermined by him. Otherwise he would be changeable, and that would be a great imperfection in him. And since this predetermination by him must be from eternity, and since in eternity there is neither before nor after, it follows inevitably from this that God was not able before to predetermine things in a way different from that in which they are now determined from eternity, and that before or without these determinations God could not have been.

[4] Furthermore, if God should omit doing something, that must result either from a cause in him or from none. If the former, then it is necessary that he must omit doing it. If the latter, then it is necessary that he must not omit doing it. This is clear in itself.

Again, in a created thing it is a perfection to exist and to have been produced by God, for the greatest imperfection of all is not being; and because God wills the salvation[1] and perfection of everything, if God willed that this thing did not exist, the salvation and perfection of the thing would consist in not existing. This is self-contradictory. So we deny that God can omit doing what he does.

[5] Some consider this a slander and belittling of God. But such talk comes from a misconception of what true freedom consists in. For it is not at all what they think, viz. being able to do or to omit something good or evil.[2] True freedom is nothing but [being] the first cause, which is not in any way constrained or necessitated by anything else, and only through its perfection is the cause of all perfection. So if God could omit doing this, he would not be perfect. For to be able to omit doing good or bringing about perfection in what he produces can only be through a defect.

That God alone is the only free cause is clear, not only from what has just been said, but also from the fact that outside him there is no external cause which would force or necessitate him. This is not true of created things.

[6] Against this our opponents argue in the following way: the good is only good because God wills it.[3] Since this is so, he can always

---

[1] *Heil.* Wolf: "welfare." See the glossary entry on *salvation*. Translating in this fashion involves taking sides in the dispute between Kneale and Donagan as to whether Spinoza is committed to the 'hideous hypothesis' of universal salvation. Cf. Grene, 239-240, 257-258.

[2] Wolf 2, 195, cites, as characteristic scholastic definitions, passages from Burgersdijk and Heereboord. But Aquinas' position (Aquinas 1, 5:44-46) seems to be more complex, as is Descartes' (AT VII, 57).

[3] This doctrine is characteristic of the reformers (v. Luther 1, 209; Calvin 1, 949) but in the seventeenth century was associated also with Descartes (because of the doctrine

make the evil become good. This reasoning is as sound as if I said that God is God because he wills that he is God, therefore it is in his power not to be God. This is absurdity itself.

Furthermore, if men do something, and one asks them why they do that, the answer is: because justice requires it. If one then asks why justice or rather, the first cause of everything that is just, requires it, the answer must be: because justice wills it so. But would justice, indeed, be able to omit being just? Not at all, for then it could not be justice.

But those who say that God does everything he does because it is good in itself may think they do not differ from us. That is far from being true. For they assume something prior to God, to which he is obligated or bound, viz. a cause [by] which [he] has a desire that this [which] is good, and again, that [which] is just should exist.[4]

[7] Now there arises the further problem: if God had from eternity created all things in a different way, or had ordered or predetermined them differently than they are now, would he, then, be equally perfect?

It will serve as an answer to this, that if Nature had been created from all eternity in another way than it is now, it would necessarily have to follow—according to the position of those who ascribe to God will and intellect—that God had both a different will and a different intellect then, according to which he would have made it differently. So one would then be compelled to think that God is different now than he was then, and was different then than he is now. So if we maintain that he is supremely perfect now, we are compelled to say that he was not then, when he would have created everything differently. All of these are things which involve palpable absurdities in themselves, and cannot in any way be ascribed to God, who is now, ever has been, and will remain to all eternity, immutable.

[8] We also prove this from the definition we have given of a free cause, which is not one which can both do and not do something, but only one which does not depend on anything else. So whatever God does, he does and produces as the supremely free cause. [If, then, he had made things differently before than they are now, it must follow that at some time he was imperfect. And so that is false.][5] For since

---

of the creation of the eternal truths) and Hobbes (v. Hobbes 1, LW III, 256). Cf. II/76/8ff.

[4] This passage has been much emended. I follow (partly) suggestions made by Wolf and Gebhardt. Mignini defends the manuscript reading, by reasoning I am unable to follow.

[5] Gebhardt thought the sentences bracketed here, and below (ll. 28-29), were mis-

20 God is the first cause of all things, there must be something in him through which he does what he does, and does not omit doing it. Because we say that freedom does not consist in [being able to] do something or not do it, and because we have also shown that what makes [God] do something can be nothing other than his own perfec-
25 tion, we conclude that if it was not his perfection which made him do it, the things would not exist, or could not have come to be what they are now. [This is just as if one said that if God were imperfect, things would now be different than they are now.]

30 [9] So much for the first 'attribute'; we shall now pass to the second one that we call a *proprium* in God, and see what we have to say about that, and so on to the end.

I/40

CHAPTER V

OF GOD'S PROVIDENCE

[1] The second 'attribute' which we call a *Proprium* is Providence, which according to us is nothing but that striving we find both in the
5 whole of Nature and in particular things, tending to maintain and preserve their being. For it is evident that no thing, through its own nature, could strive for its own destruction, but that on the contrary, each thing in itself has a striving to preserve itself in its state, and bring itself to a better one.[1]
10 [2] So according to this definition of ours, we posit a universal and a particular Providence. The universal is that through which each thing is produced and maintained insofar as it is a part of the whole of Nature. The particular Providence is that striving which each partic-
15 ular thing has for the preservation of its being insofar as it is considered not as a part of Nature, but as a whole.

This may be explained by the following example. All man's limbs are provided and cared for, insofar as they are parts of man: That is
20 universal providence. The particular is that striving that each particular limb (as a whole, not as a part of man) has to preserve and maintain its own well-being.

---

placed, marginal notes that had crept into the text. Though they do seem to interrupt the train of thought, Mignini retains them without comment.

[1] The Pléiade editors (Pléiade, 1372) observe that Spinoza's procedure in this chapter is characteristic: he takes a popular term and gives it an entirely new sense derived from his system. For a more traditional approach, cf. Calvin 1, I, xvi. Note that in this, its first appearance in Spinoza's writings, the striving is not merely a conservative tendency, but a progressive one.

Chapter VI

Of God's Predestination[1]

25   [1] The third 'attribute,' we say, is divine Predestination.

1. We have already proven above that God cannot omit doing what he does, viz. that he has created everything so perfect, that it cannot be more perfect.

2. And moreover, that without him no thing can be or be under-
30   stood.

[2] It remains now to consider whether there are any contingent things in Nature, viz. whether there are any things that can happen
I/41   and also can not happen. And again, whether there is any thing of which we cannot ask why it is? That there are no contingent things we prove as follows:

If something has no cause of its existence, it is impossible for it to
5   exist. Something that is contingent has no cause. Therefore.

The first [premise] is beyond all dispute. The second we prove as follows:

If something that is contingent has a determinate and certain cause of its existence, then it must exist necessarily. But that something should be both contingent and necessary is self-contradictory. There-fore.

10   [3] Perhaps someone will say that, indeed, something contingent has no determinate and certain cause, but a contingent cause.

If that were so, it would be either in a divided sense or in a com-posite one, viz. either the existence of that cause is contingent (but not its being a cause), or it is contingent that that thing (which itself would
15   necessarily exist in Nature) should be a cause of the production of the contingent thing. But in either sense, this is false.

For as far as the first is concerned, if the contingent thing is contin-

---

[1] The Pléiade editors (Pléiade, 1373) point out that throughout almost the whole of the seventeenth century the topic of predestination was the subject of fierce struggles between the various Dutch Protestant sects. In accepting a strict doctrine of predesti-nation Spinoza would tend to alienate the liberal (Mennonite and Collegiant) groups from which most of his Christian friends came. But in giving the doctrine a wholly philosophic turn he would offend the Dutch national Church.

Whether the editors are equally correct in ascribing to the reading of Calvin a decisive influence on the young Spinoza is another matter. Not only are central notions reinter-preted, but the style of argument is quite different. Cf. Calvin 1, III, xxi, 2: "To seek any other knowledge of predestination than what the Word of God discloses is not less insane than if one should purpose to walk in a pathless waste."

gent because its cause is contingent [with respect to its existence], then
20   that cause must also be contingent because the cause that produced it
is also contingent [with respect to its existence,] and so on, to infinity.
And because we have already proven *that everything depends on one single
cause*, then that cause would also have to be contingent. And this is
plainly false.

25   As for the second, if that cause were not more determined to produce the one rather than the other, i.e., either to produce this *something*, or to omit producing it, then it would at the same time be
impossible both that it should produce it and that it should omit producing it. This is an outright contradiction.

30   [4] Regarding our second question: whether there is any thing in
Nature of which one cannot ask why it exists? our saying this indicates
that we must investigate through what cause a thing exists. For if that
[cause] did not exist, it would be impossible for this something to
exist.

I/42   We must seek this cause, then, either in the thing or outside it. But
if someone asks what rule we should follow in this investigation, we
say it does not seem that any at all is necessary. For if existence belongs to the nature of the thing, then certainly we must not seek the
5   cause outside it. But if existence does not belong to the nature of the
thing, then we must always seek its cause outside it. And since the
former is true only of God, this shows (as we have already proven
before) that God alone is the first cause of everything.

10   [5] And from this it is also evident, then, that this or that will of
man must also have an external cause by which it is necessarily produced (for the will's existence does not belong to its essence). This is
also clear from everything we have said in this chapter. And it will be
15   even more evident when we treat of man's freedom in the second part.

[6] Against all this, others object: how is it possible that God, who
is said to be supremely perfect, and the only cause, disposer and pro-
20   vider of all things, nevertheless permits such a confusion to be seen
everywhere in Nature? And also, why has he not created man so that
he could not sin?

[7] First, then, it cannot rightly be said that there is confusion in
Nature, since no one knows all the causes of things, and so no one
25   can judge them.

But this objection arises from ignorance, from the fact that men
have formed universal Ideas, with which they think the particulars
must agree in order to be perfect. They maintain, then, that these
30   Ideas are in God's intellect, as many of **Plato's** followers have said,

viz. *that these universal ideas* (such as *rational animal*, etc.) *have been created by God.*

And though Aristotle's followers say, of course, that these things are not actual, but only beings of reason, nevertheless they very often regard them as things. For they have said clearly that [God's] providence does not extend to particulars, but only to kinds.[2] E.g., God has never exercised his providence over Bucephalus, but only over the whole genus Horse. They say also that God has no knowledge of particular and corruptible things, but only of universals, which in their opinion are incorruptible.[3]

But we have rightly regarded this as indicating their ignorance; for all and only the particulars have a cause, not the universals, because they are nothing.

God, then, is a cause of, and provider for, only particular things. So if particular things have to agree with another nature, they will not be able to agree with their own, and consequently will not be able to be what they truly are. E.g., if God had created all men like Adam was before the fall, then he would have created only Adam, and not Peter or Paul. But God's true perfection is that he gives all things their essence, from the least to the greatest; or to put it better, he has everything perfect in himself.

[8] As for the question, why did God not create men so that they would not sin? the following reply will serve: whatever is said about sin is said only in respect to our knowledge, as when we compare two things with each other, or [consider one thing][4] in different respects. For example, if someone has made a clock precisely to strike and show the time, and that mechanism agrees well with its maker's intention, one says it is good; if not, one says it is bad, notwithstanding the fact that then it could also be good, provided his intention had been to make it confused and so that it did not strike at the hour.

[9] We conclude, then, by saying that Peter must agree with the Idea of Peter, as is necessary, and not with the Idea of Man; good and evil, or sins, are nothing but modes of thinking, not things, or anything that has existence. Perhaps we shall show this more fully in what follows.

For all things and actions which are in Nature are perfect.

---

[2] Aristotle's followers clearly do not include Aquinas (cf. *Summa theologiae* I, 22, 2) and apparently not Maimonides (Maimonides 1, 286). Appuhn ascribes the position here attacked to Averroes.

[3] Cf. I/262/30.

[4] Adopting a suggestion of Wolf's, which Gebhardt does not consider. Wolf also points out that the example is Cartesian (cf. Meditation Six, AT VII, 84).

CHAPTER VII

OF THE 'ATTRIBUTES' WHICH DO NOT BELONG TO GOD

[1] Here we shall begin to discuss those 'attributes'[a] which are commonly ascribed to God, but which do not belong to him, and also those through which they try in vain to define God.[2] We shall also speak of the rules of true definition.

[2] To do this, we shall not trouble ourselves much with the things men commonly imagine about God; we shall only investigate briefly what the philosophers can tell us about him.

They have defined God as a *being existing of himself, cause of all things, omniscient, omnipotent, eternal, simple, infinite, the greatest good, of infinite compassion*, etc.

But before we enter into this investigation, let us first see what they allow us [to say about God].

[3] First, they say that no true or legitimate definition of God can be given; for they think there can be no definition except by genus and difference, and since God is not a species of any genus, he cannot be properly or legitimately defined.[3]

[4] Next, they say again that God cannot be defined because the definition must represent the thing absolutely and affirmatively, and in their view one cannot know God affirmatively, but only negatively.[4] So no legitimate definition of God can be given.

[5] Moreover, they also say that God can never be proven a priori

---

[a] Regarding the attributes of which God consists, they are nothing but infinite substances, each of which must, of itself, be infinitely perfect. Clear and distinct reason convinces us that this must, necessarily, be so. So far,[1] however, only two of all these infinite attributes are known to us through their essence: Thought and Extension. All other things commonly ascribed to God are not attributes, but only certain modes, which may be attributed to him either in consideration of everything (i.e., all his attributes) or in consideration of One attribute. For example, that God is one, eternal, existing through himself, infinite, the cause of everything, immutable—these things are attributed to God in consideration of all his attributes. That God is omniscient and wise, etc., are attributed to him in consideration of the attribute of thought. And that he is omnipresent and fills all, etc., are attributed to him in consideration of the attribute of extension.

[1] This is one of two passages in which Spinoza implies that the unknown attributes are not unknowable. Cf. I/17/36-47.

[2] There does appear to be some confusion in the manuscript, since chapters III-IV have already discussed God's 'attributes.' Cf. I/27/11ff., and Freudenthal 2, 258-259. Mignini, however, defends the manuscript and also rejects Gebhardt's emendation of l. 6. About the latter, at least, i.e., the substitution of *beschrijven* for *bewijzen*, I believe Gebhardt must be right.

[3] Cf. *Summa theologiae* I, 3, 5. The view was a common one among scholastics and Spinoza's source is likely to have been Heereboord 1, 1:147.

[4] Cf. Maimonides 1, 81-83, with *Summa theologiae* I, 13, 12.

(because he has no cause), but only probably, or through his effects.[5]

Because they have sufficiently conceded, by these doctrines, that they have a very slight and inconsiderable knowledge of God, we may now go on to investigate their definition.

[6] First, we do not see that they give us here any Attributes through which it is known what the thing (God) is, but only *Propria*, which indeed belong to a thing, but never explain what it is. For though *existing of itself, being the cause of all things, the greatest good, eternal,* and *immutable*, etc., are proper to God alone, nevertheless through those *propria* we can know neither what the being to which these *propria* belong is, nor what attributes it has.

[7] It is time now also to look at those things which they ascribe to God, and which, nevertheless, do not belong to him,[b] such as being *omniscient, compassionate, wise,* etc. Because these things are only certain modes of the thinking thing, they can neither be nor be understood without that substance of which they are modes. That is why they cannot be attributed to him, who is a being existing of himself, without anything else.

[8] Finally, they call him the greatest good. But if by that they understand anything other than what they have already said, viz. that God is immutable, and a cause of all things, then they are confused in their own concept or have not been able to understand themselves. This arises from their error regarding good and evil, since they think man himself, and not God, is the cause of his sins and evil. But according to what we have already proven, this cannot be, unless we are compelled to maintain that man is also a cause of himself. But this will be still clearer when we treat, afterwards, of man's will.

[9] Now we must untangle the sophistries by which they try to excuse their lack of knowledge of God.

First, then, they say *that a legitimate definition must be by genus and difference.* But though all the logicians admit this, I do not know where they get it from.

Certainly if this must be true, then one can know nothing. For if we can only know a thing perfectly through a definition consisting of genus and difference, then we can never know perfectly the highest genus, which has no genus above it. Now if the highest genus, which

---

[b] I.e., in consideration of all that he is, or all his attributes. On this, see the note to [I/44/3]. [Gebhardt rejects this note as meaningless. Mignini defends it as an accurate explication of the text.]

[5] Cf. I/18/17ff. It is not clear, however, that St. Thomas would accept Spinoza's identification of proof through effects with probable argument. Cf. *Summa theologiae* I, 2, 2, ad 3.

is the cause of the knowledge of all other things, is not known, the other things which are explained by that genus are much less known or understood.

However, since we are free, and do not consider ourselves in any way bound to their positions, we shall produce, according to the true Logic, other laws of definition, guided by the division of Nature we make.

[10] We have already seen that the attributes (or as others call them substances) are things, or, to put it better and more properly, a being existing through itself; and that this being therefore makes itself known through itself. We see that other things are only modes of those attributes, and without them can neither exist nor be understood.

So definitions must be of two kinds:[6]

1. Of attributes, which are of a self-existing being; these require no genus, or anything else through which they are better understood or explained; for since they, as attributes of a being existing through itself, exist through themselves, they are also known through themselves.

2. Of those things which do not exist through themselves, but only through the attributes of which they are modes, and through which, as their genus, they must be understood.

And this is what we have to say about their position on definitions.

[11] Regarding their second claim, that we cannot know God with an adequate knowledge, Descartes has answered this satisfactorily, in his reply to the objections regarding this.[7]

[12] And as for their third contention—that God cannot be proven a priori—we have already answered that previously. Since God is the cause of himself, it is enough that we prove him through himself, and such a proof is much more conclusive than an a posteriori one, which usually proceeds only by external causes.[8]

---

[6] Cf. Hobbes, *De Corpore*, VI, 13.

[7] Cf. AT VII, 368.

[8] In this sentence the copyist first wrote "a priori," but immediately crossed it out and wrote "a posteriori." The question is whether he was correcting a mistake he himself had made in copying or attempting a textual emendation. The reading the copyist preferred is certainly an easier one, but I find it suspiciously so. The first sentence refers us to a prior reply to the objection that God's existence cannot be proven a priori. Probably the reference is to I, i, 10. Just possibly it is to I, vii, 5. In both passages, however, the objection assumes the usual seventeenth-century concept of an a priori proof, that it proceeds from cause to effect. (Though the text of I, i, 10 is disputed, ll. 25-28 are not.) If the objector also assumed that cause and effect are always distinct, he might take Spinoza to be implying that God has an external cause. And Spinoza might well reply that, although an a priori proof *usually* (I/47/16) proceeds from an external

Chapter VIII

Of *Natura naturans*

20   Here, before we proceed to anything else, we shall briefly divide the whole of Nature into *Natura naturans* and *Natura naturata*. By *Natura naturans* we understand a being that we conceive clearly and distinctly through itself, without needing anything other than itself (like all the
25   attributes which we have so far described), i.e., God. The Thomists have also understood God by this phrase, but their *Natura naturans* was a being (as they called it) beyond all substances.[1]

We shall divide *Natura naturata* in two: a universal and a particular.
30   The universal consists in all those modes which depend on God immediately. We shall treat them in the next chapter. The particular consists in all those singular things which are produced by the universal modes. So *Natura naturata* requires some substances in order to be conceived properly.

I/48

Chapter IX

Of *Natura naturata*

[1] Turning now to universal *Natura naturata*, or those modes or creatures which immediately depend on, or have been created by God—
5   we know only two of these: Motion[a] in matter, and Intellect in the thinking thing. We say, then, that these have been from all eternity, and will remain to all eternity, immutable, a work truly as great as the greatness of the workman.

10   [2] With regard particularly to Motion, it belongs more properly to a treatise on Natural science than here, [to show] that it has been from

---

cause, it does not always do so, viz. not when the entity is *causa sui*. I assume that some such dialectic lies behind both I, i, 10, and I, vii, 12. But if so, then the text of I, vii, 12 is defective in a way that cannot be repaired simply by substituting "a priori" for "a posteriori."

I/48   [a] Note: What is said here of Motion in matter is not said seriously. For the Author
30   still intends to discover its cause, as he has already done, to some extent, a posteriori. But it can stand as it is here, because nothing is built on it, or depends on it. [The style and content of this note suggest that, while probably not written by Spinoza himself, it probably was written in his lifetime, by someone privy to his plans. It is unclear what portion of the text Spinoza intends to disavow, possibly the use of the language of creation. Gebhardt regards this note as evidence that the manuscript originated in a dictation, and points out that the problem here mentioned concerned Spinoza to the end of his life. Cf. Letters 82 and 83.]

[1] Gueroult points out (1, 1:564-568) that although the use of the phrase *Natura naturans* to designate God was current among seventeenth-century Scholastics, there is reason to dissociate Thomas himself from this usage.

all eternity, and will remain to all eternity, immutable, that it is infinite in its kind, that it can neither exist nor be understood through itself, but only through Extension. So we shall not treat any of these things here, but shall say only that it is a Son,[1] product or effect, created immediately by God.

[3] As for Intellect in the thinking thing, this too is a Son, product or immediate creature of God, also created by him from all eternity, and remaining immutable to all eternity. Its sole property is to understand everything clearly and distinctly at all times. From this arises immutably a satisfaction infinite, or most perfect, since it cannot omit doing what it does. And though what we have just said is sufficiently clear through itself, we shall nevertheless prove it more clearly later when we treat of the Affections of the Soul. So we shall say no more about it here.

Chapter X

What Good and Evil are

[1] To say briefly now what good and evil are in themselves, we begin as follows:

Some things are in our intellect and not in Nature; so these are only our own work, and they help us to understand things distinctly. Among these we include all relations, which have reference to different things. These we call *beings of reason*.

[2] So the question now is whether good and evil should be regarded as *beings of reason* or as *real beings*. But since good and evil are nothing but relations, they must, beyond any doubt, be regarded as *beings of reason*. For one never says that something is good except in respect to something else that is not so good, or not so useful to us as something else. So one says that a man is bad only in respect to one who is better, or that an apple is bad only in respect to another that is good, or better. None of this could possibly be said if there were not something better, or good, in respect to which [the bad] is so called.

[3] Therefore, if one says that something is good, that is nothing but saying that it agrees well with the universal Idea which we have of such things. But as we have already said, things must agree with their particular Ideas, whose being must be a perfect essence, and not with universal ones, because then they would not exist.

[4] [As for confirming what we have just said, the thing is clear to

---

[1] The Pléiade editors (Pléiade, 1375) observe that the use of traditional religious language here is neither a mark of Christian influence, nor a concession to the sensibilities of his audience, but a desacralization of an important theological concept. Cf. I/117-18.

us, but to conclude what we have said we shall add the following proofs.

30   All things which exist in Nature are either things or actions.
Now good and evil are neither things nor actions.
Therefore, good and evil do not exist in Nature.

I/50   For if good and evil were things or actions, they would have to have their definitions. But good and evil, say, Peter's goodness and Judas's evil, have no definitions apart from the [particular] essence[s] of Judas and Peter, for these [essences] alone [are] in Nature, and without them [the goodness of Peter and the evil of Judas] cannot be defined. There-
5   fore, as above, it follows that good and evil are not things or actions which are in Nature.][1]

I/51

The Second Part
On Man and What Pertains to Him

PREFACE TO THE SECOND PART

[1] Because we have spoken in the First Part of God, and of the universal and infinite things, in this Second Part we shall now proceed to
10   treat of particular and limited things—not of all of them, since they are innumerable, but only of those that concern man. And first we shall consider what man is, insofar as he consists of certain modes (contained in those two attributes which we have noted in God).

15   [2] I say of certain modes because I do not at all think that man,
I/52   insofar as he consists of a mind, soul, or body, is a substance. For we have shown previously, at the beginning of this book;[1]

    1. *That no substance can begin*;
    2. *That one substance cannot produce another*;
    and finally,
I/53   3. *That there cannot be two equal substances.*

---

  [1] Gebhardt brackets this concluding section as doubtful. This represents the consensus among students of the *Short Treatise* who have considered the question (e.g., Sigwart, Freudenthal, Wolf). But their main reason for bracketing seems to be that nothing like this argument is found elsewhere in Spinoza. Whether that is true or not, it seems an insufficient reason for rejecting the authenticity of the passage. Mignini cites various passages supporting the authenticity of the assumption that all things (*dingen*) existing in Nature are either things (*zaaken*) or actions, e.g., I/43/35, II/24/28, IV/311/16-17.

  [1] The reference is evidently to I/19/7ff.

[3] Since man, then, has not existed from eternity, is limited, and equal to[2] many men, he cannot be a substance, so that whatever he has of thinking are only modes of the attribute of thought which we ascribe to God. And again, whatever he has of form, motion, etc., are similarly modes of that other attribute which is ascribed to God.

[4] And though some try to prove that man is a substance from the fact that the nature of man can neither exist nor be understood without those attributes which we ourselves concede to be substance, nevertheless, this has no other foundation than false suppositions.

For because the nature of matter or body has existed before the form of this human body existed, that nature cannot be peculiar to the human body, because it is clear that at that time when man did not exist, it could not have belonged to man's nature.

[5] And we deny what they make a fundamental principle: *that that belongs to the nature of a thing without which the thing can neither exist nor be understood.* For we have already proven that without God no thing can either exist or be understood. I.e., God must first exist and be understood before these particular things exist and are understood. Also, we have shown that genera do not belong to the nature of definition but that such things, which cannot exist without others, also cannot be understood without them. Since this is so, what rule do we lay down, by which one will know what belongs to the nature of a thing?

The rule is this: That belongs to the nature of a thing without which the thing can neither exist nor be understood: but this is not sufficient; it must be in such a way that the proposition is always convertible, viz. that what is said also can neither be nor be understood without the thing.

We shall begin, then, to treat of these modes of which man consists at the start of the first chapter, which follows.

✳

I/51/16   1.[3] Our soul is either a substance or a mode; not a substance, for we have already proven that there can be no limited substance in Nature. Therefore, a mode.

---

[2] *Gelijk met.* Here Wolf's "like" seems more natural, though sense can be given to "equal to," e.g., "has as much reality as." Cf. above, note to I/19/32.

[3] What follows is generally printed as a note to the first sentence of section 2 of this Preface, but no one has really thought that placement correct; the manuscript does not give any indication of where the "note" should go. Freudenthal suggested that it was probably intended to replace or supplement a passage originally appearing at the beginning of Chapter I, where there seems to be a gap in the manuscript.

If it is placed between the main content of the Preface and the main content of

2. Being a mode, then, it must be a mode either of substantial extension or substantial thought; not of extension because etc.; therefore, of thought.

3. Because substantial thought cannot be limited, it is infinitely perfect in its kind, and an attribute of God.

4. A perfect thought must have a knowledge, idea, mode of thinking, of each and every thing that exists, both of substances and of modes, without exception.

5. We say "that exists" because we are not speaking here of a knowledge, Idea, etc., which knows the whole of Nature, the connection of all beings according to their essences, without knowing their particular existence, but only of the knowledge, Idea, etc., of particular things which continually come into existence.

6. This knowledge, Idea, etc., of each particular thing which comes to exist, is, we say, the soul of this particular thing.

7. Each and every particular thing that comes to exist becomes such through motion and rest. The same is true of all modes in the substantial extension we call body.

8. The differences between [one body and another] arise only from the different proportions of motion and rest, by which this one is so, and not so, is this and not that.

9. From this proportion of motion and rest, then, there comes to exist also this body of ours, of which (no less than of all other things) there must exist a knowledge, Idea, etc., in the thinking thing. This Idea, knowledge, etc., then, is also our soul.

10. But our body had a different proportion of motion and rest when we were unborn children, and later when we are dead, it will have still another. Nevertheless, there was before our birth, and will be after our death, an Idea, knowledge, etc., of our body in the thinking thing, as there is now. But it was not, and will not be at all the same, because now it has a different proportion of motion and rest.

11. To produce in substantial thought an Idea, knowledge, mode of thinking, such as [this soul of] ours now is, not just any body whatever is required (for then it would have to be known differently than it is),

---

Chapter I, we do get an order approximating that of Part II of the *Ethics*. Sections 1 to 3 of the Preface to Part II of the *Short Treatise* would correspond to the Preface of Part II of the *Ethics*, P10, P10S, and P10C; sections 4 and 5, to P10CS; the 'note' (or at least its first thirteen paragraphs) would correspond to the section beginning with IIP11 and ending with P16C1 (though paragraphs 3 and 4 go back to IIP1 and P3); and Chapter I would correspond to the presentation in the *Ethics* of the three kinds of knowledge, beginning with IIP17 and ending with P47S.

but one which has this proportion of motion and rest and no other. For as the body is, so is the soul, Idea, knowledge, etc.

12. So if such a body has and preserves its proportion—say of 1 to 3—the soul and the body will be like ours now are; they will, of course, be constantly subject to change, but not to such a great change that it goes beyond the limits of from 1 to 3; and as much as it changes, so also the soul changes each time.

13. And this change, which arises in us from the fact that other bodies act on ours, cannot occur without the soul's becoming aware of it, since it, too, changes constantly. And this change [i.e., in the soul] is really what we call sensation.

14. But if other bodies act on ours with such force that the proportion of motion [to rest] cannot remain 1 to 3, that is death, and a destruction of the soul, insofar as it is only an Idea, knowledge, etc. of a body having this proportion of motion and rest.

15. However, because it is a mode in the thinking substance, it has been able to know and love this [substance] also, as well as that of extension; and uniting itself with these substances (which always remain the same), it has been able to make itself eternal.[4]

I/54

CHAPTER I

OF OPINION, BELIEF AND SCIENCE

[1] To begin our discussion of the modes[a] of which man consists, we shall say: 1. what they are, 2. what their effects are, and 3. what their cause is.

Regarding the first, let us begin with those which are first *known*

---

[a] The modes of which man consists are perceptions, divided into opinion, true belief, and clear and distinct knowledge, produced by objects, each according to its own kind. [Gebhardt relegates this and the other five ms. notes in this chapter to his textual commentary, on the ground that they are clearly a reader's comments. This second part of the work contains a great many notes of this kind: appearing in the margin of the ms., summarizing the content of the paragraph next to which it stands, and typically not being keyed to any word or phrase in the paragraph. Generally they read like a student's notes and Gebhardt's policy is to mention them only in his textual commentary. Mignini reproduces all of them in the margins of his text. I reproduce in bracketed footnotes all those which I think might illuminate the text in any way.]

[4] Wolf thought this final section of the note both inaccurate and inessential, and doubted whether it came from Spinoza. Gebhardt saw nothing against its authenticity. I find it no more problematic than any of Spinoza's other pronouncements on the eternity of the mind.

to us, viz. certain perceptions,[1] or the consciousness, of the knowledge of ourselves and of those things that are outside us.[2]

✳

[2] We acquire these [2]perceptions, then, either 1. simply through 'belief'[b] (which comes either from experience or from report), or 2. through a true belief, or 3. through a clear and distinct concept.

The first is commonly subject to error. The second and third, though they differ from one another, cannot err.

[3] To make this somewhat more clearly understood, we shall use an example taken from the rule of three.

Someone[c] has merely heard someone else say that if, in the rule of three, you multiply the second and third numbers, and divide the product by the first, you then find the fourth number, which has the same proportion to the third as the second has to the first. And in spite of the fact that the one who told him this could have been lying, he still governed his actions according to this rule, without having had any more knowledge of the rule of three than a blind man has of color.

---

[b] The perceptions of this 'belief' are put first at [I/55/18]; also it is here and there called opinion, which it also is. [This seems to be a reader's attempt to clarify a distinction blurred by the translation. According to a conjecture by Sigwart, now generally accepted, the translator used *geloof* for *opinio* at I/54/10, decided later that it was required for *fides*, and adopted *waan* for *opinio*, without making the change consistently. I mark nonstandard uses of *geloof* by putting single quotes around *belief*.]

[c] [This one only opines, or is commonly said, 'believes' only from report.]

[1] The manuscript has *begrippen*, which I think must here correspond to *perceptiones* rather than *ideas* or *conceptus* or *conceptiones*. Cf. II/10/3 and II/122/2ff. Though this *may* be the earliest of Spinoza's various divisions of knowledge, the initial division is like that of the *Ethics* (and unlike that of the *Treatise on the Intellect*) in recognizing three main species of knowledge, with a subdivision of the first, rather than four species of knowledge. As Freudenthal pointed out, there is, in the *Short Treatise* as a whole, a good deal of variation in Spinoza's treatment of the division. For example, in II, iii, 4, the three-fold division is into knowledge from report, from opinion, and from true perception. More important, it is unclear whether true belief (= belief in II, ii, 1 = reason in II, xiv, 2 and E IIP40S2) can lead us to the knowledge and love of God which constitute our highest happiness or whether only science (= clear and distinct conception = clear knowledge in II, ii, 1 = intuitive science in E II P40S2) can have this effect. Contrast II, iv, 3; II, v, 7; and II, xviii with II, xiv, 2; II, xix, 2; II, xxii, 1; II, iv, 2; II, xxvi, 6.

[2] I have translated the ms. reading of this sentence, which is retained by Mignini. But many scholars have felt that it required emendation and have conjectured mistranslations of the original Latin. Here are the main alternatives: "viz. from certain ideas, or from the knowledge of ourselves, and then let us treat of things outside us" (Freudenthal); "viz. from certain ideas or from the knowledge of ourselves, *or* consciousness, and of things outside us" (Appuhn); "viz. certain perceptions of those things which are outside us and the knowledge of ourselves, *or* consciousness" (Gebhardt).

The ellipsis space marks the place where Gebhardt (following Freudenthal) believes the note from the Preface should come. See I/51/16ff.

So whatever he may have been able to say about it, he repeated, as a parrot repeats what it has been taught.

A second person,[d] of quicker perception, is not content in this way with report, but tests it with some particular calculations, and finding that these agree with it, he gives his 'belief' to it. But we have rightly said that this one too is subject to error. For how can he be sure that the experience of some particular [cases] can be a rule for him for all.

A third,[e] being satisfied neither with report, because it can deceive, nor with the experience of some particular [cases], because it cannot be a rule, consults true reason, which has never, when properly used, been deceptive. Reason tells him that because of the property of proportionality in these numbers, this is so, and could not have been, or happened, otherwise.

But a fourth,[f] who has the clearest knowledge of all, has no need either of report, or of experience, or of the art of reasoning, because through his penetration he immediately sees the proportionality in all the calculations.[3]

Chapter II

What Opinion, Belief and clear Knowledge are

[1] We shall now come to treat of the effects of the different kinds of knowledge of which we have spoken in the preceding chapter, and as in passing, say again what opinion, belief and clear knowledge are.[1]

[2] We call the first opinion because it is subject to error, and has no place in anything of which we are certain, but only where guessing and speculating are spoken of.

[a]We call the second belief, because the things we grasp only through

---

[d] [This one opines or 'believes' not only through hearsay, but through experience. These are two kinds of opining.]

[e] [This one is certain through true belief, which can never deceive him. He is properly called a believer.]

[f] [But this last one never opines or believes, but sees the thing itself, not through something else, but in itself.]

[a] See the definition of belief, p. 2; and where the affirmation, taken for the *will*, is

[3] The manuscript reads: "the proportionality and all the calculations." Modern editors follow Monnikhoff, as I have. But even with that emendation, the expression does not seem very exact. The thought, presumably, is: "he immediately sees the proportionality of the numbers in [*all* those?] problems which others solve by calculation." Cf. II/12/11-14.

[1] Freudenthal 2, 262, thought it incredible that, having explained his view clearly and distinctly in II, i, Spinoza should have repeated it in a modified and less clear manner here.

25 reason, we do not see, but know only through a conviction in the intellect that it must be so and not otherwise.

But we call that clear knowledge which comes not from being convinced by reasons, but from being aware of and enjoying the thing itself. This goes far beyond the others.

30 [3] This said, let us come now to their effects. From the first, we say, come [3]all the passions which are contrary to good reason; from I/56 the second, the good [4]Desires; and from the third, true and genuine [5]Love, with all that comes of that.

[4] [6]So we maintain that knowledge is the proximate cause of all the
5 'Passions' of the soul.[2] For we consider it quite impossible that if someone neither perceives nor knows in any of the preceding ways, he should be able to be moved to Love, or Desire, or any other modes of will.

Chapter III

Of the origin of the Passions

in opinion

10 [1] Let us now see how the Passions arise, as we have said, from opinion. And to make this more intelligible, we shall take some par-
15 ticular cases, and prove what we say by using them as examples.

[2] Let us take Wonder [7]first. This is found in one who knows the thing in the first way, for because he draws a universal conclusion from some particular [cases],[1] he is astonished when he sees something
20 that goes against this conclusion of his[a]—like someone who has never

---

distinguished from belief, p. 2. [A marginal note. The first page reference would presumably be to I/59/23-36; the second, to I/80/24-34.]

[2] As Sigwart pointed out, this seems to be aimed explicitly at Descartes, PA I, 27, where motions of the animal spirits are made the cause of the passions. Appuhn calls attention to E IIA3 as a parallel passage, but questions whether *passion* is not too narrow a term to use for *lijding* here. *Lijding* may translate *passio* in section 3, but perhaps renders *affectus* in section 4. See the Glossary-Index on *passion*.

[1] Wolf has "from a few particulars" here, but I take it that what is in question is *any* inference from some to all. (One might see a great many sheep before seeing one with a long tail.)

I/56 [a] This does not mean that a formal inference must always precede wonder; it also
25 occurs without that, as when we tacitly presume that the thing is so, and not different from the way we are used to seeing, hearing or understanding it.

For example, when Aristotle says that *the dog is a barking animal*, he concludes therefore that whatever barks is a dog. But when a peasant says *a dog*, he tacitly understands just the same thing Aristotle does with his definition. So when the peasant hears bark-
30 ing, he says *a dog*. Hence, if they once heard another animal barking, the peasant, who had drawn no conclusion, would be as astonished as Aristotle, who had drawn a conclusion.

seen any sheep without short tails, and wonders at those from Morocco, which have long ones.

I/57   Similarly, they tell of a Peasant who deluded himself into thinking that, outside his fields, there were no others. But one day he missed one of his cows, and had to go far away in search of her. He was astonished that outside his own small farm there were so very many

5   others.

[3] Many Philosophers must also be like that. They have deluded themselves into thinking that beyond this plot of ground, or little globe, on which they are, there is nothing more (because they have seen nothing else). But there is no wonder in him who draws true conclu-

10   sions. This is one [passion].

[4][b] The [8]second will be love.[2] Since this arises either from true perceptions, or from opinion, or finally, also from mere report, we shall first see how [it arises] from opinion, and then how [it arises] from [true] perceptions. For the first tends to our destruction, and the

15   second to our supreme salvation. And then [we shall see how it arises] from the last.

[5] Regarding the first, it is such that whenever someone sees something good, or thinks he does, he is always inclined to unite himself with it, and for the sake of the good that he perceives in it, he chooses

20   it as the best, apart from which he then knows nothing better or more pleasant.

But whenever it happens (as it usually does in these cases) that he comes to know something better than this good he now knows, then his love turns immediately from the first to the second. We shall make

25   all of this more evident when we discuss man's freedom.

[6] Since this is not the place to speak of the love that arises from

---

I/56   Again, when we come to perceive something of which we have never thought before, it is still not as though we had never known anything like it before, as a whole or in

35   part; it is only that it was not so constituted in every respect, or that we have never been affected by it in this way, etc.

[b] That Love comes from opinion, clear knowledge, and report. This is the foundation of all good and evil. See p.——, chap. 14. [A marginal note relegated to the textual commentary by Gebhardt and probably stemming from a reader, but interesting nonetheless for the forward reference to I/77/24.]

[2] Many scholars have found the order of this and the next three paragraphs illogical and have preferred the arrangement in Monnikhoff, who gives us first the discussion of love arising from report (§ 7), then the discussion of love arising from opinion (§ 5), and finally the passing over of love arising from true perceptions (§ 6), with appropriate rewriting of § 4 (but also omitting the third sentence of § 4). Gebhardt retains the order of the manuscript, though he finds it confused. Mignini finds the order of the manuscript defensible.

true perceptions,[c] we shall pass over them now, and speak of the third and last, viz. the love that comes from mere report.

30 [7] We usually observe this in children in relation to their father. Because he says that this or that is good, they are inclined to it, without knowing anything more about it.

We also see it in those who, out of love, give up their lives for the Fatherland, and also in those who, because of a report about something, come to fall in love with it.

I/58 [8] [9]Hate, then, the direct opposite of Love, arises from that error which comes from opinion. For if someone has drawn the conclusion that something is good, and someone else does something to harm that thing, then the first person will acquire a hatred of the second. This 5 could never happen if one knew the true good, as we shall indicate later. For in comparison with the true good, whatever is, or is thought, is nothing but misery itself. And is not someone who loves misery in this way more worthy of compassion than of hate?

10 Finally, Hate also comes from mere report—as we see in the Hate the Turks have against the Jews and the Christians, the Jews against the Turks and the Christians, and the Christians against the Jews and Turks, etc. For how ignorant most of these are of one another's religion and customs.

15 [9] As for [10]desire—whether it consists (as some maintain) in an appetite or inclination to get what one lacks, or (as others contend), to preserve the things we already enjoy[d]—certainly it cannot be found to have occurred in anyone except for something which has seemed good.[3]

20 [10] So it is clear that Desire, like the Love spoken of here, comes from the first kind of knowledge. For someone who hears that a thing is good acquires an appetite or inclination for it. This may be seen in a sick man, who, simply on hearing from the Doctor that such and such a remedy is good for his illness, is immediately inclined toward 25 it.

Desire comes also from experience,[e] as may be seen in the practice

---

[3] According to Wolf, this doctrine would be rejected in E IIIP9S. Not so, however, according to Gueroult 2, 2:492-495.

[c] Love that comes from true perceptions or clear knowledge is not treated here because it does not come from opinion. But see ch. XXII. [Gebhardt rejects this marginal note.]

I/58 [d] The first definition is the best, for when the thing is enjoyed, the desire ceases; so 35 the inclination which we then have to retain that thing is not desire but fear of losing the thing we love. [Gebhardt brackets this note as a critical, but imperceptive, reader's interpolation. Mignini defends it as thoroughly Spinozistic, but the passages he cites (most notably, I/84/22) do not seem very satisfactory.]

[e] It comes also from experience, according to the second definition, which does not

of Doctors. When they have found a certain remedy to be good in some cases, they usually regard it as something infallible.

30   [11] All that we have just said about these passions can equally be said of all the others, as is clear to everyone. And since, in what follows, we shall begin to investigate which ones are rational for us, and which ones are irrational, we shall leave this topic for now and add no more.[4]

I/59

Chapter IV

What Comes from Belief [and of Man's Good and Evil][1]

[1] In the preceding chapter we have shown how the passions arise
5   from the error of opinion. So now let us see the effects of the two other ways of knowing. First, of that which we have called *true belief*.[a]

[2] *[12]*This shows us, indeed, what it belongs to the thing to be, but not what it truly is. That is why it can never unite us with the thing
10   we believe. I say, then, that it teaches us only what it belongs to the thing to be, not what it is. There is a great difference between the two. For as we have said in our example of the rule of three, if someone can discover through proportionality a fourth number that agrees

---

please me. [A marginal note, relegated by Gebhardt to his textual commentary but regarded by Mignini as Spinoza's. See Mignini 3,270-271.]

I/59   [a] Belief is a strong proof based on reasons, by which I am convinced in my intellect
25   that the thing truly is, outside my intellect, such as I am convinced in my intellect that it is.
      I say a strong proof based on reasons, to distinguish it thereby both from opinion, which is always doubtful and subject to error, and from science, which does not consist in conviction based on reasons, but in an immediate union with the thing itself.
30   I say that the thing truly is such, outside my intellect; *truly*, because the reasons can not deceive me in this, otherwise they would not differ from opinion; *such*, because it can only indicate to me what it belongs to the thing to be, not what it truly is, otherwise it would not differ from science; *outside*, because it makes us enjoy intellectually, not what is in us, but what is outside us. [Gebhardt brackets this note, on the ground (dubious in this instance) that it adds nothing really new to what is said in the text. Joel had pointed out parallel passages in Crescas' *The Light of the Lord*, II, v, 5.]

      [4] Freudenthal observed (2, 262) that after Chapter III and the early sections of Chapter IV, we would expect it to be proven that the ethically superior affects arise from the higher kinds of knowledge. Instead they are distinguished more by the objects which produce them than by the kind of knowledge they originate from (II, iv, 10; II, v). Instead of showing how these affects arise from these kinds of knowledge, Spinoza enumerates their effects and reviews the whole series of Descartes' Passions of the Soul. Affects already discussed—wonder, love, hate, and desire—are once again discussed, as if this had not been done. Freudenthal plausibly infers that we have here two presentations of a moral psychology, stemming from different times and juxtaposed by an unknown editor. This is confirmed by the difficulties mentioned above (II, i, 1, n. 1).

      [1] The addition to the title is supplied from the table of chapters.

15 with the third as the second does with the first, then (having used multiplication and division) he can say that the four numbers must be proportional; but if this is so, then he speaks about it just as of a thing that is outside him. But if he comes to see the proportionality, as we

20 have shown in the fourth example, then he says that the thing is truly such, since then it is in him, not outside him. So much for the first effect of true belief.

I/60 [3] The second is that it brings [13]us to a clear understanding, through which we love God, and makes us perceive intellectually those things which are not in us, but outside us.

5 [4] The third effect is that it provides [14]us with the knowledge of good and evil, and shows us all the passions that are to be destroyed. And because, as we have already said, those passions which come from opinion are subject to great evil, it is worth the trouble to see

10 how they are sifted by this second kind of knowledge, to see what is good and what is evil in them.

[b]To do this conveniently, let us use the same method as before, and examine them closely, so as to know which we must choose and which

15 reject. But before we come to that, let us first say briefly what man's good and evil are.

[5] We have already said before that all things are necessitated, and that *in Nature there is no good and no evil*. So whatever we require of

20 man, must relate only to his genus, and this is nothing but *a being of reason*. And when we have conceived an Idea of a [15]perfect man in our intellect, that [Idea] [16]could be a cause of our seeing (when we examine ourselves) whether we have any means of arriving at such a perfection.

25 [6] [17]Therefore, whatever helps us to attain that perfection, we shall call good, and whatever hinders our attaining it, or does not assist it, we shall call evil.

[7] [17]I say, then, that I must conceive a perfect man, if I want to say anything regarding man's good and evil. For if I discussed the

30 good and evil of, say, Adam, I would confuse a real being with a being of reason—something a true Philosopher must [18]scrupulously avoid, for reasons we shall expound later, or on some other occasion.

[8] Since we are not aware of Adam's end, or of that of any other

I/61 particular creature, except through the outcome, it follows that what we can say of man's end[c] must be grounded on the concept in our

---

[b] On the fourth effect of true belief see p.—— It shows us what truth and falsity consist in. [A marginal note, probably stemming from a reader. The forward reference would be to I/78/16.]

[c] For one cannot have an idea that is perfect from any particular creature; for the very perfection of this Idea, [i.e., the judgment by which one decides] whether it is perfect or not, must be deduced from a perfect universal Idea, or *Being of Reason*. [Geb-

intellect of a perfect man, whose end we can indeed know, because it is a being of reason. We can also, as we have said, know his good and evil, which are only modes of thinking.

[9] To come gradually to the point, then, we have already indicated how the soul's emotions, its passions and actions, arise from perception. We have divided perception into four kinds: *report alone, experience, belief*, and *clear knowledge*. And since we have now seen the effects of all of these, it is evident from this that the fourth, [19]clear knowledge, is the most perfect of all. For opinion often leads us into error; true belief is good only because it is the way to true knowledge, awakening us to things that are truly worthy of love, so that the final end we seek, and the most excellent thing we know, is true knowledge.

[10] [20]But this true knowledge is also distinguished according to the objects presented to it. So the better the object with which it comes to unite itself, the better is this knowledge. [21]And therefore, the most perfect man is the one who unites with the most perfect being, God, and thus enjoys him.

[11] So to discover what is good and evil in the Passions, let us take them separately, as we have said. [22]And first, Wonder. Because this arises either from ignorance or from prejudice, it is an imperfection in the man who is subject to this emotion. I say an imperfection, because Wonder through itself does not lead to any evil.

I/62

Chapter V

Of Love

[1][3][1] Love, then, arises from the perception and knowledge which we have of a thing, and as the thing shows itself to be greater and more magnificent, so also is our Love greater and greater.

[4] It is possible to rid ourselves of Love in two ways, either by knowledge of a better thing, or by finding that the thing we have loved, and have regarded as something great and magnificent, brings much misery with it.

[2][5] But Love is also such that we never strive to free ourselves of it (as we do of wonder and the other passions). This is for two reasons:

---

hardt brackets this note as doubtful, on the ground that it merely repeats what is said in the text. The bracketed emendation is a suggestion of Appuhn's.]

[1] Gebhardt, following a suggestion of Meijer's, rearranges the first five sections of this chapter so that they come in what he sees as a more logical order and make a smoother transition to section six. Mignini defends the arrangement of the ms. I have followed Gebhardt's arrangement, but to allow readers to reconstruct easily the order of the ms. I have introduced Mignini's paragraph numbers in italics.

(1) because it is impossible; (2) because it is necessary that we not be free of it.

[3] It is impossible because it does not depend on us, but only on the good or advantage we find in the object. If we did not want to love it, it would be necessary for us not to have known it before. And this does not depend on us or on our freedom. For if we knew nothing, certainly we also were nothing.

[4] So it is necessary that we not be free of it, because, given the weakness of our nature, we could not exist if we did not enjoy something to which we were united, and by which we were strengthened.

[1] Love, then, is nothing but enjoying a thing and being united with it.[2] We divide it according to the qualities of the object man seeks to enjoy and unite with.

[5][2] [24]Some objects are corruptible in themselves; [25]others, through their cause, are not corruptible; but there is a third [object] which, solely through its own power and capacity, is eternal and incorruptible.

The corruptible, then, are all the singular things, which have not existed from all time, or have had a beginning.

[a]The next are all those modes which we have said are the cause of the singular modes.

But the third is God, or what we take to be one and the same thing, the Truth.

[6] Which of these three kinds of object should we choose, and which reject?

[27]As far as the corruptible are concerned—because, as we have said, the weakness of our nature requires us to love something, and to unite ourselves with it, in order to exist—certainly loving them, and [28]uniting ourselves with them, does not strengthen our nature at all. For they are weak, and the one cripple cannot support the other. And not only do they not help us, but they are even harmful to [29]us.

For we have said that Love is a union with an object that our intellect judges to be good and magnificent; and by that we understand a union such that the lover[3] and the loved come to be one and the same

---

[a] Which are incorruptible only through their cause. See p. 53f. [A marginal note, probably due to a reader. The reference is to a ms. page number corresponding to I/47f.]

[2] Though this is similar to the Cartesian formula rejected in the *Ethics* (II/192/22ff.), the conception is still not Cartesian, since the Love defined in PA II, 79, is a passion caused by motion of the animal spirits. Appuhn's interpretation of the religious significance of this transitional conception of love deserves consideration. Cf. Appuhn 1, 1:408-409.

[3] The ms. has *de Liefde* (the love), which Mignini, like most scholars, emends to *de lievende*. Gebhardt defended the text with an appeal to passages in Leone Ebreo's *Dia-*

thing, or to form a whole together. So he who unites with corruptible things is always miserable. For because they are outside his power and subject to many accidents, it is impossible that, when they are acted on, he would be able to be freed of them.

20 Consequently, we conclude that if they are so miserable who love corruptible things (which still have some essence), how miserable will they be who love honor, wealth, and sensual pleasure, which have no essence?[4]

25 [7] Let this be enough, then, to show how [30]Reason teaches us to separate ourselves from things so corruptible. For what we have just said indicates clearly to us the poison and the evil that lie hidden in the love of these things. But we shall see this incomparably more 30 clearly when we note how magnificent and excellent is the good from which we separate ourselves by enjoying these things.

[8] [b]We said previously that the things that are corruptible are outside our power. Let us be properly understood. We do not mean that I/64 we are a free cause, depending on nothing else. When we say that some things are in our power, and others outside it, we understand by those which *are in our power* those which we bring about through the order of, or together with, Nature, of which we are a part. By 5 those which *are not in our power* we understand those which, being outside us, do not undergo any changes through us, since they are very far removed from our actual essence, as it is constituted by Nature.

[9] Next we come to the second kind of objects. Though these are 10 eternal and incorruptible, they still are not such through their own power. [31]And if we examine the question briefly, we shall immediately become aware that these are nothing but [c]modes which depend im-

---

loghi de amore where the love, the lover, and the loved are all identified. Spinoza possessed a copy of this work in a Spanish translation, and Gebhardt devoted a long article to his relation to Spinoza (Gebhardt (2)). Wolfson thought his influence on Spinoza had been exaggerated (Wolfson (1), II, 277). See also Bidney (1), 178, 180. I follow Mignini.

[4] The very negative evaluation of honor (*eer* = *honor?* or *gloria?*) implied here seems to mark this passage as belonging to a different stratum than II, xii. Cf. Spinoza's account of his development in the *Treatise on the Intellect*, §§ 1-11.

[b] What we understand by things which are outside our power or do not depend on us. P. 80. So we must also not unite with those objects which are incorruptible through their cause, which are the second kind of objects we posited. [A marginal note. The ms. page reference = I/62/19-63/1. This note seems to go beyond anything said explicitly in the text. Is it by Spinoza?]

[c] Because they are only modes which depend immediately on God, [we] cannot unite with them. Because we cannot know them without [knowing] God, and knowing God, would not possibly love them. For knowing God, we cannot but love him immediately. [Again a marginal note which goes beyond anything in the text. Meijer ascribed it to Spinoza, Gebhardt didn't. I see no impossibility in Meijer's view.]

mediately on God. Because that is their nature, we shall not be able
to conceive them unless we have at the same time a concept of God.
Because he is perfect, our Love must necessarily rest in him. In a
word, it will be impossible for us, if we use our intellect well, not to
love God.

[10] The reasons why are clear:

First, because we find that God alone has being, and all other things
have no being, but are modes. And since modes cannot be understood
properly without the being on which they immediately depend, and
we have already shown that when we who love something come to
know something better than what we love, we always fall on it at
once, and leave the first thing, it follows incontrovertibly that when
we come to know God, who has all perfection in himself alone, we
must love him.

[11] Second, if we use our intellect well in the knowledge of things,
we must know them in their causes. Now since God is a first cause
of all other things, the knowledge of God is prior, according to the
nature of things, to the knowledge of all other things, because the
knowledge of all other things must follow from knowledge of the first
cause.

True love comes always from knowledge that the thing is splendid
and good. What else, then, can follow, but that love will be able to
pour forth more powerfully on the lord ³²our God than on anyone
else? For he alone is magnificent, and a perfect Good.

[12] So we see, then, how we make Love powerful,⁵ and also how
it must rest only in God. What we had to say further about Love, we
shall try to do when we treat of the last kind of knowledge. Now we
shall return to our promised investigation of which 'passions'⁶ we have
to accept, and which reject.

Chapter VI

Of Hate

[1] Hate is an Inclination to avoid something which has caused us some
evil.¹

⁵ Meijer, appealing to I/63/7-10, proposed emending to: "make ourselves more powerful through love."

⁶ The Pléiade editors conjecture that the Latin was *affectus*, rather than *passio*, and
that the Dutch translator did not respect the distinction between these two, "perhaps
because the teaching of his church declared human nature to be always corrupted."

¹ This definition of hate, like the earlier definition of love, is closer to Descartes' (PA,
II, 79) than to Spinoza's definition in the *Ethics* (E III Def Aff 7). In II, vi, 4, the
definition will be narrowed in a way which one might have expected to find paralleled
in Descartes, though it is not.

Here we note that we perform our actions in two ways, viz. with or without passions. A common example of an action with passions occurs in the treatment masters accord their servants who have done wrong, for this is commonly accompanied by anger. Socrates, they say, provides us with an example of action without the passions. For when he was obliged to correct his servant by punishing him, he did not do this so long as he was aware of being angry at him.

[2] Because we see now that we perform our actions either with or without passions, we [33] consider it clear that such things as are, or have been, an obstacle to us can be removed, if necessary, without emotion on our part. So which is better: that we should shun things with Aversion and Hate? or that through the power of reason we should endure them without emotion (for we consider this possible)?

First, it is certain that when we do the things we must without passion, then no evil can come of that. And as there is no mean between good and evil, we see that if it is evil to act with passion, it must be good to act [34] without it.

[3] But let us see whether there is anything evil in shunning things with Hate and Aversion.

As for the Hate which stems from opinion, certainly that should have no place in us. For we know that one and the same thing is at one time good for us, at another, bad for us (as is always the case with medicinal herbs).

So in the end, it comes to this: does Hate arise in us only through opinion, or sometimes also through true reasoning? To answer this, it seems good to us to explain clearly what Hate is, and to distinguish it from aversion.

[4] I say, then, that Hate is an emotion of the soul against someone who has knowingly and willingly done us some ill. But aversion is that emotion against a thing which arises in us from some trouble or injury which we either understand or opine it to cause by its nature.

I say by nature, for if we do not think so, then we are not averse to it, even though we have received some hindrance or injury from it, because, on the contrary, we expect some advantage from it—as someone who has been hurt by a stone or a knife does not, on that account, have any aversion to it.

[5] This being noted, let us look briefly at the effects of both of these. From Hate, then, comes sadness; [36] and if the Hate is great, it produces anger, which strives not only (like Hate) to shun what is hated, but also to destroy it, if possible. This great Hate also produces Envy.

But [37] Aversion produces some sadness because we strive to deprive ourselves of something which, being real, must always have also its own essence and perfection.

[6] From what we have said, then, it can easily be understood that, when we use our reason well, we can have no Hate or Aversion toward anything, because in [having such emotions] we deprive ourselves of the perfection that is in each thing. And so we also see through reason that we can never have any Hate toward anyone, because if we will something regarding anything in Nature, we must always change it for the better, either for ourselves or for the thing itself.

[7] And because a perfect man is the best of all that we presently know, or have before our eyes, then it is by far the best, both for us and for everyone individually, that we strive at all times to bring [men] to that perfect state. For only then can we have from them, and they from us, the greatest benefit.

The way to do this is for us always to treat them as our good Conscience constantly teaches and exhorts us to do. For this never prompts us to our destruction, but always to our salvation.

[8] In conclusion we say that Hate and Aversion have in them as many imperfections as love has perfections. For love always produces improvement, strengthening, and increase, which is perfection.[2] Hate, on the other hand, always leads to desolation, weakening, and destruction, which is imperfection itself.

CHAPTER VII
OF JOY AND SADNESS[1]

[1][a] We have seen that hate and wonder are such that we may freely say that they can have no place in those who use their intellect as they

---

[a] Of Desire and Joy. What the third effect of belief will show us about them.

Each of the following is a certain species of joy: 1. Hope, though it is mingled with some sadness; 2. Confidence; 3. Laughter; 4. Honor. [A marginal note. The marginalia in this chapter seem to foreshadow the reductionist program of the *Ethics*.]

[2] After II, v, 6, this is most surprising.

[1] Three things are particularly noteworthy about this chapter: a) from the point of view of the *Ethics* the order of the chapters is anomalous, since love and hate, the subjects of the two preceding chapters, will in the *Ethics* be reduced to species of joy and sadness; b) the marginal notes attached to the first two paragraphs (relegated to the textual commentary by Gebhardt) call attention to the role joy and sadness will play in the accounts of some of the passions to be discussed in subsequent chapters; and c) the sequence of mysterious numbers in the ms. breaks off here, to resume in Chapter IX with a repetition of n. 37. According to Mignini's hypothesis, all of these facts are connected and are a sign of the new logical order the author of the series of numbers intended to assign to the passions. See Mignini 3, 244ff. The text itself is quite vague, both about the nature of desire, joy and sadness, and about the relation of these passions to love and hate.

should. So we shall now proceed in the same way and speak of the other passions. To begin with, the first will be [b]Desire and Joy.

I/68   Since these arise from the same causes as love does, we have nothing to say about them except that we must remember what we said then. With that we leave them.

5   [2][c] To these we shall add Sadness, of which we dare say that it arises only from opinion and the error[2] which follows from that. For it comes from the loss of some good.

Now we have said before that everything we do must tend toward advancement and improvement. But it is certain that so long as we are
10   sad, we make ourselves incapable of doing such things. Therefore we must free ourselves of it. We can do this by thinking of ways to regain what we have lost, if this is in our power. If not, we must still dispel the Sadness, in order not to fall into all the misery that it necessarily
15   brings with it. Whichever we do, it must be with Joy. For it is foolish to want to recover and reclaim a lost good by an evil we ourselves have desired and fostered.

[3] Finally, he who uses his intellect properly must know God first, since God, as we have proven, is the greatest good, and all good. So
20   it follows incontrovertibly that someone who uses his intellect properly cannot fall into Sadness. For how could he? He rests in that good which is all good, and in which there is the fullness of all Joy and satisfaction.

Chapter VIII

25   ### Of Esteem and Disdain[1]

[1][a] Now we shall speak of Esteem and Disdain, of Legitimate Self-esteem and Humility, of Pride and Self-depreciation. To distinguish the good and evil in them, we shall take them one by one.

[b] These because they arise from the same cause as Love, as can be seen from pp. 70, 79. [A marginal note. The ms. page references are to KV II, iii, 4-7, and v, 1-3 (Mignini numbering).]

[c] Of Sadness. It arises only from opinion and it is necessary to be freed of it, because it hinders us. Each of the following is a certain species of sadness: 1. Despair; 2. Remorse and Repentance; 3. Shame; 4. Longing. [A marginal note.]

[a] What division the third effect of belief makes in these six, viz. [A marginal note.]

[2] *Waan*, as it is normally used in the *Short Treatise*, does not seem to connote error, but to be a synonym for *opinie*. This context, like I/69/28, is exceptional.

[1] The technical terminology in this chapter is more than usually difficult to translate
• with confidence, mainly because it is hard to be sure how the Dutch terms are related to their Latin analogues in Descartes' *Passions of the Soul*, which was Spinoza's model, and in the *Ethics*, whose analysis of the passions Spinoza has not yet achieved. See the Glossary entries on *esteem, disdain, legitimate self-esteem, humility*, etc.

[2] Esteem and Disdain occur only when we judge something to be great or small, whether this great or small thing is inside us or outside us.[2]

[3] Legitimate Self-esteem does not extend to things outside us and is only attributed to one who knows his perfection according to its true worth, without passion, and without regard to [others'] esteem of him.

[4] Humility exists when someone knows his own imperfection, without regard to [others'] disdain of him; it does not extend to anything outside the humble man.

[5] Pride exists when someone attributes to himself a perfection that is not to be found in him.

[6] Self-depreciation exists when someone attributes to himself an imperfection that does not belong to him.

Here I am talking not about hypocrites, who depreciate themselves to deceive others, without meaning what they say, but about those who believe themselves to be as imperfect as they say they are.

[7] From what we have now noted, it is clear enough what there is of good and evil in each of these 'passions.'

As far as Legitimate Self-esteem and Humility are concerned, through themselves they show their excellence. For we say that he who has these knows his perfection or imperfection according to its worth. And this, as reason teaches us, is the chief means of attaining our perfection. For if we know our power and perfection accurately, we thereby see clearly what we must do to attain our good end. And again, if we know our defect and lack of power, we see what we must avoid.

[8] As for Pride and Self-depreciation, their definitions indicate that they arise from a kind of error.[3] For we said that Pride is attributed to one who ascribes to himself some perfection, which does not belong to him. And Self-depreciation is the direct opposite.

[9] This said, it is evident that Legitimate Self-esteem and true

---

One striking feature of Spinoza's treatment here is the comparatively favorable evaluation of *nederigheid* (humility), which Appuhn took as evidence of Christian influence (Appuhn 1, 1:28). The Pléiade editors point out that in the *Short Treatise* humility and legitimate self-esteem are not opposites, but naturally associated with one another, as *humilité* and *générosité* are in Descartes. Moreover, though the *Ethics* will provide a generally negative evaluation of *humilitas*, Spinoza does recognize even there that it has some instrumental value (E IV P54S).

[2] Wolf's translation of this passage implies that our judgment of the thing's perfection or imperfection is not merely accurate, but known to be so. But I take it that both legitimate self-esteem and pride are intended to be species of esteem, and both humility and self-depreciation to be species of disdain.

[3] *Waan.* But cf. the note at I/68/6.

Humility⁴ are as good and salutary as Pride and Self-depreciation are evil and destructive. For the former not only put their possessor in a very good state, but they are also the true stairway on which we climb to our highest salvation.

I/70   The latter two, on the other hand, not only prevent us from attaining our perfection, but lead us to total destruction. Self-depreciation is what prevents us from doing what we should otherwise have to do
5   to become perfect. We see this in the Skeptics, who deny that man can have any truth, and by that denial, deprive themselves of having truth. Pride is what causes us to undertake things that tend directly to our destruction. We see this in all those who have been, or are, deluded into thinking that they stand wonderfully well with God;
10   standing in awe of no danger, ready for everything, they brave fire and water in their pride, and so die most miserably.

[10] As for Esteem and Disdain, there is no more to say of these, except to keep in mind what we have said of love.⁵

15   CHAPTER IX

                        OF HOPE, FEAR, ETC.

[1]ᵃ We shall now begin to speak of Hope and Fear, Confidence, Despair, and Vacillation, Strength of Character, Tenacity and Emulation, Cowardice, Consternation, [and Jealousy]. As usual, we shall
20   take them one by one, and then indicate which of these are a hindrance and which can be advantageous.

We shall be able to do all this very easily, provided we take note of the conceptions which we can have of a thing which is to come, whether
25   it is good or evil.

[2] The conceptions we have in respect to the thing itself are either that we regard the thing as contingent, i.e., as able to happen or not happen, or that we regard it as happening necessarily. This is in respect to the thing itself.
30   With respect to him who conceives the thing, [we conceive] either

---

ᵃ What belief shows us in the following ten, viz., that they arise from the conceptions we have of a thing. [A marginal note.]

⁴ I take it that the qualification *true* here implies a correct estimate of one's imperfections and not merely that the humility is unfeigned. So it is simply the (nonculpable) humility of § 4.

⁵ Wolf cites II, v, ii, with the thought, apparently, that Spinoza is implying that we should esteem God more than anything else. Other sections in that chapter (e.g., 6, 7, 10, 12) might suggest that we should esteem only God and disdain all singular things. In any case, the very cursory treatment of esteem and disdain is puzzling.

that he must do something to further the thing's happening, or that he must do something to prevent it.

[3] From these conceptions all these 'passions' come, in the following way. If we conceive that a future thing is good, and that it could happen, then from this the soul acquires a form that we call Hope. This is nothing but a certain kind of joy, mixed, however, with a certain sadness.

And again, if we judge that the thing possible in the future is evil, the soul acquires from this the form we call Fear.

But if we conceive the thing to be good, and at the same time as necessarily to come, then from this there comes into the soul that tranquillity which we call Confidence. This is a kind of joy which is not, as hope is, mixed with sadness.

But if we conceive a thing to be evil, and as necessarily to come, from this there arises in the soul Despair, which is nothing but a certain kind of sadness.

[4] So far our definitions of the passions considered in this Chapter have been put in an affirmative way, and we have thus said what each of them is. But we can reverse the procedure and define them negatively, as follows: we hope that the evil will not come; we fear that the good will not come; we are confident that the evil will not come; we despair that the good will not come.

[5] This will suffice for the passions insofar as they come from conceptions in respect to the thing itself. We must now speak of those which arise from conceptions in respect to him who conceives the thing:

If we must do something to bring the thing about, and [can] make no decision about the thing, then the soul acquires a form we call Vacillation.

But if it decides in a manly way to bring the thing about, and this can be done, then this is called Strength of Character. And if the thing is difficult to bring about, it is called Tenacity, or Bravery. When, however, someone decides to do a thing because someone else has done it before him with success, that is called Emulation.

If someone knows what decision he must make, to further a good thing and prevent an evil one, and nevertheless does not do this, one calls this Cowardice, and if it is very great, Consternation.

Finally, Jealousy is an anxiety one has about being allowed to enjoy and preserve exclusively something that has already been acquired.

[6] Because we now know how these 'passions' arise, it will be quite easy for us to show which are good and which are evil.

As for Hope, Fear, Confidence, Despair, and Jealousy, it is certain

10 that they arise from an incorrect opinion. For as we have already proven, all things have their necessary causes and must happen as they do happen.

And though [37]Confidence and Despair seem to have a place in the inviolable order and series of causes (for there everything is inviolable and unalterable), nevertheless when we examine the matter rightly, we find that is far from being the truth. For Confidence and Despair never exist unless Hope and Fear have previously existed (for they have their being from them).

20 For example, if someone thinks something he is waiting for is good, he acquires in his soul that form we call Hope; and if he is assured of what he thinks is good, then his soul acquires that satisfaction we call Confidence.

What we have just said about Confidence must also be said about 25 Despair. But according to what we said about love, these [passions] can have no place in a perfect man: because they presuppose things we must not attach ourselves to, since they are subject to change (as is noted in relation to the definition of love).

30 Nor may we have an aversion to them (as is shown in relation to the definition of hate). Nevertheless, the man who has these passions is always subject to such attachments and aversions.

[7] [38]As for Vacillation, Cowardice, and Consternation, their very kind and nature indicates their imperfection. For whatever they con- I/73 tribute to our advantage comes from actions of their nature only neg- atively. For example, someone hopes for something which he thinks is good, but which is not good. Nevertheless, because of his Vacilla- tion or Cowardice, he happens to lack the Strength of Character re- 5 quired to carry it out. So, negatively, or by chance, he is freed of the evil he thought was good.

These, then, also cannot have any place in the man who is led by true reason.

[8] Finally, regarding Strength of Character, Tenacity and Emula- 10 tion, there is nothing else to say about them except what we have already said about love and hate.

Chapter X

Of Remorse and Repentance

[1][a] Now we shall speak of Remorse and Repentance, but only briefly. 15 These occur only by surprise;[1] for Remorse proceeds only from our

[a] What belief tells us about Remorse and Repentance. And what they arise from. [A marginal note.]
[1] Because of a miscalculation regarding good and evil.

114

doing something of which we afterwards doubt whether it is good or evil, while Repentance proceeds from our having done something evil.

[2] And because many people who use their intellect well sometimes go astray, lacking the discipline required to always use their intellect properly, some might perhaps think that Remorse and Repentance would bring them to the right path, and conclude, as the whole world does,[2] that these are good.

But if we consider them correctly, we shall find that they are not only not good, [39]but on the contrary, injurious, and consequently evil. For it is manifest that we always come to the right path more through reason and love of truth than through Remorse and Repentance. And because they are species of sadness, which we have already proven to be injurious, and which we must therefore strive to avoid, as an evil, these too are injurious, evil, and to be shunned and fled.

CHAPTER XI

OF MOCKERY AND RIDICULE

[1][a] Mockery and Ridicule rest on a false opinion and indicate an imperfection in him who mocks and ridicules.

They rest on a false opinion, because one thinks that he who is mocked is the first cause of his actions, and that they do not (like other things in Nature) depend necessarily on God.

They indicate an imperfection in him who mocks because either what is mocked is ridiculous or it is not. If not, the mockery shows that he is ill-natured, mocking what does not deserve to be mocked. If it is ridiculous, then the mockery shows that he recognizes in the one mocked an imperfection which he ought improve with good reasons, not mockery.[1]

[2] Laughter is not related to another, but only to the man who notices something good in himself; and because it is a certain kind of joy, there is nothing to say about it which has not already been said about joy.

I am speaking here of such laughter as is produced by a certain idea which rouses one to laugh, not of the laughter produced by a motion

---

[a] What belief says that Mockery and Ridicule depend on, viz., on a false opinion, what that [false opinion] is and what it arises from. [A marginal note.]

[2] Spinoza's close contacts with members of the Collegiant sect, and some of the themes of the *Short Treatise*, have suggested a possible Christian influence on him at this stage of his development. But in his attitude toward repentance, he is even more critical than in the *Ethics*. Cf. the first Dialogue, where repentance is cited as one of the two mortal enemies of the human race (in company with hate), with E IVP54S.

[1] Descartes, by contrast, had held that a moderate use of mockery could correct vices by making them appear ridiculous (PA III, 180).

of the [animal] spirits.[2] Since the latter has no relation to good or evil, it would be out of place to speak of it here.

[3] We shall say nothing here about Envy, Anger, and Indignation,
25 except to recall what we have previously said about hate.

Chapter XII

Of Love of Esteem, Shame and Shamelessness

[1][a] We shall now speak briefly about Love of Esteem,[1] Shame and Shamelessness.

30 The first is a certain kind of joy which everyone feels in himself when he becomes aware that his conduct is esteemed and praised by others, without regard to any advantage or profit they have in view.

I/75 Shame is a certain sadness which arises in someone if he comes to see that his conduct is disdained by others, without regard to any disadvantage or injury they have in view.

5 Shamelessness is nothing but a lack or rejection of Shame, not through reason, but either through ignorance of Shame (as in children, savages, etc.), or through having been so greatly disdained that one now will do anything without regard to criticism.

[2] Now that we know these passions, we also know the vanity and
10 imperfection they have in them. For not only are Love of Esteem and Shame not advantageous, according to what we have noted in their definitions, they are also injurious and objectionable, insofar as they are built on self-love, and on an error, that man is a first cause of his own actions, and consequently deserving of praise and blame.

15 [3] But I don't mean that one must live among men as one would live without them, where Love of Esteem and Shame have no place. On the contrary, I grant that we are permitted not only to use [these passions] for men's advantage and improvement, but also to do this even if it involves a restriction of our own freedom, which is otherwise
20 complete and lawful.

For example, if someone dresses expensively in order to be honored

---

[a] What belief shows us in these and what Love of Esteem is. [A marginal note.]
[2] Cf. PA II, 124-127.
[1] Wolf renders *eer* by "glory," pointing out the agreement between the definition given here and the definition of *gloria* in E III Def. App 20. Appuhn contends that the *eer* of the *Short Treatise* does not correspond to the *gloria* of the *Ethics* because the evaluation of *gloria* at E IVP58 is more favorable than that of *eer* here. But I take it that this is a sign of a change of view about the same affect, not a sign that these are two different affects.

for that, then he seeks an Esteem that arises from self-love, not from any regard for his fellow men: But if someone sees that men disdain
25 his wisdom, by which he could be helpful to his fellow men, and trample it under foot because he dresses badly, then he does well if he provides himself with clothing that will not shock them, thereby becoming like his fellow men in order to win them over and help them.

30 [4] As for Shamelessness, this shows itself to be such that we need only its definition to see its deformity. And that will be enough for us.

I/76
Chapter XIII
Of Favor, Gratitude and Ingratitude.[1]

[1] We come now to Favor, Gratitude and Ingratitude. As for the first two, they are inclinations the soul has to desire and to do some good
5 to its fellows. To desire, I say, when to one who has done some good, good is done in return; to do, I say, when we ourselves have obtained or received some good.[2]

[2] I know, of course, that all men judge these passions to be good.
10 But notwithstanding that, I dare say they can have no place in a perfect man. For a perfect man is moved to help his fellow man only by necessity, without any other cause. And therefore he finds himself all the more obliged to help the most godless, since he sees that they have
15 the greater misery and need.

[3] Ingratitude is a disdain for Gratitude (as shamelessness is for shame), arising not from reason, but either from greed or from an all too great love of oneself. That is why it can have no place in a perfect
20 man.

---

[1] The manuscript does not indicate clearly where the division between Chapters XIII and XIV falls. Gebhardt puts the discussion of longing in Chapter XIII as the fourth section, modifies the title given to Chapter XIII in the table of contents and makes up a new title for Chapter XIV. Mignini (in company with most editors before Gebhardt) puts the discussion of longing in Chapter XIV and preserves the titles given to these chapters in the table of contents. I follow Mignini.

[2] To my knowledge no one has questioned the text here. But comparison with the definitions of *favor* and *gratitude* in the *Ethics* (E III Def. Aff. 19, 34) or in *Passions of the Soul* (PA II, 192, 193) suggests that there may be some confusion. We would expect something like: "The former [i.e., favor], I say, when we desire that good be done in return to one who has done some good; the latter [gratitude], I say, when we desire that good be done to someone who has done some good we ourselves have obtained or received."

Chapter XIV

Of Longing

[1]ᵃ We shall conclude our treatment of the passions by speaking about Longing. Longing is a kind of sadness arising from the consideration of some good that we have lost and that there is no hope of our regaining.

It manifests its imperfection to us in such a way that as soon as we examine it, we find it to be bad. For we have already proven that it is bad to tie ourselves to things which can easily, or at some time, fail us, and which we cannot have when we will. And because it is a certain kind of sadness, we have to avoid it, as we noted before, when we were treating of sadness.

[2] I think I have now indicated sufficiently, and proven, that it is only true belief or reason that leads us to the knowledge of good and evil. So when we prove that the first and principal cause of all these 'passions' is knowledge, then it will be clearly evident that when we use our intellect and reason properly, we can never fall into one of those we are to reject. I say our intellect, for I do not think that reason alone has the power to free us from all of these, as we shall prove later, in its place.

[3] But we must note here an excellent thing about the 'passions,' viz. we see and find that all those 'passions' which are good are of such a kind and nature that without them we can neither be nor persist, and they belong to us, as it were, essentially. Such are love, desire, and everything that is proper to love.

But it is quite the contrary with those which are evil, and to be rejected by us. Not only can we be very well without them, but also only when we have made ourselves free of them, can we be properly what it belongs to us to be.

[4] To make all of this still clearer, note that the foundation of all good and evil is love falling on a certain object. For whenever we do not love that object which alone is worthy of being loved, i.e. (as we have already said), God, but love those things which through their own kind and nature are corruptible, there follow necessarily from that hate, sadness, etc., according to the changes in the object loved (because the object is subject to many accidents, indeed to destruction itself). Hate: when someone takes the thing he loves away from him. Sadness: when he loses it. Love of Esteem: when he depends on love of himself. Favor and Gratitude: when he does not love his fellow man for the sake of God.

ᵃ The last passion regarding which the third effect of belief shows us the difference between good and evil is Longing. [A marginal note.]

I/78 [47]If, on the other hand, a man comes to love God, who always is and remains immutable, it is impossible for him to fall into this bog of the passions. And therefore, we maintain it as a fixed and unshakeable rule, [48]that God is the first and only cause of all our good, and one who frees us from all our evil.

[5] [49]We must note, finally, that only Love, etc., are unlimited, viz. the more it increases, the more excellent it becomes, since it falls on an object that is infinite. That is why it can always increase, which is not possible with any other thing. [b]And perhaps this will later give us material from which we shall prove the immortality of the soul, and how that can be.[1]

[6] Having spoken up to now of everything which the third kind of effect of true belief shows us, we shall now proceed to speak of the fourth and last effect, which we did not mention on p. [I/60].[2]

CHAPTER XV
OF THE TRUE AND THE FALSE

[1] Let us now examine the True and the False, which indicate to us the fourth and last effect of true belief. To do this, we shall first state the definitions of truth and falsity:

Truth, then, is an affirmation (or denial) which one makes concerning a thing and which agrees with the thing itself.[1]

Falsity is an affirmation (or denial) about a thing which does not agree with the thing itself.

[2] [50]But this being so, it will seem either that there is no distinction between the false and the true Idea, or that there is no real distinction between them, [51]but only a distinction of reason, because affirming or denying this or that are only modes of thinking, and have no other

[b] And also the immortality of the soul as that will subsequently be proven on the same basis in Chapter 23. [A marginal note.]

[1] This topic will come up for treatment again in Chapter XXIII, but the "perhaps" is an indication of the character of this work as not having received a final revision. There were similar instances earlier at I/43/33 and I/60/33. Cf. also Freudenthal 2, 259-260.

[2] This sentence occurs as a note in the manuscript. Gebhardt rejects it. Mignini accepts it as the conclusion of the chapter. The style of the note suggests that Mignini is right.

[1] Appuhn observes correctly that Spinoza here defines truth by what he will later call an extrinsic denomination, the agreement of the idea with its object (cf. E II D4). What Appuhn adds, however, seems incorrect: that Spinoza will exclude this extrinsic denomination formally from the definition of the true idea. In the passage cited Spinoza is defining adequacy, not truth. As late as Letter 60 Spinoza seems to think that a proper definition of truth is in terms of agreement. Cf. also I/246/15ff. The anomalous passage seems to be II/26/15ff.

distinction between them than that the one agrees with the thing and the other does not.

And if that should be so, one could rightly ask [52]what advantage one man has with his Truth, and what harm the other has through his Falsity? [53]And how will the one know that his concept or Idea agrees more with the thing than the other's does? Finally, how is it that the one errs and the other does not?

[3] To this we may answer, first, that the things which are clearest of all make known both themselves and also Falsity, so that it would be very foolish to ask how one can be aware of them.[a] For because they are said to be the clearest of all, there can never be any other clarity through which they could be explained. So it follows that Truth manifests both itself and falsity. For Truth becomes clear through Truth, i.e., through itself, as Falsity is also clear through Truth. But Falsity is never manifested or indicated through itself.

So someone who has the Truth cannot doubt that he has it. But someone who is stuck in Falsity or error can indeed think that he has the Truth. Similarly, someone who is dreaming can think that he is awake, but no one who is awake can ever think that he is dreaming.

(Having said this, we have to some extent explained also our previous statement that God is Truth, or that the Truth is God himself.)

[4] Why, then, is the one more aware of his Truth than the other? Because the Idea of affirmation (or denial) [in the first][2] agrees completely with the nature of the thing, and consequently has more essence.

[5] To grasp this better, note that the intellect (though the word sounds otherwise) is wholly passive,[3] i.e., that our soul is changed in such a way that it acquires other modes of thinking it did not have before. Now if someone, because the whole object has acted in him, acquires such forms or modes of thinking, it is clear that he acquires a completely different sense of the form or quality of the object than another who has not had so many causes, and so is moved to affirm or deny by a different, and slighter action (since he becomes aware of it in himself by a few, or lesser, affections).

[6] From this we see the perfection of one who has the Truth, as opposed to one who doesn't have it. Because the one easily changes, and the other does not, it follows that the one has more constancy and

---

[a] That it is foolishness to ask how one knows that one knows. [A marginal note.]

[2] Gebhardt incorporates the bracketed phrase into the text, following the reading in Monnikhoff (and Meijer and Appuhn). Mignini rejects it as not necessary and even confusing.

[3] Cf. II, xvi, 5 and the note thereto.

I/80   essence than the other. And so also, because those modes of thinking which agree with the thing have had more causes, they have more constancy and essence in them also. Because they agree completely with the thing, it is impossible that at some time they can be differ-

5   ently affected by the thing, or undergo any change. For as we have said before, the essence of a thing is immutable. None of this is true of Falsity.

And with this the questions above are satisfactorily answered.[4]

10
Chapter XVI[1]
Of the Will

[1][a] Now that we know what good and evil, and truth and falsehood are, and also what the well-being of a perfect man consists in, it is time to begin investigating ourselves, [54]and to see whether we arrive

15   at such a well-being freely or by necessity. For this purpose it is necessary for us to investigate what the Will is, according to those who posit the Will, and how it is distinguished from Desire.

[2] Desire, we have said, is that inclination which the Soul has toward something it considers good. From this it follows that before our

20   Desire extends externally to something, a decision has already taken place in us that such a thing is good. This affirmation, then, or taken generally, the power of affirming and denying, is called the Will.[b]

I/80   [a] What true belief has taught us according to the third effect, and also the fourth. [A marginal note.]

25   [b] The Will, taken as the affirmation, or the decision, differs from true belief in this: that it extends also to what is not truly good, because the conviction is not such that the thing is clearly seen not to be able to be otherwise; but the conviction is always of this kind, and must be, in true belief, because nothing but good Desires proceed from it.

30   But [the will] differs from opinion also, in that it can sometimes be infallible and certain; in opinion, which consists of guessing and conjecturing, [such certainty] has no place.

So one could call it a belief, insofar as it is capable of certainty, and opinion, insofar as it is capable of error.

[4] Freudenthal (2, 278) contended that the third of Spinoza's questions in II, xv, 2 ("how is it that the one errs and the other does not?") has not yet been answered and will not be answered until we reach II, xvi, 7, which he thought ought to be placed near the end of II, xv. Against this is the fact that II, xvi, 7 addresses an objection based on a doctrine first enunciated in II, xvi, 5. I suggest that Spinoza considered his third question to have been answered in II, xv, 5.

[1] Freudenthal (2, 278) thought that II, xvi-xviii ought to come after II, xix-xx, partly on the ground that II, xvi, 1 alludes to a previous discussion of the well-being of a perfect man, a discussion which, Freudenthal maintained, came only in II, xix-xx. But all of Spinoza's other references to a perfect man come in earlier chapters (II, iv, vi, ix, and xiii).

I/81   [3] The question now is whether this affirmation of ours happens
          freely or by necessity, i.e., whether we affirm or deny something of
          a thing without ⁵⁵any external cause compelling us to do so. But we
5   have already proven that a thing which is not explained through itself,
          or whose existence does not belong to its essence, must necessarily
          have an external cause, and that a cause which is going to produce
          something must produce it necessarily. So it must also follow that the
          particular willing this or that, the particular affirming or denying this
I/82   or that of a thing, must proceed from some external cause; and the
          definition we have given of a cause is that it cannot be free.

I/81/10   [3a]² It is certain that the particular willing must have an external
          cause through which it is. For since existence does not belong to its
          essence, it must necessarily exist through the existence of something
          else.

          Some say: the efficient cause [of the particular willing] is not an
15   Idea,³ but the Will itself in the man; and the intellect is a cause with-
          out which the Will can do nothing;⁴ therefore, the Will, taken as un-
          determined, and also the intellect, are not beings of reason, but real
          beings.

          But I say: when I consider them attentively, they seem to me to be
          universals, and I cannot attribute anything real to them. But even if
20   they are real beings, nevertheless, one must grant that the Volition is
          a modification of the Will, and the Idea a modification of the intellect.
          It follows necessarily that the intellect and the Will are different and
          really distinct substances. For the substance is modified, not the mode
          itself. If the soul is said to govern these two substances, then there is
          a third substance.

25   All this confuses things so that it is impossible to have a clear and
          distinct perception of them. For because the Idea is not in the Will,
          but in the intellect, then according to the principle that the mode of
          one substance cannot pass into another substance, no love can arise in

---

² What appears here as section [3a] is printed by Gebhardt as a note to "the particular
willing" in l. 9, though as he observes, the manuscript does not indicate where the note
should go. I follow Meijer in introducing it into the text.
³ The manuscript reads: "the Idea of its efficient cause is not an Idea." Most subsequent editors (including Mignini) have followed Monnikhoff in deleting the initial phrase.
Gebhardt thinks the text can be defended, and would understand: "the idea that each
particular volition must have an efficient cause is not an idea which can be conceived,
i.e., is an absurdity."
⁴ Meijer proposed to emend this to: "without which the idea cannot exist," a reading
which both Appuhn and Dunin-Borkowski preferred to the text. The objection Spinoza
rebuts would thus see the intellect as the cause of particular ideas, as the will is the
cause of particular volitions. Gebhardt defends the text, arguing that Spinoza's reply
presupposes an objection which represents the intellect as determining the will.

30   the Will. For it involves a contradiction that one should will something
the idea of which is not in the power which wills.

If you say that the Will, because of its union with the intellect, also
perceives the same thing the intellect understands, and therefore also
loves it, [the reply is that] because perceiving is also a concept and a
35   confused Idea, it too is a mode of the intellect, and according to the
preceding, cannot be in the Will, even if there were a union like that
of soul and body. For assume that the body is united with the soul,
according to the common doctrine of the Philosophers; nevertheless,
I/82/17 the body never senses, nor is the soul extended. For then a Chimera,
in which we conceive two substances, would be able to become one.
And that is false.

If one says that the soul governs both the intellect and the Will,
20   that cannot be conceived. For in so doing we seem to deny that the
Will is free, which is contrary to their position.

To conclude, then, I have no desire to bring up all the objections I
have against positing a created finite substance. But I shall only show
briefly that Freedom of the Will is completely inconsistent with a
25   continuous creation, viz. that the same action is required in God to
preserve [a thing] in being as to create it, and that without this action
the thing could not exist for a moment. If this is so, nothing can be
attributed to [the will].⁵ But one must say that God has created it as
it is; for since it has no power to preserve itself while it exists, much
30   less can it produce something through itself. If someone should say,
therefore, that the soul produces the volition of itself, I ask: from what
power? Not from that which was, for that no longer exists. Nor from
that which it now has, for it does not have any by which it could exist
or endure for the least moment, because it is continuously created. So
35   because there is no thing which has any power to preserve itself or to
produce anything, the only conclusion left is that God alone is, and
must be, the efficient cause of all things, and that all Volitions are
determined by him.

I/82/5   [4] Possibly this will not satisfy some, who are accustomed to occupy themselves more with *Beings of Reason*⁶ than with the particular
things which are truly in Nature. In doing this, they consider the
Being of Reason not as what it is, but as *a Real Being*. For because man
has now this, now that Volition, he forms in his soul a universal mode
10   which he calls the Will, just as he forms the Idea of man from this
and that man. And because he does not sufficiently distinguish real

⁵ Ms.: "it." Meijer, followed by Appuhn and Francès, would gloss: "freedom of the
will."

⁶ The italicized phrases are in Latin in the text.

123

beings from beings of reason, it comes about that he considers the beings of reason as things that are truly in Nature, and thus posits himself as a cause of some things.

This happens not infrequently in treating the matter of which we speak. For if you ask someone why man wills this or that, the answer is: because he has a Will. But since, as we have said, the Will is only an Idea of this or that volition (and therefore only a mode of thinking, a *Being of Reason*, not a *Real Being*), nothing can be produced by it. *For nothing comes of nothing.* So I think that when we have shown that the Will is no thing in Nature, but only a fiction, we do not need to ask whether it is free or not.

[5] I say this not only of the universal Will, which we have shown to be a mode of thinking, but also of the particular willing this or that, which some have posited in affirmation or denial. This will be clear to anyone who only attends to what we have already said.ᶜ For we have said that the intellect is wholly passive, i.e., a perception in the soul of the essence and existence of things. So it is never we who affirm or deny something of the thing; it is the thing itself that affirms or denies something of itself in us.[7]

[6] Some, perhaps, will not grant this, because it seems to [56]them that they can affirm or deny of the thing something other than what they are aware of. But they think this only because they have no conception of the concept which the soul has of the thing, without or apart from words. It is, of course, true that we can (when there are reasons which move us to do so) indicate to others, by words or other means, something other than what we are aware of. But we shall never bring it about, either by words or by any other means, that we think differently about the things than we do think about them. That is impossible, as is clear to all, once they attend only to their intellect, apart from the use of words or other symbols.

[7] [57]But against this, some could perhaps say that if it is not we, but only the thing, which affirms or denies [something] of itself in us, then nothing can be affirmed or denied except what agrees with the thing. So there is no falsity. For we have said that falsity is affirming (or denying) something of a thing that does not agree with the thing, i.e., that the thing does not affirm or deny that of itself.

ᶜ For those who only consider the definition we gave of the intellect on [ms.] p. 112. [A marginal note. The ms. page reference = I/79/10-27.]

[7] The doctrine that the intellect is wholly passive appears to be rejected in the *Ethics* IIIP1), but so much of what Spinoza says in this and the next section is retained in his later attacks on the Cartesian doctrine of judgement, that Wolf is probably right to attempt a reconciliation. Cf. Pléiade 1384-85.

But I think that if only we attend properly to what we have already said about truth and falsity, we shall immediately see that this objection has been satisfactorily answered. For we have said that *the object is the cause of what is affirmed or denied of it,*[8] *whether it is true or false,* i.e., *because we perceive something coming from the object, we imagine that the object affirms or denies this of itself as a whole (even though we perceive very little of it).* This occurs most in weak souls which very easily receive a mode or idea through a slight action of the object on them. Apart from this there is no other affirming or denying in them.

[8] [58]Finally, someone could also object to us that there are many things which we will and do not will, e.g., to affirm something of a thing and[9] not to affirm it, to speak the truth, and not to speak it, etc.

But this [objection] arises because Desire is not sufficiently distinguished from Will. For according to those who posit the Will, Will is only that action of the intellect by which we affirm or deny something of a thing,[10] without regard to good or bad. But Desire is a form in the soul to acquire or do something, with regard to the good or bad which are seen in it. So even after the affirmation or denial which we have made of a thing, the Desire still remains; that is, after we have found or affirmed a thing to be good (which, according to them, is the Will), only after that does one acquire the Desire, that inclination to pursue the thing. So according to their own statements, the Will can indeed exist without the Desire, but the Desire cannot exist without the Will, which must have preceded it.

[9] All the actions, then, which we have spoken of above (since they are either done by reason, as seeming good, or prevented by reason, as seeming evil), can only be conceived under those inclinations which are called Desires, and only most improperly under the name of Will.

---

[8] The ms. reading, retained by Mignini, would be translated: "the object is the cause of that of which something is affirmed or denied." I have accepted an emendation of the text advocated by Gebhardt, Appuhn and Wolf. Even if sense can be made of the ms. as it stands, anyone who retains that reading must assume the burden of finding a place where something like that has previously been said. The emenders can apeal to II, xv, 5. (A marginal note refers us to ms. pp. 110-111 (=I/78/11-79/10), but it is difficult to see the relevance of that citation.)

[9] Ms.: "or." I follow Monnikhoff, who is surely right to emend here, though not, as Wolf suggests, because the things in question are ones we sometimes want and sometimes do not want. Rather the objection envisages conflicts of desire, in which we, at one and the same time, both want and do not want the same thing.

[10] If this is intended to represent Descartes' position, it does not seem very accurate, since Descartes would not want to characterize the will as an action of the intellect. But perhaps Spinoza would regard the argument of § 3a as justifying the denial of the distinction Descartes wants to make.

CHAPTER XVII

[THE DISTINCTION BETWEEN WILL AND DESIRE]

[1]¹ Because it is now clear that we have no Will to affirm or to deny, let us see the correct and true distinction between Will and Desire, or what that Will may really be which the Latins called *voluntas*.

[2] According to Aristotle's definition, Desire seems to be a genus comprising under it two species.² For he says the Will is that appetite or tendency which one has for what seems good. From this it seems to me that he thinks Desire (or *cupiditas*) includes all inclinations, whether to good or bad.

But when the inclination is only to the good, or the man who has such inclinations has them for what seems good, he calls that *voluntas*, or good will.

But if it is bad, i.e., if we see in someone else an inclination toward something that is bad, he calls that *voluptas*, or bad will. So the inclination of the soul is not to affirm or to deny something, but only an inclination to acquire something that seems good, and to avoid something that seems bad.

[3] It remains now to ⁵⁹examine whether this Desire is free or not. Besides what we have already said, viz. that *Desire depends on the perception of things*, and that *the intellect must have an external cause*, and also what we have said about the Will, it remains to be shown that Desire is not free.

[4] Though many men see, indeed, that the knowledge man has of various things is a means by which his appetite or tendency passes from one thing to another, nevertheless they do not consider what it might be that happens to draw the appetite from the one to the other in this way.

---

¹ Freudenthal found the first two sections of this chapter a cursory and completely unsatisfactory discussion of topics already treated more fully and carefully in the preceding chapter, and suggested that they were a first draft of material for Chapter XVI, which an unknown (and imperceptive) editor had incorporated into the text. Many subsequent editors have essentially agreed. Mignini nevertheless suggests an important distinction between the two discussions, viz. that Chapter XVI is primarily a critique of Cartesian doctrines, while Chapter XVII, 1-2, is primarily an exposition of Aristotelian doctrines.

Gebhardt also took this passage to be a remnant of the original Dutch dictation which he hypothesized, on the ground that it would be unnatural for Spinoza to refer to the Latin language as he does here if he were writing in Latin. Mignini points out parallels in works which we know Spinoza composed in Latin.

A marginal note reads: "What belief tells us about the distinction between Will and Desire. According to the fourth effect."

² The reference appears to be to *De Anima* III, 10, though, as Wolf observes, Spinoza's comments are probably based on Scholastic intermediaries.

30 But to show that in our view this inclination is not free, and to make quite vivid what it is to pass over and be drawn from one thing to the other, we shall imagine a child who comes to perceive a certain thing for the first time. For example, I hold before him a little bell

I/86 which makes a pleasant sound in his ears, by which he acquires an appetite for it. Let us see now whether he could omit having this appetite or Desire? If you say yes, I ask: by what cause? Not by

5 something he knows to be better, for this is all he knows. Nor because it seems bad to him, for he knows nothing else, and that pleasure is the best that has ever come to him.

But perhaps he has a freedom to put aside that appetite which he has? From this it would follow that this appetite could indeed begin

10 in us without our freedom, but that we would equally have a freedom in us to put it aside. But this freedom cannot stand up to examination. For what would it be that would destroy this appetite? The appetite itself? Certainly not. For nothing by its own nature seeks its own destruction.

15 What, then, might it finally be that could lead him away from this appetite? Nothing else except that by the order and course of Nature he is affected by something that is more pleasant to him than the first thing.

[5] And therefore, as we said in treating of the Will, that *the Will in*

20 *man is nothing but this or that Will*, so also is there in him nothing but this or that Desire, which is caused by this or that perception. That [universal] Desire is not something that is really in Nature, but is only abstracted from this or that particular desire. Not really being something, it cannot really cause anything.

25 So if we say that the desire is free, it is just as if we said that this or that Desire was a cause of itself, i.e., that before it was, it brought it about that it would exist. This is absurdity itself, and cannot be.

30 ## CHAPTER XVIII
[OF THE ADVANTAGES OF THE PRECEDING]

[1] We see then that because man is a part of the whole of Nature, depends on it, and is governed by it, he can do nothing, of himself,

I/87 toward his salvation and well-being. So let us see what advantages there are for us in these propositions of ours. This is all the more necessary, because we have no doubt that they will seem rather shocking to some people.

5 [2] First, it follows from this that we are [60]truly God's servants—indeed, his slaves—and that our greatest perfection is to be such nec-

essarily. For if we were left to ourselves, and so did not depend on God, there would be very little, or nothing, that we could accomplish, and we would rightly find in that a cause of sadness. But that would be quite the contrary to what we now see, viz. that we depend on what is most perfect in such a way that we are a part of the whole, i.e., of him, and so to speak contribute our share to the accomplishment of as many well-ordered and perfect works as are dependent on him.

[3] Second, this knowledge also has the result that after the accomplishment of something excellent ⁶¹we do not pride ourselves on this. Such pride causes us—when we think ourselves to be something great already, and to not require anything further—to stand still. So it is directly contrary to our perfection, which consists in this, that we must always strive to attain more and more. But on the contrary, [if we have this knowledge,] we ascribe everything we do to God, who is the first and only cause of all that we accomplish.

[4] ⁶²Third, in addition to the true love of one's fellow man which this knowledge gives us, it disposes us so that we never hate him, or are angry with him, but are instead inclined to help him and bring him to a better condition. Those are the actions of men who have a great perfection or essence.

[5] ⁶³Fourth, this knowledge also serves to further the common Good, for through it a judge will never be able to favor one more than another, and being required to punish one in order to reward the other, he will do this with insight, so as to help and improve the one as much as the other.

[6] ⁶⁴Fifth, this knowledge frees us from sadness, despair, envy, fright, and other evil passions, which, as we shall say later,¹ are the real hell itself.

[7] ⁶⁵Sixth, this knowledge brings us to the point where we do not fear God, as others fear the devil, whom they have feigned, so that he will not do anything evil to them. For how could we fear God, who is himself the greatest good, and through whom all things that have any essence—and we who live in him—are what they are?

[8] [Finally], this knowledge ⁶⁶also brings us to the point where we attribute everything to God, love him alone, because he is most mag-

---

¹ Freudenthal noted that we do not get the promised later discussion of the real hell as domination by bad passions, and he cited this as evidence that our manuscript of the *Short Treatise* represents an unfinished draft. Gebhardt suggests that the reference might be to I/108/6-17. Though the doctrine of eternal punishment was widely questioned in the seventeenth century, Spinoza would appear to be considerably more radical than most of his contemporaries. Cf. Walker (1).

nificent and supremely perfect, and offer ourselves entirely to him.
For that is what true religion and our eternal salvation and happiness
really consist in. For the only perfection and the final end of a slave
and an instrument is to fulfill properly the task imposed on them.

For example, if a carpenter, in making some work, finds himself
well-served by his axe, that axe has thereby attained its end and perfection. But if he should think, this axe has now served me so well
that I shall let it rest and exact no more service from it, then the axe
would be separated from its end, and would no longer be an axe.

[9] Similarly, man, so long as he is a part of Nature, must follow
the laws of Nature. That is [true] religion.[2] So long as he does this,
he has his well-being. But if God, so to speak, willed that man should
no longer serve him, that would be just as if he were to deprive him
of his well-being and destroy him. For all that he is consists in this,
that he serves God.

CHAPTER XIX[1]

OF OUR BLESSEDNESS

[1][a] Having seen the advantages of this true belief, we shall now strive
to fulfill the promise we have made: to investigate whether, through
the [67]knowledge we already have (such as, what good and evil are,
what truth and falsity are, and what, in general, the advantages of all
these are) we can attain our well-being, i.e., the Love of God, which,
as we have observed, is our greatest blessedness, and also how we can
be free of those passions which we have judged to be evil?[b]

[a] Whether we can attain our supreme salvation and be free of evil passions through
true belief. [A marginal note.]

[b] All the passions which are contrary to good reason arise (as we have previously
indicated) from opinion. True belief indicates to us everything that is good or bad in
them. But neither of these, either separately or together, is powerful enough to free us
from them. Only the third way, true knowledge, makes us free of them. Without this
it is impossible for us ever to be able to be freed of them, as will be shown later.

[2] Godsdienst, the ordinary term in Dutch for religion, is literally "service to God."
That etymology is so central to the thought of this passage that one might find grounds
here for suspecting that the passage was not written originally in Latin. But perhaps
the explanation is simply that Spinoza was addressing an audience whose native language was Dutch.

[1] Freudenthal contended that this (and the immediately following chapter, which is
closely tied to it) should be placed between II, xv and xvi, partly because the epistemological discussions of xvi-xvii are a digression from the ethical discussions of the
chapters which surround them, partly because the opening of II, xix presupposes that
the discussion of the advantages of true belief has just been concluded, and partly for
reasons already discussed (see the note to II/80/10). Meijer, Appuhn, and Gebhardt
reject his contention, because they find the structure of the chapters of the Short Treatise
as we have it analogous to that of the last two books of the Ethics.

[2] To speak first to the second question, whether we can become free of the passions, I say that if we suppose that they have no other causes than those we have posited, then if only we use our intellect well—as we can very easily[c] do, now that we have a measure of truth and falsity—we shall never fall into them.

[3] [68]But what we must now prove is that they have no other causes; for this it seems to me to be required that we investigate ourselves completely, both with respect to the body and with respect to the mind.

And [69]first [we have] to show that there is in Nature a body by whose form and actions[2] we are affected, so that we perceive it. We do this because if we come to see the actions of the body and what they produce, we shall then also find the first and principal cause of all these passions, and at the same time, the means by which all these passions can be destroyed. From this we can then see whether that can possibly be done through reason. Then we shall go on to speak of our Love of God.

[4] To show, then, that there is a body in Nature cannot be difficult for us, since we know already that God is, and what God is. For we have defined him as *a being of infinite attributes, of which each is infinite and perfect.* And since extension is an attribute which we have shown to be infinite its kind, it must also, necessarily, be an attribute of that infinite being. And because we have also proven already that *this infinite being is real*, it follows at the same time that this attribute is also real.

[5] Moreover, since we have also shown that apart from Nature, which is infinite, there is and can be no further being, it is evident that this effect of body through which we perceive [it] can come from

---

Would this not be what others, using other terms, say and write so much about? For who does not see how well we can understand by opinion, sin, by belief, the law that points out sins, by true knowledge, the grace that frees us of sin? [The note comes at this point in the manuscript, but without any indication of what it is supposed to amplify here. It concludes with the instruction that it should be placed in II, xxii. Gebhardt, in company with most editors, leaves it here, as the more appropriate location, though he does not think that as a whole it offers any "enrichment" of the text. Meijer suspected the second paragraph of being an interpolation by the Christian copyist. Gebhardt brackets the whole note as inauthentic, and probably introduced by Jelles. I see no reason to reject the first paragraph. Mignini attaches it to I/100/8.]

   [c] That is, if we have a thorough knowledge of good and evil, truth and falsity. For then it is impossible to be subject to what the passions arise from. For when we know and enjoy the best, the worst has no power over us. [Gebhardt brackets this note, which occurs as a footnote rather than as a marginal note, as being probably an editorial gloss, essentially similar to other notes relegated to the textual commentary.]

   [2] Generally *uitwerking* must translate *effectus*, but here it seems best (following Meijer and Wolf) to treat it as equivalent to *werking*.

nothing other than extension itself, and not from anything else that (as some maintain) has that extension *eminently*. For as we have already shown in the first Chapter,[3] this does not exist.

[6][d] So we should note that all the effects which we see depend necessarily on extension must be attributed to this attribute, e.g., Motion and Rest. For if the power to produce these effects were not in Nature, it would be impossible for them to be able to exist (even though many other attributes might also be in Nature). For if one thing produces another, there must be some being in it through which it can produce that rather than something else.

What we say here about extension, we say also about thought, and everything there is.

[7] We must note further that nothing is in us unless there is a power in us to be aware of it. So if we find nothing else to be in us but the effects of the thinking thing, and those of extension, we may say with certainty that nothing more is in us.

To understand clearly the actions of both of these, we shall take each of them, first separately, and then together, along with the effects of each.

[8] [70]When we consider extension alone, we perceive nothing else in it except motion and rest, from which we find that all its effects derive. [71]And such are these two[e] modes in body, that there can be no other thing which can change them, except themselves. E.g., if a stone is lying at rest, it is impossible that it should be able to be moved by the power of thinking, or anything else but motion, as when another stone, having more motion than this has rest, makes it move. Similarly, a stone in motion will not come to rest except through something else that moves less. So it follows, then, that no mode of thinking will be able to produce either motion or rest in the body.

[9] [72]But according to what we perceive in ourselves,[4] it can indeed

---

[d] What now comes into consideration is of great consequence. [A marginal note, relegated by Gebhardt to the textual commentary.]

[e] Two modes because rest is certainly not Nothing. [Gebhardt brackets this footnote as a reader's note.]

[3] Wolf suggests that the reference is to the first Dialogue in Part I and to I, ii, but perhaps it is to I, i, 8.

[4] A marginal note at this point reads: "What we, notwithstanding this, perceive to be able to happen in us. Followed by what is on [ms.] p. 132." The reference is to section 12. On the strength of this note and the order of the mysterious numbers in the ms., Mignini places section 12 immediately after section 9. This does seem to me a more logical ordering of the materials, and I have followed it. Mignini takes this as confirmation that Spinoza himself was the author of the numerical sequence in the ms. and that he is here correcting his own first draft. Cf. Mignini 3,259. If this hypothesis is correct, then the doubts some editors have had about the authenticity of this passage

happen that a body which is now moving in one direction comes to move in another direction—e.g., when I stretch out my arm, and

25 thereby bring it about that the spirits, which previously were moving in a different direction, now however have this one—though [this does] not always [happen], but according to the constitution of the spirits, as will be said later.

The cause of this is, and can only be, that the soul, being an Idea

30 of this body, is so united with it, that it and this body, so constituted, together make a whole.

I/92/27 [12] [74]Furthermore, the soul's power to move the spirits can also be hindered, either because the motion of the spirits is much decreased, or because it is much increased. It is decreased, for example, when

30 we have run a great deal. In doing this, we bring it about that the spirits give so much more motion than usual to the body, and lose so much motion, that they are necessarily much weakened. This can also happen through taking too little food. It is increased, for example, when we drink too much wine or other strong drink, thereby becoming merry, or drunk, and destroying the soul's power to govern the

I/93/2 body.

I/91/32 [10] [75]The principal effect of the other attribute is a perception of things which, depending on the way that [the soul] comes to conceive

I/92 them, generates love or hate, etc. This effect, then, since it does not involve any extension, can also not be ascribed to extension, but only

5 to thought. So the cause of all the changes which arise in these modes must be sought only in the thinking thing, not in extension.

We can see this in love; for whether it is to be destroyed or to be aroused, such a change must be produced through the perception itself, which happens (as we have already said) because one comes to

10 know either that there is something bad in the object or that something else is better.

[11] So when these attributes come to act on one another, there arises from this a passion produced in the one by the other; e.g., through the determination of motion, which we have the power to

15 make go where we will. The actions, then, by which the one comes to be acted on by the other, are as follows: the soul [acting] on the body,[5] as we have already said, can bring it about that the spirits

---

(and others in which Spinoza seems to accept a measure of mind-body interaction) would be misplaced. See Wolf, 2, 227-229 for an interesting discussion of the relevant passages.

[5] The ms. reads: "the soul and the body." Gebhardt retains the ms. reading, though Sigwart had challenged it on the strength of a marginal note attached to "soul" which reads: "Understand: each particular, or also the soul acting on the body can indeed bring it about etc." Mignini adopts the emendation (reading "in" for "en", but also changing "konnen" to "kan"), calling attention to the beginning of § 13.

which would otherwise have moved in one direction, should now, however, move in another.

And because these spirits can also be moved by the body, and so determined [in their direction], it can often happen that having their motion in one direction because of the body, and in another because of the soul, they bring about those anxieties which we often perceive in ourselves, without knowing the reasons why we have them. For otherwise the reasons are usually well known to us.

[13] Having said this much about the actions of the soul on the body, let us now examine the actions of the body on the soul. We maintain that [76]the principal one is that it causes the soul to perceive it, and thereby to perceive other bodies also. This is caused only by Motion and Rest together. For there are no other things in the body through which it could act.

[14] So whatever else apart from this perception happens to the soul cannot be produced through the body. And because the first thing the soul comes to know is the body, the result is that the soul loves the body and is united to it. But since, as we have already said, the cause of love, hate, and sadness must be sought not in the body, but only in the soul (for all the actions of the body must proceed from motion and rest), and because we see clearly and distinctly that the one love is destroyed by the perception of something else that is better, it follows from this clearly that if we once come to know God (at least with as clear a knowledge as we have of our body), we must then come to be united with him even more closely than with our body, and be, as it were, released from the body.

I say more closely, for we have already proven before that without him we can neither be nor be understood. This is because we know him, and must know him, not through anything else (as is the case with all other things), but only through himself (as we have already said before). Indeed, we know him better than we know ourselves, because without him we cannot know ourselves at all.

[15] From what we have so far said, it is easy to infer what are the principal causes of the passions. For regarding the body, and its effects, Motion and Rest, they cannot act on the soul otherwise than to make themselves known to it as objects. And according to the appearances they present to it, whether of good or bad,[f] so the soul is also

[f] But how does it come about that we know the one to be good and the other bad? Answer: since it is the objects which make us perceive them, we are affected differently by the one than by the other. Those by which we are moved most moderately, according to the proportion of motion and rest of which they consist,[6] are most pleasant to
[6] Gebhardt emended the text here to read: "of which we consist" (reading "wij" for "sij"), arguing that consistency with the subjectivistic aesthetic of E I App. required this. Mignini retains the ms. reading, arguing that it is not inconsistent with E I App.

affected by them, not insofar as [the body] is a body (for then the body would be the principal cause of the passions), but insofar as it is an object, like all other things, which would also have the same effects if they presented themselves to the soul in the same way.

[16] (But by this I do not mean that the love, hate, and sadness which proceed from the consideration of incorporeal things would have the same effects as those which arise from the consideration of corporeal things. For as we shall say later, the former have still other effects, according to the nature of the thing whose conception arouses the love, hate, sadness, etc., in the soul considering the incorporeal things.)

[17] So, to return to our previous topic, if something else should present itself to the soul more magnificently than the body does, it is certain that the body would then have no power to produce such effects as it now does.

From this it follows not only that the body is not the principal cause of the passions,g but also that even if there were something else in us, apart from what we have now considered to be capable of producing the passions, such a thing, if it existed, would be able to act on the soul neither more, nor differently than the body now does. For it could never be other than such an object as would be completely different from the soul, and consequently it would show itself to be such, and not otherwise (as we have also said of the body).

[18] So we may conclude truly that love, hate, sadness, and the other 'passions' are produced in the soul in various ways, according to the kind of knowledge the soul has each time, And consequently, if it can once come to know also the most magnificent being of all, it will then be impossible for any of these passions to produce the least disturbance in it.

---

us, and as they depart further and further from [such moderation], they are most unpleasant.

And from this there arise all the kinds of feelings which we are aware of in ourselves and which, when they are produced by corporeal objects, acting on our body, as they often are, we call *impulses*. For example, one can make someone who is sad laugh or be merry by tickling him, or having him drink wine, etc. The soul indeed is aware of this, but does not act. For when the soul acts, its merriment is of another kind. Then body does not act on body, but the intellectual soul uses the body as an instrument. Consequently, the more the soul acts, the more perfect the feeling is.

g It is not necessary to hold that the body alone is the principal cause of the passions, but any other substance, if it came to exist, would be able to produce them, and not something else or more; for it could not differ more in nature than this one [the body], which is completely different from [the soul]. And it is from this difference of the objects that the change in the soul arises. [Gebhardt prints this note, which most editors have suppressed. But he does not think it genuine. Meijer does ascribe it to Spinoza.]

CHAPTER XX

CONFIRMATION OF THE PRECEDING

[1] The following difficulties could be raised against what we have said in the preceding chapter:

[77]First, if motion is not the cause of the passions, how can one nevertheless drive out sadness by [certain] means, as is often accomplished by wine?

[2] To this we may reply that a distinction must be drawn[a] between the perception of the soul when it first becomes aware of the body and the judgment it directly makes as to whether it is good or bad for it.

The soul, then, being constituted as has now mediately been said,[1] we have shown before that [it] has [the] power to move the [animal] spirits where it will; but this power can nevertheless be taken from it, as when, through other causes, arising from the body in general, the proportion [of motion of rest] established in the spirits is taken from them, or changed; and when the soul becomes aware of this, a sadness arises in it, according to the change the spirits then receive. This sadness[b] results from the love and the union it has with the body.

---

[a] That is, between the intellect taken generally, and the intellect as having a regard for the good or bad of the thing. [A marginal note, bracketed by Gebhardt as probably not genuine.]

[b] The sadness is produced in man by an opinion that something bad is happening to him, i.e., the loss of some good. When he has such a perception, the result is that the spirits gather around the heart, and with the help of other parts press against it and enclose it, just the opposite of what happens in joy. The soul in turn is aware of this pressure, and is pained.

Now what is it that medicines or wine bring about? This: that by their action they drive these spirits from the heart and make room again. When the soul becomes aware of this, it gets relief, in that the opinion that something bad is occurring is diverted by the different proportion of motion and rest which the wine produces; so it turns to something else, in which the intellect finds more satisfaction. This cannot be an immediate action of the wine on the soul, but only an action of the wine on the spirits [and thereby on the soul].

[1] So the manuscript reads. There is a consensus that the text is corrupt, but no consensus as to its emendation. Earlier editors tended to read the phrase translated by "now mediately" (*nu mediate*) as a slip for "immediately" (*immediate*). Gebhardt omits the *nu* and transfers *mediate* to the next line, producing a text that would be translated: "The soul, then, being constituted as has been said, we have shown before that it has mediately the power etc." He refers to 99/3-4 as a corresponding passage. It would be more convincing if Gebhardt had cited an earlier rather than a later passage. Perhaps Spinoza's backward reference here is to xix, 9, where he does seem to ascribe to the soul an indirect control over the motions of the animal spirits. Mignini finds this interpretation impossible and suggests an emendation which would be translated: "The soul, then, being mediately constituted as has been said, we have shown before that [it] has [the] power etc." The idea seems to be that, although the soul is a mode of thought, because it is also the idea of the body, undergoing changes corresponding to those in the body, its powers are in a certain sense derivative from those of the body.

That this is so can easily be inferred from the fact that the sadness can be relieved in one of two ways: either by restoration of the spirits to their original form, i.e., by freeing him of that pain, or by being convinced by good reasons to make nothing of this body. The first is temporary and [the pain always threatens] to come again. But the second is eternal, constant, and immutable.

[3] The [78]second possible objection is this: we see that the soul, though it has nothing in common with the body,[c] nevertheless can bring it about that the spirits, which would have moved in one direction, now however move in another direction—why, then, could they

[c2] There is no difficulty here as to how this one mode, which differs infinitely from the other, acts on the other. For it is a part of the whole, because the soul has never existed without the body, nor the body without the soul. We arrive at this as follows:
  1. There is a perfect being. [I/20/1]
  2. There cannot be two substances. [I/23/14ff.]
  3. No substance can begin. [I/19/39-43]
  4. Every attribute is infinite in its kind. [I/19/6]
  5. There must also be an attribute of thinking. [I/51/22-23]
  6. There is no thing in Nature of which there is not, in the thinking thing, an idea proceeding from it according to its essence and its existence together. [I/51/24]
  7. Consequently,
  8. Since the essence, without existence, is conceived as belonging to the meanings of things, the Idea of the essence cannot be considered as something singular. That can only happen when the existence is there together with the essence, and that because then there is an object which did not exist before. E.g., when the whole wall is white, then there is no this or that in etc.
  9. This Idea then, considered alone, apart from all other Ideas, can be no more than an Idea of such a thing; it does not have an idea of such a thing. Because such an idea, so considered, is only a part, it cannot have the clearest and most distinct concept of itself and its object; but the thinking thing, which alone is the whole of Nature, can. For a part, considered apart from its whole, cannot etc.[3]
  10. Between the Idea and the object there must necessarily be a union, because the one cannot exist without the other. For there is no thing of which there is not an Idea in the thinking thing, and no idea can exist unless the thing also exists.
  Further, the object cannot be changed unless the Idea is also changed, and vice versa, so that no third thing is necessary here which would produce the union of soul and body.
  But it should be noted that here we are speaking of such Ideas as necessarily arise in God from the existence of things, together with their essence, not of those Ideas which things now actually present to us[4] [or] produce in us. Between these two there is a great difference. For in God the Ideas arise from the existence and essence [of the things], according to all they are—not, as in us, from one or more of the senses (with the result that we are nearly always affected by things only imperfectly and that my Idea and yours differ, though one and the same thing produces them in us.).[5]
  [2] There is no indication in the ms. as to where this note goes. For each of the first six propositions the ms. has an incomplete reference in the form: "p.———." Some scholars have contended that the missing page references could not be supplied from the *Treatise* as we have it, and have therefore conjectured a lost section, or sections. The bracketed page references are given by Gebhardt, following suggestions by Meijer.
  [3] Meijer suggests glossing "etc." as "be conceived."
  [4] So Wolf, and this does seem to me the most natural way of taking the Dutch. But Appuhn, followed by the Pléiade editors, has: "things, actually existing, present to us." And Gebhardt has: "things, as they now exist, present to us."
  [5] Here I follow Meijer and Appuhn. One might compare II, xv, 5.

not also make a body which is completely at rest begin to move? Similarly, why could it not also move wherever it will all other bodies that already have motion?

[4] But if we recall what we have already said about the thinking thing, we will be able to remove this difficulty very easily. We said then that *although Nature has different attributes, it is nevertheless only one unique Being, of which all these attributes are predicated.* We added that the thinking thing is also unique in Nature and that it is expressed in infinite Ideas, according to the infinite things that are in Nature. For if the body receives one mode, such as, for example, Peter's body, and again another, such as Paul's body, the result of this is that there are two different ideas in the thinking thing: One Idea of Peter's body, which makes the soul of Peter, and another of Paul['s body], which makes Paul's soul. So then, the thinking thing can indeed move Peter's body, through the Idea of Peter's body, but not through the Idea of Paul's body. So Paul's soul can indeed move his own body, but not that of someone else, such as Peter.[d]

And for this reason it also cannot move a stone which is at rest. For the stone makes another Idea again in the thinking thing.[8] Hence it is no less clear that it is impossible for a body completely at rest to be able to be moved by any mode of thought, for the reasons given above.

[5] The third possible [79]objection is this: we seem to be able to see clearly that we can nevertheless produce a certain rest in the body. But after we have moved our spirits a long time, we find that we are tired. This is nothing but a rest in the spirits, brought about by us.

[6] We answer that the soul is indeed a cause of this rest, but only indirectly. For it does not bring the motion to rest immediately, but only through other bodies which it has moved, and which must have lost as much rest as they communicated to the spirits. So it is clear on all sides that in Nature there is one and the same kind of motion.

[d6] It is clear that since man had a beginning, no attribute is to be found in him other than those which were already in Nature. And since he consists of a body such that there must necessarily be an Idea of it in the thinking thing, and that Idea must necessarily be united with the body, we affirm without hesitation that his soul is nothing but this Idea, in the thinking thing, of this body of his. And because this body has a [proportion of] motion and rest which is determined and continually[7] changed by external objects, and because no change can occur in the object, unless the same thing also actually occurs in the Idea, the result is that people feel (reflexive idea). I say "because it has a proportion of motion and rest," because no action can occur in the body without these two concurring.

[6] Previous editors have attached this note to 98/15, as I have. Mignini, without explanation, but with some plausibility, attaches it to 98/3.

[7] Adopting a suggestion of Meijer's. Cf. I/52/25-29.

[8] So Gebhardt's text reads. The ms. has "in the soul." Mignini retains the ms. reading, since he thinks it unlikely that it represents a copyist's error. But he agrees that Gebhardt's reading reproduces the true sense of the text.

Chapter XXI

Of Reason

[1] Now we have to inquire how it is that sometimes, [80]though we see that a thing is good or bad, we nevertheless find no power in ourselves to do the good, or omit the bad, while at other times we do [find this power in ourselves].

[2] We can easily grasp this, if we take into consideration the causes we have given of opinions, which we said were the causes of all the passions. These [causes] we said, are *either report or experience*. And because whatever we find in ourselves has more power over us than anything which comes from outside, it follows that Reason can be a cause of the destruction of those opinions[a] which we have only from report (because Reason has not come to us from outside), but not [a cause of the destruction] of those which we have through experience.

[3] For the power the thing itself gives us is always greater than that we get as a result of a second thing. We noted this difference when speaking of reasoning and of clear understanding [I/54] where we illustrated it with the rule of three. For we have more power if we understand the proportion itself than if we understand the rule of proportion. That is why we have already said so often that one love is destroyed by another that is greater, because by that we did not at all want to refer to the desire which proceeds from reasoning.

Chapter XXII

Of true Knowledge, Rebirth, etc.

[1] Since reason,[1] then, has no power to bring us to our well-being, it remains for us to investigate whether we can attain it by the fourth and [81]last kind of knowledge.

We have said that this kind of knowledge is not a consequence of anything else, but an immediate manifestation of the object itself to

[a] It will be the same whether we use the word *opinion* here, or *passion*. And so it is clear why we cannot conquer by Reason those which are in us through experience; for these are nothing else in us but an enjoyment of, or immediate union with, something we judge to be good, and though Reason shows us something that is better, it does not make us enjoy it. Now what we enjoy in ourselves cannot be conquered by what we do not enjoy and what is outside us, as what Reason shows us is. But if it is to be conquered, there must be something that is more powerful, like an enjoyment of, and immediate union with, what is known to be better than the first and enjoyed more. And when this is present, the conquest is always inevitable. Or [the conquest can come] also from the experience of an evil known to be greater than the good enjoyed and immediately following on it. But experience teaches us that this evil does not always follow necessarily, for etc. See pp. [62/20-63/1; 88/30-89/13].

[1] See Spinoza's note at I/89/22ff.

the intellect. And if the object is magnificent and good, the soul necessarily becomes united with it, as we have also said of the body.

[2] From this it follows incontrovertibly that this knowledge is what produces love; so if we come to know God in this way, then we must necessarily unite with him, for he cannot manifest himself, or be known by us, as anything but the most magnificent and best of all. As we have already said, our blessedness consists only in this union with him.

I do not say that we must know him as he is;[2] it is enough for us to know him to some extent in order to be united with him. For even in the knowledge we have of the body we do not know it as it is, or perfectly. And yet, what a union! what a love!

[3] That this fourth [kind of] knowledge, which is the knowledge of God, is not the consequence of anything else, but immediate, is evident from what we have previously proven, viz. that he is the cause of all knowledge which is known through itself alone, and not through any other thing. But in addition to that, it is also evident from the fact that by Nature we are so united with him that without him we can neither be nor be understood. For this reason, then, because there is so close a union between God and us, it is evident that we can only understand him immediately.

[4] We shall now try to explain the union we have with him by Nature and by love. We have already said that there can be nothing in Nature of which there is not an idea in the soul of the same thing.[a] And as the thing is more or less perfect, so also are the union of the Idea with the thing, or with God himself, and the effect [of that union] more perfect.[3] [5] For since the whole of Nature is one unique substance, whose essence is infinite, all things are united through Nature, and united into one [being], viz. God.

And because the body is the very first thing our soul becomes aware of—for as we have said, there can be nothing in Nature whose Idea does not exist in the thinking thing, the idea which is the soul of that

[a] This explains what we said in the first part, viz. that the infinite intellect must exist in Nature from all eternity, and why we called it the son of God. For since God has existed from eternity, so also must his Idea be in the thinking thing, i.e., exist in itself from eternity; this Idea agrees objectively with him. See p. [I/48].

[2] Of the ten marginal notes in this chapter only one seems to contain anything of interest. Just above this passage is a note reading: "This knowledge need not be adequate, and why." What is interesting here is the use of the term *adequate* (*evenmatig*), which otherwise does not seem to occur in the *Short Treatise*.

[3] Gebhardt emends the text to read: "the union of the idea with the thinking thing . . ." in order to avoid an equation between the thing and God. Mignini points out that the equation of the thinking thing with God would be no more acceptable. To read the "or" as indicating an equivalence is probably to miss the point of the passage, which foreshadows the argument for immortality in II, xxiii.

thing—that thing must, then, necessarily be the first cause of the idea.[b]

I/102   But this Idea cannot find any rest in the knowledge of the body, without passing over into knowledge of that without which neither the body nor the Idea itself can either exist or be understood. Hence, as soon as it knows that being, it will be united with it by love.

[6] To grasp this union better and infer what it must be, we must consider the effect [of the union] with the body. In this we see how, by knowledge of and passions toward corporeal things, there come to arise in us all those effects which we are constantly aware of in our body, through the motion of the spirits; and so (if once our knowledge and love come to fall on that without which we can neither exist nor be understood, and which is not at all corporeal) the effects arising from this union will, and must, be incomparably greater and more magnificent. For these [effects] must necessarily be commensurate with the thing with which it[4] is united.

[7] [83]When we become aware of these effects, we can truly say that we have been born again. For our first birth was when we were united with the body. From this union have arisen the effects and motions of the [animal] spirits. But our other, or second, birth will occur when we become aware in ourselves of the completely different effects of love produced by knowledge of this incorporeal object. This [love of God] is as different from [love of the body] as the incorporeal is from the corporeal, the spirit from the flesh.

This, therefore, may the more rightly and truly be called Rebirth, because, as we shall show, an eternal and immutable constancy comes only from this Love and Union.

Chapter XXIII

Of the Immortality of the Soul

[1] If we once consider attentively what the Soul is, and where its change and duration arise from, we shall easily see whether it is mortal or immortal.

I/103   We have said, then, that the Soul is an Idea which is in the thinking thing, arising from the existence of a thing which is in Nature. From this it follows that as the duration and change of the thing are, so also

---

[b] I.e., our soul being an Idea of the body, it has its first being from the body, for it is only a representation of the body, both of the whole and of the parts, in the thinking thing. [Bracketed by Gebhardt, and generally regarded as a reader's comment.]
    [4] The reference of the pronoun may be either to the idea, as Mignini thinks (cf. §§ 4 and 5) or to the soul, as Meier thought (cf. § 1). In any case, there seems to be no need to emend the text, as Gebhardt and others have done, to read: "we are united."

the duration and change of the Soul must be. Moreover, we have noted that the Soul can be united either with the body of which it is the Idea or with God, without whom it can neither exist nor be understood.

[2] From this, then, one can easily see that:

1. if it is united with the body only, and the body perishes, then it must also perish; for if it lacks the body, which is the foundation of its love, it must perish with it; but that

2. if it is united with another thing, which is, and remains, immutable, then, on the contrary, it will have to remain immutable also. For through what would it then be possible that it should be able to perish? Not through itself, for as little as it was able, when it did not exist, through itself to begin to exist, so little is it able, now that it exists, [through itself]¹ to change or perish. So what alone is the cause of [the Soul's] existence [i.e., God], would also, when [the Soul] came to perish, have to be the cause of its nonexistence, because it [i.e., God] changed or perished.²

¹ A suggestion of Monnikhoff's.

² The manuscript here, if it is correct, might be translated: "So what is alone the cause of its essence must also be (when it comes to perish) the cause of its non-essence, because it itself comes to perish." Everyone agrees that the ms. cannot be right as it stands. Most editors (Wolf, Meijer, Appuhn, Sigwart, Mignini, and Gebhardt himself in his translation) have emended "essence" (*wezenheid*) and "non-essence" (*niet wezenheid*) to "existence" (*wezenlijkheid*) and "non-existence" (*niet wezenlijkheid*).

In his edition, however, Gebhardt (followed by the Pléiade editors) retained "essence" and "non-essence," and changed "because" (*omdat*) to "if" (*indien*). His reasoning seems to have been as follows: (1) if the phrase "what is alone the cause" referred to the body, "essence" would have to be emended to "existence" and "because" would be unobjectionable; (2) but if the phrase refers to God, then "essence" is correct and "because" cannot be right; (3) since the context suggests that the reference is to God, "essence" should be retained and the last clause made conditional (apparently conjecturing a mistranslation of a *cum* in the Latin original).

Mignini contends that (4) since God can never change or perish, "what is alone the cause" cannot refer to God, but must refer in general to the cause of the soul's existence; (5) only the existence of the body can be the cause of the soul's existence; (6) the essences of things are eternal; and (7) the copyist often writes *wezenheid* instead of *wezenlijkheid*. Mignini thus seems to accept Gebhardt's (1) and (2).

I would say that while "essence" is possible, other things equal, if "what is alone the cause" refers to God, since God is the sole cause of the essences of things, it is not necessary, since the argument is proceeding on the assumption that in appropriate circumstances God can also be the sole cause of a thing's existence. I take it that the whole passage (from l. 12) is conducted on the hypothesis of union with God, which is equivalent to hypothesizing that God is the only cause of the soul's existence. These hypotheses represent possibilities. That God should change or perish is admittedly an impossibility. But the point of the argument, I think, is to deduce from that impossibility the impossibility of the soul's perishing if it can unite itself with God. For further discussion, relating this argument to what I claim is a revised and improved version of it in II, xxvi, and to the Second Dialogue, which I suggest is a response to its problems, see Curley 1.

Chapter XXIV

Of God's Love for Man

25 [1] So far we think we have sufficiently shown what our love of God is, and its effect, our eternal duration. [85]So we do not consider it necessary to say anything here about other things, such as joy in God, peace of mind, etc., since from what has been said one can easily see what should be said about them.

30 [2] But[1] since we have spoken up to now only of our love for God, it remains to be seen whether there is also a love of God for us. [86]I.e., whether God also loves men, and whether he does this when they love him?

I/104 First, we have said that no modes of thought can be ascribed to God except those which are in creatures, so that it cannot be said that God loves men, much less that he loves them because they love him, 5 and hates them because they hate him. For if that were so, one would have to suppose that men do such a thing freely and that they do not depend on a first cause. This we have already proven to be false. Moreover, this would also have to produce a great mutability in God. 10 Where previously he had neither loved nor hated, he would now begin to love and to hate, and would be caused to do this by something that would be outside him. But this is absurdity itself.

[3] When[2] we say, however, that God does not love man, that must 15 not be understood as if he left man, as it were, to proceed on his own; [we mean] rather, that because man, together with all there is, is so in God, and God so consists of all of these, there cannot be in him any real love toward something else, since everything consists in one unique thing which is God himself.

20 [4] From[3] this it follows also that God does not give man laws in order to reward him when he fulfills them. To put it more clearly, God's laws are not of such a nature that they could ever be transgressed. For the rules that God has established in Nature, according 25 to which all things come to be and endure—if we want to call them laws—are such that they can never be transgressed. E.g., *that the weakest must yield to the strongest, that no cause can produce more than it has in itself*, etc., are of such a kind that they never change, never begin, but that everything is disposed and ordered under them.

---

[1] A marginal note (relegated by Gebhardt to the textual commentary) at this point reads: "What then remains for me to treat, viz. whether there is a love of God for man."

[2] A marginal note at this point reads: "How this nevertheless must not be understood to seem an absurdity."

[3] A marginal note at this point reads: "Thus God also does not makes laws for man, to reward him when he has performed them. For the laws of God, if one wants to call by this name the rules that are in Nature, can not be transgressed."

[5] To say something about them briefly, [88]all laws that cannot be transgressed are divine laws. For whatever happens is, not contrary to, but according to his own decree. All laws that can be transgressed are human laws. For everything that man decides for his own well-being is not necessarily for the well-being of the whole of Nature also. On the contrary, it may be destructive of many other things.

[6] [89]When the laws of Nature are more powerful, the laws of man are destroyed.[4] [90]The divine laws are the ultimate end, on account of which they exist, and are not subordinated. Not so human laws. For notwithstanding the fact that men make laws for their own well-being, and have no other end than to advance their own well-being thereby, this end of theirs—being subordinated to other ends, which another has in view, who is above them and lets them so act, as being parts of Nature—can also serve the end that it concurs with those eternal laws that God has established from eternity and that in this way it contributes to produce everything.

For example, bees, in all their work, and in the order they maintain among themselves, have no other end in view than to provide a certain supply for the winter. Nevertheless, man, who is above them, has a completely different end in maintaining and caring for them, viz. to get honey for himself.

So also man, as a particular thing, has no further purpose than his limited essence can attain; but as a part and instrument of the whole of Nature, this end of his cannot be the ultimate end of Nature, because it is infinite and must use man, along with all other things, as its instrument.

[7] So far, then, we have spoken of the law established by God. [91]But we should also note that man is also aware of two kinds of law in himself (I mean the man who uses his intellect properly, and comes to knowledge of God): one produced by the community he has with God, the other by the community he has with the modes of Nature.

[8] Of these, the one is necessary, the other not.

For regarding the law arising from community with God, because he cannot fail to be always necessarily united with God, he has, and must always have before his eyes, the laws according to which he must live for and with God.

But as for the law arising from community with modes, since he can separate himself from men,[5] this is not so necessary.

---

[4] So the text runs. Gebhardt, in company with others, saw it as needing the following explanation: "When the laws of Nature come in conflict with those of man, then since the laws of Nature are more powerful, the laws of man are destroyed."

[5] This passing remark is strikingly different from the general tone of the *Ethics*. Cf., for example, E IVP35C1, C2 and S. One might see in this difference a symptom of Spinoza's mood at the time of composing this work. Cf. Feuer 1, chap. 2.

[9] Because we maintain such a community between God and man, one might rightly ask how God can make himself known to man, and whether this happens, or could happen, through spoken words, or immediately, without using any other thing to do it?

[10] We answer: not in any case by words. For then man would have had to know already the meanings of those words before they were spoken to him. For example, if God had said to the Israelites: *I am Jehovah your God*,[6] they must have known previously, without the words that he was God, before they could be sure that it was he.[7] For they knew that that voice, thunder and lightning were not God, though the voice said that it was God.

And what we say here about words, we want applied to all other external signs. So we consider it impossible that God could make himself known to men by means of any external signs.

[11] [93]We also consider it unnecessary that this should happen through anything other than God's essence alone and man's intellect. For since that in us which must know God is the intellect, and the intellect is so immediately united with him that it can neither exist nor be understood without him, it is incontrovertibly clear that no thing can ever be joined to the intellect as God himself is.

[12] [94]It is also impossible to be able to know God through anything else:[8]

1. Because such a thing would then have to be better known to us than God himself, which is plainly contrary to everything which we have clearly shown up to this point, viz. that God is a cause both of our knowledge and of all essence, and that all particular things not only cannot exist without him, but also cannot even be understood.

2. That we can never attain to the knowledge of God through any other thing whose being is necessarily limited, even if it was better known to us. For how is it possible that we could infer an infinite and unlimited thing from one that is limited?

[6] Spinoza probably has in mind Exodus 20:2, a text he will also discuss in the TTP III/18/21ff.), though there are certainly other candidates (e.g., Exodus 6:7). Francès, comparing the discussion in the KV with that in the TTP, comments that the former is direct, but summary, whereas the latter is so diplomatic and conciliatory that some commentators have mistaken Spinoza's true thought.

[7] Monnikhoff has: ". . . they must have known previously that God existed before they could be sure that it was God [who was speaking to them]." Most editors seem to have favored the ms. reading, but I think Monnikhoff has made an improvement.

[8] Freudenthal 2, 247, notes the inconsistency of this section (and II, xix, 14) with I, i, which allows the possibility of an a posteriori proof of God's existence. He offers this as evidence of the unfinished state of the *Short Treatise*.

[13] For though we observed some effects or some work in Nature whose cause was unknown to us, nevertheless, it is impossible for us to infer from that that there must be an infinite and unlimited thing in Nature to produce this effect. For how can we know whether many causes concurred to produce it, or there was only one? Who will tell us that? So we conclude, finally, that to make himself known to man, God neither can, nor need, use words, miracles, or any other created thing, but only himself.

CHAPTER XXV
OF DEVILS

[1] [95]We shall now say something briefly about whether or not there are Devils:

If the Devil is a thing that is completely contrary to God and has nothing from God, then he agrees precisely with Nothing, of which we have already spoken previously.

[2] If, as some do, we maintain that he is a thinking thing that neither wills nor does anything at all that is good, and so completely opposes himself to God, then certainly he is quite miserable, and if prayers could help, we should pray for his conversion.

[3] But let us just see whether such a miserable thing could exist for even a single moment. If we consider this, we shall immediately find that it cannot. For all the duration of a thing arises from its perfection, and the more essence and divinity they have in them, the more constant they are.[1] Since the Devil has the least perfection in himself, how, I wonder, could he exist? Moreover, constancy or duration in the mode of the thinking thing only arise through the union which such a mode has with God, a union produced by love. Since the exact opposite of this is posited in Devils, they cannot possibly exist.

[4] But because there is no necessity to posit Devils, why should they be posited? [96]For we have no need, as others do, to posit Devils in order to find causes of hate, envy, anger, and such passions. We have come to know them sufficiently without the aid of such fictions.

---

[1] The phrase "essence and divinity" is unusual and the Pléiade editors conjecture a possible misreading of *divinitas* for *realitas* on the part of the Dutch translator, though they acknowledge that the manuscript may well have read *divinitas*. Opinion is divided on the question whether Spinoza's doctrine here is consistent with E IIP30D. Cf. Wolf 2, 234 and Appuhn, 1:414.

Chapter XXVI

Of true Freedom etc.

[1] By what we have maintained in the preceding, we wanted to in-dictate not only that there are no devils, [97]but also that the causes (or to put it better, what we call sins) which prevent us from attaining our perfection are in ourselves.

[2] We have also shown in the preceding how, both by reason[1] and by the fourth kind of knowledge, we must attain our blessedness, and how the passions must be destroyed: not in the way commonly said, that they must be subdued before we can attain to the knowledge, and consequently to the love, of God—that would be like maintaining that someone who is ignorant should first put aside his ignorance before he could arrive at knowledge—on the contrary, only knowledge [of God] is the cause of the destruction [of the passions],[2] as is evident from everything we have said.

Similarly, it may also be inferred clearly from the preceding that without virtue, or to put it better, without being governed by the intellect, everything leads to ruin, without our being able to enjoy any peace, and we live as if out of our element.

[3] So even if the power of knowledge and divine love did not bring the intellect to an eternal peace, as we have shown, but only to a temporary one, it is our duty to seek even this, since it is such that one who enjoys it would not want to exchange it for anything else in the world.

[4] Since this is so, we can, with reason, regard as most absurd what is said by many, who are otherwise considered great theologians: that if the love of God did not lead to eternal life, they would then seek what is best for themselves. As if they could find anything better than God! This is as silly as if a fish (which cannot live outside the water) should say: if no eternal life is to come to me after this life in the water, I want to leave the water for the land.[3] But what else can those who do not know God say to us?

[5] So we see that to reach the truth of what we maintain as estab-lished regarding our salvation and peace, we need no principle other

---

[1] Monnikhoff has simply "how, by the fourth kind of knowledge." Wolf conjectured that this was because he had noticed that it had *not* been shown how our happiness might be attained through reason. Freudenthal saw the mention of reason as an editor's attempt to resolve the contradiction mentioned in II, i, 1, n. 1.

[2] The ms. does not make clear what is being destroyed. Some translators (Appuhn, the Pléiade editors, Gebhardt) have supposed that it was simply ignorance. I follow Meijer.

[3] An echo of a Talmudic parable (Babylonian Talmud, Berachot 61b), details of which are given in Wolf 2, 235.

than that of seeking our own advantage, something which is very natural in all things. And since we find that pursuing sensual pleasures, lusts, and worldly things leads not to our salvation but to our destruction, we therefore prefer to be governed by our intellect.

But because this can make no progress unless we have first arrived at the knowledge and love of God, it is most necessary to seek him. And because, after the preceding reflections and considerations, we have found him to be the greatest good of all goods, we must stand firm here, and be at peace. For we have seen that outside him, there is nothing that can give us any salvation. True freedom is to be and to remain bound by the lovely chains of the love of God.[4]

[6] Finally, we see also that reasoning is not the principal thing in us, but only like a stairway, by which we can climb up to the desired place, or like a good spirit which without any falsity or deception brings tidings of the greatest good, to spur us thereby to seek it, and to unite with it in a union which is our greatest salvation and blessedness.

[7][5] To bring this work to an end, it remains now to indicate briefly what human freedom consists in. To do this, I shall use the following propositions as things which are certain and proven.

1. The more essence a thing has, the more it also has of action and the less of passion. For it is certain that the agent acts through what he has, and that the one who is acted on is acted on through what he does not have.

2. All passion, whether it is from not being to being, or from being to not being, must proceed from an external agent, and not from an internal one. For no thing, considered in itself, has in itself a cause enabling it to destroy itself (if it exists) or to make itself (if it does not exist).

3. Whatever is not produced by external causes can also have nothing in common with them, and consequently will not be able to be changed or transformed by them.

---

[4] It is most natural, perhaps, to take *syne liefde* to refer to God's love for man. But previously (I/103-104) we have had a denial that God can properly be said to love man and the contrary is not plainly asserted elsewhere in this work. If our ms. is indeed a translation of a Latin original, the Latin would probably be ambiguous. In the *Ethics*, Spinoza's consistency on this point is disputed. Cf. A. E. Taylor.

[5] Meijer thought that this and the following two sections were probably later insertions. Linguistic symptoms of this, perhaps, are: the use of the term *gewrocht*, the normal translation of *effectus* in Spinoza's other works, but rare in the *Short Treatise* (occurring otherwise only in Second Dialogue, which is also thought to be a later addition and which comments on these sections, and at I/107/8); the use of the term *doening* for *actio* (rather than *werking*), which occurs only here. Cf. Curley 1.

From these last two [propositions], I infer the following fourth proposition.

4. No effect of an immanent or internal cause (which is all one, according to me) can possibly perish or change so long as its cause remains. For just as such an effect has not been produced by external causes, so also it cannot be changed [by them] (by the third proposition). And because nothing can be destroyed except through external causes, it is impossible that this effect should be able to perish so long as its cause endures (by the second proposition).

5. The freest cause of all, and the one most suited to God, is the immanent. For the effect of this cause depends on it in such a way that without it, [the effect] can neither exist nor be understood; nor is [the effect] subjected to any other cause. Moreover, [the effect] is also so united with [the cause] that together they form a whole.

[8] So let us see now what we have to conclude from these propositions. First, then,

1. Since God's essence is infinite, it has an infinite action, and an infinite negation of passion (by the first proposition); consequently, the more things, through their greater essence, are united with God, the more they also have of action, and the less of passion, and the more they are also free of change and corruption.

2. The true intellect can never come to perish, for in itself it can have no cause to make itself perish (by the second proposition). And because it has not proceeded from external causes, but from God, it cannot receive any change from him (by the third proposition). And since God has produced it immediately, and he alone is an internal cause, it follows necessarily that it cannot perish, so long as this, its cause, remains (by the fourth proposition). Now this, its cause, is eternal. Therefore, it too [is eternal].

3. All the effects of the intellect which are united with him are the most excellent, and must be valued above all others. For because they are internal effects, they are the most excellent of all (by the fifth proposition); moreover, they also must be eternal, for their cause is eternal.

4. All the effects which we produce outside ourselves are the more perfect the more they are capable of being united with us to make one and the same nature, for in this way they are nearest

148

to internal effects. For example, if I teach my fellow men to love sensual pleasure, esteem, and greed, then whether I also love these things or not, I am hacked or beaten.[6] This is clear. But [this will] not [be the result] if the only end I strive to attain is to be able to taste union with God, produce true ideas in myself, and make all these things known to my fellow men also.[7] For we can all share equally in this salvation, as happens when this produces in them the same desire that is in me, bringing it about thereby that their will and mine are one and the same, and producing one and the same nature, agreeing always in all things.

[9] From all that has been said, it can now be very easily conceived what human freedom[a] is. I define it as follows: it is a firm existence, which our intellect acquires through immediate union with God, so that it can produce ideas in itself, and outside itself effects agreeing well with its nature, without its effects being subjected, however, to any external causes by which they can be changed or transformed.

At the same time, from what has been said it is also clear which things are in our power and are subjected to no external causes; similarly we have also proven here, and in a different way than before, the eternal and constant duration of the intellect, and finally, which effects we have to value above all others.

[10][8] To bring all this to an end, it remains only for me to say to

---

[a] The bondage of a thing consists in being subjected to external causes; freedom, on the contrary, in being freed of them, not subjected to them. [Bracketed by Gebhardt as probably a reader's summary.]

[6] I render this literally, at the suggestion of an anonymous reader of the ms. of this translation, who thought it desirable to "bring out the Pauline resonance perhaps intended by Spinoza."

[7] A marginal note at this point reads: "The reader should attend well to this and also to what follows from it, for on it depend things of great importance regarding the conduct of man's life."

[8] This concluding section of the work makes it clear that it was written in the first instance, not for publication but for circulation among Spinoza's friends. It also appears that the friends would be at some distance from Spinoza, prompting the hypothesis that at least the concluding portions of the work, and possibly all of it, were written after Spinoza took up residence in Rijnsburg, for the benefit of friends in Amsterdam. This much, I think, would be generally agreed.
There is, however, a marginal note at this point which has led to much theorizing, but no consensus: "The author's request to those for whom, at their request, he has dictated [?*gedicteert*] this treatise, and with it the conclusion of everything." This note was a key item in Gebhardt's theory that our manuscript of the *Short Treatise* had its origin in a dictation. (See Preface, p. 50.) Mignini argues at length (Mignini 1, 432-435) that *dicteren* may not have its literal meaning here, that it may be a literal translation of the Latin *dictare*, which may also mean *compose* or *have written out*, as well as *dictate*. If this conjecture is correct, it would have the advantage of removing an apparent contradiction between the note (which does not appear to be by Spinoza) and the text on which it comments, according to which the work is one Spinoza *wrote*.

149

the friends to whom I write this: do not be surprised at these novelties, for you know very well that it is no obstacle to the truth of a thing that it is not accepted by many.

25 And as you are also aware of the character of the age in which we live, I would ask you urgently to be very careful about communicating these things to others. I do not mean that you should keep them altogether to yourselves, but only that if you ever begin to communicate

30 them to someone, you should have no other aim or motive than the salvation of your fellow man, and make as sure as possible that you will not work in vain.

I/113 Finally, if in reading through this you encounter any difficulty regarding what I maintain as certain, I ask you not to hasten, on that account, immediately to refute it before you have given enough time

5 and reflection to meditating on it. If you do this, I feel sure you will attain the enjoyment of the fruits you promise yourselves from this tree.

THE END

I/114

[Appendix I][1]

AXIOMS

A1: Substance is, by its nature, prior to all its modifications.[2]

5 A2: Things that are different are distinguished either really or modally.

A3: Things that are distinguished really either have different attributes, like thought and extension, or are related to different attributes,

10 like understanding and motion, of which the one belongs to thought, the other to extension.

[1] This appendix is not designated as such in the manuscript and is generally believed to be posterior to the main body of the *Treatise*. As Appuhn remarks, it is not so much an addition to the *Treatise* as the first draft of another work, explaining similar ideas in a different form (cf. also Letter 2). Meijer thought, on grounds of style, that Spinoza might have written this appendix in Dutch. (We have Spinoza's own testimony that he did not write Dutch very fluently, and the style of the appendix is awkward.) On the other hand, others (Gebhardt and Sigwart) have seen in this appendix errors to be explained by mistranslation of the Latin original. (Three of the eleven passages Gebhardt cites and Boehm disputes come from this appendix.)

[2] The ms. has *toevallen*—the usual term for *accidens*—followed by the Latin term *modificationes* in parentheses. There is also a hint that our ms. at this stage may not be the work of a copyist. The ms. has: "Substance is prior to by its nature prior to all its modification." The first "prior to" is then crossed out.

A4: Things that have different attributes, as well as those that belong to different attributes, have nothing in themselves the one from the other.[3]

A5: What has nothing in itself from another thing can also not be the cause of the existence of such another thing.

A6: What is a cause of itself could not possibly have limited itself.

A7: That by which things are distinguished[4] is by its nature prior to such things.

[PROPOSITIONS]

P1: *To no substance which really exists can we relate the same attribute that is related to another substance, or (what is the same) in Nature there cannot be two substances unless they are distinguished really.*[5]

Dem.: If the two substances are two, they are different. And consequently (by A2) are distinguished, either really or modally. Not modally, for then (by A7)[6] the modifications by their nature would be prior to the substance (contrary to A1). Therefore, really. Hence what can be said of the one cannot (by A4) be said of the other. This is what we were trying to prove.

P2: *One substance cannot be the cause of the existence of another substance.*

Dem.: Such a cause can have nothing in itself of such an effect (by P1), for the difference between them is real, and consequently (by A5) it cannot produce it (existence).

P3: *Every attribute, or substance, is by its nature infinite, and supremely perfect in its kind.*

Dem.: No substance is produced by another (P2); consequently, if it exists, it is either an attribute of God or it has been a cause of itself outside God. If the first, then it is necessarily infinite and supremely perfect in its kind, as are all God's other attributes. If the second, it also must be such; for (by A6) it could not have limited itself.

P4: *Existence belongs, by nature, to the essence of every substance, so much so that it is impossible to posit in an infinite intellect the idea of the essence of a substance which does not exist in Nature.*

---

[3] I.e., they have nothing in common with one another.

[4] The manuscript has: "are maintained" which has seemed to some to make A7 an idle repetition of A1. Meijer, adverting to the note at I/119/34-35, proposed reading "distinguished" (*onderscheiden* for *onderhouden*) and this emendation has been accepted by both Gebhardt and Mignini. Wolf suspected A7 of being a reader's comment on A1, inadvertently incorporated in the text by an uncritical copyist. But this was based partly on the (incorrect) belief that A7 is not used in what follows (see I/115/4).

[5] Monnikhoff: "or (what is the same) in nature, no two substances of one and the same nature can be posited." This makes P1 much closer to its analogue in the *Ethics* (E IP5).

[6] This reference is omitted in Van Vloten and Land and in Wolf.

Dem.: The true essence of an object is something which is really distinct from the Idea of that object, and this something (by A3)[7] either exists really, or is contained in another thing which exists really and from which one cannot distinguish this essence really, but only modally; such are all the essences of things we see which, when they did not previously exist, were contained in extension, motion and rest, and which, when they do exist, are distinguished from extension not really, but only modally. And also it involves a self-contradiction to maintain that the essence of a substance is contained in another thing in this way, since in that case it would not be distinguished from it really (contrary to P1); also, it could then be produced by the subject which contains it (contrary to P2); and finally, it could not be infinite through its nature and supremely perfect in its kind (contrary to P3). Therefore, because its essence is not contained in any other thing, it must be a thing that exists through itself.

Cor.: Nature is known through itself, and not through any other thing. It consists of infinite attributes, each of which is infinite and perfect in its kind. Existence belongs to its essence, so that outside it there is no essence or being. Hence it agrees exactly with the essence of God, who alone is magnificent and blessed.

I/117

[Appendix II]

OF THE HUMAN SOUL

[1] Since man is a created, finite thing, etc., it is necessary that what he has of thought, and what we call the soul, is a mode of that attribute we call thought, without any thing other than this mode belonging to his essence; so much so that if this mode perishes, the soul is also destroyed, although the preceding attribute remains immutable.

[2] Similarly, what he has of extension, which we call the body, is nothing but a mode of the other attribute we call extension. If this mode too is destroyed, the human body no longer exists, though the attribute of extension remains immutable.

[3] To understand now what this mode is, which we call soul, how it has its origin from the body, and also how its change depends (only) on the body (which I maintain to be the union of soul and body), we must note:

1. That the most immediate mode of the attribute we call thought

---

[7] The ms. has A3. Gebhardt and Mignini, following Boehmer, emend to A2, though it is not clear to me that this is an improvement.

20 has objectively in itself the formal essence of all things, so that if one posited any formal things whose essence did not exist objectively in the above-named attribute, it would not be infinite or supremely perfect in its kind (contrary to P3).

25 [4] And since Nature or God is one being, of which infinite attributes are said, and which contains in itself all essences of created things, it is necessary that of all this there is produced in thought an infinite Idea, which contains in itself objectively the whole of Nature, as it is in itself.[1]

30 That is why I have also called this Idea (in I, ix) a creature created immediately by God, since it has in itself objectively the formal essence of all things, without omission or addition. And this is necessarily only one, taking into consideration that all the essences of the
I/118 attributes, and the essences of the modes contained in those attributes, are the essence of only one infinite being.[2]

[5] 2. It should also be noted that all the remaining modes, such as
5 Love, Desire, and Joy, have their origin in this first immediate mode, so that if it did not precede them, there could be no Love, Desire, etc.

[6] From this it may clearly be concluded that the Natural love which is in each thing for the preservation of its body[3] can have no
10 other origin than in the Idea, or the objective essence of such a body, which is in the thinking attribute.

[7] Furthermore, since for the existence of an Idea (or objective essence) nothing is required other than the thinking attribute and the object (or formal essence), it is certain, as we have said, that the Idea,
15 or objective essence, is the most immediate[a] mode of the attribute. And consequently there can be, in the thinking attribute, no other mode which would belong to the essence of the soul of each thing, except the Idea, which must be of such a thing as really existing, and
20 which must exist in the thinking attribute. For such an Idea brings with it the remaining modes of Love, Desire, etc.

[a] The mode I call the most immediate mode of the attribute is that which, in order to exist, needs no other mode in the same attribute.
[1] This sentence seems defective in the ms. Gebhardt takes it to mean: ". . . it is necessary that of everything which is produced in thought, there is in reality an infinite idea, which contains in itself objectively the whole of Nature, as it is in itself." But Monnikhoff's reading seems more likely to me and I have followed it, in company with most other editors. For argument see Mignini 1, 435.
[2] In the ms. this paragraph comes at I/119/20, after ". . . of one infinite being." Gebhardt, following Freudenthal, argues that it belongs here. Mignini argues for retaining the order of the ms.
[3] The ms. here adds in parentheses an explanation which many editors, including Gebhardt and Van Vloten and Land, have omitted: "I mean the modification." Mignini restores it to the text.

Now since the Idea proceeds from the existence of the object, then if the object changes or is destroyed, the Idea itself also changes or is destroyed in the same degree; this being so, it is what is united with the object.[4]

[8] Finally, if we should wish to proceed to ascribe to the essence of the soul that by which it can exist, we would not be able to find anything other than that attribute, and the object of which we have just spoken, and neither of these can belong to the essence of the soul. For the object has nothing of thought, and is really distinct from the soul. And as for the attribute, we have already proven that it cannot belong to the above-mentioned essence. From what we have subsequently said, this should be seen even more clearly; for the attribute, as attribute, is not united with the object, since it neither changes nor is destroyed, though the object changes or is destroyed.

[9] Therefore, the essence of the soul consists only in the being of an Idea, or objective essence, in the thinking attribute, arising from the essence of an object which in fact exists in Nature. I say *of an object that really exists*, etc., without further particulars, in order to include here not only the modes of extension, but also the modes of all the infinite attributes, which have a soul just as much as those of extension do.[5]

[10] To understand this definition in more detail, it will help to consider what I have already said in speaking of the attributes. I have said[b] that the attributes are not distinguished according to their existence, for they themselves are the subjects of their essences;[6] that the essence of each of the modes is contained in the attributes just mentioned; and finally, that all the attributes are attributes of One infinite being.

[11] But it should be noted in addition that these modes, when considered as not really existing, are nevertheless equally contained in

[b] For things are distinguished by what is first in their nature, but this essence of things is prior to their existence, therefore. [This note, which was omitted by Sigwart, Vloten-Land, and Wolf, and retrieved by Meijer, is printed without brackets by Gebhardt. Appuhn takes its sense to be that the existence of attributes, unlike that of modes, follows necessarily from their essence.]

[4] Monnikhoff has: "as being thus united with its object." Some (e.g., Sigwart, Appuhn) have thought that originally the text may have read: "and in this its union with the object consists."

[5] This suggests that as early as the *Short Treatise* Spinoza conceived of thought as coextensive with all the other attributes, and hence more 'extensive' than any one taken singly—i.e., that what some have seen as a damaging admission made in response to the criticism of Tschirnhaus was an acknowledged part of the theory all along. Cf. Joachim 1, 134f. But see below I/119/24n.

[6] As Appuhn suggests, this probably means that because the attributes exist through themselves, in them essence and existence are identical.

their attributes. And because there is no inequality at all in the attributes,[7] nor in the essences of the modes, there can be no particularity in the Idea, since it is not in Nature. But whenever any of these modes put on their particular existence, and by that are in some way distinguished from their attributes (because their particular existence, which they have in the attribute, is then the subject of their essence), then a particularity presents itself in the essences of the modes, and consequently in their objective essences, which are necessarily contained in the Idea.

[12] This is why we have used these words in the definition, that *the soul is an Idea arising from an object which exists in Nature*. And with this we consider that we have sufficiently explained what kind of thing the soul is in general, understanding by this expression not only the Ideas that arise from corporeal modes, but also those that arise from the existence of each mode of the remaining attributes.

[13] But since we do not have, of the remaining attributes, such a knowledge as we have of extension, let us see whether, having regard to the modes of extension, we can discover a more particular definition, which is more suited to express the essence of our soul. For this is our real intention.

[14] Here, then, we shall suppose as a thing proven, that there is no other mode in extension than motion and rest, and that each particular corporeal thing is nothing but a certain proportion of motion and rest, so much so that if there were nothing in extension except motion alone, or nothing except rest alone, there could not be, or be indicated, in the whole of extension, any particular thing. The human body, then, is nothing but a certain proportion of motion and rest.

[15] So this existing proportion's objective essence in the thinking attribute is the soul of the body. Hence when one of these modes (motion or rest) changes, either by increasing or by decreasing, the Idea also changes correspondingly. For example, if the rest happens to increase, and the motion to decrease, the pain or sadness we call *cold* is thereby produced. On the other hand, if this [increase] occurs in the motion, then the pain we call *heat* is thereby produced.

[16] And so when the degrees of motion and rest are not equal in all parts of our body, but some have more motion and rest than others, there arises a difference of feeling (e.g., from this comes the different kind of pain we feel when we are struck with a little stick in the eyes or on the hands).

---

[7] Both Appuhn and the Pléiade editors have: "there is no inequality between the attributes." Gueroult (1, 2: 99n) rejects this, partly on linguistic grounds, partly because he takes the attributes to be incommensurable.

I/121   When the external causes which bring changes about differ in themselves, and do not all have the same effects, there arises a difference
of feeling in one and the same part (e.g., the difference of feeling from
a blow with a piece of wood or iron on the same hand).

5   And again, if the change which happens in a part is a cause of its
returning to its original proportion, from this there arises the joy we
call peace, pleasurable activity, and cheerfulness.

[17] Finally, because we have now explained what feeling is, we can
10   easily see how from this there arises a reflexive Idea, or knowledge of
oneself, experience, and reasoning.

And from all of this (as also because our soul is united with God,
and is a part of the infinite Idea arising immediately from God) we
can see clearly the origin of clear knowledge, and the immortality of
15   the soul. But for the present what we have said will be enough.

Letters

AUGUST 1661–AUGUST 1663

EDITORIAL PREFACE

SPINOZA'S correspondence, as the editors of his *Opera posthuma* recognized, makes a very important contribution to our understanding of his work. Just how important is well illustrated in the letters in this first section. We find transitional sketches of the material later contained in Part I of the *Ethics*, showing considerable development from the axiomatic appendix to the *Short Treatise* (Letters 2-4) and helping us to understand how (at one stage, at least) Spinoza understood such key definitions as those of substance and attribute (Letters 2, 4, and 9), discussions of the nature of definition (Letters 3, 4, and 8-10), and an important letter on the problem of infinity (Letter 12).[1] These letters also remind us that in the seventeenth-century correspondence was not always a private communication between the sender and the receiver. Important letters (like 6, 9, and 12) often had considerable circulation and should be regarded as the forerunners of today's journal articles.

But beyond what they add to our understanding of works intended for formal publication, the letters also shed light on sides of Spinoza we would know little or nothing about from these other works. We find him communicating (via Oldenburg) with Boyle about the latter's work in chemistry (Letters 6, 11, 13, and 16); we learn about an unrealized plan to publish the *Short Treatise*, in conjunction, probably, with the *Treatise on the Emendation of the Intellect* (Letter 6), and why he chose instead to publish his exposition of Descartes first (Letter 13); and we get considerable insight into his relations with his friends (Letters 8, 9, 12a, 13, and 15). The picture that emerges is not that of the recluse often portrayed, but of a man who maintained a lively interest in current intellectual affairs and close connections, by letters and frequent visits, with a small but devoted band of friends in Amsterdam. (For most of this period Spinoza lived in Rijnsburg, a small village near the important university center of Leiden; in late April 1663 he moved to Voorburg, a suburb of The Hague.)

The correspondence presented in this section is effectively with four men:

Henry Oldenburg (c. 1618-1677) was born in Bremen, where he stud-

---

[1] The subject of a long appendix in Gueroult 1, 1:500-528. It should be noted that Gueroult preferred the revised version published in English translation in Grene: "The mathematical formulas I used in appendix 9 do not satisfy me, for they are faulty. I had wished to avoid the formulas of the differential calculus because it had not been invented when Spinoza wrote his 12th Letter. But his thought can only be rendered by the formulas of this calculus. You will find them in the English translation. . . ." (personal correspondence, 21 December 1970).

ied theology, receiving his master's degree in 1639, with a thesis on the relations between Church and state. Most of his adult life was spent in England, where he was occupied partly in diplomatic work, partly in teaching (one of his pupils being a nephew of Boyle), but mainly with the secretaryship of the Royal Society, a position he held from 1662 until his death.

His meeting with Spinoza on a trip to the Continent in 1661 is thought to have been suggested by a relative, Johannes Koch (Coccejus), a professor of theology at the University of Leiden. We have far more letters between Spinoza and Oldenburg than we do between him and any other correspondent, but there was a long break in their correspondence between 1665 and 1675, and the tone of Oldenburg's letters changes markedly after 1675. In the interim he had spent two months imprisoned in the Tower of London for espionage and had read Spinoza's *Theological-Political Treatise*, neither very pleasant experiences, it seems.

At this writing nine volumes of his extensive correspondence have been published (see Oldenburg in the bibliography). These cover the period from 1662-1673, and the first volume contains a substantial biographical sketch.

Robert Boyle (1627-1691), the seventh son of the Earl of Cork, and thus a member of a large, wealthy, and influential family, was the leading British scientist of the period between Bacon and Newton. An 'amateur' scientist in the best sense of that term, he was, from about 1654, a member of the group of Baconians centered in Oxford who were subsequently to be incorporated as the Royal Society.

His first important scientific publication, *New Experiments Physico-Mechanial, Touching the Spring of the Air and its Effects* (Boyle 1), stemmed from his interest in von Guericke's recently discovered air pump. A model of the experimental method, and soon to lead Boyle to the law relating the pressure and volume of gases which bears his name, this work is most helpfully discussed in Conant. It is on this work that his reputation as a scientist is most securely based.

More characteristic, however, is the work Oldenburg sent to Spinoza, *Certain Physiological Essays* (Boyle 2), with its attempt to illustrate the principles of the mechanical philosophy by chemical experiments. On this general program, and for an excellent overview of Boyle's life and work, see Hall 1. A more detailed treatment, concentrating on Boyle's work in chemistry, and his role in paving the way for the eighteenth-century revolution in that field, is Hall 2. For a specific discussion of the interchange between Boyle and Spinoza, see Hall 3.

In addition to his scientific interests, Boyle was much concerned

160

with the relation between science and religion (he held that science was not only compatible with Christianity but encouraged an appreciation of God's works) and with the propagation of (preferably Protestant) Christianity. The Boyle lectures established in his will were to defend the truth of that religion against infidels. As Wolf observes, at least two series of Boyle lectures were directed against Spinoza, Samuel Clarke's in 1704 and B. Guerdon's in 1721-1722.

Simon de Vries (c. 1633-1667) was a well-to-do Amsterdam merchant, who belonged, as did many of Spinoza's closest friends, to the Collegiants, a sect of Quaker-like dissenters, who were persecuted by the dominant Calvinist clergy. His regard for Spinoza is indicated by two stories, each told by both of Spinoza's early biographers, Colerus and Lucas.

On one occasion de Vries wanted to give Spinoza 2,000 florins to enable him to live more comfortably. Spinoza declined on the ground that he needed no money and that if he received so large a sum, it would divert him from his studies.

Later, approaching death and having neither wife nor children, de Vries wanted to make Spinoza his sole heir. Spinoza again declined, this time on the ground that the money ought, in justice, to go to de Vries' brother. After failing to get Spinoza to accept an annuity of 500 florins from the estate, he finally prevailed on him to accept 300 (or 250, on some accounts). The classic work on such members of the Spinoza circle is Meinsma.

Lodewijk Meyer (1629-1681) was born in Amsterdam and from 1654 studied philosophy and medicine at the University of Leiden, where he became an ardent Cartesian. After receiving doctorates in both subjects in 1660, he practiced medicine in Amsterdam and played an important part in Dutch letters. In 1654 he had assisted with the second edition of Hofman's *Nederlandsche woordenschat*, a dictionary of foreign terms used in Dutch. From the fifth edition of this much used work (1669), it appeared under his name, and in the judgment of Thijssen-Schoute, "codified a scientific language of great purity." A writer of poetry and plays and an admirer of French classicism, from 1665 to 1669 he was director of the Amsterdam theater. In 1669, in company with others, he formed an artistic society, *Nil Volentibus Arduum* (Nothing is difficult for those who have the will).

Meyer's association with Spinoza began, perhaps, as early as the days when Spinoza assisted van den Enden in the teaching of Latin. Meyer may have helped not only with the publication of *Descartes' Principles* (see Letters 12a, 13, and 15, and his preface to that work), but also with the publication of the *Opera posthuma*. His *Philosophia S.*

Scripturae interpres, first published anonymously in 1666, and in 1674 published bound with Spinoza's *Theological-Political Treatise*, argued a thesis Spinoza rejected in his own work: that the true philosophy is an infallible norm for the interpretation of Holy Scripture. According to some reports he was present at Spinoza's death.

Apart from the work of Meinsma, see Thijssen-Schoute 1 and 2.

Spinoza's correspondence presents special problems for the editor. Of the eighty-eight letters contained in the most recent edition of his correspondence (AHW), we possess autographs of twenty, thirteen of them from Spinoza and seven to Spinoza. Some of these give us an additional source for letters already known through the OP and the NS. This is helpful in that it gives us an insight into the work done by the editors on Spinoza's manuscript, but it also raises difficult problems about the relative authority of the various versions. Gebhardt regarded Spinoza as being, in effect, the editor of his own correspondence, as having himself reworked and prepared for publication the Latin versions of letters written originally in Latin, and as having translated into Latin some of the letters written originally in Dutch (including some letters written *to* him in Dutch). While there is no doubt that some of the variations between the autographs and the published letters are Spinoza's work (e.g., in Letter 6), it seems unlikely that Spinoza did anywhere near as much work on the published versions as Gebhardt assumed. In some cases—in the opinion of Akkerman, Hubbeling and Westerbrink, whose judgment on this point I accept—Gebhardt's view is demonstrably incorrect.

What, then, did Spinoza's first editors contribute?[2] They made the letters ready for the press by (i) introducing a heading giving the number of the letter and the names and titles of the author and the recipient (though often shortening the name to initials, sometimes deleting it altogether, and always indicating Spinoza by his initials); (ii) formalizing the salutation; (iii) introducing punctuation and capital letters (Spinoza's punctuation is unorthodox and in his autographs he rarely uses capitals even for the beginning of a sentence); (iv) correcting the spelling and polishing the style;[3] (v) omitting details of biographical rather than philosophical interest; and (vi) suppressing the names of

---

[2] In what follows I summarize the conclusions of Akkerman, in AHW, 11-13.

[3] Spinoza's spelling often betrays the fact that he seems to have been more at home in Spanish than in Latin or Dutch (on this see IV/95/12 and the note thereto). On his knowledge of Latin, see Leopold. Spinoza's Latin is not always strictly correct, but as Leopold points out, it has a terse elegance and compares favorably, both stylistically and grammatically, with much of the Latin written by his contemporaries. In the judgment of Akkerman, Spinoza wrote a Dutch which was awkward, when measured by strict standards regarding style and choice of words, but not without a certain charm.

third parties. Since Spinoza's Dutch was less accurate than his Latin, the Dutch letters required more substantial reworking than the Latin ones, but the NS's Dutch versions of letters written originally in Dutch were not the result of translating back into Dutch the Latin translation.

All the letters presented in this section were written originally in Latin. For Letters 1-5, 7, 10, 11, 13, 14, and 16, our sources are the OP and the NS, and in these cases I translate the text of the OP, noting occasional variations in the NS.

Letters 12a (a very recent discovery) and 15 are known only through autographs.

For Letters 6, 8, and 9 we have three sources: the OP, the NS and an autograph. For Letter 12 our third source is a copy made by Leibniz. Where there is a third source for one of Spinoza's letters, Gebhardt generally prints it beneath the OP text, which results in fewer lines of text per page. For Letter 8, Gebhardt gives only the autograph. Following AHW I translate the OP text of Letters 6 and 12 and the autograph text of Letters 8 and 9. Interesting variations from the autograph of 6 and from Leibniz's copy of 12 are introduced by 'A' and 'LC.'

V/5

LETTER 1

HENRY OLDENBURG TO THE ESTEEMED B.D.S.

Esteemed Sir, Dear Friend,

When I visited you recently in your retreat at Rijnsburg, I found it so difficult to tear myself away from your side, that now that I am back in England I hasten to reunite myself with you, so far as is possible, even if it is only by correspondence. Knowledge of things of enduring importance, combined with kindness and graciousness (all of which Nature and your own Diligence have most abundantly enriched you with), have in them such charms that they must win for themselves the love of any honorable man, educated as becomes a free man. Come, then, most Excellent Sir, let us bind ourselves to one another in unfeigned friendship, and let us cultivate that friendship assiduously, with every kind of good will and service. What I, in my weakness, can provide, you may consider yours. As for the gifts of mind which you possess, let me claim a share in them, since that can be done without loss to you.

In Rijnsburg we talked about God, about infinite Extension and Thought, about the difference and agreement of these attributes, about the way the human soul is united with the body, and about the Prin-

5

20

25

IV/6

163

ciples of the Cartesian Philosophy and of the Baconian. But since we
spoke then as if through a lattice[1] and only in passing about matters
of such great importance, and in the meantime those things all torment
me, I now undertake, by right of the friendship we have entered into,
to engage you in discussion, and cordially ask you to explain to me
somewhat more fully your views concerning the subjects I have mentioned.

In particular I should like to be instructed on these two points: first,
in what do you place the true distinction between Extension and
Thought; second, what defects do you find in the Philosophy of Descartes and [in that] of Bacon, and how do you judge that they can be
removed and replaced by sounder views. The more frankly you write
to me on these and similar matters, the more closely you will bind me
to you, and oblige me very strongly to return like services, if only I
can.

Here there is now in the press a work, *Certain Physiological Essays*,
written by an English Noble of exceptional learning.[2] It treats of the
nature of air and its Elasticity, proved by forty-three experiments; of
Fluidity, Solidity and the like. As soon as it has been printed, I shall
see that it is delivered to you by a Friend, who may be crossing the
sea.

Meanwhile, farewell, and remember your friend, who is

Yours in all love and devotion,

London 16/26 August 1661 Henry Oldenburg

IV/7

LETTER 2

B.D.S. TO THE VERY NOBLE AND LEARNED

H. OLDENBURG

Reply to the preceding

Esteemed Sir,

How pleasing your friendship is to me, you yourself will be able to
judge if only you can prevail on your modesty to allow you to consider

---

[1] *Quasi per transennam*. AHW explain that a *transenna* was a lattice used by merchants
to allow prospective customers to look at their merchandise without being able to examine it too closely. From this and other indications (cf. IV/6/12, IV/8/13, IV/11/27-
12/1), it appears that Spinoza was somewhat guarded in his initial conversation with
Oldenburg.

[2] Oldenburg refers here to Robert Boyle, who did indeed publish in 1661 a work
titled *Certain Physiological Essays*. These were essays in physics or chemistry, rather than
anything we would now call physiology. But Oldenburg misdescribes the contents of
the work actually published under that title. Though it treated of fluidity and solidity,

the excellences in which you abound. When I consider them, I seem
to myself rather presumptuous, to dare to enter into friendship with
you (particularly when I think that friends must share all things,[3] especially spiritual things). Nevertheless, this step must be ascribed to
your courtesy and good will, rather than to me. The former is so great
that you have been willing to belittle yourself, the latter so abundant
that you have been willing to enrich me, that I might not fear to enter
into the close friendship you continue to offer me and deign to ask of
me in return. I shall take great care to cultivate it zealously.

As for any mental endowments I may possess, I would gladly let
you claim them for yourself, even if I knew that it would be greatly
to my detriment. But lest I seem in this way to wish to deny you
what you ask of me, by the right of friendship, I shall try to explain
what I think concerning the matters we discussed, though I do not
think this will be a means of binding you more closely to me, unless
your generosity intervenes.

I shall begin, then, by speaking briefly about

[D1] God, whom I define as a Being consisting of infinite attributes, each of which is infinite, *or* supremely perfect in its kind.

Here it should be noted that

[D2] By attribute I understand whatever is conceived through
itself and in itself, so that its concept does not involve the concept
of another thing.[4]

For example, Extension is conceived through itself and in itself, but
motion is not. For it is conceived in another and its concept involves
Extension.

That [D1] is a true definition of God is clear from the fact that by
God we understand a Being supremely perfect and absolutely infinite.
Moreover, it is easy to demonstrate from this definition[5] that such a

---

it did not describe Boyle's experiments on the elasticity of air. The latter had been
published in 1660. Oldenburg appears to be referring to a projected Latin work which
would have combined translations of the pneumatic essays with translations of the work
on fluidity and solidity (or 'firmness,' to use Boyle's term). See p. 7 of the Preface to
the Essays on Nitre (Saltpetre) in Boyle 2.

[3] AHW note that this proverb is traceable to Pythagoras, and already appears as a
familiar saying in Terence's *Adelphi*, 803.

[4] The numbers for definitions, propositions and axioms here and in footnote 5 are
added to the text for convenience. It should be noted that the formula use here to define
attribute will be used in Letter 4 to define substance. See IV/13/32-34 and compare IV/
46/2-6.

[5] The phrase "this definition" might refer to D1 or to what appears to be an alternative
definition in ll. 2-3, that God is a being supremely perfect and absolutely infinite. If,

being exists. Since this is not the place for it, I·shall omit the demonstration. But what I must show here, to answer satisfactorily your first question [concerning the true distinction between extension and thought] are the following:

[P1] That two substances cannot exist in nature unless they differ in their whole essence;

[P2] That a substance cannot be produced, but that it is of its essence to exist;

[P3] That every substance must be infinite, *or* supremely perfect in its kind.

Once I have demonstrated these things, then (provided you attend to the definition of God), you will easily be able to see what I am aiming at, so it is not necessary to speak more openly about these matters. But I can think of no better way of demonstrating these things clearly and briefly than to prove them in the Geometric manner and subject them to your understanding. So I send them separately with this letter and await your judgment regarding them.[6]

---

as Hubbeling thinks (55), Spinoza does, at this stage, regard the latter as a satisfactory alternative, he will later change his mind. See Letter 60, IV/271/2-7.

[6] At this point the OP has a note (presumably by the editors) referring the reader to the beginning of the *Ethics* through EIP4. But the lost geometric enclosure sent to Oldenburg in fact represents a transitional stage between the *Short Treatise* and the *Ethics*. From Letter 4 we can reconstruct at least some of its assumptions. (Cf. Wolf 3, 371-373, and Hubbeling.) There would have been a further definition:

[D3] By modification, *or* accident, I understand what is in another and is conceived through that in which it is. (Cf. IV/13/34)

And four axioms:

[A1] Substance is by nature prior to its accidents. (Cf. IV/14/1)
[A2] Except for substances and accidents there is nothing real, *or* outside the intellect. (Cf. IV/14/2)
[A3] Things which have different attributes have nothing in common with one another. (Cf. IV/14/6)
[A4] If two things have nothing in common with one another, one cannot be the cause of the other. (Cf. IV/14/9)

In most respects this is much closer to the first appendix to the *Short Treatise* than to the *Ethics*. The propositions of the enclosure correspond to the propositions of the *Short Treatise* and axioms 1, 3, and 4 correspond to axioms in the *Short Treatise*. There is, however, evidence of development. The enclosure gives considerable prominence to definitions, which do not occur in the *Short Treatise*, and though a new axiom has been added, the overall number of axioms has been reduced.

The *Ethics* shows still further development. Presumably in response to Oldenburg's objections (IV/10-11), the axioms of the enclosure become propositions in the *Ethics* (A1, 3, and, 4 = E IP1, 2, and 3; A2 is not stated as a proposition in the *Ethics*, but occurs in E IP4D and follows readily from E ID3, D5, and A1). And substance and attribute are defined by different formulas. Hubbeling (65-67) attempts a reconstruction of the demonstrations of the propositions, in which he suggests that Spinoza's proof of P1

You ask next what errors I find in the Philosophy of Descartes and of Bacon. Though it is not my custom to uncover the errors of others, I do also want to comply with your wishes. The first and greatest error is that they have wandered so far from knowledge of the first cause and origin of all things. Second, they did not know the true nature of the human Mind. Third, they never grasped the true cause of error. Only those lacking any education or desire for knowledge will fail to see how necessary the true knowledge of these three things is. That they have wandered from knowledge of the first cause and of the human Mind may easily be inferred from the truth of the three propositions mentioned above, so I restrict myself to showing the third error.

I shall say little about Bacon, who speaks quite confusedly about this, and proves hardly anything, but only makes assertions. For he supposes:

(1) That in addition to the deceptiveness of the senses, the human intellect is deceived simply by its own nature, and feigns everything from the analogy of its own nature, not from the analogy of the universe, so that in relation to the rays of things it is like an uneven mirror, which mixes its own nature with the nature of things, etc.[7]

(2) That the human intellect, of its own nature, is inclined to abstractions, and feigns to be constant things which are fleeting, etc.[8]

(3) That the human intellect is unquiet, and can neither take a stand nor rest.[9]

The other causes he assigns can all easily be reduced to the one Descartes gives: the human will is free and wider than the intellect, *or*, as Bacon himself says, more confusedly (Aphorism 49), the intellect is not a dry light, but is fueled by the will. (It should be noted here that Bacon often takes the intellect for the Mind, in which respect he differs from Descartes.)

---

assumed two further principles: that every definition, or clear and distinct idea, is true (cf. IV/13/12-13) and Leibniz's principle of the identity of indiscernibles.

[7] The reference may be to Bacon's *Novum Organum* I, 41, though in some respects Spinoza's paraphrase is closer to a passage in "The Plan of the Work" (Bacon, I, 138-139). On Bacon's use of the terms *analogia* and *radius* see Ellis' notes at pp. 130, 138.

[8] Gebhardt, following a marginal note in the NS, emends the OP's *fluxa* to *fluida*, but as Wolf points out, *fluxa* is Bacon's term in the passage Spinoza is quoting, *Novum Organum* I, 51.

[9] *Novum Organum* I, 48.

10   Disregarding the other causes, as being of no importance, I shall show that this cause is a false one, which they themselves would easily have seen, if only they had attended to the fact that the will differs from this or that volition in the same way as whiteness differs from this or that white thing, or humanity differs from this or that man.

15   So it is as impossible to conceive that the will is the cause of this or that volition as to conceive that humanity is the cause of Peter and Paul. Since the will, then, is only a being of reason and ought not in any way to be called a cause of this or that volition, since particular volitions cannot be called free (because they require a cause in order to exist) but must be as their causes have determined them to be, and

20   finally since, according to Descartes, the errors themselves are particular volitions, it follows necessarily that the errors (i.e., particular volitions) are not free, but determined by external causes, and not at all by the will. This is what I promised to demonstrate, etc.
[Rijnsburg, September 1661]

IV/10   **LETTER 3**

HENRY OLDENBURG TO THE ESTEEMED B.D.S.

Excellent Sir, and Dearest Friend,
    I have received your very learned letter, and read it through with great pleasure. I approve very much of your geometric style of proof, but at the same time I blame my own obtuseness that I do not follow so easily the things you teach so exactly. Please, then, let me give you

10   evidence of my slowness by putting the following Problems to you, and seeking their solutions.
    First, do you understand clearly and without doubt that, merely from the definition you give of God, it is demonstrated that such a Being exists? When I reflect that definitions contain only our Mind's

15   concepts, that our Mind conceives many things which do not exist, and that it is most fruitful in multiplying and increasing things once they have been conceived, I do not yet see how I can infer God's existence from the concept I have of him. To be sure, from the mental

20   collection of all the perfections I find in men, animals, vegetables, minerals, etc., I can form a conception of some one substance which really possesses all those virtues; indeed my Mind is capable of multiplying and increasing them to infinity, so that it can conjure up in itself a most perfect and excellent Being. But from this one cannot at

25   all infer the existence of such a Being.
    Second, are you certain that Body is not limited by Thought nor Thought by Body? For the controversy about what Thought is, whether

it is a corporeal motion or some spiritual act, entirely different from the corporeal, is still unresolved.

Third, do you regard the axioms you communicated to me as indemonstrable Principles, known by the light of Nature and requiring no proof? Perhaps the first is of that kind, but I do not see how the other three can be so regarded. The second supposes that nothing exists in Nature except Substances and Accidents, but many maintain that time and place are neither. I am so far from conceiving clearly your third axiom—*Things which have different attributes have nothing in common with one another*—that the whole universe of Things seems rather to prove its contrary. For all Things known to us both differ from one another in some respects and agree in others. Finally, the fourth axiom—*If things have nothing in common with one another, one cannot be the cause of the other*—is not so evident to my dull intellect that it does not need more light shed on it. Surely God has nothing formally in common with created things, yet nearly all of us regard him as their cause.

Since I do not find these Axioms beyond any shadow of a doubt, you will easily guess that the Propositions you have built on them cannot but totter. And the more I consider them, the more I am overwhelmed by doubts concerning them. For regarding the first, I consider that two men are two Substances, and have the same attribute, since each has the capacity to reason; from that I conclude that there are two Substances of the same attribute. Regarding the second, *That a Substance cannot be produced, not even by another Substance*, I consider that we can hardly grasp how this could be true, since nothing can be its own cause. This Proposition sets up every Substance as its own cause, and makes them all independent of one another, makes them so many Gods. In this way it denies the first cause of all Things.

I readily confess that I cannot grasp this unless you do me the favor of revealing to me somewhat more straightforwardly and fully your Opinion concerning this lofty matter and teaching me what is the origin and production of Substances, the dependence of things on one another, and their subordination to one another. I entreat you, by the friendship we have entered into, to deal openly and confidently with me in this matter, and I ask you most earnestly to be fully persuaded that whatever things you are pleased to share with me will be safe, and that I will take care that none of them become known to your harm or disadvantage.

In our Philosophical Group[10] we devote ourselves as energetically as we can to making experiments and observations, and are much

---

[10] The Philosophical Group referred to here was an informal gathering of scientists of Baconian inclinations, who began to meet in London and Oxford in about 1645. It

occupied with putting together a History of the Mechanical Arts. For
we regard it as settled that the forms and qualities of things can best
be explained on Mechanical Principles, that all Nature's effects are
produced by motion, shape, and texture, and their various combina-
tions, and that there is no need for us to seek a refuge for our ignorance in inexplicable forms and occult qualities.

I shall pass along to you the book I promised as soon as your Dutch
Ambassadors here send a messenger to The Hague (as they often do),
or as soon as some other Friend to whom I can safely entrust it goes
that way.

Please excuse my prolixity and frankness; in particular, I ask you to
take in good part, as is the custom between friends, the objections I
have freely put to you, without any glossing over or courtly refine-
ments. Believe that I am, without pretense or cunning,

Your most devoted,

London, 27 September 1661   Henry Oldenburg

LETTER 4

B.D.S. TO THE MOST NOBLE AND LEARNED
HENRY OLDENBURG

Reply to the preceding

Esteemed Sir,

While I was preparing to go to Amsterdam, to spend a week or two
there, I received your very welcome letter and saw your objections to
the three Propositions I sent you. I shall try to satisfy you only on
those points, omitting the rest for lack of time.

To the first, then, I say that it is not from the definition of any
thing whatever that the existence of the thing defined follows; it follows only (as I demonstrated in the Scholium I attached to the three
Propositions) from the definition, *or* idea, of some attribute, i.e. (as I
explained clearly in relation to the definition of God), of a thing which
is conceived through itself and in itself. In the Scholium just mentioned, I have also, unless I am mistaken, stated clearly enough the
reason for this difference—especially for a Philosopher, who is supposed to know the difference between a fiction and a clear and distinct
concept, and the truth of the Axiom that every definition, *or* clear and
distinct idea, is true. Once these things are noted, I do not see what
more is lacking for the solution to the first problem.

---

was soon to be incorporated under a royal charter whereupon it became the Royal
Society (see Letter 7, IV/37/23).

So I proceed to the solution of the second, where you seem to concede that if Thought does not pertain to the nature of Extension, then Extension will not be limited by Thought, since you raise a doubt only concerning the example. But please note: if someone says that Extension is limited not by Extension, but by Thought, is that not the same as saying that Extension is infinite not absolutely, but only so far as it is Extension? I.e., he does grant me that Extension is not infinite absolutely, but only insofar as it is Extension, i.e., in its own kind.[11]

But, you say, perhaps thought is a corporeal act. So be it (though I do not grant this). Still, you will not deny that extension, insofar as it is extension, is not thought, which is enough to explain my definition and demonstrate my third proposition.

Your third objection against the things I proposed is that the Axioms ought not to be counted as common Notions.[12] I have no quarrel with that. But you also doubt their truth; indeed you seem to want to show that their contrary is more likely. So please attend to the definitions I gave of Substance and of Accident, from which all these [axioms] are derived. For by Substance I understand what is conceived through itself and in itself,[13] i.e., that whose concept does not involve the concept of another thing; but by modification, *or* Accident, what is in another and is conceived through what it is in. From this it is clear that:

[A1] Substance is by nature prior to its Accidents, for without it, they can neither be nor be conceived.

[A2] Except for Substances and Accidents, nothing exists in reality, *or* outside the intellect,

for whatever there is, is conceived either through itself or through another, and its concept either does or does not involve the concept of another thing,

[A3] Things which have different attributes have nothing in common with one another,

for I have explained that an attribute is that whose concept does not involve the concept of another thing.

---

[11] AHW regard the Latin text of this sentence, which is lacking in the NS, as doubtful.

[12] Oldenburg did not use the term *notio communis*, but had asked whether the axioms were indemonstrable principles, known by the natural light and requiring no proof. Spinoza's introduction of the term in his reply gives us a gloss on his own usage. See also the Glossary-Index on *axiom*.

[13] NS: which is through itself and is conceived in itself.

[A4] If two things have nothing in common with one another,
10   one cannot be the cause of the other,

for since there would be nothing in the effect which it had in common with the cause, whatever the effect had, it would have from nothing.

As for your contention that God has nothing formally in common with created things, etc., I have maintained the complete opposite of this in my definition. For I have said that God is a Being consisting of infinite attributes, of which each is infinite, *or* supremely perfect in its kind.

As for your objection to the first Proposition, I ask you, my friend, to consider that men are not created, but only generated, and that their bodies already existed before, though formed differently. It may, indeed, be inferred, as I cheerfully acknowledge, that if one part of matter were annihilated, the whole of Extension would also vanish at the same time.

Moreover, the second Proposition does not make many Gods, but only one, consisting of infinite attributes, etc.

[Rijnsburg, October 1661]

LETTER 5

HENRY OLDENBURG TO THE ESTEEMED B.D.S.

Dearest Friend,

Here is the little book I promised you. Do let me know your judgment of it, particularly regarding the Experiments he has included on Niter, and on Fluidity and Solidity.

Thank you very much for your learned second letter, which I received yesterday. I am very sorry, however, that your trip to Amsterdam prevented you from answering all my doubts. I beg you to send me what you then omitted as soon as your leisure permits. Your last letter illuminated much for me, but not so much as to dispel all the darkness, a result which I believe will happily come to pass when you instruct me clearly and distinctly regarding the true and first origin of things. For so long as it is not clear to me by what cause and how things have begun to be, and by what connection they depend on the first cause (if there is any first cause), everything I hear and read seems to be thrown into confusion. So, Most Learned Sir, I ask you eagerly to hold out a torch for me in this, and not to doubt my loyalty and gratitude.

Your most devoted,
Henry Oldenburg

London, 11/21 October 1661

LETTER 6

B.D.S. TO THE MOST NOBLE AND LEARNED

HENRY OLDENBURG

Reply to the Preceding, containing Comments on the Most Noble
Robert Boyle's book on Niter, Fluidity and Solidity

Esteemed sir,

I have received the very able Mr. Boyle's book,[14] and read through
it, as much as time allowed. Thank you very much for this gift. I see
that I was not wrong to conjecture, when you first promised me this
book, that you would trouble yourself so only about matters of great
importance. Meanwhile, Most Learned Sir, you want me to send you
my judgment of what he has written, which I shall do, as far as my
modest capacities allow, by noting certain things which seem to me
obscure, or inadequately demonstrated. But because of my other occupations I have not yet been able to read through everything, much
less examine it. Here, then, is what I [A: so far] find noteworthy
regarding Niter, etc.

On Niter

First, he infers from his experiment concerning the reconstitution
of Niter that Niter is something heterogeneous, consisting of fixed and
volatile parts, whose nature (so far as the Phenomena are concerned,
at least) is nonetheless very different from the nature of the parts of
which it is composed, though it arises solely from the mixture of these
parts.[15] But I would say that for this conclusion to be regarded as

---

[14] This would not have been the English edition of *Certain Physiological Essays* (Boyle
2) (since Spinoza could not read English, see Letter 26), but the Latin translation of
those essays (Boyle 3) also published in 1661 (not, *pace* Wolf, 1665).

[15] In his experiment on the 'redintegration' or reconstitution of niter Boyle melted
niter in a crucible, added a live coal which kindled the niter, and continued adding
coals until the kindling stopped. The mixture was then heated further until all 'the
volatile part' escaped. The remaining 'fixed niter' was then divided into two parts. Boyle
dissolved one part in water, then added drops of 'spirit of niter.' This was continued
until the effervescence stopped. The other part was treated similarly, except that the
fixed niter was not first dissolved in water. Each solution was then set to evaporate near
an open window. The first solution crystallized in a few hours, yielding niter. The
second solution crystallized very slowly, but after water was added and the solution
was evaporated, niter crystals were also produced.

Boyle had two main interests in performing this experiment. First, according to the
Scholastic theory of substantial forms, the properties of a natural substance like niter
were supposed to be accounted for by its possession of a 'form,' which would be destroyed if the substance underwent substantial change. The redintegration of niter was
intended to show that such substances could be broken up into more elementary constituents and then made whole again by reuniting the constituents. So the properties of

173

IV/17   valid, a further experiment seems to be required, which would show that Spirit of Niter is not really Niter and cannot be solidified or crystallized without the aid of the alkaline salt.[16] Or at least it was necessary to ask whether the quantity of the fixed salt that remains in the crucible is found to be always the same when the quantity of Niter

5   is the same and to vary in proportion to the quantity of the Niter.

    As for what the Distinguished Author says he observed with the aid of the scale (§ 9),[17] and the fact that the Phenomena of the spirit of Niter are so different from those of the Niter (and indeed, in some cases contrary to them), in my opinion at least, these do nothing to confirm his conclusion.

10   To make this clear, I shall set out briefly what occurs to me as the simplest explanation of this [A, NS: phenomenon] of the reconstitution of Niter, and at the same time add two or three quite easy experiments which to some extent confirm this explanation. To explain this Phenomenon as simply as possible, then, I shall posit no other

15   difference between the spirit of Niter and the Niter itself except what is manifest enough: the particles of the Niter are at rest, whereas those of the spirit of Niter, having been considerably stirred up, keep one another in motion.

    I shall suppose that the fixed salt does nothing to constitute the essence of Niter, but shall consider it to be the impurities of Niter

IV/18   (from which I find that not even the spirit of Niter is [A: completely] free: though [A: much] reduced in size, the impurities float in it abundantly enough).

---

the whole were to be explained, not by its possession of a form, but by the composition of its parts.

    Second, Boyle wanted to show that the secondary qualities of things (taste, smell, temperature, etc.) were caused by primary qualities (size, shape, arrangement, motion) of their constituents. So, for example, the fact that the constituents of niter differed markedly in taste and smell from one another and from the compound was to show that these qualities of the various substances depended on the size, shape, arrangement and motion of their parts. Spinoza has no quarrel with these general aims (cf. IV/25/5, IV/64/27).

    Boyle's 'niter' is generally identified with potassium nitrate, his 'fixed niter' with potassium carbonate, and his 'spirit of niter' with nitric acid. Crommelin gives equations for the reactions, which, if correct, illustrate the role of carbon in the experiment (unsuspected by Boyle) and indicate that the 'fixed niter' was not, as he thought, simply a part of the niter. But it is doubtful that Boyle was dealing with pure substances, and the equations probably oversimplfy the situation. If Boyle was right in identifying the 'volatile part' given off in the first reaction with the spirit of niter added in the second, there must have been a source of hydrogen.

    [16] I.e., the 'fixed niter,' which on Spinoza's hypothesis is an impurity in the niter (IV/17-18).

    [17] In § 9 Boyle reports having weighed the spirit of niter necessary to fully dissolve the fixed niter and having compared that weight with the weight lost by the niter when it was separated from its spirit. The weights were nearly, but not quite equal.

This salt, *or* these impurities, have pores, *or* passages, hollowed out in them, of the size of the particles of Niter. But when the particles of niter were driven out of them by the force of the fire, some of the passages became narrower and consequently others were forced to dilate, and the very substance, *or* walls, of these passages were made rigid, and at the same time very brittle. So when the spirit of Niter was dropped on the salt, some of the spirit's particles began to penetrate forcibly through those narrower passages. And since the particles are of unequal thickness (as Descartes has demonstrated, not badly),[18] they first bent the rigid walls of the passages like a bow, and then broke them. When they broke them, they forced those fragments to spring back; since they retained the motion they had, they remained as incapable of solidifying or crystallizing as before. Some [A, NS: particles of the spirit of niter] penetrated through wider passages; since they did not touch the walls of these passages, they were necessarily surrounded by a very fine matter, were driven upwards by it (in the same way the parts of wood are by flame or heat) and flew off in smoke. If they were plentiful enough, or if they mixed with the fragments of the walls and the particles entering through the narrower passages, they formed droplets flying upwards. But if, with the aid of water[a] or air, the fixed salt is loosened and made more flexible, then it is sufficiently able to restrain the impetus of the particles of [A: spirit of] Niter and to force them to lose the motion they had, and come to rest again (just as a cannonball loses its motion when it hits sand or mud). The reconstitution of Niter consists simply in this coming to rest of the particles of spirit of Niter. To bring it about, the fixed salt is used [A: only] as an instrument, as is plain from this explanation.

So far we have spoken about the reconstitution. Now, if you please, let us see (i) why the Niter and the spirit of Niter differ so in taste, and (ii) why the Niter is inflammable and the spirit of Niter is not in any way.

(i) To understand the first, it must be noted that bodies in motion never meet other bodies with their largest surfaces, whereas bodies at rest lie on others on their largest surfaces. So if the particles of Niter

---

[a] If you ask why there was effervescence when the spirit of niter was dropped on the dissolved fixed salt, read the note regarding § 24. [When Boyle dropped spirit of niter on the fixed niter, he found that "the saline particles of these liquors toss one another (or are tossed by some brisk invisible substance) to the height of divers fingers breadth up into the air, whence most of them fall back into the vessel like a thick shower of little drops of rain . . . the particles thus thrown into the air appear to be most of them saline by this observation . . . soon after the fall of the fore-mentioned showers, you shall find the sides of the glass . . . all embroidered with little grains of salt, left there by those wandering drops that fell beside the liquor."]

[18] See Descartes, *Principles of Philosophy* IV, 110.

175

IV/20   are put on the tongue while they are at rest, they lie on it on their largest surfaces. In this way they block its pores, which is the cause of the cold. Moreover the Niter cannot be dissolved by the saliva into such small particles [A: as it is with the help of the fire]. But if these particles are put on the tongue while they are in violent motion, they

5   will meet it on their more pointed surfaces and will penetrate through its pores. The more violent their motion, the more sharply they will prick the tongue. The different sensations are produced in the same way as if a needle encountered the tongue point-first, or lay on it lengthwise.

     (ii) The reason why the Niter is inflammable, whereas the spirit is

10   not, is that it is more difficult for the fire to carry the particles of Niter upwards when they are at rest than when they have their own motion in all directions. So when they are at rest, they resist the fire until it separates them from one another and surrounds them on every side. But when it surrounds them, it takes them with it this way and that,

15   until they acquire their own motion and go up in smoke. But since the particles of the spirit of Niter are already in motion and separated from one another, they are [A: immediately] spread out over a greater

IV/21   volume by a little heat from the fire. So before they are completely surrounded by the flame some go up in smoke and others penetrate through the matter which feeds the fire. Hence they extinguish the fire rather than maintain it.

     I shall proceed now to the experiments that seem to confirm this

5   explanation [A: of the phenomenon]. First, I find that the particles of Niter that go up in smoke with a crackling noise are pure niter. More than once when I melted the Niter until the crucible was hot enough to be glowing and kindled it with a live coal, I collected its smoke in a cold glass flask until the flask was moist with smoke[19] and afterwards

10   moistened it further with my breath. Finally I put it out in the cold air[b] to let it dry. When it was dry, little icicles of Niter appeared here and there in the flask.

     It might be suspected that this did not occur from the volatile particles alone, but that perhaps the flame carried with it (to speak according to the Distinguished Gentleman's opinion) whole

IV/22   parts of the Niter, and drove out fixed particles together with the volatile, before they were dissolved. To remove this suspicion, I made the smoke go up through a chimneylike tube more than a foot long (like A), so that the heavier parts would stick to

---

[b] When I tried this, the air was very clear. [A: NB This ought to be done in clear weather.]

[19] A: "I moistened a glass flask with its smoke (taking care that the flask was cold enough)."

5 the tube, and I would collect only the more volatile ones passing through the more narrow opening B [A: and I also took a small quantity of niter, so that the flame would be lower and less violent]. The experiment turned out as I have said.

But I did not wish to stop here. To examine the matter further, I took a larger quantity of Niter, melted it, and ignited it with a live 10 coal. As before, I put the tube, A, over the crucible. As long as the flame lasted, I held a piece of a mirror close to the opening, B. A certain material stuck to it, which became liquid when it was exposed to the air [A: from which I immediately conjectured that it consisted only of fixed parts]. Though I waited several days, I could not observe [A: any little icicle of niter, nor] any effect of Niter. But after I poured 15 in spirit of Niter, it was [A: immediately] changed into Niter.

From this I seem to be able to infer: (i) that in the melting the fixed V/23 parts are separated from the volatile parts and that the flame drives them upward, still separated from one another; (ii) that after the fixed parts are separated from the volatile ones with a crackling noise, they cannot be reunited; from this I infer (iii) that the parts which stuck to the flask and coalesced into little icicles were not fixed, but only volatile.[20]

The second experiment seems to show that the fixed parts are only impurities in the Niter; I find that the more it is purified, the more volatile it is, and the more apt to crystallize. For when I put crystals of purified or filtered Niter in a glass goblet, like A, and poured in a little cold water, it 0 partly evaporated with the cold water, and those particles which escaped stuck to the rim of the glass and coalesced into little icicles.

The third experiment seems to indicate that, when the particles of spirit of Niter lose their motion, they are made inflammable. I trickled 5 drops of spirit of Niter in a damp paper bag and then added sand. The spirit of Niter immediately penetrated through the openings in the sand. After the sand had absorbed all, or nearly all, of the spirit of Niter, I dried it thoroughly over a fire in the same bag. That done, I removed the sand and put the paper on a live coal. As soon as it V/24 caught fire it gave off sparks in the same way it usually does when it has absorbed Niter itself.

[20] In A the conclusions are formulated as follows: "(i) that in the melting the parts of niter are separated from that fixed salt, and though the flame drives off the fixed parts also, it drives them off only separated from what the distinguished author calls the volatile parts; (ii) that after these volatile parts have once been separated from the fixed salt, they cannot penetrate through its pores again because their motion is less violent; from which it follows (iii) that the parts of the smoke which stuck to the flask and hardened into little circles of niter in the cold air were parts of niter, separated from the fixed salt, and that the niter into which they formed was crystals, which consisted only of volatile parts."

If I had had the opportunity to experiment further, I would have added other things, which perhaps would make the matter completely clear. But because I am entirely occupied with other matters, with your indulgence I shall put this off till another time and proceed to the other things to be noted.

In § 5, where the Distinguished Gentleman deals in passing with the shape of the particles of Niter, he finds fault with Modern Writers for having misrepresented it. I don't know whether he means Descartes also, but if so, perhaps he criticizes Descartes because of what others have said. For Descartes was not speaking of particles such as can be seen with the eyes. Nor do I think [A: And I would really be surprised if] the Distinguished Gentleman means that if the little icicles of Niter were rubbed until they were changed into parallelepipeds, or into any other shape, they would [A: lose their own nature and] cease to be Niter.[21] But perhaps he is referring to some of those Chemists who admit nothing but what they can see with their eyes or touch with their hands.

Regarding § 9, if this experiment could be made accurately, it would completely confirm what I wished to infer from the first experiment mentioned above.

In §§ 13-18 the Distinguished Gentleman tries to show that all the tangible qualities[22] depend only on motion, shape, and the remaining mechanical affections. Since he does not present these demonstrations as Mathematical, it is not necessary to examine whether they are completely convincing.[23] But meanwhile, I don't know why the Distinguished Gentleman strives so anxiously to infer this from his experi-

[21] The Halls note that "Boyle was one of the first to recognize that salts normally crystallize in regular and characteristic figures, which cannot be altered." (Oldenburg, 1:468).

[22] Boyle in fact refers to "those more secondary affections of bodies which are wont to be called sensible qualities." 'Tactile qualities,' like heat and cold, are among these, but so are sound, color, taste and smell.

[23] The Halls remark at this point that: "Nothing better illustrates the gulf of incomprehension separating Spinoza from an experimental philosopher like Boyle than this and the following statement—expressing a position with which Leibniz was later to agree. Needless to say, many of Spinoza's errors arise precisely from his inability to realize that pure ratiocination could not solve all the mysteries of the physical world." (Oldenburg, 1: 468). The reference to Leibniz is presumably to the following passage: "Mr. Boyle spends too much time, to be truthful, drawing from an infinity of splendid experiments no other conclusions than those which he could have taken for principles of nature . . . which one can certify to be true from reason alone, whereas experiments, no matter how numerous, cannot prove them." (Quoted in Hall 1, 43).

It is not, however, clear that Spinoza's position is identical with Leibniz's. Both are clearly impatient with Boyle's belaboring a point they regard as evident. But where Leibniz talks of certifying the point by reason alone, Spinoza seems to regard it as demonstrated by the less recondite 'experiments' adduced by Bacon and Descartes. For more on this theme, see IV/50/14ff., and IV/66/32ff. Since Spinoza has begun his cri-

ment, since it has already been more than adequately demonstrated by Bacon and later by Descartes. Nor do I see that this experiment offers us more illuminating evidence than others which are readily enough available.

For as far as heat is concerned, is the same [conclusion][24] not just as clear from the fact that if two pieces of wood are rubbed together, though they are cold, they produce a flame simply from that motion? or that if lime is sprinkled with water, it becomes hot? As for sound, I do not see that anything more remarkable is to be found in this experiment[25] than in the boiling of ordinary water and in many other things. Regarding the Color [A: which was changed when the spirit of niter was added], to restrict myself to things which are provable, I shall say only that we see all green plants changing into so many and such different colors. Again, if bodies that give off a foul·smell are shaken, they give off a still more offensive smell, particularly if they become somewhat warm. Finally, sweet wine is changed into vinegar, and similarly with many other things.

So (*if one may use Philosophic freedom*)[c] I would judge all these things to be superfluous. *I say this because I fear that others, who love the Distinguished Gentleman less than they should, may judge him wrongly.*

§ 24. I have already spoken about the cause of this Phenomenon [see IV/18/15-19/6]. Here I add only that I have also found by experience that particles of the fixed salt float in those saline drops. For when they flew upwards, they struck against the piece of glass I had made ready for this and had warmed somewhat, so that any volatile [particle] that stuck to the glass would fly off. When this was done, I observed a thick whitish material sticking to the glass here and there.

In § 25[26] the Distinguished Gentleman seems to wish to demon-

---

tique of Boyle by complaining that Boyle had not done enough experiments to prove his conclusions (IV/16/14ff.), it is ironic that he should be criticized for trying to solve all the mysteries of the physical world by pure ratiocination.

[c] In the letter I sent I deliberately omitted these words [i.e., those in italics].

[24] Boyle found that when he put the 'parts' of the niter together again, they immediately "agitated each other with great vehemency," producing a considerable heat, which lasted as long as the agitation lasted. Boyle inferred that heat was "nothing but a various and nimble motion of the minute particles of bodies."

[25] The reunion of the parts of the niter was also accompanied by "a very audible sound, not unlike the hissing produced by the quenching of a live coal in water. . . . This sound seemed to proceed from the nimble and smart percussions of the ambient air, made by the swift and irregular motions of the particles of the liquors."

[26] "There seems to be a very nimble agitation in the particles of the spirit of nitre, by this, that upon the pouring of aqua fortis (whose active part is little else than spirit of nitre) upon a solution of salt of tartar in fair water, in which divers small lumps of the salt remained yet undissolved, we have observed the acid spirit to sever the particles of the salt with such impetuosity that the numberless little bubbles produced upon their conflict, and hastily ascending in swarms from some of the little lumps, made them

strate that the alkaline parts are carried here and there by the impulse[27]
of the saline particles, but that the saline particles raise themselves
into the air by their own impulse.

In explaining this Phenomenon I have said that the particles of Spirit
of Niter acquire a more violent motion because, when they enter wider
passages, they must necessarily be surrounded by a very fine matter
and driven upwards by it, as particles of wood are by fire, but that
the alkaline particles receive their motion from the impulse of particles
of Spirit of Niter penetrating through the narrower passages. Here I
add that pure water cannot so easily dissolve and loosen the fixed
parts. So it is no wonder that when you drop Spirit of Niter on the
solution of that fixed salt dissolved in water, there is an effervescence
such as the Distinguished Gentleman recounts in § 24. Indeed, I think
this effervescence will be more violent than if the Spirit of Niter is
dropped on the fixed salt while it is still intact. For in the water it is
dissolved into very minute molecules, which can be divided more easily and moved more freely than when all the parts of the salt lie on
one another and adhere firmly to one another.

§ 26. I have already spoken of the taste of the acid Spirit. So only
the alkali remains to be discussed. When I put it on my tongue, I felt
heat, followed by a prickling. This indicates to me that it is some kind
of lime. For in the same way that lime becomes hot with the aid of
water, so this salt becomes warm with the aid of saliva, or sweat, or
Spirit of Niter, or perhaps even of moist air.[28]

§ 27. It does not immediately follow that if a particle of matter is
joined to another it acquires a new shape; it only follows that it becomes larger, and this suffices to bring about what the Distinguished
Gentleman is inquiring about in this section [A: that it corrodes gold].[29]

---

emulate so many little, but rapidly rising, springs . . . after the two contrary salts had
by their mutual conflict tired each other, (or rather had been upon their occursions
fastened to one another) there would follow no further ebullition or skipping up and
down of little drops of the liquors, upon the putting in of more spirit of nitre, unless
there were added likewise more of the alkalizate liquor."

[27] OP, A: *impulsus*, NS: *drift/impetus*. (This is only one of a number of variations in
the marginal notes at this point.)

[28] The Halls note that: "Spinoza . . . failed to understand what an alkali (or acid)
might be. Boyle was the first chemist who was able to establish the modern classification
of substances into acid, alkaline, and neutral." (Oldenburg, 1:468).

[29] "It is not barely an indefinite nimbleness of motion and activity of the particles of
saline liquors that enables them to perform each of their particular effects: for to the
production of some of these there seems requisite, besides perhaps a modification of
their motion, a determinate figure of the corpuscles, answerable to that of the pores of
the body to be dissolved; as spirit of nitre corrodes silver, but not gold; which nevertheless its particles associated with those of sal-ammoniac, and thereby acquiring a new
figure, and perhaps a differing motion, will readily dissolve."

§ 33. I shall say what I think of the Distinguished Gentleman's manner of philosophizing, after I see the Dissertation mentioned here and in the Proemial Essay, p. 23.[30]

On Fluidity

§ 1: *It is manifest enough that [fluidity and firmness [i.e., solidity]] are to be reckoned among the most general affections [of the conventions or associations of several particles of matter into bodies of any certain denomination, there being scarce any distinct portion of matter in the world that is not either fluid, or else stable or consistent.][31]* I would think that notions derived from ordinary usage, or which explain Nature, not as it is in itself, but as it is related to human sense perception, ought neither to be counted among the chief kinds, nor to be mixed (not to say confused) with pure notions, which explain Nature as it is in itself. Of the latter kind are motion, rest, and their laws; of the former are visible, invisible, hot, cold, and as I will say at once, also fluid and solid, etc.

§ 5: *The first is the smallness of the bodies that compose it, for certainly in larger . . . [parcels of matter, besides the greater inequalities or roughnesses that are usual upon their surfaces, and may hinder the easy sliding of those bodies along one another, . . . the bulk itself is apt to make them so heavy that they cannot be agitated by the power of those causes (whatever they be) that make the minute parts of fluid bodies move so freely up and down among themselves . . .].[32]* Even though bodies are small, they nevertheless have

---

[30] In § 33 (Latin edition only), Boyle writes: "We shall never be able to investigate so thoroughly the subtle workings of nature that there will not remain many natural phenomena which cannot be explained on the principles of the Atomical philosophy." The English version (which, of course, Spinoza did not see) is more cautious, saying only that perhaps men will not be able to give intelligible (i.e., mechanical) explanations of all things. Cf. Boyle 2, with Boyle 3.

In the Proemial Essay (p. 21 of Boyle 2), Boyle writes: ". . . I elsewhere declare that there are some things, as particularly the origin of local motion, of which even by the Atomical Doctrine no physical cause can well be rendered, since either such things must be ascribed to God, who is indeed the true, but the supernatural cause of them, or else it must be said that they did ever belong to matter, which, considering that the notion of matter may be compleat without them, is not to give a physical cause of the things in question, but in effect to confess that they have no causes." I assume that it is to this passage (which does not differ materially in the Latin version) that Spinoza means to refer when he cites p. 23 of the Proemial Essay, though this passage in fact occurs on p. 21 in Boyle 3 also.

[31] Here and in the following pages I have expanded Spinoza's quotations from Boyle to make them more intelligible.

[32] In the passage in question Boyle is proposing a theory of fluidity alternative to that of the Epicureans, for whom fluid bodies were thought to be composed of smooth, round atoms which could easily be separated from one another (he quotes Lucretius, *De rerum natura* II, 451-456). Boyle allows that in some liquids the component particles may be smooth and round, and that this would contribute to their fluidity, but argues that the qualities of some other fluids indicate a different shape in the components. He

(or can have)[33] surfaces which are uneven and rough. Hence if large bodies should so move that the proportion of their motion to their bulk is the same as that between the motion and bulk of minute bodies, they too would have to be called fluid, if the word fluid did not mean something extrinsic and were not taken over from ordinary usage to mean those moved bodies whose smallness and intervals escape human sense perception. So to divide bodies into fluid and solid will be the same as dividing them into visible and invisible.

In the same section: *[. . . whereas it would scarce be believed how much the smallness of parts may facilitate their being easily put into motion, and kept in it,] if we were not able to confirm*[34] *it by Chemical experiments.* No one will ever be able to 'confirm' this by Chemical experiments, nor by any others, but only by demonstration and computation.[35] For it is by reasoning and calculation that we divide bodies to infinity, and consequently also the Forces required to move them. But we can never 'confirm' this by experiments.

IV/30   § 6: *[And to show yet more particularly] that great bodies are too unwieldy to constitute fluid ones; [we may further observe, how as well nature as art, when either of them makes bodies of considerable bulk fluid, is wont, in order thereunto, to make a comminution of them . . .].*[36] Whether or not one understands by fluid what I have just said, nevertheless, the thing is manifest [A: enough] through itself. But I do not see how the Distinguished Gentleman 'confirms' this by the experiments reported in this section. For (since we want to doubt concerning a thing certain)[37] although bones are unsuitable for composing Chyle and similar fluids, perhaps they will be suitable enough for composing some new kind of fluid [A: unknown to us].

---

suggests three conditions of fluidity: (i) smallness of the component particles, (ii) the existence of empty spaces or "some yielding matter" around the component particles, or at least around those on the surface of the fluid, and most importantly (iii) the motion of the component particles.

[33] The qualification in parenthesis occurs in the OP, but not in A.

[34] *Comprobare.* See the Glossary-Index on *confirm*.

[35] A: "by reasoning and calculation." What Spinoza here is saying cannot be proven by experiment seems to be not so much "the particulate structure of matter" (cf. Hall 3, 244), as the slightness of the force required to put particles in motion. Spinoza's view seems to be that, if bodies are infinitely divisible, the force required to move their parts may be indefinitely small. The infinite divisibility of bodies is not an experimental question, so neither is the calculation that effective forces may be indefinitely small.

[36] Boyle goes on to cite a number of examples, the first of which is the dissolution of bones into minute parts by the stomach juices of dogs to form chyle and blood.

[37] Gebhardt reproduces the reading of the OP: "concerning a thing uncertain." AHW reinstate the reading of A and NS, and I have followed them. I take it that Spinoza is somewhat diffident about offering arguments in favor of a thesis he regards as sufficiently clear without argument: that fluidity is not a function of size.

§ 10:[38] *By making them less pliant than formerly [or giving them a figure more easy to be entangled with the neighbouring corpuscles, or else by making their surfaces less smooth and slippery than before].* The parts driven into the Receiver could have coagulated into another body, more solid than oil, without any change of the parts, but only because they were separated from the remaining parts. For bodies are lighter or heavier according to the kinds of fluid in which they are immersed.

So when particles of butter are floating in milk, they compose part of the liquid. But after the milk, from being stirred, acquires a new motion, to which all the parts composing the milk cannot equally accommodate themselves, this by itself brings it about that some parts become heavier and drive the lighter ones upwards. But because these lighter parts are so much heavier than air that they cannot compose a liquid with it, they are driven downwards by it; and because they are unable to move, they alone cannot also make a fluid, but lie on one another and stick to one another.[39]

Vapors, too, when they are separated from the air, are changed to water, which can be called solid by comparison with air [A: and similarly with many other things].

§ 13:[40] *And I take as an example a Bladder distended by water rather than one full of air [because, though this latter will also emulate a hard body, yet*

[38] In this section Boyle describes an experiment designed to show that the shape as well as the size of its component particles may be a hindrance to a body's fluidity. He distilled olive oil slowly in a glass retort and found that about a third of the oil driven into the receiver coagulated into "a whitish body almost like butter. So that although it seemed manifest by the strong smell and very piercing taste of this white substance that the oil which afforded it had its particles, as it were, torn in pieces, and though distillation be wont to obtain liquors even from consistent bodies, yet in our experience of a concrete that is naturally fluid, the distilled liquor itself proves not to be so; of which no cause seems more obvious than that the newly acquired shape of the dissipated parts of the oily corpuscles makes them unfit for motion, either absolutely speaking, or at least in respect of one another. . . ." Then follows the phrase Spinoza quotes.

[39] In A this paragraph reads: "So when particles of butter are floating in the whey, they compose part of the milk. But after the milk or cream acquires a new motion, to which not all the parts composing the whole milk can accommodate themselves so easily as to their first motion, the parts of the butter become too light to be able to compose a fluid with the whey, and they are also too heavy to compose a fluid with the air. And because they have an irregular shape, as is evident from the fact that they could not accommodate themselves to the motion of the particles of whey, they alone can not constitute a fluid. Hence they lie on one another and are entangled with one another."

[40] In this section Boyle argues that vacant spaces (or yielding matter) around the component particles of a body contribute to fluidity, adducing the example of water compressed in a bladder, "so that its exterior particles have not about them as before the yielding air to give way to them." Instead of giving way to a body pressing in on it, the water "emulates a hard body and resists such motions as otherwise it would readily yield to." The Halls observe that the example is not a happy one, and that Boyle's other example (comparing new-fallen snow and snow which has been packed into a hard ball) is better.

in this case the tension of the bladder would perhaps be ascribed to a kind of spring, which divers experiments have taught us to belong to the air]. Since the particles of water are always moving unceasingly in every direction, it is clear that if they are a not restrained by surrounding bodies, the water will be extended in every direction [A: or what is the same thing, it has an elastic force].

Further, I confess that I cannot yet perceive how the distention of a bladder full of water helps to confirm his view about the small spaces. For the reason why the particles of water do not yield when the sides of the bladder are pressed by a finger (as they would do otherwise, if they were free) is that there is no equilibrium, *or* circulation, as there is when some body, say our finger, is surrounded by a fluid or by water. But however much the water is pressed by the bladder, nevertheless its particles will yield to a stone which is also enclosed in the bladder in the same way they usually do outside the bladder.

In the same section: *[Yet I will not say that it were altogether absurd to question] whether there is a portion of matter [consisting of parts so minute and so agitated, and consequently so easy to be either crumbled into yet smaller parts, or squeezed into any figure as occasion requires, that they may incessantly change places among themselves, and thereby constitute a most fluid body, without any vacuities, receptacles, or yielding matter about them . . .].*[41] The affirmative must be maintained unless we are willing instead to embark on an infinite regress, or to grant (what is the height of absurdity) that there is a vacuum.

§ 19:[42] *[The humidity of a body is but a relative thing, and depends chiefly upon the congruity or incongruence of the component particles of the liquor in reference to the pores of those particular bodies that it touches: for sometimes the little eminencies and pores of the surface of the dry body . . . are of such magnitudes and figure] that the particles of the liquor find admittance into those pores, and are detained there, by which means [they usually soften it; and sometimes the pores and asperities of the dry bodies are so incommensurate in bigness and figure to the particles of the liquor that they glide over the surface without sticking or adhering firmly to any part of it].*

[41] The Halls note that Boyle is here being skeptical about "The Cartesian 'first matter,' whose particles are very small and very flexible, so that they can fit between the particles of greater matter . . . and prevent the formation of a vacuum."

[42] In this section Boyle distinguishes between those fluids which can and those which cannot be regarded as "moist," "wetting" or "humid": "The air, the aether and even flame itself may properly be called fluid bodies, according to the notion of fluidity hitherto made out, and yet will scarce by any man be called moist liquors; and saltpetre, whilst in fusion is really a liquor, and so is every melted metal; and yet these wet not the bodies they touch, as do water and other wetting liquors. . . ."

10   This must not be affirmed absolutely of all fluids which find an entry into the pores of other [bodies]. For if the particles of Spirit of Niter enter the pores of white paper, they make it stiff and brittle; one can test this by pouring
15   a few drops in a glowing iron cup, like A, and channeling the smoke through a paper cover, like B. Further, the same Spirit of Niter makes leather soft, but not wet; on the contrary, it shrinks it, just as fire also does.

In the same section: *[And even water,[43] that wets almost all other animal and vegetable, and many mineral bodies . . . seems not a humid body in relation to the feathers of ducks, swans and other waterfowl;] since nature [A: has designed] them both for flying and for swimming [she providently makes their feathers of such a texture that they do not, like the feathers of other birds, admit the water, which imbibed would make them unfit for the use of flying].*

20   He seeks the cause in the purpose.[44]

§ 23: *[Let us return to visible liquors and endeavor to prove . . . that their insensible parts may be every way agitated,] though their motion is rarely seen by us. Take then [what quantity you please of aqua fortis, and dissolve in it as much as you please of ordinary coined silver . . . pour the colored solution into twelve or fifteen times as much fair water, and then decant or filtrate the mixture that it may be very clear. If you look upon this liquor, the parts of it will seem to be all of them as perfectly at rest as those of common water, nor will your eye be able to distinguish any corpuscles of silver swimming in the liquor . . . that there are such metalline corpuscles agitated to and fro with and by those of the water will quickly appear if you immerse into it a flatted piece of clean copper. For by that time you have held it two or three minutes . . . in the liquor, you shall see the particles of silver that were roving up and down the liquor, fasten themselves in such swarms to the copper plate that they will . . . cover it with a loose case of silver].*

V/33   The matter is sufficiently evident without this experiment and without any expense, from the fact that in winter we see [A: clearly] enough that our breath moves, whereas in summer or in a heated room we cannot see that it moves.

Further, if in summer the wind cools suddenly, then since the new density of the air prevents vapors arising from the water from being dispersed through it so easily as they were before it cooled, they are gathered again over the surface of the water in such abundance that we can see them [A: clearly] enough.

---

[43] Boyle has just pointed out that quicksilver, which will not wet most substances, will wet certain metals, like gold and tin.

[44] Unlike most of the mechanical philosophers, Boyle did not reject final causes. Cf. Hall 1, 51. To Spinoza, as to Descartes, this is anathema.

Again, we can infer from the sundial and the shadow of the Sun that motion is often too slow for us to see it, and from a lighted piece of tinder, moved swiftly in a circle, that it is very often too fast for us to see it. In the latter case we imagine that the fiery part is at rest at every point on the circumference which it describes by its motion. I would recount here the causes of this, if I did not judge it superfluous.

Finally, let me say in passing that to understand the nature of a fluid in general it suffices to know that we can move our hand [A: in it] in all directions without any resistance, with a motion proportionate to the fluid. This is evident enough to those who attend sufficiently to those Notions which explain Nature as it is in itself, not as it is related to human sense perception.[45] Not that on that account I scorn this history[46] as useless. On the contrary, if this were done concerning each fluid, as accurately and reliably as possible, I would judge it very useful for understanding their special differences. This is something all Philosophers ought greatly to desire, as being very necessary.[47]

On Solidity

§ 7: *[Upon what account soever the atomists have omitted to reckon for a cause of firmness that which we have newly been speaking of (i.e., that the body's component parts are at rest in relation to one another), yet . . . if two bodies be at rest against one another, it seems] consonant to the universal laws of Nature [that they should continue in that state of rest till some force capable to overpower their resistance puts them out of it].*

This is Descartes' demonstration, and I do not see that the Distinguished Gentleman brings to light any genuine demonstration drawn from his experiments or observations.

I had noted many things here and in what follows, but afterwards I saw that the Distinguished Gentleman corrected himself.

Section 16:[48] *[The marbles being skilfully wetted and kept by . . . wires*

---

[45] Instead of this sentence, A has simply: "This one observation, I say, indicates completely the nature of a fluid."

[46] The title of this part of Boyle's work is "The History of Fluidity and Firmness." It is a history in the Baconian sense of a collection of experimental data relating to some phenomenon. Cf. IV/12/4.

[47] A: "very useful, indeed, absolutely necessary to understand the special properties of fluids and to master them."

[48] Boyle has been arguing (Boyle 2, 187ff.) that the pressure of the air is a probable explanation of the fact that smooth bodies will stick together "upon bare juxtaposition or contact." E.g., if one piece of flat glass is placed against another, parallel to the ground, the lower piece will not drop down, though it will very easily slide along the surface of the upper piece. In the present section he describes an experiment designed to estimate how great the presence of the air is. Boyle took two pieces of marble of 1½ inches in diameter, "as flat and smooth as we could get," moistened them with spirit of wine to prevent air from coming between them, and attached a scale to one.

from slipping aside, we cast into the scale fastened to the lower of them divers weights at several times, and by nimbly pulling up the higher stone, tried many times how much we could draw up with the lower, and did sometimes take up above an hundred ounces,] and once an hundred thirty-two[49] ounces [Troy, besides the scale that contained them, and the marble itself. . .].

If one compares it with the weight of the quicksilver enclosed in the tube,[50] it comes very near the true weight. But I would consider it worth the trouble to examine these things so that one may obtain, as far as possible the ratio between the pressure of the air along a line 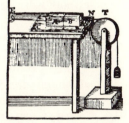 parallel to the Horizon and that along a line perpendicular to the Horizon.[51] I think it can be done in this way. Let CD in figure 6 be a flat mirror, very smoothly polished, on which lie two pieces of marble, A and B, immediately touching one another; let A be attached to a hook, E; let B be attached to a cord [A: sufficiently strong silk thread], N; let T be a pulley and G a weight which will show the force which is required to pull B away from A along a line parallel to the Horizon.

In figure 7 let F be a sufficiently strong silk thread by which the marble, B, is tied to the floor; let D be a pulley and G a weight which will show the force which is required to pull apart A and B [A: which  touches A immediately] along a line perpendicular to the horizon.[52]

[A: It is not necessary to explain these things more fully. With this, my dear friend, you have what I so far find worth noting about Mr. Boyle's experiments.

V/35

V/36

V35/28

---

[49] As Wolf notes, the figure that Spinoza quotes (432 ounces) is a mistake introduced by Boyle's Latin translator.

[50] A reference to another experiment described in Boyle 2, 188-189: "If you take a small open-mouthed glass and plunge it into a vessel full of quicksilver with the mouth upward, that the quicksilver may fill it without leaving any air in it, and if then, whilst it is under the quicksilver, you turn the mouth downwards, and so keeping it upright, lift it up till the mouth be almost to the top of the mercury, you shall perceive that the glass will remain almost full of quicksilver. . . . Of which the reason seems to be that the glass hinders the quicksilver in it from the pressure of the incumbent air, whereas the quicksilver in the vessel being exposed to it must by it necessarily be forced up against the surface of the inverted bottom of the glass . . . that it is not nature's abhorrency of a vacuum that keeps the quicksilver from descending till some air can come to succeed in its room, the famous experiment invented by Torricellius, . . . touching the descent of quicksilver in any tube of above two foot and a half long, seems clearly to evince." On the Torricellian experiment, see Letter 14 and Conant.

[51] Spinoza evidently does not realize that the vertical and horizontal pressures are the same, though this had been shown by Pascal.

[52] Here the OP and NS break off with the remark that the rest is lacking.

IV/36/8 As for your first questions, when I look through my replies, I see nothing that I have omitted. And if by chance I have put something obscurely (as I often do for lack of words), I ask you to be so good as to indicate it to me. I shall do my best to explain it more clearly.

10 As for your new question, how things have begun to be, and by what connection they depend on the first cause, I have composed a whole short work devoted to this matter and also to the emendation of the intellect.[53] I am engaged in transcribing and emending it, but sometimes I put it to one side because I do not yet have any definite

15 plan regarding its publication. I fear, of course, that the theologians of our time may be offended and with their usual hatred attack me, who absolutely dread quarrels.

I shall look for your advice regarding this matter, and to let you know what is contained in this work of mine which might somewhat offend the preachers, I say that I regard as creatures many 'attributes'

20 which they—and everyone, so far as I know—attribute to God. Conversely, other things, which they because of their prejudices regard as creatures, I contend are attributes of God, which they have misunderstood. Also, I do not separate God from nature as everyone known

25 to me has done. So I look for your advice, regarding you as a most faithful friend, whose honesty it would be wrong to doubt.

Farewell, and as you have begun, continue to love me, who am,

Yours entirely,

[Rijnsburg, April 1662]   Benedictus Spiñoza][54]

[53] It seems clear from the description of the contents that follows that the work referred to here would have corresponded more closely to the *Short Treatise* than to anything else we possess. It is unclear, however, just how closely our ms. of the *Short Treatise* resembles the ms. Spinoza was working with at this stage. Certainly the axiomatic systems of the early correspondence seem more mature than does the first appendix of the KV.

The major question, however, is whether the work here referred to would have included the *Treatise on the Intellect* as a part. Gebhardt 3 argued that it would have. One difficulty with that theory is that Spinoza's language here suggests a work completed at least in a rough draft. Joachim 2,7, suggested that "Spinoza, writing hurriedly at the end of an extremely long letter, has given a not quite accurate summary of a complicated situation," since one part of the work (the KV) existed in a complete, if rough draft, while the other (the TdIE) was incomplete (though it may have embodied most of what he wanted to say on the emendation of the intellect). Mignini 1, 231-233, influenced partly by this difficulty and partly by his conviction that the TdIE represents an earlier stage in Spinoza's thought than the KV does, suggests that we might regard the second part of the KV as a treatise on the emendation of the intellect. And while this may seem unlikely (on the ground that the KV II is more concerned with the effects of the intellectual improvement than with its causes), it strikes me as not impossible (cf. KV II, xix, 2-3).

[54] Gebhardt notes that in this, the earliest signature we have from him, Spinoza gives his first name in a Latinized form, but his family name in a form more Portuguese than Latin. Mignini 2 argues that this letter was probably written toward the end of 1661, rather than at the later date usually assumed.

Letter 7

Henry Oldenburg to the Esteemed B.d.S.

It is many weeks ago, Distinguished Sir, since I received your very welcome letter, with its learned comments on Boyle's book. The Author himself joins me in thanking you very much for the reflections you have shared with us. He would have indicated this more quickly if he had not hoped that he would soon be relieved of the mass of business with which he is burdened, so that he could send you his answer along with his thanks. But he finds that so far his hope has been in vain; he has been so distracted, both by public and by private business, that for now he can only convey his gratitude to you, and is forced to put off till another time his opinion regarding your Notes.

Moreover, two Opponents[55] have attacked him in print and he considers himself bound to reply to them as soon as possible. Those Writings are not aimed at his Treatise on Niter, but at another book of his, containing his Pneumatic Experiments, which prove the Elasticity of the Air. As soon as he has freed himself from this work, he will disclose his thoughts regarding your Objections. Meanwhile he asks you not to take this delay amiss.

That Group of Philosophers I had mentioned to you has now, by our King's favor, been converted into a Royal Society, protected by a public Charter, which grants it special Privileges. There is great hope that it will be endowed with the necessary income.

I would advise you, without reservation, not to grudge scholars what you have learnedly arrived at by the acuteness of your understanding, both in Philosophy and in Theology. Let it be published, whatever rumblings there may be among the foolish Theologians. Your Republic is very free, and gives great freedom for philosophizing. And your own prudence will suggest to you that you express your concepts and your opinion as moderately as possible. For the rest, leave the outcome to Fate.

Come, then, excellent Sir, banish all fear of arousing the pygmies of our time. Long enough have we appeased ignorant triflers. Let us set full sail for true knowledge, and penetrate more deeply into Nature's mysteries than anyone yet has. Among your people, I think, your meditations can be published with impunity, nor should you fear that they will give any offense to the Wise. If you find such to be your Patrons and Supporters—and I guarantee without reservation that you will—why should you fear an ignorant Momus. I will not leave you in peace, honored Friend, until I prevail on you, nor will I

[55] Thomas Hobbes and Franciscus Linus. See Letter 14 and Conant.

ever, so far as it depends on me, allow your Thoughts, which are of
such great weight, to be concealed in eternal silence. I ask you urgently to take the trouble to let me know, as soon as you conveniently
15   can, what resolution you form on this.

Perhaps things will occur here which will be worth your knowing.
Certainly the Society I have mentioned will now press on more vigorously with its work, and perhaps, provided that the Peace on these
shores lasts, it will contribute to the Republic of Letters with distinction.

20   Farewell, excellent Sir, and believe that I am
                              Your very Devoted and Dear Friend,
[London, July 1662]   Henry Oldenburg

LETTER 8

SIMON DE VRIES TO THE DISTINGUISHED B.D.S.

Most Upright Friend,

For some time now I have been anxious to visit you, but the weather
and the long winter have prevented me. Sometimes I complain about
IV/39 my lot, because the distance between us keeps us apart for so long.
Fortunate, indeed, most Fortunte, is your companion, Casearius, who
lives under the same roof with you, and can talk to you about the
most important matters at breakfast, at dinner, and on your walks.
5   But though our bodies are separated from one another by such a distance, nevertheless you have very often been present in my mind,
especially when I meditate on your writings and hold them in my
hands. But since not everything is clear enough to the members of our
group—which is why we have begun meeting again—and so that you
10   will not think I have forgotten you, I have set myself to write this
letter.

As for our group, it is arranged in this way: one of us (but each one
takes his turn) reads through, explains according to his own conceptions, and then proves everything, following the sequence and order
of your propositions. Then if it happens that one cannot satisfy the
15   other, we have thought it worthwhile to make a note of it and to write
to you, so that, if possible, it may be made clearer to us, and under
your guidance we may be able to defend the truth against those who
are superstitiously religious and Christian, and to stand against the
attacks of the whole world.[56]

---

[56] Much of this letter is omitted in the OP and the NS: for example, the reference to
Casearius in the first paragraph, the whole of the next two paragraphs describing the
Amsterdam Spinoza circle, and the final paragraph. Similarly, first person plurals are
changed to singulars.

So since, when we first read through and explained the definitions, they did not all seem clear to us, we did not agree about the nature of definition. In your absence we consulted a certain author, a mathematician named Borelli.[57] When he discusses the nature of a definition, an axiom and a postulate, he also introduces the opinions of others regarding this matter. His own opinion is as follows:

> Definitions are used in a demonstration as premises. So it is necessary for them to be known evidently, otherwise scientific, *or* very evident, knowledge cannot be acquired from them.

And elsewhere:

> The basis for a construction, or the essential, first and best known property of a subject, must be chosen, not rashly, but with the greatest care. For if the construction or the property named is impossible, then a scientific definition will not result. For example, if someone were to say: "Let two straight lines enclosing a space be called 'figurals,' " this would be a definition of a nonbeing, and would be impossible. So ignorance rather than knowledge would be deduced from it.
>
> Next, if the construction or property named is indeed possible and true, but unknown to us, or doubtful, then it will not be a good definition; for conclusions drawn from what is unknown and doubtful will also be uncertain and doubtful. So they will produce suspicion or opinion, but not certain knowledge.

Tacquet[58] seems to disagree with this opinion, for as you know, he maintains that one can proceed directly from a false proposition to a true conclusion.

But Clavius,[59] whose opinion [Borelli] also introduces, thinks that

> Definitions are technical terms, and it is not necessary to give a reason why a thing is defined in this or that way. It is enough if one never asserts that the thing defined agrees with something unless one has first demonstrated that the definition given agrees with it.

So Borelli maintains that the definition of a subject must consist of a property or construction which is first, essential, best known to us, and true, whereas for Clavius it does not matter whether it is first or

---

As AHW note, it is unclear whether "superstitiously" is meant to modify only "religious" or "Christian" as well. Gebhardt takes this passage as establishing that those who are closest to Spinoza no longer regarded themselves as Christians.

[57] Giovanni Alfonso Borelli (1608-1679) was an Italian mathematician and physicist who published an edition of Euclid, *Euclides restitutus*, in 1658. On his work in mechanics, see Westfall, 213-229.

[58] Andreas Tacquet (1612-1660) was a Belgian mathematician whose *Elementa geometricae planae ac solidae* was published in 1654.

[59] Christopher Clavius (1537-1612) was a German mathematician who published an edition of Euclid with commentary in 1574.

best known or true or not, so long as the definition we have given is not asserted to agree with something unless we have first demonstrated that the definition given does agree with that thing.

We prefer Borelli's opinion, but we do not really know, Sir, which of the two you agree with, or whether you agree with neither. Since there are such various disputes about the nature of definition, which is numbered among the principles of demonstration, if the mind is not freed of difficulties regarding this, then it will also be in difficulty regarding those things deduced from it. So if we are not making too much trouble for you, and if you have the time, we would very much like you, sir, to write to us, giving us your opinion about this matter, and also about what the distinction is between axioms and definitions. Borelli, in fact, admits no true distinction between them, except as regards the name. But I believe you maintain another distinction.

Next, the third definition[60] is not sufficiently clear to us. As an example, I reported what you, Sir, said to me at The Hague, that a Thing can be considered in two ways, either as it is in itself or as it has a relation to something else. For example, the intellect can be considered either under thought or as consisting of ideas. But we do not see clearly what this distinction would be. For we think that if we conceive thought rightly, we must comprehend it in relation to ideas, since if all ideas were removed from it, we would destroy thought itself. So since the example is not clear enough to us, the thing itself still remains somewhat obscure, and we require further explanation.

Finally, at the beginning of P8S3 you write:

> From these [propositions] it is evident that although two attributes may be conceived to be really distinct (i.e., one may be conceived without the aid of the other), they do not, on that account, constitute two beings or two different substances. The reason is that it is of the nature of a substance that all of its attributes (I mean each of them) should be conceived through themselves, since they have [always][61] been in it together.

In this way you seem, Sir, to suppose that the nature of substance is so constituted that it can have more than one attribute, which you have not yet demonstrated, unless you depend on the fifth[62] definition of an absolutely infinite substance, *or* God. Otherwise, if I should say that each substance has only one attribute, and if I had the idea of

---

[60] Cf. IV/46/2-5.

[61] As AHW suggest, this word seems to have been inadvertently omitted. Cf. E IP10S.

[62] This reference, like the reference to P8S3 above, reflects an earlier stage in the development of the *Ethics*. In the OP and the NS the references are corrected to D6 and P10S.

two attributes, I could rightly conclude that, where there are two different attributes, there are two different substances. We ask you for a clearer explanation of this too.

Next, I thank you very much for your writings, which were imparted to me by P. Balling and which have given me great joy— particularly P19S.[63] If I can help you here in anything that is in my power, I am at your service. You have only to let me know. I have entered an anatomy course, and am about half through. When it is finished, I shall begin chemistry, and following your advice, go through the whole Medical Course. I break off now, and await your reply. Receive the greetings of

Your very Devoted,

Amsterdam, 24 February 1663   S. J. De Vries

V/42

LETTER 9

B.D.S. TO THE VERY LEARNED YOUNG MAN, SIMON DE VRIES[64]

Reply to the preceding
[NS: On the Nature of Definition and Axiom]

I have received your letter, which I had long looked for, and I thank you very much for it and for your feeling toward me. The length of your absence has been no less burdensome to me than to you. Meanwhile, however, I am glad that my nightly studies are of use to you and our friends. For in this way, while you are far from me, I who am absent speak to all of you.

There is no need for you to envy Casearius.[65] No one is more troublesome to me, and there is no one with whom I have to be more on my guard. So I should like to warn you and all our friends not to communicate my views to him until he has reached greater maturity. He is still too childish and unstable, more anxious for novelty than for truth. But I hope that in a few years he will correct these youthful

---

[63] AHW conjecture that the reference is to what is now P28S. Certainly it is hard to see why the present P19S should arouse special enthusiasm.

[64] The first two paragraphs of this letter are omitted in the OP and NS, as is the reference to the Amsterdam Spinoza circle in the next paragraph. Similarly, the second person plurals are changed to singulars.

[65] Casearius (1641 or 1642-1677) was enrolled as a student in theology at the nearby University of Leiden in 1661. In 1665 he was ordained as a minister of the Reformed Church in Amsterdam; and subsequently served in the Dutch East Indies, where he died. It was he Meyer was later to refer to as the pupil to whom Spinoza taught the Cartesian philosophy (I/129-130).

25   faults. Indeed, as far as I can judge from his native ability, I am almost certain that he will. So his talent induces me to like him.

As for the questions proposed in your group (which is very sensibly organized), I see that you are in these perplexities because you do not distinguish between different kinds of definition—between one which
30   serves to explain a thing whose essence[66] only is sought, as the only thing there is doubt about, and one which is proposed only to be examined. For because the former has a determinate object, it ought to be true. But the latter does not require this.

IV/43   For example, if someone asks me for a description of the Temple of Solomon, I ought to give him a true description of the temple [NS: as
20   it was] unless I want to talk nonsense to him. But if I have constructed in my mind some temple which I want to build, and if I infer from its description that I must buy land of such a kind and so many thousand stones and other materials, will anyone in his right mind tell me that I have drawn a bad conclusion because I have perhaps used a
25   false definition? Or will anyone require me to prove my definition? To do so would be to tell me that I have not conceived what I have conceived, or to require me to prove that I have conceived what I have conceived. Surely this is trifling.

So a definition either explains a thing as it is [NS: in itself] outside
30   the intellect—and then it ought to be true and to differ[67] from a proposition or axiom only in that a definition is concerned solely with the essences of things or of their affections, whereas an axiom or a proposition extends more widely, to eternal truths as well—or else it explains a thing as we conceive it or can conceive it—and then it also differs from an axiom and a proposition in that it need only be con-
35   ceived, without any further condition, and need not, like an axiom [NS: and a proposition] be conceived as true.[68] So a bad definition is
IV/44   one that is not conceived.

To help you understand this, I shall take Borelli's example. Suppose
20   someone says "Let two straight lines enclosing a space be called figurals." If he understands by a straight line what everyone understands by a curved line, then his definition will be a good one, provided he does not subsequently understand [by it] squares and other figures.
25   (By that definition would be understood figures like ⓐ and the like.)

[66] A has: "a thing outside us," and then the words "outside us" are crossed out and replaced by "whose essence." (There are a number of such indications of revision during the course of composition in this ms.)

[67] Following AHW, I read *differre* for *differt* here and *hoc* for *hae* in l.32.

[68] In the NS this paragraph, down to here, comes earlier, replacing the passage from IV/42/29 to IV/43/18.

But if by a straight line he understands what we commonly understand, the thing is completely inconceivable. So it is no definition. Borelli, whose opinion you are inclined to embrace, confuses all these things completely.

I shall add another example, the one you bring up at the end. If I say that each substance has only one attribute, that is only a proposition and requires a demonstration. But if I say "By substance I understand what consists of one attribute only," that will be a good definition, provided that afterwards beings consisting of more attributes than one are designated by a word other than substance.

But you say that I have not demonstrated that a substance (*or* being) can have more attributes than one. Perhaps you have neglected to pay attention to my demonstrations. For I have used two: *first*, that nothing is more evident to us than that we conceive each being under some attribute, and that the more reality or being a being has the more attributes must be attributed to it; so a being absolutely infinite must be defined, etc.; *second*, and the one I judge best, is that the more attributes I attribute to a being the more I am compelled to attribute existence to it; that is, the more I conceive it as true. It would be quite the contrary if I had feigned a Chimaera, or something like that.

As for your contention that you do not conceive thought except in relation to ideas (because if you remove the ideas, you destroy thought), I believe this happens to you because when you, as a thinking thing, do this, you put aside all your thoughts and concepts. So it is no wonder that when you have done so, nothing afterwards remains for you to think of. But as far as the thing itself is concerned, I think I have demonstrated clearly and evidently enough that the intellect, though infinite, pertains to *natura naturata*, not to *natura naturans*.

However, I still do not see what this has to do with understanding D3, nor why it should be a problem. Unless I am mistaken, the definition I gave you was as follows:

By substance I understand what is in itself and is conceived through itself, i.e., whose concept does not involve the concept of another thing. I understand the same by attribute, except that it is called attribute in relation to the intellect, which attributes such and such a definite nature to substance.

I say that this definition explains clearly enough what I wish to understand by substance, *or* attribute.

Nevertheless, you want me to explain by an example how one and the same thing can be designated by two names (though this is not necessary at all). Not to seem niggardly, I offer two: (i) I say that by

Israel I understand the third patriarch; I understand the same by Jacob, the name which was given him because he had seized his broth-
30 er's heel; (ii) by flat I mean what reflects all rays of light without any
change; I understand the same by white, except that it is called white
in relation to a man looking at the flat [surface].

IV/46/15 [NS: With this I consider that I have answered your questions.
Meanwhile, I shall wait to hear your judgment. If there is still something which you find to be not well or clearly enough demonstrated,
don't hesitate to point it out to me, etc.]

[Rijnsburg, March 1663]

IV/47

LETTER 10

B.D.S. TO THE VERY LEARNED YOUNG MAN,
SIMON DE VRIES

5 Cherished Friend,

You ask me whether we need experience to know whether the Definition of any Attribute [NS: any thing] is true. To this I reply that
we need experience only for those things which cannot be inferred
from the definition of the thing, as, for example, the existence of Modes
(for this cannot be inferred from the definition of the thing); but not
10 for those things whose existence is not distinguished from their essence, and therefore is inferred from their definition. Indeed no experience will ever be able to teach us this, for experience does not
teach any essences of things. The most it can do is to determine our
15 mind to think only of certain essences of things. So since the existence
of the attributes does not differ from their essence, we will not be able
to grasp it by any experience.

You ask, next, whether also things or their affections are eternal
truths. I say certainly. If you should ask why I do not call them
20 eternal truths, I answer, to distinguish them (as everyone generally
does)[69] from those which do not explain any thing or affection of a
thing, as, for example, *nothing comes from nothing*. These and similar
Propositions, I say, are called absolutely eternal truths, by which they
want to signify nothing but that such [propositions] have no place
outside the mind, etc.

[Rijnsburg, March (?) 1663]

[69] The reference seems to be to Descartes' *Principles of Philosophy* I, 49. Cf. Gueroult
1, 1:86.

LETTER 11

HENRY OLDENBURG TO THE DISTINGUISHED B.D.S.

Reply to Letter 6

Most Excellent Sir, Dearest Friend,

I could offer many excuses for my long silence to you, but I shall limit myself to two chief ones: the ill health of the very noble Boyle and the pressures of my own affairs. The former prevented Boyle from answering your Comments on Niter more quickly; the latter have kept me so busy for many months that I have hardly been my own master, so that I could not discharge the duty I confess I owe you. I rejoice that, for a while at least, both obstacles have been removed, so that I may renew my correspondence with so great a Friend. Indeed, I do this now with the greatest pleasure, and am resolved (God willing) that henceforth our communication by letters shall not be interrupted for so long.

But before I deal with the matters that particularly concern you and me, let me take care of what is due to you in Mr. Boyle's name. He has received, with his usual kindness, the notes you assembled on that little Chemical-Physical Treatise of his and he thanks you very much for your Examination of it. Meanwhile, he wants me to advise you that his purpose was not so much to show that this is a truly Philosophic and perfect Analysis of Niter, as to explain that the common doctrine of Substantial Forms and Qualities, received in the Schools, rests on a weak foundation, and that what they call the specific differences of things can be referred to the size, motion, rest, and position of the parts.

Having noted this first, our Author then says that his Experiment with Niter was more than enough to show that the whole body of Niter was resolved by Chemical Analysis into parts differing from one another and from the whole, but that afterwards it was reunited out of the same parts and so reconstituted that only a little of the original weight was lacking. He adds that he has shown *that* the thing occurs thus, but has not discussed *how* it occurs, which seems to be the subject of your conjecture. Nor has he determined anything about it, since that was beyond his purpose.

Meanwhile, he thinks what you suppose about *how* it occurs—that you consider the fixed salt of Niter to be its impurities, and other such things—is said gratuitously and without proof. With regard to your assertion that these impurities, *or* this fixed salt, has passages hollowed out according to the measure of the particles of Niter, our Author

notes that just as Spirit of Niter combines with its own fixed salt to
constitute Niter, so it combines with salt of potash to produce Niter.[70]
From this he thinks it clear that similar pores are found in bodies of
that kind, from which Nitrous Spirits are not given off.

Nor does our Author see that the necessity of that very fine matter
which you also allege is proved from any phenomena. Rather it is
assumed simply from the Hypothesis that a vacuum is impossible.

The Author denies that he is affected by what you say about the
causes of the differences in taste between Niter and Spirit of Niter.
As for what you relate about the inflammability of Niter and the non-
inflammability of Spirit of Niter, he says it supposes Descartes' doctrine of Fire,[71] with which he declares he is not yet satisfied.

With regard to the Experiments by which you think to confirm your
explanation of the Phenomenon [of reconstitution of Niter] the Author
replies that (i) materially, indeed, Spirit of Niter is Niter, but not
formally, since they differ very greatly in their qualities and powers,
viz. in taste, smell, volatility, power of dissolving metals, of changing
the colors of vegetables, etc.; (ii) as for your contention that certain
particles which have been carried upwards join to form Crystals of
Niter—he maintains that this happens because the nitrous parts are
driven off together with the Spirit of Niter by the fire, just as happens
with soot; (iii) to what you maintain about the effect of purification
the Author replies that in that purification the Niter is for the most
part freed of a certain salt, which looks like common salt, but that
rising up and forming little icicles is common to it and other salts, and
depends on the pressure of the air and on certain other causes, which
must be discussed elsewhere, since it does not contribute to the present Problem; (iv) what you say about your third Experiment, the Author says happens also with certain other salts; he maintains that when
the paper is actually alight, it causes the rigid and solid particles which
composed the salt to vibrate and in this way produces a sparkling.

Regarding the fifth section, where you think that the Noble Author
is criticizing Descartes, he believes that you are the one at fault here.
He says he had not referred to Descartes at all, but to Gassendi and
others who ascribe a Cylindrical shape to the particles of Niter, when
it is really prismatic. Nor was he was speaking about any shapes other
than those which are visible.

To your comments on §§ 13-18 he replies only that he had written

---

[70] If the usual identification of Boyle's substances is correct (see above, n. 15), then
Boyle's fixed salt of niter *was* potash (potassium carbonate), though he seems not to have
realized it.
[71] See the *Principles of Philosophy*, IV, 80-132.

these things primarily to show the usefulness of Chemistry for confirming the Mechanical principles of Philosophy, and that he had not found these matters treated so clearly by others. Our Boyle is one of those whose trust in reason is not so great that they have no need for the Phenomena to agree with their reason.

Furthermore, he says that there is a great difference between readily available experiments (where we do not know what Nature contributes and what things intervene) and experiments where it is definitely known what things are brought in.[72] Wood is a much more composite body than the subject our Author deals with. And in the boiling of ordinary water an external fire is added, which is not used in producing our sound. The reason why green plants change into so many and such different colors is still being sought, but that [in some substances] it arises from a change of parts is indicated by this experiment, in which it is evident that the color has been changed by adding Spirit of Niter. Finally, he says that Niter has neither a foul nor a pleasant smell, but it acquires a foul smell simply by being decomposed, and loses it when it is reconstituted.

To what you note about § 25 (for he says that none of the other things touch him) he replies that he has used the Epicurean principles which hold that motion is innate in the particles because it was necessary for him to use some Hypothesis to explain the Phenomenon. Nevertheless, he does not on that account make it his own, but uses it to sustain his own opinion against the Chemists and the Schools, by showing that at least the matter can be well explained on the Hypothesis mentioned.

To what you add in the same place about the inability of pure water to dissolve the fixed parts, our Boyle replies that the Chemists generally observe and assert that pure water dissolves alkaline salts more quickly than others.

There has not yet been time for the Author to consider your comments on Fluidity and Solidity. I am sending you these things I have recorded, so that I may no longer be deprived of correspondence with you. But I ask you most strenuously to take in good part what I pass on to you in this disjointed and mutilated way, and to attribute its defects to my haste rather than to the renowned Boyle's ability. I have put it together more from friendly talk on the subject with him than from any written out and Methodical reply from him. So doubtless many things he said have escaped me—things perhaps more substan-

---

[72] Boyle here shows the sophistication about experiments that made him a great scientist. But it is ironic that he did not in fact grasp the contribution made to his experiment by the coal he used to kindle the niter. See above, n. 15.

tial and more neatly put than those I have here recalled. I therefore
take all the blame on myself, and absolve the Author entirely.

I proceed now to the things which are between you and me. And
right away may I ask whether you have finished that little work of
20   such great importance, in which you treat of the origin of things, their
dependence on the first cause, and the Emendation of our intellect. I
certainly believe, Dearest Sir, that to Men who are really learned and
wise nothing will be more pleasant or more welcome than a Treatise
of that kind. A Man of your talent and understanding must look to
25   that rather than to the things that please the Theologians of our age
and fashion. For they have an eye more to their own interest than to
truth. So by the compact of friendship between us, and by every duty
of increasing and spreading [knowledge of] the truth, I adjure you not
to begrudge or deny us your writings on these matters. Nevertheless,
30   if something of greater importance than I foresee prevents you from
publishing that work, I beg you to be good enough to share a summary of it with me in your letters. If you do me this service, you will
find me a grateful friend.

The Very Learned Boyle is soon to publish other works,[73] which I
shall send you by way of compensation. To these I shall also add
35   others which will describe the whole Purpose of our Royal Society,
IV/52   to whose Council I belong (with twenty others) and whose secretary
I am (with one other).

Lack of time prevents me from digressing now about other matters.
Promising you all the loyalty that can come from an honest heart, and
all the readiness to do you services that my weakness is capable of, I
5   am, Most Excellent Sir,

Yours entirely,
London, 3 April 1663   Henry Oldenburg

Letter 12

B.d.S. to the Very Learned and Expert
Lodewijk Meyer, Doctor of Medicine
and Philosophy

[NS: On the Nature of the Infinite]

Special Friend,

15   I have received your two Letters, one dated 11 January [1663] and
delivered to me by our friend N. N., the other dated 26 March [1663]

---

[73] In 1663 Boyle published his *Considerations touching the usefulness of experimental natural
philosophy* and *Experiments and considerations upon colours.*

and sent to me from Leiden by some friend, I know not whom. Both were very welcome to me, especially when I learned from them that everything is quite well with you and that you often think of me. For your kindness to me and for the honor you have always been willing to do me, I return, as I am bound to do, very hearty thanks. At the same time I ask you to believe that I am no less devoted to you, as I shall always try to show at every opportunity, as far my slight abilities allow. To begin [showing my devotion], I shall take some pains to answer the question you put to me in your Letters. You ask me to tell you what I have discovered about the Infinite, which I shall most gladly do.

[53]   Everyone has always found the problem of the Infinite very difficult, indeed insoluble. This is because they have not distinguished between what is infinite as a consequence of its own nature, *or* by the force of its definition, and what has no bounds, not indeed by the force of its essence, but by the force of its cause. And also because they have not distinguished between what is called infinite because it has no limits and that whose parts we cannot explain or equate [NS: determine or express] with any number, though we know its maximum and minimum [NS, LC: *or* it is determined]. Finally, they have not distinguished between what we can only understand, but not imagine, and what we can also imagine.

If they had attended to these distinctions, I maintain that they would never have been overwhelmed by such a great crowd of difficulties. For then they would have understood clearly what kind of Infinite cannot be divided into any parts, *or* cannot have any parts, and what kind of Infinite can, on the other hand, be divided into parts without contradiction. They would also have understood what kind of Infinite can be conceived to be greater than another Infinite, without any contradiction,[74] and what kind cannot be so conceived. This will be clear from what I am about to say. But first let me briefly explain these four [concepts]: Substance, Mode, Eternity, and Duration.

[54]   The points I want you to consider about Substance are: (i) that existence pertains to its essence, i.e., that from its essence and definition alone it follows that it exists (if my memory does not deceive me, I have previously demonstrated this to you in conversation, without the aid of any other Propositions); (ii), which follows from (i), that

---

[74] In E IP15S, where Spinoza is discussing the arguments of those opponents who contend that extended substance cannot be infinite, he lets pass, without challenging it, their assumption that it is absurd to suppose that one infinite can be greater than another. This tempts us to think that Spinoza accepts that part of the opponent's argument. This passage warns us not to argue from silence in that way.

Substance is not one of many, but that there exists only one of the same nature; and finally, (iii) that every Substance can be understood only as infinite.

I call the Affections of Substance Modes. Their definition, insofar as it is not the very definition of Substance, cannot involve any existence. So even though they exist, we can conceive them as not existing. From this it follows that when we attend only to the essence of modes, and not to the order of the whole of Nature [LC: matter], we cannot infer from the fact that they exist now that they will or will not exist later, or that they have or have not existed earlier. From this it is clear that we conceive the existence of Substance to be entirely different from the existence of Modes.

The difference between Eternity and Duration arises from this. For it is only of Modes that we can explain the existence by Duration. But [we can explain the existence] of Substance by Eterntiy, i.e., the infinite enjoyment of existing, *or* (in bad Latin) of being.

From all this it is clear that when we attend only to the essence of Modes (as very often happens), and not to the order of Nature, we can determine as we please their existence and Duration, conceive it as greater or less, and divide it into parts—without thereby destroying in any way the concept we have of them. But since we can conceive Eternity and Substance only as infinite, they can undergo none of these without our destroying at the same time the concept we have of them.

Hence they talk utter nonsense, not to say madness, who hold that Extended Substance is put together of parts, *or* bodies, really distinct from one another. This is just the same as if someone should try, merely by adding and accumulating many circles, to put together a square or a triangle or something else completely different in its essence. So that whole array of arguments by which Philosophers ordinarily labor to show that Extended Substance is finite falls of its own weight. For they all suppose that corporeal Substance is composed of parts. Similarly there are others, who, after they have persuaded themselves that a line is composed of points, have been able to find many arguments by which they would show that a line is not divisible to infinity.

But if you ask why we are so inclined, by a natural impulse, to divide extended substance, I reply that we conceive quantity in two ways: either abstractly, *or* superficially, as we have it in the imagination with the aid of the senses; or as substance, which is done by the intellect alone. So if we attend to quantity as it is in the imagination, which is what we do most often and most easily, we find it to be divisible, finite, composed of parts, and one of many. But if we attend to it as it is in the intellect, and perceive the thing as it is in itself, which is very difficult, then we find it to be infinite, indivisible and unique, as [NS: if I am not mistaken] I have already demonstrated sufficiently to you before now.

Next, from the fact that when we conceive Quantity abstracted from Substance and separate Duration from the way it flows from eternal things, we can determine them as we please, there arise Time and Measure—Time to determine Duration and Measure to determine Quantity in such a way that, so far as possible, we imagine them easily. Again, from the fact that we separate the Affections of Substance from Substance itself and reduce them to classes so that as far as possible we imagine them easily, arises Number, by which we determine [these affections of substance].

You can see clearly from what I have said that Measure, Time, and Number are nothing but Modes of thinking, or rather, of imagining. So it is no wonder that all those who have striven to understand the course of Nature by such Notions—which in addition have been badly understood—have so marvelously entangled themselves that in the end they have not been able to untangle themselves without breaking through everything and admitting even the most absurd absurdities. For since there are many things which we cannot at all grasp by the imagination, but only by the intellect (such as Substance, Eternity, etc.), if someone strives to explain such things by Notions of this kind, which are only aids of the Imagination, he will accomplish nothing more than if he takes pains to go mad with his imagination.

And if the Modes of Substance themselves are confused with Beings of reason of this kind, *or aids of the imagination*, they too can never be rightly understood. For when we do this, we separate them from Substance, and from the way they flow from eternity, without which, however, they cannot be rightly understood.

To see this still more clearly, take this example. When someone has conceived Duration abstractly, and by confusing it with Time begun to divide it into parts, he will never be able to understand, for example, how an hour can pass. For if an hour is to pass, it will be necessary for half of it to pass first, and then half of the remainder, and then half of the remainder of this. So if you subtract half from the remainder in this way, to infinity,[75] you will never reach the end of the hour. Hence many, who have not been accustomed to distinguish Beings of reason from real beings, have dared to hold that Duration

---

[75] NS: *onbepaaldelijk/indeterminaté*, LC: *indefinité*, indefinitely.

is composed of moments. In their desire to avoid Charybdis, they have run into Scylla [NS: or gone from bad to worse]. For composing Duration of moments is the same as composing Number merely by adding noughts.

From what has just been said it is sufficiently evident that neither Number, nor Measure, nor Time (since they are only aids of the imagination) can be infinite. For otherwise Number would not be number, nor Measure measure, nor Time time. Hence it is clear why many who confused these three with the things themselves, because they were ignorant of the true nature of things, denied an actual Infinite. But let the Mathematicians judge how wretchedly these people have reasoned—such Arguments have never deterred the Mathematicians from the things they perceived clearly and distinctly. For not only have they discovered many things which cannot be explained by any Number—which makes quite plain the inability of numbers to determine all things—they also know many things which cannot be equated with any number, but exceed every number that can be given. Still they do not infer that such things exceed every number because of the multiplicity of their parts, but because the nature of the thing cannot admit number without a manifest contradiction.

For example, all the inequalities of the space between two circles, A and B,[76] and all the variations which the matter moving in it must undergo, exceed every number. That is not inferred from the excesive size of the intervening space. For however small a portion of it we take, the 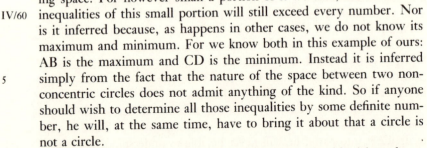 inequalities of this small portion will still exceed every number. Nor is it inferred because, as happens in other cases, we do not know its maximum and minimum. For we know both in this example of ours: AB is the maximum and CD is the minimum. Instead it is inferred simply from the fact that the nature of the space between two non-concentric circles does not admit anything of the kind. So if anyone should wish to determine all those inequalities by some definite number, he will, at the same time, have to bring it about that a circle is not a circle.

Similarly, to return to our theme, if someone should wish to determine all the motions of matter there have been up to now by reducing them and their Duration to a definite number and time, he will certainly be striving for nothing but depriving corporeal Substance (which we can not conceive except as existing) of its Affections and bringing it about that it does not have the nature which it has. I could dem-

[76] Following AHW who here follow the NS more closely than either of the Latin texts. The example recurs in *Descartes' Principles* (I/198-199), and is discussed by Tschirnhaus and Spinoza in Letters 80 and 81 and by Gueroult in Grene, 203-209.

onstrate this clearly here—as well as many other things I have touched on in this Letter—but I judge it to be unnecessary.

From everything now said, it is clear that some things are infinite by their nature and cannot in any way be conceived to be finite, that others [are infinite] by the force of the cause in which they inhere, though when they are conceived abstractly they can be divided into parts and regarded as finite, and that others, finally, are called infinite, or if you prefer, indefinite, because they cannot be equated with any number, though they can be conceived to be greater or lesser. For if things cannot be equated with a number, it does not follow that they must be equal. This is manifest enough from the example adduced, and from many others.

I have, finally, set out briefly the causes of the errors and confusions which have arisen concerning the Problem of the Infinite, and unless I am mistaken, I have so explained all of them that I do not think any Problem about the Infinite remains which I have not touched on here or which cannot be solved very easily from what I have said. So I don't regard it as worthwhile to detain you any longer with these matters.

But in passing I should like to note here that the more recent Peripatetics have, as I think, misunderstood the demonstration by which the Ancients tried to prove God's existence. For as I find it in a certain Jew, called Rab Chasdai,[77] it runs as follows: if there is an infinite regress of causes, then all things that are will also have been caused; but it does not pertain to anything which has been caused, to exist necessarily by the force of its own nature; therefore, there is nothing in Nature to whose essence it pertains to exist necessarily; but the latter is absurd; therefore, the former is also. Hence the force of this argument does not lie in the impossibility of there being an actual infinite or an infinite regress of causes, but only in the supposition that things which do not exist necessarily by their own nature are not determined to exist by a thing which does necessarily exist by its own nature [NS: and which is a cause, not something caused.]

Because time forces me to hasten, I would now pass to your second Letter, but I will be able to answer the things contained in it more conveniently when you are good enough to visit me. So I ask you, if you can, to come as soon as possible. For the time of my moving approaches rapidly. That is all. Farewell, and remember me, who am, etc.

[Rijnsburg, 20 April 1663]

[77] Chasdai Crescas (c.1340-c.1410), a Spanish critic of the Aristotelian Maimonides. See Wolfson 3.

LETTER 12A[78]

B.D.S. TO LODEWIJK MEYER

Dearest Friend,

Yesterday I received your very welcome letter in which you ask (i) whether in part I, chapter 2 of the appendix you have correctly indicated all the propositions, etc., which are cited there from part I of the principles? (ii) whether what I say in part II, that the son of god is the father himself, should not be deleted? and finally (iii) whether my statement that I do not know what the theologians understand by the word personality should not be changed?

To this I reply, (1), that everything you have indicated in chapter 2 of the appendix you have indicated correctly. But in chapter 1 of the appendix, page 1, you have indicated P4S, and nevertheless I would prefer you to have indicated P15S, where I explicitly discuss all modes of thinking.[79] Next, on page 2 of the same chapter, you have written in the margin these words *why negations are not ideas*. In place of this word *negations* should be put *beings of reason*, for I am speaking of the being of reason in general, and saying that it is not an idea.

(2) I think what I have said, that the son of god is the father himself, follows very clearly from this axiom, things which agree in a third thing agree with one another. But because this matter is of no importance to me, if you think this can offend certain theologians, do as it seems best to you.[80]

(3) and finally, what theologians understand by the term personality escapes me, but not what philologists understand by that word. Meanwhile, because the manuscript is with you, you can decide these things better. If it seems to you that they should be changed, do so as you please.[81]

Farewell, Special friend, and remember me, who am

Your most devoted,

Voorburg, 26 July 1663   B. de Spinoza

---

[78] This most recent addition to the Spinozistic corpus was discovered in 1974 and published in the following year. See Offenburg. That edition contains a reproduction of the original letter, written in Latin in Spinoza's own hand, a transcription, a modern Dutch translation, and a commentary. It is interesting, among other things, as illustrating that Meyer's role in the publication of *Descartes' Principles of Philosophy* and the *Metaphysical Thoughts* did not consist simply in writing a preface and improving Spinoza's Latin style.

[79] This reference was not corrected in the text, but was corrected in the errata of the first edition. Similarly with the marginal correction.

[80] See the note at I/271/30.

[81] See the note at I/264/14.

LETTER 13
B.D.S. TO THE VERY NOBLE
AND LEARNED HENRY OLDENBURG
REPLY TO LETTER 11

Most Noble Sir,

At last I have received the letter I had long desired from you, and also have the opportunity to answer it. But before I undertake that, let me say briefly what has prevented me from writing back to you before now.

When I moved my furniture here in April, I went to Amsterdam, where some of my friends asked me to make them a copy of a Treatise containing a concise account of the Second Part of Descartes' *Principles*, demonstrated in the Geometric style, and of the main points treated in Metaphysics. Previously I had dictated this to a certain young man to whom I did not want to teach my own opinions openly.[82] Then they asked me to prepare the first Part also by the same Method, as soon as I could. Not to disappoint my friends, I immediately undertook to do this and finished it in two weeks. I delivered it to my friends, who in the end asked me to let them publish the whole work. They easily won my agreement, on the condition that one of them, in my presence, would provide it with a more elegant style and add a short Preface warning Readers that I did not acknowledge all the opinions contained in this treatise as my own, *since I had written many things in it which were the very opposite of what I held,*[d] and illustrating this by one or two examples. One of my friends, to whose care the publishing of this little book has been entrusted, has promised to do all this and that is why I stayed for a while in Amsterdam. Since I returned to this village where I am now living, I have hardly been my own master because of the friends who have been kind enough to visit me.

Now at last, dearest Friend, I have some time to myself to communicate these things to you, and at the same time tell you why I am letting this Treatise see the light of day: perhaps it will induce some who hold high positions in my country to want to see other things I have written, which I acknowledge as my own, so that they would see to it that I can publish without any danger of inconvenience. If

---

[d] [NS only] In the letter I sent I omitted this and everything else printed in italics. [This presumably refers to the italicized passages at 63/24-25, 67/4-5, 67/25-26, but not to that at 66/9.]

[82] Casearius, on whom see IV/42/19ff.

this happens, I have no doubt that I will publish certain things immediately. If not, I shall be silent rather than force my opinions on
10 men against the will of my country and make them hostile to me. I
beg you, then, honored Friend, not to mind waiting for that. Then
you will have either the printed Treatise itself, or a summary of it, as
you request. If, meanwhile, you wish to have one or two copies of
the work now in the press, I shall comply with your wish as soon as
15 I learn of it and of a way I can conveniently send the work to you.

I turn now to your Letter, and thank you and the Very Noble
Boyle, as I must, for the kindness and generosity you have clearly
shown me. For the many affairs of great importance in which you are
20 involved could not make you forget your Friend; indeed you kindly
promise to take every care that our correspondence will henceforth
not be interrupted for so long. I am also quite grateful to the Very
Learned Mr. Boyle for being so good as to reply to my Notes, even
if he does so in passing, and as if doing something else. For my part,
25 I confess that they are not so important that that Most Learned
Gentleman should waste in replying to them the time he can spend
on higher thoughts.

I did not think, indeed I could not have persuaded myself, that this
Most Learned Gentleman had no other object in his Treatise on Niter
30 than to show the weak foundations of that childish and frivolous doctrine of Substantial Forms and Qualities. I had persuaded myself,
rather, that the Distinguished Gentleman wanted to explain the nature
of Niter to us, that it is a heterogeneous body, consisting of fixed and
volatile parts. So I wanted by my explanation to show—and I think I
did show more than adequately—that we can very easily explain all
35 the Phenomena of Niter, or at least all the Phenomena that I know,
IV/65 even if we don't grant that Niter is a heterogeneous body, but regard
it as homogeneous. Hence it was not my task to show that the fixed
salt is an impurity in Niter, but only to suppose it, to see how the
Distinguished Gentleman could show me that that salt is not an im-
5 purity but is absolutely necessary to constitute the essence of Niter,
without which Niter could not be conceived. For as I say, that is what
I thought the Distinguished Gentleman wanted to show.

Regarding my statement that the fixed salt has passages hollowed
out according to the measure of the particles of Niter, I did not require
10 this to explain the reconstitution of Niter. For from what I have said—
that the reconstitution of niter consists only in the solidification of its
spirit—it is clear that every calx whose passages are too narrow to be
able to contain the particles of Niter and whose walls are weak is
suitable for checking the motion of the particles of Niter, and so, on

my Hypothesis, for reconstituting the Niter itself. Hence it is no wonder that there are other salts, say, of tartar and of potash, with whose
aid Niter can be reconstituted.

But I only said that the fixed salt of Niter has passages hollowed
out according to the measure of the particles of Niter to give a reason
why the fixed salt of Niter is more suitable for reconstituting Niter so
that it lacks little of its former weight. Indeed, from the fact that other
salts are found by which Niter can be reconstituted I thought to show
that calx of Niter is not required to constitute the essence of Niter, if
the Distinguished Gentleman had not said that there is no salt more
universal than Niter, so that it could have been concealed in tartar
and potash.[83]

When I said further that the particles of Niter in the larger passages
are surrounded by a finer matter, I inferred that from the impossibility
of a vacuum, as the Distinguished Gentleman notes. But I do not
know why he calls the impossibility of a vacuum a Hypothesis, since
it follows very clearly from the fact that nothing has no properties.
And I am surprised that the Distinguished Gentleman doubts this,
since he seems to maintain that there are no real accidents. I ask whether
there would not be a real accident if there were Quantity without
Substance?

As for the causes of the difference in taste between Niter and spirit
of Niter, I was obliged to propose them to show how I could very
easily explain its Phenomena from the only difference I was willing to
allow between Niter and spirit of Niter, without taking any account
of the fixed salt.

What I said about the inflammability of Niter and the noninflam-
mability of Spirit of Niter supposes only that to arouse a flame in any
body requires a matter which separates and sets in motion the parts
of the body. I think reason and daily experience adequately teach both
these lessons.

I pass now to the experiments I offered to confirm my explanation—
not absolutely, but as I expressly said [at IV/17/13] *to some extent*. So
against the first experiment I offered the Distinguished Gentleman
brings nothing except what I myself very expressly noted. But of the
other things I attempted, to remove the suspicion the Distinguished
Gentleman joins me in noting, he says nothing at all.

What he offers next, against the second experiment—that by purification Niter is for the most part freed of a certain salt resembling

---

[83] NS: "and that he might therefore say that it could be concealed in tartar and
potash."

ordinary salt—he only says, but does not prove. For as I expressly said, I did not offer these experiments that they might confirm absolutely what I said. It was only that these experiments, which I had said and showed to agree with reason, seemed to confirm those things to some extent. As for his contention that the rising to form little icicles is common to this and other salts, I do not know what this matters. For I grant that other salts also have impurities and are made more volatile if they are freed of them.

I also do not see that anything touching me is brought against the third experiment.

In the fifth section I thought the noble author was criticizing Descartes, which he has certainly done elsewhere, by the liberty of Philosophizing granted to anyone, without any harm to the Nobility of either. Perhaps others who have read both Descartes' *Principles* and Mr. Boyle's writings will think the same thing I did, unless they are expressly warned.[84]

Nor do I yet see that the Distinguished Gentleman explains his opinion very clearly. For he does not yet say whether Niter would cease to be Niter if its visible icicles (of which alone he says he is speaking) were rubbed until they were changed into parallelipeds or some other shape.

But I leave these matters and pass to what the Distinguished Gentleman [NS: answers to the things I noted on] §§ 13 to 18. I willingly confess that this reconstitution of Niter is indeed an excellent experiment for investigating the very nature of Niter when we first know the Mechanical principles of Philosophy and that all the variations of bodies happen according to the Laws of Mechanics. But I deny that these things follow more clearly and evidently from the experiment just mentioned than from many other readily available experiments, *from which, however, this is not proven*.

The Distinguished Gentleman says he has not found these things to be so clearly taught and discussed in others. Perhaps he has something which I cannot see to allege against the reasonings of Bacon and Descartes by which he thinks he can refute them. I do not recount their reasonings here, because I do not think the Distinguished Gentleman is unfamiliar with them. But I will say this: they too wanted the Phenomena to agree with their reason; if they nevertheless erred in some things, they were men, and I think nothing human was alien to them.[85]

[84] NS: ". . . which perhaps others, who had read Descartes' *Principles* and to whom I have also shown his letter, after I received it, have thought."
[85] An allusion to the well-known line from Terence's *Heautontimorumenos*, 77.

He says, further, that there is a great difference between those experiments (the readily available and doubtful ones I have adduced), where we don't know what Nature contributes and what things intervene, and those regarding which it is established with certainty what things are contributed. But I do not yet see that the Distinguished Gentleman has explained to us the Nature of the things used in this matter, the calx of Niter and its Spirit. So these two things seem no less obscure than those I have adduced, ordinary lime and water [NS: from whose combination heat arises]. As for wood, I grant that this body is more composite than Niter. But so long as I do not know the Nature of either, and the way heat arises in each, what, I ask, does it matter?

Again, I do not know why the Distinguished Gentleman is bold enough to maintain that he knows what Nature contributes in the matter we are speaking of. *By what reasoning, I ask, will he be able to show us that that heat has not arisen from some very fine matter?* Was it perhaps because so little of the original weight was lacking? But even if none was lacking, one could, in my judgment at least, infer nothing. For we see how easily a thing can be imbued with a color from a very small quantity of matter, and not on that account become sensibly heavier or lighter. So it is not without reason that I can doubt whether perhaps certain things have concurred which could not have been observed by any sense perception—especially so long as we do not know how all those Variations which the Distinguished Gentleman observed in experimenting could have come about from the bodies mentioned. Indeed I regard it as certain that the heat and the effervescence the Distinguished Gentleman recounts have arisen from foreign matter.

Next, I think I can infer that movement of the air is the cause of sound more easily from the boiling of water (not to mention its agitation) than I can from this experiment, where the nature of things that concur is completely unknown and where heat is also observed, without our knowing how or from what causes it has arisen.

Finally, there are many things which give off no smell at all, though if their parts are stirred up and become warm, they will give off a smell immediately, and if they are cooled again, they have no smell again (at least as far as human sense perception is concerned). Amber is an example, and there are others, though I don't know whether they too are more composite than Niter.

The things I noted regarding § 24 show that spirit of Niter is not a pure Spirit, but abounds in calx of Niter and other things. So I doubt whether the Distinguished Gentleman has been able to observe carefully enough what he says he detected with the aid of the scales, that the weight of the Spirit of Niter which he added almost equaled the weight of what had been lost during the detonation.

Finally, although as far as the eye is concerned pure water can dissolve alkaline salts more quickly [than other salts], nevertheless, since it is a more homogeneous body than air is, it cannot, as air can, have so many kinds of particles which can penetrate through the pores of every kind of calx. So since water consists mostly of certain particles of one kind, which can dissolve a calx up to a certain limit, but air does not, it follows that water will dissolve the calx to that limit far more quickly than air does. But since air, on the other hand, consists of both thicker and much finer particles, and particles of every kind, which can penetrate in many ways through far narrower pores than those the particles of water can penetrate, it follows that though air cannot dissolve calx of Niter so quickly as water does (because air cannot consist of so many particles of each kind), nevertheless it can dissolve it far better and more finely, and make it weaker and hence better able to halt the motion of the particles of the Spirit of Niter. For so far the experiments do not force me to recognize any other difference between Spirit of Niter and Niter itself than that the particles of Niter are at rest, whereas those of the Spirit of Niter, having been very much stirred up, are in motion among themselves. So there is the same difference between Niter and its Spirit as there is between ice and water.

I dare not detain you any longer on these matters. I fear I have been too prolix already, though I have tried to be as brief as I could. If I have, nonetheless, been burdensome, I beg you to overlook it and to take in good part what is said freely and sincerely by a Friend. For I judged it unwise, now that I write to you again, to be completely silent on these matters. Still, to praise to you what was less pleasing would be sheer flattery. Nothing, I think, is more destructive and harmful in Friendships than that. I resolved, therefore, to explain my mind as frankly as possible, and thought nothing would be more welcome to Philosophers than that.

Meanwhile, if it seems more advisable to you to consign these thoughts to the fire rather than pass them on to the Very Learned Mr. Boyle, do as you please, provided you believe me to be very devoted and loving to you and to the Very Noble Boyle. I am sorry my slender means prevent me from showing this otherwise than by words; however, etc.

[Voorburg, 17/27 July 1663]

LETTER 14
HENRY OLDENBURG TO THE DISTINGUISHED B.D.S

Distinguished Sir, Most Cherished Friend,

I find much happiness in the renewal of our correspondence; know, then, with what gladness I received your letter to me of 17/27 July, especially since it both gives evidence of your well-being and makes me more certain of your friendship towards me. If that were not enough, you report that you have entrusted to the press the first and second part of *Descartes' Principles*, demonstrated in the Geometric style, and very generously offer me one or two copies of it. I accept the gift most willingly and ask you, if you will, to send me the Treatise now in the press via Mr. Pieter Serrarius, of Amsterdam.[86] I have instructed him to receive such a package and forward it to me by a friend traveling in this direction.

For the rest, permit me to tell you that I bear impatiently your continued suppression of those writings you acknowledge as your own, especially in a Republic so free that there you are permitted to think what you will and say what you think. I wish you would break through those barriers, particularly since you can conceal your name, and so put yourself beyond any chance of danger.

The noble Boyle has gone away. As soon as he is back in the City, I shall communicate to him that part of your very learned Letter which concerns him and write you his opinion of your views as soon as I have obtained it. I think you have already seen his *Sceptical Chymist*, which for some time now has been published in Latin and distributed abroad.[87] It contains many Chemico-Physical Paradoxes and subjects the so-called Hypostatic principles of the Spagyrists to a severe examination.

Recently he has published another booklet, which perhaps has not yet reached your Booksellers. So I send it to you enclosed with this letter, and ask you, cordially, to take this little gift in good part. As you will see, this booklet contains a defense of the Elastic power of air against a certain Francis Linus who tries to explain the phenomena Mr. Boyle recounts in his *New Physicomechanical Experiments*, by a certain little thread which escapes the intellect as much as it does all sense

---

[86] Pieter Serrarius was a Belgian who lived in Amsterdam and traveled frequently to London. A collegiant, who expected the second coming of Christ, he was to publish in 1667 a reply to Meyer's *Philosophy the Interpreter of Holy Scripture*.

[87] Boyle's *Sceptical Chymist* was first published in English in 1661 and in Latin in 1662. For an account of Boyle's critique of Spagyrist theories of matter, see Hall 2.

perception.[88] Read this booklet, weigh it, and let me know your opin-
30   ion of it.

Our Royal Society is vigorously pursuing its goal with all its power, keeping itself within the bounds of experiments and observations, and avoiding all the intricacies of Disputations.

Recently an excellent experiment has been performed which greatly distresses those who affirm
35   a vacuum, but very much pleases those who deny
IV/71 one. It proceeds as follows. Let a glass Flask A,
filled to the top with water, be inverted with its
mouth in a glass jar, B, containing water, and placed
in the Receiver of Mr. Boyle's New Air Pump.
5   Then let the air be pumped out of the Receiver.
Bubbles will be seen to rise in great abundance
from the water into the Flask, A, and to expel all
the water from there into the jar B, below the sur-
10   face of the water contained there. Let the two ves-
sels be left in this condition for a day or two, the
air being evacuated from the Receiver repeatedly
by frequent pumpings. Then let them be taken out
15   of the Receiver, let A be filled with this water from

which the air has been removed and inverted again in B, and let each vessel be enclosed again in the Receiver. When the Receiver has been
20   emptied again by the required pumping, perhaps a little bubble will be seen to rise from the neck of A. As it comes up at the top and expands with the continued pumping, it will expel all the water from the Flask, as before. Then the Flask is to be taken out of the Receiver
25   again, filled to the top with water from which air has been removed, inverted as before, and put in the Receiver. The air is then to be duly evacuated from the Receiver, and if this has been done properly and completely, the water will remain suspended in the Flask in such a way that it does not descend at all.

In this experiment the cause which, according to Boyle, sustains the
30   water in the Torricellian experiment (the air lying on the water in the jar, B) seems to be completely removed, but the water in the Flask does not descend.[89]

[88] For an account of Boyle's experiments and Linus' ad hoc counterhypothesis, see Conant.
[89] As the Halls note, this experiment is one of several 'anomalous suspensions' much discussed at the time (Huygens had performed a similar experiment). Most of these perplexing experiments depended on the then unknown properties of surface tension and capillarity. They constitute a salutary reminder that the controversy between those who denied and those who affirmed the possibility of a vacuum was not a straightfor-

I had meant to add more here, but friends and business call me away. [NS: I shall only mention this: if you would like to send me the things you are having printed, please address your letters and packages in the following way, etc.]

I cannot conclude this letter without urging you once again to publish your own meditations. I shall never stop exhorting you until you grant my request. Meanwhile, if you were willing to share with me some of the main results, how much would I love you! how closely would I judge myself to be bound to you! May everything prosper with you, and may you continue to love me as you do,

Your Most Devoted and Friendly,

London, 31 July[/10 August] 1663   Henry Oldenburg

Letter 15

B. de Spinoza offers cordial greetings
to Mr. Lodewijk Meyer

Dearest Friend,

The preface you sent me by our friend de Vries I return to you by him. As you will see, I have noted a few things in the margin, but a few still remain, which I thought it more advisable to tell you of by letter.

First, when you advise the reader on p. 4 of the occasion on which I composed the first part, I wish you would also advise, either there or elsewhere, as you please, that I composed it within two weeks. For with this warning no one will think I have set these things out so clearly that they could not be explained more clearly, and therefore they will not be held up by a word or two if here and there they happen to find something obscure.

Second, I wish you would point out to them that I demonstrate many things in a way different from the way Descartes demonstrated them, not to correct Descartes, but to retain my own order better and not increase the number of axioms so much, and that for the same reason I demonstrate many things Descartes asserts without any demonstration, and have had to add others Descartes omitted.

Finally, dearest friend, I ask you most urgently to omit—to delete entirely—what you have written at the end against that petty man.[90] Many reasons incline me to ask this of you, but I shall mention only

---

ward conflict between those who relied on a priori argument and those who relied on experiment.

[90] So far no one has been able to suggest a target of Meyer's attack.

IV/73 one. I would wish everyone to be convinced without difficulty that these things are published for the benefit of all men, that in publishing this little book you are possessed only by a desire to spread the truth, that you are taking the greatest care to make this little work pleasing
5 to everyone, that you are generously and with good will inviting men to study the true philosophy, and are aiming at the advantage of all. Everyone will easily believe this when he sees that no one is injured and that nothing is put forward that could be offensive to anyone. If afterwards, however, that man wants to show his malice, then you
10 will be able to portray his life and character, and not without approval. So I ask you to let yourself be persuaded to wait till then, and not to mind doing so.

Believe that I am most devoted to you,

Yours with all good will,

Voorburg, 3 August 1663   B. de Spinoza

15   Our friend de Vries had promised to take this with him, but because he does not know when he will return to you, I am sending it by someone else. With it I enclose part of IIP27S, as it begins on p. 75, for you to give to the printer, so that it can be set again. What I
20 am sending you here must be printed again, and 14 or 15 lines must be added. These can easily be inserted.

LETTER 16

HENRY OLDENBURG TO THE DISTINGUISHED B.D.S.

Most Excellent Sir, and Cherished Friend,

Hardly three or four days have passed since I sent you a Letter by the ordinary post. In that letter I mentioned a certain booklet written by Mr. Boyle, which I wanted to send you. I did not then hope to
IV/74 find so quickly a friend who would take it. Since then someone has appeared more quickly than I had expected. So receive, now, what I could not send then, together with the courteous greetings of Mr. Boyle, who has now returned to the City from the country.
5   He asks you to consult the Preface to his Experiments on Niter, to understand the true goal he had set himself in that Work: to show that the teachings of a more solid Philosophy, which is now appearing again,[91] can be illustrated by clear experiments, and that these [exper-

---

[91] Boyle welcomed the revival of Epicureanism by writers like Gassendi. But notwithstanding certain differences between the atomists and the Cartesians, their disagreement "about the notion of body in general, and consequently about the possibility of a true vacuum, as also about the origin of motion, the indefinite divisibleness of matter, and some other points of less importance," he considered that because they

iments] can be explained very well without the forms, qualities and
futile elements of the Schools. But he did not at all take it on himself
to teach the nature of Niter nor even to reject what anyone can maintain about the homogeneity of matter and about the differences of
bodies arising only from motion, shape, etc. He says he had only
wished to show that the various textures of bodies produce their various differences, that from these proceed quite different effects, and
that so long as the resolution to prime matter has not been accomplished, Philosophers and others rightly infer some heterogeneity from
this. I should not think that there is any fundamental difference between you and Mr. Boyle here.

But as for your contention that every calx whose passages are too
narrow to be able to contain the particles, and whose walls are weak,
is suitable to check the motion of the particles of Niter, and so to
reconstitute the Niter, Boyle replies that if spirit of Niter is mixed
with other calxes, it will nevertheless not compose true Niter with
them.

With regard to the Reasoning you use to overthrow a vacuum, Boyle
says he is familiar with it and has seen it before, but is not at all
satisfied with it. He says there will be an opportunity to speak about
this elsewhere.

He has requested me to ask you whether you can supply him with
an example in which two odorous bodies combined into one compose
a completely odorless body, as Niter is. He says that the parts of Niter
are such that its Spirit gives off a very foul smell and that fixed Niter
is not without any smell.

He asks next that you consider carefully whether you have made a
proper comparison between ice and water, on the one hand, and Niter
and its Spirit, on the other, since all the ice is resolved only into water,
and the odorless ice, when it has become water again, remains odorless. But spirit of Niter and the fixed salt of Niter are found to have
different qualities, as the printed Treatise abundantly teaches.

I gathered these and similar things from conversation about this
with our Illustrious Author, though I am certain that with my weak
memory I recollect them to his disadvantage rather than to his credit.
Since the two of you are in agreement on the main point, I do not

---

agreed "in deducing all the phenomena of nature from matter and local motion . . .
they might be thought to agree in the main, and their hypotheses might, by a person
of reconciling disposition, be looked on as . . . one philosophy, which because it expli-
cates things by corpuscles, or minute bodies, may be called corpuscular" (Preface to the
Essay on Nitre (Saltpetre), pp. 3-4, in Boyle 2. Hence, Oldenburg's stress below on
the fundamental agreement between Boyle and Spinoza.

want to enlarge further on this. I would rather encourage you both to unite your abilities in cultivating eagerly a genuine and solid Philosophy. May I advise you especially to continue to establish the principles of things by the acuteness of your Mathematical understanding, as I constantly urge my Noble friend Boyle to confirm and illustrate this philosophy by experiments and observations, repeatedly and accurately made.

You see, Dearest Friend, what I am striving for. I know that in this Kingdom our native Philosophers will not shirk their experimental duty. I am no less convinced that you in your Country will zealously do your part, however much the mob of Philosophers or Theologians may growl, whatever accusations they may make. Since in past letters I have already urged you to this many times, I restrain myself now, so as not to become tedious.

I do at least ask this much in addition: please be so kind as to send me as quickly as possible, by Mr. Serrarius, whatever you have already had printed, whether it is your commentary on Descartes or what you have produced from the resources of your own intellect. You will bind me that much more closely to you, and will understand that at every opportunity, I am

Your most devoted,
Henry Oldenburg

London, 4 August 1663

The Expositor of Descartes

EDITORIAL PREFACE

THE WORKS presented in this section have suffered unwarranted neglect at the hands of some Spinoza scholars. Wolfson, for example, dismisses them by saying that "If these two works are not to be altogether disregarded by the student of the *Ethics*, they may be considered only as introductory to it." (1, 1:32) The first he characterizes as a summary of the first two parts of Descartes' *Principles*, together with a fragment of the third; the second, as a "summary of certain philosophic views of scholastic origin." But this is most misleading. Though there is much in both works that Spinoza would not accept, in neither work is Spinoza *merely* summarizing anyone's views.

In *Descartes' Principles*, as Meyer remarks in his preface, Spinoza frequently offers proofs different from Descartes'—or offers proofs where Descartes had indulged in mere assertion. He makes use of other Cartesian works—notably the *Correspondence*, the *Dioptrique*, and the *Meditations* (including the *Replies* to objections)—to help interpret Descartes where Descartes is obscure or too brief. And sometimes he criticizes Descartes, though rarely does he do so openly.

The most important acknowledged points of difference are probably those Meyer notes (at Spinoza's request) at the end of his preface (I/132): Spinoza does not think the will is distinct from the intellect, or endowed with the liberty Descartes ascribes to it; he does not think that the mind is a substance; and he does not think there is anything that surpasses our understanding, provided that we seek the truth in a way different from Descartes'. (See also the interesting Scholium to IP7.)

But there is a good deal of thinly veiled criticism in Spinoza's exposition of the *Principles*. In the Introduction, for example, Spinoza comments that Descartes' reply (or what he takes to be Descartes' reply) to the charge of reasoning in a circle "will not satisfy some people." He does not say who will be dissatisfied, or why, but immediately goes on to offer an answer of his own. In so doing, he subtly invites the reader to put his own critical faculties to work. Similar instances occur at IP8D, IP9S, IP15S, IP21Note, IIP2CS, and in the *Metaphysical Thoughts* at I/239, 255, 274, 276, and 277-281.

And quite apart from exposition, interpretation, and criticism of Descartes, there is much, particularly in the *Metaphysical Thoughts*, which is simply independent of Descartes. According to Meyer's Preface (I/131) it was Spinoza's intention—both in his exposition of the *Principles* and in the Appendix—to set out Descartes' opinions, and their demonstrations, as they would be found in his writings *or as they ought to be deduced validly from the fundamental principles of Descartes' philosophy.* But it would take a very generous interpretation of this last clause to justify everything that appears here. Spinoza's discussions of Zeno's paradoxes (IIP6S), or of truth (I/246-247), or of good and evil (I/247-248), go well beyond Descartes' sketchy reflections on those topics. The reader who is familiar with Spinoza's mature philosophy will find many passages which foreshadow the *Ethics* or the *Theological-Political Treatise* (e.g., at I/240-243, 250-252, 264-265, 266). And it is all the more interesting to see these anticipations developed as deductions from Cartesian principles.

The frequency with which Spinoza's own opinions emerge in the *Metaphysical Thoughts* gave rise, at the turn of the century, to an interesting debate among German scholars about the relation of that work to *Descartes' Principles*. Kuno Fischer (I:285) saw the *Metaphysical Thoughts* as having been written against Descartes, for the purpose of clarifying and emphasizing the disagreements which Meyer had alluded to in his Preface.[1] Freudenthal, however, showed (i) that this work was certainly written before the first part of the *Principles*, and quite probably before any of the *Principles* (though, of course, it would have been revised somewhat before being printed), and (ii) that it was directed more against the scholastics than against Descartes.

And indeed, if Spinoza did write these works in the order suggested, there would be a certain logic to the presentation. The *Metaphysical Thoughts* begin with the definition of being and its division into those beings whose essence does, and those whose essence does not, involve existence, the latter being subdivided into substances and modes. There follows a discussion of various putative beings, which do not in fact qualify as beings (time, truth, etc.). The second part deals principally with the nature of the one infinite substance, God, and his relation to the world, but closes with a brief discussion of the nature of finite thinking substances. And the second part of the *Principles* completes the discussion by describing the most general features of finite corporeal substances. The work would thus be an introduction to modern philosophy, written from a broadly Cartesian point of view, for someone who already had some familiarity with the scholastic philosophy still dominant in Dutch universities.[2] It would then be the

---

[1] Fischer modified his position in later editions of his history but not sufficiently to escape further criticism from Freudenthal (see Freudenthal 4, 304ff.). See also Lewkowitz.

[2] On the introduction of Cartesian philosophy into the Dutch universities, see Bouillier, Thijssen-Schoute 2 and 3, and Dibon.

first part of the *Principles*, not the "appendix," which would be the afterthought.

Freudenthal (in Freudenthal 3) provided a great service to students of Spinoza by identifying some of the medieval and late scholastic authors who formed the background for the *Metaphysical Thoughts*: Aquinas and Maimonides, of course, were part of that background, but of the better-known scholastics Suarez was probably the most important. Also important were two now obscure Dutch writers, Burgersdijk and Heereboord.

Burgersdijk was a professor of philosophy at the University of Leiden from 1620 to 1635, and the author of a number of manuals which had a considerable influence on the teaching of philosophy in Holland. Dibon (277) comments that while, for Burgersdijk, Aristotle remained the master, "true fidelity to the spirit of Aristotle required each philosopher to adapt the traditional philosophy to the requirements of his own reflection, taking account of what preceding thinkers had contributed." Burgersdijk's openness to change clearly inspired his pupil Heereboord to be receptive to the new philosophy.

Heereboord was a professor of logic and ethics at Leiden from 1641 until his death in 1661. Like many Dutch philosophers of his time, he hoped to achieve a synthesis of the new philosophy and the old. By comparison with a Descartes or a Spinoza, he appears a reactionary figure. But he was, in fact, one of the reasons why the University of Leiden became known as a center of Dutch Cartesianism (see Bouillier, I, 270-271). Thijssen-Schoute (2, 96-105) reports that he embarrassed Descartes by his excessive praise of him.

Since there is some reason to think that Spinoza may have studied at the University of Leiden after his excommunication (see Revah 1, 32, 36), and since Heereboord may have been one of his teachers, the man and his work deserve to be less obscure. Spinoza frequently seems to have Heereboord in mind when he criticizes unnamed opponents, and Heereboord shares with Aristotle the distinction of being one of only two opponents to be both named and quoted. Nor does Spinoza refer to Heereboord only to disagree with him. Sometimes he adopts from Heereboord doctrines and distinctions which are of great importance in his mature philosophy (at I/240-241, for example). Whether or not Heereboord was formally his teacher, Spinoza learned from him.

So there is far more in these works than mere summary of Cartesian and scholastic doctrine. They are of the greatest importance for the study of Spinoza's development. But they also hold much that is of interest to the student of Descartes. No less a scholar than Gilson has

223

commended Spinoza as "an incomparable commentator" (Gilson 2, 68ff.) To say that Spinoza is always faithful to Descartes' thought would be to claim too much, even if we considered only those passages where Spinoza intends merely to expound Descartes' view.[3] But even the errors of a Spinoza are interesting.

Finally, a word about Balling's Dutch translation of this work. This appeared in 1664, the year after the first Latin edition. It is more than a translation, though something rather less than the second edition Meyer hoped for (cf. his Preface I/131). A number of new passages have been added, which were not consistently taken into account by any of Spinoza's editors before Gebhardt. There seems to be no reasonable ground for doubting that these additions were made by Spinoza.

"EP" designates the reading of the first edition, "B" a reading taken from Balling's translation.

PARTS I AND II OF DESCARTES'
PRINCIPLES OF PHILOSOPHY

Demonstrated in the geometric manner,

By Benedictus de Spinoza, of Amsterdam.

To which are added his

Metaphysical Thoughts

In which are briefly explained the more difficult problems which arise both in the general and in the special part of Metaphysics.

Amsterdam,
Johannes Riewerts,
1663

To the Honest Reader Lodewijk Meyer Presents His Greetings

I/127   Everyone who wishes to be wiser than is common among men agrees that the best and surest Method of seeking and teaching the truth in

---

[3] On this theme, see Gueroult's criticism of Spinoza's interpretation of the *cogito* (in Gueroult 2, 64-78) and Curley 7. In the latter article I take up what still seems to me a great paradox about Spinoza's geometric exposition of Descartes, viz. (if we are to believe the *Conversation with Burman*) Spinoza is undertaking in this work to put into synthetic geometric form a work which according to Descartes was already in that form. This would imply that Spinoza misunderstood Descartes' distinction between analysis and synthesis. See Cottingham, 12, and, for criticism of my interpretation, Garber and Cohen, 141-147.

the Sciences is that of the Mathematicians, who demonstrate their Conclusions from Definitions, Postulates, and Axioms. Indeed, this opinion is rightly held. For since a certain and firm knowledge of anything unknown can only be derived from things known certainly beforehand, these things must be laid down at the start, as a stable foundation on which to build the whole edifice of human knowledge; otherwise it will soon collapse of its own accord, or be destroyed by the slightest blow.

No one who has even the most cursory acquaintance with the noble discipline of Mathematics will be able to doubt that the things which are there called Definitions, Postulates, and Axioms, are of that kind. For Definitions are nothing but the clearest explanations of the words and terms by which the things to be discussed are designated; and Postulates and Axioms, or common Notions of the mind, are Propositions so clear and evident that no one can deny his assent to them, provided only that he has rightly understood the terms themselves.

But in spite of this you will find hardly any sciences, other than Mathematics, treated by this Method. Instead the whole matter is arranged and executed by another, almost totally different, Method, in which Definitions and Divisions are constantly linked with one another, and problems and explanations are mixed in here and there. For almost everyone has been convinced, and many who have applied themselves to founding and writing about the sciences still are convinced, that the Mathematical Method is peculiar to the Mathematical disciplines, and does not apply to any of the rest.

The result is that none of the things they produce are demonstrated by conclusive reasonings, but that they try to construct only probable arguments, foisting on the public a huge heap of huge books, in which you will find nothing that is firm and certain. All of their works are full of strife and disagreement, and whatever is corroborated by some slight, insufficient reasoning is soon rebutted by another, and destroyed and torn apart by the same weapons. So the mind, which has longed for an unshakable truth, and thought to find a quiet harbor, where, after a safe and happy journey, it could at last reach the desired haven of knowledge, finds itself tossed about on a violent sea of opinions, surrounded everywhere by storms of dispute, hurled up and dragged down again endlessly by waves of uncertainty, without any hope of ever emerging from them.

Nevertheless, there have been some who have thought differently, and, taking pity on the wretched plight of Philosophy, have departed from the common way of treating the sciences, and entered on an arduous new path, one beset indeed with many difficulties, that they might leave to posterity the other parts of Philosophy, beyond Math-

225

ematics, demonstrated by the mathematical Method and with mathematical certainty. Some of these have put into mathematical order and communicated to the world of letters the Philosophy already received and customarily taught in the school; others have done this with a new philosophy, discovered through their own struggle.

25 And though many undertook that task for a long time without success, at last there appeared that brightest star of our age, René Descartes. By this new Method he first brought out of darkness and into the light, whatever in Mathematics had been inaccessible to the ancients, and whatever could be desired in addition to that by his own Contemporaries. Then he uncovered firm foundations for Philosophy, foundations on which a great many truths can be built, with Mathematical order and certainty, as he himself really demonstrated, and as manifests itself more clearly than the Noon light to anyone who diligently studies those writings of his, which can never sufficiently be praised.

Although the Philosophical writings of this most Noble and Incomparable Man contain a Mathematical manner and order of demonstra-
I/129 tion, nevertheless they are not written in the style commonly used in Euclid's *Elements* and in the works of other Geometricians, the style in which the Definitions, Postulates, and Axioms are set out first, followed by the Propositions and their Demonstrations. Instead they are written in a very different manner, which he calls the true and
5 best way of teaching, the Analytic. For at the end of his *Reply to the Second Objections*, he recognizes two ways of demonstrating things conclusively, by Analysis, "which shows the true way by which the thing was discovered, methodically, and as it were a priori,"[1] and by Synthesis, "which uses a long series of definitions, postulates, axioms,
10 theorems, and problems, so that if a reader denies one of the consequences, the presentation shows him that it is contained immediately in the antecedents, and so forces his assent from him, no matter how stubborn and contrary he may be."

But though a certainty which is placed beyond any risk of doubt is found in each way of demonstrating, they are not equally useful and
15 convenient for everyone. For since most men are completely unskilled in the Mathematical sciences, and quite ignorant, both of the Synthetic Method, in which they have been written, and of the Analytic, by which they have been discovered, they can neither follow for themselves, nor present to others, the things which are treated, and dem-

---

[1] AT VII, 155 (cf. AT IX, 121). See the Glossary-Index on *a priori*. Descartes' contrast between the analytic and the synthetic method has been the subject of much discussion by Cartesian scholars. See, for example, Gueroult 3, 1: 22-28; Gouhier, 104-112; Alquié, 2: 581-585; Curley 7; and Garber and Cohen.

onstrated conclusively, in these books. That is why many who have been led, either by a blind impulse, or by the authority of someone else, to enlist as followers of Descartes, have only impressed his opinions and doctrines on their memory; when the subject comes up, they know only how to chatter and babble, but not how to demonstrate anything, as was, and still is, the custom among those who are attached to Aristotle's philosophy.

To bring these people some assistance, I have often wished that someone who was skilled both in the Analytic and the Synthetic order, and possessed a thorough knowledge of Descartes' writings and Philosophy, would be willing to take on this work, to render in the Synthetic order what Descartes wrote in the Analytic, and to demonstrate it in the manner familiar to the geometricians. Indeed, I myself, though quite unequal to so great a task, and fully conscious of my weakness, frequently thought of doing this, and even began it. But other occupations distracted me so often that I was prevented from completing it.

Therefore I was very pleased to learn from our Author that he had dictated, to a certain pupil of his, whom he was teaching the Cartesian Philosophy, the whole Second Part of the *Principles*, and part of the Third, demonstrated in that Geometric manner, along with some of the principal and more difficult questions which are disputed in Metaphysics, and had not yet been resolved by Descartes,[2] and that in response to the entreaties and demands of his friends, he had agreed that, once he corrected and added to them, these writings might be published. So I too commended this project to him, and at the same time gladly offered my help in publishing, if he should require it.

Moreover, I advised him—indeed entreated him—to render also the first part of the *Principles* in a like order, and set it before what he had already written, so that by having been arranged in this manner from the beginning, the matter could be better understood and more pleasing. When he saw the soundness of this argument, he did not wish to deny both the requests of a friend and the utility of the reader. And he entrusted to my care the whole business of printing and publishing, since he lives in the country, far from the city, and so could not be present.[3]

This, then, honest Reader, is what we give you in this little book:

[2] This statement is particularly important for what it tells us about the status of the work now known as the *Cogitata Metaphysica*, viz. that it was originally composed as a part of the project of teaching Casearius the Cartesian philosophy. But since Meyer describes it as treating of questions which had not been resolved by Descartes, we are warned not to expect straightforward exposition, but a treatment of traditional problems in a Cartesian spirit.

[3] In spite of what Meyer says here, it does appear from Spinoza's correspondence

227

15   the first and second parts of Descartes' *Principles of Philosophy*, together with a fragment of the third, to which we have attached, as an Appendix, our Author's *Metaphysical Thoughts*. But when we say, and when the title of the book promises, the first part of the *Principles*, we do not mean that everything Descartes says there is demonstrated here
20   in Geometric order, but only that the main matters which concern Metaphysics, and were treated by Descartes in his *Meditations*, have been taken from there (leaving aside whatever is a matter of Logic, or is recounted only historically).[4]

    To do this more easily, our Author has carried over, word for word,
25   almost all the things which Descartes put in Geometrical order at the end of his *Reply to the Second Objections*—beginning with all of Descartes' Definitions and inserting Descartes' Propositions among his own, but not annexing the Axioms to the Definitions without interruption. He has placed the Axioms taken from Descartes after the fourth Proposition and altered their order, so they could be demonstrated more
30   easily. He has also omitted certain things which he did not require.

    Our Author realizes that these Axioms could be demonstrated as Theorems (as Descartes himself says in the 7th postulate), and that they would be more elegantly treated as Propositions. And though we
I/131   asked him to do this, more important business in which he was involved allowed him only two weeks in which to complete this work. So he was unable to satisfy his desire and ours. Annexing at least a brief explanation, which can take the place of a proof, he has put off
5   a fuller explanation, complete in every respect, till another time. Perhaps, after this printing is exhausted, a new one will be prepared. If so, we shall also try to get him to enrich it by completing the Third Part, On the visible World (we have added here only a fragment of that Part, since our Author ended the instruction of his pupil at that point, and we did not wish to deprive the reader of it, however little
10   it was). For this to be done properly, it will be necessary to introduce certain Propositions concerning the nature and properties of Fluids in the Second Part. I shall do my best to see that our Author accomplishes this at that time.

    Our Author quite frequently departs from Descartes, not only in

---

that he had the opportunity to see page proofs of this work, and to make corrections and additions. See Gebhardt I/610, and Letter 12a.

   [4] The matters of logic are presumably those questions about universals and about the various kinds of distinction which Descartes takes up in *Principles* I, 58-62. The things recounted only historically are perhaps things like Descartes' explanation of why people have failed to distinguish mind from body properly (I, 12), why they fail to see the force of the ontological argument (I, 16), and various other explanations of error which Descartes offers (e.g., I, 71-74). Cf. Spinoza's note c at I/159/4.

the arrangement and explanation of the Axioms, but also in the demonstration of the Propositions themselves, and the rest of the Conclusions; he often uses a Proof very different from Descartes'. Let no one take this to mean that he wished to correct that most distinguished Man in these matters; it was done only so as to better retain the order he had already taken up, and not to increase unduly the number of Axioms. For the same reason he has also been forced to demonstrate quite a number of things which Descartes asserted without any demonstration, and to add others which he completely omitted.

Nevertheless, I should like it to be particularly noted that in all these writings—not only in the first and second parts of the *Principles*, and in the fragment of the third part, but also in his *Metaphysical Thoughts*—our Author has only set out the opinions of Descartes and their demonstrations, insofar as these are found in his writings, or are such as ought to be deduced validly from the foundations he laid. For since he had promised to teach his pupil Descartes' philosophy, he considered himself obliged not to depart a hair's breadth from Descartes' opinion,[5] nor to dictate to him anything that either would not correspond to his doctrines or would be contrary to them. So let no one think that he is teaching here either his own opinions, or only those which he approves of. Though he judges that some of the doctrines are true, and admits that he has added some of his own, nevertheless there are many that he rejects as false, and concerning which he holds a quite different opinion.

An example of this—to mention only one of many—is what is said concerning the will in the *Principles* IP15S and in the Appendix, II, 12, although it seems to be proved with sufficient diligence and preparation. For he does not think that the will is distinct from the Intellect, much less endowed with such freedom. Indeed in asserting these things—as is evident from the *Discourse on Method*, Part IV, the Second Meditation, and other places—Descartes only assumes, but does not prove that the human mind is a substance thinking absolutely. Though our Author admits, of course, that there is a thinking substance in nature, he nevertheless denies that it constitutes the essence of the human Mind; instead he believes that just as Extension is determined by no limits, so also Thought is determined by no limits. Therefore, just as the human Body is not extension absolutely, but only an extension determined in a certain way according to the laws of extended nature by motion and rest, so also the human Mind, *or* Soul, is not thought absolutely, but only a thought determined in a certain way

---

[5] Reading (with Akkerman and Van Vloten and Land): *sententiâ*.

according to the laws of thinking nature by ideas, a thought which, one infers, must exist when the human body begins to exist. From this definition, he thinks, it is not difficult to demonstrate that the Will is not distinct from the intellect, much less endowed with that liberty which Descartes ascribes to it; that that faculty of affirming and denying is a mere fiction; that affirming and denying are nothing but ideas; and that the rest of the faculties, like Intellect, Desire, etc., must be numbered among the fictions, or at least among those notions which men have formed because they conceive things abstractly, like humanity, stone-hood, and other things of that kind.

Again we must not fail to note that what is found in some places— viz. *that this or that surpasses the human understanding*—must be taken in the same sense, i.e., as said only on behalf of Descartes. For it must not be thought that our Author offers this as his own opinion. He judges that all those things, and even many others more sublime and subtle, can not only be conceived clearly and distinctly, but also explained very satisfactorily—provided only that the human Intellect is guided in the search for truth and knowledge of things along a different path from that which Descartes opened up and made smooth. The foundations of the sciences brought to light by Descartes, and the things he built on them, do not suffice to disentangle and solve all the very difficult problems that occur in Metaphysics. Different foundations are required, if we wish our intellect to rise to that pinnacle of knowledge.

Finally—to put an end to prefacing—we wish our Readers to know that all the things treated here are published with no purpose except that of searching out and propagating the truth, and rousing men to strive for a true and genuine Philosophy; so in order that men may be able to harvest that rich fruit which we sincerely desire each of them to have, we warn them, before they set themselves to read this book, to insert in their place certain things which have been omitted, and to correct accurately the Typographical errors which have crept in. For some of them could be an obstacle to a correct perception of the Author's intention, and the force of the Demonstration, as anyone who inspects them will easily see.

The Principles of Philosophy
Demonstrated In the Geometric Manner

Part I

PROLEGOMENON

Before we come to the Propositions themselves and their Demonstrations, it seems desirable to explain concisely why Descartes doubted everything, how he brought to light solid foundations for the sciences, and finally, by what means he freed himself from all doubts. We would have reduced even all these things to Mathematical order, if we had not judged that the prolixity required by such a presentation would prevent them from being understood as they ought to be. For they should all be seen in a single act of contemplation, as in a picture.

Descartes, then, in order to proceed as cautiously as possible in the investigation of things, attempted

(1) to lay aside all prejudices,
(2) to discover the foundations on which all things
ought to be built,
(3) to uncover the cause of error,
(4) to understand all things clearly and distinctly.

That he might be able to attain the first, second and third of these, he sought to call all things into doubt, not as a Skeptic would, who has no other end than doubting, but to free his mind from all prejudices, so that in the end he might discover firm and unshakable foundations of the sciences. In this way, if there were any such foundations, they could not escape him. For the true principles of the sciences must be so clear and certain that they need no proof, that they are beyond all risk of doubt, and that nothing can be demonstrated without them. These he found, after a long period of doubting. And after he had discovered these principles, it was not difficult for him to distinguish the true from the false, to uncover the cause of error, and so to put himself on guard against assuming something false and doubtful as true and certain.[1]

To obtain the fourth and last, i.e., that he might understand all things clearly and distinctly, his chief rule was to enumerate and examine separately all the simple ideas of which all the rest of his ideas

---

[1] B: "something false as true or something doubtful as certain."

were compounded. For when he could perceive the simple ideas clearly and distinctly, he would undoubtedly understand, with the same clarity and distinctness, all the rest, which have been constructed from those simple ideas.

15   With this as preface, we shall explain briefly how he called all things into doubt, discovered the true principles of the Sciences, and extricated himself from the difficulties of his doubts.

Doubt concerning all things

First, then, he considered all those things which he had received from the senses, viz. the heavens, the earth, and the like, and even his

20   own body. All these he had till then thought to exist in nature. And he came to doubt their certainty because he had realized that the senses sometimes deceived him, because in dreams he had often persuaded himself of the existence outside himself of many things, concerning which he afterwards discovered himself to have been deluded, and

25   finally, because he had heard others claim, even while awake, that they felt pain in limbs which they had long lacked.[2] So it was not without reason that he was able to doubt the existence of his own body.

From all this he was able to conclude truly that the senses are not that most firm foundation on which every science should be built (for

30   they can be called into doubt), but that certainty depends on other principles, of which we are more certain.

To investigate such principles then, he considered second all universals, such as corporeal nature in general, and its extension, figure,

I/143   quantity, and also all Mathematical truths. And though these seemed more certain to him than all those he had derived from the senses, nevertheless he discovered a reason for doubting them: for others had erred even about these matters, and most important, deeply rooted in

5   his mind was an old opinion, according to which there is a God who can do all things and by whom he was created such as he was. Perhaps this God had made him so that he would be deceived even about those things that seemed clearest to him. And this is the way he called all things in doubt.

The discovery of the foundation of the whole science

To discover the true principles of the sciences, he asked next whether

10   he had called into doubt everything which could fall under his thought. His purpose was to examine whether, perhaps, there was not some-

---

[2] The first two grounds are offered both in the First Meditation and in the *Principles* I, 4. The third is not offered until the Sixth Meditation.

thing remaining which he had not yet doubted. And if he did, by doubting in this way, discover something which could be called into doubt by none of the preceding reasons, nor by any other, he rightly judged that he should set it up as the foundation on which he might build all his knowledge.

And though it seemed that he had already doubted everything—for he had doubted both the things he had derived from the senses and those he had perceived by the intellect alone—nevertheless, there was something remaining which should be examined, viz. he himself who was doubting in this way. Not himself insofar as he consisted of a head, hands, and the other members of the body, since he had doubted these things, but only himself insofar as he was doubting, thinking, etc.

And when he considered it accurately, he discovered that he could not doubt it for any of the previously mentioned reasons. For whether he thinks waking or sleeping, he still thinks and is. And though others, and even he himself had erred concerning other things, since they were erring, they were. Nor could he feign any author of his nature so cunning[3] as to deceive him about this. For it will have to be conceded that he exists, so long as it is supposed that he is deceived. Finally, whatever other reason for doubting might be thought up, none could be mentioned that did not at the same time make him most certain of his existence. Indeed, the more reasons for doubting are brought up, the more arguments are brought up that convince him of his existence. So in whatever direction he turns in order to doubt, he is forced to break out with these words: *I doubt, I think, therefore I am.*

Hence, because he had laid bare this truth, he had at the same time also discovered the foundation of all the sciences, and also the measure and rule of all other truths: *Whatever is perceived as clearly and distinctly as that is true.*[4]

That there can be no other foundation of the sciences than this, is more than sufficiently evident from the preceding. For we can call all the rest in doubt with no difficulty, but we can not doubt this in any way.

But what we must note here, above all else concerning this foundation, is that this formula, *I doubt, I think, therefore I am,* is not a syllogism in which the major premise is omitted. For if it were a

---

[3] B: "powerful."

[4] In deriving this rule directly from the *cogito*, Spinoza follows the *Discourse* rather than the *Meditations* or *Principles*. But Descartes' version of the rule there is slightly different: "Whatever things we conceive very clearly and very distinctly are true" (AT VI, 32).

syllogism, the premises would have to be clearer and better known
than the conclusion itself, *therefore I am.* And so, *I am* would not be
the first foundation of all knowledge. Moreover, it would not be a
certain conclusion. For its truth would depend on universal premises
which the Author had previously put in doubt. So *I think, therefore I
am* is a single proposition which is equivalent to this, *I am thinking.*[5]

Next, to avoid confusion in what follows, we need to know what
we are (for this is a matter that ought to be perceived clearly and
distinctly). Once we do understand it clearly and distinctly, we shall
not confuse our essence with others. To deduce it from the above, our
Author proceeded as follows.

He recalled all the thoughts which he had formerly had of himself,
e.g., that his soul was something tenuous, like wind, or fire, or air,
infused throughout the grosser parts of his body, that the body was
better known to him than the soul, and that he perceived it more
clearly and distinctly. And he observed that all these thoughts are
clearly incompatible with those which up to this point he had understood. For he was able to doubt his own body, but not his own essence, insofar as he was thinking. Moreover, he perceived these thoughts
neither clearly nor distinctly, and consequently, according to the rule
of his method, he was obliged to reject them as false.

Since he could not understand such things to pertain to himself,
insofar as he was known to himself up to this point, he proceeded to
inquire further what did properly pertain to his essence, which he
could not put in doubt, and on account of which he was forced to
infer his existence. But these were such things as: *that he wished to take
care lest he be deceived; that he desired to know many things; that he doubted
all things which he could not understand; that so far he affirmed only one
thing; that he denied all the rest and rejected them as false; that he imagined
many things, even though unwilling to; and finally that he perceived many
things as if coming from the senses.* Since he could infer his existence from
each of these things equally clearly, and could count none of them
among those which he had called in doubt, and finally, since they can
all be conceived under the same attribute, it followed that all these
things were true and pertained to his nature. So when he said, *I think,*
all these modes of thinking were understood, viz. *doubting, understanding, affirming, denying, willing, not willing, imagining,* and *sensing.*[6]

---

[5] Spinoza's account of the *cogito* follows very closely that which Descartes gives in his
Reply to the Second Objections (AT VII: 140-141). I have argued for a different reading of
Descartes, stressing *Principles* I, 7 and 10, in Curley 8, chap. 4.

[6] Spinoza's list of the various modes of thought is drawn from the Second Meditation,
AT VII, 28.

But here the chief things to be noted—because they will be very useful later, when we deal with the distinction between mind and body—are (i) that these modes of thinking are understood clearly and distinctly without the rest, concerning which there is still doubt, and (ii) that the clear and distinct concept we have of them is made obscure and confused, if we wish to ascribe to them any things concerning which we still doubt.

Liberation from all doubts

Finally, in order to become certain of the things he had called in doubt and to remove all doubt, Descartes proceeded to inquire into the nature of the most perfect Being, and whether such a Being existed. For when he discovers that there is a most perfect being, by whose power all things are produced and conserved, and with whose nature being a deceiver is incompatible, then that reason for doubting which he had because he was ignorant of his cause will be removed. He will know that a God who is supremely good and veracious did not give him the faculty of distinguishing the true from the false so that he might be deceived. Hence neither Mathematical truths nor any of those that seem most evident to him can be at all suspected.

Next, to remove the remaining causes of doubt, he went on to ask how it happens that we sometimes err. When he discovered that this occurs because we use our free will to assent even to things we have perceived only confusedly, he was able to conclude immediately that he could guard against error in the future, provided he gave his assent only to things perceived clearly and distinctly. Each of us can easily accomplish this by himself, since each has the power of restraining the will, and so of bringing it about that it is contained within the limits of the intellect.

But because we have absorbed at an early age many prejudices from which we are not easily freed, he went on next to enumerate and examine separately all the simple notions and ideas of which all our thoughts are composed, so that we might be freed from our prejudices, and accept nothing but what we perceive clearly and distinctly. For if he could take note of what was clear and what obscure in each, he would easily be able to distinguish the clear from the obscure and to form clear and distinct thoughts. In this way he would discover easily the real distinction between the soul and the body, what was clear and what obscure in the things we have derived from the senses, and finally, how a dream differs from waking states. Once this was done, he could no longer doubt his waking states nor be deceived by the senses. So he freed himself from all the doubts recounted above.

But before we finish, it seems we must satisfy those who make the following objection. Since God's existence does not become known to us through itself, we seem unable to be ever certain of anything; nor will we ever be able to come to know God's existence. For we have said that everything is uncertain so long as we are ignorant of our origin, and from uncertain premises, nothing certain can be inferred.

To remove this difficulty, Descartes makes the following reply.[7] From the fact that we do not yet know whether the author of our origin has perhaps created us so that we are deceived even in those things that appear most evident to us, we cannot in any way doubt the things that we understand clearly and distinctly either through themselves or through reasoning (so long, at any rate, as we attend to that reasoning). We can doubt only those things that we have previously demonstrated to be true, and whose memory can recur when we no longer attend to the reasons from which we deduced them and, indeed, have forgotten the reasons. So although God's existence cannot come to be known through itself, but only through something else, we will be able to attain a certain knowledge of his existence so long as we attend very accurately to all the premises from which we have inferred it. See *Principles* I, 13; *Reply to Second Objections*, 3, and Meditation 5, at the end.

But since this answer does not satisfy some people, I shall give another.[8] When we previously discussed the certainty and evidence of our existence, we saw that we inferred it from the fact that, wherever we turned our attention—whether we were considering our own nature, or feigning some cunning deceiver as the author of our nature, or summoning up, outside us, any other reason for doubting whatever—we came upon no reason for doubting that did not by itself convince us of our existence.

So far we have not observed this to happen regarding any other matter. For though, when we attend to the nature of a Triangle, we

---

[7] Spinoza here presents as Descartes' answer to the objection of circularity, a reply that hinges on his exempting from the scope of the doubt propositions so evident that they do not require proof. And certainly Descartes does, in the passage cited, seem to rely on such an exemption. But Descartes also, in other passages (e.g., AT VII, 21 and 36), says that the hypothesis of a deceiving God casts doubt on all his former beliefs, no matter how evident. Spinoza's verbal reminiscences of those passages (at I/143/6f, I/145/32f, and I/146/30ff) suggest an awareness that Descartes cannot consistently take that line of defense. Cf. Spinoza's note f at I/171/14.

[8] The answer Spinoza here goes on to offer, not as Descartes' own answer, but presumably as one at least consistent with Cartesian principles (cf. I/131/25ff.), relies on a distinction between having a clear and distinct idea of God and knowing that God exists. This second reply does have certain affinities to what I believe to be Descartes' best line of defense (cf. Curley 8, chap. 5). In the *Treatise on the Intellect* (§ 79) Spinoza adopts this reply as his own.

are compelled to infer that its three angles are equal to two right angles, nevertheless we cannot infer the same thing from [the supposition] that perhaps we are deceived by the author of our nature. But from [this supposition] we did most certainly infer our existence. So here we are not compelled, wherever we direct our attention, to infer that the three angles of a Triangle are equal to two right angles. On the contrary, we discover a ground for doubting, viz. because we have no idea of God which so affects us that it is impossible for us to think that God is a deceiver. For to someone who does not have a true idea of God (which we now suppose ourselves not to have) it is just as easy to think that his author is a deceiver as to think that he is not a deceiver. Similarly for one who has no idea[9] of a Triangle, it is just as easy to think that its three angles are equal to two right angles, as to think that they are not.

So we concede that we can not be absolutely certain of anything, except our own existence, even though we attend properly to its demonstration, so long as we have no clear and distinct concept of God that makes us affirm that he is supremely veracious, just as the idea we have of a Triangle compels us to infer that its three angles are equal to two right angles. But we deny that we cannot, therefore, arrive at knowledge of anything.

For as is evident from everything we have said just now, the crux of the whole matter is that we can form a concept of God which so disposes us that it is not as easy for us to think that he is a deceiver as to think that he is not, but which now compels us to affirm that he is supremely veracious. When we have formed such an idea, that reason for doubting Mathematical truths will be removed. Wherever we then direct our attention in order to doubt some one of them, we shall come upon nothing from which we must not instead infer that it is most certain—as happened concerning our existence.

E.g., if, after we have discovered the idea of God, we attend to the nature of a Triangle, the idea of this will compel us to affirm that its three angles are equal to two right angles; but if we attend to the idea of God, this too will compel us to affirm that he is supremely veracious, and the author and continual conserver of our nature, and therefore that he does not deceive us concerning that truth. Nor will it be less impossible for us to think that he is a deceiver, when we attend to the idea of God (which we now suppose ourselves to have discovered), than it is for us to think that the three angles of a Triangle do not equal two right angles, when we attend to the idea of a Triangle.

---

[9] B: "no clear idea."

And just as we can form such an idea of a Triangle, even though we do not know whether the author of our nature deceives us, so also we

30 can make the idea of God clear to ourselves and put it before our eyes, even though we still doubt whether the author of our nature deceives us in all things. And provided we have it, however we have acquired it, it will suffice to remove all doubt, as has just now been shown.

Therefore, from these premises we reply as follows to the difficulty

I/149 raised. We can be certain of nothing—not, indeed, so long as we are ignorant of God's existence (for I have not spoken of this)—but as long as we do not have a clear and distinct idea of him.

So if anyone wishes to argue against me, his objection will have to

5 be this: *we can be certain of nothing before we have a clear and distinct idea of God; but we cannot have a clear and distinct idea of God so long as we do not know whether the author of our nature deceives us; therefore, we can be certain of nothing so long as we do not know whether the author of our nature deceives us, etc.*

10 To this I reply by conceding the major and denying the minor. For we have a clear and distinct idea of a Triangle, although we do not know whether the author of our nature deceives us; and provided we have such an idea (as I have just shown abundantly), we will be able

15 to doubt neither his existence, nor any Mathematical truth.

With this as preface, let us now come to the matter itself.

Definitions[10]

D1: Under the word *thought* I include everything which is in us and of which we are immediately conscious.

20 *So all operations of the will, the intellect, the imagination and the senses are thoughts. But I have added* immediately *to exclude those things that follow from thoughts, e.g., voluntary motion does have thought as its principle, but it is still not itself a thought.*

D2: By the term *idea* I understand that form of each thought through

25 the immediate perception of which I am conscious of the thought itself.

So if I understand what I say, I cannot express anything in words, without its being certain from this that there is in me an idea of what is signified by those words.[11] And so I do not call only images depicted in the fantasy ideas.

---

[10] The definitions, apart from the exceptions noted, follow very closely those given by Descartes in the geometric presentation of his thought at the end of the *Second Replies* (AT VII, 160-162).

[11] B: "an idea of what I want to signify by those words."

238

Indeed I do not here call them ideas at all, insofar as they are depicted in the corporeal fantasy, i.e., in some part of the brain, but only insofar as they give form to the mind itself which is directed toward that part of the brain.

D3: By the *objective reality of an idea* I understand the being of the thing represented by the idea, insofar as it is in the idea.

In the same way, one can speak of objective perfection, or objective artifice, etc. For whatever we perceive as in the objects of the ideas is in the ideas themselves objectively.

D4: The same things are said to be *formally* in the objects of the ideas when they are in the objects as we perceive them, and *eminently* when they are in the objects, not indeed as we perceive them, but to such an extent as to be able to take the place of such things.

Note that when I say the cause contains the perfections of its effect eminently, I mean that the cause contains the perfections of the effect more excellently than the effect itself does. See also A8.

D5: Everything in which there is immediately, as in a subject, *or* through which there exists, something we perceive, i.e., some property, *or* quality, *or* attribute, of which there is a real idea in us, is called *Substance.*[12]

For of substance itself, taken precisely, we have no idea, other than that it is a thing in which exists formally or eminently that something which we perceive, or, which is objectively in one of our ideas.[13]

D6: A substance in which thought is immediately is called a *Mind.*

I speak here of mind [mens] rather than soul [anima], because the word soul is equivocal and is often taken for a corporeal thing.[14]

D7: A substance which is the immediate subject of extension[15] and of accidents which presuppose extension, like figure, position, local motion, etc., is called a *body.*

---

[12] The definition of *substance* given here follows that in the *Second Replies.* Later (PPII, D2, I/181) Spinoza will give another definition modeled on *Principles* I, 51-52 (AT VIII, 24-25).

[13] The explanation comes from Descartes, but Descartes adds: "because it is known to the natural light that nothing can have no real attribute."

[14] The explanation comes from Descartes, who further explains to Mersenne (21 April 1641) that "in good Latin *anima* means *air* or *breath*" and that its use for *mind* is a transferred one. Balling uses *ziel* for *mens* and replaces the explanation by: "What Descartes adds to this definition concerns only the word *mens,* which expresses his meaning more clearly because it is not ambiguous in Latin and does not signify something corporeal. But since in our language we find no such word, which does not at the same time signify something corporeal, one word would not express the meaning more clearly than another. So it would be useless to translate that here."

[15] Descartes: "of local extension."

But whether the substance called mind is one and the same as that called body, or whether they are two different substances, will need to be asked later.

35 D8: The substance which we understand to be through itself[16] supremely perfect, and in which we conceive nothing which involves any defect or limitation of perfection, is called *God*.

I/151 D9: When we say that something is contained in the nature or concept of something, that is the same as saying that it is true of that thing, i.e., can be truly affirmed of it.[17]

D10: Two substances are said to be really distinct when each of them can exist without the other.

5 *We have omitted Descartes' postulates here, because we infer nothing from them in what follows. Still we earnestly ask the reader to read through them, to consider them, and to meditate on them carefully.*

Axioms[18]

A1: We do not arrive at knowledge and certainty of an unknown thing
10 except by the knowledge and certainty of another thing which is prior[19] to it in certainty and knowledge.

A2: There are reasons which make us doubt the existence of our body.
15 *This has been shown in the Prolegomenon, and so it is made an axiom here.*

---

[16] Spinoza has added "through itself" to Descartes' definition. Cf. P10D.

[17] Spinoza has added "truly" to Descartes' definition. In each of the preceding definitions some word or phrase has been italicized to show what term is being defined. In D9 and D10 (both here and in Descartes), nothing is italicized. In the case of D10, it is clear that "really distinct" is being defined. Here the most natural assumption is that "being contained in the nature or concept of" is being defined.

However, there is some plausibility in taking D9 as a definition of truth, and as an attempt to define truth in such a way that it will make sense to speak of truths about nonexistent objects, or objects whose existence is problematic. Descartes' and Spinoza's views about mathematical objects would make such an account desirable, as would their common endeavor to defend the ontological argument. We might regard D9 as a first step toward a Leibnizian theory of truth, though in Leibniz there is the further concern to understand God's knowledge of future contingents.

[18] Once again Spinoza relies on the Geometrical Exposition, but he is much freer in his treatment of Descartes' axioms (AT VII, 164-166) than in his treatment of the definitions. Some are carried over verbatim A4 = Desc. A6, A7 = Desc. A3, A8 = Desc. A4, A9 = Desc. A5), some are reproduced only approximately (A5, A6, A10, and A11 correspond to Descartes' A7, A10, A2, and A1, respectively), some are omitted (Descartes' A8 and A9, which Spinoza will later query at IP7S), and new axioms are introduced (A1-A3). A1 is arguably an assumption Descartes makes in defending the *cogito* against the charge of being a syllogism with a suppressed major premise; A2 corresponds very roughly to Descartes' first postulate; A3 corresponds to nothing I know of in Descartes.

[19] B: "prior in us." Cf. P2D.

A3: If we have anything beyond a mind and a body, it is less known to us than the mind and the body.

It should be noted that these axioms make affirmations concerning no things outside us, but only concerning those things which we find in us, insofar as we are thinking things.[20]

20

PROPOSITIONS

P1: *We cannot be absolutely certain of anything, so long as we do not know that we exist.*

Dem.: This proposition is evident through itself. For whoever absolutely does not know that he is, equally does not know that he is affirming or denying, i.e., that he certainly affirms or denies.[21]

But it should be noted here that although we affirm and deny many things with great certainty without attending to the fact that we exist, nevertheless, unless this is presupposed as indubitable it is possible for everything to be called in doubt.

I/152   P2: I am *must be known through itself.*

Dem.: If you deny this, then it will not become known except through something else, the knowledge and certainty of which (by A1) will be prior in us to this proposition, *I am.* But this is absurd (by P1). Therefore, it must be known through itself, q.e.d.

P3: I, *insofar as I am a thing consisting of a body,* am, *is not the first thing known, nor is it known through itself.*

Dem.: There are certain things which make us doubt the existence of our body (by A2); therefore (by A1), we shall not arrive at certainty of [the existence of our body] except through the knowledge and certainty of another thing, which is prior to it in knowledge and certainty. Therefore, the proposition that *I*, insofar as I am a thing consisting of a body, *am,* is not the first thing known, nor is it known through itself, q.e.d.

P4: I am *cannot be the first thing known except insofar as we think.*

Dem.: The proposition *I am a corporeal thing or one consisting of a body* is not the first thing known (P3). Nor am I certain of my existence

---

[20] This stipulation regarding the nature of axioms evidently has its origin in passages like *Principles* I, 10 and I, 49. While it plausibly holds of the axioms just enumerated, it is not clear that it holds of all the axioms which follow P4S, which come more directly from Descartes. While Spinoza sometimes appears to accept such a stipulation in his own usage (e.g., in Letter 10), it is far from clear that all the axioms in the *Ethics* satisfy this condition.

[21] Cf. the TdIE, §§ 47-48.

I/153 insofar as I consist of anything else besides a mind and a body. For if we consist of anything else different from the mind and the body, this is less known to us than the body (A3). So *I am* can not be the first thing known except insofar as we think, q.e.d.

5 Cor.: Hence it is evident that the mind, *or* thinking thing, is better known than the body. *For a fuller explanation, see Principles* I, 11 and 12.

10 Schol.: Everyone perceives most certainly that he affirms, denies, doubts, understands, imagines, etc., or that he exists doubting, understanding, affirming, etc., or in a word, *thinking*. Nor can this be

15 called in doubt. So the proposition *I think*, or *I am Thinking* is the unique (P1) and most certain foundation of the whole of Philosophy.

Now to be completely certain of matters in the sciences nothing more can be sought or desired than to deduce all things from the firmest principles and to render them as clear and distinct as the prin-

20 ciples from which they are deduced. So clearly whatever is equally evident to us, whatever we perceive as clearly and distinctly as the principle we have already discovered, and whatever so agrees with this principle, and so depends on it that if we should wish to doubt it we would have to doubt this principle as well, must be held most true.[22]

25 But to proceed as cautiously as possible in examining these matters, I shall admit in the beginning, as equally evident and as perceived by us with equal clarity and distinctness, only those things that each of us observes in himself, insofar as he is thinking. E.g., that he wills

30 this and that, that he has ideas of a certain sort, that one idea contains in itself more reality and perfection than another, that the idea which contains objectively the being and perfection of substance is far more

I/154 perfect than the one which contains only the objective perfection of some accident, and finally that the idea of a supremely perfect being is the most perfect of all. These, I say, we perceive not only with equal evidence and clarity, but even, perhaps, more distinctly. For

5 they affirm not only that we think, but also how we think.

Next we shall also say that those [propositions] agree with this principle which cannot be called into doubt unless at the same time this unshakable foundation of ours should be put in doubt. E.g., if someone should wish to doubt whether something comes from nothing, he

10 will at the same time be able to doubt whether we exist when we think. For if I can affirm something of nothing—viz. that it can be the cause of something—I shall be able at the same time, with the same

---

[22] B: "most certain."

right, to affirm thought of nothing, and to say that I am nothing when I think. But since I cannot do that, it will also be impossible for me to think that something may come from nothing.

Having considered these matters, I decided to set out here, in order, the things which at present seem necessary to enable us to go further, and to add to the number of Axioms. They are put forward as axioms by Descartes, at the end of the Replies to the Second Objections, and I do not wish to be more accurate than he is.[23] Nevertheless, so as not to depart from the order already begun, I shall try to make them somewhat clearer and to show how one depends on the other and how they all depend on this principle—*I am thinking*—or agree with it in evidence and reason.

Axioms Taken from Descartes

A4: There are different degrees of reality, *or* being: for a substance has more reality than an accident or mode, and the infinite substance more than a finite; accordingly there is more objective reality in the idea of a substance than in that of an accident, and in the idea of the infinite substance than in that of a finite [substance].

This axiom comes to be known just from the contemplation of our ideas, of whose existence we are certain, because they are modes of thinking. For we know how much reality or perfection the idea of substance affirms of a substance, and how much the idea of mode affirms of a mode.[24] *Hence we necessarily find that the idea of substance contains more objective reality than that of some accident.* See P4S.

A5: If a thinking thing knows any perfections which it lacks, it will immediately give them to itself, if they are in its power.

Everyone observes this in himself, insofar as he is a thinking thing. Consequently (by P4S) we are most certain of it. And for the same reason we are no less certain of the following, viz.,

A6: Existence—either possible or necessary—is contained in the idea, *or* concept, of every thing (see Descartes, A10). *Necessary existence, in the concept of God, or of a supremely perfect being (for otherwise he would be conceived as imperfect, contrary to what is supposed to be conceived); but contingent, or possible, in the concept of a limited thing.*

---

[23] Descartes remarks (AT VII, 164) that some of his axioms could have been presented as theorems if he had wished to be more accurate.

[24] Note that Spinoza's explanation of Descartes' axiom relies on a doctrine Spinoza held in opposition to Descartes: that ideas involve an element of affirmation. Cf. E IIP49 and Meditation IV.

A7: No actually existing thing and no actually existing perfection of a thing can have nothing, *or* a thing not existing, as the cause of its existence.

20 *In P4S I have demonstrated that this axiom is as evident to us as* I am thinking.

A8: Whatever reality, *or* perfection, there is in any thing, exists formally or eminently in its first and adequate cause.

25 *I understand that the reality is in the cause* eminently *when the cause contains the whole reality of the effect more perfectly than the effect itself, but* formally *when it contains it as perfectly.*

This axiom depends on the preceding one. For if it were supposed that there was either nothing in the cause, or less in the cause than in the effect, then the
30 *nothing in the cause would be the cause of the effect. But this (by A7) is absurd. So not anything can be cause of an effect, but only that in which there is every perfection which is in the effect either eminently or at least formally.*

A9: The objective reality of our ideas requires a cause in which the
I/156 same reality itself is contained, not only objectively, but formally or eminently.

Though many people misapply this axiom, it is acknowledged by everyone. For whenever anyone has conceived something new, there is no one who does
5 *not look for the cause of that concept,* or *idea. When they can assign one which contains formally or eminently as much reality as that concept contains objectively, they are satisfied. This is explained adequately by the example of the machine which Descartes uses in the* Principles *(I, 17).*

Again, if anyone should ask from what source a man has the ideas of his
10 *thought and of his body, no one fails to see that he has them from himself, as containing formally all that the ideas contain objectively. So, if a man were to have some idea which contained more objective reality than he contained formally, we would be driven by the natural light to look for another cause, outside the man himself, which contained all that perfection formally or emi-*
15 *nently. Nor has anyone ever assigned any other cause, except this one, which he conceived as clearly and distinctly.*

As for the truth of this axiom, it depends on the preceding one. For (by A4) there are different degrees of reality or being in ideas, and therefore by (A8)
20 *the more perfect they are, the more perfect the cause they require. But the degrees of reality which we perceive in our ideas are not in the ideas insofar as they are considered as modes of thinking, but rather insofar as one represents a substance and another represents only a mode of substance—or, in a word, insofar as they are considered as images of things.[a] So clearly, there can be no*

[a] We are certain of this too because we experience it in ourselves insofar as we are thinking. See preceding schol.

244

other first cause of ideas except that which (as we have just shown) everyone understands clearly and distinctly by the natural light: viz., one in which there is contained either formally or eminently the same reality which the ideas have objectively.

That this conclusion may be more clearly understood, I shall explain it with one or two examples. Suppose someone sees two books—one the work of a distinguished philosopher, the other that of some trifler, but both written in the same hand. If he attends to the meaning of the words (that is, does not attend to them insofar as they are like images), but only to the handwriting and to the order of the letters, he will recognize no inequality between them which compels him to look for different causes. They will seem to him to have proceeded from the same cause in the same way. But if he attends to the meaning of the words and the discourses,[25] he will find a great inequality between them. And so he will conclude that the first cause of the one book was very different from the first cause of the other, and really more perfect than it in proportion to the differences he finds between the meaning of the discourses of each book, or between the words considered as images. I speak of the first cause of the books; there must be a first cause, though I concede—indeed I assume—that one book can be copied from another, as is obvious in itself.

The same [axiom] can also be explained clearly by the example of a portrait—say of some Prince. For if we attend only to its materials, we shall find between it and other portraits no inequality which would force us to look for different causes. On the contrary, nothing will prevent us from being able to think that it has been painted from another picture, and that one again from another, and so on to infinity. For we shall discern [clearly] enough that no other cause is required for drawing it. But if we attend to the image insofar as it is an image we shall immediately be forced to look for a first cause which contains, formally or eminently, what the image contains by representation. I do not see what more could be desired for the confirmation and clarification of this axiom.

A10: No less a cause is required for preserving a thing than for first producing it.

From the fact that we are thinking now, it does not necessarily follow that we shall be thinking afterwards. For the concept which we have of our thought does not involve, or contain, the necessary existence of the thought. I can conceive the thought clearly and distinctly even though I suppose that it does not exist.[b]

But the nature of every cause must contain or involve in itself the perfection of its effect (by A8). From this it follows clearly that there must be something,

---

[b] Everyone discovers this in himself, insofar as he is a thinking thing.

[25] EP: *orationum*, B: *redenen* (= *rationum*), so perhaps "reasons." Similarly in l. 5.

either in us or outside us, which we have not yet understood, whose concept,
30   or *nature, involves existence and which is the cause of our thought's having*
begun to exist, and also of its continuing to exist. For though our thought has
begun to exist, its nature and essence does not on that account involve necessary
existence any more than before it existed. So it needs the same power to persevere
I/158   *in existing as it needed to begin existing. And what we say here about thought,*
must also be said about anything whose essence does not involve necessary exist-
ence.

A11: Nothing exists of which it cannot be asked, what is the cause,
or reason, why it exists. See Descartes' A1.
5   *Since existing is something positive, we cannot say that it has nothing as its*
cause (by A7). Therefore we must assign some positive cause, or reason, why
[a thing] exists—either an external one, i.e., one outside the thing itself, or an
internal one, i.e., one comprehended in the nature and definition of the existing
thing itself.

10

The following four propositions are taken from Descartes.

P5: *God's existence is known from the consideration of his nature alone.*
15   Dem.: To say that something is contained in the nature, *or* concept,
of something is the same as saying that it is true of that thing (by D9).
But necessary existence is contained in the concept of God (by A6).
So, it is true to say of God that necessary existence is in him, *or* that
he exists.
20   Schol.: Many excellent things follow from this proposition. Indeed,
almost all that knowledge of God's attributes through which we are
led to the love of him, *or* the highest blessedness, depends on this
alone: that existence pertains to the nature of God, *or* that the concept
of God involves necessary existence, as the concept of a triangle in-
25   volves that its three angles are equal to two right angles, *or* that his
existence, no less than his essence, is an eternal truth. So it would be
I/159   very desirable for the human race at last to embrace these things with
us.
        I confess, of course, that there are certain prejudices that stand in
the way of everyone's understanding this so easily.[c] But if anyone
5   moved by a good intention and by the simple love of the truth and of
his own true advantage, should wish to examine the matter and to
weigh carefully the things considered in the Fifth Meditation and at
the end of the *Replies to the First Objections*, as well as what we say
about eternity in our Appendix (II, 1), he will doubtless understand

---

[c] Read *Principles* I, 16.

it as clearly as possible, and no one will be able to doubt whether he
has an idea of God, which, of course, is the first foundation of human
blessedness. For he will see that the idea of God is very different from
the ideas of other things as soon as he understands that God differs in
every way from other things, with respect both to his essence and to
his existence. So there is no need to detain the Reader longer about
these matters.

P6: *God's existence is demonstrated a posteriori from the mere fact that there
is an idea of him in us.*

Dem.: The objective reality of any of our ideas requires a cause in
which the very same reality is contained, not only objectively, but
formally or eminently (by A9). But we have an idea of God (by D2
and D8), and the objective reality of this idea is not contained either
formally or eminently in us (by A4); nor can it be contained in any
other thing except God himself (by D8). So this idea of God which is
in us requires God as its cause, God, therefore, exists (by A7).

Schol.: There are some who deny that they have any idea of God,
and who nevertheless (so *they* say) worship and love him. And though
you may put before them a definition of God, and God's attributes,
you will still gain nothing by it, no more than if you labored to teach
a man blind from birth the differences between the colors, just as we
see them. But unless we should wish to regard them as a new kind of
animal, between men and the lower animals, we must not bother too
much about their words. How, I ask, can we make the idea of any
thing known except by propounding its definition and explaining its
attributes? Since we offer this concerning the idea of God, there is no
reason for us to be delayed by the words of men who deny that they
have an idea of God merely because they can form no image of him
in their brain.

Next we should note that when Descartes cites A4 to show that the
objective reality of our idea of God is not contained in us, either formally or eminently, he supposes that everyone knows that he is not
an infinite substance—i.e., supremely intelligent, powerful, etc. He is
entitled to suppose this because he who knows that he thinks, knows
also that he has doubts about many things and does not understand
everything clearly and distinctly.

Finally, we must note that it also follows clearly from D8 that there
can not be more than one God, as we clearly demonstrate in P11 and
in our Appendix, II, ii.

P7: *The existence of God is also demonstrated from the fact that we ourselves
who have an idea of him exist.*

247

Schol.: To demonstrate this proposition Descartes assumes these two axioms: (1) *What can bring about the greater, or more difficult, can also bring about the lesser*; (2) *It is greater to create, or (by A10) to preserve, a substance than the attributes, or properties, of a substance.* But what he means by this I do not know. What does he call easy, and what difficult? Nothing is said to be easy or difficult absolutely, but only in relation to a cause. So one and the same thing can at the same time be called both easy and difficult in relation to different causes.[d]

But if he calls difficult those things that can be accomplished [by a cause] with great labor, and easy, those that can be accomplished by the same cause with less labor—as a force which can lift 50 pounds will be able to lift 25 pounds twice as easily—then of course, the axiom will not be absolutely true, nor will he be able to demonstrate from it what he wants to. For when he says [AT VII, 168], *if I had the power of preserving myself, I would also have the power of giving myself all the perfections I lack* (because they do not require such a great power), I would concede this to him. The powers I expend in preserving myself could bring about many other things far more easily, if I did not require them for preserving myself. But so long as I use them for preserving myself, I deny that I can expend them to bring about other things, even though they are easier, as is clear in our example.

It does not remove the difficulty if it is said that since I am a thinking thing I would necessarily have to know whether I spend all my powers in preserving myself, and also whether this is the cause of my not giving myself the remaining perfections. The dispute now does not concern this, but only how the necessity of this proposition follows from this axiom. Moreover, if I knew it, I would be greater, and perhaps would require greater powers to preserve myself in that greater perfection than those I have.[26]

And then I do not know whether it is a greater work to create (*or*

---

[d] Take as one example the spider, which easily weaves a web that men could weave only with the greatest difficulty. On the other hand, how many things do men do with the greatest ease which are perhaps impossible for angels? [In a letter to Mesland, 2 May 1644, AT IV, 110-20. Descartes replies to a similar objection: "I confess that in physical and moral causes, which are particular and limited, one often finds that those which produce some effect are incapable of producing many others which seem less to us. So a man, who can produce another man, cannot produce an ant; and a king, who can make a whole people obey him, sometimes cannot make a horse obey him. But when it is a question of a universal and unlimited cause, it seems to me a very evident common notion that *what can do more, can also do less*, as evident as *the whole is greater than its part*." This letter was number 115 in Volume I of Clerselier's edition of Descartes' correspondence. Since Spinoza elsewhere refers to letter 118 of that volume (at I/195/32), it seems natural to assume that he had read the letter to Mesland. It is therefore surprising that he makes no reference to Descartes' reply.]

[26] B: "than those I now have to preserve myself in my present condition."

preserve) a substance than to create (*or* preserve) attributes. To speak more clearly and Philosophically, I do not know whether a substance does not require its whole power and essence, by which it perhaps preserves itself, for preserving its attributes.[27]

But let us leave these things to examine further what our most noble Author means here, i.e., what he understands by easy and difficult. I do not think, nor can I in any way persuade myself, that by difficult he understands what is impossible (so that it cannot in any way be conceived how it happens), and by easy, what implies no contradiction (so that it can easily be conceived how it happens). It is true that he seems at first glance to mean this, when he says in the Third Meditation [AT VII, 48]: *I must not think that perhaps the things I lack are more difficult to acquire than those now in me. On the contrary, it is evident that it was far more difficult for me—i.e., a thing, or substance, which thinks— to emerge from nothing than,* etc. But that would not be consistent with the author's words and would not be worthy of his genius.

For, to pass over the first consideration, there is nothing in common between the possible and the impossible, *or* between the intelligible and the unintelligible, just as there is nothing in common between something and nothing; and power does not agree with impossibilities any more than creation and generation do with nonexistent things, so they ought not to be compared in any way. Moreover, I can compare things with one another and know the relation between them only if I have a clear and distinct concept of each of them. Hence I deny that it follows that if someone can do the impossible, he should also be able to do what is possible.

What sort of conclusion is this? If someone can make a square circle, he will also be able to make a circle all of whose radii are equal, or, if someone can bring it about that nothing[28] is acted on, and can use it as a material from which to produce something, he will also have the power to make something from some [B: other] thing. As I have said, between these and similar things there is neither agreement, nor proportion, nor comparison, nor anything whatsoever in common. Anyone can see this, if he gives the matter any attention at all. I think Descartes was too intelligent to have meant that.

But when I consider the second axiom of the two just cited, it seems that by greater and more difficult he means more perfect, and by less

---

[27] Cf. I/163.

[28] EP: *To nihil*, B: *het niet*. See the Glossary-Index on *nothing*. Spinoza is somewhat more open here in his criticism of the doctrine of creation *ex nihilo* than he will be when he treats it later in the Appendix (CM II, x). His comparison here indicates his belief that creation *ex nihilo* involves a contradiction.

and easier, more imperfect. But this is also very obscure. There is the same difficulty here as before. I deny, as before, that he who can do the greater, should be able at the same time and by the same work (as must be supposed in the Proposition) to do the lesser.

Again, when he says: *it is greater to create* or *preserve a substance than to create* or *preserve its attributes*, he can surely not understand by attributes what is contained formally in substance and is distinguished from substance itself only by reason.[29] For then creating a substance is the same as creating its attributes. For the same reason he also cannot understand [by attributes] the properties of a substance which follow necessarily from its essence and definition.

Much less can he understand what he nevertheless seems to mean, viz. the properties and attributes of another substance. So, for example, if I say that I have the power of preserving myself, a finite thinking substance, I cannot on that account say that I also have the power of giving myself the perfections of the infinite substance which differs in its whole essence from my essence. For the power, *or* essence,[e] by which I preserve myself in my being differs entirely from the power, *or* essence, by which the absolutely infinite substance preserves itself, from which its powers and properties are only distinguished by reason. Hence, even though I were to suppose that I preserve myself, if I should wish to conceive that I could give myself the perfections of the absolutely infinite substance, I would be supposing nothing but this—that I can reduce my whole essence to nothing and create afresh an infinite substance. This, of course, would be much greater than only supposing that I can preserve myself, a finite substance.

[e] Note that the power by which the substance preserves itself is nothing but its essence, and differs from it only in name. This will be discussed mainly when we treat of God's power in the Appendix. [In fact the identity of *vis* and *essentia* does not come into CM II, 9, though it is mentioned in II, 6.]

[29] Descartes maintains that the distinction between substance and attribute is a distinction of reason in *Principles* I, 62. The similarity of the objection made in this and the following paragraph to those made by Burman (AT V, 154-155) naturally raises the question whether Spinoza knew the *Conversation with Burman*. Caillois thinks he certainly did (Pléiade, 1407). Lachièze-Rey (91-93) more cautiously judges that he probably did. I think it unlikely.

The similarity has relatively little weight, since the objections might occur easily enough to a careful student of the *Principles*. Descartes often seems to identify substance and attribute. Cf. *Principles* I, 63, and II, 9 helpfully annotated in Alquié, III, 133 and 154.

Perhaps Spinoza's apparent ignorance of Descartes' replies is also of little weight, since elsewhere he ignores replies Descartes made in works we know he had access to cf. note d at I/161/7). But apart from the fact that his accounts of the *cogito* and the circle might well have been different, had he known the *Entretien*, there is also the fact that there Descartes says the *Principles* were written in the synthetic mode (AT V, 153), whereas here Spinoza takes himself to be expounding synthetically a work Descartes had written in the analytic mode (I/129/25).

Since, then, he can understand none of these things by attributes or properties, nothing else remains, except the qualities that the substance itself contains eminently (as, this or that thought in the mind, which I clearly perceive to be lacking in me), but not those another substance contains eminently (as, this or that motion in extension; for such perfections are not perfections for me, a thinking thing, and so are not lacking to me). But then Descartes cannot in any way infer from this axiom the conclusion he wants to demonstrate; i.e., that if I preserve myself, I also have the power of giving myself all the perfections that I clearly find to pertain to a supremely perfect being.

This is quite evident from what has just been said. But not to leave the matter undemonstrated, and to avoid all confusion, it seemed best to demonstrate the following lemmas first, and afterwards to construct a demonstration of P7 on that basis.

Lemma 1: *The more perfect a thing is by its own nature, the greater and more necessary is the existence it involves; conversely, the more necessary the existence it involves by its own nature, the more perfect it is.*

Dem.: Existence is contained in the idea, *or* concept, of everything (by A6). Let A be a thing that has ten degrees of perfection. I say that its concept involves more existence than it would if it were supposed to contain only five degrees of perfection. For since we can affirm no existence of nothing (see P4S), then the more we take away its perfection in thought, and so the more we conceive it as participating in nothing,[30] the more possibility of existence we also deny it. Hence, if we should conceive its degrees of perfection to be diminished infinitely to zero, it will contain no existence, *or* absolutely impossible existence. On the other hand, if we increase its degree [of perfection] infinitely, we shall conceive it as involving existence in the highest degree, and therefore as involving supremely necessary existence. This was the first thing to be proven.

And the second thing proposed for demonstration follows clearly from the fact that these two things [necessary existence and perfection] cannot be separated in any way (as is sufficiently established by A6, and by this whole first part).

Note 1. Although many things are said to exist necessarily from the mere fact that there is a determinate cause to produce them, we are not speaking about these things here, but only about that necessity and possibility which follow solely from the consideration of the nature, or essence, of the thing, without regard to any cause.

Note 2. We are not speaking here about beauty and the other 'perfections' which men have wished, in their superstition and ignorance, to call perfections.

[30] B: "comes nearer and nearer to Nothing."

251

5   *By perfection I understand only reality, or being. E.g., I perceive that more reality is contained in substance than in modes, or accidents. Hence I understand clearly that it contains a more necessary and perfect existence than accidents do, as is plain enough from A4 and A6.*

10   Cor.: Hence it follows that whatever involves necessary existence is a supremely perfect being, *or* God.

     Lemma 2: *The nature of him who has the power of conserving himself involves*
15   *necessary existence.*

     Dem.: Whoever has the power to preserve himself also has the power to create himself (by A10), i.e. (as everyone will readily concede), he requires no external cause in order to exist; rather, his own nature
20   alone will be a sufficient cause of his existing, either possibly (see A10) or necessarily. But he does not exist possibly. For then (by what we have demonstrated concerning A10), from the fact that he existed now, it would not follow that he would exist afterwards (which is contrary to the hypothesis). So he exists necessarily, i.e., his nature involves
25   necessary existence, q.e.d.

     Demonstration of P7: If I had the power to preserve myself, I would
I/166   be of such a nature that I would involve necessary existence (by L2). So (by L1C) my nature would contain all perfections. But I find in myself, insofar as I am a thinking thing, many imperfections—that I doubt, desire, etc.—of which I am certain (P4S). Therefore, I have
5   no power to preserve myself. I cannot say that the reason I now lack those perfections is that I wish to deny them to myself, for that would clearly be incompatible with L1 and with what I clearly find in myself (by A5).

     Next, I cannot now exist without being preserved as long as I exist,
10   either by myself, if in fact I have that power, or by another who has it (by A10 and A11). But I exist (by P4S) and nevertheless I do not have the power to preserve myself, as was just now proved. Therefore, I am preserved by another. But not by another who does not have the power to preserve himself (by the same reasoning by which
15   I just demonstrated that I cannot preserve myself). So I am preserved by another who has the power of preserving himself, i.e. (by L2), whose nature involves necessary existence, i.e. (by L1C), who contains all the perfections which I understand to pertain clearly to a su-
20   premely perfect being. And therefore a supremely perfect being, i.e. (by D8), God, exists, as was to be demonstrated.

     Cor.: *God can bring about whatever we clearly perceive, as we perceive it.*
25   Dem.: All these things clearly follow from the preceding Proposition. For it is proved there that God exists from the fact that there must exist someone who has all the perfections of which there is some

idea in us. But there is in us the idea of a power so great that the heaven, and the earth, and all the other things which I understand to be possible, can be made, unaided, by him in whom the power exists. So all these things have been proved about God together with his existence.

P8: *Mind and body are really distinct.*

Dem.: Whatever we perceive clearly can be made by God as we perceive it (P7C). But (by P3 and P4) we clearly perceive the mind, i.e. (by D6), a thinking substance, without the body, i.e. (by D7), without any extended substance. Conversely, we perceive the body clearly without mind (as everyone will readily concede). So the mind can exist without the body and the body can exist without the mind—at least by divine power.

Now substances which can exist without one another are really distinct (by D10). But the mind and the body are substances (by D5, 6, and 7), which can each exist without the other (as we have just proven). So the mind and the body are really distinct.

See Descartes' P4 (at the end of the *Replies to the Second Objections*) and the *Principles* I, 22-29. For I do not judge it worthwhile to transcribe here the things said there.[31]

P9: *In the highest degree, God understands.*

Dem.: If you deny this, then God will understand either nothing, *or* not everything, *or* only certain things.

But to understand only certain things and be ignorant of others supposes a limited and imperfect intellect, which it is absurd to ascribe to God (by D8).

But that God should understand nothing would indicate either that he lacks any intellection, as men do when they understand nothing, and so would involve imperfection, which cannot be in God (by D8), or that his understanding something would be incompatible with his perfection.

Since intellection would thus be denied to him altogether, he would not be able to create any intellect (by A8). But since we perceive intellect clearly and distinctly, God can be its cause (P7C). Hence it

---

[31] This proof and that of the immediately preceding corollary are taken almost word for word from the end of the *Second Replies* (AT VIII, 169-170). Note the role played by definitions in the proof of P8 and cf. Meyer's preface, I/132/5. The sections of the *Principles* which Spinoza cites deal with God's attributes and various topics concerning which Descartes invokes the limits of the human intellect—e.g., the mysteries of the incarnation and the trinity, the indefinite extension of the physical world, and God's purposes. Cf. Meyer's preface, I/132/25. Some of these topics will later be taken up by Spinoza in his own way. Cf. P9, P16.

is not at all true that it is incompatible with God's perfection for him to understand something.

10   Consequently, he will, in the highest degree, understand, q.e.d.

Schol.: Although it must be conceded that God is incorporeal, as is demonstrated in P16, still this must not be taken to mean that all the

15 perfections of Extension are to be denied him. Extension is to be rejected only insofar as its nature and properties involve some imperfection. The same thing must also be said about God's intellection, as everyone who wants to be wiser than the ordinary run of Philosophers

20 confesses. This will be explained fully in our Appendix (II, vii).[32]

P10: *Whatever perfection is found in God, is from God.*

Dem.: If you deny this, suppose there is some perfection in God

25 which is not from God. It will be in God, either from itself or from something different from God. If it is from itself, then it will have necessary, *or* not [merely] possible, existence (by P7L2).[33] And so (by P7L1C) it will be something supremely perfect, and therefore (by D8) God. Accordingly, if it should be said that there is something in God

I/169 which is from itself, it is said at the same time to be from God, q.e.d. But if it is from something different from God, then God cannot be conceived as supremely perfect through himself, contrary to D8. Therefore, whatever perfection is found in God is from God, q.e.d.

5   P11: *There is not more than one God.*[34]

Dem.: Suppose you deny this. Conceive, if possible, that there is more than one God, e.g., A and B. Then both A and B must, in the

10 highest degree, understand (by P9), i.e., A understands everything, including both himself and B, and B, in turn, will understand himself

---

[32] It is interesting that whereas Descartes treats God's omniscience as known from examination of our idea of God (*Principles* I, 22), Spinoza offers a proof in which God's role as a creator of other intellects is stressed. This procedure inevitably provokes the question of God's corporeality, and Spinoza's qualification of his concession in the scholium is suggestive of his own doctrine that corporeal substance, insofar as it is substance, is indivisible. Cf. II/55-60.

Note that in the *Short Treatise* (I/45/23) omniscience is included on a list of properties traditionally but improperly ascribed to God. In the *Ethics* Spinoza will argue that intellect pertains to *natura naturata*, not *natura naturans* (E IP31).

[33] EP: *necessariam, sive minimè possibilem . . . existentiam.* Appuhn wanted to suppress *sive minimè possibilem* as an inadvertent addition. If the phrase had to be translated as it has been by some (e.g., Hayes, Caillois): "or at least possible," then that emendation would be correct. But Balling's version, which I follow, makes good sense of the text as it stands. I assume that here (as, e.g., at I/155/16) *possibilis* is used as a synonym for *contingens*. We have the same construction at I/179/25.

[34] Descartes does not attempt to prove this proposition in the *Principles*, but does offer an argument for it in the *Conversation with Burman* (AT V, 161) apropos of a statement made in the Fifth Meditation (AT VII, 68).

and A. But since A and B exist necessarily (by P5), then the cause of
the truth and necessity of the idea of B which is in A, is B. Conversely, the cause of the truth and necessity of the idea of A which is
in B is A. Consequently, there will be a perfection in A which is not
from A, and one in B which is not from B. So (by P10) neither A nor
B will be Gods. Therefore, there is not more than one God, q.e.d.

*It should be noted here that it follows necessarily from the mere fact that
some thing involves necessary existence from itself (as God does) that it is unique.
Everyone will be able to see this for himself, provided he meditates attentively.
I could also have demonstrated it here, but not in a way perceptible by everyone, as has been done in this proposition.*

P12: *Whatever exists is preserved by the power of God alone.*

Dem.: If you deny this, let it be supposed that something preserves
itself. Then (by P7L2), its nature involves necessary existence, and so
it would be God (by P7L1C). There would thus be more than one
God, which is absurd (by P11). So nothing exists which is not preserved by the power of God alone, q.e.d.

Cor. 1: *God is the creator of all things.*

Dem.: God (by P12) preserves all things, i.e. (by A10), he has
created whatever exists, and even now continuously creates it.

Cor. 2: *Things have no essence from themselves which might be the cause of
God's knowledge; rather, God is the cause of things even with respect to their
essences.*

Dem.: Since no perfection is found in God which is not from God
(by P10), things will have no essence from themselves which could be
the cause of God's knowledge. On the contrary, since God has not
generated everything from something else, but has created all things
completely (P12 and P12C1), and since that act of creation admits of
no cause except the efficient (for so I define creation), which is God,
it follows that things were nothing at all before the creation; and so
God was also the cause of their essence, q.e.d.

It should be noted that this corollary is also evident from the fact
that God is the cause, *or* creator, of all things (by C1) and that the
cause must contain in itself all the perfections of the effect (by A8), as
everyone can easily see.

Cor. 3: From this it clearly follows that God does not sense or,
strictly speaking, perceive. For his intellect is not determined by anything outside itself. Rather, all things proceed from him.

Cor. 4: God is prior in causality to the essence and to the existence
of things, as follows clearly from Corollaries 1 and 2 of this Proposition.

P13: *God is supremely veracious, and not at all a deceiver.*

10   Dem.: We can attribute nothing to God (by D8) in which we find any imperfection. Now (as is known through itself) every deception, or will to deceive, proceeds only from malice or fear.[f] Fear implies a

15   lesser power, and malice a privation of goodness. So no deception, or will to deceive, ought to be ascribed to God, i.e., to a being supremely powerful and supremely good. On the contrary, he must be said to be supremely veracious, and not at all a deceiver, q.e.d. See the *Replies to the Second Objections*, No. 4.

25   P14: *Whatever we perceive clearly and distinctly is true.*

Dem.: The faculty of distinguishing the true from the false, which (as everyone discovers in himself and can be seen from all that we

I/172   have now demonstrated) is in us, has been created, and is continuously preserved by God (by P12 with its corollary), i.e. (by P13), by a being supremely veracious and not at all a deceiver. Nor has he given us (as everyone discovers in himself) any faculty of holding back from, *or*

5   not assenting to, those things we perceive clearly and distinctly. So if we were deceived concerning them, we would be deceived entirely by God, and he would be a deceiver, which (by P13) is absurd. Therefore, whatever we perceive clearly and distinctly is true, q.e.d.

10   Schol.: Since the things to which we must necessarily assent, when we perceive them clearly and distinctly, must be true, and since we have the faculty of not assenting to those that are obscure and doubtful, *or* that are not deduced from most certain principles (as everyone

15   discovers in himself), it clearly follows that we can always prevent ourselves from falling into errors and from ever being deceived, provided that we decide resolutely to affirm nothing we do not perceive clearly and distinctly, *or* which is not deduced from principles clear and certain through themselves. This will be understood even more

20   clearly from what follows.

P15: *Error is not something positive.*[35]

Dem.: If error were something positive, it would have God alone

25   as its cause, by whom it would be continuously created (by P12). But this is absurd (by P13). So, error is not something positive, q.e.d.

I/173   Schol.: Since error is not something positive in man, it can be noth-

---

[f] I have not counted this axiom among the axioms, because it was not at all necessary. I only required it for demonstrating this proposition, and also because, so long as I did not know God's existence, I did not want to assume anything to be true except what I could deduce from the first thing known; that *I am* (as I warned in P4S). Again, I have not put definitions of fear and malice among the definitions, because no one is ignorant of these definitions, and I do not require them except for this one proposition.

[35] Cf. Descartes, *Principles* I, 29-30.

ing but a privation of the proper use of liberty (by P14S). So God should not be called the cause of error, except in the sense in which we say that the absence of the Sun is the cause of darkness, or that God is the cause of blindness, because he has made a child like others, except in respect of vision. For he has given us an intellect that extends only to a few things.

To understand this more clearly, and to understand as well how error depends solely on the misuse of our will and, finally, how we can guard against error, we should recall the modes of thinking that we have. They can all be grouped into two kinds: modes of perceiving (like sensing, imagining, and purely understanding) and modes of willing (like desiring, shunning, affirming, denying, and doubting).

It must be noted about these [modes of thinking]:

(1) that the mind can be deceived neither insofar as it understands things clearly and distinctly and assents to them (by P14), nor insofar as it merely perceives things and does not assent to them. For though I may now perceive a winged horse, it is certain that this perception contains no falsity, so long as I do not assent to its being true that there is a winged horse, nor also so long as I doubt whether there is a winged horse. And since assenting is nothing but determining the will, it follows that error depends solely on the use of the will.

To make this still clearer, note:

(2) that we have the power of assenting not only to those things which we perceive clearly and distinctly, but also to those which we perceive in any other way. For our will is not determined by any limits. Anyone can see this clearly, provided he attends to the fact that if God had wished to make our faculty of understanding infinite, he would not have needed to give us a greater faculty of assenting than the one we now have in order for us to be able to assent to everything we understand. The same faculty we now have would suffice to our assenting to infinitely many things. And we know from our experience that we assent to many things that we have not deduced from certain principles.

Again, it is clear from these considerations that we should never fall into error (by P14) if either the intellect extended itself as widely as the faculty of willing, or if the faculty of willing could not extend itself more widely than the intellect, or finally, if we could contain the faculty of willing within the limits of the intellect.

But we have no power to bring about the first two. For it involves a contradiction both that the will should not be infinite and that the created intellect should not be finite. There remains, then, the third possibility to be considered, viz., whether we have the power to con-

tain our faculty of willing within the limits of the intellect. Now since
15 the will is free to determine itself, it follows that we do have the power
to contain our faculty of assenting within the limits of the intellect,
and so can bring it about that we do not fall into error. Hence it is
quite evident that it depends entirely on the use of the freedom of the
20 will that we are ever deceived. That our will is free is demonstrated
in *Principles* I, 39 and in the Fourth Meditation.[36] We have also shown
it fully in the last chapter of our Appendix.

And though we cannot but assent to a thing when we perceive it
clearly and distinctly, that necessary assent does not depend on the
weakness of our will, but only on its freedom and perfection. For to
25 assent is truly a perfection in us (as is known sufficiently by itself),
and the will is never more perfect or more free than when it completely determines itself. Since this can happen when the mind understands something clearly and distinctly, it will necessarily give that
perfection to itself immediately (by A5). So it is far from being the
30 case that we understand ourselves to be less free from the fact that we
are not at all indifferent in embracing the truth. On the contrary, we
have established it as certain that the more we are indifferent, the less
we are free.

All that remains to be explained, therefore, is how error is nothing
I/175 but a privation in relation to man, but is only a negation in relation
to God. We shall see this easily if we first observe that because we
perceive many things in addition to those we understand clearly[37] we
are more perfect than we would be if we did not perceive them. This
5 is clearly established by the fact that if we could perceive nothing
clearly and distinctly, but only confusedly, we would have nothing
more perfect than perceiving things confusedly. Nor could anything
else be desired for our nature. Next, assenting to things, even to confused things, is a kind of action, and as such, it is a perfection. This
10 will also be plain to anyone who supposes (as above) that perceiving

---

[36] In fact the passage cited from the *Principles* does not offer a proof of the freedom
of the will, but claims that it is so manifest that it should be numbered among the
common notions, and that it is known by experience. In the Fourth Meditation it is
also said to be known by experience (AT VII, 57), and the following account is given:
"[The freedom of the will] consists only in this, that we can do or not do a thing (that
is, affirm or deny it, pursue or flee it), *or rather* that in affirming or denying, or pursuing
or fleeing, what is proposed to us by the intellect, we are so impelled that we feel
ourselves to be determined toward it by no external force." Cf. Spinoza, Ep. 58, IV/
266: "This is that human freedom which all men boast that they have, and which
consists only in this, that they are conscious of their appetites, but ignorant of the causes
by which they are determined." See also E IIP35S, and IIIP2S. The passage cited from
the Appendix (I/278/5) offers no argument for the freedom of the will, but at the critical
point refers the reader back to the Fourth Meditation.
[37] B: "clearly and distinctly."

things clearly and distinctly is contrary to man's nature. For then it will be evident that it is far better for man to assent even to confused things and to exercise his freedom, than to remain always indifferent, i.e. (as we have just shown), in the lowest degree of freedom. And if we also consider what is needed and advantageous in human life, we shall find it absolutely necessary, as daily experience sufficiently teaches everyone.

Since, then, all the modes of thinking we have are perfect, insofar as they are considered in themselves alone, what constitutes the form of error cannot be in them, considered in themselves. But if we consider the modes of willing, as they differ from one another, we shall discover that some are more perfect than others, insofar as some render the will less indifferent, i.e., more free, than others. Next we shall also see that, so long as we assent to confused things, we make the mind less fit to distinguish between the true and the false, and bring it about that we lack the best liberty. So assenting to confused things, insofar as it is something positive, contains neither any imperfection [B: in itself], nor the form of error; [it contains imperfection] only insofar as we thereby deprive ourselves of the best freedom, which belongs to our nature and is in our power. So the whole imperfection of error will consist solely in the privation of the best freedom, which is called error. It is said to be a Privation because we are deprived of a perfection which is suited to our nature; but [it is said to be] Error because we lack that perfection through our own fault, insofar as we do not contain the will within the limits of the intellect to the extent that we can.

Since, then, error is nothing, in relation to man, but a privation of the perfect, *or* right, use of freedom, it follows that it is not placed in any faculty which man has from God, nor in any operation of faculties, insofar as it depends on God. Nor can we say that God has deprived us of a greater intellect than he could have given us, and so has brought it about that we can fall into error. For nothing is such that its nature can require anything of God, nor does anything pertain to anything except what the will of God has willed to bestow on it. For nothing existed prior to the will of God, nor can anything be conceived prior to it. (This is fully explained in our Appendix, II, vii and 8.) So God has no more deprived us of a greater intellect, *or* a more perfect faculty of understanding, than he has deprived a circle of the properties of a sphere or its circumference of the properties of a spherical surface.

Therefore, since none of our faculties, however it is considered, can show any imperfection in God, it clearly follows that that imperfec-

20   tion in which the form of error consists, is a privation only in relation to man. But considered in relation to God as its cause, it cannot be called a privation, only a negation.

P16: *God is incorporeal.*

25   Dem.: Body is the immediate subject of local motion (by D7). So if God were corporeal, he would be divided into parts. Since this clearly involves an imperfection, it is absurd to affirm it of God (by D8).

I/177   Alternative Dem.: If God were corporeal, he could be divided into parts (by D7). Now each part could either subsist through itself, or it could not. If the latter were the case, then it would be like the other

5   things created by God, and so, like every created thing, would be created continually by God by the same power (by P10 and A11), and would no more pertain to the nature of God than the other created things do. But that is absurd (by P5). On the other hand, if each part exists through itself, then each one must also involve necessary exist-

10   ence (by P7L2), and consequently each one would be a supremely perfect being (by P7L2C). But that is also absurd (by P11). Therefore, God is incorporeal, q.e.d.

P17: *God is an entirely simple being.*

15   Dem.: If God were composed of parts, the parts would have to be at least prior in nature to God (as everyone will easily concede). But that is absurd (by P12C4). Therefore, he is an entirely simple being, q.e.d.

20   Cor.: From this it follows that God's intellect and his will, *or* his Decree, and his power, are only distinguished by reason from his essence.[38]

I/178   P18: *God is immutable.*

Dem.: If God were mutable, he could not be changed only in part,

5   but would have to be changed in respect to his whole essence (by P17). However, the essence of God exists necessarily (by P5, 6, and 7). Therefore, God is immutable, q.e.d.

P19: *God is eternal.*

10   Dem.: God is a supremely perfect being (by D8), from which it follows (by P5) that he exists necessarily. If we now ascribe a limited existence to him, the limits of his existence must be understood—at least by God himself, if not by us, because he understands in the

15   highest degree (by P9). So beyond those limits God will understand himself (i.e., a supremely perfect being, by D8) as not existing. That

---

[38] Cf. Descartes' Letter to Mersenne, 27 May 1630.

is absurd (by P5). So God has, not a limited, but an infinite existence, which we call eternity. See our Appendix, II, 1. Therefore, God is eternal, q.e.d.

P20: *God has preordained all things from eternity.*

Dem.: Since God is eternal (by P19), his understanding is eternal, because it pertains to his eternal essence (by P17C). But his intellect is not really distinct from his will, *or* decree (by P17C). So when we say that God has understood things from eternity, we are saying at the same time that he has willed, *or* decreed, them so from eternity, q.e.d.[39]

Cor.: From this Proposition it follows that God is supremely constant in his works.

P21: *Substance extended in length, breadth and depth really exists; and we are united to one part of it.*[40]

Dem.: The extended thing, as we perceive it clearly and distinctly, does not pertain to God's nature (by P16), but can be created by God (by P7C and P8). Now we perceive clearly and distinctly (as everyone finds in himself, insofar as he thinks) that extended substance is a sufficient cause for producing in us pleasure, pain, and similar ideas, *or* sensations. These are continually produced in us, even though we are unwilling. But if we wish to feign some other cause of our sensations, beyond extended substance—say God or an Angel—we immediately destroy the clear and distinct concept which we have. Hence, so long as we attend rightly to our perceptions,[g] so that we admit nothing but what we have perceived clearly and distinctly, we shall be wholly disposed (*or* not at all indifferent) to assent that extended substance is the only cause of our sensations. Hence [we will be wholly

---

[g] See P14D and P15S.

[39] Whereas Descartes derives God's preordination of things from God's power (*Principles* I, 40), Spinoza derives it from the eternity of God's intellect (cf. E IP33S2). And whereas Descartes asserts that free will is compatible with God's preordination, though we cannot understand how (*Principles* I, 41), Spinoza passes over this problem in silence (apart from what he says through Meyer at I/132/25ff.).

[40] In the *Principles* Descartes' analogues of this proposition occur as sections 1 and 2 of Part II. In the Latin version Descartes does not speak of 'extended substance,' but of "the extended thing which we call body or matter" and "a certain matter [thing] extended in length, depth and breadth." In the French version, where the term 'substance' is introduced, it is still treated as a general term ("a certain substance," "this substance"). But in Spinoza's version extended substance seems to be treated as a singular term, hence my avoidance of articles. Though Descartes is not consistent in his usage, there is Cartesian authority for the doctrine that ultimately there is only one extended substance, even by the somewhat relaxed standards for substancehood which Descartes allows in *Principles* I, 52 (cf. The Synopsis of the *Meditations*, AT VII, 13-14).

disposed] to affirm that the extended thing created by God exists.[41]
And in this we can surely not be deceived (by P14 and P14S). So it
is affirmed truly that substance extended in length, breadth, and depth
exists. This was the first thing to be demonstrated.

Next, we observe that among our sensations, which must be produced in us by extended substance (as we have now demonstrated),
there is a great difference, viz. when I say that I sense, *or* see, a tree,
and when I say that I am thirsty or in pain. But I clearly see that I
cannot perceive the cause of this difference unless I first understand
that I am closely united to one part of matter and not to others. Since
I understand this clearly and distinctly and cannot perceive it in any
other way, it is true that I am united to one part of matter (by P14
and P14S). This was the second thing to be demonstrated.

*Note: Unless the Reader here considers himself only as a thinking thing,
lacking a body, and puts to one side, as prejudices, all the reasons he previously
had for believing that body exists, any effort to understand this proof will be
in vain.*

Principles of Philosophy
Demonstrated in the Geometric Manner
Part II

POSTULATE: Here I ask only that everyone attend to his perceptions
as accurately as possible, so as to be able to distinguish the clear from
the obscure.

DEFINITIONS

D1: *Extension* is what consists of three dimensions; but by extension
we do not understand the act of extending, or anything distinct from
quantity.[1]

D2: By *substance* we understand what requires only the concurrence of
God to exist.[2]

D3: An *atom* is a part of nature which is, by its nature, indivisible.[3]

---

[41] I.e., that the extended thing which God was able to create he did create.
[1] Cf. *Principles* II, 5.   [2] Cf. *Principles* I, 51-52.
[3] Cf. *Principles* II, 20.

D4: *Indefinite* is that whose limits (if it has any) cannot be discovered by the human intellect.[4]

D5: A *vacuum* is extension without corporeal substance.[5]

D6: We make only a distinction of reason between *space* and extension, *or* they are not really distinct. Read *Principles* II, 10.

D7: What we understand to be divided in thought is at least potentially *divisible*.[6]

D8: *Local motion* is the transfer of one part of matter, *or* one body, from the vicinity of those bodies that touch it immediately, and are considered as resting, to the vicinity of others.

82   *Descartes uses this definition to explain local motion. To understand it properly, we must consider:*

(1) That he understands by a part of matter whatever is transferred at the same time, even though it, in turn, may consist of many parts.[7]

(2) That for the sake of avoiding confusion he speaks in this definition only of what is constantly in the mobile thing, viz. the transfer, in order not to confuse this, as others frequently do, with the force or action which moves it. It is commonly thought that this force or action is required only for motion, and not for rest. But those who so think are thoroughly deceived. For as is known through itself, the force which is needed to impart certain degrees of motion to a body at rest is also required to take away those certain degrees of motion from the body so that it is wholly at rest.

Indeed this is also proved by experience. For we use nearly the same force to put in motion a boat resting in still water as we use to check suddenly the same boat when it is moving. The force would surely be exactly the same if we were not aided in checking the motion by the weight and resistance of the water the boat displaces.

(3) That he says the transfer takes place from the vicinity of contiguous bodies into the vicinity of others, and not from one place to another.[8] For place, as he has explained in II, 13, is not something real, but depends merely on our thought, so that the same body can be said at the same time both to change and not to change place. But it cannot be said at the same time both to be transferred and not to be transferred from the vicinity of a contiguous body. For only certain bodies can be contiguous to the same mobile [thing] at the same moment of time.

(4) That he does not say absolutely that the transfer takes place from the vicinity of contiguous bodies, but only from the vicinity of those which are regarded as being at rest. If

[4] Cf. *Principles* I, 26-27.   [5] Cf. *Principles* II, 16.   [6] Cf. *Principles* II, 20.

[7] Cf. *Principles* II, 25.   [8] Cf. *Principles* II, 28.

30

I/183

5

10

15

20

25

30

body A is transferred from body B, which is at rest, the same force and action are required on the one part as on the other.[9] *This is evident from the example of a boat which is stuck in mud or sand at the bottom of the water. To free it, the force exerted on the bottom will have to equal that exerted on the boat. So the force by which bodies must be moved is expended equally on the body which is moved and on the one at rest. The transfer is, in fact, reciprocal; for if the boat is separated from the sand, the sand is also separated from the boat.*

Therefore, if we should wish to ascribe equal motions absolutely to two bodies which are separated from one another—one in one direction, the other in another—and should wish not to regard one as being at rest, simply because the same action which is in one is in the other, then we would also be compelled to ascribe just as much motion to bodies which everyone takes to be at rest (like the sand from which the boat is separated) as we do to the bodies which move. For as we have shown, the same action is required on the one part as on the other and the transfer is reciprocal. But this would be too inconsistent with the ordinary manner of speaking. Still, even though those bodies from which others are separated are regarded as being at rest, and are so spoken of, nevertheless we shall remember that whatever is in the body in motion, in virtue of which it is said to move, is also in the body at rest.

(5) Finally, it is also clear from the Definition that each body has only one motion proper to it, since it is understood to depart from certain bodies only, viz. those that are contiguous to it and at rest. Nevertheless, if the body in motion is a part of other bodies, having other motions, we understand clearly that it can also participate in countless other motions. But because we cannot easily understand so many at once, or even recognize all of them, it will suffice to consider in each body that one motion which is proper to it. Read Principles *II, 31*

D9: By the *circle of moved bodies* we understand only what occurs when the last body which is moved on account of the impulse of another body immediately touches the first of the bodies in motion, even though the line which is described by all the bodies at once through the impulse of one motion may be very twisted.[10]

Axioms

A1: Nothing has no properties.[11]

A2: If something can be removed from a thing, while that thing remains intact, it does not constitute the thing's essence, but if some-

---

[9] Cf. *Principles* II, 29, and the Letter to More, 15 April 1649. On the relation between the Cartesian and Newtonian laws of motion, see Ellis, Westfall, Koyré 3, and Herivel.
[10] Cf. *Principles* II, 33.   [11] Cf. *Principles* I, 11.

thing, on being taken away, takes the thing away, it does constitute the thing's essence.[12]

184 A3: The senses do not indicate anything to us in hardness, nor do we understand anything clearly and distinctly about it, except that the parts of hard bodies resist the motion of our hands.[13]

A4: If two bodies move, either toward one another or away from one another, they will not, on that account, occupy more or less space.

A5: Whether a part of matter moves away or resists, it does not, on that account, lose the nature of body.

A6: Motion, rest, figure and the like cannot be conceived without extension.[14]

A7: Beyond the sensible qualities there is nothing in body except extension and its affections, enumerated in Part I of the *Principles*.[15]

A8: One space, *or* extension, cannot be larger at one time than at another.[16]

A9: Every extension can be divided, at least in thought.[17]

No one who has learned even the elements of Mathematics doubts the truth of this axiom. For the space between a circle and a line tangent to the circle can always be divided by infinitely many other larger circles. The same thing is also evident from the Asymptotes of the Hyperbola.

A10: No one can conceive the limits of any extension, *or* space, unless at the same time he conceives other spaces beyond them, i.e., immediately following them.[18]

A11: If there were more than one sort of matter and one did not touch the other immediately, each would be comprehended within limits beyond which there is no matter.[19]

A12: The smallest bodies yield easily to the motion of our hands.

A13: One space does not penetrate another, nor is it larger at one time than at another.

A14: If a pipe, A, is of the same length as another pipe, C, but C is twice as wide as A, and some fluid matter passes twice as quickly through A as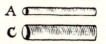

---

[12] Spinoza will criticize this Cartesian conception of essence in the *Ethics* II P1OCS.
[13] Spinoza's acceptance of this Cartesian doctrine (*Principles* II, 3-4) lies behind his criticism of Boyle at IV/28.
[14] Cf. *Principles* I, 53.
[15] Cf. *Principles* I, 66-70.
[16] *Principles* II, 19.
[17] *Principles* II, 20.
[18] *Principles* II, 21.
[19] *Principles* II, 22.

I/185 what passes through C, the quantity of matter which passes through A in a given interval of time will be the same as that which passes through C. And if the same quantity passes through A as through C, the former will move twice as quickly.[20]

A15: If two things agree with a third, they agree with one another. And if they are each double the same third thing, they are equal to one another.

A16: Matter that moves in various ways has at least as many parts into which it is actually divided as the different degrees of speed that are observed in it at the same time.

A17: The shortest line between two points is a straight line.

A18: If a body, A, in motion from C toward B, is repelled by an opposite impulse, it will be moved along the same line toward C.

A19: When two bodies which have opposite modes come into contact with one another, either both are constrained to suffer some variation, or else at least one of them is.

A20: A variation in any thing proceeds from a stronger force.

A21: If, when body 1 moves toward body 2 and sets it in motion, body 8 is moved toward body 1 by this impulse, bodies 1, 2, and 3, etc., cannot be in a straight line, but all of them will form a whole circle, up to body 8. See D9.

L1: *Where there is Extension, or Space, there is necessarily a Substance.*
   Dem.: Extension, *or* space, cannot be a pure nothing (by A1). Therefore, it is an attribute, which must necessarily be attributed to some thing. But not to God (by IP16); therefore to a thing which requires only the concurrence of God to exist (by IP12), i.e. (by D2), to a substance, q.e.d.

I/186 L2: *We conceive Rarefaction and Condensation clearly and distinctly, even though we do not grant that bodies occupy a larger space when rarefied than when condensed.*
   Dem.: We can clearly and distinctly conceive Rarefaction and Condensation as occurring when the parts of a body merely move away from one another or approach one another. Therefore (by A4) they will not occupy a larger or smaller space; for if the parts of a body—

---

[20] *Principles* II, 33.

266

say, a sponge—by, approaching one another expel the bodies which fill the intervals between the parts, this in itself renders that body more dense, and its parts will not on that account occupy a smaller space than before (by A4). And if they should move away from one another again and their path should be filled by other bodies, rarefaction will take place, and yet they will not occupy a larger space. What we perceive clearly in a sponge with the aid of the senses, we can conceive by the intellect alone concerning all bodies, even though the intervals between their parts completely escape our senses [B: on account of their smallness]. So we do conceive Rarefaction and Condensation clearly and distinctly, etc., q.e.d.

It seemed desirable to set these things out first so that the intellect might lay aside its prejudices about Space, Rarefaction, etc., and be made suited to understand the things that follow.

P1: *Even though the hardness, weight, and the rest of the sensible qualities are separated from a body, the nature of the body will still remain whole.*

Dem.: Sensation does not indicate anything else to us in the hardness of, say, this stone than that the parts of hard bodies resist the motion of our hands, nor do we clearly and distinctly understand anything else about it (by A3). So hardness will also be nothing else than that (by IP14). But if that body should be reduced to as fine a powder as possible, its parts will move away easily (by A12), and nevertheless it will not lose the nature of body (by A5), q.e.d.

The proof proceeds in the same way for weight and the rest of the sensible qualities.

P2: *The nature of Body, or Matter, consists in extension alone.*

Dem.: The nature of the body is not taken away when the sensible qualities are taken away (by P1). Therefore, they do not constitute its essence (by A2). Nothing remains, then, except extension and its affections (by A7), [B: which (by A6) cannot be conceived without extension]. So if extension is taken away, nothing will remain that pertains to the nature of the body, but it will be entirely taken away. Therefore, the nature of Body consists in extension alone (by A2), q.e.d.

Cor.: *Space and body do not really differ.*

Dem.: Body and extension do not really differ (by P2), and space and extension do not really differ (by D6); therefore (by A15) space and body do not really differ, q.e.d.

Schol.: Though we say that God is everywhere, we do not thereby concede that God is extended,[a] i.e. (by P2), corporeal. For being

[a] On this, see the fuller explanation in the Appendix, II, iii and ix.

5   everywhere is related only to God's power and concurrence, by which
he preserves all things, so that God's omnipresence is related no more
to extension, *or* body, than to angels or human souls. But it should be
noted that when we say that his power is everywhere, we do not
exclude his essence. For where his power is, there his essence is also
10   (by IP17C). We exclude only corporeality, i.e., God is everywhere
not by some corporeal power, but by the divine power, *or* essence,
which is common to the preservation both of extension and of thinking
things (by IP17). For God would not really have been able to preserve
15   the latter if his power, i.e., his essence, were corporeal.[21]

P3: *It involves a contradiction that there should be a vacuum.*
Dem.: By a vacuum is understood extension without corporeal sub-
20   stance (by D5), i.e. (by P2), body without body, which is absurd.
For a fuller explanation, and to correct the prejudice about the vacuum,
Principles II, 17-18 should be read. The main point there is that bodies
25   *between which nothing lies must touch one another, and also that nothing has*
no properties.

I/189 P4: *One part of a body does not occupy a larger space at one time than at*
another; conversely, the same space does not contain more body at one time
than at another.
5   Dem.: Space and body do not really differ (P2C). So when we say
that a space is not larger at one time than at another (by A13), we are
saying thereby that a body cannot be larger, i.e., occupy a larger
space, at one time than at another. That was the first thing to be
10   proven. Next, from the fact that space and body do not really differ,
it follows that when we say that the body cannot occupy a larger space
at one time than at another, we are saying thereby that the same space
cannot contain more body at one time than at another.
15   Cor.: *Bodies which occupy equal space—say, gold and air—have just as*
much matter, or *corporeal substance.*
Dem.: Corporeal substance does not consist in the hardness of the
20   gold, nor in the softness of the air, nor in any of the sensible qualities
(by P1); it consists rather in extension alone (by P2). But since (by
Hypothesis) there is as much space, *or* (by D6) extension, in the one
as in the other, there will also be as much corporeal substance, q.e.d.

I/190 P5: *There are no atoms.*
Dem.: Atoms are parts of matter which are, by their own nature,
5   indivisible (by D3). But since the nature of matter consists in exten-

---

[21] If the corporeality of God's essence would be a barrier to his conservation of thinking things, it is natural to wonder why God's being a thinking thing would not be a
barrier to his conservation of corporeal things. In this scholium Spinoza seems again to
be making use of the correspondence with More. See the letter of 15 April 1649.

sion (by P2), which is, by its nature, divisible, however small it may be (by A9 and D7), a part of matter, however small, is, by its nature, divisible. I.e., there are no Atoms, *or* parts of matter which are, by their nature, indivisible, q.e.d.

Schol.: The dispute about Atoms has always been an important and complicated one. Some maintain that there are Atoms on the ground that one infinite cannot be greater than another. If two quantities, A and its double, should be divisible to infinity, they will also be able to be actually divided into infinitely many parts by the power of God, who understands their infinitely many parts in one intuition. Therefore, since, as has been said, one infinite is not greater than another, quantity A will be equal to its double, which is absurd. Again, they also ask whether half of an infinite number is also infinite, whether it is even or odd, and the like.

To all these questions Descartes replies that we must not reject the things that fall under our intellect and therefore that we conceive clearly and distinctly, because of others that exceed our intellect, or grasp, and that we therefore perceive only quite inadequately.[22] But the infinite, and its properties, exceed the human understanding, which is finite by nature. So it would be foolish to reject as false, *or* to doubt, what we conceive clearly and distinctly about space, because we do not comprehend the infinite. For this reason Descartes considers those things in which we do not perceive any limits—like the extension of the world, or the divisibility of parts of matter—as indefinite. Read *Principles* I, 26.

P6: *Matter is indefinitely extended and the matter of the heavens is one and the same as that of the earth.*[23]

Dem.: (1) We cannot imagine any limits to extension, i.e. (by P2), to matter, unless we conceive other spaces which follow immediately beyond them (by A10), i.e. (by D6), extension *or* matter, and that indefinitely. This was the first thing to be proven.

(2) The essence of matter consists in extension (by P2), and it is indefinite (by part 1), i.e., cannot perceived by the human intellect under any limits (by D4). So (by A11) there is not more than one kind of matter, but it is one and the same everywhere. This was the second thing to be proven.

Schol.: So far we have dealt with the nature, *or* essence, of extension. That it exists, created by God just as we conceive it, we have demonstrated in IP21. From IP12 it follows that it is now preserved

---

[22] We know from Meyer's Preface (I/132/25), that Spinoza would not give this answer himself. It seems, from Letter 12 (IV/53/14), that he would deny that one infinite cannot be greater than another.

[23] *Principles* II, 22.

by the same power by which it was created. We have also demonstrated in IP21 that, insofar as we are thinking things, we are united to a part of that matter, with the aid of which we perceive that all those variations actually exist, which we know matter to be capable of from merely contemplating it. E.g., divisibility and local motion, *or the passage of one part from one place to another.*[24] We perceive local motion clearly and distinctly, provided that we understand that other parts of matter take the place of those that are moving.

We conceive this division and motion in infinite ways, and so can conceive infinite variations of matter. I say that we conceive them clearly and distinctly so long as we conceive them as modes of extension, but not as things really distinct from extension. This is fully explained in Part I of the *Principles.*[25] And though philosophers have feigned many other motions, we who admit nothing we do not conceive clearly and distinctly, must admit no motion except local motion, since we clearly and distinctly understand that extension is not capable of any motion except local motion, nor can we even imagine any other motion.

Zeno, they say, denied local motion, because of various arguments, which were refuted by Diogenes the Cynic in his fashion—i.e., by walking about the School in which Zeno was teaching these doctrines and thus disturbing those who were listening to Zeno. When he perceived that one of the listeners was holding him back to prevent his walking, he reproached him, saying "How is it that you have thus dared to refute your master's arguments?"[26]

Nevertheless, someone who is deceived by Zeno's argument might think that the senses show us something (viz. motion) which the intellect finds absolutely contradictory, so that the mind would be deceived even about those things that it perceives clearly and distinctly with the aid of the intellect. To prevent any such confusion, I shall set out here Zeno's main arguments and show that they rest only on false prejudices, because he did not have a true concept of matter.

First, then, Zeno is reported to have said[27] that if there were local motion, the motion of a body moving circularly with the greatest speed,

24 Cf. IP21 with *Principles* II, 1.

25 Cf. *Principles* I, 64, 69; II, 24.

26 This anecdote goes back to Diogenes Laertius VI, 39, but along the way some colorful and inaccurate details have been added. As Bayle pointed out (354ff.), Diogenes the Cynic was not a contemporary of Zeno. In view of Spinoza's criticisms of Zeno here, it is ironic that Bayle treats the Eleatic philosophy of Parmenides and Melissus as a species of Spinozism (387).

27 The argument recounted here is not to be found in any of our ancient sources of knowledge of Zeno. It is unclear what Spinoza's source was.

30 would not differ from rest. But the latter is absurd, so the former is also. He proves the consequence as follows. If all of the points of a body remain continuously in the same place, it is at rest. But all the points of a body moving circularly with the greatest speed remain continuously in the same place. Therefore, etc.

I/193 They say he explained this by using the example of a wheel—say ABC. If it moves around its center with a certain speed, point A will complete the circle through B and C more quickly than it would if it 5 moved more slowly. Suppose that when it begins to move slowly, after an hour has passed it is in the same place as that from which it began. If it should move twice as quickly, it would be in that place after the passage of half an hour. If it should move four 10 times as quickly, then after a quarter of an hour. And if we conceive this speed to be increased to infinity and the time diminished to a moment, then when point A is at that greatest speed it will be at every moment, or continuously, in the place from which it began[28] to be moved; so it will always remain in the same place. What we under-5 stand to be the case concerning A, must also be understood to apply to all the points of this wheel. So all the points, when at that greatest speed, remain continuously in the same place.

To answer this argument, I must call attention to the fact that it is more an argument against the greatest speed of motion than against 0 motion itself. We shall not examine here whether Zeno argues rightly, but shall rather uncover his prejudices, on which this whole argu-ment—insofar as he thinks that it attacks motion—rests. He supposes, first, that bodies can be conceived to move so quickly that they cannot 5 move more quickly, and second, that time is composed of moments, just as others have conceived that quantity is composed of indivisible points.

Both assumptions are false. For we can never conceive a motion so fast that we do not at the same time conceive a faster one. Our intellect 0 finds a contradiction in conceiving a motion so fast that there cannot be a faster one, no matter how short its course may be. The same is true of slowness. The concept of a motion so slow that there cannot be a slower one also implies a contradiction. We maintain the same thing about time, which is the measure of motion, viz. that our intel-194 lect clearly finds a contradiction in conceiving a time so short that there cannot be a shorter one.

To prove all these assertions, let us follow in Zeno's footsteps. Sup-

---

[28] EP: "begins," G: "began."

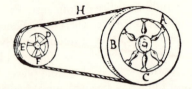

pose, therefore, as he did, that a Wheel, ABC, moves about its center with such speed that point A is at every moment in the place, A, from which it moves. I say that I clearly conceive a speed indefinitely faster than this, and so moments infinitely less than these. For suppose that while the wheel, ABC, moves around its center, with the aid of a belt it makes another wheel, DEF, move around its center. Let DEF be half the size of ABC. It is plain that in this case, DEF moves twice as fast as ABC, and consequently that at each half moment the point D is again in the place from which it began to move. Again, if we attribute the motion of DEF to ABC, DEF will move four times as fast as [ABC did][29] before. And if we again ascribe this last speed of DEF to ABC, then DEF will move eight times faster, and so on, to infinity.

But this is clearest from the concept of matter alone. For we have proven that the essence of matter consists in extension, *or* space, which is always divisible; and there is no motion without space. We have also demonstrated that one part of matter cannot occupy two spaces at the same time. For that would be the same as if we were to say that one part of matter is equal to its double, as is evident from what has been demonstrated above. So if a part of matter moves, it moves through some space, which will be divisible, no matter how small it is feigned to be. Consequently the time by which that motion is measured will also be divisible, and the duration of that motion, *or* time, will be divisible, and this to infinity, q.e.d.

Let us go on now to the other sophism which he is said to have used.[30] Viz., if a body moves, it either moves in a place in which it is or in one in which it is not. But not in a place in which it is, for if it is somewhere, then it must be at rest. And not in a place in which it is not. Therefore, the body does not move.

But this argument is just like the previous one. For it, too, supposes that there is a time than which no time is shorter. If we reply to the argument by saying that the body does not move in a place, but rather from the place in which it is to the place in which it is not, he will ask whether it has not been in the places in between. We may reply by drawing a distinction: if by *has been* he understands *has rested*, then

---

[29] Following Vloten-Land.
[30] This second argument is sometimes (e.g., by Appuhn and Caillois) identified with the 'flying arrow' argument reported by Aristotle (*Physics* 239b30). But the identification is questionable (cf. Barnes, 1:276). A more likely source is Diogenes Laertius IX, 72, though the account there is very incomplete.

we deny that it has been anywhere while it was moving; but if by *has been* he means *has existed*, we say that, while it was moving, it must have existed.

Again, he will ask, where has it existed, while it was moving? We may reply once more: if by *where has it existed?* he means *what place has it stayed in?* while it was moving, we say that it did not stay in any. But if he means *what place has it changed?* we say that it changed whatever places he might wish to assign in the space through which it was moving.

He will continue by asking whether it could, at the same moment of time, both occupy a place and change it. To this we will reply finally, by drawing this distinction: if by a moment of time he understands a time than which none can be shorter, he asks something which has been adequately shown to be unintelligible and hence unworthy of an answer. But if he takes time in the sense I have explained above, i.e., in its true sense, he can never assign a time so short that, even though an indefinitely shorter one might be supposed, a body could not both occupy and change its place. This is sufficiently plain to anyone who pays attention. So what we were saying above is now clearly evident—that he is supposing a time so short that there can not be a shorter one. Hence, he proves nothing.

In addition to these two, still another argument of Zeno's is commonly mentioned. This can be read, together with its refutation in the next to the last of Descartes' Letters, Volume one.[31]

But here I should like my Readers to note that I have opposed my reasonings to Zeno's reasonings, and therefore that I have refuted him by reason, not by the senses, as Diogenes did. For the senses cannot provide anything else to one who is seeking the truth except the Phenomena of Nature, by which he is determined to investigate their causes. They can never show him that something is false that the intellect has clearly and distinctly found to be true. For so we judge. And therefore, this is our Method: to demonstrate the things we put forward by reasons perceived clearly and distinctly by the intellect, and to regard as negligible whatever the senses say that seems contrary to those reasons. As we have said, the senses can only determine the intellect to inquire into this matter rather than that one. They cannot convict it of falsity, when it has perceived something clearly and distinctly.

96

---

[31] The reference is to Letter 118 of the Clerselier edition of Descartes' correspondence, a letter to Clerselier of June or July 1646.

P7: *No body enters the place of another unless at the same time that other body* 15 *enters the place of some other body.*

Dem.: If you deny this, assume (if it can be done) that body A[b] enters the place of body B, which, I also assume, is equal to A and does not yield its place. Therefore the space which used to contain 20 only B, now contains (by Hypothesis) both A and B. So it contains twice as much corporeal substance as before, which (by P4) is absurd. Therefore no body enters the place of another unless, etc., q.e.d.[32]

25 P8: *When any body enters the place of another, at the same moment of time* *the place left by it is occupied by another body which touches it immediately.*

I/197 Dem.: If body B moves toward D, then either bodies A and C will, at the same moment of time, approach and touch one another or they will not. If they should approach and touch one another, then what we have 5 maintained is conceded. But if they should not approach one another, then the whole space left by B would lie between A and C. Therefore, a body equal to B lies between A and C (by P2C and 10 P4C). But (by Hypothesis) the body is not identical with B. Therefore, it is another body which enters B's place at the same moment of time. And since it enters at the same moment of time, it can be none other than one which is immediately touching. For in P6S we demonstrated that there is no motion from one place to another which does not 15 require a time such that there is always a shorter one. From this it follows that body B's space cannot be occupied at the same moment of time by another body which would have to move through some space before it entered B's place. So only a body which touches B 20 immediately enters its place at the same moment of time, q.e.d.

Schol.: Since the parts of matter are really distinct from one another (by *Principles* I, 61), one can exist without another (by IP7C), and they 25 do not depend on one another. So all those fictions about Sympathy and Antipathy are to be rejected as false. Moreover, since the cause of an effect must always be positive (by IA8), it should never be said that a body moves in order that there not be a vacuum. A body moves only on account of the impulse of another body.

I/198 Cor.: *In every motion a whole Circle of bodies moves at the same time.*[33]

Dem.: At the same time that body 1 enters the 5 place of body 2, body 2 must enter the place of another body, say 3, and so on (by P7). Next, at the same moment of time at which body 1 enters the place

---

b See the figure for P8 [Fig. 17].
32 Cf. the Letter to More of 15 April 1649.   33 Cf. *Principles* II, 33.

of body 2, the place left behind by body 1 must be occupied by another body (by P8), say 8, or another, which touches 1 immediately. Since this happens only on account of the impulse of another body (by P8S) which is here taken to be 1, not all of these bodies can be in motion in the same straight line (by A21); instead they describe a whole circle (by D9), q.e.d.

P9: *If a circular pipe, ABC, is full of water, and is four times as wide at A as at B, when the water (or other fluid body) which is at A begins to move toward B, the water which is at B will move four times as fast.*[34]

Dem.: Since all the water which is at A moves toward B, at the same time just as much water must enter its place from C, which immediately touches A (by P8). And as much water will have to enter C's place from B (by P8). Therefore (by A14), it will move four times as quickly, q.e.d.

What we say here about a circular pipe must also be understood to be true of all the unequal spaces through which bodies which move at the same time are forced to pass. For the demonstration will be the same in the other cases.

Lemma: If two semicircles are described about the same center, as A and B are, the space between their perimeters will be equal everywhere. But if they are described about different centers, as C and D are, the space between their perimeters will be unequal everywhere.

The demonstration is obvious from the definition of the circle alone.

P10: *A fluid body moving through a pipe, ABC,[c] receives indefinite degrees of speed.*

Dem.: The space between A and B is unequal everywhere (by the preceding Lemma). So (by P9), the speed with which a fluid body moves through a pipe, ABC, will be unequal everywhere. Now, since we conceive in thought indefinite spaces between A and B, which are always less and less (by P5), we shall also conceive the inequalities, which are everywhere, as indefinite. Hence (by P9), the degrees of speed will be indefinite, q.e.d.

P11: *There is a division into indefinite parts in the matter which flows through a pipe, ABC.[d]*

---

[c] See the figure for P9 [Fig. 19].   [d] See the figure for P9 [Fig. 19].
[34] Cf. *Principles* II, 33.

I/200 Dem.: The matter that flows through the pipe, ABC, acquires at the same time indefinite degrees of speed (by P10). Therefore (by A16), it has indefinite parts which are really divided, q.e.d. Read

5 *Principles* II, 34 and 35.[35]

Scholium: So far we have dealt with the nature of motion. Now it is necessary for us inquire into its cause, which is twofold. There is the primary, *or* general, cause, which is the cause of all the motions

10 that there are in the world, and there is the particular cause, by which it comes about that the individual parts of matter acquire motions that they did not have before. As far as the general cause is concerned, since nothing is to be admitted except what we perceive clearly and distinctly (by IP14 and P15S), and since we do not clearly and dis-

15 tinctly understand any other cause except God (i.e., the creator of matter), it is evident that no other general cause except God should be admitted.[36] And what we say here about motion should also be understood to be true of rest.

20 P12: *God is the principal cause of motion.*
Dem.: Examine the immediately preceding Scholium.

P13: *God still preserves, by his concurrence, the same quantity of motion and*
25 *rest which he first imparted to matter.*[37]

I/201 Dem.: Since God is the cause of motion and of rest (by P12), he still preserves them by the same power by which he created them (by

5 IA10), and indeed, in that same quantity in which he first created them (by IP20C), q.e.d.

Schol.: (1) Although it may be said in Theology that God does many things from his good pleasure and to show his power to men,

10 nevertheless, since those things which depend only on his good pleasure do not become known except by divine revelation, they are not to

---

[35] Those who follow Spinoza's instructions here will find that, according to Descartes, this is an instance of a truth which our mind perceives but does not comprehend.

[36] Cf. *Principles* II, 36. In II, 37 Descartes contrasts the primary or general cause of motion (God) with "the secondary and particular causes" of the different motions, which he identifies with "certain rules or laws of nature." In II, 40, he observes that "all the particular causes of changes which happen to bodies are contained in" his third law of motion, which states that in cases of impact the quantity of motion is conserved. Though Spinoza will go on to deduce Descartes' laws of motion, he suppresses Descartes' reference to them as secondary causes. Perhaps the explanation for this omission is that, according to Spinoza's own philosophy God's power of acting is to be identified with the laws of nature (cf. II/138/11ff. and Curley 3, 47). In 1.13 I follow an emendation of Hubbeling's. Both EP and B cite "IP14 & IP17S," which cannot be right.

[37] Cf. *Principles* II, 36.

be admitted in Philosophy, where we inquire only into what reason
tells us, lest Philosophy be confused with Theology.[38]

15   (2) Although motion is nothing in the matter that moves but a mode
of it, nevertheless it has a certain determinate quantity. How this is
to be understood will be evident from what follows. Read *Principles*
II, 36.

20   P14: *Each thing, insofar as it is simple, undivided, and considered in itself
alone, always perseveres in the same state as far as it can.*[39]

This proposition is like an axiom to many; nevertheless, we shall
demonstrate it.

25   Dem.: Since nothing is in any state except by God's concurrence
alone (IP12) and God is supremely constant in his works (IP20C), if
we attend to no external, i.e., particular causes, but consider the thing
by itself, we shall have to affirm that insofar as it can it always per-

30   severes in the state in which it is, q.e.d.

I/202   Cor.: *Once a body moves, it always continues to move unless it is impeded
by external causes.*

5   Dem.: This is obvious from P14. Nevertheless, to correct the prejudice about motion, read *Principles* II, 37-38.

P15: *Every body in motion tends of itself to continue to move in a straight
line, not in one which is curved.*[40]

0   It would be proper to number this proposition among the axioms,
but I shall demonstrate it as follows from what has been shown above.

Dem.: Because the motion has only God as its cause (P12),[41] it never

5   has any power to exist of itself (IA10), but is as it were created by
God at every moment (by those things which are demonstrated concerning the axiom just cited). Hence, so long as we attend only to the
nature of the motion, we shall never be able to attribute to it, as

---

[38] Considering Descartes' position in the *Principles* (I, 76; IV, 207), we must read this
scholium as a muted criticism of him. The implication, I take it, is that, if we conceive
of God's power as being like that of a king, as Descartes did (cf. the Letter to Mersenne,
15 April 1630 with E II P3S), we destroy the foundation of our physics.

[39] Cf. *Principles* II, 37. The phrase here translated "as far as it can," *quantum in se est*,
is used both by Descartes, in stating his law of inertia, and by Newton, in his definition
of inertial force. Cohen traces it back to Lucretius and concludes that it connotes what
a body can do by its own natural force, in the absence of any external forces, with the
additional implication that the body's own natural force is limited. Spinoza will use the
same phrases in stating his own *conatus* principle (E III P6). Cf. Curley 4, 367-368.

[40] Cf. *Principles* II, 30. Spinoza's proof is quite different from Descartes', which seems
to require the concept of motion at an instant, while denying that there can be such a
thing.

[41] IIP12 does not quite say what it is made to say here. Cf. IIP8S and IIP11S.

277

20 pertaining to its nature, a duration that can be conceived to be greater than another. But if it should be said to pertain to the nature of a body in motion that it describes a curved line by its own motion, a greater duration would be attributed to the nature of the motion than when it is supposed to be of the nature of the moving body to tend to

25 continue to move in a straight line (A17). But since (as we have just demonstrated) we cannot attribute such a duration to the nature of the motion, neither can we assert that it is of the nature of the moving body to continue to move in a curved line, but only in a straight line, q.e.d.

I/203 Scholium: To many, perhaps, it will seem that this Demonstration shows no more that it does not pertain to the nature of motion to describe a curved line, than that it does pertain to the nature of motion

5 to describe a straight line. For no straight line can be assigned such that there is none shorter, whether straight or curved, nor any curved line such that there is not also another shorter curve. But though I have considered these things, I still judge that the demonstration proceeds correctly. It reaches the conclusion proposed for demonstration

10 from the universal essence, *or* essential difference, of lines, not from the quantity of anything, *or* not from an accidental difference.

But to demonstrate a thing already clear enough in itself might make it more obscure. So I shall refer the Readers simply to the definition of motion [D8], which affirms nothing of motion except that it is the

15 transfer of one part of matter from the vicinity, etc., into the vicinity of others, etc. So unless we conceive this transfer most simply, i.e., as occurring in a straight line, we add something to the motion which is not contained in its definition, *or* essence. So it does not pertain to its nature.

20 Cor.: From this proposition it follows that every body which moves in a curved line continuously deviates from the line along which it would, of itself, go on moving; and this occurs by the force of some external cause (P14).

25 P16: *Every body which moves in a circle, as for example, a stone in a sling, is continuously determined to go on moving along a tangent.*[42]

I/204 Dem.: A body that moves in a circle is continuously prevented by an external force from continuing to move in a straight line (by P15C). If this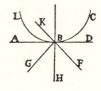

5 force ceases, the body of itself will continue to move in a straight line (by P15). I say, moreover, that a body moving in a circle is determined by an exter-

---

[42] Spinoza's argument in these two demonstrations is at best suggested by Descartes'

nal cause to continue to move along a tangent. For, if you deny this, suppose there is a stone at B which is determined to move by a sling, not along the tangent BD, but along another line from the same point, a line conceived as either outside the circle or within it—say, along BF, when the sling is assumed to come from L toward B, or along BG, if it is supposed to come from C toward B (I understand BG and BF to form equal angles with the line BH which is drawn from the center of the circle and cuts the circumference at B). But if the stone at B is supposed to be determined by the sling, which is moving in a circle from L toward B, so that the stone continues to move toward F, then necessarily (by A18) when the sling moves in an opposite direction, from C toward B, the stone will be determined to continue to move along the same line, BF, in an opposite direction. Hence, it will tend toward K, not toward G. But this is contrary to the hypothesis. And since, except for the tangent, there can be no line drawn through B which makes equal angles with the line BH (as DBH and ABH do),[e] there can be none except the tangent which can preserve the hypothesis, whether the sling moves from L toward B or from C toward B. So there can be no line except the tangent along which it tends to move, q.e.d.

Alt. Dem.: Conceive, instead of a circle, a Hexagon, ABH, inscribed in a circle, and a body C at rest on one side, AB. Then conceive that a ruler, DBE (with one end fixed in the center at D and the other end movable) moves around the center, continuously cutting the line AB. It is evident that if the ruler, DBE, while it is conceived to move in this way, meets body C at the time when it cuts the line AB at right an-

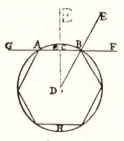

gles, the ruler will determine C by its impulse, to continue to move toward G along the line FBAG, i.e., along the line AB extended indefinitely.

But because we have assumed a Hexagon at our pleasure, we shall have to say the same of any other figure which we conceive can be inscribed in this circle—i.e., that when a body, C, lying at rest on one side of the figure, is struck by a ruler, DBE, at the same time

---

arguments in the relevant sections of the *Principles* (II, 39, and III, 57-59). It is not clear that Spinoza's exposition is even consistent with Descartes', since Spinoza treats the sling as a cause of the stone's tendency to continue along a line tangential to the circle in which it is moving (I/206/6-8), whereas Descartes treats the sling as an impediment to a tendency to rectilinear motion which is in the stone itself (AT VIII-1, 108-109).

[e] This is evident from propositions 18 and 19 of Book III of Euclid's *Elements*.

DBE cuts the side at right angles, it will be determined by that ruler to continue to move along that side produced indefinitely. Conceive, then, instead of a Hexagon, a rectilinear figure of infinitely many sides (i.e., a circle, according to Archimedes' definition). It is evident that the ruler, DBE, whenever it meets C, always meets it at that time when it cuts some side of the figure at right angles. Hence it will never meet C without determining it at the same time to continue to move along that side. And since any side, extended in any direction, must always fall outside the figure, this side, indefinitely extended, will be tangent to a figure of infinitely many sides, i.e., a circle. Therefore, if we conceive, instead of a ruler, a sling moving in a circle, it will continuously determine this stone to go on moving along a tangent, q.e.d.

Here it should be noted that both of these demonstrations can be adapted to any curved figure.

P17: *Every body that moves in a circle strives to move away from the center of the circle that it describes.*[43]

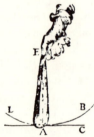

Dem.: As long as a body moves in a circle, it is compelled by an external cause. When this ceases, it continues at the same time to move along a tangent (by P16), all of whose points, except that which touches the circle, fall outside the circle (by Euclid's *Elements* III P16), and so are further away from its center. So when a stone which moves in a circle in the sling EA is at point A, it strives to continue along a line whose points are all further away from the center, E, than are all of the points of the circumference LAB. Doing this is nothing but striving to move away from the center of the circle which it describes, q.e.d.

P18: *If a body, say A, moves toward another body at rest, B, and nevertheless B does not lose any of its rest on account of the impetus of A, then A will also not lose any of its motion, but it will retain entirely the same quantity of motion that it had before.*[44]

---

[43] Cf. *Principles* II, 39. In Spinoza's version of the proposition *conari* replaces Descartes' *tendere*. But the *conatus ad motum* is a thoroughly Cartesian concept. Cf. I/229/21.

[44] B: "*then A will also not lose any of its motion, and if A loses none of its motion, then B will also lose none of its rest.*" In the corresponding passage of the *Principles* (II, 40), Descartes does not mention rest as a quantity subject to his conservation law. But cf. *Principles* II, 26-27, and *Le monde*, vii (AT XI, 40). See also Gueroult 2, viii, and Koyré 3, 76-77.

Dem.: If you deny this, suppose that body A loses
some of its motion, and nevertheless does not transfer
what it has lost to another, say to B. Then, when this
happens, there will be a lesser quantity of motion in nature than there
was before, which is absurd (P13). The Demonstration proceeds in
the same way with respect to the rest in body B. So if the one transfers
nothing to the other, B will retain all its rest, and A will retain all its
motion, q.e.d.

P19: *Motion, considered in itself, is different from its determination in some
definite direction; nor is it necessary that a moving body be at rest for a time,
in order to move in an opposite direction, or be repelled.*[45]

Dem.: Assume, as in the preceding proposition, that body A is
moving in a straight line toward B, and is prevented by B from continuing further. Therefore (P18) A will retain its whole motion, and
will not be at rest for any interval of time, however small. Nevertheless, although it continues to move, it does not move in the same
direction in which it was moving before. For it is supposed to be
prevented by B. Hence since its motion remains intact, and its former
determination [in a certain direction] is lost, it will move in the opposite direction, and not in any other (by those things said in chap. 2
of the *Dioptric*). Hence (by A2) its determination [in a certain direction]
does not pertain to the essence of the motion, but differs from it. Nor
does a moving body, when it is repelled, remain at rest for some time,
q.e.d.

Cor.: From this it follows that motion is not contrary to motion.

P20: *If body A meets body B, and takes B with it, A will lose as much motion
as B acquires because of its meeting with A.*[46]

Dem.: If you deny this, suppose that B acquires
more or less motion from A than A loses. That whole
difference will have to be added to or subtracted from
the quantity of motion of the whole of nature, which is absurd (by
P13). Since, therefore, body B can acquire neither more nor less motion, it will acquire as much as A loses, q.e.d.

P21: *If body A is twice as large as B[f] and is moving with equal speed, A will
also have twice as much motion as B, or twice as much force for retaining a
speed equal to B's.*

[f] See the figure for P20 [Fig. 25].

[45] Cf. *Principles* II, 41; *Dioptric*, ii (AT VI, 94-96). See Westfall, 64-68, on the role,
in Cartesian physics, of the distinction between motion and its determination.

[46] Cf. *Principles* II, 40.

25

I/209

Dem.: Let twice B be put in place of A, i.e. (by Hypothesis), one A divided in two equal parts; each B has a force for remaining in the state in which it is (P14), and that force is equal in each of them (by Hyp.); now if these two Bs are joined, their speed remaining the same, there will result one A, whose force and quantity will be equal to two Bs, *or* twice one B, q.e.d.

5

Note that this also follows simply from the definition of motion; for the greater a moving body is, the more matter there is which is separated from other matter; there is, therefore, more separation, i.e. (by D8), more motion. See our fourth note on the definition of motion [I/182ff.].

10

P22: If body A is equal to body B, and A is moving twice as fast as B, the force, or motion, in A will be twice that of B.[g]

15

20

Dem.: Assume that when B first acquired a certain force for moving, it acquired four degrees of speed. If nothing comes near it, it will continue to move (by P14) and to persevere in its state. Suppose it again acquires, from some new impulse, another new force equal to the first, so that it acquires, in addition to the first four, four more degrees of speed, which it will also maintain (by P14). I.e., it will move twice as quickly as before, i.e., as quickly as A; and it will at the same time have twice the force, i.e., a force equal to A's. So the motion in A is twice that in B, q.e.d.

25

Note that here, by force in moving bodies, we understand a quantity of motion, which must be greater, in bodies of equal size, as the speed of motion is greater, insofar as the equal bodies are, by that speed, separated more, in the same time, from bodies immediately touching them, than they would be if they were moving more slowly. Therefore (by D8) they also have more motion. But in bodies at rest we understand by force of resisting a quantity of rest.[47] *From which it follows that*

30

I/210

Cor. 1: *The more bodies are moving slowly, the more they participate in rest.* For they offer more resistance to bodies moving more quickly which meet them and have less force than they. They are also separated less from bodies which touch them immediately.

5

Cor. 2: *If body A moves twice as quickly as body B, and B is twice as large as A, there is just as much motion in the larger B as in the smaller A; and hence there is also an equal force.*

Dem.: Let B be twice as large as A, and A move twice as quickly

[g] See the figure for P20 [Fig. 25].
[47] Spinoza interprets the principle of inertia as implying that bodies at rest have a resistance to motion. Cf. I/223/7. Descartes is not consistent on this point. Cf. *Principles* II, 43; the Letter to More of August 1649; the Letter to Morin of 13 July 1638; and Westfall, 69-72.

as B; next, let C be half as large as B, and move with half the speed of A. Then B (by P21) will have a motion twice as great as C's, and A (by P22) will have a motion twice as great as C's. Therefore (by A15) B and A have equal motion, for the motion of each is twice that of the same third thing, C, q.e.d.

Cor. 3: From these it follows that *motion is distinguished from speed.* For we conceive that of bodies which have equal speed, one can have more motion than another (P21); and on the other hand, those which have unequal speed can have equal motion (by P22C2). This can also be inferred just from the definition of motion. For it is nothing but the transfer of one body from the vicinity, etc.

But here it should be noted that this third Corollary is not inconsistent with the first. For we conceive of speed in two ways: either insofar as a body is separated more or less in the same time from the bodies immediately touching it (and to that extent it participates more or less in motion or rest) or insofar as it describes a greater or lesser line in the same time (and to that extent it is distinguished from motion).

211 *I could have added other propositions here to explain P14 more fully, and to explain the forces of things in each state, as we have done here concerning motion. But it will be enough to read over* Principles *II, 43, and to annex one proposition which is necessary for understanding those which follow.*

P23: *When the modes of a body are forced to suffer variation, that variation will always be the least that there can be.*

Dem.: This proposition follows clearly enough from P14.

P24, Rule 1: *If two bodies, A and B, absolutely equal, and moving in a straight line toward each other with equal speed,[h] meet, each will be reflected in the opposite direction without losing any part of its speed.*[48]

In this hypothesis it is clearly evident that, to remove the contrariety of these two bodies, either each of them must be reflected in an opposite direction, or one must take the other with it. For they are contrary to one another only with respect to their determination in a certain direction, not with respect to their motion.

Dem.: When A and B meet, they must undergo some variation (by A19). But since motion is not contrary to motion (by P19C), they will

---

[h] See the figure for P20 [Fig. 25].

[48] Cf. *Principles* II, 46. Note that Descartes prefaces his laws of impact with a warning that they are laws bodies would observe in ideal conditions, viz. if they were perfectly hard and isolated from other bodies which might impede or assist their motion (II, 45). Spinoza defers the warning to P31S. In 1665 Spinoza expressed only limited disagreement with Descartes' laws (see the fragment of Letter 30 first published in Wolf 4). By 1676 he was prepared to be more critical (see Letter 81).

25   not be forced to lose any of their motion (by A19). Hence the change
will occur only in the determination [in a certain direction]. But we
cannot conceive that the determination of only one—say B—is changed,
unless we should suppose that A, by which it would have to be changed,
I/212 has more force (by A20). But this would be contrary to the hypothesis.
Therefore, since the change of determination in a certain direction
cannot occur only in one, it will occur in each of them, with both A
and B moving off in an opposite direction (but not in just any other
5   direction—according to what is said in chapter 2 of the *Dioptric* and
retaining its motion intact, q.e.d.[49]

P25, Rule 2: *If two bodies are unequal in bulk, B being larger than A, and
the rest assumed to be as before,[i] then only A will be reflected, and each will*
10   *continue to move with the same speed.*[50]

Dem.: Since A is supposed to be smaller than B, it will also have
less force than B (P21). But since, in this hypothesis (as in the preceding one), there is contrariety only in the determination [in a certain
15   direction], then, as we demonstrated in P24, the variation must occur
only in the determination [in a certain direction]. It will occur in A
and not in B (A20). So only A will be reflected in the opposite direction by B, which has more force, with A retaining its speed intact,
q.e.d.

20   P26: *If two bodies are unequal both in bulk and speed, B being twice as large
as A, but the motion in A being twice as fast as that in B, and the rest
assumed to be as before,[j] then each will be reflected in an opposite direction,*
25   *and each will retain the speed it had.*

Dem.: When A and B move toward each other, according to the
hypothesis, there is just as much motion in the one as in the other
(P22C2), and[51] the motion of the one will not be opposed to that of
I/213 the other (P19C), and the forces in each are equal (P22C2). Hence this
hypothesis is just like the hypothesis of P24. Therefore, A and B are
5   reflected in an opposite direction, each retaining its motion intact (by
the demonstration of P24), q.e.d.

Cor.: From these three preceding propositions it is clear that to

---

[i] See the figure for P27 [Fig. 26].
[j] See the figure for P27 [Fig. 26].
[49] Descartes' laws of impact are generally asserted without supporting arguments in
the Latin version of the *Principles*. In the French version more of an attempt is made to
justify them. Spinoza's demonstrations show no sign of his having used the French
version, though, as this demonstration illustrates, he does make use of the *Dioptric*.
[50] Cf. *Principles* II, 47.
[51] Following B.

change a body's determination [in a certain direction] requires a force
equal to that required to change its motion.[52] From which it follows
that a body which loses more than half of its determination [in a certain direction] and more than half its motion, suffers more change than
one which loses its whole determination [in a certain direction].

P27, Rule 3: *If two bodies are equal in bulk, but B is moving a little more
quickly than A, not only will A be reflected in the opposite direction, but also
B will transfer to A half of its excess speed, and both will proceed to move in
the same direction at the same speed.*[53]

Dem.: By hypothesis A is opposed to B not only
in its determination [in a certain direction], but also
in its slowness, insofar as it participates in rest (by
P22C1). So even if it were reflected in the opposite direction, and only
its determination [in a certain direction] were changed, not all of the
contrariety of the two bodies would thereby be removed. So (by A19)
the variation must occur both in the determination and in the motion.
But since B (by hypothesis) moves more quickly than A, B will have
more force than A (P22). So (by A20) the change in A will proceed
from B, from which A will be reflected in the opposite direction. This
was the first thing to be proved.

Next, so long as A moves more slowly than B, it is opposed to B
(by P22C1); therefore, the variation must occur (by A19) until it does
not move more slowly than B. But that A should move faster than B
is something which, in this hypothesis, is not compelled by any cause
of enough force. [B: For if B could impel A so that it moved more
quickly than B, these bodies would suffer more variation than was
necessary to remove their contrariety. It really was removed (as we
proved just now) when A did not move more slowly than B; so (by
P23) B cannot impel A to move faster than B.] Since, therefore, when
A is impelled by B, it can move neither more slowly than B, nor faster
than B, it will proceed to move as fast as B.

Next, if B should transfer less than half its excess speed to A, then
A would proceed to move more slowly than B. But if B should transfer more than half its excess speed to A, A would proceed to move
faster than B. But each of these is absurd, as we have already demonstrated. Therefore, the variation will occur just until B has transferred to A half its excess speed, which (by P20) B must lose. So both

---

[52] This is not Descartes' view of the matter. Cf. the *Dioptric*, ii (AT XI, 94) and
Westfall, 66-67.
[53] Cf. *Principles* II, 48.

will proceed to move in the same direction with equal speed without any contrariety, q.e.d.

Cor.: From this it follows that, the faster a body is moving, the more it is determined to continue moving in the direction in which it is moving; and conversely, the slower it is moving, the less determination [in a certain direction] it has.

Schol.: So that my Readers do not here confuse the force of determination [in a certain direction] with the force of motion, it seems desirable to add a few words to explain this distinction. If two bodies, A and C, should be conceived as equal, and as moving in a straight line toward one another with

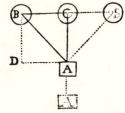

equal speed, they will be reflected in the opposite direction and retain their motion intact (P24). But if C is at B, and is moving obliquely toward A, it is clear that it is less determined to move along the line BD, or CA. So although it has a motion equal to A's, C's force of determination when moving directly toward A (which is equal to A's force of determination) is greater than its force of determination when moving from B toward A, and is as much greater as the line BA is longer than the line CA. For the longer line BA is in relation to CA, then (when B and A are moving with equal speed, as we assume here) the more time B requires to be able to move along the line BD or CA, through which it is opposed to the determination of body A. Therefore, when C meets A obliquely, from B, it will be determined as if it would proceed to move along the line AB toward B (which I assume to be as far from C as C is from B when it is at the point where line AB intersects the extended line BC). But A, retaining its motion and determination intact, will continue to move toward C and will drive body B[54] with it, since B, so long as it is determined to motion along the diagonal AB, and is moving with a speed equal to A's, requires more time than A to describe any part of the line AC by its own motion. And to that extent it is opposed to the determination of body A, which has more force.

But for C's force of determination, when it is moving from B to A (insofar as it participates in the line CA), to be equal to its force of determination when moving directly toward A (i.e., by hypothesis, to be equal to A's force of determination), B will have to have more degrees of motion than A in proportion as the line BA is longer than

---

[54] B: *body C*; B errata: *body B*. The text of the EP frequently has 'B' where we might have expected 'C'.

the line CA. And then, when it meets body A obliquely, A will be reflected in the opposite direction, toward A, and B toward B, each retaining its motion intact.

But if the excess of B over A is greater than the excess of the line BA over the line CA, then B will drive A back toward A, and transfer a part of its motion to A, until the motion of B is related to the motion of A, as the line BA is to the line CA, and B will continue to move in the direction in which it was moving before, losing as much motion as it transferred to A. E.g., if line AC is to line AB as 1 to 2, and the motion of body A is to the motion of body B as 1 to 5, then B will transfer to A one degree of its motion, drive it back in the opposite direction, and continue to move in the same direction in which it was tending before, with the four remaining degrees of motion.

P28, Rule 4: *If body A is completely at rest and a little larger than B,*[k] *then no matter how fast B moves toward A, it will never move A, but will be driven back by it in the opposite direction, without loss of motion.*[55]

Note that the contrariety of these bodies is removed in three ways: either one takes the other with it, and afterwards they continue to move in the same direction at equal speeds; or one is reflected in the opposite direction, and the other [B errata: which is at rest] retains its rest intact; or one is reflected in the opposite direction, and transfers some of its motion to the other, which was at rest. But there is no fourth way (by P13). Therefore it will have to be demonstrated now (by P23) that, in accordance with our hypothesis, the least change occurs in these bodies.[56]

Dem.: If B were to move A until they both proceeded to move with the same speed, then (by P20) it would have to transfer as much of its motion to A as A acquires, and (by P21) it would have to lose more than half of its motion. Consequently (by P27C) it would have to also lose more than half of its determination [in a certain direction]. Hence, (by P26C) it would suffer more change than if it lost only its determination [in a certain direction]. And if A should lose some of its rest, but not so much that it proceeded to move as fast as B, then the contrariety of these two bodies would not be removed. For A, by its slowness, insofar as it participates in rest, will be opposed to the speed of B (by P22C1). There B will still have to be reflected in the opposite direction, and will lose its whole determination [in a certain direction]

---

[k] See the figure for P27 [Fig. 26].

[55] Cf. *Principles* II, 49.

[56] This note, and the one immediately following P29, are set in smaller type in the first edition, indicating that they were additions made in proof. Cf. Letter 15.

35   and part of its motion, which it transferred to A. This is also a greater
I/217 change than if it were to lose only its determination [in a certain di-
rection]. Therefore since the change is only in the determination, it
is, in accordance with our hypothesis, the least which can occur in
these bodies. Hence, no other change occurs (by P23), q.e.d.

5   *It should be noted that in the demonstration of this Proposition (as in other
demonstrations) we have not cited P19, in which it is demonstrated that* the
whole determination can be changed, while the whole motion remains
intact. *Nevertheless you must attend to this proposition to rightly perceive the
force of the demonstration. For in P23 we did not say that* the variation will
10   always be absolutely the least, but the least there can be. *It is evident
from P18, P19, and P19C that such a change as we have assumed in this
demonstration, i.e., one consisting only in the determination, can occur.*

15   P29, Rule 5: *If a body at rest, A, is smaller than B, then no matter how
slowly B moves toward A,*[1] *it will move it with it, and transfer a part of its
motion to A, so that afterwards both will move with equal speed. (Read Principles II, 50.)*

20   In this Rule also, as in the preceding one, we can conceive only
three cases in which this contrariety would be removed. Indeed we
shall demonstrate that, in accordance with our hypothesis, the least
change happens in these bodies. Therefore (by P23), they also must
be changed in such a way.

25   Dem.: According to our hypothesis, B transfers to A (by P21) less
than half its motion, and (by P27C)[57] less than half its determination
[in a certain direction]. If B did not take A with it, but were reflected
in the opposite direction, it would lose its whole determination, and a
30   greater variation would occur (by P26C)—much greater, if it were to
lose its whole determination, and at the same time, part of its motion,
as is supposed in the third case. Hence the variation [B: which occurs
in these bodies] is, in accordance with our hypothesis, the least, q.e.d.

I/218 P30, Rule 6: *If body A, which is at rest, were exactly equal to body B, which
is in motion toward it, [A] would partly be impelled by [B], and partly drive
[B] back in the opposite direction.*[58]

5   Here also, as in the preceding proposition, only three cases can be

---

[1] See the figure for P30 [Fig. 28].

[57] EP and B both cite P17C, which cannot be right. Hubbeling (following Van Vloten
and Land) emends to P27C.

[58] Both EP and B have: "*and partly be driven back by [B] in the opposite direction.*" But
this is neither what Descartes said (*Principles* I, 51) nor the conclusion Spinoza will reach
at the end of the demonstration.

conceived. Therefore we shall have to demonstrate that we assert here the least variation that there can be.

Dem.: If body B takes body A with it, until both proceed to move with equal speed, then there will be as much motion in the one as in the other (P22) and (by P27C) it must lose half of its determination, and also (by P20) half of its motion. But if it is driven back by A in the opposite direction, then it will lose all of its determination and retain all of its motion (by P18). The second variation is equal to the first (by P26C). But neither of these can happen. For if A were to keep its state, and could change B's determination, it would necessarily have more force than B (by A20), which is contrary to the hypothesis. And if B were to take A with it until both were moving with equal speed, B would have more force than A, which is also contrary to the hypothesis. Therefore, since neither of these cases can happen, the third will, i.e., B will set A in motion a little[59] and be driven back by A, q.e.d. Read *Principles* II, 51.

P31, Rule 7: *If B and A should be moving in the same direction, A more slowly, and B following after it more quickly, so that B finally strikes A, and if A should be larger than B, but the excess of speed in B should be greater than the excess of size in A,[m] then B would transfer so much of its motion to A that afterwards they both proceed in the same direction, with the same speed. But if, on the other hand, the excess of size in A should be greater than the excess of speed in B, [B] would be reflected in the opposite direction, retaining all of its motion.*

Read *Principles* II, 52. Here, as in the preceding propositions, only three cases can be conceived.

Dem.: Of part 1: B, which is supposed to have more force than A (by P21 and P22), cannot be reflected in the opposite direction by A (by A20). Therefore, since B has more force, it will move A with it, and indeed, in such a way that they proceed to move with equal speed. For then the least change will occur, as is easily apparent from the preceding.

Of part 2: B, which is supposed to have less force than A (by P21 and P22), cannot impel A (by A20), nor give it any of its own motion. So (by P14C) B will retain all of its motion, [but] not in the same

---

[m] See the figure for P30 [Fig. 28].

[59] Cf. *Principles* I, 51. Descartes claims that if B approaches A with four degrees of speed, it will transfer one degree to A and be reflected with three degrees. This is the law to which Spinoza takes exception in Letters 30 and 32. It is difficult to see why the quantity of motion should be conserved in just that way.

direction, since it is supposed to be impeded by A. Therefore (by what is said in *The Dioptric*, chap. 2) it will be reflected in the opposite direction—not in any other direction—retaining all of its motion (by P18), q.e.d.

25   *Note that here and in the preceding Propositions we have assumed as demonstrated that every body which directly meets another, by which it is completely prevented from going further in the same direction, must be reflected in the opposite direction, not in any other direction. To understand this, read chap. 2 of the* Dioptric.[60]

30   Schol.: Up till now, to explain the changes of bodies that arise from the impulse of one on the other, we have considered two bodies as

I/220 divided from all bodies, and taken no account of the bodies surrounding them on all sides.[61] But now we shall consider their state and changes, taking into account the surrounding bodies.

5   P32: *If body B is surrounded on all sides by particles in motion, which are striking it in every direction at once with equal force, then so long as no other cause occurs, it will remain in the same place unmoved.*

10   Dem.: This proposition is evident in itself. For if it were moved in any direction by the impulse of particles coming from one direction, the particles that moved it would strike it with greater force than the others that were striking it at the same time in an opposite direction and could not have their effect (by A20),[62] which would be contrary

15 to the hypothesis.

   P33: *Body B, in the same conditions as assumed above, can be moved in any direction whatever by any external force, no matter how small.*[63]

20   Dem.: Because all bodies touching B immediately are in motion (by Hyp.), and B remains unmoved (by P32), those bodies are reflected in another direction, retaining all of their motion, as soon as they touch B (by P28). So body B is automatically, and continuously, left by the

25 bodies touching it immediately. Therefore, however large B is feigned

---

[60] Descartes remarks of this law, in the Latin version of the *Principles*, that it is so manifest as to require no proof, and in the French version, that the demonstrations of it are so certain that even if experience should seem to be against it, we should trust our reason more than our senses.

[61] Cf. *Principles* II, 45, 53. Here Spinoza begins his version of Descartes' account of the nature and properties of fluids (cf. *Principles* II, 56), a section which, according to Meyer, would have required further elaboration if a true second edition had been prepared (I/131/10-12). In Cartesian physics the difference between solid and fluid bodies is simply that the minute parts of fluids are already in motion, whereas the parts of solid bodies are at rest. Cf. *Principles* II, 54-55 (and Alquié's notes thereto) and IIP37S.

[62] Gebhardt (following EP) has 'A29,' which is impossible. Van Vloten and Land (following B) have 'A20,' as do AHMPS.

[63] Cf. *Principles* II, 56.

to be, no action is required to separate it from the bodies immediately touching it (by what we have noted in section 4 concerning D8). So no external force, no matter how small it is feigned to be, can be thrust against it, which is not greater than the force which B has for remaining in the same place (for we have just now demonstrated that it has no force for adhering to the bodies immediately touching it); nor can there be any external force which is not also greater than the force of the other particles striking B in an opposite direction, when it is added to the impulse of the particles which at the same time drive B in the same direction as the external force does (for it was supposed that without the external force, the forces of the particles were equal). Therefore (by A20), body B will be moved in any direction whatever by this external force, however slight it is feigned to be, q.e.d.

P34: *Body B, in the conditions assumed above, cannot move more quickly than it is driven by an external force, even though the particles by which it is surrounded may be agitated far more rapidly.*

Dem.: The particles that strike body B at the same time and in the same direction as the external force, even though they may be agitated much more rapidly than the external force can move B, nevertheless (by hyp.) do not have a greater force than the bodies which drive B back in the opposite direction. Hence, they expend all their forces of determination merely in resisting these, without (by P32) yielding any of their speed to it. Therefore, since no other circumstances, *or* causes, are supposed, B will receive a quantity of speed from no cause other than the external force. So (by IA8)[64] it will not be able to be moved more quickly than it is driven by the external force, q.e.d.

P35: *When body B is thus moved by an external impulse, it receives the greatest part of its motion from the bodies by which it is continuously surrounded, not from the external force.*[65]

Dem.: Even though body B may be feigned to be very large, it must be moved by any impulse, no matter how slight (by P33). Let us conceive, therefore, that B is four times larger than the external body by whose force it is set in motion. Since (by P34) both bodies must move with equal speed, there will be four times as much motion in B as in the external body by which it is set in motion (by P21). So (by IA8) it does not have the principal part of its motion from the external force. And because, beyond this, no other causes are supposed except

---

[64] In *Principles* II, 60, Descartes states the causal principle relied on here in somewhat less metaphysical terms than Spinoza does in IA8. But he emphasizes that it is "one of the chief things to be observed in philosophizing."

[65] See *Principles* II, 59.

the bodies by which it is continuously surrounded (for B is supposed to be, of itself, unmoved), it receives the chief part of its motion solely from the bodies (by IA7) by which it is surrounded, not from the external force, q.e.d.

Note that here we cannot say, as we did above, that the motion of the
15 *particles coming from one direction is required to resist the motion of the par-*
ticles coming from the opposite direction. For bodies moving toward one another
with an equal motion (as these are here supposed to be) are contrary only in
their determination [in a certain direction], not in their motion (by P19C).
Therefore they expend only their determination in resisting each other, but not
20 *their motion.*[n] *For this reason, body B can receive no determination, and con-*
sequently (by P27C) no speed (insofar as speed is distinguished from motion)
from the bodies surrounding it. But it can receive motion. Indeed, as the
external force approaches, B must necessarily be moved by them, as we have
demonstrated in this Proposition, and as you can clearly see from the way we
25 *have demonstrated P33.*

P36: *If any body, e.g., our hand, can move with equal motion in any direction*
whatever, so that it does not in any way resist any bodies, and no other bodies
30 *resist it in any way, then, in that space through which it would thus move,*
there will necessarily be as many bodies moving in one direction as in any
other, and each will move with a force of speed equal to that of any other and
to that of our hand.

I/223   Dem.: A body can move through no space which is not full of bodies (by P3). Therefore I say that the space through which our hand
5 can thus move is filled by bodies which will move under the same conditions that I have indicated. If you deny this, suppose that they are either at rest or moving in some other way.

If they are at rest, they will necessarily resist the motion of our hand (by P14) until its motion is communicated to them so that in the end they are moving in the same direction that it is, and with an equal
10 speed (P20). But in the hypothesis, they are assumed not to resist. Therefore, these bodies are moving, which was the first thing to be proved.

Next, they must be moving in all directions. For if you deny this, assume that they are not moving in some direction, say from A toward
15 B. Therefore, if the hand is moving from A toward B, it will meet bodies which are moving (by the first part of this demonstration), and moving (according to your hypothesis) with a determination different

[n] See P24, where it is demonstrated that two bodies expend their determination, but not their motion, in resisting one another.

from that of the hand. So they will resist it (by P14) until they are moving in the same direction as our hand (by P24 and P27S). But (by Hyp.) they do not resist our hand. Therefore, they will be moving in every direction, which was the second thing to be proved.

Again, these bodies will be moving in every direction with a force of speed which is equal in each of them. For if they were supposed to be moving with an unequal force of speed, then let it be assumed that those which are moving from A toward B are not moving with so great a force of speed as those which are moving from A toward C. So if the hand should move from A to B with the same speed with which bodies are moving from A to C (for it is supposed to be able to move with an equal motion in every direction without resistance), then the bodies moving from A toward B will resist the hand (by P14) until they are moving with a force of speed equal to that of the hand (by P31). But this is contrary to the hypothesis. Therefore, they will move in every direction with an equal force of speed, which was the third thing to be proved.

Finally, if the bodies are moving with a force of speed not equal to that of the hand, the hand will move either more slowly, or with less force of speed, or more rapidly, or with a greater force of speed, than the bodies do. If the former, then the hand will resist the bodies following it in the same direction (by P31); if the latter, then the bodies which our hand follows, and with which it is moving in the same direction, will resist it (by P31). But each of these is contrary to the hypothesis. Therefore, since our hand can move neither more quickly nor more slowly, it will move with a force of speed equal to that of the bodies, q.e.d.

If you ask, why I say "with an equal force of speed," and not, uncondition-ally, "with equal speed," read P27CS. If you then ask whether the hand, while it is moving, for example, from A to B, does not resist the bodies moving at the same time, with equal force, from B to A, read P33. From that you will understand that their force is balanced by the force of the bodies which are moving at the same time with the hand from A to B (for the latter force, by the 3rd part of this proposition, is equal to the former).

P37: *If a body, say A, can be moved in any direction whatever, by any force, no matter how small, it must be surrounded by bodies each moving with a speed equal to that of the others.*

Dem.: Body A must be surrounded on every side by bodies (by P6), moving equally in every direction. For if they were at rest, body A could not be moved in any direction whatever, by any force, no

30   matter how small (as is supposed in the hypothesis), but only by a force great enough to be able to move with it the bodies immediately touching A (by A20).

Next, if the bodies by which A is surrounded

I/225   were moving with a greater force in one direction than in another—say from B to C rather than from C to B—since it is surrounded on every side by moving bodies (as we have just now demonstrated), the

5   bodies moving from B to C would necessarily bear A with them in the same direction (by what we have demonstrated in P33). So not any small force would suffice to move A toward B, but only one great enough to make up for the excess of motion of the bodies coming from

10   B to C (by A20). So they must be moving with an equal force in every direction, q.e.d.

Schol.: Since these things happen concerning those bodies which are called Fluid, it follows that fluid bodies are those which are divided into many small particles, moving with equal force in all directions.

15   And although those particles cannot be seen by an eye, no matter how sharpsighted, nevertheless what we have just clearly demonstrated should not be denied. For such minuteness of nature, which cannot be determined or reached by any thought (not to mention the senses), is sufficiently proven from the previously stated PP10 and 11.

20   Again, since it is also sufficiently established from the preceding, that bodies resist other bodies only by their rest, and that we perceive nothing else in hardness, as the senses indicate, than that the parts of hard bodies resist the motion of our hands, we clearly infer that those bodies whose particles are all at rest in relation to each other are hard.

25   Read *Principles* II, 54-56.

I/226

Principles of Philosophy Demonstrated Geometrically Part III

HAVING thus set out the most universal principles of natural things, we must now proceed to explain those things that follow from them. But since the things that follow from these principles are more than

10   our mind can ever survey in thought, and since we are not determined by them to consider some rather than others, we should first set out a brief history of the main Phenomena whose causes we shall investi-

gate here.[1] But you have this in *Principles* III, from article 5 up to article 15. And from article 20 to article 43 Descartes proposes the hypothesis that he judges most convenient, not only to understand the Phenomena of the heavens, but also to investigate their natural causes.

Next, since the best way to understand the nature of Plants and of Man is to consider how they gradually come to be and are generated from seeds, we shall have to devise such principles as are very simple and very easy to know, from which we may demonstrate how the stars, earth and finally all those things that we find in this visible world, could have arisen, as if from certain seeds—even though we may know very well that they never did arise that way. For by doing this we shall exhibit their nature far better than if we only described what they now are.[2]

I say that we seek principles that are simple and easy to know; for if they are not, we shall not need them. We only ascribe seeds to things fictitiously, in order to get to know their nature more easily, and in the manner of the Mathematicians, to ascend from the clearest things to the more obscure, and from the simplest to the more composite.[3]

Next, we say that we seek principles from which we may demonstrate how the stars, earth, etc., could have arisen. For we do not seek causes that suffice only to explain the Phenomena of the heavens (as the Astronomers usually do), but causes that will lead us also to a knowledge of the things on earth. For we judge that whatever we observe to happen on the earth ought to be counted among the Phenomena of nature.

To discover such principles, we must observe the following requirements for a good hypothesis:

1. Considered only in itself, it should imply no contradiction.
2. It should be the simplest there can be.
3. It should be the easiest to know (this follows from the second requirement).
4. Everything which is observed in the whole of nature should be capable of being deduced from it.[4]

We have said, finally, that we are permitted to assume a hypothesis from which, as from a cause, we can deduce the Phenomena of nature,

---

[1] Here Spinoza follows *Principles* III, 4 very closely. Cf. Letter 10. The 'history' of the phenomena in Descartes is a description of various features of the solar system, such as the distances and relative sizes of the sun, moon, planets, and fixed stars.

[2] Cf. *Principles* III, 45. Descartes is there concerned to excuse his departure from the creationist account in the Bible.

[3] Cf. the *Discourse*, ii, AT VI, 19.   [4] Cf. *Principles* III, 42-44; IV, 204-206.

even though we may know very well that they have not arisen in this way.

So that you may understand this, I shall use the following example. If someone should find drawn on a paper the curved line we call a
25 Parabola, and wish to investigate its nature, it is all the same whether he supposes that line to have been, first cut from some Cone, and then pressed on the paper, or to have been described by the motion of two straight lines, or to have arisen in some other way—provided that he demonstrates all the properties of the Parabola from what he supposes.
30 Indeed, even though he may know it to have come to be from the pressing of a Conic section on the paper, he will nevertheless be able to feign any other cause he pleases, which seems to him most convenient to explain all the properties of the Parabola. Similarly we are permitted to assume any hypothesis we please to explain the features
I/228 of nature, provided that we deduce all the Phenomena of nature from it by Mathematical consequences.

And what is more worthy of note, is that we shall hardly be able to assume anything from which the same effects could not be deduced, though perhaps with more difficulty, through the Laws of nature ex-
5 plained above.

For since matter, with the aid of these Laws, successively takes on all the forms of which it is capable, if we consider those forms in order, we will be able, in the end, to arrive at [the form] of this world. So no error is to be feared from a false hypothesis.[5]

10 Post: We ask it to be conceded: [i] that in the beginning God divided all that matter of which this visible world is composed into particles which were, as nearly as possible, equal to one another (not, indeed, into spheres, for several spheres joined together do not fill a continu-
15 ous space, but) into parts shaped in another way and of medium size, *or* of a size intermediate among all those of which the heavens and stars are now composed; [ii] that these particles had just as much motion among themselves as is now found in the world, and were moving equally—both each one around its own center and separately from
20 one another (so that they would make up a fluid body, such as we think the heavens to be) and also many together around certain other centers, equally removed from one another, and distributed in the same way that the centers of the fixed stars now are; [iii] that they were also moved around several other

[5] Cf. *Principles* III, 47.

points, which equal the number of the Planets; and [iv] that they would thus make as many different vortices as there now are stars in the world.[6] See the Figure for *Principles* III, 47.[7]

This hypothesis, considered in itself, does not imply any contradiction. For it does not ascribe to matter anything except divisibility and motion, modifications which, as we have demonstrated above, really exist in matter; and because we have shown that indefinite matter is one and the same as the matter of the heavens and the earth, we can suppose these modifications to have been in the whole of matter, without worrying about any contradiction.[8]

Next, this hypothesis is the simplest, because it supposes inequality or dissimilarity neither in the particles into which matter was divided in the beginning, nor in their motion. From this it follows that this hypothesis is also the easiest to know. This is also evident from the fact that, according to this hypothesis, nothing is supposed to have been in matter except what becomes known by itself to anyone from the concept of matter alone, viz. divisibility and local motion.

Moreover, we shall try to show that, from this hypothesis, everything observed in nature can really be deduced, to the extent that such a deduction is possible. We shall adopt the following order. First, we shall deduce the fluidity of the Heavens from it, and explain how this is a cause of light. Next we shall proceed to the nature of the Sun, and at the same time, to those things observed in the fixed Stars. Afterwards, we shall speak of the Comets, and finally, of the Planets and their Phenomena.

DEFINITIONS

D1: By *Ecliptic* we understand that part of the vortex which, when it rotates around its axis, describes the greatest circle.

D2: By *Poles* we understand the parts of the vortex which are most remote from the ecliptic, or which describe the smallest circles.

D3: By *Striving for motion* we do not understand any thought, but only that a part of matter is so placed and stirred to motion, that it really would go somewhere if it were not prevented by any cause.[9]

D4: By *Angle* we understand whatever projects beyond a spherical shape in any body.[10]

---

[6] Cf. *Principles* III, 46, 48.

[7] Spinoza's text does not reproduce fig. 31, which is here reproduced from AT VIII-1, 102.

[8] Cf. IIP6.   [9] Cf. *Principles* III, 56.   [10] Cf. *Principles* III, 48.

Axioms

A1: Several spheres joined together cannot occupy a continuous space.

30
I/230
A2: A portion of matter divided into parts which have angles requires more space if its parts move around their own centers than if all of its parts are at rest and all their sides touch one another immediately.

A3: The smaller a part of matter is, the more easily it is divided by
5 the same force.[11]

A4: The parts of matter that are in motion in the same direction, and do not depart from one another by their motion, are not actually divided.[12]

10 P1: *The parts into which matter was first divided were not round, but had angles.*[13]

Dem.: The whole of matter was divided from the beginning into equal and similar parts (by the Postulate). Therefore (by A1 and IIP2)
15 they were not round, and so (by D4) had angles, q.e.d.

P2: *The force which brought it about that the particles of matter would move around their own centers, brought it about at the same time that the angles of*
20 *the particles would be worn away by their meeting one another.*

Dem.: The whole of matter was divided in the beginning into parts which were equal (by the Postulate) and had angles (by P1). Therefore if, as soon as they began to move around their centers, their angles
25 had not been worn away, then necessarily (by A2) the whole of matter would have had to occupy more space than when it was at rest. But this is absurd (by IIP4); therefore their angles were worn away as soon as they began to move, q.e.d.

The rest is lacking.

[11] Cf. *Principles* III, 50.
[12] Cf. I/182/3f.
[13] For this and the following proposition, cf. *Principles* III, 48.

Appendix
Containing Metaphysical Thoughts
Part I

IN WHICH are briefly explained the chief things that commonly occur in the general part of Metaphysics, concerning Being and its Affections.
[B: The end and purpose of this Part is to show that the common Logic and Philosophy serve only to train and strengthen the memory, so that we rightly remember the things which are presented to us, through the senses, randomly and without order or connection, and by which we can be affected only through the senses; but these disciplines do not serve to train the intellect.]

CHAPTER I
OF REAL BEINGS, FICTITIOUS BEINGS,
AND BEINGS OF REASON

I shall say nothing concerning either the definition of this Science or the things it is concerned with; my intention here is only to explain the more obscure things which are commonly treated by Writers on Metaphysics.

The definition of Being
    Let us begin, therefore, with Being, by which I understand *Whatever, when it is clearly and distinctly perceived, we find to exist necessarily, or at least to be able to exist.*

Chimaeras, Fictitious Beings, and Beings of reason are not beings
    From this definition, or if you prefer, description, it follows that *Chimaeras, Fictitious Beings*, and *Beings of reason* can not in any way be classed as beings. For a *Chimaera*,[a] of its own nature, cannot exist. But a *Fictitious Being* cannot be clearly and distinctly perceived, because in that case a man, from his sheer freedom alone, knowingly and intentionally (and not, as in the case of the false, unknowingly) connects what he wishes to connect and disjoins what he wishes to disjoin. Finally, a *Being of reason* is nothing but a mode of thinking, which

---

[a] By the term *Chimaera*, here and in what follows, I understand that whose nature involves an explicit contradiction, as is explained more fully in Chapter 3.

helps us to more easily *retain, explain, and imagine* the things we have understood. Note that by a mode of thinking we understand, as we have already explained in IP15S, all affections of thought, such as
35   intellect, joy, imagination, etc.

I/234 *By what modes of thinking we retain things*
     That there are certain modes of thinking which help us to *retain* things more firmly and easily, and when we wish, to recall them to mind or keep them present to the mind, is sufficiently established for those who use that well-known rule of Memory, by which to *retain*
5   something very new and imprint it on the memory, we recall something else familiar to us, which agrees with it, either in name or in reality. Similarly, the Philosophers have reduced all natural things to certain classes, to which they recur when anything new presents itself
10   to them. These they call *genus, species*, etc.

By what modes of thinking we explain things
     We also have modes of thinking which serve to *explain* a thing by determining it through comparison to another. The modes of thinking by which we do this are called *time, number*, and *measure*, and perhaps
15   there are other besides. Of these, time serves to explain duration, number discrete quantity, and measure continuous quantity.

By what modes of thinking we imagine things
     Finally, since we are accustomed to depict in our fantasy also images of whatever we understand, it happens that we *imagine* nonenti-
20   ties positively, as beings. For the mind, considered in itself, since it is a thinking thing, has no greater power of affirming than of denying. But as imagining is nothing but being aware of the traces found in the brain from the motion of the spirits aroused in the senses by objects,
25   such an awareness can only be a confused affirmation.[1] Hence it happens that we imagine as if they were beings all those modes which the mind uses for negating, such as blindness, extremity *or* limit, term, darkness, etc.

Why beings of reason are not Ideas of things and are nevertheless taken to be ideas
     So it is evident that these modes of thinking are not ideas of things, and can not in any way be classed as ideas. So they also have no object

---

[1] The conception of imagination as involving an awareness of traces made in the brain by the animal spirits is Cartesian (cf. the *Traité de l'Homme*, AT XI, 174-177). But the notion that this awareness involves affirmation seems to be a Spinozistic deduction from

that exists necessarily, or can exist. Moreover, the reason why these modes of thinking are taken for ideas of things is that they arise from the ideas of real beings so immediately that they are quite easily confused with them by those who do not pay very close attention. So these people also give names to them, as if to signify beings existing outside our mind, which Beings, or rather Nonbeings, they have called beings of reason.

Being is badly divided into real being and being of reason

From this it is easy to see how improper is the division of being into real being and being of reason.[2] For they divide being into being and nonbeing, or into being and mode of thinking. Nevertheless, I do not wonder that Philosophers preoccupied with words, *or* grammar, should fall into such errors. For they judge the things from the words, not the words from the things.

In what sense Beings of reason can be called a mere nothing, and in what sense they can be called real Beings

Nor do they speak less improperly who say that a being of reason is not a mere nothing.[3] For if anyone looks outside the intellect for what is signified by those words, he will find it to be a mere nothing. But if he means the modes of thinking themselves, they are indeed real beings. For when I ask, what is a species, I seek nothing but the nature of that mode of thinking, which is really a being and distinguished from another mode of thinking.

Still, these modes of thinking cannot be called ideas, nor can they be said to be true or false, just as love cannot be called true or false, but [only] good or bad. So when Plato said that man is a featherless biped, he erred no more than those who said that man is a rational animal. For Plato was no less aware than anyone else that man is a rational animal. But he referred man to a certain class so that, when he wished to think about man, he would immediately fall into the thought of man by recalling that class, which he could easily remember. Indeed Aristotle erred very seriously if he thought that he had adequately explained the human essence by that definition of his. Whether, indeed, Plato did well, one can only ask. But this is not the place for these matters.

Cartesian premises rather than anything Descartes explicitly maintained. Cf. the Letter of Mersenne of July 1641 and Curley 5.

[2] Cf. Heereboord 2, 222 and 225. The doctrine that beings of reason are modes of thinking is in Suarez, 2:1016.

[3] Heereboord would be among those open to this criticism. Cf. Heereboord 2, 222.

30 *In the investigation of Things real Beings must not be confounded with beings of reason*

From all that has been said above, it is clear that there is no agreement between a real being and the objects of a being of reason. From this also it is easy to see how carefully we should be on guard in the investigation of things, lest we confound real beings with beings of reason. For it is one thing to inquire into the nature of things, and another to inquire into the modes by which things are perceived by I/236 us. Indeed, if these things are confounded, we shall be able to understand neither the modes of perceiving, nor nature itself. Moreover, and this is most important, we shall, on that account, fall into great 5 errors, as has happened to many before us.

How the being of reason is distinguished from the fictitious being

It ought also to be noted that many confound beings of reason with fictitious beings.[4] For they think that a fictitious being is also a being of reason because it has no existence outside the mind. But if one attends correctly to the definitions just given of beings of reason and 10 fictitious beings, he will discover a great difference between them, both with respect to the cause, and also with respect to their nature, without regard to the cause. For we said that a fictitious being is nothing but two terms connected by a sheer act of the will alone, without any guidance from reason. So a fictitious being can be true 15 by chance. But a being of reason does not depend on the will alone, nor does it consist of any terms connected with one another, as is sufficiently obvious from the definition.

If anyone asks, therefore, whether a fictitious being is a real being or a being of reason, we need only to go back and repeat what we have already said, that being is badly divided into real being and being 20 of reason, and that therefore the question is ill-founded. For it is supposed that all being is divided into real being and being of reason.

The division of being

But let us return to our proposition, from which we seem to have strayed somewhat. From the definition of being already given (or if 25 you prefer, from the description), it is easy to see that being should be divided into being which exists necessarily by its own nature, *or* whose essence involves existence, and being whose essence involves only possible existence. This last is divided into Substance and Mode,

---

[4] According to Freudenthal (3, 108), Thomas, Cajetan, and Suarez would be among those under attack here, whereas Heereboord (2, 225) would agree with Spinoza.

whose definitions are given in the *Principles of Philosophy* I, 51, 52, and 56. So it is not necessary to repeat them here.

I only wish it to be noted, concerning this division, that we say expressly that being is divided into Substance and Mode, and not into Substance and Accident. For an Accident is nothing but a mode of thinking, inasmuch as it denotes what is only a respect. E.g., when I say that the triangle is moved, the motion is not a mode of the triangle, but of the body which is moved. Hence the motion is called an accident with respect to the triangle. But with respect to the body, it is called a real being, *or* mode. For the motion cannot be conceived without the body, though it can without the triangle.[5]

So that you may understand better what has already been said, and what will follow, we shall try to explain what should be understood by *the being of essence, the being of existence, the being of idea*, and *the being of power*. We are moved to do this by the ignorance of certain people who recognize no distinction between essence and existence, or who, if they do recognize such a distinction, confuse *the being of essence* with *the being of idea* or *the being of power*. We shall explain this matter as distinctly as we can in what follows, both to satisfy them, and for its own sake.

Chapter II

What are the being of Essence, the being of Existence, the being of Idea and the being of Power

To perceive clearly what should be understood by these four, it is necessary only to consider what we have already said about uncreated substance, *or* God:

That creatures are in God eminently

(1) That God contains eminently what is found formally in created things, i.e., that God has attributes in which all created things are contained in a more eminent way. See IA8 and P12C1. E.g., we conceive extension clearly without any existence, and therefore, since it has, of itself, no power to exist, we have demonstrated that it was created by God (IP21). And since there must be at least as much

---

[5] Cf. Descartes, *Principles* I, 61, and Gueroult 1, 1:65n.

303

perfection in the cause as there is in the effect, it follows that all the perfections of extension are in God. But because we saw afterward that an extended thing, by its very nature, is divisible, i.e., contains an imperfection, we could not attribute extension to God (IP16). So we were constrained to allow that there is some attribute in God which contains all the perfections of matter in a more excellent way (IP9S) and can take the place of matter.

(2) That God understands himself and all other things, i.e., that he also has all things objectively in himself (IP9).

(3) That God is the cause of all things, and that he acts from absolute freedom of the will.

What are the being of essence, of existence, of idea and of power[6]

From this, one may see clearly what should be understood by those four. For first, *being of Essence* is nothing but that manner in which created things are comprehended in the attributes of God. *Being of Idea* is spoken of insofar as all things are contained objectively in God's idea. *Being of Power* is spoken of only with respect to God's power, by which he was able to create all things not yet existing from the absolute freedom of his will. Finally, *being of Existence* is the essence itself of things outside God, considered in itself. It is attributed to things after they have been created by God.

These four are only distinguished from one another in creatures

From this it is evident that these four are only distinguished from one another in created things, but not at all in God. For we do not conceive God to have been in another by his power, and his existence and his intellect are not distinguished from his essence.

Reply to certain questions concerning essence

Hence we can easily reply to the questions that are usually raised concerning essence. These questions are as follows: whether essence is distinguished from existence? and if it is distinguished, whether it is anything different from the idea? and if it is something different from an idea, whether it has any being outside the intellect? The last of these must surely be granted.

To the first question we reply by making a distinction: in God essence is not distinguished from existence, since his essence cannot be conceived without existence; but in other things it does differ from and certainly can be conceived without existence. To the second we

---

[6] Cf. Suarez, Disp. 31, sec. 1, and Heereboord 2, 342-345.

say that a thing that is conceived clearly and distinctly, *or* truly, outside the intellect is something different from the idea.

But again it is asked whether that being outside the intellect is by itself or has been created by God. To this we reply that the formal essence neither is by itself nor has been created, for both these presuppose that the thing actually exists. Rather it depends on the divine essence alone, in which all things are contained. So in this sense we agree with those who say that the essences of things are eternal.

Still, it could be asked how we understand the essences of things, when the nature of God is not yet understood. For these essences, as we have just said, depend on the nature of God alone. To this I say that it arises from the fact that the things have already been created. For if they had not been created, then I should concede fully that it would be impossible to understand the essences of things without an adequate knowledge of the nature of God—just as impossible as knowing the nature of the coordinates of a Parabola prior to a knowledge of its nature (or even more so).

Why the author recurs in the definition of essence to the attributes of God

Next it is to be noted that, although the essences of nonexistent modes are comprehended in their substances, and their *being of essence* is in their substances, nevertheless we wished to recur to God in order to explain generally the essence of modes and of substances, and also because the essence of modes has only been in their substances after the creation of the substances and we were seeking the eternal *being of essences*.

Why he has not recounted the definitions of others

I do not think it worthwhile to refute here those Authors who think differently than we do, nor to examine their definitions or descriptions of essence and existence. For in this way we should render a clear thing more obscure. Since we can give no definition of anything without at the same time explaining its essence, what do we understand more clearly than what essence is, and what existence is?

How the distinction between essence and existence is easily learned

Finally, if any Philosopher still doubts whether essence is distinguished from existence in created things, he need not labor greatly over definitions of essence and existence to remove that doubt. For if he will only go to some sculptor or woodcarver, they will show him how they conceive in a certain order a statue not yet existing, and after having made it, they will present the existing statue to him.

305

CHAPTER III

CONCERNING WHAT IS NECESSARY, IMPOSSIBLE, POSSIBLE, AND CONTINGENT

What is to be understood here by affections

Having explained in this way the nature of being, insofar as it is being, we pass to the explanation of some of its affections. It should be noted, that by affections we here understand what Descartes has elsewhere called attributes (*Principles* I, 52). For being, insofar as it is being, does not affect us by itself alone, as substance. It must, therefore, be explained by some attribute, from which, nevertheless, it is distinguished only by a distinction of reason. So I cannot sufficiently admire the very subtle cleverness of those who have sought—not without great harm to the truth—for a middle ground between being and nothing.[7] But I shall not stay to refute their error, since they themselves vanish entirely in their empty subtlety when they struggle to give definitions of such affections.

The definition of affections

Let us, therefore, attend to our own business. We say that *affections of being* are *certain attributes, under which we understand the essence or existence of each thing, [the attributes,] nevertheless, being distinguished from [being] only by reason.* I shall try here to explain certain things concerning these attributes (for I do not undertake to treat them all), and also to distinguish them from denominations, which are affections of no being. First I shall treat of what is *necessary*, and what is *impossible*.

In how many ways a thing is said to be necessary, and impossible

A thing is said to be necessary or impossible in two ways: either in respect to its essence or in respect to its cause.[8] We know that God exists necessarily in respect to his essence, for his essence cannot be conceived without existence. And it is impossible that a chimaera exist in respect to its essence, which involves a contradiction.

[Other] things—e.g., material ones—are called either impossible or necessary in respect to their cause. For if we consider only their essence, we can conceive it clearly and distinctly without existence. Therefore, they can never exist by the power and necessity of their

---

[7] Cf. Heereboord 2, 225

[8] This distinction has been referred to Heereboord 2, 99. But the earlier scholastic distinction between what is necessary or impossible *per se* and what is necessary or impossible *per accidens* is clearly analogous, and Heereboord is clearly only reporting a common division. Cf. Aquinas, *Summa theologiae* Ia. 25, 4.

essence, but only by the power of their cause, God, the creator of all things. And so, if it is in the divine decree that some thing exists, it will necessarily exist; but if not, it will be impossible that it should exist. For it is evident in itself that if a thing has neither an internal nor an external cause for existing, it is impossible that it should exist. Nevertheless, such a thing is assumed in this second hypothesis:[9] one that could exist without either the power of its own essence (which is what I understand by an internal cause), or the power of the divine decree (the only external cause of all things). It follows that things of the sort described by us in the second hypothesis cannot exist.

Chimaeras properly called verbal beings

First, it should be noted that we may properly call a Chimaera a verbal being because it is neither in the intellect nor in the imagination. For it cannot be expressed except in words. E.g., we can, indeed, express a square Circle in words, but we cannot imagine it in any way, much less understand it. So a Chimaera is nothing but a word, and impossibility cannot be numbered among the affections of being, for it is only a negation.

Created things depend on God both for essence and existence

Second, it should be noted that not only the existence of created things, but also their essence and nature depend on the decree of God alone, as we shall demonstrate very clearly below in the second part.[10] From this it clearly follows that created things have no necessity of themselves. For they have no essence of themselves, nor do they exist by themselves.

The necessity which is in created things from their cause is either of essence or of existence, but these two are not distinguished in God

Finally, it should be noted that necessity, as it is in created things by the power of their cause, is said either in respect to their essence or in respect to their existence. For these two are distinguished in created things. The former depends on the eternal laws of nature, the latter on the series and order of causes. But in God, whose essence is not distinguished from his existence, necessity of essence is also not distinguished from necessity of existence.

---

[9] I.e., that the thing whose essence does not involve existence is not in the divine decree. Here, and in what follows, the doctrine is certainly not Cartesian, though Spinoza could claim, with some plausibility, to be deriving this denial of contingency from Cartesian premises (such as IA11, P12 and P12C1).

[10] Cf. I/261-262 and I/170.

30   It follows from this that if we were to conceive the whole order of nature, we should discover that many things whose nature we perceive clearly and distinctly, that is, whose essence is necessarily such, can not in any way exist. For we should find the existence of such things in nature to be just as impossible as we now know the passage of a

I/242 large elephant through the eye of a needle to be, although we perceive the nature of each of them clearly. So the existence of those things would be only a chimaera, which we could neither imagine nor understand.

5   *Possible and contingent are not affections of things*
    Let this be enough about necessity and impossibility. But it seems desirable to add a few words about the *possible* and the *contingent*; for these are taken by some to be affections of things. Nevertheless, they are nothing but a defect in our understanding, as I shall show clearly,

10 after I have explained what is to be understood by these two.

    What possibility and contingency are
    A *thing* is called *possible*, then, *when we understand its efficient cause, but do not know whether the cause is determined.* So we can regard it as possible, but neither as necessary nor as impossible. If, however, we

15 attend *to the essence of the thing alone, and not to its cause,* we shall call it *contingent.* That is, we shall consider it as midway between God and a chimaera, so to speak, because we find in it, on the part of its essence, neither any necessity of existing (as we do in the divine essence)

20 nor any impossibility *or* inconsistency (as we do in a chimaera).
    And if anyone wishes to call *contingent* what I call *possible*, or *possible* what I call *contingent*, I shall not contend with him. For I am not accustomed to dispute about words. It will suffice if he grants us that these two are nothing but a defect in our perception, and not anything

25 real.

    That possibility and contingency are only a defect of our understanding
    Moreover, if anyone wishes to deny this, his error can be demonstrated to him with no difficulty. For if he attends to nature and how it depends on God, he will find that there is nothing *contingent* in things, that is, nothing which, on the part of the thing, can either

30 exist or not exist, or as is commonly said, be a *real contingent.*
    This is readily apparent from what we have taught (IA10), viz. that as much power is required for creating a thing as for preserving it. So, no created thing does anything by its own power, just as no cre-

I/243 ated thing has begun to exist by its own power. From this it follows that nothing happens except by the power of the cause who creates all things, namely God, who produces all things at each moment by his concurrence.

Moreover, since nothing happens except by the divine power alone, it is easy to see that whatever happens, happens by the power of God's decree and his will. But since in God there is no inconstancy or change (IP18 and P20C), he must have decreed from eternity that he would produce those things which he now produces. And since nothing is more necessary in its existence than what God has decreed would exist, it follows that a necessity of existing has been in all created things from eternity. Nor can we say that those things are contingent because God could have decreed otherwise. For since in eternity there is no when, nor before, nor after, nor any other affection of time, it follows that God never existed before those decrees so that he could decree otherwise.

[B: In order that this proof may properly be understood, we must note what is said in the second part of this appendix concerning the will of God, namely, that God's will or constant decree is only understood when we conceive the thing clearly and distinctly. For the essence of the thing, considered in itself, is nothing other than God's decree, or his determinate will. But we also say that the necessity of really existing is not distinct from the necessity of essence (II, ix). That is, when we say that God has decided that the triangle shall exist, we are saying nothing but that God has so arranged the order of nature and of causes that the triangle shall necessarily exist at such a time. So if we understood the order of causes as it has been established by God, we should find that the triangle must really exist at such a time, with the same necessity as we now find, when we attend to its nature, that its three angles are equal to two right angles.]

The reconciliation of the freedom of our will and of God's predestination surpasses the human understanding

As for the freedom of the human will (which we have said is free, IP15S), that also is preserved by the concurrence of God, nor does any man will or do anything but what God has decreed from eternity that he would will and do. How this can happen and human freedom still be preserved is beyond our grasp.

But we should not reject what we perceive clearly because we are ignorant of something. For if we attend to our nature, we understand clearly and distinctly that we are free in our actions and that we de-

liberate about many things, simply from the fact that we will [to do
so]. Also if we attend to the nature of God, we perceive clearly and
distinctly, as we have just shown, that all things depend on him and
that nothing exists whose existence has not been decreed by God from
eternity. But how the human will is produced by God at each moment
in such a way that it remains free we do not know. For there are many
things exceeding our grasp which we nevertheless know to have been
done by God—e.g., there is that real division of matter into indefinite
particles, which we have already demonstrated quite clearly (IIP11),
though we do not know how that division occurs.

Note that we here take it as something known that these two notions, *possible* and *contingent*, signify only a defect in our knowledge
about a thing's existence.

Chapter IV
Of Duration and Time

What eternity is; What duration is

From our earlier division of being into being whose essence involves
existence and being whose essence involves only possible existence,
there arises the distinction between eternity and duration. Of *eternity*
we shall speak more fully later. Here we say only that it is *an attribute
under which we conceive the infinite existence of God*. But *duration is an
attribute under which we conceive the existence of created things insofar as they
persevere in their actuality*. From this it clearly follows that duration is
only distinguished by reason from the whole existence of a thing. For
as you take duration away from the thing, you take away just as much
of its existence.[11]

What time is

But to determine this duration, we compare it with the duration of
other things which have a certain and determinate motion. *This comparison* is called *time*. Time, therefore, is not an affection of things,
but only a mere mode of thinking, *or*, as we have already said, a being
of reason. For it is a mode of thinking that serves to explain duration.
We should also note here—since it will be of use later, when we speak
of eternity—that duration is conceived as being greater or lesser, and
as composed of parts, and finally, that it is only an attribute of existence, and not of essence.

[11] Cf. Descartes, *Principles* I, 55-57.

Chapter V

Of Opposition, Order, etc.

What Opposition, Order, Agreement, Difference, Subject, Adjunct, etc. are

From the fact that we compare things with one another certain notions arise which nevertheless are nothing outside the things themselves but modes of thinking. This is clear from the fact that if we wish to consider them as things posited outside of thought [B: outside the intellect], we immediately render confused the clear concept which we otherwise have of them. These are such notions as *Opposition, Order, Agreement, Difference, Subject, Adjunct,* and whatever others are like these. We perceive them clearly enough, I say, insofar as we conceive them not as something different from the essences of the things opposed, ordered, etc., but only as modes of thinking by which we retain or imagine the things themselves more easily. So I do not judge it necessary to speak more fully about them. Instead I pass to the terms usually called transcendental.

Chapter VI

Of the One, True, and Good

These terms are taken by nearly all Metaphysicians to be the most general Affections of Being; for they say that every being is one, true and good, even though no one thinks of these things. But we shall see what should be understood concerning them when we have examined each of these terms separately.

What unity is

So let us begin with the first, viz. *One.* They say that this term signifies something real outside the intellect. But what this adds to being they cannot explain, which shows sufficiently that they confound beings of reason with real being; by doing this they render confused what they understand clearly. We say, however, that *Unity* is not in any way distinguished from the thing itself, or that it adds nothing to the being, but is only a mode of thinking by which we separate the thing from others which are like it or agree with it in some way.[12]

---

[12] Cf. Descartes, *Principles* I, 58.

What multiplicity is; in what respect God can be called one,
in what respect unique

To unity is opposed *multiplicity*, which, of course, also adds nothing
to things, is nothing but a mode of thinking, as we understand clearly
and distinctly. I do not see what more remains to be said about a
thing so clear. All that need be noted here is that God can be called
one insofar as we separate him from other beings. But insofar as we
conceive that there cannot be more than one of the same nature, he is
called unique. Indeed, if we wished to examine the matter more accurately, we could perhaps show that God is only very improperly
called one and unique. But this does not matter greatly, or even at all,
to those who care about things and not about words. So we shall leave
this behind and pass on to the second topic, and at the same time we
shall say what the false is.[13]

What the true and the false are, both among ordinary people
and among Philosophers

To perceive these two, the *true* and the *false* rightly, we shall begin
with the meaning of the words, from which it will be plain that these
are only extrinsic denominations of things and are not attributed to
things except metaphorically. But since ordinary people first invent
words, which afterwards are used by the Philosophers, it seems desirable for one seeking the original meaning of a term to ask what it first
denoted among ordinary people—particularly where we lack other causes
that could be used to investigate that [meaning], causes drawn from
the nature of language.

The first meaning of *true* and *false* seems to have had its origin in
stories: a story was called true when it was of a deed that had really
happened, and false when it was of a deed that had never happened.

Afterwards the Philosophers used this meaning to denote the agreement of an idea with its object and conversely. So an idea is called
true when it shows us the thing as it is in itself, and false when it
shows us the thing otherwise than it really is. For ideas are nothing
but narratives, *or* mental histories of nature. But later this usage was
transferred metaphorically to mute things, as when we call gold true
or false, as if the gold which is presented to us were to tell something
of itself that either was or was not in it.

I/247   *True not a transcendental term*

So they are thoroughly deceived who judge *true* to be a transcen-

---

[13] In Descartes the nearest approach to what follows seems to be in the Letter to
Mersenne of 16 October 1639.

dental term, *or* affection of being. For it can only be said improperly—or if you prefer, metaphorically—of the things themselves.

Truth and a true idea, how they differ

If you should ask what truth is beyond a true idea, ask also what whiteness is beyond a white body. For they are related to each other in the same way.

The cause of the true and of the false, we have already dealt with previously. So nothing remains to be noted—even what we have said would not have been worth the trouble of noting, if writers had not so entangled themselves in trifles of this kind that afterwards they have not been able to untangle themselves, finding difficulties where none exist.

What are the properties of truth? Certainty is not in things

The properties of truth, or of a true idea, are (1) that it is clear and distinct, and (2) that it removes all doubt, *or* in a word, that it is certain. Those who seek certainty in the things themselves are deceived in the same way as when they seek truth in them. And although we say that the thing is uncertain, this is a figure of speech which takes the object for the idea. In the same way we call a thing doubtful, except perhaps that then we understand by uncertainty contingency, or a thing which inspires uncertainty or doubt in us. There is no need to delay longer concerning these, so we shall proceed to the third term, and at the same time we shall explain what should be understood by its contrary.

Good and bad are only said in respect to something

No thing is said to be either *good* or *evil* considered alone, but only in respect to another [thing], to which it is advantageous in acquiring what it loves, or the contrary.[14] So each thing can be said at the same time to be both good and evil in different respects. E.g., the counsel given by Achitophel to Absalom is called good in Sacred Scripture; nevertheless it was very bad for David, at whose death it aimed.[15]

And indeed many other things are good, which are not good for all. So salvation is good for men, but neither good nor evil for animals or plants, to which it has no relation. To be sure, God is called supremely good, because he acts to the advantage of all, preserving, by his concurrence, each one's being, than which nothing is dearer. But there is no absolute evil, as is evident through itself.

[14] The doctrine that follows seems quite independent of Descartes.
[15] 2 Samuel 17:14.

I/248 *Why some have maintained a Metaphysical good*

However, those who eagerly seek some Metaphysical good, needing no qualification, labor under a false prejudice, for they confuse a distinction of reason with a real or modal distinction. They distinguish
5 between the thing itself and the striving that is in each thing to preserve its being, although they do not know what they understand by striving. For though the thing and its striving to preserve its being are distinguished by reason, or rather verbally (which deceives these people very greatly), they are not in any way really distinct.

10 *How the thing and the striving it has to persevere in its state are distinguished*

To make this clear, let us take an example of a very simple thing. Motion has a force of persevering in its state; this force is really nothing other than the motion itself—that is, the nature of motion is such. For if I say that in this body, A, there is nothing but a certain quantity of motion, it follows clearly from this that, so long as I attend to A, I
15 must always say that it is moving. For if I were to say that it was losing, of itself, its force of moving, I should necessarily have to attribute to it something else, besides what we have supposed in the hypothesis, through which it was losing its nature.

If this reasoning seems somewhat obscure, let us concede that that
20 striving to move itself is something beyond the laws themselves and nature of motion. Since, therefore, you suppose this striving to be a metaphysical good, this striving will necessarily also have a striving to persevere in its being, and this again will have another, and so on to infinity.[16] I know of nothing more absurd which could be feigned. But
25 the reason why some distinguish the thing's striving from the thing itself is that they find in themselves a longing to preserve themselves and they imagine such a [longing] in each thing.

Whether God could be called good before creation of things

Nevertheless, it is asked whether God could be called good before he created things. It seems to follow from our definition that God had
30 no such attribute, because we say that a thing can be called neither good nor evil, if it is considered in itself alone. This will seem absurd to many; but I do not know why. For we ascribe to God many attributes of this sort, which could only be ascribed to him potentially

 16 B: "But since this striving is assumed to be something, it must also be called good, and therefore must in turn have a striving to persevere in its state, and this striving in turn another, and so on, to infinity."

before things were created, as when he is called creator, judge, compassionate, etc.[17] So such arguments should not cause us any delay.

How perfection may be ascribed in a certain respect, and how absolutely
Next, just as good and bad are said of a thing only in a certain respect, so also is perfection, except when we take perfection for the very essence of the thing. In that sense we said previously that God has infinite perfection, that is, infinite essence *or* infinite being.

It is not my intention to add more to this. I think the rest of what pertains to the general part of Metaphysics is sufficiently known, and so not worth the trouble of pursuing further.

Part II of the Appendix Containing Metaphysical Thoughts

IN WHICH are briefly explained the chief things which commonly occur in the special part of Metaphysics about God, his Attributes, and the human Mind.

[B: In this Chapter God's existence is explained quite differently from the way in which men commonly understand it; for they confuse God's existence with their own, so that they imagine God as being somewhat like a Man and do not take note of the true idea of God which they have, or are completely ignorant of having it. As a result, they can neither prove God's existence a priori, i.e., from his true definition, or essence, nor prove it a posteriori, from the idea of him, insofar as it is in us. Nor can they conceive God's existence.

In this Chapter, therefore, we shall attempt to show as clearly as we can that God's existence differs entirely from the existence of created things.]

CHAPTER I
OF GOD'S ETERNITY

The division of substances
We have already pointed out that there is nothing in Nature but substances and their modes. So it is not to be expected here that we

---

[17] Cf. Descartes, who asserts in the Third Meditation that there is nothing merely potential in the idea of God. AT VII, 47.

should say anything about substantial forms and real accidents, for these things, and others of the same kind, are clearly absurd.

I/250 We have divided substances into two chief kinds, extension and thought; thought we have divided into created, *or* the human Mind, and uncreated, *or* God. His existence we have demonstrated more than sufficiently, both a posteriori, from the idea which we have of 5 him, and a priori, or from his essence as the cause of his existence. But since we have treated certain of his attributes more briefly than the dignity of the argument requires, we have decided to return to them here, to explain them more fully, and at the same time to resolve some problems.

10 *That duration is not attributed to God*

The chief attribute, which deserves consideration before all others, is God's *Eternity*, by which we explain his duration. Or rather, so as not to ascribe any duration to God, we say that he is eternal. For as we have noted in Part I, duration is an affection of existence, and not 15 of the essence of things.[1] But since God's existence is of his essence, we can attribute no duration to him. Whoever attributes duration to God distinguishes his existence from his essence.

Nevertheless, there are those who ask whether God has not existed longer now than he had when he created Adam. It seems to be clear enough to them that he has and they hold that duration should in no 20 way be taken away from God.[2]

But they beg the question. For they suppose that God's essence is distinguished from his existence and ask whether God, who has existed until Adam, shall not have existed for more time from the creation of Adam until us. So they ascribe to God a greater duration each 25 day and think of him as if he were created continuously by himself. If they did not distinguish God's existence from his essence, they would not ascribe duration to him at all, since duration cannot in any way pertain to the essences of things. For no one will ever say that the essence of a circle or a triangle, insofar as it is an eternal truth, 30 has endured longer now than it had in the time of Adam.

Again, since duration is conceived as being greater or lesser, *or* as composed of parts, it follows clearly that no duration can be ascribed to God: for since his being is eternal, i.e., in it there can be nothing

---

[1] In B, the beginning of this paragraph is revised as follows: "The chief attribute, which deserves consideration before all others, is God's eternity, through which we explain his existence, in order not to confuse it with the existence of created things; for we cannot in any way explain his existence through duration, since duration is an affection of the existence and not of the essence of things (as was shown in the first part)."

[2] Cf. Suarez, 2:922ff., and Descartes, AT V, 148-149.

1/251 which is before or after, we can never ascribe duration to him, without at the same time destroying the true concept which we have of God. I.e., by attributing duration to him, we divide into parts what is infinite by its own nature and can never be conceived except as infinite. [B: We divide his existence into parts, or conceive it as divisible, when we attempt to explain it by duration. See I, iv.]

The reasons why Writers have attributed duration to God
The reason why these Writers have erred is threefold: first, because they have attempted to explain eternity without attending to God, as if eternity could be understood without contemplation of the divine essence—or as if it were something beyond the divine essence; and this again has arisen because we are accustomed, on account of a defect of words, to ascribe eternity also to things whose essence is distinguished from their existence, as when we say that it does not involve a contradiction for the world to have existed from eternity; also we attribute eternity to the essences of things so long as we conceive the things as not existing, for then we call them eternal; secondly, they have erred because they have ascribed duration to things only insofar as they judged them to be subject to continuous variation and not, as we do, insofar as their essence is distinguished from their existence; thirdly, they have erred because they have distinguished God's essence from his existence, just as they do in the case of created things.

These errors, I say, have provided them with the occasion for further error. For the first error resulted in their not understanding what eternity is, but rather considering it as if it were a species of duration. The second, in their not being able to discover easily the difference between the duration of created things and the eternity of God. And the last, as we have said, in their ascribing duration to God, although duration is only an affection of existence and they have distinguished his existence from his essence.

What is eternity?
In order that we may better understand what *Eternity* is, and how it cannot be conceived without the divine essence, we need to consider what we have already said before, viz. that created things, *or* all things except God, always exist only by the power, *or* essence, of God, and not by their own power. From this it follows that the present existence of things is not the cause of their future existence, but only God's immutability is. So we are compelled to say that when God has first created a thing, he will preserve it afterwards continuously, *or* will continue that same action of creating it.

From this we conclude: (1) that the created thing can be said to

317

enjoy existence, because existence is not of its essence; but God cannot be said to enjoy existence, for the existence of God is God himself, as is his essence also; from which it follows that created things enjoy duration, but that God does not in any way; (2) that all created things, while they enjoy present duration and existence, altogether lack future duration and existence, because it must continually be attributed to them; but nothing similar can be said of their essence. But we cannot ascribe future existence to God, because existence is of his essence; for the same existence which he would have then ought even now to be ascribed to him actually, or, to speak more properly, infinite actual existence pertains to God in the same way as infinite actual intellect pertains to him. And I call this infinite existence *Eternity*, which is to be attributed to God alone, and not to any created thing, even though its duration should be without beginning or end.

So much for eternity. Of the necessity of God I say nothing. There is no need, since we have demonstrated his existence from his essence. Let us proceed then to his unity.

Chapter II
Of God's Unity

We have often wondered at the worthless arguments by which Writers try to prove God's Unity, such as, *If one could create the world, others would be unnecessary*, and *If all things tend toward the same end, they are all produced by one maker*, and similar arguments drawn from relations or extrinsic denominations.[3] Leaving all these to one side, we shall here put forward our own proof as clearly and briefly as we can.[4]

That God is unique

Among the attributes of God we have numbered also supreme understanding, and we have added that he has all his perfection from himself and not from another. If now you say that there are many Gods, *or* supremely perfect beings, they will all have to understand, in the highest degree. To satisfy that condition, it is not sufficient that each one should understand only himself; for since each one must understand all things, he will have to understand both himself and the

[3] Both these arguments may be found in Burgersdijk (I, vi). The first is discussed by Maimonides (1, I, lxxv) as one of the arguments of the Mutakallemim, but rejected by him in favor of arguments derived from the Aristotelian tradition.
[4] The argument which follows goes back to Scotus, I, ii, 3. But the addition made in B suggests that Spinoza did not find it ultimately satisfactory. E IP31 suggests a reason why Spinoza would not find it satisfactory.

rest. From this it would follow that the perfection of each one's intellect would depend partly on himself and partly on another. Therefore, there could not be any supremely perfect being, i.e., as we have just noted, any being that has all its perfection from itself and not from another. Nevertheless we have already demonstrated that God is a supremely perfect being and that he exists. From this we can now conclude that he is unique. For if there were more than one, it would follow that a most perfect being has an imperfection, which is absurd. [B: But although this proof is completely convincing, nevertheless it does not explain God's *Unity*; therefore I advise the Reader that by right we infer God's Unity from the nature of his existence, which is not distinguished from his essence, or which necessarily follows from his essence.] This will suffice on God's Unity.

CHAPTER III

OF GOD'S IMMENSITY

How God is called infinite, how immense
We have explained previously that no being can be conceived as finite and imperfect, that is, as participating in nothing, unless we first attend to the perfect and infinite being, i.e., to God. So only God is to be called absolutely infinite, insofar as we find that he really consists of infinite perfection. But he can also be called immense, *or* interminable, insofar as we consider the fact that there is no being by which God's perfection can be limited.

From this it follows that God's *Infinity*, in spite of what the term suggests, is something most positive. For we call him infinite insofar as we are attending to his essence, *or* supreme perfection. But *Immensity* is only ascribed to God in a certain respect. For it does not pertain to God insofar as he is considered absolutely, as a most perfect being, but only insofar as he is considered as the first cause, which, even if it were only most perfect in respect to secondary beings, would still be no less immense. For there would be no being, and consequently, no being could be conceived, more perfect than him, by which he could be limited or measured.[a]

What is commonly understood by the immensity of God
Nevertheless, usually when authors deal with God's *Immensity*, they seem to ascribe quantity to him.[5] For from this attribute they wish to

---

[a] For a fuller discussion of this, see IA9.
[5] Cf. Burgersdijk, 267.

conclude that God must necessarily be present everywhere, as if they thought that if there were some place which God was not in, then his quantity would be limited.

15 This is even clearer from the other argument they bring forward to show that God is infinite, *or* immense (for they confuse these two), and also that he is everywhere. If God, they say, is pure act, as indeed he is, he must be everywhere and infinite. For if he were not everywhere, either he would not be able to be wherever he wishes to be, or he would necessarily—note this—have to move. From this it is clear that

20 they ascribe *Immensity* to God insofar as they regard him as having a certain quantity; for they seek to argue for God's *Immensity* from the properties of extension, which is most absurd.

A proof that God is everywhere

If you should now ask how we shall prove that God is everywhere,
25 I reply that we have already demonstrated this more than sufficiently when we showed that nothing can exist for even a moment that is not produced by God at each moment.[6]

God's omnipresence cannot be explained

Now, of course, for God's *omnipresence* or *presence in each thing* to be properly understood, it would be necessary for us to know fully the
30 inmost nature of the divine will, by which he has created things and continually produces them. Since this is beyond man's grasp, it is impossible to explain how God is everywhere.

[B: Here we should note that whenever ordinary people say that God is everywhere they introduce Him as a spectator at a Play. From this what we say at the end of this Chapter is evident, viz. that People
35 usually confuse the Divine nature with Human nature.]

I/255 *That God's Immensity is said by some to be threefold, but wrongly*

Some claim that God's *Immensity* is threefold: immensity of essence, of power, and of presence;[7] but that is foolish, for they seem to distinguish between God's essence and his power.

5 *That God's power is not distinguished from his essence*

But others have also asserted the same thing more openly, when they say that God is everywhere through his power, but not through

---

[6] The principle is Cartesian, but similar arguments occur in Aquinas 1, I, 8, 1, and Suarez, 2:95-96.
[7] Cf. Aquinas 1, I, 8, 3; Heereboord 2, 138.

his essence[8]—as if the power of God were distinguished from all of his attributes, *or* his infinite essence. Nevertheless it cannot be anything else. For if it were something else, it would be either some creature or something accidental to the divine essence, which the divine essence could be conceived to lack. But both alternatives are absurd. For if it were a creature, it would require the power of God in order to be conserved, and so there would be an infinite regress. And if it were something accidental, God would not be a most simple being, contrary to what we have demonstrated above.[9]

Nor is his Omnipresence

Finally, by *Immensity* of presence they seem also to mean something beyond the essence of God, through which things have been created and are continually preserved. Such is the absurdity into which they have fallen, through confusing the divine intellect with the human and frequently comparing his power with the power of kings.

CHAPTER IV
OF GOD'S IMMUTABILITY

What Change is; What Transformation is

By *Change* we understand here whatever variation there can be in a subject while the very essence of the subject remains intact; commonly the term is taken in an even broader sense, signifying the corruption of things, not an absolute corruption but one which at the same time includes the generation following corruption, as when we say that peat is changed into ashes, or men into beasts. But Philosophers use a different term to denote this, viz. *Transformation*. Here we are speaking only of that change in which there is no transformation of the subject, as when we say that Peter has changed his color, or his ways.

Transformation cannot be ascribed to God

We must see now whether such changes can be ascribed to God; for there is no need to say anything about *transformation*, after we have explained that God exists necessarily—i.e., that God could not cease to be, *or* be transformed into another God. For then he would cease to exist, and at the same time there could be many gods, both of which we have shown to be absurd.

[8] Cf. Descartes, Letter to More, 15 April 1649; Aquinas 1, I, 25, 5.
[9] Cf. IP17. See also the note at I/258/14.

What are the causes of Change

In order to understand more distinctly the things which remain to be said here, we need to consider that every *change* proceeds either from external causes (with the subject either willing or unwilling), or from an internal cause and the choice of the subject himself. E.g., that a man becomes darker, becomes ill, grows, and the like all proceed from external causes, the two former against the subject's will, the last in accordance with it; but that he wills to walk,[10] to display anger, etc., these result from internal causes.

That God is not changed by another

The first sort of *change*, which proceeds from external causes, can not be ascribed to God, since he is the sole cause of all things and is acted on by no one. Add to this the fact that no created thing has in itself any power of existing, much less any power of producing any effect outside itself or on its cause. And although it is often found in Holy Scripture that God has been angry or sad on account of men's sins, in such places the effect is taken for the cause—just as we say that the Sun in summer is stronger and higher than in winter, although it has not changed its position or renewed its strength. And that such things are often taught in Holy Scripture may be seen in Isaiah—for he says (59:2), when he is reproaching the people: '*Your iniquities separate you from your God.*'

Nor by himself

Let us, therefore, go on to ask whether there is any change in God from God himself. We do not concede that there is such a change in God—indeed, we deny it completely. For every change which depends on the will occurs in order that its subject may change into a better state. But this cannot occur in a most perfect being. Also there is no change except for the sake of avoiding some disadvantage or acquiring some good which is lacking, neither of which can occur in God. So we conclude that God is an immutable being.

[B: Note that this can be much clearer if we consider the nature of God's will and his decrees. For as I shall show in what follows, God's will, through which he has created things, is not distinct from his intellect, through which he understands them. So to say that God understands that the three angles of a triangle are equal to two right angles is the same as saying that God has willed or decreed that the

---

[10] So the EP would be translated. Gebhardt follows B, which would be translated: "wills, walks, displays anger . . ." Hubbeling appeals to I/256/28-31 in defense of the EP reading.

three angles of a triangle should equal two right angles. For this reason, it will be as impossible for us to conceive that God can change his decrees as it is for us to think that the three angles of a triangle are not equal to two right angles. Moreover, this proposition—that there can be no change in God—can also be proven in other ways; but because we are trying to be brief, we prefer not to pursue this further.]

Note that I have here deliberately omitted the common divisions of change, although in a way we have encompassed them too. For there was no need to show of each one that God is free of it, since we have demonstrated (IP16) that God is incorporeal and those common divisions include only changes of matter.

CHAPTER V
OF GOD'S SIMPLICITY

The threefold Distinction of Things: Real, Modal, of Reason
We proceed to the Simplicity of God. In order to understand this attribute of God rightly, we need to recall what Descartes has taught (*Principles* I, 48, 49), viz. that there is nothing in nature but substances and their modes. From this a threefold distinction of things is deduced (I, 60-62), viz. *real*, *modal*, and *of reason*.

That distinction is called *real* by which two substances are distinguished from one another, whether they have the same or different attributes, e.g., thought, and extension, or the parts of matter. This is known from the fact that each can be conceived, and consequently, can exist, without the aid of the other.

The *modal* distinction is shown to be twofold: there is that between a mode of a substance and the substance itself, and that between two modes of one and the same substance. We know the latter from the fact that, although either mode may be conceived without the aid of the other, nevertheless neither may be conceived without the aid of the substance whose modes they are. The former is known from the fact that, although the substance can be conceived without its mode, nevertheless, the mode cannot be conceived without the substance.

258   Finally, that distinction is said to be *of reason* which exists between substance and its attribute, as when duration is distinguished from extension. And this is also known from the fact that such a substance cannot be understood without that attribute.

Whence all composition arises, how many kinds there are
From these three all composition arises. The first sort of composition is that which comes from two or more substances which have the

same attribute (e.g., all composition which arises from two or more bodies) or which have different attributes (e.g., man). The second comes from the union of different modes. The third, finally, does not occur, but is only conceived by the reason as if it occurred, so that the thing may be the more easily understood. Whatever is not composed in these first two ways should be called simple.

That God is a most simple Being

It must be shown, therefore, that God is not something composite, from which we shall be able to conclude that he is a most simple being. This we shall accomplish easily. For since it is clear through itself that component parts are prior in nature at least to the thing composed, those substances by whose coalition and union God is composed will necessarily be prior in nature to God himself, and each one will be able to be conceived through itself, although it is not attributed to God. Then, since they must be really distinguished from one another, each one will also necessarily be able to exist through itself without the aid of the others; and so, as we have just said, there could be as many gods as there are substances from which God would be supposed to be composed. For since each one is able to exist through itself, it will have to exist of itself, and therefore will also have the power of giving itself all the perfections which we have shown to be in God (as we have already explained more fully in IP7, where we have demonstrated the existence of God). But since nothing more absurd than this can be said, we conclude that God is not composed of a coalition and union of substances.[11]

That there is also in God no composition from different modes is sufficiently demonstrated from the fact that there are no modes in God. For modes arise from the alteration of substance (*Principles* I, 56).

Finally, if anyone wishes to feign another manner of composition, from the essence of things and their existence, we will not contradict him at all. But it should be remembered that we have already sufficiently shown that these two are not distinct in God.

That God's Attributes are distinguished only by reason

And from this we can now clearly conclude that all the distinctions we make between the attributes of God are only distinctions of rea-

---

[11] It is disputed whether Spinoza is speaking for himself here or for Descartes. Cf. Wolfson 1, 1:112-121, and Gueroult 1, 1:446-447. The argument is reminiscent of E IP12D. But note that in 'proving' God's simplicity Spinoza refers us back to a proposition which was followed, not by a demonstration, but by a long, critical scholium.

son—the attributes are not really distinguished from one another. Understand such distinctions of reason as I have just mentioned, which are recognized from the fact that *such* a substance cannot exist without *that* attribute. So we conclude that God is a most simple being. For the rest, we pay no attention to the hodgepodge of Peripatetic distinctions but go on to God's life.

Chapter VI
Of God's Life

What the Philosophers commonly understand by life

In order that this attribute, the *Life* of God, may be rightly understood, it is necessary for us to explain generally what in each thing is denoted by its life. First, we shall examine the opinion of the Peripatetics. By life they understand *the persistence of the nutritive soul with heat* (see Aristotle, *De Respiratione*, I, 8).[12] And because they have feigned three souls, vegetative, sensitive, and intellective, which they ascribe only to plants, the lower animals, and men, it follows, as they themselves confess, that all other things are without life.

But in the meantime they did not dare to say that minds and God lack life. Perhaps they were afraid that they would fall into its contrary, i.e., that if minds and God lacked life, they might be dead. So Aristotle (*Metaphysics* XI, vii) gives another definition of life, which is peculiar to minds, viz. *Life is the actuality of the intellect.*[13] In this sense he attributes life to God, who understands and is pure act.

We shall not take much trouble to refute these doctrines. We have already proven sufficiently that those three souls they attribute to plants, the lower animals, and men are only fictions, for we have shown that there is nothing in matter but mechanical constructions and operations. As far as God's life is concerned, I do not know why [Aristotle] should call it an action of the intellect more than an action of the will and of similar things. But because I expect no reply from him, I pass to the explanation promised, i.e., what life is.

To what things life can be attributed

Although this term if often taken in an extended sense, to signify the conduct of some person, we shall explain briefly only what is denoted by it philosophically. Note that if life ought to be attributed

---

[12] The reference is apparently to 474a25: "life and the possession of soul depend on some degree of heat" (Hett). Cf. *De anima* 415a23-25.
[13] The reference is in fact to *Metaphysics* XII, vii (1072b27-29), though as Appuhn notes, Aristotle does not appear to be offering a definition of life there.

to corporeal things also, nothing will be without life. But if it should be attributed only to those things in which a soul is united to a body, then it will have to be ascribed only to men, and perhaps also to the lower animals, but not to minds or to God. But since the term life is commonly used more widely than this, there is no doubt but what it should also be ascribed to corporeal things not united to minds and to minds separated from the body.

What life is, and what it is in God

So we understand by *life* the *force through which things persevere in their being*. And because that force is different from the things themselves,[14] we say properly that the things themselves have life. But the power by which God perseveres in his being is nothing but his essence. So they speak best who call God life. Some Theologians think it was for this reason, i.e., that God is life, and is not distinguished from life, that the Jews, when they swore, said *chay yëhowah, living Jehovah*, but not *chey yëhowah, the life of Jehovah*, as Joseph, when he swore by the life of the Pharaoh, said *chey phar'oh*.[15]

CHAPTER VII
OF GOD'S INTELLECT

[B: From what is proven in these next three chapters, in which we treat of God's *intellect, will* and *power*, it follows very clearly that the essences of things, and the necessity of their really existing from a given cause, are nothing but God's determinate will, or decree. Therefore God's will is clearest to us when we conceive things clearly and distinctly. So it is ridiculous for the Philosophers to take refuge in the will of God whenever they are ignorant of the causes of things. We often see this happen: for example, when they say that the things whose causes are unknown to them have happened solely by God's pleasure and from his absolute decree.

Ordinary people too have found no stronger proof of God's providence and rule than that based on the ignorance of causes. This shows clearly that they have no knowledge at all of the nature of God's will, and that they have attributed a human will to him, i.e., a will really distinct from the intellect. I think this misconception has been the sole cause of superstition, and perhaps of much knavery.]

[14] Bidney, 97, questions whether this does not contradict I/248/4-5, and whether the same difficulty does not occur in the *Ethics* (between IP24 and IIIP7).
[15] Zac, 19, refers this passage to one in Maimonides 2, 43. The scriptural reference is to Gen. 42:15-16.

That God is Omniscient

Among the attributes of God we have previously numbered *Omniscience*, which is quite certainly ascribable to God. For knowledge involves perfection, and God, as the supremely perfect being, must lack no perfection. So we shall have to attribute to God knowledge in the highest degree, i.e., such as presupposes, or supposes, no ignorance, *or* privation of knowledge. For then there would be an imperfection in the attribute itself, *or* in God. From this it follows that God has never had a potential intellect, nor does he conclude anything by reasoning.

The objects of God's knowledge not things outside God

It also follows from God's perfection that his ideas are not determined, as ours are, by objects placed outside God. On the contrary, the things which have been created outside God by God are determined by God's intellect.[b] For otherwise the objects [of his knowledge] would have their own nature and essence through themselves, and would be prior, at least in nature, to the divine intellect. But that is absurd.

Because some people have not taken sufficient note of this, they have fallen into very great errors, and have maintained that there is matter outside God, coeternal with him, existing of itself. According to some, God, in understanding, only reduces this matter to order; according to others, he impresses forms on it. And then some have maintained that things are, of their own nature, either necessary, or impossible, or contingent, and that God, therefore, also knows them as contingent and is completely ignorant of whether they exist or not. Finally, others have said that God knows contingents from their circumstances, perhaps because he has had long experience of them. In addition to these, I could mention here still other errors of this kind, if I did not judge it superfluous. From what has been said, their falsity should be evident without further discussion.

But God himself

Let us return then to our thesis, viz. that outside God there is no object of his knowledge, but that he himself is the object of his knowledge, or rather is his own knowledge. Those who think that the world is also the object of God's knowledge are far less discerning than those who would have a building, made by some distinguished Architect, be considered the object of his knowledge. For the builder is forced

[b] From this it clearly follows what God's intellect, by which he understands created things, and his will and power by which he has determined them, are one and the same.

to seek suitable material outside himself, but God sought no matter outside himself. Both the essence and the existence of things have been made from his intellect *or* will.

How God knows sins, and beings of reason, etc.

The question now arises whether God knows evils, *or* sins, and beings of reason, and the like. We reply that God must understand those things of which he is the cause, particularly since they could not even exist for a moment without his concurrence. Therefore, since evils and sins are nothing in things, but are only in the human mind, which compares things with one another, it follows that God does not know them outside human minds. We have said that beings of reason are modes of thinking, and in this way must be understood by God, i.e., insofar as we perceive that he preserves and produces the human mind, in whatever way it is constituted. But we do not mean that God has such modes of thinking in himself in order to retain more easily the things he understands. And if only the little we have said here is rightly attended to, it will not be possible to propose any difficulty concerning God's intellect which cannot be very easily resolved.

How he knows singular things and universals

But in the meantime, we must not pass over the error of those writers who say that God knows only eternal things, such as the angels, the heavens, etc., which they have feigned to be, by their nature, unsusceptible either to generation or to corruption, but that he knows nothing of this world, except species, inasmuch as they also are not subject to generation or corruption. These writers seem determined to go astray and to contrive the most absurd fantasies. For what is more absurd than to deprive God of the knowledge of singular things, which cannot exist even for a moment without God's concurrence. Then they maintain that God is ignorant of the things that really exist, but fictitiously ascribe to him a knowledge of universals, which neither exist nor have any essence beyond that of singular things. We, on the contrary, attribute a knowledge of singular things to God, and deny him a knowledge of universals, except insofar as he understands human minds.

In God there is only one simple idea

Finally, before we put an end to this argument, we must deal satisfactorily with the question whether there is more than one idea in God, or only one, absolutely simple idea. To this I reply that the idea

328

of God in virtue of which he is called omniscient is unique and absolutely simple.[16] For really, God is called omniscient only because he has the idea of himself, which idea or knowledge has always existed with God. For it is nothing but his essence, nor could it exist in any other way.

What God's knowledge concerning created things is
But God's knowledge concerning created things cannot so properly be referred to God's knowledge; for if God had willed it, created things would have had another essence, which has no place in the knowledge God has concerning himself. Nevertheless, it may be asked whether what is (properly or improperly) called knowledge of created things is manifold or one.

But, we may reply, this question is like those which ask whether God's decrees and volitions are many or not, and whether God's omnipresence, *or* the concurrence by which he preserves singular things, is the same in all things. And we have already said that we can have no distinct knowledge concerning these.

Nevertheless, we know most evidently that just as God's concurrence, if it is referred to his omnipotence, must be unique, although it is manifested variously in its effects, so also his volitions and decrees (for so it pleases us to call his knowledge of created things), considered in God, are not many,[17] although they are expressed variously through created things, or rather, in created things.

Finally, if we attend to the proportion of the whole of nature,[18] we can consider it as one being, and consequently there will only be one idea of God, *or* decree concerning *natura naturata*.

CHAPTER VIII
OF GOD'S WILL

That we do not know how God's Essence, his intellect, by which
he understands himself, and his will, by which he loves himself,
are distinguished
God's will, by which he wills to love himself, follows necessarily from his infinite intellect, by which he understands himself. But how are these three things—God's essence, his intellect, by which he understands himself, and his will, by which he wills to love himself—distinguished? We do not know. Not that we are ignorant of the term *personality*, which the Theologians commonly use to explain this matter.

---

[16] Cf. Suarez, 2:180.   [17] B: "cannot be many."   [18] Cf. II/101-102.

But though we are familiar with the term, we do not know its meaning, nor can we form any clear and distinct concept of it. Nevertheless, we believe firmly that God will reveal this to his own, in the most blessed vision of God which is promised to the faithful.

God's Will and Power, as far as externals are concerned, are not distinguished from his intellect

God's *Will* and *Power*, as far as externals are concerned, are not distinguished from his intellect, as has already been well-established above. For we have shown that God decreed, not only that things would exist, but also that they would exist with such a nature. That is, that their essence and their existence had to depend on the will and power of God. From which we perceive clearly and distinctly that God's intellect, and his power and will, by which he has created, understood, and preserves, *or* loves, created things, are not distinguished from one another in any way, except in regard to our thought.[19]

God is improperly said to hate things, and love others

But when we say that God hates some things and loves others, this is said in the same sense Scripture uses in maintaining that the earth disgorges men, and other things of that kind. That God is angry with no one, that he does not love things in the way in which ordinary people persuade themselves he does—these propositions may be inferred sufficiently from Scripture itself. Isaiah says, and the apostle Paul to the Romans more clearly, *For when they* (namely the sons of Isaac) *had not yet been born and had done neither good nor evil, it was said to her* [Rebekah] *that in order that God's purpose should be maintained according to his choice, not because of works, but because of his call, the elder would serve the younger, etc.*[20] And a little later, *Therefore, he has pity on whom he will, and hardens whom he will. You will say to me—What does he still complain of? For who resists his will? But, who are you, man, to answer God thus? Will what is made say to him who made it—Why have you made me in this way? Does the potter not have power over his clay, to make, from the same mass, one vessel for honor, and another for dishonor? etc.*[21]

Why God warns men, why he does not save without warning, and why the impious are punished

If you should ask now, why does God warn men? the answer is

---

[19] B: "intellect."

[20] Romans 9:11-12. The passage continues: "As it is written, 'Jacob I loved, but Esau I hated.' " The prophecy to Rebekah occurs at Gen. 25:23. Relevent passages in Isaiah occur at 29:16 and 45:9.

[21] Romans 9:18-21.

easy, viz. that God has decreed from eternity to warn men at that time, in order that those whom he willed to be saved might be converted. If you ask next, whether God could not save them without that warning, we reply that he could have.

Why, then, does he not save? you will perhaps ask again. I shall answer this after you have told me why God did not render the Red Sea passable without a strong east wind, and why he does not bring about all singular motions without others, and infinitely many other things which God does by mediating causes.

You will ask again, why are the impious punished? For they act from their own nature, and according to the divine decree. But I answer that it is also from the divine decree that they are punished. If only those were fit to be punished whom we feign to sin only from freedom, why do men try to exterminate poisonous snakes? For they only sin from their own nature, nor can they do otherwise.

Scripture teaches nothing which contradicts the natural light

Finally, if any other passages which give rise to scruples still occur in Sacred Scripture, this is not the place to explain them. For here we are inquiring only after those things that we can grasp most certainly by natural reason. It suffices that we demonstrate those things clearly for us to know that Sacred Scripture must also teach the same things. For the truth does not contradict the truth, nor can Scripture teach such nonsense as is commonly supposed. For if we were to discover in it anything that would be contrary to the natural light, we could refute it with the same freedom which we employ when we refute the Koran and the Talmud. But let us not think for a moment that anything could be found in Sacred Scripture that would contradict the natural light.[22]

CHAPTER IX
OF GOD'S POWER

How God's Omnipotence should be understood

We have already proven sufficiently that God is omnipotent. Here we shall only attempt to explain briefly how this attribute is to be

---

[22] Spinoza here seems to adopt (ironically, in my view) the position of Maimonides which he will contest in the *Theological-Political Treatise*, vii, III/113ff. Certainly by the time he wrote that work he thought Scripture did teach things contrary to the natural light, e.g., that God is liable to passions, like jealousy (cf. TTP vii, III/100-101, and KV II, 24).

Nevertheless the passage here is sometimes taken as expressing Spinoza's own view, e.g., by Caillois, Pléiade, 1417, and by Harris 1, 211. Cf. also IV/126/22ff.

5   understood. For there are many people who speak of it neither piously enough nor according to the truth. They say that some things are possible, others impossible, and still others necessary, by their own nature, and not by God's decree. And they say that God's omnipotence applies only to possible things.

10   But we, who have already shown that all things depend absolutely on God's decree, say that God is omnipotent. Moreover, after we have understood that he decreed certain things from the sheer freedom of his will, and then that he is immutable, we say now that he can do nothing against his own decrees, and that this is impossible for the

15   sole reason that it is incompatible with God's perfection.

All things are necessary with respect to God's decree, but it is not the case that some are necessary in themselves, and others with respect to his decree

But perhaps someone will argue that we find some things to be necessary only by attending to God's decree, and others to be necessary without attending to his decree. For example, that Josiah would burn the bones of the idolators on Jeroboam's altar.[23] If we attend

20   only to Josiah's will, we shall regard the matter as possible, nor shall we call it necessarily future in any way, except from the fact that the prophet had predicted it from God's decree. But that the three angles of a triangle must equal two right angles, the thing itself shows.

Those who say this surely feign distinctions in things out of their

25   own ignorance. For if men understood clearly the whole order of Nature, they would find all things just as necessary as are all those treated in Mathematics. Yet because this is beyond human knowledge, we judge certain things to be possible, but not necessary. Accordingly,

30   we must say either that God can do nothing, since all things are really necessary, or that he can do all things, and that the necessity we find in things has resulted from the decree of God alone.

I/267   *If God had made a different nature of things, he would have had to give us a different intellect*

Suppose someone asks now: what if God had decreed otherwise and had made false those things which are now true? would we not, nevertheless, admit them as quite true? Yes indeed, if he had left us with

5   the nature which in fact he has given us; but then he would also have been able, if he had so willed, to give us such a nature as he has now given us, by which we would understand the nature of things, and their laws, as God would have decreed them. Indeed, if we attend to God's veracity, [we shall see that] he must have given us such a nature.

[23] 1 Kings 13:2, 2 Kings 23:16.

The same conclusion is also evident from what we said above, viz. that the whole *natura naturata* is only one being. From this it follows that man is a part of Nature, which must be coherent with the other parts. Accordingly, it would also follow from the simplicity of God's decree that, if God had created things in another way, he would at the same time have constituted our nature so that we would understand things just as they had been created by God. So though we wish to retain the same distinction concerning the power of God that the Philosophers commonly teach, nevertheless, we are forced to explain it differently.

The subdivisions of God's Power: absolute, ordained, ordinary, extraordinary; what they are

We divide the *power of God*, therefore, into *absolute and ordained*, and we call God's *power absolute*, when we consider his omnipotence without attending to his decree, but *ordained*, when we do consider his decrees.

Then there is the *ordinary* power of God, and his *extraordinary* power. The *ordinary* is that by which he preserves the world in a certain order; the *extraordinary* is exercised when he does something beyond the order of nature, e.g., all miracles, such as the speaking of an ass, the appearance of angels, and the like.

Concerning this last there could, not without reason, be considerable doubt. For it seems a greater miracle if God always governs the world with one and the same fixed and immutable order, than if, on account of human folly, he abrogates the laws which (as only one thoroughly blinded could deny) he himself has most excellently decreed in nature, from sheer freedom. But we leave this for the Theologians to settle.

We omit the other questions commonly raised about God's power, viz. *whether it extends to the past, whether he can do better what he does, whether he can do more than he has done.*[24] For after what we have said above, such questions are very easily answered.

CHAPTER X
OF CREATION

What creation is

That God is the creator of all things we have already established. Now we shall try to explain what should be understood by creation.

---

[24] Cf. Aquinas, *Summa theologiae* Ia, 25, 4 and 6. On the distinctions in God's power, see Ia, 25, 5, and Suarez, Disp. XXX, sect. xvii, 32-36.

10   Then we shall answer as well as we can the questions commonly raised
concerning creation. We say, therefore, that *creation* is *an activity in
which no causes concur except the efficient*, or *a created thing is that which
presupposes nothing except God in order to exist.*[25]

The common definition of creation rejected

There are several things which need to be noted here: (1) we omit
those words which the philosophers commonly use, viz. *ex nihilo*, as
15   if nothing was the matter from which things were produced. The
reason why philosophers speak this way is that when things are generated, they customarily suppose something prior to the things, out of
which the things are made; consequently they were not able to omit
that particle *ex* in creation.

The same thing has happened concerning matter. Because they see
20   that all bodies are in a place and are surrounded by other bodies, when
they ask themselves where the whole of matter would be, they reply,
in some imaginary space. So there is no doubt that they have not
considered *nothing* as the negation of all reality, but have feigned or
imagined it to be something real.[26]

25   *The author's own definition explained*

(2) I say that in creation no other causes concur beyond the efficient.
I could, indeed, have said, that creation *denies, or excludes*, all causes
except the efficient. Still, I preferred *concur*, so as not to be forced to
answer those who ask whether God had set no end before him, on
30   account of which he created things.

Furthermore, to explain the matter better, I have added the second
definition, viz. that a created thing presupposes nothing except God.
I/269   Surely if God had some end before him, it was not outside God. For
there is nothing outside God by which he might be roused to action.

That accidents and modes are not created

(3) From this definition it follows that there is no creation of accidents and modes; for they presuppose a created substance in addition
5   to God.

There was no time or duration before creation

(4) Finally, we can imagine neither time nor duration before creation; but these latter have begun with things. For time is the measure
of duration, or rather, is nothing but a mode of thinking. Conse-

[25] Cf. Aquinas, *Summa theologiae* Ia, 45, 1; Suarez, 1:745.
[26] Cf. Heereboord 2, 49, 993-997.

quently it presupposes, not just any created thing whatever, but particularly, thinking men. Moreover, duration ceases when created things cease to be, and begins when created things begin to exist.

I say *created things*, for we have already shown quite unmistakably that no duration, but only eternity, is ascribable to God. Wherefore, duration presupposes, or at least, supposes created things. Those, however, who imagine duration and time before created things labor under the same prejudice as those who invent a space outside matter. That is evident enough through itself. This will suffice concerning the definition of creation.

God's activity is the same in creating the world as in preserving it

Again, there is no need for us to repeat here what we demonstrated in IA10, viz. that as much power is required for creating a thing as for preserving it,[27] i.e., that God's activity is the same in creating the world as in preserving it.

With these matters noted, we pass to the second thing we promised. We need to ask (1) what has been created, and what is uncreated? and (2) whether the created could have been created from eternity?

What created things are

To the first, we reply that the created is everything whose essence is conceived clearly without any existence, and is nevertheless conceived through itself. E.g., matter, of which we have a clear and distinct concept, when we conceive it under the attribute of extension, and we conceive it equally clearly and distinctly whether it exists or not.

How God's thought differs from ours

But perhaps someone will say that we perceive thought clearly and distinctly without existence, and nevertheless, ascribe it to God. To this, however, we reply that we do not ascribe to God a thought such as ours is, i.e., susceptible of being acted on, and limited by the nature of things, but one that is pure act, and therefore involves existence, as we have demonstrated above at sufficient length. For we have shown that God's intellect and will are not distinguished from his power and essence, which involves existence.

There is not something outside God, and coeternal with him

Therefore, since all those things whose essence involves no existence

[27] The doctrine is Cartesian, of course, but as Freudenthal points out, was common among the scholastics. Cf., e.g., Aquinas, *Summa theologiae* I, 104, 1-2.

10 must be created by God in order to exist, and must be continuously preserved by the creator himself, as we have explained above, many times, we shall not waste time in refuting the opinion of those who have set up the world, or chaos, or matter devoid of all form, as coeternal with God, and therefore independent of him.[28] So we pass
15 to the second question and ask whether what has been created could have been created from eternity.[29]

What is denoted here by the words: from eternity
   To understand the question rightly, we must attend to this manner of speaking: *from eternity.* For by this we wish to signify here something altogether different from what we explained previously when
20 we spoke of God's eternity. Here we understand nothing but a duration without any beginning of duration, or a duration so great that, even if we wished to multiply it by many years, or tens of thousands of years, and this product in turn by tens of thousands, we could still
25 never express it by any number, however large.

A proof that there could not have been something created from eternity
   But that there can be no such duration is clearly demonstrated. For if the world were to go backward again from this point, it could never have such a duration. Therefore the world also could not have arrived at this point from such a beginning.
30   You will say, perhaps, that to God nothing is impossible, for he is omnipotent, and therefore could make a duration such that there can not be a greater. We reply that God, because he is omnipotent, will never create a duration such that he cannot create a greater. For the nature of duration is such that, for any given duration, a greater or
I/271 lesser can always be conceived, just as is the case with number.
   You will insist, perhaps, that God has existed from eternity, and therefore has endured up to this time. So there is a duration than which a greater cannot be conceived. But in this way you attribute to God a duration consisting of parts, which we have already refuted
5 more than adequately, when we showed that, not duration, but eternity pertains to God. Would that men had considered this rightly! For then they could have extricated themselves very easily from many disputes and absurdities, and would have occupied themselves entirely with the most blessed contemplation of this being, to their very great
10 delight.

[28] Suarez 1:749, ascribes this heresy to (among others) Plato, the Pythagoreans, the Peripatetics, and the Stoics.
[29] Cf. Aquinas, *Summa theologiae* Ia, 46; Suarez, 1:779-785.

But let us proceed to reply to the arguments of certain writers[30] who try to show the possibility of such an infinite prior duration.

From the fact that God is eternal, it does not follow that his effects can also exist from eternity

First, they contend, *a thing produced can exist at the same time as its cause, but since God has existed from eternity, his effects could also have been produced from eternity.* And this they confirm further *by the example of the son of God, who has been produced by the father from eternity.* But from what we have previously said, it is clear that they confuse *eternity* with duration and only attribute duration to God from eternity, as is also evident from the example they use. For the same eternity they ascribe to the son of God they hold to be possible for creatures. Again, time and duration are imagined prior to the establishment of the world and they wish to set up a duration without created things, just as others invent an eternity outside God. We have already shown both views to be very far from the truth.

We reply, therefore, that it is quite false that God can communicate his eternity to creatures. Nor is the son of God a creature; rather like the father, he is eternal. So when we say that the father has begotten the son from eternity, we mean only that he has always communicated his eternity to the son.[31]

That God, if he acted necessarily, is not infinitely powerful

Secondly, they argue *that God is not less powerful when he acts freely, than when he acts necessarily; but if God acted necessarily, since his power is infinite, he would have had to create the world from eternity.* Still, we can reply very easily to this argument also if we pay attention to its basis. For those good men[32] suppose that they can have different ideas of a being of infinite power. For they conceive God to be of infinite power, both when he acts from the necessity of nature and when he acts freely.

But we deny that God, if he acted from the necessity of nature, would be of infinite power. We may deny this now, and indeed they

---

[30] According to Freudenthal, these arguments come to Spinoza from Pereira, via Heereboord 2, 105-107.

[31] It was presumably to the original version of this passage that Meyer took exception in the letter to which Letter 12a is a reply. When we compare the version we now have with the statement at issue in that correspondence, it appears that Meyer did take advantage of the permission given him by Spinoza to alter the passage so as to lessen the offense it might give to certain theologians.

[32] B: "These [sc. men]."

are obliged to concede it, after we have demonstrated that the most perfect being acts freely and can only be conceived as unique.

They may reply that it can, nevertheless, be posited that God, when he acts from the necessity of nature, is of infinite power, even though what is supposed is impossible. Our answer is that it is no more legitimate to suppose that, than to suppose a square circle in order to infer that not all lines drawn from its center to its circumference are equal. And this is adequately established by what we have said just now, so that there is no need to repeat what was said earlier. For we have just demonstrated that there is no duration such that its double, or a greater or lesser duration cannot be conceived, and that therefore, for any given duration, a greater or lesser can always be created by God, who acts freely with infinite power. But if God acted from the necessity of nature, that would not follow at all. For he could produce only that [duration] which would result from his nature, and not infinitely many others greater than the given [duration].

Briefly, we argue thus: if God created a greatest duration, such that he himself could not create a greater one, then he would necessarily diminish his power. But the latter is false, for his power does not differ from his essence. Therefore, etc. Again, if God acted from the necessity of nature, he would have to create a duration such that he himself cannot create a greater; but if God creates such a duration, he is not of infinite power, for we can always conceive a duration greater than any given duration. Therefore, if God acted from the necessity of nature, he would be of infinite power.

How we have the concept of a greater duration than the world has

But here perhaps a difficulty will occur to some, viz. how is it that—seeing that the world was created five thousand years ago, or more, if the calculation of the chronologists is correct[33]—we can nevertheless conceive a greater duration, which we said could not be understood without created things. That difficulty can be very easily removed, if it is noted that we do not understand this duration from the mere contemplation of created things, but from the contemplation of God's infinite power of creating. For creatures cannot be conceived as existing, *or* enduring, through themselves, but as existing through God's infinite power, from which alone they have all their duration. See IP12 and its corollary.

[33] The accuracy of the Scriptural chronology was a traditional problem in Jewish thought, since other civilizations claimed to have histories going back much further. Cf. Wolfson 2, 237-241. It also appears to have been one of the problems which concerned the small group of heterodox Jews with whom Spinoza associated at the time of his excommunication. Cf. Revah 2, 378.

Finally, in order not to waste time here replying to worthless arguments, the following things only are to be noted: the distinction between eternity and duration, and that duration is not in any way intelligible without created things, nor eternity without God. If we perceive these things rightly, we can reply to all the arguments very easily. So we do not think it necessary to dwell on them further.

CHAPTER XI

OF GOD'S CONCURRENCE

Little or nothing remains to be said about this attribute, after we have shown that at each moment God continually creates a thing, anew as it were. From this we have demonstrated that the thing, of itself, never has any power to do anything or to determine itself to any action, and that this applies not only to things outside man, but also to the human will itself. Then we reply also to certain arguments concerning this; and though many other arguments are usually brought forward, our intention here is to ignore them, since they pertain principally to Theology.

Nevertheless, because there are many who admit God's concurrence, but in quite a different sense from that in which we maintain it, we must, in order to uncover their fallacy most readily, take note here of what we have proven previously. Viz. that the present time has no connection with the future time (see IA10), and that we perceive this clearly and distinctly. And if only we attend properly to this, we will be able, without any difficulty, to answer all of the arguments they can draw from Philosophy.

How God's Preservation is related to his determination of things to act

Still, in order not to mention this question uselessly, we shall reply in passing to the query, *whether it adds something to God's preservation, when he determines a thing to act.* When we spoke of motion, we already suggested an answer to this. For we said that God preserves the same quantity of motion in nature. So if we attend to the whole nature of matter, nothing new is added to it. But with respect to particular things, it can in a sense be said that something new is added to them. It does not seem that this applies also to spiritual things; for it is not evident that they depend on one another in this way.

Finally, since the parts of duration have no connection with one another, we can say, not so much that God preserves things as that he creates them. So if a man now has a determinate freedom to do something, it must be said that God has created him thus at this time.

20 Nor is it an objection to this that the human will is often determined by things outside it, and that in turn all things in nature are determined by one another to activity. For they have been determined so by God. No thing can determine the will, nor can the will in turn be determined,[34] except by the power of God alone. But how this is
25 compatible with human freedom, i.e., how God can do this and human freedom still be preserved, we confess that we do not know, as we have already frequently remarked.

That the common division of God's attributes is more nominal than real
These are the things I had decided to say about God's attributes. So far I have given no division of them. But that division Writers
30 generally give—that God's attributes are divided into the communicable and the incommunicable—to confess the truth, that division seems more nominal than real. For God's knowledge agrees no more with human knowledge than the Dog that is a heavenly constellation agrees with the dog that is a barking animal. And perhaps even much less.[35]

I/275 *The Author's own division*
But we give this division. There are some attributes of God which explain his active essence, others which explain nothing of his action, but only his manner of existing.[36] Unity, eternity, necessity, etc., are
5 of the latter sort, but understanding, will, life, omnipotence, etc., of the former. This division is sufficiently clear and evident, and includes all of God's attributes.

Chapter XII
Of the Human Mind

10 We must go on now to created substance, which we have divided into extended and thinking. By extended substance we understood matter, *or* corporeal substance. But by thinking substance we understood only human minds.

Angels are a subject for theology, but not for metaphysics
And though the Angels have also been created, nevertheless, be-
15 cause they are not known by the natural light, they do not concern

[34] Appuhn makes the passive reflexive: "nor can the will determine itself." That makes sense of an otherwise very obscure passage.
[35] Cf. E IP17S, and in particular the note to II/63/32. According to Heereboord 2, 964, the communicable attributes are those which in some way are also found in creatures (e.g., goodness, intellect, and will), the incommunicable are those which in no way are found in creatures (e.g., immensity, eternity).
[36] Cf. I/33-34.

Metaphysics. For their essence and existence are known only by revelation, and so pertain solely to Theology. Since theological knowledge is altogether other than, *or* completely different in kind from, natural knowledge, it ought not to be mixed with it in any way. So no one will expect us to say anything about angels.

The human mind is not transmitted but created by God, though we do not know when

Let us return, then, to human minds, about which few things now remain to be said, apart from reminding you that we have said nothing about the time of the human mind's creation.[37] Our reason is that it is not sufficiently established at what time God creates it, since it can exist without body. It is sufficiently certain that it is not *by transmission*.[38] For that occurs only in things which are generated, i.e., in the modes of some substance. But substance itself cannot be generated; it can only be created by the Omnipotent alone, as we have proven fully in the preceding.

In what sense the human soul is mortal

But let me add something concerning its immortality. Quite certainly we cannot say of any created thing that its nature is such that it would involve a contradiction for the thing to be destroyed by God's power; he who has the power of creating a thing, has also the power of destroying it. Moreover, as we have already fully demonstrated, no created thing can exist by its own nature for even a moment, but each is created continually by God.

In what sense immortal

In spite of this, we see clearly and distinctly that we have no idea by which we conceive that a substance is destroyed, as we have ideas of the corruption and generation of modes. For we conceive clearly, when we attend to the structure of the human body, that such a structure can be destroyed. But when we attend to corporeal substance,[39] we do not conceive clearly that it can be annihilated.

Again, a Philosopher does not ask what God can do by his supreme power, but judges the nature of things from the laws that God has placed in them. So he judges to be fixed and settled what is inferred

---

[37] But cf. I/132/14-17.

[38] I.e., by some form of propagation from the soul(s) of one or both of the parents. Cf. Heereboord 2, 61-64.

[39] On the avoidance of definite articles in connection with corporeal (or extended) substance, see the note at I/179/10. Descartes does not consistently hold that there is only one corporeal substance (cf. AT VII, 44, 222-223), but the doctrine was apparently to be central to his proof of immortality (cf. AT VII, 12-14).

from those laws to be fixed and settled, though he does not deny that God can change those laws and everything else.[40] Hence we also do not ask, when we speak of the soul, what God can do, but only what follows from the laws of nature.[41]

20 *Its immortality is demonstrated*
Moreover, since it clearly follows from these laws that a substance can be destroyed neither through itself nor through another created substance (as we have already proven abundantly, unless I am mistaken), we are compelled, from the laws of nature, to maintain that the mind is immortal.
And if we wish to look into the matter still more thoroughly, we 25 shall be able to demonstrate most evidently that it is immortal. For as we have just demonstrated, it follows clearly from the laws of nature that the soul is immortal. But those laws of nature are God's decrees, revealed by the natural light, as is also established most plainly by the preceding. Now we have also already demonstrated that God's decrees 30 are immutable. From all this we infer clearly that God's immutable will concerning the duration of souls has been manifested to men not only by revelation, but also by the natural light.

God acts, not against nature, but above nature; what this is, according to the author
Nor does it matter if someone objects that God sometimes destroys those natural laws to bring about miracles. For most of the more pru-
I/277 dent Theologians[42] concede that God does nothing against nature, but only acts above nature. I.e. (as I explain it), that God also has many laws of acting which he has not communicated to the human intellect. But if these laws had been communicated to the human intellect, they 5 would be just as natural as the rest.
So it is quite clearly established that minds are immortal, and I do not see what remains to be said here about the human soul in general. Nor would there remain anything to be said in particular about its functions, if the arguments of certain Authors did not summon me to

[40] This is surely not Descartes' doctrine. For though Descartes holds that the eternal truths (which include the laws of nature) are what they are because God has willed them, as a king establishes the laws of his kingdom, he denies that they are changeable, on the ground that God's will cannot change. Cf. the letter to Mersenne of 15 April 1630, and Curley 10.
[41] Note that when Descartes argues for the real distinction between mind and body, he contends that each can exist without the other "at least by the divine power" (AT VII, 170). The *Ethics* will deny any distinction between God's power of acting and the laws of nature (II/138/11ff.).
[42] Cf. Aquinas, *Summa theologiae* III, 4, 2.

342

10   reply to them. For they try, by these arguments, to bring it about
that they do not see and think what they do see and think.

Why some think the will is not free

Some think they can show that the will is not free, but is always
determined by something else. And they think this because they understand by will something distinct from the soul, something they
15   consider as a substance whose nature[43] consists entirely in that it is
indifferent. To remove all confusion, we shall first explain [what the
will is]. Once this is done, we shall lay bare the fallacies of their
arguments very easily.

What the will is

We have said that the human mind is a thinking thing; it follows,
'0   accordingly, that, from its own nature alone, considered in itself, it
can do something, viz. think, i.e., affirm and deny. But these thoughts
are determined either by things existing outside the mind, or by the
mind alone. For it is a substance from whose thinking essence many
5   acts of thought can and must follow. But those acts of thought which
recognize no other cause of themselves than the human mind are called
volitions. And the human mind, in so far as it is conceived as a sufficient cause for producing such actions, is called the *will*.

That there is a will

)   But that the soul has such a power, although determined by no
external things, can be explained most conveniently by the example
of Buridan's ass. For if we put a man, instead of an ass, in such a
condition of equilibrium,[44] the man will rightly be considered, not a
thinking thing, but a most shameful ass, if he should perish from
hunger and thirst.

278   The same conclusion is also evident from the fact that, as we have
said before, we willed to doubt all things, and indeed, not just to judge
doubtful those things which can be called in question, but to reject
them as false. (See Descartes *Principles* I, 39.)

And that it is free

Next, it must be noted that, although the soul is determined by
external things to affirming or denying something, it is not so determined as if it were compelled by external things, but it always remains
free. For no thing has the power of destroying its essence. So what

---

[43] Gebhardt has *naturâ*, but the EP has *natura*.
[44] B: "indifference."

the soul affirms and denies, it always affirms and denies freely, as is explained sufficiently in the fourth Meditation. Hence, if anyone asks why the soul wills this or that, or does not will this or that, we shall reply, because the soul is a thinking thing, i.e., a thing which, of its own nature, has the power of willing and not willing, of affirming and denying. For this is what it is to be a thinking thing.

And should not be confused with wanting

With these matters explained, let us now look at our opponents' arguments. (1) The first is as follows: *If the will can will contrary to the last dictate of the intellect, if it can want what is contrary to the good pre-scribed by the last dictate of the intellect, it will be able to want evil as evil. But the latter is absurd. Therefore the former is also.*

From this argument it is plain that they do not understand what the will is. For they confuse it with the appetite which the soul has after it has affirmed or denied something. This they have learned from their Master, who has defined the will as an appetite for what seems good.[45]

But we say that the will is *the affirming that this is good, or the contrary*. We have already explained this fully in dealing with the cause of error, which we have shown to arise from the fact that the will extends more widely than the intellect. But if the mind had not affirmed from the fact that it is free, that this is good, it would want nothing.

So we reply to the argument by conceding that the mind can will nothing contrary to the last dictate of the intellect, i.e., that it can will nothing insofar as it is supposed not to will it. And that is what is supposed here, when it is said that the mind has judged something evil, i.e., it has not willed it. Nevertheless, we deny that the mind absolutely could not have willed what is evil, i.e., judged it good. That would be contrary to experience. For we judge good things that are evil, and evil many things that are good.

Nor is the will anything except the mind itself

(2) The second argument—or if you prefer, the first, since so far there has been none—is this: *If the will is not determined to willing by the last judgment of the practical intellect, then it will determine itself. But the will does not determine itself, because of itself and by its nature it is indeterminate.* So they go on to argue thus. *If the will, of itself and by its own nature, is indifferent to willing and not willing, it cannot be determined by itself to willing. For what determines must be as determinate as what is*

---

[45] Their 'Master,' of course, is Aristotle and Spinoza might have in mind a passage in the *Rhetoric* (1369a1-4). But he might equally well be relying on a scholastic source, like Aquinas (e.g., *Summa theologiae* Ia, 59, 4). Cf. I/85/7ff.

determined is indeterminate. But the will, considered as determining itself, is as indeterminate as it is when it is considered as to be determined. For our opponents posit nothing in the determining will which is not the same in the will which either is to be determined or has been determined. Nor indeed, can they posit such a thing here. Therefore, the will cannot be determined by itself to willing. And if not by itself, then it is determined by another.

These are the very words of Professor Heereboord of Leiden.[46] They show plainly that he understands by will, not the mind itself, but something else either outside the mind or in the mind, like a blank tablet, lacking all thought, and capable of receiving any picture whatever. Or rather he conceives it as a balance in a state of equilibrium, which is moved in either direction you like by any weight whatever, as the added weight is determined [in a certain direction], or finally, as something that neither he nor any mortal can grasp by any thought.

But we have just said, indeed we have shown clearly, that the will is nothing except the mind itself, which we call a thinking thing, i.e., one that affirms and denies. From this we clearly infer, when we attend to the nature of the mind alone, that it has an equal power of affirming and of denying. For this, I say, is thinking.

So if we conclude that the mind has the power of affirming and denying from the fact that it thinks, why then do we seek adventitious causes of the production of what follows from the nature of the thing alone? You will say that the mind is no more determinate toward affirming than toward denying. Therefore, you will conclude, we must seek a cause by which it is determined.

But I argue on the contrary, that if the mind, of itself and by its own nature, were determined only to affirming (although it is impossible to conceive this, as long as we think it is a thinking thing), then of its own nature alone it could only affirm, and never deny, no matter how many causes concurred; if it is determined neither to affirming nor to denying, then it will be able to do neither; and finally, if it has the power to do each, as we have just shown it to have, then it will be able to bring about each one, of its own nature alone, with no other cause assisting.

This will be quite evident to all those who consider the thinking thing as a thinking thing, i.e., who in no way separate the attribute

---

[46] See Heereboord 2, 713. But the first argument is equally a direct quote from Heereboord 2, 712-713. Descartes' teaching concerning the will led to his being accused of Pelagianism, and in 1647 the curator of the University of Leiden forbade his name or doctrines to be mentioned, either favorably or unfavorably, in disputes there.

It is difficult to believe that Spinoza did not have considerable sympathy with the criticism of Descartes he purports to rebut here, though of course he could not accept the alternative that the will is determined by the last judgment of the practical intellect.

of thought from the thinking thing itself, from which it is only distinguished by reason. Our opponents do make this separation when they strip the thinking thing of every thought and feign it as that prime matter of the Peripatetics.

20 So I reply thus to the argument. First, to its major premise. If by will one understands a thing stripped of every thought, we grant that the will is, of its nature, indeterminate. But we deny that the will is something stripped of every thought. On the contrary, we maintain that it is a thought, i.e., a power of doing each one, of affirming and

25 of denying. By a power of doing each one, of course, nothing else can be understood than a cause sufficient for each one.

Next, we also deny that, if the will were indeterminate, i.e., deprived of every thought, some adventitious cause (except God, by his

30 infinite power of creating) would be able to determine it. For to conceive a thinking thing without any thought is the same as wishing to conceive an extended thing without extension.

Why Philosophers have confused the mind with corporeal things

There should, finally, be no need to examine many arguments here. I give warning only that our Opponents, because they have not under-

I/281 stood the will and have had no clear and distinct concept of the mind, have confused the mind with corporeal things. This has happened because they have used words that they are accustomed to use for corporeal things to signify spiritual ones which they did not understand. For they have been accustomed to call indeterminate those bod-

5 ies which are propelled in opposite directions by equivalent and opposite external causes. So when they say that the will is indeterminate, they seem to conceive it also as a body in equilibrium. And because

10 those bodies have nothing but what they have received from external causes (from which it follows that they must always be determined by an external cause), they think the same thing follows in the will. But we have already explained sufficiently how the matter really stands, so we make an end of it here.

15 Of extended substance we have already said enough previously, and beyond these two, we recognize no others. As for real accidents and other qualities, they have already been rejected adequately and it is not necessary to spend our time refuting them. So here we bring our work to a close.

The End

Letters

EDITORIAL PREFACE

SPINOZA'S correspondence in this period is dominated by the figure of Willem van Blijenbergh (1632-1696), not, it must be admitted, one of Spinoza's most acute correspondents. A grain broker by profession, van Blijenbergh was already an author himself when his reading of *Descartes' Principles* and the *Metaphysical Thoughts* prompted him to write to Spinoza. In 1663 he had published a work whose title alone suggests how little he and Spinoza really had in common:

> Theology and Religion defended against the views of Atheists, wherein it is shown by natural and clear arguments that God has implanted and revealed a Religion, that God wants to be worshipped in accordance with it, and that the Christian Religion not only agrees with the Religion revealed by God but also with the Reason which is implanted in us.

In 1674 he was to write a defense of the Christian religion and of the authority of Holy Scripture against the arguments of the irreligious— "a refutation of that blasphemous book called the *Theological-Political Treatise.*" In 1682 there followed a 'refutation' of the *Ethics.*

Van Blijenbergh is a tedious fellow, obscure, repetitious, and slow to see the point. His doctrine that Scripture must be the ultimate authority (IV/96-98) is not a very promising basis for discussion with Spinoza. But he is not an utter fool. Some of his difficulties arise from the fact that in the beginning he knows Spinoza only through a work which is primarily an exposition of the thought of Descartes. Although there are many hints in that work of Spinoza's own position, it is much easier to see their implications if you know the *Ethics,* or the *Short Treatise.* In any case, the basic questions he raises are important: is there such a thing as evil? if so, how is it compatible with God's creation and continual conservation of the world? what does it mean to say that evil is only a negation in relation to God? what sense can Spinoza attach to the traditional language of theology which he persists in using? how can we distinguish between Spinoza's own views and Descartes' in the geometrical demonstration and its appendix? what does Spinoza's view about the relation between mind and body imply about the immortality of the soul? While we may sympathize with Spinoza for losing his patience with van Blijenbergh, we cannot help wishing that he had been as forthcoming and instructive in his answers to some of these questions as he was to others.

Apart from the philosophical interest these letters contain, they may also have had an important effect on Spinoza's life. We know from occasional remarks in the correspondence that the bulk of the *Ethics* was written between about 1662 and 1665. A draft of Part I was evidently circulating by early 1663 (Letter 8) and a draft of the final part, called at that stage Part III, was nearly ready to circulate by June of 1665 (Letter 28). In mid-1663 Spinoza had interrupted his work on the *Ethics* to write *Descartes' Principles* and the *Metaphysical Thoughts*, in the hope that this work would arouse interest in the *Ethics* and allow him to publish it safely (Letter 13). The reference to his *Ethics* as "not *yet* published" (Letter 23, IV/151) and the plans for a Dutch translation (Letter 28) suggest that by mid-1665 he was nearly ready to go ahead.

But the next letters in the correspondence, which are reserved for Volume II, indicate a change of focus. A lost letter to Oldenburg of 4 September 1665 prompts its recipient to remark that Spinoza is not so much philosophizing as theologizing: "You are recording your thoughts about Angels, prophecy and miracles. But perhaps you are doing this philosophically." (Letter 29, IV/165) In the following letter Spinoza announces that he is writing a treatise on his judgment regarding Scripture. Among the reasons he gives for doing this are:

(1) The prejudices of the theologians, for I know of no greater obstacle to men's applying their minds to philosophy. . . .

(2) The opinion ordinary people have of me. They never stop accusing me of atheism, and I am forced to rebut this accusation as much as I can. . . . (Letter 30, IV/166)

It will be years before we hear more of the *Ethics* in the correspondence.

Now why does Spinoza put to one side a treatise he thinks of as nearly finished in order to start on another, which, as it turns out, will take some five years to complete? Note that I am not asking "Why did Spinoza feel it worthwhile to write the *Theological-Political Treatise* at all?" The answer to that involves a complicated story, having much to do with political and social conditions in the Netherlands at that time.[1] I ask, instead, "Why did Spinoza defer publication of the one (nearly finished) work until after he had published the other?" And I conjecture that the correspondence with van Blijenbergh may have been a factor, that Spinoza may have come to think that the time was not yet ripe for his *Ethics*, that another work was required which would help to further prepare the way for the *Ethics* by freeing people from their reliance on Scripture as a guide to the truth about speculative matters. If that was his motivation, then Spinoza badly misjudged his

[1] See Freudenthal 5, 1:148ff.

public. For the *Theological-Political Treatise* generated a storm which made publication of the *Ethics* virtually impossible, not easier.

Apart from van Blijenbergh, there are two other new correspondents in this period:

(1) Pieter Balling (b. ?; d. c. 1664-1669) was a Mennonite and the agent in Amsterdam of various Spanish merchants. As a result he knew Spanish well. That is one reason for the suspicion that Letter 17 may have been written originally in Spanish.[2] A work entitled *The Light on the Candlestick* (1662), which "attacked dogmatism and advocated a simple religion based on the inward light of the soul," has been attributed to him, but there is some doubt about the accuracy of this attribution.[3] He was, in any case, the translator into Dutch of *Descartes' Principles* and the *Metaphysical Thoughts*, and perhaps of other works as well.[4]

(2) Johannes Bouwmeester (1630-1680) was a close friend both of Lodewijk Meyer and of Spinoza. Trained in medicine and philosophy at the University of Leiden, he was a fellow member with Meyer of the society *Nil volentibus arduum* and codirector of the Amsterdam theater in 1677. On commission from that society he translated (from a Latin translation, not from the Arabic) Ibn Tophail's novel, *The Life of Hai Ibn Yokdan*, a work which purported to show how one could attain knowledge of oneself and of God, without any association with other people or instruction.[5]

For Letters 17, 25, and 26 our only sources are the OP and the NS. In each of those cases I translate the OP text, as reproduced in Gebhardt. Letter 28 (a draft of the letter actually sent) was known to the editors of the OP, but omitted by them as being of no value, so our only source there is the draft itself, reproduced in Gebhardt.

For the correspondence with van Blijenbergh the situation is more complicated. The OP and NS published four letters from van Blijenbergh to Spinoza (18, 20, 22, and 24). Of these we possess autographs of the last three, which Gebhardt reproduces (not too exactly) at the top of the page, with the OP text underneath. In these cases I translate the autograph text, as emended by AHW. Gebhardt gives priority to the NS text of Letter 18, which is the text I translate.

---

[2] A stronger reason, perhaps, is the fact that we know that Spinoza preferred not to write in Dutch (IV/95) and that Balling had a good knowledge of Latin. See AHW, 459-460.

[3] Wolf 3, 51; AHW, 45.

[4] Akkerman (2, 145-160) makes a very strong case for regarding Balling as the translator of EI-II in the NS, and Gebhardt has suggested him as the translator of the KV.

[5] AHW, 47.

There are also four letters from Spinoza to van Blijenbergh (19, 21, 23, and 27). Of these, we possess autographs of the last two. Gebhardt does not give priority to the autographs, since he takes Spinoza to be responsible for the Latin translation which appeared in the OP, but he does print them below the OP text. I translate Gebhardt's autograph text, as emended by AHW. In the case of Letter 21 we are dependent on the OP and the NS. I translate the OP text, which is the only one Gebhardt reproduces. For Letter 19, our sources are the OP, the NS and François Halma, who published a copy of the original in *De boekzaal der geleerde wereld*, an eighteenth-century periodical. Since Halma also published a copy of Letter 27, of which we possess an autograph, we can establish that his work was trustworthy. I translate Halma's text, which Gebhardt reproduces below the OP text. For Letter 27, I translate the autograph text, though Gebhardt gives priority to the OP text.

IV/76

LETTER 17

B. D. S. TO THE VERY LEARNED AND PRUDENT PIETER BALLING

Version[1]

Dear friend,

Your last letter, written, if I am not mistaken, on the 26th of last month, has reached me safely. It has caused me no little sadness and anxiety, though that has greatly decreased as I consider the prudence
10 and strength of character with which you are able to scorn the blows of fortune, or rather opinion, when they attack you with their strongest weapons. For all that, my anxiety increases daily, and therefore by our friendship I beseech and implore you to take the trouble to write to me at length.
15 As for the omens you mention—that when your child was still healthy and well, you heard sighs like those he made when he was ill and shortly afterwards passed away—I should think that this was not a true sigh, but only your imagination. For you say that when you sat up and set yourself to listen, you did not hear them so clearly as
20 before, or as afterwards, when you had gone back to sleep. Surely this shows that those sighs were only sheer imagination, which, when it was unfettered and free, was able to imagine certain sighs more

---

[1] This subheading in the OP generally signals a translation from the Dutch. But AHW plausibly conjecture that in this case the original may have been written in Spanish. Cf. the Preface, p. 351.

effectively and vividly than when you sat up to focus your hearing on a certain place.

I can confirm, and at the same time explain, what I say here by an incident that happened to me last winter in Rijnsburg.[2] One morning, as the sky was already growing light, I woke from a very deep dream to find that the images which had come to me in my dream remained before my eyes as vividly as if the things had been true—especially [the image] of a certain black, scabby Brazilian whom I had never seen before. For the most part this image disappeared when, to divert myself with something else, I fixed my eyes on a book or some other object. But as soon as I turned my eyes back away from such an object without fixing my eyes attentively on anything, the same image of the same Black man appeared to me with the same vividness, alternately, until it gradually disappeared from my visual field.

I say that the same thing which happened to me in my internal sense of vision happened to you in hearing. But since the cause was very different, your case, but not mine, was an omen. You will understand this clearly from what follows.

The effects of the imagination arise from the constitution either of the Body or of the Mind. To avoid being tedious, I shall prove this for now by experience alone. We find by experience that fevers and other corporeal changes are causes of madness, and that those whose blood is thick imagine nothing but quarrels, troubles, killings, and things like these. We see that the imagination is also determined by the constitution of the soul alone; for as we find by experience, it follows the traces of the intellect in everything and links its images and words together in order, as the intellect does its demonstrations, so that we can hardly understand anything of which the imagination does not form some image from a trace.

Because of this, I say, none of the effects of the imagination which proceed from corporeal causes can ever be *omens* of future things, because their causes do not involve any future things. But the effects of the imagination (or the images which have their origin in the constitution of the Mind) can be *omens* of a future thing, because the Mind can confusedly be aware, beforehand, of something which is future. Hence it can imagine it as firmly and vividly as if a thing of that kind were present.

To take an example like yours, a father so loves his son that he and his beloved son are, as it were, one and the same. According to what I have demonstrated on another occasion, there must be in thought an

---

[2] Since Spinoza moved from Rijnsburg to Voorburg in April 1663, he is probably referring to the winter of 1662-1663, rather than the winter just ended.

idea of the son's essence, its affections, and its consequences. Because of this, and because the father, by the union he has with his son, is a part of the said son, the father's soul must necessarily participate in the son's ideal essence, its affections, and consequences (as I have dem-
35 onstrated elsewhere at greater length).

IV/78   Next, since the father's soul participates ideally in the things which follow from the son's essence, he (as I have said) can sometimes imagine something of what follows from [the son's] essence as vividly as if he had it in his presence—if, at least, the following conditions concur:
5 (i) If the incident which will happen to the son in the course of his life will be remarkable; (ii) if it will be of the kind that we can imagine very easily; (iii) if the time when this incident will happen is not very remote; and finally (iv) if his body is not only well constituted as regards health, but also free and void of all cares and troubles that disturb the senses externally.

10   It can also be of assistance in this if we think of those things which for the most part arouse ideas like these. For example, if, while we are speaking with this or that man, we hear sighs, it will generally happen that when we think again of that same man, the sighs we heard when we spoke with him will come into our memory.

15   This, dear friend, is my opinion about the Problem you raise. I confess I have been very brief, but intentionally, so that I might give you an occasion for writing back to me at the first opportunity, etc.
Voorburg, 20 July 1664

IV/79   LETTER 18

WILLEM VAN BLIJENBERGH TO THE
DISTINGUISHED B.D.S.

Sir and unknown friend,

    I have now had the honor of reading through, frequently and attentively, your recently published Treatise, together with its Appendix.[3] It will be more proper for me to express to someone else, rather than
10 yourself, the great solidity I have found there and the satisfaction I have received from this reading. But I cannot refrain from saying that the more often I run through it attentively, the more it pleases me. I continually find something there I had not noticed before. However,
15 having no wish to seem a flatterer, I do not want to marvel too much at the author in this letter. I know what price in toil the gods exact for what they give.[4]

[3] I.e., Descartes' *"Principles"* and the *Metaphysical Thoughts.*
[4] An allusion to a line from the Greek poet Epicharmus (AHW).

But lest I keep you wondering too long who it is, and how it happens that someone unknown dares to take such liberty in writing to
you, I shall tell you that he is one who, driven only by a desire for
pure truth in this short and transitory life, strives to plant his feet
firmly in knowledge, as far as the human intellect allows, someone
who, in his search for truth, has no other end than the truth, who
seeks to acquire, by science, neither honor nor riches, but only truth,
and peace of mind as an effect of truth, who, among all truths and
sciences, takes pleasure in none more than in those of *Metaphysics* (if
not in all of it, then at least in some of its parts), and who finds his
whole life's pleasure in devoting what free time he has to its study.
(But not everyone is so fortunate, or not everyone is so industrious as
I imagine you to be, and so not everyone attains the level of perfection
I see already in your work.) In a word, it is one whom you will be
able to know better, if you are willing to oblige him so much as to
help open and pierce through his tangled thoughts.

But to return to your Treatise. As I have found many things in it
which were very palatable to me, so also have I found some I could
not easily digest. Not knowing you, it would not be right for me to
object to them, all the more because I do not know whether this will
be pleasing to you or not. So I send this ahead, to ask whether, on
these winter evenings, you will have the time and the disposition to
oblige me so much as to answer the difficulties I still find in your
Book, and whether you will let me send you some of them, though
on the condition that it should not hinder you in your more necessary
and pleasant pursuits.

For above all else I want what is promised in your Book, a fuller
publication of your own views. (I would rather have communicated to
you in person what I at last entrust to writing, but first my ignorance
of where you lived, then the epidemic, and finally my profession have
caused me to keep postponing a visit to you.)

But that this letter may not be entirely empty, and in the hope that
it will be agreeable to you, I shall present only this one [difficulty]
here. Both in the *Principles* and in the *Metaphysical Thoughts* you generally maintain—whether as your own opinion or to explain M. Descartes, whose Philosophy you were teaching—that creation and preservation are one and the same thing (which is so clear in itself, for
those who have thought about it, that it is a first notion) and that God
has created not only substances, but also the motions in substances,
i.e., that God not only preserves substances in their state by a continuous creation, but also preserves their motion and striving. For example, God not only makes the Soul exist longer and persevere in its

355

state by his immediate willing or activity (whichever one is pleased to
call it), but that he also stands in a like relation to the motion of the
Soul, i.e., as God's continuous creation makes things exist longer, so
also the striving or motion of things happens in them by the same
cause, since outside God there is no cause of motion. So it follows
that God is the cause not only of the Soul's substance, but also of the
Soul's every Motion or Striving, which we call will, as you maintain
throughout.

From this assertion it also seems to follow necessarily, either that
there is no evil in the Soul's motion or will, or else that God himself
does that evil immediately. For the things we call evil also happen
through the Soul, and consequently through such an immediate influence and concurrence of God. For example, Adam's Soul wants to eat
the forbidden fruit. According to the proposition above, that will of
Adam happens through God's influence—not only that [Adam] wills,
but that he wills in this way, as will be shown immediately. So either
Adam's forbidden act is no evil in itself, insofar as God not only moved
his will, but also moved it in such a way, or else God himself seems
to do what we call evil.

Nor does it seem to me that either you or M. Descartes solve this
problem by saying that evil is a *nonbeing* [I/262/20], with which God
does not concur. For where, then, did the will to eat come from? Or
the Devil's will to pride? As you rightly note [I/279/28], the will is not
something different from the Soul, but is this or that motion or striving of the Soul. Hence, it has as much need of God's concurrence for
the one motion as for the other.

Now as I understand it from your writings [I/274/14ff.?], God's
concurrence is nothing but a determining of the thing in this or that
way by his will. It follows, then, that God concurs with (that is,
determines) the evil will, insofar as it is evil, as much as the good. For
his will, which is an absolute cause of everything that exists, both in
the substance and in the striving, seems then to be also a first cause
of the evil will insofar as it is evil.

Next, there is no determination of the will in us which God has not
known from eternity (unless we ascribe an imperfection to God). But
how did God know those determinations except from his decrees?
Therefore, his decrees are causes of our determinations. So it seems
again to follow either that the evil will is no evil, or that God causes
that evil immediately.

And here the Theologians' distinction between the act and the evil
adhering to the act cannot be applied. For God has decreed not only
the deed, but also the manner of the deed, i.e., God has decreed not

only that Adam shall eat, but also that he shall necessarily do so contrary to the command. So again it seems to follow either that Adam's eating the apple contrary to the command is no evil, or that God himself caused it.

For the present, Worthy Sir, I mention only this, of the things I cannot penetrate in your Treatise. For the extremes on both sides are hard to maintain. But I expect from your penetrating judgment and diligence a reply that will satisfy me, and I hope to show you in the future how much you will thereby put me under obligation to you.

Be assured, Worthy Sir, that I ask these things only from a desire for the truth, not from any other Interest. I am a free person, not dependent on any profession, supporting myself by honest trade and devoting my spare time to these matters. I also humbly ask you to find pleasure in my difficulties, and if you are of a mind to write me the answer I look forward to so anxiously, please write to W.v.B. etc. Meanwhile, I shall be and remain, sir,

Your devoted servant,
Dordrecht, 12 December 1664   Willem van Blijenbergh

LETTER 19

B.d.S. TO THE VERY LEARNED AND PRUDENT
WILLEM VAN BLIJENBERGH

Reply to the preceding

Sir, and very welcome friend,

I did not receive your letter of the 12th (enclosed with another of the 21st of December) until the 26th of that month, while I was at Schiedam. From it I learned of your great love for the truth, and that it alone is the object of all your inclinations. Since I too aim at nothing else, this made me resolve not only to grant completely your request (that I should be willing to answer, to the best of my ability, the questions you send now and will send in the future), but also to do everything on my part to bring us to a closer acquaintance and genuine friendship.

To me, of the things outside my power, I esteem none more than being allowed the honor of entering into a pact of friendship with people who sincerely love the truth; for I believe that of things outside our power we can love none tranquilly, except such people. Because the love they bear to one another is based on the love each has for knowledge of the truth, it is as impossible to destroy it as not to embrace the truth once it has been perceived. Moreover, it is the greatest

357

25 and most pleasant that can be given to things outside our power, since
nothing but truth can completely unite different opinions and minds.
I shall not describe the very considerable advantages which follow
from it, so as not to detain you longer with things you undoubtedly
30 well know yourself. I have done so up to now, the better to show how
pleasant it is to me, and will be in the future, to be allowed the opportunity to show my ready service.

To seize the moment, I shall try to answer your question, which
35 turns on this: it *seems* clearly to follow, both from god's providence,
IV/88 which does not *differ* from his will, and from his concurrence and
continuous creation of things, either that there are no sins and no evil,
20 or that god does those sins and that evil. But you do not explain what
you mean by evil. As far as I can see from the example of Adam's
determinate will, it appears that by evil you understand the will itself
insofar as one conceives it *to be determined in such a way, or insofar as it*
25 *would be contrary to god's prohibition.* And therefore it seems a great
absurdity (as I too would grant, if it were so) to maintain either of
these, i.e., that god himself produced things that were contrary to his
will, or that they would be good, notwithstanding the fact that they
were contrary to god's will. But for myself, I cannot grant that *sins*
30 *and evil are something positive, much less that something would exist or happen*
contrary to god's will. On the contrary, I say not only that sin is not something
positive, but also that when we say that we sin against god, we are speaking
inaccurately, or in a human way, as we do when we say that men anger god.
35 For regarding the first [that sin and evil are not something positive],
IV/89 we know that whatever there is, considered in itself, without relation
to any other thing, involves perfection, which always extends, in each
thing, as far as the thing's essence does. For essence is nothing other
20 [than perfection]. As an example, I too take Adam's decision, or determinate will, to eat the forbidden fruit. That decision, or determinate will, considered only in itself, involves as much perfection as it
expresses of essence. We can understand this from the fact we can
25 conceive no imperfection in things unless we consider others which
have more essence. Therefore, we will be able to find no imperfection
in Adam's decision, if we consider it in itself, without comparing it
with others which are more perfect, or show a more perfect state.
Indeed, we can compare it with infinitely many other things which
30 are much more imperfect in relation to that, such as stones, logs, etc.
And in fact everyone grants this. For the same things we detest in
men, and look on with aversion there, we all look on with admiration
and pleasure in animals. For example, the warring of bees, the jeal-
35 ousy of doves, etc. We detest these things in men, but we judge ani-

358

V/90 mals more perfect because of them. This being so, *it follows clearly that sins, because they indicate nothing but imperfection, cannot consist in something that expresses essence,* as Adam's decision or its execution do.

Furthermore [regarding the second, that nothing exists or happens contrary to god's will], we also cannot say that Adam's will was in
5 conflict with god's will, and that it was, therefore, evil, because it was displeasing to god. For apart from the fact that it would posit a great imperfection in god if anything happened contrary to his will, or if he wished for something he did not get, or if his nature were so limited that, like his creatures, he had sympathy with some things and an
10 antipathy for others—apart from all that, it would be completely contrary to the nature of god's will. For because it does not differ from his intellect, it is as impossible for something to happen contrary to his will as it would be for something to happen contrary to his intellect. I.e., what would happen contrary to his will must be of such a nature that it conflicts with his intellect, like a square circle.

15 So because the will or decision of Adam, considered in itself, was
V/91 not evil, nor, properly speaking, contrary to god's will, it follows that god can be its cause—indeed, according to the reasoning you call attention to, he must be—but not *insofar as it was evil, for the evil that was in it was only a privation of a more perfect state,* which Adam had to
5 lose through that act. It is certain that privation is nothing positive, and that it is said only in relation to our intellect, not in relation to god's intellect. This arises because we express all the singular things of a kind (e.g., all those which have, externally, the shape of man) by one and the same definition, and therefore we judge them all to be
10 equally capable of the highest perfection which we can deduce from such a definition. When we find one whose acts are contrary to that perfection, we judge him to be deprived of it and to be deviating from his nature. *We would not do this, if we had not brought him under such a*
V/92 *definition and fictitiously ascribed such a nature to him. But because god* does not know things abstractly, and does not make such general definitions, because he does not attribute more essence to things than the divine intellect and power endow them with, and in fact give them, it
5 follows clearly *that that privation can be said only in relation to our intellect, not in relation to god's.* By this, in my opinion, the problem is completely solved.

But to make the path smooth and to remove every objection, I must still answer the two following questions: (1) Why does Scripture say that god wants the godless to repent, and why did he forbid Adam to eat of the tree when he had decided the opposite? (2) From what I say, it seems to follow that the godless, with their pride, greed, de-

spair, etc., serve god as well as the pious do, with their legitimate self-
esteem, patience, love, etc., because they also follow god's will.

*To answer the first, I say that scripture, since it is intended mainly to serve
ordinary people, continually speaks in a human fashion.* For the people are
not capable of understanding high matters. Therefore, I believe that
all the things which god has revealed to the prophets to be necessary
for salvation are written in the manner of laws. And in this way the
prophets wrote a whole parable. First, because god had revealed the
means to salvation and destruction, and was the cause of them, they
represented him as a king and lawgiver. The means, which are nothing but causes, they called laws and wrote in the manner of laws.
Salvation and destruction, which are nothing but effects which follow
from the means, they represented as reward and punishment. They
have ordered all their words more according to this parable than according to the truth. Throughout they have represented god as a man,
now angry, now merciful, now longing for the future, now seized by
jealousy and suspicion, indeed even deceived by the devil. So the
Philosophers, and with them all those who are above the law, i.e.,
who follow virtue not as a law, but from love, because it is the best
thing, should not be shocked by such words.

The prohibition to Adam, then, consisted only in this: god revealed
to Adam that eating of that tree caused death, just as he also reveals
to us through the natural intellect that poison is deadly to us. And if
you ask for what purpose he revealed it to him, I answer: to make him
that much more perfect in knowledge. So to ask god why he did not
also give him a more perfect will is as absurd as to ask him why he
did not give the circle all the properties of the sphere. This follows
clearly from what is said above; I have also demonstrated it in IP15S
[of *Descartes' Principles*].

As for the second difficulty, it is indeed true that the godless express
God's will in their fashion. But they are not on that account to be
compared with the pious. For the more perfection a thing has, the
more it has of godliness, and the more it expresses God's perfection.
So since the pious have inestimably more perfection than the godless,
their virtue cannot be compared with that of the godless. They lack
the love of God which comes from knowledge of God and through
which alone we are said, according to our human understanding, to
be servants of God. Indeed, since they do not know God, they are
nothing but a tool in the hand of the master, that serves unknowingly,
and is consumed in serving. The pious, on the other hand, serve
knowingly, and become more perfect by serving.

That, Sir, is all that I can now say in answer to your question. I wish for nothing more than that it may satisfy you. But if you still find some difficulty, I ask you to let me know it, to see whether I can remove it. For your part, you need not hesitate, but as long as it seems to you that you are not satisfied, I want nothing more than to know the reasons for it, so that the truth may finally become evident.

I wish that I could write you in the language in which I was raised.[5] Perhaps I could express my thoughts better. Please excuse it, correct the mistakes yourself, and consider me

Your devoted Friend and Servant,

The Long Orchard   B. de Spinoza
5 January 1665

I shall be at this address three or four weeks longer, and then I intend to return to Voorburg. I believe that I shall receive an answer from you before then, but if your occupations do not permit it, please write to Voorburg at the following address: To be delivered in the church lane, at the house of Mr. Daniel Tydeman, the painter.

/96

LETTER 20

TO THE VERY DISTINGUISHED B.D.S.

WILLEM VAN BLIJENBERGH

Reply to the Preceding

Sir and worthy friend,

When I first received your letter and read through it quickly, I intended not only to reply immediately, but also to criticize many things in it. But the more I read it, the less I found to object to in it. My pleasure in reading it was as great as my longing to see it had been.

Before I proceed to ask you to resolve certain other difficulties, you should know that I have two general rules according to which I always try to philosophize: the clear and distinct conception of my intellect and the revealed word, or will, of God. According to the one I strive to be a lover of truth, according to the other, a Christian philosopher.

/97 Whenever it happens, after a long investigation, that my natural knowledge either seems to contradict this word, or is not easily reconciled with it, this word has so much authority with me that I sus-

[5] Probably this language was Spanish, the language used in the Amsterdam Jewish community for instruction in the schools, and for literary and religious discussions. Portuguese was the language of daily life and of business; Hebrew, the language of prayer. See AHW, Wolf, Roth and Freudenthal 5, 1:316.

5   pect the conceptions I imagine to be clear, rather than put them above
       and against the truth I think I find prescribed to me in that book. And
       no wonder, since I want to persist steadfastly in the belief that that
       word is the word of God, i.e., that it has proceeded from the highest
10   and most perfect God, who contains many more perfections than I
       can conceive, and who perhaps has willed to predicate of himself and
       of his works more perfections than I, with my finite intellect, can
       conceive today. I say 'can conceive today,' for it is possible that through
       my own action I have deprived myself of a greater perfection, and
15   therefore that, if I perhaps had that perfection of which I have been
       deprived by my own action, I would be able to conceive that every-
       thing that is presented and taught to us in that word agrees with the
       soundest conceptions of my mind. But since I now suspect myself of
20   having deprived myself of a better state through continued error, and
       since, as you maintain (*Principles* IP15), even our clearest knowledge
IV/98 still involves some imperfection, I rather incline toward that word,
       even without reason, merely on the ground that it has proceeded from
       the most perfect being (I presuppose this now, because the proof of it
       would be out of place or would take too long) and therefore I must
5   accept it.
            If I should now judge your letter only by the guidance of my first
       rule, excluding the second, as if I did not have it, or as if it did not
       exist, I would have to grant a great many things (as I do, too) and
10   admire your penetrating Conceptions. But the second rule causes me
       to differ more from you. Within the limits imposed by a letter I shall
       examine your conceptions under the guidance of each of these rules.
            First, according to the former rule, I have asked whether, from your
15   doctrines that creation and preservation are one and the same, and
       that God makes, not only things, but also the motions and modes of
       things, to persevere in their state (i.e., concurs with them), it does not
       seem to follow that *there is no evil* or *that God himself does evil*, relying
20   on this rule, that nothing can happen contrary to God's will, otherwise
       it would involve an imperfection, or else the things God does (among
IV/99 which seem to be included those we call evil) would also have to be
       evil? But this also involves a Contradiction. However I turned, I could
       not avoid a Contradiction. Therefore I had recourse to you, who should
5   be the best interpreter of your own Conceptions.
            In reply you say that you persist in that first presupposition, namely,
       that nothing happens, or can happen, contrary to God's will. But then
       to the difficulty, whether God then does evil or not, *you say that sin is*
10   *nothing positive, but also that we can only very improperly be said to sin*
       against God. And in I, vi, of the Appendix, you say that "there is no absolute

evil, as is manifest through itself."[6] But whatever exists, considered in itself, without relation to any other thing, involves perfection, which always extends as far, in each thing, as the thing's essence. Therefore it clearly follows that because sins denote nothing but imperfections, they cannot consist in something that expresses essence. If sin, evil, error, or whatever you please to call it, is nothing but the loss or the privation of a more perfect state, it seems to follow, doesn't it, that existing is neither an evil nor an imperfection, but that something evil can arise in the existing thing. For

/100 what is perfect will not lose a more perfect state through an equally perfect act, but through the fact that we incline toward something imperfect, because we do not sufficiently use the power given to us. This you seem to call, not an evil, but a lesser good, because the things considered in themselves involve perfection. Furthermore, because, as you say, no more essence belongs to the things than the divine intellect and power have ascribed to them, and in fact given them, and therefore they can display no more existence in their actions than they have received essence. For if I can bring about neither greater nor lesser acts than I have received existence,[7] there can be no privation of a more perfect state. For if nothing happens contrary to God's will, and if only as much happens as essence has been given for, in what conceivable way can there be an evil, which you call the privation of a better state? How can anyone lose a more perfect state through an act so determined and dependent? So it seems to me that you must maintain one of two things: either there is an evil, or if there is no evil, that there can be no privation of a better state. For that there is no evil, and that there is privation of

/101 a better state, seems to me to be a Contradiction.

But you will say, that in privation we decline from a more perfect state to a lesser good, not to an absolute evil. Still, you have taught me (Appendix I, iii) that we must not quarrel over words. So, whether or not it may be called an absolute evil, I am not now disputing, but only whether the decline from a better to a worse state is not called by us, and may not rightly be called, a more evil state, or a state which is evil.

But you will say that this evil state still contains much good. Still, I ask whether that man, who, through his imprudent act, caused the privation of a more perfect state, and consequently is now less than he was before, may not be called evil.

To escape the above reasoning, since some difficulties still seem to remain concerning it, you say that there is indeed evil, and that there was

---

[6] Here van Blijenbergh quotes in Latin from the *Metaphysical Thoughts* (I/247/34-35).
[7] So A and NS; the OP corrects to: "essence."

indeed evil in Adam, but that it is not something positive, and is said only in
relation to our intellect, and not in relation to God's intellect; that that [evil]
20 *is a privation in relation to us,*[8] *but a negation in relation to God.*
IV/102 But let us examine here whether what you call evil, if it were evil
only in relation to us, would be no evil, and next, whether evil, considered as what you maintain it to be, must be called only a negation
in relation to God.
5 The first question I seem to have already answered, to some extent,
in what I said above. And though I granted that being less perfect
than another being can posit no evil in me, because I can demand no
better state from the creator, and it makes me differ only in degree,
nevertheless I will not on that account be able to grant that, if I am
10 now more imperfect than I was before, and if I have brought this on
myself through my own misdeed, I am not to that extent worse. I
must acknowledge that I am worse. I.e., if I consider myself before I
ever declined into imperfection, and compare myself then with others
15 who have more perfection than I, then that lesser perfection is no evil,
but a lesser degree of good. But if I compare myself after I have
declined from a more perfect state, and have deprived myself, through
my own imprudence, of my first form, with which I came forth from
the hand of my creator, in a more perfect form, then I must judge
20 myself to be more evil than before. For it was not the creator, but I
IV103 myself, who brought me to this state. As you acknowledge, I had
enough power to restrain myself from error.
The second question is whether evil, which you maintain to consist
5 in the privation of a better state, which not only Adam, but all of us
have lost, by a hasty and disorderly act, whether in relation to God
that evil is only a negation? To examine this soundly, we must see
how you conceive of man and make him dependent on God before all
error, and how you conceive of the same man after error.
10 Before error you describe him as having no more essence than the
divine intellect and power attributed to him, and in fact gave him.
I.e., unless I misunderstand you, man can have neither more nor less
perfection than God has endowed him with essence. That is to make
15 man dependent on God in the way the elements, stones, and plants
are. But if that is your opinion, I cannot understand what is meant
by the following:

[8] At this point van Blijenbergh quotes in parentheses from the Latin text of *Principles*
P15S (I/175/29-31): "but [assenting to confused things contains imperfection] only insofar as we thereby deprive ourselves of the best liberty, which belongs to our nature
and is in our power."

Now, since the will is free to determine itself, it follows that we do have the power to contain our faculty of assenting within the limits of the intellect, and so can bring it about that we do not fall into error.[9]

/104 Does this not seem a contradiction, to make the will so free that it can restrain itself from error, and at the same time to make it so dependent on God that it can manifest neither more nor less perfection than God has given it essence?

As for how you conceive of man after error, there you say that man has deprived himself of a more perfect state by a too hasty deed, namely, by not restraining his will within the limits of his intellect. But it seems to me that here (as also in the *Principles*) you ought to have shown in more detail the two extremes of this privation: what he possessed before the privation and what he retained after the loss of that perfect condition (as you call it). You say what we have lost, but not what we have retained:

> So the whole imperfection of error will consist solely in the privation of the best liberty, which is called error.[10]

Let us examine both of these, as you maintain them.

You hold not only that there are such different modes of thinking in us, that we call some willings and others understandings, but also that between these there is such an order that we must not will things without first having a clear understanding of them. [OP: you affirm also that] if we keep our will within the limits of our intellect, we shall never err, and finally that it is within our power to keep the will /105 within the limits of the intellect.

When I reflect seriously on this, certainly one of two things must be true: either everything that has been maintained is a fiction, or else God has impressed this same order on us. But if God has impressed that order on us, would it not be absurd to say that it happened for no purpose, and that God does not want us to have to observe and follow that order? For that would posit a contradiction in God. And if we must practice the order placed in us, how can we then be and remain so dependent on God? For if no one has more or less perfection than he has received essence, and this power must be known from its effects, he who lets his will go beyond the limits of his intellect did not receive so much power from God, or else he would also put it into

---

[9] Here van Blijenbergh quotes again from the Latin text of *Principles* IP15S (I/174/14-17).

[10] A quotation from *Principles* IP15S (I/175/31-33).

15   effect. Consequently, he who errs must not have received from God the perfection of not being able to err, or he would never err. For according to what you maintain, there is always as much essence given as there is perfection produced.

    Next, if God has given us so much essence that we are able to
20   maintain that order, as you hold that we can maintain it, and if we always produce as much perfection as we have essence, how does it
IV/106 happen that we transgress that order? How does it happen that we *can* transgress it, and that we do not always restrain the will within the limits of the intellect?

    Thirdly, if, as I have shown above that you hold, I am so dependent
5   on God that I can restrain the will neither within, nor outside the intellect, unless God has first given me just so much essence, and has, through his will, first determined one or the other, how, if we consider this thoroughly, can I ever use this freedom of the will? Indeed, doesn't it seem to posit a Contradiction in God, that he should give us an
10   order to restrain our will within the limits of our intellect, and not give us enough essence or perfection that we can put it into effect? And if, on your view, he has given us so much perfection, certainly we could never err. For we must produce as much perfection as we
15   have essence, and always display the power we are given in our actions. But our errors are a proof that we do not have such a power that is so dependent on God as you hold. So one of these two must be true, either that we are not so dependent on God, or that we do
20   not have in us the power of being able not to err. But on your view we have the power of not erring. Therefore, we can not be so dependent.

IV/107   From what has been said, it seems to me now clear that it is impossible that evil, or being deprived of a better state, should be a negation in relation to God. For what is meant by being deprived, or losing a more perfect state? Is it not passing from more to less perfec-
5   tion, and consequently, from more to less existence,[11] and being placed by God in a certain measure of perfection and essence? Is that not to will that we can acquire no other state without his perfect knowledge, unless he had decided and willed otherwise? Is it possible that this
10   creature, produced by that omniscient and perfect being, who willed that it retain such a state of essence, indeed, a creature with which God is continually concurring to maintain it in that essence—is it possible that such a creature should decline in essence, i.e., become

---

[11] So A and NS; the OP again corrects to: "essence."

less perfect without God's knowledge? This seems to me to involve an absurdity.

Is it not absurd to say that Adam lost a more perfect state, and consequently was incapable of the order God had put in his soul, and that God had no knowledge of that loss and of that imperfection, no knowledge of how much perfection Adam had lost? Is it conceivable that God would constitute a being so dependent that it would only produce such an action, and that then [this being] should lose a more perfect state through that action (of which, moreover, [God] would be an absolute cause) and that God should have no knowledge of it?

I grant that there is a distinction between the act and the evil adhering to the act. But I cannot conceive that "evil in relation to God is a negation," that God would know the act, determine it, concur with it, and yet that he would not know the evil that is in that act, nor know what outcome it would have. That seems to me to be impossible in God.

Note, with me, that God concurs with my act of procreation with my wife, for that is something positive, and consequently, he has a clear knowledge of it. But insofar as I misuse that act with another woman, contrary to my promise and oath, evil accompanies that act. What would be negative here in relation to God? Not that I perform that act of procreation, for insofar as it is something positive, God concurs with it. So the evil that accompanies the act must be only that, contrary to my agreement, or else to God's prohibition, I do it with such a woman, with whom such an act is not allowed. But is it really conceivable that God should know our actions, that he should concur with them, and that he should not know with whom we engage in those actions (particularly since God also concurs with the act of that woman with whom I transgress)? It seems hard to think this of God.

Consider the act of killing. Insofar as it is a positive act, God concurs with it. But the effect of that act, i.e., the dissolution of a being and the destruction of God's creature, he would not know—as if he did not know his own effects. (I fear that here I must not properly understand your meaning, for your conceptions seem to me too penetrating for you to commit such a grave error.)

Perhaps you will reply that all those acts, as I represent them, are simply good, and that no evil accompanies them. But then I cannot grasp what it is that you call evil, on which the privation of a more perfect state follows. Also the whole world would then be put in an eternal and lasting confusion, and we men would be made like the beasts. Just see what advantage such an opinion would bring the world.

You also reject the usual definition of man, but want to ascribe to each man only as much perfection of action as God in fact has given 20 him to exercise. But then I can't see that you don't maintain that the godless serve God with their acts as well as the godly do. Why? Be-IV/110 cause neither of them can perform actions more perfect than they have been given essence for, and than they show through their effects. And it doesn't seem to me that you answer this question satisfactorily when you say:

5 The more perfection a thing has, the more it has of godliness and the more it expresses God's perfection. So since the pious have inestimably more perfection than the godless, their virtue cannot be compared with that of the godless . . . for the latter, like a tool in the hand of the master, serve unknowingly and are consumed in serving. The pious, on the other hand, serve know-10 ingly and are consumed in serving.[12]

This, however, is true of both, that they cannot do more. For the more perfection the one displays in comparison with the other, the more essence he has received in comparison with the other. Don't the godless, then, serve God with their slight perfection as much as the 15 godly do? For on your view, God wants no more of the godless, otherwise he would have given them more essence. But he hasn't given them more essence, as is evident from the effects. Therefore, he wants no more of them. And if each of them, in his species, does neither 20 more nor less than God wills, why should those who do less, but still as much as God desires of them, not please God as well as the godly?

IV/111 Moreover, as on your view, we lose a more perfect state, by our imprudence, through the evil which accompanies the act, so you also seem to want to maintain that, by restraining our will within the limits 5 of our intellect, we not only remain as perfect as we are, but that we also become more perfect by serving. It seems to me to involve a contradiction, if we are so dependent on God that we can do neither more nor less than we have been given essence for, i.e., than God has 10 willed, and yet we can become worse through imprudence or better through prudence. So far as I can see, if man is as you describe him, the godless serve God with their actions as much as the godly do with theirs. And in this way, we are made as dependent on God as the 15 elements, Plants, stones, etc. What use is our intellect to us? What use, then, is that power of restraining our will within the limits of our understanding? Why has that order been impressed on us?

Consider, on the other side, what we deprive ourselves of, viz. the

---

[12] Van Blijenbergh here quotes a passage from IV/94/27ff.; but not accurately.

368

0   anxious and serious meditation aimed at making ourselves perfect according to the rule of God's perfection and according to the order he V/112 has impressed on us. We deprive ourselves of prayer and aspiration toward God, by which we have so often felt that we received extraordinary strength. We deprive ourselves of all religion, and all that hope, all that satisfaction which await us from prayer and religion. For surely if God has no knowledge of evil, it is hardly credible that he will punish evil. What reason do I have for not eagerly committing all sorts of knavery (provided I can escape the judge). Why not enrich myself 0   through abominable means? Why should I not do, without making any distinction, whatever I like and the flesh inclines me towards?

    You will say: because we must love virtue for its own sake. But how can I love virtue? So much essence and perfection has not been given me. And if I can take as much satisfaction from the one as from 5   the other, why should I make the effort to restrain my will within the limits of the intellect? Why not do what my passions lead me to? Why not secretly kill the man who gets in my way? See what an opening we give to all the godless, and to godlessness. We make ourselves like logs, and all our actions just like the movements of a clock.

/113   From what has been said, it seems to me that it is very hard to maintain that we can only improperly be said to sin against God. For what, then, is the significance of that power which is given to us to restrain our will within the limits of our intellect, so that when we transgress it, we sin against that order?

    Perhaps you will say: that is no sin against God, but only something against ourselves, for if we were properly said to sin against God, then we would also have to say that something happens contrary to God's will. But that is impossible, on your view. Hence, sin is impossible too. One of these two must be true: either that God wills that or that he does not will it. But if God wills it, how can it be evil in relation to us? And if he does not will it, then, on your view, it would not happen.

    But though this, on your view, involves some absurdity, to admit, for that reason, all the absurdities mentioned above seems very dangerous to me. Who knows whether, if we spent much meditation on it, we would not find an expedient to reconcile this in some measure?

    With this I will conclude my examination of your letter according to the guidance of my first general rule. But before I pass to examining it according to the second rule, I will mention here two more things which concern this Conception in your letter, both maintained by you in your *Principles* IP15.

114   First, you "affirm that we can retain the power of willing and judg-

ing within the limits of the intellect."[13] But I cannot absolutely grant this. For if that were true, then certainly, out of countlessly many men, at least one would be found who would show through its effects that he had that power. Also, everyone can find in himself that, no matter how much of his power he exercises, he cannot reach that goal. And if anyone doubts this, let him examine himself and see how often, in spite of his own intellect, his passions master his reason, even when he exerts the greatest force against them.

You will say that we don't do that, not because it is impossible for us, but because we do not use enough diligence. To which I reply that if it were possible, wouldn't we find at least one out of so many thousands [who had done it]? But of all these men, there has been, or is, not even one who would dare boast of not falling into error. What more certain proof of this can we adduce than these examples? If there were even a few, there would be one [and that would show that the thing is possible]. But when there is not even one, then there is also no proof.

But you will persist, saying: if it is possible that I, by suspending judgment and keeping my will within the limits of my intellect, can once bring it about that I do not err, then why could I not always have that effect, when I use the same diligence? I reply that I cannot see that today we have so much power as to be able to continue always. If I put all my effort into it, I can cover two leagues in an hour, but I cannot do that always. So with great diligence I can refrain from error once at least, but I don't have enough power to be able to do that always. It seems clear to me that the first man, proceeding from the hand of that perfect craftsman, did have that power, but (and in this I agree with you) by not using that power sufficiently, or by misusing it, he lost that perfect state of being able to do what previously was in his power. I could adduce various arguments to prove this, if it would not take too long.

And in this it seems to me that the whole essence of holy Scripture consists, and that on this account we ought to hold it in very high esteem, since it teaches us what our natural intellect so clearly establishes: a fall from our initial perfection, caused by our imprudence. What is more necessary than to reform that fall as much as possible? That is also the sole aim of holy Scripture, to bring fallen man back to God.

The second point to be mentioned from *Principles* IP15 is that you "affirm that understanding things clearly and distinctly is contrary to

---

[13] A not very exact quotation of I/174/15-16.

the nature of man" [I/175/11ff.]. From this you ultimately conclude that it is far better to assent to things [though] confusedly, and to be free, than to always remain indifferent, which is the lowest degree of freedom. I don't find this clear enough to grant it. For to suspend our judgment keeps us in the state in which we were created by our creator. But to assent to things that are confused is to assent to what we do not understand. In doing this we assent as easily to the false as to the true. And if (as M. Descartes teaches somewhere)[14] we don't use that order in assenting which God has given between our intellect and will, viz. not to assent unless we understand clearly, even though by chance we obtain the true, we still sin because we do not embrace the true with the order with which God has willed that we should embrace it. Consequently, just as not assenting preserves us in the state in which God put us, so assenting to things that are confused puts us in a worse state. For it lays the foundation for the errors through which we then lose our perfect state.

But, I hear you say, is it not better to make ourselves more perfect by assenting to things, though they are confused, than by not assenting to keep ourselves always at the lowest degree of perfection and freedom? But apart from the fact that we deny that, and in some measure have shown that we have made ourselves not better, but worse, it also seems to us impossible, and like a contradiction, that God should make the knowledge of things he himself determined extend further than the knowledge he gave us, indeed that God then would involve an absolute cause of our error. Nor does it go against this that we cannot complain that God should give us more than he has, because he was not bound to. It is, indeed, true that God was not obliged to give us more than he did. But God's supreme perfection posits also that the creature that proceeds from him can involve no contradiction, as would then appear to follow. For nowhere in created nature do we find knowledge, except in our intellect. For what other purpose can that be given us than to contemplate and know God's works? And what seems to follow more evidently than that there must be an agreement between our intellect and the things that must be known?

But if I were to examine your letter by the guidance of my second general rule, we would differ more than we do when I examine it by the first. For it seems to me (but if I am mistaken, please tell me) that you do not ascribe that infallible truth and godliness to holy Scripture that I believe to be in it. It is true that you say you believe that God has revealed the things in holy Scripture to the prophets, but in such

---

[14] AT VII, 59-60.

an imperfect way that, if it was done in the way you maintain, it would involve a Contradiction in God. For if God has revealed his word and will to men, he has done so for a certain end, and clearly.
10 Now if the prophets had feigned a parable from the word they received, then God would have had either to will that also or not to will it. If God had willed that they should feign a parable from his word, i.e., depart from his meaning, then God was the cause of that error, and willed something contradictory. If God did not will it, then it was
15 impossible that the prophets should have been able to feign a parable from them. Moreover, it seems credible, if it is presupposed that God gave his word to the prophets, that he gave it to them in such a way that they, in receiving it, would not have erred. For in giving his
20 word, God had to have a certain end. But God's end could not be to
IV/119 lead men into error by giving them his word, for that would be a Contradiction in God. Also, man could not err contrary to the will of God, for on your view that is impossible. In addition to all this, it is not credible that that most perfect God would allow that his word,
5 given to the prophets to explain to the people, should be given to the prophets in another sense than God willed. For if we maintain that God gave the prophets his word, we maintain at the same time that God appeared to the prophets in an extraordinary way, or spoke with
10 them. Now, if the prophets feigned a parable from the word given them, i.e., gave it another meaning than the one God has willed that they should give it, God would surely tell them about it. Also, it is both impossible in relation to the prophets, and a Contradiction in relation to God, that the prophets could have another meaning than
15 God willed that they should have.

I see, also, very little proof that God would have revealed his word in the way you maintain, i.e., that he would have revealed only salvation and destruction, that he decreed certain means to [those ends],
20 and that salvation and destruction are nothing more than the effects of those means he decreed. For surely if the prophets had received
IV/120 God's word in that sense, what reason would they have had to give it another sense? But I also don't see that you adduce any proof capable of convincing us that this view should be placed above that of the
5 prophets. If you think it is a proof that otherwise that word would involve many imperfections and contradictions, I say that that is only an assertion, not a proof. Who knows which opinion would involve fewer imperfections, if they were both put on the carpet? Finally, that
10 supremely perfect being knew very well how much the people could understand, and therefore what the best way was to instruct them.

As far as the second part of your first question is concerned, you

372

ask yourself why God forbade Adam to eat of the tree when he had decreed the opposite. And you answer that the prohibition to Adam consisted only in this: that God revealed to Adam that eating of that tree caused death, as he reveals to us, through the natural intellect, that poison is deadly for us. If it is established that God has forbidden something to Adam, what reasons are there that I should have to believe in the manner of prohibition you maintain rather than that of the prophets, to whom God himself has also revealed the manner of prohibition?

/121   You will say: my way of prohibition is more natural, and therefore agrees better with the truth and with God. But I deny that. I also cannot conceive that God has revealed to us through the natural understanding that poison is deadly, and I see no reason by which I would ever know that something is poisonous, if I had not seen or heard evil effects of the poison in others. Daily experience teaches us how many men, because they are not acquainted with a poison, eat it unknowingly and die.

You will say: if the people knew that it was poison, they would know that it is evil. But I answer that no one is acquainted with poison, or can be, unless he has seen or heard that someone has hurt himself by using it. And if we maintained that until now we had never seen or heard that anyone had hurt himself by using it, not only would we not know it now, but we would use it, without fear, to our detriment. Such truths are taught us every day.

What can give an upright intellect more pleasure in this life than the contemplation of that perfect godhead? For as it is concerned with the most perfect [being] it must also involve in itself the most perfect

/122 [thing] that can fall under our finite intellect. I also have nothing in my life that I would want to exchange for that pleasure. I can spend much time in it, with a heavenly joy. But at the same time I can also be deeply saddened when I see that my finite intellect lacks so much. I soothe that sadness with the hope I have, which is dearer to me than life, that I shall exist again, and remain, and shall contemplate this godhead with more perfection than I do today. When I consider this short and fleeting life, in which I see that my death may occur at any moment, if I had to believe that I would have an end, and be cut off from that holy and glorious contemplation, certainly I would be the most miserable of all creatures, who have no knowledge that they will end. For before my death, my fear of death would make me wretched, and after my death, I would entirely cease to be, and hence be wretched because I would be separated from that divine contemplation. And this is where your opinions seem to me to lead: that when I come to an end here, then I will come to an end for eternity. Against this, God's word and will fortify me with his inner witness in my soul that after this life I shall, in a more perfect state, enjoy myself in the contemplation of that most perfect godhead of all. Certainly even if that hope were ultimately found to be a false one, it makes me happy while I have it. This is the only thing I desire of God, and will desire with prayers, sighs, and earnest wishes (Oh that I could contribute more to it!), so long as there is breath in this body: that through his goodness he should be pleased to make me so fortunate that, when this body is dissolved, I might still remain as an intellectual being, to continue contemplating that perfect godhead. If only I get that, it is a matter of indifference to me what men believe here, what they persuade one another of, and whether it is something founded on our natural intellect and can be grasped, or not. That and that alone is my wish, my desire, and my constant prayer, that God should only establish that assurance in my soul. Oh, if I lack it, I am most miserable! And if I have it, then my soul cries out from desire: "As a hart cries for fresh brooks, so longs my soul for thee, the living God. Oh, when will the day come when I will be with you and behold you?" [Ps. 42:2-3] If only I obtain that, then I will have the whole end and desire of my soul.

But those hopes do not appear to me, on your view, because our service is not pleasing to God. I also cannot grasp why, if God takes no pleasure in our service and praise (if at least I may speak of him in so human a way), why he should produce us and preserve us? But if I mistake your view in this, then I wish you would explain how.

I have delayed myself, and perhaps also you, too long with this. Seeing that my time and paper are running out, I shall end. This is what I would still like to see solved in your letter. Perhaps here and there I have drawn some conclusions from your writing that by chance will not be your opinion. But I would like to hear your explanations of them.

I have busied myself recently with reflection on some of God's attributes. Your Appendix has given me no little help with these. Indeed I have only paraphrased your views, which seem to me nothing short of demonstrations. So I am astonished that L. Meyer says, in his preface, that this is not your opinion, but that you were obliged so to instruct your student, whom you had promised to teach the philosophy of Descartes. He says that you have a completely different view both of God and of the soul, particularly of the soul's will. I also see it said in that preface that you will shortly publish these *Metaphysical Thoughts* in an expanded form. I have a very great longing for

374

/125 both of these, for I expect something special from them. But it is not my custom to praise someone to his face.

This is written in sincere friendship, as your letter requests, so that we may discover the truth. Forgive me for having written more than I intended to. If I receive an answer to this, you will oblige me very much. As for being allowed to write in the language in which you were brought up, I cannot refuse you, so long, at least, as it is Latin or French. But I ask to receive the answer to this letter in Dutch. I have understood your meaning in it very well, and perhaps in Latin I would not understand it so clearly. If you do this, you will oblige me so that I shall be, and remain, Sir,

Your most devoted and dutiful,
Dordrecht, 16 January 1665   Willem van Blijenbergh

In your reply I would like to be somewhat more fully informed what you really understand by a negation in God.

/126

LETTER 21

B.D.S. TO THE VERY LEARNED AND DISTINGUISHED
WILLEM VAN BLIJENBERGH

Reply to the preceding

Version

Sir and friend,

When I read your first Letter, I thought our opinions nearly agreed. But from the second, which I received on the 21st of this month, I see that I was quite mistaken, and that we disagree not only about the things ultimately to be derived from first principles, but also about the first principles themselves. So I hardly believe that we can instruct one another with our Letters. For I see that no demonstration, however solid it may be according to the Laws of Demonstration, has weight with you unless it agrees with that explanation which you, or Theologians known to you, attribute to sacred Scripture. But if you believe that God speaks more clearly and effectively through sacred Scripture than through the light of the natural intellect, which he has also granted us, and which, with his Divine Wisdom, he continually preserves, strong and uncorrupted, then you have powerful reasons for bending your intellect to the opinions you attribute to sacred Scripture. I myself could hardly do otherwise.

But as for myself, I confess, clearly and without circumlocution, that I do not understand Sacred Scripture, though I have spent several

25 years on it. And I am well aware that, when I have found a solid
demonstration, I cannot fall into such thoughts that I can ever doubt
it. So I am completely satisfied with what the intellect shows me, and
entertain no suspicion that I have been deceived in that or that Sacred
Scripture can contradict it (even though I do not investigate it). For
30 the truth does not contradict the truth, as I have already indicated
clearly in my Appendix. (I cannot cite the chapter [I/265/30] for I do
IV/127 not have the book here with me in the country.) And if even once I
found that the fruits which I have already gathered from the natural
intellect were false, they would still make me happy, since I enjoy
them and seek to pass my life, not in sorrow and sighing, but in peace,
joy, and cheerfulness. By so doing, I climb a step higher. Meanwhile
5 I recognize something which gives me the greatest satisfaction and
peace of mind: that all things happen as they do by the power of a
supremely perfect Being and by his immutable decree.

But to return to your letter, I am, sincerely, very grateful to you
10 for revealing to me in time your manner of Philosophizing. But I do
not thank you for attributing to me the things you want to draw from
my letter. What occasion did my letter give you for ascribing these
opinions to me: that men are like beasts, that men die and perish as
beasts do,[15] that our works are displeasing to God, etc.? (On this last
15 point we may differ very much, for if I understand you, you think
that God takes pleasure in our works, as someone who has attained
his end is pleased because things have turned out as he wished.) As
for me, I have said quite clearly that the pious honor God, and by
continually knowing him, become more perfect, and that they love
20 God. Is this to make them like beasts? or to say that they perish like
beasts? or, finally, to say that their works do not please God?

If you had read my letter more attentively, you would have seen
clearly that our disagreement is located in this alone: whether God as
God—i.e., absolutely, ascribing no human attributes to him—com-
25 municates to the pious the perfections they receive (which is what I
understand), or whether he does this as a judge (which is what you
maintain). That is why you defend the impious, because, in accordance with God's decree, they do whatever they can, and serve God as
much as the pious do. But according to what I said, that does not
follow at all. For I do not introduce God as a judge. And therefore I

---

[15] Westerbrink notes that there is an echo of Ecclesiastes here: "I said in my heart
with regard to the sons of men that God is testing them to show them that they are but
beasts. For the fate of the sons of men and the fate of beasts is the same; as one dies,
so dies the other" (3:18-19 RSV). Westerbrink thinks Spinoza is not conscious of setting
himself in opposition to scripture, though this seems doubtful to me.

30 value works by their quality, and not by the power of the workman, and the wages which follow the work follow it as necessarily as from the nature of a triangle it follows that its three angles must equal two right angles. Everyone will understand this, provided only that he is aware that our highest blessedness consists in love toward God, and

35 that that love flows necessarily from the knowledge of God which is
IV/128 so greatly commended to us. Moreover, this can easily be proven in general, provided only that one attends to the nature of God's Decree, as I explained in my Appendix. But I confess that anyone who confuses the Divine Nature with human nature is quite incapable of understanding this.

5 I had intended to end this letter here, so as not to be more troublesome to you in matters which serve only for joking and laughter, but are of no use (as is clear from the very devoted addition at the end of your letter). But not to reject your request entirely, I proceed further to the explanation of the terms "Negation" and "Privation." I shall

10 also give a brief explanation of what is necessary to grasp more clearly the meaning of my preceding Letter.

I say, therefore, that Privation is, not the act of depriving, but only the pure and simple lack, which in itself is nothing. Indeed, it is only a Being of reason, or mode of thinking, which we form when we

15 compare things with one another. We say, for example, that a blind man is deprived of sight because we easily imagine him as seeing, whether this imagination arises from the fact that we compare him with others who see, or his present state with his past, when he used to see. And when we consider this man in this way, by comparing his

20 nature with that of others or with his own past nature, then we affirm that seeing pertains to his nature, and for that reason we say that he is deprived of it. But when we consider God's decree, and his nature, we can no more affirm of that man than of a Stone, that he is deprived

25 of vision. For at that time vision no more pertains to that man without contradiction than it does to the stone, *since nothing more pertains to that man, and is his, than what the Divine intellect and will attribute to him.* Hence, God is no more the cause of his not seeing than of the stone's not seeing, which is a pure Negation.

30 *Similarly, when we attend to the nature of a man who is led by an appetite for sensual pleasure, we compare his present appetite with that which is in the pious, or with that which he had at another time. We affirm that this man has been deprived of a better appetite, because we judge that then an appetite*

35 *for virtue belongs to him. We cannot do this if we attend to the nature of the*
IV/129 *Divine decree and intellect; for in that regard, the better appetite no more pertains to that man's nature at that time than it does to the Nature of the*

Devil, or of a stone. That is why, in that regard, the better appetite is not a Privation, but a Negation.

So Privation is nothing but denying something of a thing which we judge to pertain to its nature, and Negation nothing but denying something of a thing because it does not pertain to its nature. From this it is evident why Adam's appetite for earthly things was evil only in relation to our intellect, but not in relation to God's. *For although God knew the past and present of Adam, he did not on that account understand that Adam was deprived of the past state, i.e., that the past state pertained to his nature.* For then God would understand something contrary to his will, i.e., contrary to his own intellect.

If you had perceived this properly, and also that I do not grant that Freedom which Descartes ascribes to the Mind (as L. M. declared in my name in the Preface), you would not have found even the least contradiction in my words. But I see that I would have done much better if, in my first Letter, I had replied in Descartes' words, by saying that we cannot know how our freedom, and whatever depends on it, is compatible with God's providence and freedom (as I have done in various places in the Appendix [NS: to *Descartes' Principles*]), so that we can find no contradiction between God's Creation and our freedom, because we cannot grasp at all how God created things or (what is the same) how he preserves them. But I thought you had read the Preface, and that, if I did not reply with my own opinion, I would have sinned against the duty of the friendship which I was offering from the heart. But these things are of no importance.

Nevertheless, because I see that you have not yet understood Descartes' Meaning, I ask you to attend to these two things:

(1) Neither I nor Descartes ever said that it pertains to our nature to contain our will within the limits of the intellect, but only that God has given us a determinate intellect and an indeterminate will, though in such a way that we do not know to what end he created us; moreover, an indeterminate or perfect will of that kind not only makes us more perfect, but also is quite necessary for us, as I shall say in what follows.

IV/130 (2) That our Freedom is placed neither in contingency nor in a certain indifference, but in a manner of affirming and denying, so that the less indifferently we affirm or deny a thing, the more free we are. For example, if God's nature is known to us, then affirming that God exists follows necessarily from our nature, just as it proceeds from the nature of a triangle that its three angles equal two right angles. Nevertheless, we are never more free than when we affirm a thing in such

378

a way. Because this necessity is nothing but God's Decree (as I have shown clearly in my Appendix [NS: to *Descartes' Principles*]), one can understand, in some measure, how we do something freely, and are the cause of it, notwithstanding the fact that we do it necessarily and from God's decree. I say that we can understand this in some measure when we affirm something which we perceive clearly and distinctly. But when we assert something which we do not grasp clearly and distinctly, i.e., when we allow our will to wander beyond the limits of our intellect, then we cannot so perceive that necessity and God's Decrees, but [can so perceive] our freedom, which our will always involves (and only in relation to our freedom are our works called good or evil). If we then strive to reconcile our freedom with God's Decree and continuous Creation, we confuse what we understand clearly and distinctly with what we do not understand. Therefore we strive for that in vain. It is enough for us, then, that we know that we are free, and that we can be such, notwithstanding God's decree, and that we are the cause of evil, in that no act can be called evil except in relation to our freedom.

These are the things that concern Descartes, which I mention to demonstrate that his position on this involves no contradiction. Now I shall turn to those things that concern me.

First I shall briefly recall the advantage that stems from my opinion. This derives chiefly from the fact that our intellect offers Mind and Body to God, free of any Superstition. Not that I deny that prayers are quite useful to us. For my intellect is too weak to determine all the means God has to lead men to love him, i.e., to salvation. Hence, it is so far from being the case that this opinion of mine will be harmful, that on the contrary, it is the only means of attaining the highest degree of blessedness for those who are not in the grip of prejudice or childish superstition.

But what you say—that I make men like elements, plants, and stones by making them so dependent on God—shows sufficiently that you understand my opinion very perversely and confuse things that concern the intellect with [those which concern] the imagination. For if you had perceived with a pure intellect what it is to depend on God, you would certainly not think that things, insofar as they depend on God, are dead, corporeal, and imperfect. Who has ever dared to speak so vilely of the supremely perfect Being? On the contrary, you would grasp that for that reason, and to that extent, they are perfect. So that we best understand this dependence and necessary operation through God's decree, when we attend not to logs and plants, but to the most

15   intelligible and perfect created things, as is clearly evident from what I have already mentioned above, under the second point about Descartes' view. You ought to have noticed this.

    I cannot suppress my astonishment at your saying that if God did not punish transgressions (i.e., punish as a judge does, with the kind of punishment that the transgression itself does not carry with it—for
20   that is all that is at issue here), what reason would prevent me from eagerly perpetrating all sorts of knavery? Certainly one who abstains from knavery only from dread of punishment (I hope this is not you) does not in any way act from love and does not at all esteem Virtue. As for myself, I abstain from those things, or try to, because they are explicitly contrary to my singular nature, and make me wander from
25   the knowledge and love of God.

    Next, if you had attended a little to human nature, if you had perceived the nature of God's decree, as I have explained it in the Appendix, and finally, if you had known how things ought to be deduced, before one arrives at a conclusion, you would not have said so
30   boldly that this opinion makes us like logs, etc. Nor would you have attributed so many absurdities to me as you imagine.

    Before you proceed to your second Rule, you say there are two things you cannot perceive. To the first I reply that Descartes is enough
35   for drawing your conclusion, viz. that if only you attend to your nature, you will find by experience that you can suspend your judgment.
IV/132 But if you say that you do not find by experience that we have so much power over reason today, that we can always continue this, to Descartes that would be the same as saying we cannot see today that as long as we exist we shall always be thinking things, or will retain
5   the nature of a thinking thing. That certainly involves a contradiction.

    Regarding the second point, I say, with Descartes, that if we could not extend our Will beyond the limits of our very limited intellect, we would be very wretched, and it would not be in our power to eat a
10   piece of bread, or take a step, or to remain still. For all things are uncertain and full of danger.

    I pass now to your second Rule, and I assert that I indeed believe that I do not attribute to Scripture that Truth which you believe to be in it. Nevertheless, I believe that I ascribe as much, if not more,
15   authority to it, and that I take care, far more cautiously than others do, not to attribute to it certain childish and absurd opinions. No one can do this unless he either understands Philosophy well or has Divine revelations. So I am not much moved by those explanations that Or-
20   dinary Theologians give of Scripture, especially if they are of the kind that always take Scripture according to the letter and external mean-

ing. Except for the Socinians,[16] I have never seen a Theologian so dense that he did not perceive that Sacred Scripture very often speaks of God in a human way and expresses its meaning in Parables.

As for the contradiction you strive—in vain, I think—to show, I believe that by a Parable you understand something quite different from what is commonly understood. For who ever heard that one who expresses his conceptions in parables wanders from his own meaning. When Micaiah said to King Ahab [1 Kings 22:19ff.] that he had seen God sitting on his throne, with the heavenly hosts standing on his right and his left, and that God asked them who would deceive Ahab, that was certainly a Parable by which the Prophet expressed sufficiently the main thing he was supposed to reveal in God's name on that occasion (which was not one for teaching lofty doctrines of Theology). So he would not depart in any way from his meaning.

So also the other Prophets revealed God's Word to the people, by God's command, in that way, as the best means (though not as the means God demanded) of leading the people to the primary goal of Scripture. According to what Christ himself taught [Matt. 22:37-40], that goal consists in this: in the love of God before all else, and of one's neighbor as oneself. Lofty speculations, I believe, concern Scripture not at all. As for me, I have learned no eternal attributes of God from Sacred Scripture, nor could I learn them.

As for your argument[17] (that the Prophets have revealed God's word in such a way), since truth is not contrary to truth, nothing remains except that I should demonstrate (as anyone who perceives the Method of Demonstrating will judge) that Scripture, just as it is, is the true revealed Word of God. I cannot have a Mathematical Demonstration of it, except by Divine Revelation. And for that reason I said "I believe"—but not "I know in a mathematical way"—"that all the things which God has revealed to the Prophets [to be necessary for salvation are written in the manner of laws.—IV/92/15-93/1]." For I firmly believe, but do not know Mathematically, that the Prophets were God's confidential Counselors and trusty Messengers. So in the things I have affirmed, there is no contradiction at all, whereas on the other side, many are found.

The rest of your Letter—viz. where you say "Finally that supremely perfect Being knew [very well how much the people could understand—IV/120/9ff.]," and next what you bring up against the

---

[16] AHW note (following Dunin-Borkowski, 4:113-117) that Spinoza's inaccurate conception of Socinianism probably stemmed from his contact with Meyer.

[17] OP: "fifth argument." I follow AHW (and the NS). I also accept Wolf's emendation of the punctuation.

example of the poison, and finally, what concerns the Appendix and what follows—none of this, I say, concerns the present Problem.

With regard to Meyer's Preface, it certainly shows both what Des-
25   cartes would still have to prove, to construct a real demonstration of Free Will, and adds that I favor the contrary opinion, and how I favor it. In its proper time perhaps I shall show this, but that is not my intention now.

I have not thought about the work on Descartes nor given any fur-
30   ther attention to it since it was published in Dutch. The reason for this would take too long to tell. So nothing more remains to be said, except that I, etc.

[Schiedam, 28 January 1665]

IV/134

LETTER 22

To the Very Distinguished B.D.S.

from Willem van Blijenbergh

Reply to the preceding

Sir and worthy Friend,

I received your letter of 28 January in good time, but occupations other than those of study have prevented me from answering before
10   now. And since your letter was interlarded here and there with touchy reproofs, I hardly knew what I should think of it. For in your first letter, of 5 January, you firmly and heartily offered me your friendship, with a protestation that not only was the letter you had received then very pleasing to you, but also that future letters would be. In-
15   deed, I was invited, amicably, to raise freely any difficulties I might still have. That is what I did, rather extensively, in my letter of 16 January. In view of your request and promise, I expected a friendly and instructive reply. But what in fact I received was a letter that does
IV/135 not sound very friendly. You say that no demonstrations, no matter how clear they are, count with me, that I do not understand Descartes' meaning, that I mix corporeal and spiritual things too much, etc., so
5   that we can no longer instruct one another by exchanging letters.

To this I reply, very amicably, that I certainly believe that you understand the above-mentioned things better than I do, and that you are more accustomed to distinguish corporeal from spiritual things, for you have already ascended to a high level in metaphysics, where I
10   am a beginner. That is why I sought to insinuate myself into your favor, to get instruction. But I never thought that by making frank objections I would give occasion for offense. I thank you heartily for

382

the trouble you have taken with both letters, and especially for the second. I think I grasped your meaning more clearly there than in the first. Nevertheless, I still cannot assent to it unless the difficulties I still think I find in it are removed. That should not, cannot, give you any reason for offense. For it is a great defect in our intellect to assent to the truth without having the grounds of assent that are necessary.
/136 Even if your conceptions were true, I should not assent to them so long as I still have any reason for obscurity or doubt, even if those doubts arise not from what you maintain, but from the imperfection of my intellect. Because you know this only too well, do not think ill of me if I again raise some objections, as I am bound to do so long as I cannot grasp the matter clearly. This happens only because I want to discover the truth, not because I want to distort your meaning, contrary to your intention. So I ask for a friendly reply to these few words.

You say *that no thing has more essence than the divine will and power attribute to it and in fact give it. And when we attend to the nature of a man who has an appetite for sensual pleasure, and compare his present appetites with those of the pious, or with those he himself had at another time, then we say that that man is deprived of a better* [OP: *appetite*] *because then we judge that the appetite for virtue belongs to him. We cannot do this if we attend to the nature of God's decree and intellect. For in relation to that, the better appetite no more pertains to the nature of that man at that time than it does to the nature of the devil, or of a stone, etc. For even though God knew the*
/137 *past and present state of Adam, he did not on that account understand that Adam was deprived of his past* [OP: *state*], *i.e., that the past [state] belonged to his present nature, etc.*[18]

From these words it seems to me (though I am subject to correction) to follow clearly that on your view nothing else pertains to an essence than what it has at that moment when it is perceived. I.e., if I have an appetite for sensual pleasure, that appetite pertains to my essence at that time, and if I have no appetite for sensual pleasure, then that lack of appetite pertains to my essence at the time when I lack that appetite. Also, consequently, it must follow infallibly that in relation to God, I involve as much perfection (different only in degree) in my actions when I have an appetite for sensual pleasure, as when I have no appetite for sensual pleasure, when I engage in all kinds of knavery, as when I practice virtue and justice. For to my essence at that time pertains only as much as I do; for on your view I can do neither more nor less than I have in fact received essence. For because the appetite

---

[18] The quotations, which are not very exact, come from IV/128/26ff.

for sensual pleasure and knavery pertains to my essence at the time when I engage in them, and at that time I receive no greater essence from the divine power, the divine power requires only such works of me. And so it seems to me to follow clearly from your position that God desires knavery in the same way he desires those things you call virtue.

Let us posit now that God, as God, and not as a Judge, gives both the pious and the impious only as much essence as he wills that they shall exercise. What reasons are there for God not to desire the act of the one in the same way as that of the other? For because God gives each the quality for his act, it follows certainly that from those to whom God has given less, he desires, in the same way, only so much; as he [desires more] from those to whom he has given more. Consequently, God, in relation to himself, wills more or less perfection from our actions, the desire for sensual pleasure and the desire for virtue, in the same way. So those who engage in knavery must necessarily engage in knavery because nothing else belongs to their essence at that time, as he who practices virtue does so because the divine power has willed that this should pertain to his essence at that time. Again, all I can see is that God wills equally, and in the same way, knavery and virtue. And insofar as he wills both, he is the cause of both, and both must be pleasing to him. I find that too hard to conceive of God.

I see, indeed, that you say that the pious serve God. But from your writings all I can see is that serving God is nothing but doing such acts as God has willed that we should do. That you ascribe also to the godless and sensual. What difference is there, then, in relation to God, between the service of the pious and of the godless? You say also that the pious serve God, and in serving continually become more perfect. But I cannot see what you understand by 'becoming more perfect' nor what 'continually becoming more perfect' means. For the godless and the pious both receive their essence, and also the preservation or continuous creation of their essence, from God, as God, not as a Judge. And they both carry out God's will in the same way, viz. according to God's decree. What distinction can there then be between the two in relation to God? For that 'continually becoming more perfect' flows not from the act, but from the will of God, so that if the godless become more imperfect through their acts, that too flows not from their acts, but only from the will of God. Both only carry out God's will. So there can be no distinction between these two in relation to God. What reasons are there, then, that the one should continually become more perfect through his acts and the other be consumed in serving?

/140   But you seem to locate the distinction of the one's acts over the other's in the fact that the one act involves more perfection than the other. I am confident that there is an error concealed here, either yours or mine. For the only rule I can find in your writings according to which a thing is called more or less perfect is that it has more or less essence.[19] But if that is now the rule of perfection, then certainly knavery, in relation to God's will, is as pleasing to him as the acts of the pious. For God, as God, i.e., in relation to himself, wills them in the same way, because they both proceed from his decree. If this alone is the rule of perfection, then errors can only improperly be so called. In fact, there are no errors, there are no acts of knavery, but everything contains just as much essence as God gives it, which always involves perfection, whatever it is. I confess that I cannot perceive that clearly.

    You must forgive me if I ask whether killing is as pleasing to God as giving charity, whether, in relation to God, stealing is as good as being just. If you say 'no,' what are the reasons? If you say 'yes,' what

/141 reasons can there be, why I should be moved to do the one act, which you call virtue, rather than the other? What law or rule forbids me the one more than the other? If you say the law of virtue itself, I must certainly confess that I see in your writings no law according to which virtue can be regulated or known. For everything depends inseparably on God's will, and consequently the one is as virtuous as the other. So I don't understand why you say that we must act from love of virtue, since I cannot grasp what, according to you, virtue, or the law of virtue, is.

    You say, indeed, that you omit vice and knavery because they are contrary to your singular nature and would make you stray from the divine knowledge and love. But in all your writings I see no rule or proof of this. Indeed, excuse me, but I must say that the opposite seems to follow from what you have written. You omit the things I call vice because they are contrary to your singular nature, but not because they contain vice in themselves. You omit doing them as we omit eating food that our nature finds disgusting. Certainly those who omit evils only because their nature finds them disgusting can pride themselves very little on their virtue.

/142   Here again the question can be raised: if there was a mind to whose singular nature the pursuit of sensual pleasure or knavery was not contrary, is there a reason for virtue which would have to move it to do good and omit evil? But how is it possible that a man should be

---

[19] A, NS: "existence." Cf. IV/100.

able to omit the appetite for sensual pleasure when that desire pertains to his essence at that time and he really has received it and cannot omit it?

I can also not see that this follows in your writings: that the acts which I call knavery should make you stray from the knowledge and love of God. For you have done only what God willed, nor could you do more, because at that time the divine power and will gave you no more essence. How can an action so determined and dependent make you stray from the love of God? To stray is to be confused and independent. And on your view that is impossible. For whether we do this or that, whether we manifest more or less perfection, we receive that for our essence, at that time, immediately from God. How, then, can we stray? I must not understand what is meant by straying. Here, and here alone, must lie the cause, either of my mistake or yours.

Here there are many other things I would still like to say and ask.

(1) Whether intellectual substances depend on God in a different way than lifeless ones do? For although intellectual beings involve more essence than the lifeless do, don't they both require God and God's decrees for their motion in general, and for such and such motions in particular? Consequently, insofar as they are dependent, are they not dependent in one and the same way?

(2) Because you do not grant the soul the freedom Descartes ascribed to it, what distinction is there between the dependence of intellectual substances and that of those without a soul? and if they have no freedom of the will, in what way do you conceive the dependence on God, and how the soul is dependent on God?

(3) If our soul does not have that freedom, is our action not God's action and is our will not God's will?

There are several other questions I would like to ask, but I dare not seek so much of you. But I shall look forward to receiving, shortly, your answer to the preceding pages. Perhaps in that way I can understand your meaning somewhat better and then we will discuss these matters in person somewhat more fully. For after I have your answer, I shall have to be in Leyden in a few weeks, and will give myself the honor of greeting you in passing, if that is agreeable with you at least. Depending on this, I send you hearty greetings, remaining

Your most devoted and dutiful
W. v. Blijenbergh

If you do not write to me under Cover, please write to Willem van Blijenbergh, Grainbroker, near the great Church, Dordrecht, 19 February 1665

In my excessive haste I have forgotten to include this question: whether by our prudence we cannot prevent what would otherwise happen to us?

LETTER 23
B.D.S. TO THE VERY LEARNED AND NOTABLE
GENTLEMAN WILLEM VAN BLIJENBERGH

Reply to the preceding

Sir and friend,

This week I received two letters from you, the one of 9 March serving only to inform me of the other, of 19 February, which was sent to me from Schiedam. In the latter I see that you complain of my having said that no demonstration is of any force with you, etc., as if I had said that with regard to my own reasonings, because they did not immediately satisfy you. That was far from my meaning. I had in mind your own words:

Whenever it happens, after a long investigation, that my natural knowledge either seems to contradict this word, or is not easily etc. this word has so much authority with me that I suspect the conceptions I imagine to be clear rather etc. [IV/97/1-5]

So I only repeated, briefly, your own words. I do not believe, therefore, that I gave the slightest reason for offense, the more so because I brought that up to show the great difference between us.

Furthermore, because you had said at the end of your second letter [IV/123/1ff.] that your only wish was to persevere in your belief and hope, and that the rest, which we can persuade one another of concerning the natural intellect, is indifferent to you, I thought, and still think, that my writing could be of no use, and that therefore it was more advisable for me not to neglect my studies—which I would otherwise have to set aside for so long—for the sake of things that can be of no use. This does not contradict my first letter because there I considered you as a pure philosopher who (as many who consider themselves Christians grant) has no other touchstone of truth than the natural intellect and not theology. But you have taught me otherwise and shown me that the foundation on which I intended to build our friendship was not laid as I thought.

Finally, as regards the rest, that happens commonly in disputation, without going beyond the bounds of politeness. For these reasons, I

have let such things pass unnoticed in your second letter, and will in
this one also. That will suffice to show that I have given you no reason
for it, much less to think that I can bear no contradiction. I shall now
35   turn to your objections to answer them again.

IV/147 *First, then, I say that God is absolutely and really the cause* of everything
that has essence, no matter what it is. If you can demonstrate now
20   that evil, error, knavery, etc., are things that express essence, then I
will grant completely that God is the cause of knavery, evil, error,
etc. As for me, it seems to me that I have shown sufficiently that what
constitutes the form of evil, error, and knavery does not consist in
something that expresses essence, and that therefore we cannot say
25   that God is the cause of it.

For example, Nero's matricide, insofar as it comprehends something
positive, was not knavery. For Orestes, too, performed the [same]
external action, and with the [same] intention of killing his mother.
Nevertheless, he is not blamed, or at least, not as severely as Nero is.
30   What, then, was Nero's knavery? Nothing but this: he showed by
that act that he was ungrateful, without compassion, and disobedient.
And it is certain that none of these things express any essence. Therefore, God was not the cause of them, but was the cause of Nero's act
and intention.

35   Next, I should like it noted here that while we are speaking philo-
IV/148 sophically we must not use theological ways of speaking. For because
theology has usually—and that not without reason—represented God
20   as a perfect man, it is appropriate in theology to say that God desires
something, that he finds sorrow in the acts of the godless and takes
pleasure in those of the pious. But in philosophy we understand clearly
that to ascribe to God those 'attributes' which make a man perfect is
25   as bad as if one wanted to ascribe to man those which make an elephant or an ass perfect. So there words of this kind have no place,
and we cannot use them without confusing our concepts very much.
Therefore, speaking philosophically, we cannot say that God desires
30   something of something, nor that something is pleasing or a cause of
sorrow to him. For those are all human 'attributes,' which have no
place in God.

Finally, I should like it noted that—though the acts of the pious
(i.e., of those who have clearly that idea of God according to which
35   all their acts and thoughts are determined), and of the godless (i.e., of
IV/149 those who do not have that idea of God, but only confused ideas of
20   earthly things, according to which all their acts and thoughts are determined), and, finally, the acts of everything there is, follow necessarily from God's eternal laws and decree, and continually depend on

God—nevertheless, they differ from one another not only in degree, but also essentially. For though a mouse depends on God as much as an angel does, and sadness as much as joy, a mouse cannot on that account be a kind of angel, nor sadness a kind of joy.

With this I think I have answered your objections (if I have understood them, for sometimes I doubt whether the conclusion you draw does not differ from the proposition that you undertake to prove). But this will be more evident if I reply, following these principles, to the questions you have proposed:

(1) Whether killing is as pleasing to God as almsgiving?

(2) Whether stealing, in relation to God, is as good as being just?

(3) If there was a mind to whose singular nature the pursuit of sensual pleasure and knavery was not contrary, is there a reason for virtue which should move it to do good and omit evil?

To the first I say that I do not know (philosophically speaking) what you mean by "pleasing to God." If the question is "Whether God does not hate the one and love the other?" or "Whether the one has not done God an injury and the other a favor?" then I answer "no." If the question is "Whether men who kill and those who give charity are equally good or perfect?" again I say "no."

To the second, I say that if "good in relation to God" means that the just man does God some good, and the thief does him some evil, I answer that neither the just man nor the thief can cause God pleasure or displeasure. But if the question is "Whether the two acts, insofar as they are something real, and caused by God, are not equally perfect?" then I say that, if we consider the acts alone, and in such a way, it may well be that both are equally perfect.

If you then *ask "Whether the thief and the just man are not equally perfect and blessed?" then I answer "no." For by a just man I understand one who constantly desires that each one should possess his own. In my Ethics, (which I have not yet published)[20] I show that this desire necessarily arises in the pious from a clear knowledge which they have of themselves and of God. And since the thief has no desire of that kind, he necessarily lacks the knowledge of God and of himself, which is the principal thing that makes us men.*

If, however, you still ask what can move you to perform the act I

---

[20] This is Spinoza's first reference in the correspondence to his *Ethics* under that title. The fact that the topic referred to is taken up only late in the *Ethics* as we have it (IVP37S2, IVP72) indicates that the work must already have been well-advanced. But neither of the passages cited is precisely parallel, an indication, as AHW suggest, that in 1665 the manuscript had not yet reached its definitive form.

call virtuous rather than the other, I reply that I cannot know what
25   way, of the infinitely many there are, God uses to determine you to
such works. It may be that God has imprinted the idea of himself
clearly in you, and through love of him, makes you forget the world
and love all men as yourself. It is clear that such a constitution of
mind is contrary to all the others which we call evil. Therefore, they
30   cannot exist in one subject.

    This is not the place to explain the foundations of Ethics, nor to
prove everything I say, because I am concerned only to answer your
objections and to turn them away from myself.

    Finally, your third question presupposes a contradiction. It is as if
35   someone were to ask: if it agreed better with the nature of someone to
IV/152 hang himself, would there be reasons why he should not hang himself? But suppose it were possible that there should be such a nature.
Then I say (whether I grant free will or not) that if anyone sees that
20   he can live better on the gallows than at his table, he would act very
foolishly if he did not go hang himself. One who saw clearly that in
fact he would enjoy a better and more perfect life or essence by being
a knave than by following virtue would also be a fool if he were not a
25   knave. For acts of knavery would be virtue in relation to such a per-
verted human nature.

    As for the other questions which you have added at the end of your
letter, since one could just as well ask a hundred in an hour, without
ever coming to the conclusion of anything, and since you yourself do
30   not press much for an answer, I shall leave them unanswered. For
now I shall say only [that I shall expect you at the time we arranged,
and that you will be very welcome to me. But I should like it to be
soon, since I am already planning to go to Amsterdam for a week or
35   two. Meanwhile, I remain, with cordial greetings,

Your friend and servant,

Voorburg, 13 March 1665   B. de Spinoza][21]

IV/153

LETTER 24

WILLEM VAN BLIJENBERGH

TO THE VERY DISTINGUISHED B.D.S.

Reply to the preceding

Sir and friend,

    When I had the honor of being with you, the time did not allow
me to stay longer with you. Still less could my memory retain every-

---

[21] The bracketed portion is not printed in the OP or NS.

thing we discussed, although immediately on leaving you I collected all my thoughts in order to be able to retain what I had heard. So in the next place I came to, I tried to put your opinions on paper myself. But I found then that in fact I had retained not even a fourth of what was discussed. So you must excuse me if once again I trouble you by asking about matters where I did not clearly understand your meaning or did not retain it well. (I wish I could do something for you in return for your trouble.) [My difficulties] were:

154 First, when I read your *Principles* and *Metaphysical Thoughts*, how shall I be able to distinguish what is stated as Descartes' opinion from what is stated as your own?

Second, is there really error, and what does it consist in?

Third, in what way do you maintain that the will is not free?

Fourth, what do you mean by what you have Meyer say in the Preface:

> Though you admit . . . that there is a thinking substance in nature, you nevertheless deny that it constitutes the essence of the human Mind; instead you maintain that just as Extension is determined by no limits, so also Thought is determined by no limits. Therefore, just as the human Body is not extension absolutely, but only an extension determined in a certain way according to the laws of extended nature by motion and rest, so also the human Soul, is not thought absolutely, but only a thought determined in a certain way according to the laws of thinking nature by ideas, a thought which, one infers, must exist when the human body begins to exist.[22]

From these words it seems to me to follow that as the human body is composed of thousands of small bodies, so also the human mind is
155 composed of thousands of thoughts; and that as the human body, when it disintegrates, is resolved again into the thousands of bodies of which it was composed, so also our mind, when separated from our body, is resolved again into that multitude of thoughts of which it was composed. And as the scattered bodies [which composed] our human body no longer remain bound to one another, but other bodies separate them, so also it seems to follow that, when our mind disintegrates, those countless thoughts of which it was composed, are no longer combined, but separated. And as our bodies, when they are broken up, remain bodies, but not human bodies, so also when, after death, our thinking substance disintegrates, the thoughts or thinking substances remain, but their essence is not what it was when it was called a human mind.

From this it continues to seem to me as if you maintained that the

---

[22] I/132/8-17. Van Blijenbergh here paraphrases Balling's Dutch translation.

thinking substance of men is changed and resolved like corporeal substances, so that some are completely annihilated and no thought of theirs remains. Indeed, if memory serves me, you maintained this
20 concerning the wicked. And just as Descartes, according to Meyer, only assumes that the mind is a substance thinking absolutely, so it
IV/156 seems to me that you and Meyer, in these words, for the most part only make assumptions. So I do not clearly grasp your meaning in this.

Fifth, you maintained, both in our conversation and in your letter of 13 March, that from the clear knowledge which we have of God
5 and of ourselves there arises in us a constant desire that each should remain in possession of his own. But it remains to be explained how the knowledge of God and ourselves causes us to have a constant desire that each should possess his own. I.e., how does it proceed from
10 the knowledge of God that we are obliged to love virtue and to omit those acts we call vicious? How does it happen—since on your view killing and stealing contain something positive in them, just as much as giving charity does—that killing does not involve as much perfection, blessedness, and satisfaction as giving charity?
15 Perhaps you will say, as you do in your letter of 13 March, that this problem belongs to the *Ethics*, and that you discuss it there. But then, without an explanation of this problem, and also of the preceding questions, I cannot clearly understand your meaning. Absurdities
20 remain which I cannot reconcile. So I ask you as a friend to answer me somewhat more fully, and especially to state some of your prin-
IV/157 cipal definitions, postulates, and axioms, on which your *Ethics*, and especially this question, rest. Perhaps the trouble will deter you, and you will excuse yourself, but I entreat you this time at least to satisfy
5 my request. Without a solution to this problem I shall never be able to grasp your meaning correctly. I wish I could offer you something in exchange. I dare not limit you to one or two weeks, but will only ask that you reply before your departure for Amsterdam. If you do
10 this, you will oblige me very much, and I shall show you that I remain, sir,

Your most devoted servant,
Dordrecht, 27 March 1665   Willem van Blijenbergh

To Mr. Benedictus de Spinosa,
staying in Voorburg
per couverto

392

Letter 25

Henry Oldenburg to the Very Illustrious B.d.S.

Very Illustrious Sir, Dearest Friend,

I was delighted to learn in a recent letter from Mr. Serrarius, that you are alive and well and remember your Oldenburg. But at the same time I complain greatly of my fortune (if it is legitimate to use that word), in that I have been deprived for so many months of that very pleasant correspondence I used to have with you. The fault lies both with a great deal of business and with frightful domestic misfortunes. My great fondness for you and my faithful friendship will always remain steadfast and unshakable through the years. Mr. Boyle and I often talk about you, your Erudition, and your profound meditations. We would like to see the fruit of your understanding published and entrusted to the embrace of the learned. We are sure that you will not disappoint us in this.

There is no need for Mr. Boyle's essay on Niter, and on Solidity and Fluidity, to be published in Holland. It has already been published in Latin here, but there is no opportunity to send you copies. I ask you, therefore, not to allow any of your printers to undertake such a thing.

Boyle has also published a notable Treatise on Colors, both in English and in Latin, and at the same time, an Experimental History of Cold, Thermometers, etc., in which there are many excellent things and many new things. Nothing but this unfortunate war[23] prevents me from sending these books to you.

Another notable publication is a Treatise on sixty Microscopic observations,[24] in which many things are discussed boldly, but Philosophically (yet according to Mechanical principles). I hope our Booksellers will find a way of sending copies of all of these to your country. For my part, I am anxious to receive, from your own hand, what you have done recently or are working on now. I am

Your most devoted and affectionate,

London, 28 April 1665   Henry Oldenburg

---

[23] In October 1664 the English had seized the Dutch colony of New Amsterdam. When Dutch protests were ignored, war broke out in March 1665.

[24] Robert Hooke's *Micrographia*.

LETTER 26
B.D.S. TO THE VERY NOBLE AND LEARNED
HENRY OLDENBURG

Most honorable friend,

A few days ago a friend of mine said he had been given your letter of 28 April by an Amsterdam Bookseller, who no doubt received it from Mr. Serrarius. I was extremely glad to be able to learn at last, from you yourself, that you were well and that you are as favorably disposed toward me as before. I, of course, as often as I could, asked about you and your health of Mr. Serrarius and Christiaan Huygens, Lord of Zeelhem, who also told me he knew you. From the same Huygens I also learned that the very learned Mr. Boyle is alive and has published that notable Treatise on Colors in English. He would lend it to me if I understood English.

So I am pleased to learn from you that this Treatise (as well as that other, on cold and Thermometers, which I had not yet heard about) has been given Latin citizenship and published. Mr. Huygens also has the book on microscopic observations, but unless I am mistaken, it is in English.

He has told me wonderful things about these microscopes, and also about certain Telescopes, made in Italy, with which they could observe Eclipses of Jupiter caused by the interposition of its satellites, and also a certain shadow on Saturn, which looked as if it were caused by a ring. These things make me astonished at Descartes' haste. He says that the reason why the Planets next to Saturn—for he thought its projections were Planets, perhaps because he never observed them touching Saturn—do not move may be that Saturn does not rotate around its own axis. But this does not agree very well with his principles, and he could have explained the cause of the projections very easily on his principles, if he had not labored under a prejudice, etc.

[Voorburg, May 1665]

LETTER 27
B.D.S. TO THE VERY COURTEOUS AND DISTINGUISHED
WILLEM VON BLIJENBERGH

Reply to Letter 24

Sir and friend,

When I received your letter of 27 March, I was about to leave for Amsterdam. So I left it at home, only half-read, intending to answer it on my return. I thought it contained only things about the first problem. Later, when I read it through, I found that its content was quite different. Not only did it ask for a proof of those things I had [Meyer] put in the Preface [OP: of my Geometric Demonstrations of Descartes' *Principles*]—but which I had him include only to indicate to everyone my own opinions, not to prove or explain them—it also asked for proof of a great part of Ethics, which, as everyone knows, must /161 be founded on metaphysics and physics. So I could not bring myself to satisfy you on this.

But I wanted the opportunity to talk with you in the friendliest way, so that I might ask you to desist from your request. Then I would, at the same time, give you a reason for my declining, and finally, show you that those things do not make for a solution of your first problem, but that, on the contrary, most of them depend on [the solution of] that problem. So it is far from being the case that you cannot understand my opinion regarding the necessity of things without the solution of these new questions, because the solution of the latter, and what pertains to them, cannot be perceived unless one first understands that necessity. For as you know, the necessity of things concerns metaphysics, the knowledge of which must always come first.

However, before I could get the desired opportunity, I received another letter this week, under cover from my host, which seems to show more displeasure at the long wait. So it is necessary for me to write these few lines, to tell you briefly my resolution and intention. That I have now done. I hope that, when you have weighed the matter, you will voluntarily desist from your request and still retain your good will toward me. For my part, I shall show, in every way that I can or may, that I am

Your well-disposed Friend and Servant,
Voorburg, 3 June 1665   B. de Spinoza

/162   LETTER 28

B.D.S. TO THE VERY LEARNED AND EXPERT
JOHANNES BOUWMEESTER

Special friend,

I don't know whether you have completely forgotten me, but many things concur that raise the suspicion. First, when I was about to leave [Amsterdam], I wanted to say goodbye to you, and since you yourself had invited me, I thought that without doubt I would find you at home. But I learned that you had gone to The Hague. I returned to

Voorburg, not doubting that you would at least visit us in passing.
20 But you have returned home, God willing, without greeting your friend.
Finally, I have waited three weeks, and in all that time I have no letter
from you.

If you want to remove this opinion of mine, you can do so easily
by a letter in which you can also indicate a way of arranging our
correspondence, of which we once talked in your house. Meanwhile,
25 I would like to ask you urgently, indeed I entreat and request you by
our friendship, to be willing to pursue serious work energetically and
with true enthusiasm, and to be willing to devote the better part of
your life to the cultivation of your intellect and soul. You must do
IV/163 this now, while there is time, before you complain of the passage of
time, indeed, the passage of yourself.

Next, to say something about our proposed correspondence so that
you will not fear to write freely to me, you should know that I have
previously suspected and am almost certain, that you have less confi-
5 dence in your ability than you should, and fear that you will ask or
propose something unbefitting a learned man. It is not proper for me
to praise you to your face and to tell you your gifts. Nevertheless, if
you fear that I will communicate your letters to others, to whom you
will subsequently be an object of mockery, I give you my word that
henceforth I will keep them scrupulously and will not communicate
10 them to any other mortal without your permission. On these conditions you can begin our correspondence, unless perhaps you doubt
my good faith. I don't believe that for a moment; nevertheless I expect
to learn your opinion about these matters from your first letter.

At the same time I also expect some of the conserve of red roses
that you promised, though for a long time now I have been better.
15 After I left [Amsterdam] I opened a vein once, but the fever did not
stop (though I was somewhat more active even before the bloodlet-
ting—because of the change of air, I think). But I have suffered two
or three times from tertian fever. By good diet, however, I have got
rid of it and sent it I know not where. My only care is that it should
not return.
20 As for the third part of our philosophy, I shall soon send some of
it either to you (if you wish to be its translator) or to friend de Vries.
Although I had decided to send nothing until I finished it, nevertheless, because it is turning out to be longer than I thought, I don't want
to hold you back too long. I shall send up to about the 80th proposition.[25]

[25] In the form in which it has come down to us, Part III of the *Ethics* contains only
fifty-nine propositions. But Spinoza is evidently close to the end of the work as he

I hear much about English affairs, but nothing certain. The people do not cease suspecting all sorts of evils. No one knows any reason why the fleet does not set sail. And indeed, the matter does not yet seem to be safe. I am afraid that our countrymen want to be too wise and cautious. Nevertheless, the event itself will finally show what they have in mind and what they are striving for. May the gods make things turn out well.

I would like to hear what people think there, and what they know for certain. But more than that, indeed more than anything, I would like to hear that you consider me, etc.

[Voorburg, June 1665]

---

conceives it at this time; since the work in this state clearly contains material which in the finished *Ethics* occurs only late in Part IV (cf. IV/151, II/136), it appears that at this stage the *Ethics* was a three-part work. On this, see Freudenthal 5, 1:147-148.

The Metaphysical Moralist

EDITORIAL PREFACE

In July 1675 Oldenburg wrote nervously to Spinoza to inquire about the prospect of publication of the *Ethics*:

> From your reply of 5 July I understand that you intend to publish that five-part Treatise of yours. Permit me, I beg you, to advise you, out of your sincere regard for me, not to include in it anything which may seem in any way whatever, to overthrow the practice of religious virtue. . . . I shall not decline to receive copies of this Treatise; I would only ask that when the time comes, they be sent by way of a certain Dutch merchant, resident in London, who will see that they are soon forwarded. There will be no need to mention that such books have been sent to me. . . . (Letter 62, IV/273)

Oldenburg need not have worried. Some time later Spinoza sent him the following reply:

> When I received your letter of 22 July, I was on the point of leaving for Amsterdam, to see to the printing of the book I wrote you about. While I was occupied with this, a rumor was spread everywhere that a book of mine about God was in the press, and that in it I strove to show that there is no God. Many people believed this rumor. So certain theologians—who had, perhaps, started the rumor themselves—seized this opportunity to complain about me to the Prince and the magistrates. Moreover, the stupid Cartesians, who are thought to favor me, would not stop trying to remove this suspicion from themselves by denouncing my opinions and writings everywhere.
>
> When I learned this from certain trustworthy men, who also told me that the theologians were everywhere plotting against me, I decided to put off the publication I was planning until I saw how the matter would turn out. . . . But every day it gets worse, and I am uncertain what to do. (Letter 68, IV/299)

Thus was the world deprived, within Spinoza's lifetime, of one of the great classics of modern philosophical thought, a work, ironically, that begins by arguing at length for God's existence, and ends with the conclusion that the knowledge and love of God are man's greatest good.

When Spinoza died, a year and a half later, his work could be published, and the slow process of recognition could begin. But not until he had been taken up by leading figures of the German enlightenment—by Lessing, Goethe, and Herder, among others—did his work receive much sympathetic attention.[1] Since then the *Ethics* has always had a wide audience, particularly—and in view of its technical difficulty and forbidding form, surprisingly—among people not them-

[1] On this process see Pollock, chap. 12, and Vernière.

selves professional philosophers, but poets, dramatists, and novelists.[2]

Much of this interest no doubt stems from the psychology and morality of the latter parts of the *Ethics*, from its serene, but remorseless dissection of human nature, and its (apparent) attempt to establish an acceptable ethic on the unpromising foundation of subjectivism, egoism, and determinism.[3] But in part the interest must come also from fascination with the difficult question whether we can really regard as religious a thinker who has rejected so forcefully so much of what has usually been regarded as essential to religion in the West.

This is not the place to try to solve the perennial problems of Spinoza's philosophy. But some attempt must be made here to disarm the resistance which the axiomatic form of his masterwork seems, inevitably, to arouse. The topic is one on which quite divergent views have been expressed.[4]

Sometimes, for example, it is suggested that Spinoza's philosophy *required* axiomatic exposition, that conceiving the world as he did, as a tightly knit deterministic system, he could not properly have expressed this conception in any other way; or that conceiving knowledge as he did, he would have regarded deduction from self-evident premises as the only suitably scientific way of presenting his philosophy. At the opposite extreme, it is sometimes held that the axiomatic exposition is merely a literary device designed to conceal the author's personality, to capitalize on the prestige of geometry, or even to avoid the temptation to quote Scripture—but having no further significance.

The truth, I suggest, is that Spinoza's choice of the axiomatic method represents nothing more, and nothing less, than an awesome commitment to intellectual honesty and clarity. Spinoza wishes to use no important term without explaining the sense in which it is to be understood, to make no crucial assumption without identifying it as a proposition taken to require no argument, to draw no conclusion without being very explicit about why that conclusion is thought to follow from his assumptions. This can be very tedious, as he well realizes (cf. E IVP18 S). But the serious reader who is prepared to use those terms as Spinoza does, and who shares Spinoza's assumptions, is forced to ask himself why he should not also accept Spinoza's conclusions. And it is only fair to point out that many of Spinoza's contemporaries

[2] E.g., Novalis, Heine, Coleridge, Wordsworth, Shelley, George Sand, George Eliot, Anatole France, and Somerset Maugham.
[3] So I read Spinoza's moral philosophy. See Curley 4. Others disagree. Cf. Mattern and Eisenberg 2.
[4] For an interesting discussion of typical views, see Mark.

did share those assumptions and did use those terms in a way very close to the way Spinoza used them.[5]

Again, it is a mistake to suppose that, when Spinoza designates something as an axiom, he really thinks that no one could question it, and is not willing to listen to argument about it. The history of his experiments with axiomatic exposition shows clearly enough that he is prepared to be flexible, and that what at one stage is treated as an axiom, may at a later stage be treated as a theorem, if experience shows that his readers resist the assumption.[6] He does, of course, think that some propositions are more suited to be axioms than others. But he is not extravagantly optimistic about the ability of his readers to see what they *should* see, and this gives him a strong incentive to reduce his assumptions to a minimum (cf. II/49/26 ff.). And any serious attempt at argument must make some assumptions which, for the time being, at least, are not questioned.

But while this line of defense may be sound enough, as far as it goes, it does not go far enough. The difficulty for the modern reader of Spinoza's *Ethics* is not so much that he finds flaws in the demonstrations (though he may, of course), nor even that he rejects the axioms (though, again, he may), but that much of the language in which the axioms and demonstrations are framed has by now fallen into disuse, so that its very meaning is quite obscure to him. The clarity the axiomatization seemed to promise is not easy to find. A glossary-index may provide a partial solution to this difficulty. But unless it is very argumentative it cannot deal with the really fundamental problem.

It must be recognized that some of the terms which are central to Spinoza's philosophy are not merely out of fashion in twentieth-century philosophy, but would be rejected by many philosophers of our time as meaningless. The term 'substance' is a good example. For many people these days it is axiomatic that the empiricist critique of this concept demonstrated its brankruptcy. (By "axiomatic" I under-

---

[5] As Mark emphasizes, in Mark, 277-280. However, the qualification "very close" is essential. Cf., for example, the discussion of the definitions of "substance" and "mode" in Curley 3, 4-28.

[6] Cf., for example, the first appendix to the *Short Treatise*, and the early correspondence with Oldenburg. This theme is emphasised both in Mark and Hubbeling. More recently Bennett (2, 20) has recommended viewing the *Ethics* as a hypothetico-deductive system ("something that starts with general hypotheses, deduces consequences from them, and checks those against the data"). Bennett would concede, of course, that Spinoza did not regard his axioms and definitions as *mere* hypotheses. "Spinoza could—and I think would—say that although his system must work on untutored minds in a hypothetico-deductive manner, when the tutoring is completed the reader will see the starting point to be certain" (21). That seems to me exactly right.

stand here something we learned when we were first introduced to philosophy.)

And yet it is arguable that this rejection has been too hasty: that the traditional use of the concept of substance was too complex to have been disposed of so simply; that there are two distinguishable strains in that use—the concept of an unknowable subject of predicates, and the concept of an independent being; that the empiricist critique touches only the first of these strains; and that only the second is of much importance for the understanding of Spinoza.[7] If this is correct and if other contentious concepts can be similarly rehabilitated, Spinoza's philosophy may once again be ripe for reevaluation.

These reflections may do something to diminish the resistance many readers have to the form of the *Ethics*. But there remains the practical problem of how even the reader of good will is to cope with a procedure that makes great demands on his patience.

On a first reading it is probably advisable to concentrate on the propositions, corollaries, scholia, prefaces, and appendices, leaving the demonstrations till later. This will make it easier to grasp the structure of the work, and give the reader some feeling for what is central and what is subsidiary. 'Corollaries' are often more important than the proposition they follow, and the scholia often offer more intuitive arguments for the propositions just demonstrated, or reply to what Spinoza regards as natural and important objections. The longer scholia, prefaces, and appendices tend to punctuate major divisions within the work and to sum up key contentions.

On a second reading, of course, it is essential to study the demonstrations carefully. Seeing how a proposition is argued for is often a useful way of clarifying its sense. It is also helpful to check the steps of a demonstration against the citations. For when Spinoza cites an axiom, definition, or proposition in a subsequent demonstration, he sometimes paraphrases it in a way that illuminates what has gone before. And in any case, it is instructive to see what Spinoza takes the implications and significance of a proposition to be. But the best advice is Spinoza's own—to proceed slowly and to abstain from judgment until everything has been read through (IIP11CS). This is not easy. Spinoza's philosophy is not easy. But as he also says, all things excellent are as difficult as they are rare (VP42S).

I close with a few observations on the probable date of composition

[7] So I have argued, at any rate, in Curley 3, chap. 1. While much of what is offered in that book as an interpretation of Spinoza is admittedly quite speculative, the conclusion relevant here seems to me almost certain. I am happy to note that Gueroult reaches a very similar conclusion in the first volume of his commentary on the *Ethics*.

of the *Ethics* and the status of our text. As we have seen, Spinoza took steps to publish this work in 1675, though it did not appear until 1677 and may have undergone some revision even after 1675. On that ground we might regard the *Ethics* as a late work, or at any rate, later than the *Theological-Political Treatise*, published in 1670. On the other hand, we can see from the early correspondence with Oldenburg that Spinoza was circulating drafts of the material for Part I as early as 1661. So we might conclude that Spinoza was occupied with writing this work, off and on, for most of his adult life.

Nevertheless, it now seems possible to be more precise than that about the composition of our text. We know from Letter 28 that toward the middle of 1665 Spinoza was near the end of a first draft of the *Ethics* (i.e., near the end of the third part of what was probably, at that stage, conceived as a three-part work). Recent research on the relation between the OP and NS versions of the *Ethics* also suggests certain conclusions about the extent of the revision the first two parts may have undergone after 1665.

Gebhardt had noted (II/315-317, 340-345) that divergences between the OP text and NS translation were much more common in the first two parts of the *Ethics* than they were in the last three, and that frequently the NS seemed to have more text than the OP had. He inferred from this that the NS translation of E I-II was done from a manuscript that represented an earlier draft of the *Ethics* and that in revising Spinoza had deliberately omitted certain passages, sometimes to avoid giving unnecessary offense.[8] He therefore incorporated many passages from the NS translation into his text. Occasionally[9] he translated his additions into Latin. One might question whether the editor of a critical edition should interfere with the text in this way, but Gebhardt believed that the practice of modern editors of Kant's first *Critique* provided a precedent for indicating (as he thought) the differences between earlier and later drafts.

I believe that Akkerman (2, 77-176) has definitively refuted this theory and shown the correctness of an alternative account of the variations: that the NS translation of E I-II is essentially the work of Balling,[10] while the NS translation of E III-V is by Glazemaker; and that

---

[8] The most plausible example of this occurs at II/81/20, but as the annotation will suggest, Gebhardt is probably wrong in his interpretation of the significance of the variation.

[9] But not usually, not on any principle that I can discern, and not, in my view, always correctly. The Latin additions he makes at 92/8, 10 seem to me to repose too much confidence in the accuracy of the marginalia.

[10] Though Glazemaker may have made some revisions in Balling's translation and probably added the marginalia. Akkerman also does not exclude the possibility that

the tendency of the NS version of E I-II to show more text than the NS version of E III-V stems from Balling's different style of translating, in particular his willingness to take greater liberties with the text than Glazemaker would take. Akkerman makes his case for this via a meticulous examination of the translating styles of the two men in other works they are known to have translated, noting differences in prose style, in the kinds of license they allow themselves, in the kinds of mistakes they are apt to make, and in the way they treat key terms. One hesitates to speak of demonstration in any matter such as this, but Akkerman's argument is very impressive.

The principal implication of his research, as far as the establishment of the text is concerned, is that where the NS seems to have more text than the OP, this is almost invariably because the translator has amplified the text to make it clearer, or used a pair of Dutch terms to render one Latin term, in the hope of better capturing the implications of the Latin, and not because the text he was translating varied from the OP text.

But Akkerman's research also, it seems to me, has implications for the study of the development of Spinoza's thought. If Balling was the author of the translation of E I-II used by the editors of the NS, and if no significant changes were made in that text after Balling translated it, then Balling's death would provide a date after which Spinoza did not significantly revise Parts I and II. We do not know precisely when Balling died. Clearly it was not before July 1664 (the date of Letter 17) and pretty certainly it was not later than 1669 (cf. AHW, 45), Akkerman (2, 152-153) thinks Balling must have died before June 1665, by which date Spinoza was writing to Bouwmeester about the possibility of his translating Part III. If this is correct, then the metaphysical and epistemological portions of the *Ethics* would have been in their final form some twelve years before they were published.

Gebhardt's additions to the text from the NS create a problem for the translator. Shirley's policy is to ignore them when they are in Dutch and to translate them when Gebhardt has translated them into Latin, but without indicating that what he is translating is an addition from the NS. But this seems to assume that Gebhardt has followed some defensible principle in deciding what to add in Dutch and what to add in Latin, an assumption I see no reason to make. In one way or another I have translated everything that Gebhardt adds from the NS (as well as some variations that Gebhardt does not seem to have

---

other friends in the Amsterdam Spinoza circle may have had some hand in Balling's translation of E I-II.

noticed). Where it has seemed to me that an addition, even though it probably came originally from the NS translator, was pretty certainly correct and useful, I have generally followed Gebhardt in adding it to the text. I assume that a translator may take liberties that the editor of a critical edition may not. Where one of Gebhardt's additions has seemed to me doubtfully correct, I have relegated it to a footnote. Wherever a bracketed addition comes from the NS, I have indicated that fact. There is some evidence that Spinoza may have had Balling's translation of E I-II at his disposal, and indeed, that the copy of that translation used by the NS editors may have been Spinoza's own (cf. Akkerman 2, 167-168). So additions made from the NS, even if they do originate from a translator, may have been seen and approved by Spinoza.

References to definitions, axioms, propositions, etc., that do not contain an explicit reference to an earlier part of the *Ethics* are to be understood as referring to the part in which they occur.

Ethics

DEMONSTRATED IN GEOMETRIC ORDER
AND DIVIDED INTO FIVE PARTS,
WHICH TREAT

I. Of God
II. Of the Nature and Origin of the Mind
III. Of the Origin and Nature of the Affects
IV. Of Human Bondage, *or* of the Powers of the Affects
V. Of the Power of the Intellect, *or* of Human Freedom[1]

First Part Of the Ethics
On God

DEFINITIONS

5   D1: By cause of itself I understand that whose essence involves existence, *or* that whose nature cannot be conceived except as existing.

D2: That thing is said to be finite in its own kind that can be limited by another of the same nature.

10   For example, a body is called finite because we always conceive another that is greater. Thus a thought is limited by another thought. But a body is not limited by a thought nor a thought by a body.

D3: By substance I understand what is in itself and is conceived through
15   itself, i.e., that whose concept does not require the concept of another thing, from which it must be formed.

D4: By attribute I understand what the intellect perceives of a substance, as constituting its essence.[2]

---

[1] The titles of the five parts are given differently in the NS: "I. Of God, II. Of the Human Mind, III. Of the Nature and Origin of the Affects, IV. Of Human Bondage, V. Of Human Freedom." Akkerman (2, 263) suggests that the order of the title of Part III in the OP is wrong (by analogy with the title of Part II), though probably the order of Spinoza's ms., and that the NS reflects Jelles's emendation of the ms.

[2] OP: "Per attributum intelligo id, quod intellectus de substantiâ percipit, tanquam

408

D5: By mode I understand the affections of a substance, *or* that which is in another through which it is also conceived.

D6: By God I understand a being absolutely infinite, i.e., a substance consisting of an infinity of attributes, of which each one expresses an[3] eternal and infinite essence.

Exp.: I say absolutely infinite, not infinite in its own kind; for if something is only infinite in its own kind, we can deny infinite attributes of it [NS: (i.e., we can conceive infinite attributes which do not pertain to its nature)];[4] but if something is absolutely infinite, whatever expresses essence and involves no negation pertains to its essence.

D7: That thing is called free which exists from the necessity of its nature alone, and is determined to act by itself alone. But a thing is called necessary, or rather compelled, which is determined by another to exist and to produce an effect in a certain and determinate manner.

D8: By eternity I understand existence itself, insofar as it is conceived to follow necessarily from the definition alone of the eternal thing.

Exp.: For such existence, like the essence of a thing,[5] is conceived as an eternal truth, and on that account cannot be explained[6] by duration or time, even if the duration is conceived to be without beginning or end.

---

ejusdem essentiam constituens." The meaning of this definition is much disputed. One important question of translation is whether *tanquam* should be rendered 'as if' or 'as.' The former would favor those who hold the 'subjective' interpretation, according to which the differences between the attributes are illusory, all the attributes being identical in substance. Cf. Wolfson 1, 1: chap. 5. The latter would be more congenial to those who think the attributes are really distinct and not merely constructions of the intellect. I think Gueroult, 1 (1: app. 3) has provided us with a definitive refutation of the subjective interpretation. But it is unclear whether his own interpretation is acceptable. See Donagan 1 and Curley 6.

Arguably the intellect referred to in this definition is the infinite intellect, not the finite (see Haserot). Note also that the NS supplies a definite article for *substantia*. Practice among modern translators and commentators varies; but I agree with Gueroult (1, 1:52) that the indefinite article is to be preferred.

[3] The NS have the indefinite article here. Cf. Gueroult 1, 1:51, 67.

[4] The gloss Gebhardt adds from the NS may be the work of the translator, as Akkerman thinks is often true in such cases, or it may be an addition by Spinoza, as Akkerman (2, 161) thinks possible here. In any case, if the NS translation of E I-II was done by Balling in the period 1663-1665, then it seems likely that Spinoza would have seen it and had an opportunity to reject any alterations he did not approve of.

[5] Parkinson (171n) suggests that while 'the essence of *a* thing' is possible, 'the essence of *the* thing' is preferable, so as to imply only that the essence of substance is eternal (anticipating E IP8S2), not that all essences are eternal. But the NS have the indefinite article. And Spinoza does not maintain that all essences are eternal only in suspect works like the *Metaphysical Thoughts*. Cf. for example, the *Treatise* (II/36-37). In any case the attributes seem to provide us with a plurality of eternal things (cf. P19).

[6] NS: "expressed."

A1: Whatever is, is either in itself or in another.

A2: What cannot be conceived through another, must be conceived through itself.

25   A3: From a given determinate cause the effect follows necessarily; and conversely, if there is no determinate cause, it is impossible for an effect to follow.

A4: The knowledge of an effect depends on, and involves, the knowledge of its cause.

30   A5: Things that have nothing in common with one another also cannot be understood through one another, *or* the concept of the one does not involve the concept of the other.

II/47   A6: A true idea must agree with its object.

A7: If a thing can be conceived as not existing, its essence does not involve existence.

5   P1: *A substance⁷ is prior in nature to its affections.*

Dem.: This is evident from D3 and D5.

P2: *Two substances having different attributes have nothing in common with*
10   *one another.⁸*

Dem.: This also evident from D3. For each must be in itself and be conceived through itself, *or* the concept of the one does not involve the concept of the other.

15   P3: *If things have nothing in common with one another, one of them cannot be the cause of the other.*

---

⁷ NS: *de zelfstandigheit*, the substance, or simply, substance. But as Appuhn says, it does not emerge until later, after the properties of substances have been established, that there is only one substance. Spinoza will continue to speak as if there could be more than one substance until P14C1.

⁸ The punctuation in both the OP and the NS, which puts commas around the participial phrase, may suggest a claim that two substances, if they are indeed two, will have to have different attributes. It seems to me not to be Spinoza's intention to claim this at this point (cf. P5). I take the force of the phrase to be conditional: "If two substances have different attributes. . . ." Leibniz's objection (I, 141), that two substances might have some attributes in common and others which were distinctive of each one (e.g., substance A has attributes C and D, substance B has attributes C and E), rests on the assumption that a substance may have more than one attribute. But (in spite of D6 and P10S) I take it that Spinoza *begins* with the Cartesian assumption (cf. *Principles* I, 53) that each substance has one attribute that constitutes its nature or essence, and that anything else that might be called an attribute would be improperly, or only loosely, so-called.

Dem.: If they have nothing in common with one another, then (by A5) they cannot be understood through one another, and so (by A4) one cannot be the cause of the other, q.e.d.

P4: *Two or more distinct things are distinguished from one another, either by a difference in the attributes of the substances or by a difference in their affections.*

Dem.: Whatever is, is either in itself or in another (by A1), i.e. (by D3 and D5), outside the intellect there is nothing except substances and their affections. Therefore, there is nothing outside the intellect through which a number of things can be distinguished from one another except substances, *or* what is the same (by D4), their attributes, and their affections,[9] q.e.d.

P5: *In nature there cannot be two or more substances of the same nature* or *attribute.*

Dem.: If there were two or more distinct substances, they would have to be distinguished from one another either by a difference in their attributes, or by a difference in their affections (by P4). If only by a difference in their attributes, then it will be conceded that there is only one of the same attribute. But if by a difference in their affections, then since a substance is prior in nature to its affections (by P1), if the affections are put to one side and [the substance] is considered in itself, i.e. (by D3 and A6), considered truly, one cannot be conceived to be distinguished from another, i.e. (by P4), there cannot be many, but only one [of the same nature *or* attribute],[10] q.e.d.

P6: *One substance cannot be produced by another substance.*

Dem.: In nature there cannot be two substances of the same attribute (by P5), i.e. (by P2), which have something in common with each

[9] Elwes, White and Shirley all omit the comma after "attributes," thereby suggesting that substance is being identified with its attributes *and* affections. But the comma appears both in the OP and the NS. On the identity of substance and attribute see Gueroult 1, 1:47-50; Curley 3, 16-18.

[10] Both the OP and the NS omit the bracketed phrase, but this is clearly only an ellipsis. Akkerman (2, 80) points out that one of the most common differences between the OP and the NS occurs at the end of demonstrations, particularly when the proof is indirect (e.g., E IIP10D) or given in two parts (e.g., E IP18D). He infers (2, 176) that, rather than constantly repeat the proposition to be demonstrated, Spinoza probably gave very summary indications of the conclusions in his mss., "which were worked out in various ways by the editors and translators."

The OP and NS also read "D3 and D6" in l. 13, but Van Vloten-Land and Gebhardt emend to "D3 and A6." Hubbeling (66) suggests that the reference may be to the principle that every definition, or clear and distinct idea, is true (cf. IV/13/12-13).

The proposition is an extremely important one, since it is the first truly radical theorem Spinoza derives from his first principles. Note the alternative demonstration in P8S2.

411

other. Therefore (by P3) one cannot be the cause of the other, *or* cannot be produced by the other, q.e.d.

Cor.: From this it follows that a substance cannot be produced by anything else. For in nature there is nothing except substances and their affections, as is evident from A1, D3, and D5. But it cannot be produced by a substance (by P6). Therefore, substance absolutely cannot be produced by anything else, q.e.d.

Alternatively: This[11] is demonstrated even more easily from the absurdity of its contradictory. For if a substance could be produced by something else, the knowledge of it would have to depend on the knowledge of its cause (by A4). And so (by D3) it would not be a substance.

P7: *It pertains to the nature of a substance to exist.*

Dem.: A substance cannot be produced by anything else (by P6C); therefore it will be the cause of itself, i.e. (by D1), its essence necessarily involves existence, *or* it pertains to its nature to exist, q.e.d.

P8: *Every substance is necessarily infinite.*

Dem.: A substance of one attribute[12] does not exist unless it is unique (P5), and it pertains to its nature to exist (P7). Of its nature, therefore, it will exist either as finite or as infinite. But not as finite. For then (by D2) it would have to be limited by something else of the same nature, which would also have to exist necessarily (by P7), and so there would be two substances of the same attribute, which is absurd (by P5). Therefore, it exists as infinite, q.e.d.

Schol. 1: Since being finite is really, in part, a negation, and being infinite is an absolute affirmation of the existence of some nature, it follows from P7 alone that every substance must be infinite. [NS: For if we assumed a finite substance, we would, in part, deny existence to its nature, which (by P7) is absurd.][13]

Schol. 2:[14] I do not doubt that the demonstration of P7 will be

[11] The NS reads: "This Proposition . . ." Gebhardt infers that the translation reflects an earlier draft. But Akkerman points out (2, 154) that the reference must be to the corollary, and concludes that the NS reading merely reflects the translator's disposition to eliminate ambiguities, a disposition which in this case leads him astray.

[12] From the perspective of Gueroult's interpretation, this phrase is highly significant, as illustrating his contention that the early propositions of Part I of the *Ethics* (P1-P8) are concerned to demonstrate properties possessed by the elements of God's essence, which are substances constituted by a single attribute, each unique in its kind, existing by itself and infinite. The problem, then, becomes one of seeing how these attributes are united in one being, i.e., how these distinct essences (P10S) can be the essences of one and the same thing.

[13] Akkerman (2, 161) takes this to be clearly a translator's addition.

[14] Because this scholium relates more to P7 than to P8, some scholars have thought it a marginal note misplaced by the original editors. But both the NS and the OP put it here, and as Gebhardt notes, it is subsequently referred to by Spinoza as the second

difficult to conceive for all who judge things confusedly, and have not been accustomed to know things through their first causes—because they do not distinguish between the modifications[15] of substances and the substances themselves, nor do they know how things are produced. So it happens that they fictitiously ascribe to substances the beginning which they see that natural things have; for those who do not know the true causes of things confuse everything and without any conflict of mind feign that both trees and men speak, imagine that men are formed both from stones and from seed, and that any form whatever is changed into any other.[16] So also, those who confuse the divine nature with the human easily ascribe human affects to God, particularly so long as they are also ignorant of how those affects are produced in the mind.

But if men would attend to the nature of substance, they would have no doubt at all of the truth of P7. Indeed, this proposition would be an axiom for everyone, and would be numbered among the common notions. For by substance they would understand what is in itself and is conceived through itself, i.e., that the knowledge of which does not require the knowledge of any other thing.[17] But by modifications they would understand what is in another, those things whose concept is formed from the concept of the thing in which they are.

---

scholium to P8. Probably the reason for its placement here is that Spinoza conceives the first eight propositions to form a natural unit, and this scholium touches on a number of the themes of that unit.

[15] Gebhardt notes that the NS has 'wijzen' with 'modi' in the margin, instead of 'modifications' as in the OP text. There are many such variations in the NS marginalia (e.g., 'affectio' for 'affectus' in l. 36) and Gebhardt takes them as a sign that the NS translation was done from an earlier state of the text. But Akkerman (2, 66-67, 163) has advanced a more plausible hypothesis, that the translator (or rather, the author of the marginalia, who in this case may not have been the translator) may not always have preserved for the Dutch reader the exact Latin word Spinoza used. The author of the marginalia may not always have taken the time to look back from the translation to the text translated, and may have been misled by the translator's (correct) treatment of 'modus' and 'modificatio' as synonyms. He may also have intended to indicate not so much the exact word, as simply a common Latin term for the Dutch term. The translation seems deliberately to avoid the use of words of foreign origin. The marginalia help to compensate for the loss entailed by that policy.

[16] Wolfson (2, 242-243) suggests a number of possible targets here: the belief that trees may speak was held by the Sabians and ridiculed by Maimonides (1, 3:29); that men may be made from stones as well as seed is implied in the Greek legend of Deucalion and Pyrrha (Ovid, *Metamorphoses*, I, 411-413), but also in Matthew 3:9; and that a thing having any one form may be changed into one having any other is illustrated both by many of the legends in Ovid, but also by many Jewish and Christian miracles (cf. Maimonides 1, 2:29, and TdIE §58).

[17] This passage is interesting partly because it provides a different gloss on the definition of substance from that offered in D3, but also because Spinoza shows clearly here that he does not take his definition of substance to be merely a report of what men ordinarily understand by that term. Cf. Curley 3, 14-16.

This is how we can have true ideas of modifications which do not exist; for though they do not actually exist outside the intellect, nevertheless their essences are comprehended in another in such a way that they can be conceived through it. But the truth of substances is not outside the intellect unless it is in them themselves,[18] because they are conceived through themselves.

Hence, if someone were to say that he had a clear and distinct, i.e., true, idea of a substance, and nevertheless doubted whether such a substance existed, that would indeed be the same as if he were to say that he had a true idea, and nevertheless doubted whether it was false (as is evident to anyone who is sufficiently attentive). Or if someone maintains that a substance is created,[19] he maintains at the same time that a false idea has become true.[20] Of course nothing more absurd can be conceived. So it must be confessed that the existence of a substance, like its essence, is an eternal truth.

And from this we can infer in another way that there is only one [substance] of the same nature, which I have considered it worth the trouble of showing here.[21] But to do this in order, it must be noted,

I. that the true definition of each thing neither involves nor expresses anything except the nature of the thing defined.

From which it follows,

[18] The NS here has an interesting variation that Gebhardt does not note: "But the object of a true idea of substances can be nothing other than the substances themselves . . . ." Akkerman (2, 166) suggests that the translator wished to eliminate the abstract term "veritas" in favor of "vera idea," which had been discussed above (l. 8). A passage in the CM(I/247/4-6) would seem to license the transformation, and that passage would have been fresh in Balling's mind if he did, as Akkerman thinks, translate E I-II around 1663. Akkerman has shown that this kind of a freedom is characteristic of Balling's work as a translator, but not of Glazemaker's.

[19] NS: "If someone maintains that a substance which was not, now begins to be."

[20] Some translators have proposed emending the text so that it would be translated 'a true idea has become false.' Gebhardt rightly rejects the emendation, though his assumption that the NS translation shows that Spinoza twice wrote "a false idea has become true" is probably incorrect. The NS translator's gloss on the beginning of the sentence helps to bring out Spinoza's point. The idea that a substance is created implies that at one time it is false of the substance that it exists and that at a later time it has become true. This is absurd because it involves conceiving an eternal truth as a temporal one.

[21] The remainder of this scholium closely parallels Letter 34, the main difference being that in the letter the argument is used to prove that there is only one God. The lost original was written in Dutch. Akkerman conjectures (2, 167-168), on the basis of a comparison of the OP version of P8S2, the NS version of P8S2, and the NS version of Letter 34, that Spinoza may have had Balling's translation of E I-II available to him when he wrote Letter 34 in 1666, and that he may have used it to help draft the letter. If this is right, it is somewhat surprising that Spinoza did not, in writing the letter, correct the NS's mistranslation of 'quòd' as 'because' in l. 32.

II. that no definition involves or expresses any certain number of individuals,[a]

since it expresses nothing other than the nature of the thing defined. E.g., the definition of the triangle expresses nothing but the simple nature of the triangle, but not any certain number of triangles. It is to be noted,

III. that there must be, for each existing thing, a certain cause[22] on account of which it exists.

Finally, it is to be noted,

IV. that this cause, on account of which a thing exists, either must be contained in the very nature and definition of the existing thing (*viz. that it pertains to its nature to exist*) or must be outside it.

From these propositions it follows that if, in nature, a certain number of individuals exists, there must be a cause why those individuals, and why neither more nor fewer, exist.

For example, if 20 men exist in nature (*to make the matter clearer, I assume that they exist at the same time, and that no others previously existed in nature*), it will not be enough (i.e., *to give a reason why 20 men exist*) to show the cause of human nature in general; but it will be necessary in addition to show the cause why not more and not fewer than 20 exist. For (by III) there must necessarily be a cause why each [NS: particular man] exists. But this cause (by II and III) cannot be contained in human nature itself, since the true definition of man does not involve the number 20. So (by IV) the cause why these 20 men exist, and consequently, why each of them exists, must necessarily be outside each of them.

For that reason it is to be inferred absolutely that whatever is of such a nature that there can be many individuals [of that nature] must, to exist, have an external cause to exist. Now since it pertains to the nature of a substance to exist (by what we have already shown in this Scholium),[23] its definition must involve necessary existence, and consequently its existence must be inferred from its definition alone. But

---

[NS: a by individuals are understood particulars which belong under a genus.]

[22] NS: "een stellige oorzaak/causa positiva," a positive cause. Perhaps, as Akkerman suggests (2, 163), this variation is to be accounted for as translator's license (cf. above at II/49/29). But it is interesting that the same variation occurs in Letter 34 (IV/179/29). If Akkerman's theory (cf. above at II/50/21) is correct, then Spinoza may have made the alteration in writing the letter, changed the NS version of P8S2 accordingly, but not taken the trouble (or remembered) to make the alteration in the Latin original.

[23] NS: "at the beginning of this scholium."

from its definition (as we have shown from II and III) the existence of a number of substances cannot follow. Therefore it follows necessarily from this, that there exists only one of the same nature, as was proposed.

P9: *The more reality or being each thing has, the more attributes belong to it.*
Dem.: This is evident from D4.

P10: *Each attribute of a substance must be conceived through itself.*
Dem.: For an attribute is what the intellect perceives concerning a substance, as constituting its essence (by D4); so (by D3) it must be conceived through itself, q.e.d.

Schol.: From these propositions it is evident that although two attributes may be conceived to be really distinct (i.e., one may be conceived without the aid of the other), we still can not infer from that that they constitute two beings, *or* two different substances.[24] For it is of the nature of a substance that each of its attributes is conceived through itself, since all the attributes it has have always been in it together, and one could not be produced by another, but each expresses the reality, *or* being of substance.

So it is far from absurd to attribute many attributes to one substance. Indeed, nothing in nature is clearer than that each being must be conceived under some attribute, and the more reality, or being it has, the more it has attributes which express necessity, *or* eternity, and infinity. And consequently there is also nothing clearer than that a being absolutely infinite must be defined (as we taught in D6) as a being that consists of infinite attributes, each of which expresses a certain eternal and infinite essence.[25]

But if someone now asks by what sign we shall be able to distinguish the diversity of substances, let him read the following propositions, which show that in Nature there exists only one substance, and that it is absolutely infinite. So that sign would be sought in vain.

[24] The usual way of rendering this into English was challenged by Bennett, who argued that *constituere* should be rendered, not by 'constitute,' but by 'characterize.' Donagan (2) replied, with reference to EID4, that 'constitute' was correct, since it might be understood as elliptical for 'constitute the essence of.' My own view is that 'constitute' is defensible without our needing to regard it as elliptical, because of the tendency in both Descartes and Spinoza to identify substance and attribute. Cf. here Spinoza's note to IP7 of his *Descartes' Principles* (I/163/5). It is true that even here Spinoza uses language apt to suggest that the attributes are properties of substance and distinct from it. But in the end I think that is only misleading.

[25] NS: "a certain kind of essence, which is eternal and infinite." Gebhardt conjectures that the variation reflects the existence of an earlier draft, Akkerman (2, 163), a free translation.

P11: *God,* or *a substance consisting of infinite attributes, each of which expresses eternal and infinite essence, necessarily exists.*

Dem.: If you deny this, conceive, if you can, that God does not exist. Therefore (by A7) his essence does not involve existence. But this (by P7) is absurd. Therefore God necessarily exists, q.e.d.

Alternatively: For each thing there must be assigned a cause, *or* reason, as much for its existence as for its nonexistence. For example, if a triangle exists, there must be a reason *or* cause why it exists; but if it does not exist, there must also be a reason *or* cause which prevents it from existing, *or* which takes its existence away.

But this reason, *or* cause, must either be contained in the nature of the thing, or be outside it. E.g., the very nature of a square circle indicates the reason why it does not exist, viz. because it involves a contradiction. On the other hand, the reason why a substance exists also follows from its nature alone, because it involves existence (see P7). But the reason why a circle or triangle exists, or why it does not exist, does not follow from the nature of these things, but from the order of the whole of corporeal Nature. For from this [order] it must follow either that the triangle necessarily exists now or that it is impossible for it to exist now.[26]

These things are evident through themselves, but from them it follows that a thing necessarily exists if there is no reason or cause which prevents it from existing. Therefore, if there is no reason or cause which prevents God from existing, or which takes his existence away, it must certainly be inferred that he necessarily exists.

But if there were such a reason, *or* cause, it would have to be either in God's very nature or outside it, i.e., in another substance of another nature. For if it were of the same nature, that very supposition would concede that God exists. But a substance which was of another nature [NS: than the divine] would have nothing in common with God (by P2), and therefore could neither give him existence nor take it away.[27]

Since, then, there can be, outside the divine nature, no reason, *or*, cause which takes away the divine existence, the reason will necessarily have to be in his nature itself, if indeed he does not exist. That is, his nature would involve a contradiction [NS: as in our second Example]. But it is absurd to affirm this of a Being absolutely infinite and supremely perfect. Therefore, there is no cause, *or* reason, either

---

[26] The NS omits "now" in both cases.

[27] Gebhardt, following the OP, reads *habere* in l. 19, i.e.: 'a substance of another nature could have nothing in common with God.' But the NS suggests that we should read *haberet*.

in God or outside God, which takes his existence away. And therefore, God necessarily exists, q.e.d.

30 Alternatively: To be able not to exist is to lack power, and conversely, to be able to exist is to have power[28] (as is known through
itself). So, if what now necessarily exists are only finite beings, then
finite beings are more powerful than an absolutely infinite Being. But
this, as is known through itself, is absurd. So, either nothing exists or
an absolutely infinite Being also exists. But we exist, either in ourselves, or in something else, which necessarily exists (see A1 and P7).
35 Therefore an absolutely infinite Being—i.e. (by D6), God—necessarily exists, q.e.d.

II/54 Schol.: In this last demonstration I wanted to show God's existence
a posteriori, so that the demonstration would be perceived more easily—but not because God's existence does not follow a priori from the
5 same foundation. For since being able to exist is power, it follows that
the more reality belongs to the nature of a thing, the more powers it
has, of itself, to exist. Therefore, an absolutely infinite Being, *or* God,
has, of himself, an absolutely infinite power of existing. For that reason, he exists absolutely.

Still, there may be many who will not easily be able to see how
10 evident this demonstration is, because they have been accustomed to
contemplate only those things that flow from external causes. And of
these, they see that those which quickly come to be, i.e., which easily
exist,[29] also easily perish. And conversely, they judge that those things
to which they conceive more things to pertain are more difficult to do,
15 i.e., that they do not exist so easily.[30] But to free them from these
prejudices, I have no need to show here in what manner this proposition—*what quickly comes to be, quickly perishes*—is true, nor whether or

---

[28] OP: "Posse non existere impotentia est, & contra posse existere potentia est." Some earlier translators thought this should read: "Non posse existere . . ." (e.g., White: "Inability to exist . . . ," Meijer: "Niet te kunnen bestaan . . ."). Gebhardt pointed out that the NS confirm the OP: "Te konnen niet zijn/Non existere/is warelijk onvermogen: in tegendeel, te konnen zijn/Existere/is vermogen." But since some persist in emending the text (e.g., Caillois, "Ne pouvoir exister . . .") it is worth observing that this makes nonsense of the following argument. Spinoza wishes to compare the power of what can exist (but cannot not exist) with the power of finite existents which (since they do in fact exist) must be able to exist, but which are also able not to exist.

Admittedly, Spinoza makes his point (that being able not to exist is not a sign of power) somewhat more difficult to grasp by speaking in the next sentence of "what . . . necessarily exists," which may suggest that these finite beings are not able not to exist. But Spinoza does not mean that their existence is an eternal truth. Considered in them-selves, they are able not to exist. It is only when they are considered in relation to an external cause that their existence is necessary. This is the force of speaking of "what *now* necessarily exists." As at 53/9-10, the NS omits the "now."

[29] NS: "which are easily able to exist."   [30] NS: "are not so easily able to exist."

not all things are equally easy in respect to the whole of Nature. It is sufficient to note only this, that I am not here speaking of things that come to be from external causes, but only of substances that (by P6) can be produced by no external cause.

For things that come to be from external causes—whether they consist of many parts or of few—owe all the perfection or reality they have to the power of the external cause; and therefore their existence arises only from the perfection of their external cause, and not from their own perfection. On the other hand, whatever perfection substance has is not owed to any external cause. So its existence must follow from its nature alone; hence its existence is nothing but its essence.

Perfection, therefore, does not take away the existence of a thing, but on the contrary asserts it. But imperfection takes it away. So there is nothing of whose existence we can be more certain than we are of the existence of an absolutely infinite, *or* perfect, Being—i.e., God. For since his essence excludes all imperfection, and involves absolute perfection, by that very fact it takes away every cause of doubting his existence, and gives the greatest certainty concerning it. I believe this will be clear even to those who are only moderately attentive.

P12: *No attribute of a substance can be truly conceived from which it follows that the substance can be divided.*

Dem.: For the parts into which a substance so conceived would be divided either will retain the nature of the substance or will not. If the first [NS: viz. they retain the nature of the substance], then (by P8) each part will have to be infinite, and (by P7)[31] its own cause, and (by P5) each part will have to consist of a different attribute. And so many substances will be able to be formed from one, which is absurd (by P6). Furthermore, the parts (by P2) would have nothing in common with their whole, and the whole (by D4 and P10) could both be and be conceived without its parts, which is absurd, as no one will be able to doubt.

But if the second is asserted, viz. that the parts will not retain the nature of substance, then since the whole substance would be divided into equal parts,[32] it would lose the nature of substance, and would cease to be, which (by P7) is absurd.

[31] Following Meijer. Both the OP and the NS have *P6*. But Gebhardt's argument that this must be right is unconvincing.

[32] The apparently gratuitous assumption that the parts would be equal has prompted various emendations. Gebhardt is probably right to suggest that Spinoza assumes that if substance can be conceived to be divided at all, then it can be conceived to be divided into equal parts. So the case of an equal division is the only one that need be considered.

20 P13: *A substance which is absolutely infinite is indivisible.*

Dem.: For if it were divisible, the parts into which it would be divided will either retain the nature of an absolutely infinite substance or they will not. If the first, then there will be a number of substances

26 of the same nature, which (by P5) is absurd. But if the second is asserted, then (as above [NS: P12]), an absolutely infinite substance will be able to cease to be, which (by P11) is also absurd.

Cor.: From these [propositions] it follows that no substance, and consequently no corporeal substance, insofar as it is a substance,[33] is

30 divisible.

Schol.: That substance is indivisible, is understood more simply merely from this, that the nature of substance cannot be conceived unless as infinite, and that by a part of substance nothing can be

II/56 understood except a finite substance, which (by P8) implies a plain contradiction.

P14: *Except God, no substance can be or be conceived.*

5 Dem.: Since God is an absolutely infinite being, of whom no attribute which expresses an essence of substance can be denied (by D6), and he necessarily exists (by P11), if there were any substance except God, it would have to be explained through some attribute of God,

10 and so two substances of the same attribute would exist, which (by P5) is absurd. And so except God, no substance can be or, consequently, be conceived. For if it could be conceived, it would have to be conceived as existing. But this (by the first part of this demonstration) is absurd. Therefore, except for God no substance can be or be

15 conceived, q.e.d.

Cor. 1: From this it follows most clearly, first, that God is unique,[34] i.e. (by D6), that in Nature there is only one substance, and that it is absolutely infinite (as we indicated in P10S).

20 Cor. 2: It follows, second, that an extended thing and a thinking thing are either attributes of God, or (by A1) affections of God's attributes.

25 P15: *Whatever is, is in God, and nothing can be or be conceived without God.*

Dem.: Except for God, there neither is, nor can be conceived, any substance (by P14), i.e. (by D3), thing that is in itself and is conceived through itself. But modes (by D5) can neither be nor be conceived

30 without substance. So they can be in the divine nature alone, and can be conceived through it alone. But except for substances and modes

II/57 there is nothing (by A1). Therefore, [NS: everything is in God and] nothing can be or be conceived without God, q.e.d.

---

[33] NS: "insofar as one conceives it as substance."
[34] On the propriety of applying this term to God, see Gueroult 1, 1:156-158.

Schol.: [I.][35] There are those who feign a God, like man, consisting of a body and a mind, and subject to passions. But how far they wander from the true knowledge of God, is sufficiently established by what has already been demonstrated. Them I dismiss. For everyone who has to any extent contemplated the divine nature denies that God is corporeal. They prove this best from the fact that by body we understand any quantity, with length, breadth, and depth, limited by some certain figure. Nothing more absurd than this can be said of God, viz. of a being absolutely infinite.

But meanwhile, by the other arguments by which they strive to demonstrate this same conclusion they clearly show that they entirely remove corporeal, *or* extended,[36] substance itself from the divine nature. And they maintain that it has been created by God. But by what divine power could it be created? They are completely ignorant of that. And this shows clearly that they do not understand what they themselves say.

At any rate, I have demonstrated clearly enough—in my judgment, at least—that no substance can be produced or created by any other (see P6C and P8S2). Next, we have shown (P14) that except for God, no substance can either be or be conceived, and hence [in P14C2][37] we have concluded that extended substance is one of God's infinite attributes. But to provide a fuller explanation, I shall refute my opponents' arguments, which all reduce to these.

[II.] *First*, they think that corporeal substance, insofar as it is substance, consists of parts. And therefore they deny that it can be infinite, and consequently, that it can pertain to God. They explain this by many examples, of which I shall mention one or two.[38]

---

[35] Wolfson's discussion of the historical background of this scholium (1, 1:262-295) is instructive, provided it is read cautiously. It should be stressed that the main theme of the scholium is the defense of the doctrine that extended substance is an attribute of God; that extended substance is infinite is a subordinate theme, relating only to the first objection Spinoza discusses (sections II, IV, and V), not to the second (sections III and VI). See also Letter 12 and Gueroult's discussion of it in Grene.

[36] We do also have 'sive' here, which is normally the 'or' of identity; but if corporeality implies finiteness (as the preceding paragraph says it does), then Spinoza ought not to identify extended substance with corporeal substance, since the latter involves a contradiction. Nevertheless, throughout this scholium Spinoza does use the terms as if they were interchangeable (e.g., at II/58/18 and at 58/34-35). Perhaps the explanation is that he adopts, for the time being, his opponents' identification of the two concepts.

[37] Gebhardt adds this from the NS. But this is not what that corollary says. As things stand, this proposition is not proven until E IIP2. Perhaps in an earlier state of the ms. the corollary did say that and perhaps the omission of this reference was deliberate, following a change in the corollary.

[38] In fact Spinoza mentions three, numbered here [i], [ii], and [iii]. That corporeal substance could be infinite was certainly denied by Aristotle (cf. *Physics* III, 5; *De Caelo* I, 5-7), though his arguments seem to have evolved considerably before they reached

[i] If corporeal substance is infinite, they say, let us conceive it to be divided in two parts.[39] Each part will be either finite or infinite. If the former, then an infinite is composed of two finite parts, which is absurd. If the latter [NS: i.e., if each part is infinite], then there is one infinite twice as large as another, which is also absurd. [ii] Again, if an infinite quantity is measured by parts [each] equal to a foot, it will consist of infinitely many such parts, as it will also, if it is measured by parts [each] equal to an inch. And therefore, one infinite number will be twelve times greater than another [NS: which is no less absurd]. [iii] Finally, if we conceive that from one point of a certain infinite quantity two lines, say AB and AC, are extended to infinity, it is certain that, although in the beginning they are a certain, determinate distance apart, the distance between B and C is continuously increased, and at last, from being determinate, it will become indeterminable. Since these absurdities follow—so they think—from the fact that an infinite quantity is supposed, they infer that corporeal substance must be finite, and consequently cannot pertain to God's essence.

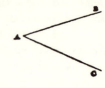

[III.] Their *second* argument is also drawn from God's supreme perfection. For God, they say, since he is a supremely perfect being, cannot be acted on. But corporeal substance, since it is divisible, can be acted on. It follows, therefore, that it does not pertain to God's essence.[40]

[IV.] These are the arguments which I find authors using, to try to show that corporeal substance is unworthy of the divine nature, and cannot pertain to it. But anyone who is properly attentive will find that I have already replied to them, since these arguments are founded only on their supposition that corporeal substance is composed of parts, which I have already (P12 and P13C) shown to be absurd. And then anyone who wishes to consider the matter rightly will see that all those absurdities (*if indeed they are all absurd, which I am not now disputing*), from which they wish to infer that extended substance is finite, do

---

the form in which Spinoza undertakes to refute them. For Descartes' attempt at compromise, see *Principles of Philosophy* I, 26-27. On the whole issue, see Koyré 1.

[39] This argument seems to require that the division be into two equal parts. Probably it is taken for granted that if any division is possible, division into equal parts is possible (cf. P12D).

[40] Descartes is generally identified as the opponent here (cf. *Principles* I, 23). Wolfson's argument to the contrary (1, 1:268) is unconvincing, but it is fair to say that Spinoza's version of the Cartesian argument in *Descartes' Principles* (IP16, I/176-177) is closer to what Descartes actually says than the argument given here. Descartes gives no reason for saying that divisibility involves imperfection. The objection Spinoza considers here makes it an imperfection because it entails the possibility of being acted on.

not follow at all from the fact that an infinite quantity is supposed, but from the fact that they suppose an infinite quantity to be measurable and composed of finite parts. So from the absurdities which follow from that they can infer only that infinite quantity is not measurable, and that it is not composed of finite parts. This is the same thing we have already demonstrated above (P12, etc.). So the weapon they aim at us, they really turn against themselves.

If, therefore, they still wish to infer from this absurdity of theirs that extended substance must be finite, they are indeed doing nothing more than if someone feigned that a circle has the properties of a square, and inferred from that the circle has no center, from which all lines drawn to the circumference are equal. For corporeal substance, which cannot be conceived except as infinite, unique, and indivisible (see P8, 5 and 12), they conceive to be composed of finite parts, to be many, and to be divisible, in order to infer that it is finite.

So also others, after they feign that a line is composed of points, know how to invent many arguments, by which they show that a line cannot be divided to infinity. And indeed it is no less absurd to assert that corporeal substance is composed of bodies, *or* parts, than that a body is composed of surfaces, the surfaces of lines, and the lines, finally, of points.

All those who know that clear reason is infallible must confess this— particularly those who deny that there is a vacuum. For if corporeal substance could be so divided that its parts were really distinct, why, then, could one part not be annihilated, the rest remaining connected with one another as before? And why must they all be so fitted together that there is no vacuum? Truly, of things which are really distinct from one another, one can be, and remain in its condition, without the other. Since, therefore, there is no vacuum in nature (a subject I discuss elsewhere),[41] but all its parts must so concur that there is no vacuum, it follows also that they cannot be really distinguished, i.e., that corporeal substance, insofar as it is a substance, cannot be divided.

[V.] If someone should now ask why we are, by nature, so inclined to divide quantity, I shall answer that we conceive quantity in two ways: abstractly, *or* superficially,[42] as we [NS: commonly] imagine it,

---

[41] OP: *de quo aliàs*. This is not specific as to time, but Appuhn is probably right to see a reference here to *Descartes' Principles* (I/188), since the topic is not mentioned again in the *Ethics*. Gueroult (1, 1:216) casts doubt on this, but on the inaccurate ground that *Descartes' Principles* is nothing more than an exposition of a philosophy Spinoza rejects. Spinoza certainly regards some of the arguments of that work as sound. Cf. E IP19S.

[42] NS: "abstracted from matter." The phrases incorporated from the NS in this sentence are perhaps no more than examples of translator's liberties.

or as substance, which is done by the intellect alone [NS: without the help of the imagination]. So if we attend to quantity as it is in the imagination, which we do often and more easily, it will be found to be finite, divisible, and composed of parts; but if we attend to it as it is in the intellect, and conceive it insofar as it is a substance, which happens [NS: seldom and] with great difficulty, then (as we have already sufficiently demonstrated) it will be found to be infinite, unique, and indivisible.

This will be sufficiently plain to everyone who knows how to distinguish between the intellect and the imagination—particularly if it is also noted that matter is everywhere the same, and that parts are distinguished in it only insofar as we conceive matter to be affected in different ways, so that its parts are distinguished only modally, but not really.

For example, we conceive that water is divided and its parts separated from one another—insofar as it is water, but not insofar as it is corporeal substance. For insofar as it is substance, it is neither separated nor divided. Again, water, insofar as it is water, is generated and corrupted, but insofar as it is substance, it is neither generated nor corrupted.

[VI.] And with this I think I have replied to the second argument also, since it is based on the supposition that matter, insofar as it is substance, is divisible, and composed of parts. Even if this [reply] were not [sufficient], I do not know why [divisibility] would be unworthy of the divine nature. For (by P14) apart from God there can be no substance by which [the divine nature] would be acted on. All things, I say, are in God, and all things that happen, happen only through the laws of God's infinite nature and follow (as I shall show) from the necessity of his essence. So it cannot be said in any way that God is acted on by another, or that extended substance is unworthy of the divine nature, even if it is supposed to be divisible, so long as it is granted to be eternal and infinite. But enough of this for the present.

P16: *From the necessity of the divine nature there must follow infinitely many things in infinitely many modes,*[43] *(i.e., everything which can fall under an infinite intellect.)*[44]

---

[43] It is unclear whether *modus* should be translated here as a technical term (Appuhn, Caillois), or as a nontechnical one (White, Elwes, Meijer, and Auerbach). The NS cannot resolve this since they use *wijz* both for technical and nontechnical uses of *modus*; but they do give the Latin in the margin, which suggests that they took it as a technical term. Gueroult (1, 1:260) suggests that it may be translated either way. For a context where the policy adopted here seems awkward, see IIP3S.

[44] NS: "that can be conceived by an infinite intellect." Similarly at ll. 29-30, and 32-

Dem.: This Proposition must be plain to anyone, provided he attends to the fact that the intellect infers from the given definition of any thing a number of properties that really do follow necessarily from it (i.e., from the very essence of the thing); and that it infers more properties the more the definition of the thing expresses reality, i.e., the more reality the essence of the defined thing involves. But since the divine nature has absolutely infinite attributes (by D6), each of which also expresses an essence infinite in its own kind, from its necessity there must follow infinitely many things in infinite modes (i.e., everything which can fall under an infinite intellect), q.e.d.

Cor. 1: From this it follows that God is the efficient cause of all things which can fall under an infinite intellect.

Cor. 2: It follows, secondly, that God is a cause through himself and not an accidental cause.[45]

Cor. 3: It follows, thirdly, that God is absolutely the first cause.

P17: *God acts from the laws of his nature alone, and is compelled by no one.*

Dem.: We have just shown (P16) that from the necessity of the divine nature alone, or (what is the same thing) from the laws of his nature alone, absolutely infinite things follow, and in P15 we have demonstrated that nothing can be or be conceived without God, but that all things are in God. So there can be nothing outside him by which he is determined or compelled to act. Therefore, God acts from the laws of his nature alone, and is compelled by no one, q.e.d.

Cor. 1: From this it follows, first, that there is no cause, either extrinsically or intrinsically, which prompts God to action, except the perfection of his nature.[46]

Cor. 2: It follows, secondly, that God alone is a free cause. For God alone exists only from the necessity of his nature (by P11 and P14C1), and acts from the necessity of his nature (by P17). Therefore (by D7) God alone is a free cause, q.e.d.

Schol.: [I.] Others[47] think that God is a free cause because he can (so they think) bring it about that the things which we have said follow from his nature (i.e., which are in his power) do not happen or are not produced by him. But this is the same as if they were to say that God

---

33. The NS's indefinite article is confirmed by the OP when Spinoza refers back to this proposition at II/83/31-32.

[45] On this corollary, cf. Wolfson 1, 1:307, with Gueroult 1, 1:253.

[46] Instead of "except the perfection of his nature," the NS have: "but he is only an efficient cause from the force of his perfection." Gebhardt adds this to the text, creating a certain redundancy. This is probably a translator's gloss, rather than a passage omitted in revision.

[47] On the medieval background of this scholium see Wolfson 1, 1:308-319, and Gueroult 1, 1:272-295.

can bring it about that it would not follow from the nature of a triangle that its three angles are equal to two right angles; *or* that from a given cause the effect would not follow—which is absurd.

Further, I shall show later, without the aid of this Proposition, that neither intellect nor will pertain to God's nature. Of course I know there are many who think they can demonstrate that a supreme intellect and a free will pertain to God's nature. For they say they know nothing they can ascribe to God more perfect than what is the highest perfection in us.

Moreover, even if they conceive God to actually understand in the highest degree, they still do not believe that he can bring it about that all the things he actually understands exist. For they think that in that way they would destroy God's power. If he had created all the things in his intellect (they say), then he would have been able to create nothing more, which they believe to be incompatible with God's omnipotence. So they preferred to maintain that God is indifferent to all things, not creating anything except what he has decreed to create by some absolute will.

But I think I have shown clearly enough (see P16) that from God's supreme power, *or* infinite nature, infinitely many things in infinitely many modes, i.e., all things, have necessarily flowed, or always follow, by the same necessity and in the same way as from the nature of a triangle it follows, from eternity and to eternity, that its three angles are equal to two right angles. So God's omnipotence[48] has been actual from eternity and will remain in the same actuality to eternity. And in this way, at least in my opinion, God's omnipotence is maintained far more perfectly.

Indeed—to speak openly—my opponents seem to deny God's omnipotence. For they are forced to confess that God understands infinitely many creatable things, which nevertheless he will never be able to create. For otherwise, if he created everything he understood [NS: to be creatable] he would (according to them) exhaust his omnipotence and render himself imperfect. Therefore to maintain that God is perfect, they are driven to maintain at the same time that he cannot bring about everything to which his power extends. I do not see what could be feigned which would be more absurd than this or more contrary to God's omnipotence.

[II.] Further—to say something here also about the intellect and will which we commonly attribute to God—if will and intellect do pertain to the eternal essence of God,[49] we must of course understand by each

[48] The NS here adds a gloss on "omnipotence": "through which he is said to be able to do everything."

[49] It must be emphasized that Spinoza does not himself think that either intellect or

426

of these attributes something different from what men commonly understand. For the intellect and will which would constitute God's essence would have to differ entirely from our intellect and will, and could not agree with them in anything except the name. They would not agree with one another any more than do the dog that is a heavenly constellation and the dog that is a barking animal. I shall demonstrate this.

If intellect pertains to the divine nature, it will not be able to be (like our intellect) by nature either posterior to (as most would have it), or simultaneous with, the things understood, since God is prior in causality to all things (by P16C1). On the contrary, the truth and formal essence of things is what it is because it exists objectively in that way in God's intellect.[50] So God's intellect, insofar as it is conceived to constitute God's essence, is really the cause both of the essence and of the existence of things. This seems also to have been noticed by those who asserted that God's intellect, will and power are one and the same.

Therefore, since God's intellect is the only cause of things (viz. as we have shown, both of their essence and of their existence), he must necessarily differ from them both as to his essence and as to his existence. For what is caused differs from its cause precisely in what it has from the cause [NS: for that reason it is called the effect of such a cause].[51] E.g., a man is the cause of the existence of another man, but not of his essence, for the latter is an eternal truth. Hence, they can agree entirely according to their essence. But in existing they must differ. And for that reason, if the existence of one perishes, the other's existence will not thereby perish. But if the essence of one could be destroyed, and become false, the other's essence would also be destroyed [NS: and become false].

So the thing that is the cause both of the essence and of the existence of some effect, must differ from such an effect, both as to its essence and as to its existence. But God's intellect is the cause both of the essence and of the existence of our intellect. Therefore, God's intellect, insofar as it is conceived to constitute the divine essence, differs from our intellect both as to its essence and as to its existence,

---

will should be ascribed to the essence of God (cf. P31). He is only discussing here what follows from a common view. This has been widely misunderstood. See Gueroult 1, 1:277-282.

[50] The NS has, for the final clause: "because God's intellect has conceived [things] as they really are." This is no doubt a translator's gloss, and not a very happy one, since it seems to cancel the text's claim that God's intellect is prior to the things understood.

[51] This passage is extremely puzzling, since it seems to contradict A5. Cf. Gueroult 1, 1:286-295.

30   and cannot agree with it in anything except in name, as we supposed. The proof proceeds in the same way concerning the will, as anyone can easily see.

P18: *God is the immanent, not the transitive, cause of all things.*

II/64   Dem.: Everything that is, is in God, and must be conceived through God (by P15), and so (by P16C1) God is the cause of [NS: all] things, which are in him. That is the first [thing to be proven]. And then

5   outside God there can be no substance (by P14), i.e. (by D3), thing which is in itself outside God. That was the second. God, therefore, is the immanent, not the transitive cause of all things,[52] q.e.d.

P19: *God is eternal,* or *all God's attributes are eternal.*

10   Dem.: For God (by D6) is substance, which (by P11) necessarily exists, i.e. (by P7), to whose nature it pertains to exist, or (what is the same) from whose definition it follows that he exists; and therefore (by D8), he is eternal.

15   Next, by God's attributes are to be understood what (by D4) expresses an essence of the Divine substance, i.e., what pertains to substance. The attributes themselves, I say, must involve it itself. But eternity pertains to the nature of substance (as I have already demonstrated from P7). Therefore each of the attributes must involve eter-

20   nity, and so, they are all eternal, q.e.d.

Schol.: This Proposition is also as clear as possible from the way I have demonstrated God's existence (P11). For from that demonstration, I say, it is established that God's existence, like his essence, is an eternal truth. And then I have also demonstrated God's eternity in

25   another way (*Descartes' Principles* IP19), and there is no need to repeat it here.

P20: *God's existence and his essence are one and the same.*

30   Dem.: God (by P19) and all of his attributes are eternal, i.e. (by D8), each of his attributes expresses existence. Therefore, the same attributes of God which (by D4) explain God's eternal essence at the

35   same time explain his eternal existence, i.e., that itself which consti-

II/65   tutes God's essence at the same time constitutes his existence. So his existence and his essence are one and the same, q.e.d.

Cor. 1: From this it follows, first, that God's existence, like his

5   essence, is an eternal truth.

Cor. 2: It follows, secondly, that God, *or* all of God's attributes, are

---

[52] For the last two sentences the NS has: "Therefore, God is not a cause of anything that is outside him. That is the second thing we proposed." Cf. the note at I/48/15. Akkerman notes similar variations in IIIP1, P2, P28, P39, and P52.

immutable. For if they changed as to their existence, they would also (by P20) change as to their essence, i.e. (as is known through itself), from being true become false, which is absurd.

P21: *All the things which follow from the absolute nature of any of God's attributes have always*[53] *had to exist and be infinite, or are, through the same attribute, eternal and infinite.*

Dem.: If you deny this, then conceive (if you can) that in some attribute of God there follows from its absolute nature something that is finite and has a determinate existence, *or* duration, e.g., God's idea[54] in thought. Now since thought is supposed to be an attribute of God, it is necessarily (by P11) infinite by its nature. But insofar as it has God's idea, [thought] is supposed to be finite. But (by D2) [thought] cannot be conceived to be finite unless it is determined through thought itself. But [thought can] not [be determined] through thought itself, insofar as it constitutes God's idea, for to that extent [thought] is supposed to be finite. Therefore, [thought must be determined] through thought insofar as it does not constitute God's idea, which [thought] nevertheless (by P11) must necessarily exist. Therefore, there is thought[55] which does not constitute God's idea, and on that account God's idea does not follow necessarily from the nature [of this thought] insofar as it is absolute thought (for [thought] is conceived both as constituting God's idea and as not constituting it). [That God's idea does not follow from thought, insofar as it is absolute thought] is contrary to the hypothesis. So if God's idea in thought, or anything else in any attribute of God (for it does not matter what example is taken, since the dem-

---

[53] It is sometimes suggested that it is inappropriate for Spinoza to characterize any mode (even an infinite one) as eternal, and so the use of temporal language here has been taken to show that the infinite modes exist at all times, but not (strictly speaking) eternally. Cf. for example, Appuhn, 3:347; Wolfson 1, 1:376-377; Curley 3, 107 and 116; and Donagan 3.

[54] OP: *idea Dei*; NS: *het denkbeelt van God* (but at l.21, and subsequently, *Gods denkbeelt*). The idea of God referred to here is generally taken to be, not the idea of God existing as a finite mode of thought in, say, some human mind, but the (infinite) idea which God has (cf. IIP3 and P7), and hence an infinite mode. I use "God's idea" and "the idea of God" to mark the distinction between the subjective and objective readings of *idea Dei*. But it must be understood that it is often very uncertain which meaning is intended.

There is disagreement as to whether God's idea should be regarded as an immediate infinite mode (Wolfson 1, 1:238ff.; Gueroult 1, 1:314ff.) or a mediate infinite mode (Pollock, 176; Joachim 1, 94). It must be realized that any interpretation of Spinoza's doctrine of infinite modes has very little evidence to work from. For example, it is usually thought that there will be one immediate infinite mode and one mediate infinite mode for each attribute. But in none of the scanty references in the *Ethics* (IP21-23), the *Short Treatise* (I, 8, 9) and the Correspondence (Letter 64) is this actually stated.

[55] The NS has an indefinite article here, but deletes it in the errata. Two lines later it has "an absolute thought," which is left unaltered.

onstration is universal), follows from the necessity of the absolute nature of the attribute itself, it must necessarily be infinite. This was the first thing to be proven.

Next, what follows in this way from the necessity of the nature of any attribute cannot have a determinate [NS: existence, *or*] duration. For if you deny this, then suppose there is, in some attribute of God, a thing which follows from the necessity of the nature of that attribute—e.g., God's idea in thought—and suppose that at some time [this idea] did not exist or will not exist. But since thought is supposed to be an attribute of God, it must exist necessarily and be immutable[56] (by P11 and P20C2). So beyond the limits of the duration of God's idea (for it is supposed that at some time [this idea] did not exist or will not exist) thought will have to exist without God's idea. But this is contrary to the hypothesis, for it is supposed that God's idea follows necessarily from the given thought. Therefore, God's idea in thought, or anything else which follows necessarily from the absolute nature of some attribute of God, cannot have a determinate duration, but through the same attribute is eternal. This was the second thing [NS: to be proven]. Note that the same is to be affirmed of any thing which, in some attribute of God, follows necessarily from God's absolute nature.

P22: *Whatever follows from some attribute of God insofar as it is modified by a modification which, through the same attribute, exists necessarily and is infinite, must also exist necessarily and be infinite.*[57]

Dem.: The demonstration of this proposition proceeds in the same way as the demonstration of the preceding one.

P23: *Every mode which exists necessarily and is infinite has necessarily had to follow either from the absolute nature of some attribute of God, or from some attribute, modified by a modification which exists necessarily and is infinite.*

Dem.: For a mode is in another, through which it must be conceived (by D5), i.e. (by P15), it is in God alone, and can be conceived through God alone. So if a mode is conceived to exist necessarily and be infinite, [its necessary existence and infinitude] must necessarily be inferred, *or* perceived through some attribute of God, insofar as that attribute is conceived to express infinity and necessity of existence, *or* (what is the same, by D8) eternity, i.e. (by D6 and P19), insofar as it

---

[56] NS: "It must be necessarily and eternally immutable."

[57] NS: "Whatever follows from one of God's attributes, insofar as it is affected with a mode that by the power of that attribute is infinite and eternal, must also be necessarily eternal and infinite." Akkerman thinks it possible that Spinoza altered the text slightly after it had been translated, but equally possible that Balling is being free with the text (licensed by the equation of eternity and necessary existence in ID8, cf. I/67/4). Backward references to IP22 vary, cf. 69/21-22 with 94/26.

is considered absolutely. Therefore, the mode, which exists necessarily and is infinite, has had to follow from the absolute nature of some attribute of God—either immediately (see P21) or by some mediating modification, which follows from its absolute nature, i.e. (by P22), which exists necessarily and is infinite, q.e.d.

P24: *The essence of things produced by God does not involve existence.*

Dem.: This is evident from D1. For that whose nature involves existence (considered in itself), is its own cause, and exists only from the necessity of its nature.

Cor.: From this it follows that God is not only the cause of things' beginning to exist, but also of their persevering in existing, *or* (to use a Scholastic term) God is the cause of the being of things. For—whether the things [NS: produced] exist or not—so long as we attend to their essence, we shall find that it involves neither existence nor duration. So their essence can be the cause neither of their existence nor of their duration, but only God, to whose nature alone it pertains to exist [,can be the cause] (by P14C1).

P25: *God is the efficient cause, not only of the existence of things, but also of their essence.*

Dem.: If you deny this, then God is not the cause of the essence of things; and so (by A4) the essence of things can be conceived without God. But (by P15) this is absurd. Therefore God is also the cause of the essence of things, q.e.d.

Schol.: This Proposition follows more clearly from P16. For from that it follows that from the given divine nature both the essence of things and their existence must necessarily be inferred; and in a word, God must be called the cause of all things in the same sense in which he is called the cause of himself. This will be established still more clearly from the following corollary.

Cor.: Particular things are nothing but affections of God's attributes, *or* modes by which God's attributes are expressed in a certain and determinate way. The demonstration is evident from P15 and D5.

P26: *A thing which has been determined to produce an effect has necessarily been determined in this way by God; and one which has not been determined by God cannot determine itself to produce an effect.*

Dem.: That through which things are said to be determined to produce an effect must be something positive (as is known through itself). And so, God, from the necessity of his nature, is the efficient cause both of its essence and of its existence (by P25 & 16); this was the first thing. And from it the second thing asserted also follows very clearly.

For if a thing which has not been determined by God could determine itself, the first part of this [NS: proposition] would be false, which is absurd, as we have shown.

P27: *A thing which has been determined by God to produce an effect, cannot render itself undetermined.*

Dem.: This proposition is evident from A3.

P28: *Every singular thing, or any thing which is finite and has a determinate existence, can neither exist nor be determined to produce an effect unless it is determined to exist and produce an effect by another cause, which is also finite and has a determinate existence; and again, this cause also can neither exist nor be determined to produce an effect unless it is determined to exist and produce an effect by another, which is also finite and has a determinate existence, and so on, to infinity.*[58]

Dem.: Whatever has been determined to exist and produce an effect has been so determined by God (by P26 and P24C). But what is finite and has a determinate existence could not have been produced by the absolute nature of an attribute of God; for whatever follows from the absolute nature of an attribute of God is eternal and infinite (by P21). It had, therefore, to follow either from God or from an attribute of God insofar as it is considered to be affected by some mode. For there is nothing except substance and its modes (by A1, D3, and D5) and modes (by P25C) are nothing but affections of God's attributes. But it also could not follow from God, or from an attribute of God, insofar as it is affected by a modification which is eternal and infinite (by P22). It had, therefore, to follow from, or be determined to exist and produce an effect by God or an attribute of God insofar as it is modified by a modification which is finite and has a determinate existence. This was the first thing to be proven.

And in turn, this cause, *or* this mode (by the same reasoning by which we have already demonstrated the first part of this proposition) had also to be determined by another, which is also finite and has a determinate existence; and again, this last (by the same reasoning) by another, and so always (by the same reasoning) to infinity, q.e.d.

Schol.: Since certain things had to be produced by God immediately, viz. those which follow necessarily from his absolute nature,

---

[58] Many commentators have wondered how the finite causality affirmed here could be consistent with the divine causality affirmed in P26 and P27. Idealist interpreters have tended to treat finite causality, and indeed, the very existence of the finite in Spinoza, as an illusion (cf. Joachim 1, 98-122), though Harris (1, 57-69) is an exception. For a realist interpretation see Curley 3, chap. 2. The criticism of this in Harris (2) seems to me to involve a confusion of epistemological issues with metaphysical ones.

and others (which nevertheless can neither be nor be conceived without God) had to be produced by the mediation of these first things,[59] it follows:

I. That God is absolutely the proximate cause of the things produced immediately by him, and not [a proximate cause] in his own kind, as they say.[60] For God's effects can neither be nor be conceived without their cause (by P15 and P24C).

II. That God cannot properly be called the remote cause of singular things, except perhaps so that we may distinguish them from those things that he has produced immediately, or rather, that follow from his absolute nature. For by a remote cause we understand one which is not conjoined in any way with its effect. But all things that are, are in God, and so depend on God that they can neither be nor be conceived without him.

P29: *In nature there is nothing contingent, but all things have been determined from the necessity of the divine nature to exist and produce an effect in a certain way.*

Dem.: Whatever is, is in God (by P15); but God cannot be called a contingent thing. For (by P11) he exists necessarily, not contingently. Next, the modes of the divine nature have also followed from it necessarily and not contingently (by P16)—either insofar as the divine nature is considered absolutely (by P21) or insofar as it is considered to be determined to act in a certain way (by P28).[61] Further, God is the cause of these modes not only insofar as they simply exist (by P24C), but also (by P26) insofar as they are considered to be determined to produce an effect. For if they have not been determined by

---

[59] The text of the OP is corrupt in this sentence. Gebhardt rightly emends on the basis of the NS (though it would be better Latin to supply *et quaedam*). Even with the emendation, however, this scholium is open to various interpretations. Some have taken "certain things" to refer to the immediate infinite modes of P21 and "others" to refer to the mediate infinite modes of P22 (Gebhardt, II/352-353; Wolfson 1, 1:390). Others (Gueroult 1, 1:342; Curley 3, 70-71) take "certain things" to refer to all the infinite modes, and "others" to refer to the finite modes. In favor of the latter interpretation (which is certainly not the most natural without reflection) it may be pointed out that (a) Spinoza's own gloss on "things produced immediately by God" is "things which follow from his absolute nature" (which applies to *all* the infinite modes), (b) at ll. 11-12 he apparently regards the latter phrase as more accurate, and (c) this reading is confirmed by the *Short Treatise* I/36, 118. The point of "nevertheless" (in l. 4) is that although the finite modes are produced by other finite modes, and do not follow from the absolute nature of God, they do still depend on him (i.e., he is not their remote cause in the sense given to that term at ll. 13-14).

[60] Gueroult's explanation (1, 1:255n) of Heereboord's use of the terms "proximate" and "remote" seems helpful in understanding this passage. See the Glossary-Index.

[61] OP, NS: P27. Gebhardt defends that reading against Meijer's proposal to read P22, but Gueroult's suggestion (1, 1:343) that we should read P28 seems right.

God, then (by P26) it is impossible, not contingent, that they should
II/71 determine themselves. Conversely (by P27) if they have been determined by God, it is not contingent, but impossible, that they should
render themselves undetermined. So all things have been determined
from the necessity of the divine nature, not only to exist, but to exist
in a certain way, and to produce effects in a certain way. There is
nothing contingent, q.e.d.

5   Schol.: Before I proceed further, I wish to explain here—or rather
to advise [the reader]—what we must understand by *Natura naturans*
and *Natura naturata*. For from the preceding I think it is already established that by *Natura naturans* we must understand what is in itself
10   and is conceived through itself, *or* such attributes of substance as express an eternal and infinite essence, i.e. (by P14C1 and P17C2), God,
insofar as he is considered as a free cause.

But by *Natura naturata* I understand whatever follows from the necessity of God's nature, *or* from any of God's attributes, i.e., all the
15   modes of God's attributes insofar as they are considered as things
which are in God, and can neither be nor be conceived without God.

P30: *An actual intellect, whether finite or infinite,*[62] *must comprehend God's
attributes and God's affections, and nothing else.*

20   Dem.: A true idea must agree with its object (by A6), i.e. (as is
known through itself), what is contained objectively in the intellect
must necessarily be in nature. But in nature (by P14C1) there is only
one substance, viz. God, and there are no affections other than those
25   which are in God (by P15) and which can neither be nor be conceived
without God (by P15). Therefore, an actual intellect, whether finite
or infinite, must comprehend God's attributes and God's affections,
and nothing else, q.e.d.

30   P31: *The actual intellect, whether finite or infinite, like will, desire, love,
etc., must be referred to* Natura naturata, *not to* Natura naturans.[63]

II/72   Dem.: By intellect (as is known through itself) we understand not
absolute thought, but only a certain mode of thinking, which mode
differs from the others, such as desire, love, etc., and so (by D5) must
5   be conceived through absolute thought, i.e. (by P15 and D6), it must
be so conceived through an attribute of God, which expresses the
eternal and infinite essence of thought, that can neither be nor be

---

[62] The text here has been variously translated, but a consensus seems to have developed in favor of this rendering. Cf. Gueroult 1, 1:354n.

[63] I.e., though thought is an attribute of God, and he is a thinking thing (IIP1), he
has neither intellect, nor will, desire nor love. This doctrine goes back to the *Short
Treatise* (cf. I/45/21ff.).

conceived without [that attribute]; and so (by P29S), like the other modes of thinking, it must be referred to *Natura naturata*, not to *Natura naturans*, q.e.d.

Schol.: The reason why I speak here of actual intellect is not because I concede that there is any potential intellect, but because, wishing to avoid all confusion, I wanted to speak only of what we perceive as clearly as possible, i.e., of the intellection itself. We perceive nothing more clearly than that. For we can understand nothing that does not lead to more perfect knowledge of the intellection.

P32: *The will cannot be called a free cause, but only a necessary one.*

Dem.: The will, like the intellect,[64] is only a certain mode of thinking. And so (by P28) each volition can neither exist nor be determined to produce an effect unless it is determined by another cause, and this cause again by another, and so on, to infinity. Even if the will be supposed to be infinite,[65] it must still be determined to exist and produce an effect by God, not insofar as he is an absolutely infinite substance, but insofar as he has an attribute that expresses the infinite and eternal essence of thought (by P23). So in whatever way it is conceived, whether as finite or as infinite, it requires a cause by which it is determined to exist and produce an effect. And so (by D7) it cannot be called a free cause, but only a necessary or compelled one, q.e.d.

Cor. 1: From this it follows, first, that God does not produce any effect by freedom of the will.

Cor. 2: It follows, secondly, that will and intellect are related to God's nature as motion and rest are, and as are absolutely all natural things, which (by P29) must be determined by God to exist and produce an effect in a certain way. For the will, like all other things, requires a cause by which it is determined to exist and produce an effect in a certain way. And although from a given will, *or* intellect infinitely many things may follow, God still cannot be said, on that account, to act from freedom of the will, any more than he can be said to act from freedom of motion and rest on account of those things that follow from motion and rest (for infinitely many things also follow from motion and rest). So will does not pertain to God's nature any more than do the other natural things, but is related to him in the same way as motion and rest, and all the other things which, as we

[64] This is only a provisional way of speaking. Cf. IIP49C. For the transition from "will" to "volition," cf. IIP48.

[65] Though the preceding sentence does not say explicitly that the will is there supposed to be a finite mode, this is implied by the reference to P28 and probably by the adjective "certain" as well. Cf. Gueroult 1, 1:362 (and contrast Wolfson 1, 1:407).

have shown, follow from the necessity of the divine nature and are determined by it to exist and produce an effect in a certain way.

P33: *Things could have been produced by God in no other way, and in no other order than they have been produced.*

Dem.: For all things have necessarily followed from God's given nature (by P16), and have been determined from the necessity of God's nature to exist and produce an effect in a certain way (by P29). Therefore, if things could have been of another nature, or could have been determined to produce an effect in another way, so that the order of Nature was different, then God's nature could also have been other than it is now, and therefore (by P11) that [other nature] would also have had to exist, and consequently, there could have been two or more Gods, which is absurd (by P14C1). So things could have been produced in no other way and no other order, etc., q.e.d.

Schol. 1: Since by these propositions I have shown more clearly than the noon light that there is absolutely nothing in things on account of which they can be called contingent, I wish now to explain briefly what we must understand by contingent—but first, what [we must understand] by necessary and impossible.

A thing is called necessary either by reason of its essence or by reason of its cause. For a thing's existence follows necessarily either from its essence and definition or from a given efficient cause. And a thing is also called impossible from these same causes—viz. either because its essence, *or* definition, involves a contradiction, or because there is no external cause which has been determined to produce such a thing.

But a thing is called contingent only because of a defect of our knowledge. For if we do not know that the thing's essence involves a contradiction, or if we do know very well that its essence does not involve a contradiction, and nevertheless can affirm nothing certainly about its existence, because the order of causes is hidden from us, it can never seem to us either necessary or impossible. So we call it contingent or possible.[66]

Schol. 2: From the preceding it clearly follows that things have been produced by God with the highest perfection, since they have followed necessarily from a given most perfect nature. Nor does this convict God of any imperfection, for his perfection compels us to affirm this. Indeed, from the opposite, it would clearly follow (as I have just shown), that God is not supremely perfect; because if things

[66] This is only provisional. Later (II/209) Spinoza will distinguish between the contingent and the possible.

had been produced by God in another way, we would have to attribute to God another nature, different from that which we have been compelled to attribute to him from the consideration of the most perfect Being.

Of course, I have no doubt that many will reject this opinion as absurd, without even being willing to examine it—for no other reason than because they have been accustomed to attribute another freedom to God, far different from that we have taught (D7), viz. an absolute will. But I also have no doubt that, if they are willing to reflect on the matter, and consider properly the chain of our demonstrations, in the end they will utterly reject the freedom they now attribute to God, not only as futile, but as a great obstacle to science. Nor is it necessary for me to repeat here what I said in P17S.

Nevertheless, to please them, I shall show that even if it is conceded that will pertains to God's essence,[67] it still follows from his perfection that things could have been created by God in no other way or order. It will be easy to show this if we consider, first, what they themselves concede, viz. that it depends on God's decree and will alone that each thing is what it is. For otherwise God would not be the cause of all things. Next, that all God's decrees have been established by God himself from eternity. For otherwise he would be convicted of imperfection and inconstancy. But since, in eternity, there is neither *when*, nor *before*, nor *after*, it follows, from God's perfection alone, that he can never decree anything different, and never could have, *or* that God was not before his decrees, and cannot be without them.

But they will say that even if it were supposed that God had made another nature of things, or that from eternity he had decreed something else concerning nature and its order, no imperfection in God would follow from that.

Still, if they say this, they will concede at the same time that God can change his decrees. For if God had decreed, concerning nature and its order, something other than what he did decree, i.e., had willed and conceived something else concerning nature, he would necessarily have had an intellect other than he now has, and a will other than he now has. And if it is permitted to attribute to God another intellect and another will, without any change of his essence and of his perfection, why can he not now change his decrees concerning

---

[67] Again it must be emphasized that (as in P17S) Spinoza is here discussing only what follows from an assumption of his opponents which he rejects. (Curley 3, 158, requires correction on this point, as De Dijn noted.) Apparent passages to the contrary in the *Metaphysical Thoughts* (e.g., I/261, 264) must be counted among those in which Spinoza is merely expounding Descartes. Cf. the note to II/71/32.

created things, and nevertheless remain equally perfect? For his intellect and will concerning created things and their order are the same in respect to his essence and his perfection, however his will and intellect may be conceived.

30   Further, all the Philosophers I have seen concede that in God there is no potential intellect,[68] but only an actual one. But since his intellect and his will are not distinguished from his essence, as they all also concede, it follows that if God had had another actual intellect, and

35   another will, his essence would also necessarily be other. And there-

II/76   fore (as I inferred at the beginning) if things had been produced by God otherwise than they now are, God's intellect and his will, i.e. (as is conceded), his essence, would have to be different [NS: from what it now is]. And this is absurd.

    Therefore, since things could have been produced by God in no

5   other way, and no other order, and since it follows from God's supreme perfection that this is true, no truly sound reason can persuade us to believe that God did not will to create all the things that are in his intellect, with that same perfection with which he understands them.

    But they will say that there is no perfection or imperfection in things;

10   what is in them, on account of which they are perfect or imperfect, and are called good or bad,[69] depends only on God's will. And so, if God had willed, he could have brought it about that what is now perfection would have been the greatest imperfection, and conversely [NS: that what is now an imperfection in things would have been the

15   most perfect]. How would this be different from saying openly that God, who necessarily understands what he wills, can bring it about by his will that he understands things in another way than he does understand them? As I have just shown, this is a great absurdity.

    So I can turn the argument against them in the following way. All

20   things depend on God's power. So in order for things to be able to be different, God's will would necessarily also have to be different. But God's will cannot be different (as we have just shown most evidently from God's perfection). So things also cannot be different.

    I confess that this opinion,[70] which subjects all things to a certain

25   indifferent will of God, and makes all things depend on his good pleasure, is nearer the truth than that of those who maintain that God does all things for the sake of the good. For they seem to place something outside God, which does not depend on God, to which God attends,

---

[68] Cf. Aquinas 1, Ia, 3, 1, and Descartes, Third Meditation, AT VII, 47.

[69] NS: "on account of which they are called perfect or imperfect, good or bad."

[70] Cf. Descartes, Sixth Replies, AT VII, 435-436, and the *Short Treatise* (I/38/11).

0 as a model, in what he does, and at which he aims, as at a certain
goal. This is simply to subject God to fate. Nothing more absurd can
be maintained about God, whom we have shown to be the first and
only free cause, both of the essence of all things, and of their existence. So I shall waste no time in refuting this absurdity.

5 P34: *God's power is his essence itself.*

I/77 Dem.: For from the necessity alone of God's essence it follows that
God is the cause of himself (by P11) and (by P16 and P16C) of all
things. Therefore, God's power, by which he and all things are and
act, is his essence itself, q.e.d.

P35: *Whatever we conceive to be in God's power, necessarily exists.*

Dem.: For whatever is in God's power must (by P34) be so comprehended by his essence that it necessarily follows from it, and there-
9 fore necessarily exists, q.e.d.

P36: *Nothing exists from whose nature some effect does not follow.*

5 Dem: Whatever exists expresses the nature, *or* essence of God in a
certain and determinate way (by P25C), i.e. (by P34), whatever exists
expresses in a certain and determinate way the power of God, which
is the cause of all things. So (by P16), from [NS: everything that
exists] some effect must follow, q.e.d.

APPENDIX

With these [demonstrations] I have explained God's nature and properties: that he exists necessarily; that he is unique; that he is and acts
from the necessity alone of his nature; that (and how) he is the free
cause of all things; that all things are in God and so depend on him
that without him they can neither be nor be conceived; and finally,
that all things have been predetermined by God, not from freedom of
the will *or* absolute good pleasure, but from God's absolute nature, *or*
infinite power.

Further, I have taken care, whenever the occasion arose, to remove
prejudices that could prevent my demonstrations from being perceived. But because many prejudices remain that could, and can, be
a great obstacle to men's understanding the connection of things in
the way I have explained it, I considered it worthwhile to submit them
78 here to the scrutiny of reason. All the prejudices I here undertake to
expose depend on this one: that men commonly suppose that all natural things act, as men do, on account of an end; indeed, they maintain as certain that God himself directs all things to some certain end,

439

5   for they say that God has made all things for man, and man that he might worship God.

So I shall begin by considering this one prejudice, asking *first* [I] why most people are satisfied that it is true, and why all are so inclined by nature to embrace it. *Then* [II] I shall show its falsity, and

10   *finally* [III] how, from this, prejudices have arisen concerning *good* and *evil, merit* and *sin, praise* and *blame, order* and *confusion, beauty* and *ugliness*, and other things of this kind.[71]

[I.] Of course this is not the place to deduce these things from the nature of the human mind. It will be sufficient here if I take as a

15   foundation what everyone must acknowledge: that all men are born ignorant of the causes of things, and that they all want to seek their own advantage, and are conscious of this appetite.

From these [assumptions] it follows, *first*, that men think themselves free, because they are conscious of their volitions and their appetite, and do not think, even in their dreams, of the causes by which they

20   are disposed to wanting and willing, because they are ignorant of [those causes]. It follows, *secondly*, that men act always on account of an end, viz. on account of their advantage, which they want. Hence they seek to know only the final causes of what has been done, and when they have heard them, they are satisfied, because they have no reason to

25   doubt further. But if they cannot hear them from another, nothing remains for them but to turn toward themselves, and reflect on the ends by which they are usually determined to do such things; so they necessarily judge the temperament of other men from their own temperament.

Furthermore, they find—both in themselves and outside them-

30   selves—many means that are very helpful in seeking their own advantage, e.g., eyes for seeing, teeth for chewing, plants and animals for food, the sun for light, the sea for supporting fish [NS: and so with almost all other things whose natural causes they have no reason to

35   doubt].[72] Hence, they consider all natural things as means to their own advantage. And knowing that they had found these means, not provided them for themselves, they had reason to believe that there was someone else who had prepared those means for their use. For after

II/79 they considered things as means, they could not believe that the things

---

[71] Wolfson's discussion of medieval doctrines concerning final causes (1, 1:422-440) is useful background to this appendix. But Gueroult is surely right to argue (1, 1:398-400) that Spinoza's antifinalism, while owing much to Descartes, is, in the end, directed against him as well as the scholastics.

[72] What Gebhardt adds here from the NS, Akkerman (2, 161) regards as a translator's gloss, though it seems to me to go beyond the sort of thing one would expect from Balling.

had made themselves; but from the means they were accustomed to prepare for themselves, they had to infer that there was a ruler, or a number of rulers of nature, endowed with human freedom, who had taken care of all things for them, and made all things for their use.

And since they had never heard anything about the temperament of these rulers, they had to judge it from their own. Hence, they maintained that the Gods direct all things for the use of men in order to bind men to them and be held by men in the highest honor. So it has happened that each of them has thought up from his own temperament different ways of worshipping God, so that God might love them above all the rest, and direct the whole of Nature according to the needs of their blind desire and insatiable greed. Thus this prejudice was changed into superstition, and struck deep roots in their minds. This was why each of them strove with great diligence to understand and explain the final causes of all things.

But while they sought to show that nature does nothing in vain (i.e., nothing which is not of use to men), they seem to have shown only that nature and the Gods are as mad as men. See, I ask you, how the matter has turned out in the end! Among so many conveniences in nature they had to find many inconveniences: storms, earthquakes, diseases, etc. These, they maintain, happen because the Gods [NS: (whom they judge to be of the same nature as themselves)][73] are angry on account of wrongs done to them by men, *or* on account of sins committed in their worship. And though their daily experience contradicted this, and though infinitely many examples showed that conveniences and inconveniences happen indiscriminately to the pious and the impious alike, they did not on that account give up their long-standing prejudice. It was easier for them to put this among the other unknown things, whose use they were ignorant of, and so remain in the state of ignorance in which they had been born, than to destroy that whole construction, and think up a new one.

So they maintained it as certain that the judgments of the Gods far surpass man's grasp. This alone, of course, would have caused the truth to be hidden from the human race to eternity, if Mathematics, which is concerned not with ends, but only with the essences and properties of figures, had not shown men another standard of truth. And besides Mathematics, we can assign other causes also (which it is unnecessary to enumerate here), which were able to bring it about that men [NS:—but very few, in relation to the whole human race—][74]

[73] What Gebhardt adds here from the NS, Akkerman (2, 161) regards as a translator's gloss.
[74] What Gebhardt adds here from the NS, Akkerman (2, 161) suggests may be a

II/80 would notice these common prejudices and be led to the true knowledge of things.

[II.] With this I have sufficiently explained what I promised in the first place [viz. why men are so inclined to believe that all things act' for an end]. Not many words will be required now to show that Nature has no end set before it, and that all final causes are nothing but
5 human fictions. For I believe I have already sufficiently established it, both by the foundations and causes from which I have shown this prejudice to have had its origin, and also by P16, P32C1 and C2, and all those [propositions] by which I have shown that all things proceed by a certain eternal necessity of nature, and with the greatest perfection.
10 I shall, however, add this: this doctrine concerning the end turns nature completely upside down. For what is really a cause, it considers as an effect, and conversely [NS: what is an effect it considers as a cause]. What is by nature prior, it makes posterior. And finally, what is supreme and most perfect, it makes imperfect.
15 For—to pass over the first two, since they are manifest through themselves—as has been established in PP21-23, that effect is most perfect which is produced immediately by God, and the more something requires intermediate causes to produce it, the more imperfect it is. But if the things which have been produced immediately by God
20 had been made so that God would achieve his end, then the last things, for the sake of which the first would have been made, would be the most excellent of all.

Again, this doctrine takes away God's perfection. For if God acts for the sake of an end, he necessarily wants something which he lacks. And though the Theologians and Metaphysicians distinguish between
25 an end of need and an end of assimilation,[75] they nevertheless confess that God did all things for his own sake, not for the sake of the things to be created. For before creation they can assign nothing except God

---

comment by Balling, "who thinks most people stupid." Akkerman is no doubt thinking of the gloss at 81/20, which probably is due to Balling. But the comment here seems to say no more than that few men are able to see common prejudices for what they are and rise above them, and that seems to be a genuinely Spinozistic view. Cf. the Preface to the TTP, III/5-6, 12. If we ascribe this line to Spinoza, we need not imagine that he deliberately omitted it in revising his first draft. If it was Spinoza's own copy of Balling's translation that Glazemaker used in compiling the NS, Spinoza may have added the line to the translation without adding it to the text, through some oversight.

[75] As Wolfson points out (1, 1:432), the distinction is to be found (among other places) in Heereboord's *Meletemata* where it is explained that in acting for the sake of an end of assimilation God acts for the benefit of other things which are outside him and are made to be like him. Heereboord does also concede there that God has done all things for his own sake.

for whose sake God would act. And so they are necessarily compelled to confess that God lacked those things for the sake of which he willed to prepare means, and that he desired them. This is clear through itself.

Nor ought we here to pass over the fact that the Followers of this doctrine, who have wanted to show off their cleverness in assigning the ends of things, have introduced—to prove this doctrine of theirs—a new way of arguing: by reducing things, not to the impossible, but to ignorance. This shows that no other way of defending their doctrine was open to them.

For example, if a stone has fallen from a roof onto someone's head and killed him, they will show, in the following way, that the stone fell in order to kill the man. For if it did not fall to that end, God willing it, how could so many circumstances have concurred by chance (for often many circumstances do concur at once)? Perhaps you will answer that it happened because the wind was blowing hard and the man was walking that way. But they will persist: why was the wind blowing hard at that time? why was the man walking that way at that same time? If you answer again that the wind arose then because on the preceding day, while the weather was still calm, the sea began to toss, and that the man had been invited by a friend, they will press on—for there is no end to the questions which can be asked: but why was the sea tossing? why was the man invited at just that time? And so they will not stop asking for the causes of causes until you take refuge in the will of God, i.e., the sanctuary of ignorance.

Similarly, when they see the structure of the human body, they are struck by a foolish wonder, and because they do not know the causes of so great an art, they infer that it is constructed, not by mechanical, but by divine, or supernatural art, and constituted in such a way that one part does not injure another.[76]

Hence it happens that one who seeks the true causes of miracles, and is eager, like an educated man, to understand natural things, not to wonder at them, like a fool, is generally considered and denounced as an impious heretic by those whom the people honor as interpreters of nature and the Gods. For they know that if ignorance[77] is taken

---

[76] As Wolfson points out (1, 1:434-436), the argument of this paragraph goes back at least as far as Cicero's *De Natura Deorum* and was used in the Middle Ages by Maimonides (1, III, 19).

[77] Gebhardt here adds a phrase from the NS which would be translated: "or rather, stupidity." He takes it that Spinoza had omitted this phrase when revising his first draft, in order to avoid unnecessary offense. But as Akkerman (2, 97) points out, it is more likely that the translator was offering a double translation of a single Latin term, to heighten the effect of lines that strongly appealed to him. The translator uses other

away, then foolish wonder, the only means they have of arguing and defending their authority is also taken away. But I leave these things,[78] and pass on to what I have decided to treat here in the *third* place.

25   [III.] After men persuaded themselves that everything that happens, happens on their account, they had to judge that what is most important in each thing is what is most useful to them, and to rate as most excellent all those things by which they were most pleased. Hence, they had to form these notions, by which they explained natural things:

30   *good, evil, order, confusion, warm, cold, beauty, ugliness.* And because they thought themselves free, those notions have arisen: *praise* and *blame, sin* and *merit.* The latter I shall explain after I have treated human nature;[79] but the former I shall briefly explain here.

    Whatever conduces to health and the worship of God, they have

35   called *good;* but what is contrary to these, *evil.*

    And because those who do not understand the nature of things, but only imagine them, affirm nothing concerning things, and take the

II/82   imagination for the intellect, they firmly believe, in their ignorance of things and of their own nature, that there is an order in things. For when things are so disposed that, when they are presented to us through the senses, we can easily imagine them, and so can easily remember

5   them, we say that they are well-ordered;[80] but if the opposite is true, we say that they are badly ordered, or confused.

    And since those things we can easily imagine are especially pleasing to us, men prefer order to confusion, as if order were anything in nature more than a relation to our imagination. They also say that

10   God has created all things in order, and so, unknowingly attribute imagination to God—unless, perhaps, they mean that God, to provide

---

double translations in this passage without provoking Gebhardt to make the corresponding additions to the text (e.g., l. 19, *interpretes/tolken en verklaarders,* l. 20, *stupor/verwondering of verbaasdheid*). Is the addition consistent with Spinoza's thought elsewhere? Akkerman notes that it is "familiar humanistic ground" that philosophers try to raise people out of their ignorance and that priests see their authority threatened by this. But does Spinoza think the people are not merely ignorant but stupid? Akkerman appeals to TTP, VII, 27 (III/319-20) to show that he does not.

  [78] Gebhardt here adds, as if it were something omitted in the Latin, what is surely (cf. Akkerman 2, 164) a translator's gloss on this first clause: "But I leave it to them to judge what force there is in such reasoning." Since Gebhardt also gives, as part of the text, the Latin which the Dutch glosses, his text is redundant.

  [79] NS: "the human mind." Akkerman (2, 169) thinks that this variation may, in fact, stem from Spinoza's altering the text after it had been translated, and that this may be a survival of the period in which Spinoza conceived the *Ethics* as having a tripartite structure (I. On God, II. On the mind, III. On human nature). The topics referred to are treated in IVP37S2 as things presently stand.

  [80] In the NS this passage is translated: "we say that they are in good order, or in order." Gebhardt assumes that something has been omitted in revision, but probably this is no more than a double translation. Cf. Akkerman 2, 88.

for human imagination, has disposed all things so that men can very easily imagine them. Nor will it, perhaps, give them pause that infinitely many things are found which far surpass our imagination, and a great many which confuse it on account of its weakness. But enough of this.

The other notions are also nothing but modes of imagining, by which the imagination is variously affected; and yet the ignorant consider them the chief attributes of things, because, as we have already said, they believe all things have made for their sake, and call the nature of a thing good or evil, sound or rotten and corrupt, as they are affected by it. For example, if the motion the nerves receive from objects presented through the eyes is conducive to health, the objects by which it is caused are called beautiful; those which cause a contrary motion are called ugly. Those which move the sense through the nose, they call pleasant-smelling or stinking; through the tongue, sweet or bitter, tasty or tasteless; through touch, hard or soft, rough or smooth, etc.; and finally, those which move the ears are said to produce noise, sound or harmony. Men have been so mad as to believe that God is pleased by harmony. Indeed there are Philosophers who have persuaded themselves that the motions of the heavens produce a harmony.

All of these things show sufficiently that each one has judged things according to the disposition of his brain; or rather, has accepted affections of the imagination as things. So it is no wonder (to note this, too, in passing) that we find so many controversies to have arisen among men, and that they have finally given rise to Skepticism. For although human bodies agree in many things, they still differ in very many. And for that reason what seems good to one, seems bad to another; what seems ordered to one, seems confused to another; what seems pleasing to one, seems displeasing to another, and so on.

I pass over the [other notions] here, both because this is not the place to treat them at length, and because everyone has experienced this [variability] sufficiently for himself. That is why we have such sayings as "So many heads, so many attitudes," "everyone finds his own judgment more than enough," and "there are as many differences of brains as of palates." These proverbs show sufficiently that men judge things according to the disposition of their brain, and imagine, rather than understand them. For if men had understood them, the things would at least convince them all, even if they did not attract them all, as the example of mathematics shows.

We see, therefore, that all the notions by which ordinary people are accustomed to explain nature are only modes of imagining, and do not

445

indicate the nature of anything, only the constitution of the imagination. And because they have names, as if they were [notions] of beings existing outside the imagination, I call them beings, not of reason, but of imagination. So all the arguments in which people try to use such notions against us can easily be warded off.

For many are accustomed to arguing in this way: if all things have followed from the necessity of God's most perfect nature, why are there so many imperfections in nature? why are things corrupt to the point where they stink? so ugly that they produce nausea? why is there confusion, evil, and sin?

As I have just said, those who argue in this way are easily answered. For the perfection of things is to be judged solely from their nature and power; things are not more or less perfect because they please or offend men's senses, or because they are of use to, or are incompatible with, human nature.

But to those who ask "why God did not create all men so that they would be governed by the command of reason?" I answer only "because he did not lack material to create all things, from the highest degree of perfection to the lowest;" or, to speak more properly, "because the laws of his nature have been so ample that they sufficed for producing all things which can be conceived by an infinite intellect" (as I have demonstrated in P16).

These are the prejudices I undertook to note here. If any of this kind still remain, they can be corrected by anyone with only a little meditation. [NS: And so I find no reason to devote more time to these matters, etc.][81]

II/84

Second Part of the Ethics
On the Nature and Origin
of the Mind

I pass now to explaining those things which must necessarily follow from the essence of God, or the infinite and eternal Being—not, indeed, all of them, for we have demonstrated (IP16) that infinitely many things must follow from it in infinitely many modes, but only those that can lead us, by the hand, as it were, to the knowledge of the human Mind and its highest blessedness.

[81] This concluding formula, which Gebhardt adds from the NS, Akkerman (2, 161) attributes to the translator.

Definitions

D1: By body I understand a mode that in a certain and determinate way expresses God's essence insofar as he is considered as an extended thing (see IP25C).

D2: I say that to the essence of any thing belongs that which, being given, the thing is [NS: also] necessarily posited and which, being taken away, the thing is necessarily [NS: also] taken away; or that without which the thing can neither be nor be conceived, and which can neither be nor be conceived without the thing.[1]

D3: By idea I understand a concept of the Mind that the Mind forms because it is a thinking thing.

Exp.: *I say concept rather than perception, because the word perception seems to indicate that the Mind is acted on by the object. But concept seems to express an action of the Mind.*

D4: By adequate idea I understand an idea which, insofar as it is considered in itself, without relation to an object, has all the properties, *or* intrinsic denominations of a true idea.

Exp.: *I say intrinsic to exclude what is extrinsic, viz. the agreement of the idea with its object.*

D5: Duration is an indefinite continuation of existing.

Exp.: *I say indefinite because it cannot be determined at all through the very nature of the existing thing, nor even by the efficient cause, which necessarily posits the existence of the thing, and does not take it away.*

D6: By reality and perfection I understand the same thing.

D7: By singular things I understand things that are finite and have a determinate existence. And if a number of Individuals[2] so concur in one action that together they are all the cause of one effect, I consider them all, to that extent, as one singular thing.

Axioms

A1: The essence of man does not involve necessary existence, i.e., from the order of nature it can happen equally that this or that man does exist, or that he does not exist.

---

[1] Spinoza's conception of essence is stricter than the Cartesian conception he expounds in *Descartes' Principles* IIA2 (I/183). His reason for not defining essence so broadly is given in P10CS (II/93/20-94/12).
[2] What Gebhardt adds here from the NS (which might be translated: "or singulars") is probably only a double translation.

25 A2: Man thinks.[3]

II/86 A3: There are no modes of thinking, such as love, desire, or whatever is designated by the word affects of the mind, unless there is in the same Individual[4] the idea of the thing loved, desired, etc. But there can be an idea, even though there is no other mode of thinking.

5 A4: We feel that a certain body[5] is affected in many ways.

A5: We neither feel nor perceive any singular things [NS: or anything of *natura naturata*],[6] except bodies and modes of thinking. *See the postulates after P13.*

10 P1: *Thought is an attribute of God,* or *God is a thinking thing.*

Dem.: Singular thoughts, *or* this or that thought, are modes that express God's nature in a certain and determinate way (by IP25C). 15 Therefore (by ID5) there belongs to God an attribute whose concept all singular thoughts involve, and through which they are also conceived. Therefore, Thought is one of God's infinite attributes, which expresses an eternal and infinite essence of God (see ID6), *or* God is a thinking thing, q.e.d.

20 Schol.: This Proposition is also evident from the fact that we can conceive an infinite thinking being. For the more things a thinking being can think, the more reality, *or* perfection, we conceive it to contain. Therefore, a being that can think infinitely many things in 25 infinitely many ways is necessarily infinite in its power of thinking. So since we can conceive an infinite Being by attending to thought alone, Thought (by ID4 and D6) is necessarily one of God's infinite attributes, as we maintained.

---

[3] What Gebhardt adds here from the NS (which may be translated: "or, to put it differently, we know that we think") he regards as a gloss from the first draft which Spinoza later suppressed because it "limited" his teaching. But as Akkerman contends (2, 97-100, 145-146), it is hard to see what limitation is involved and it is clear that the gloss goes well beyond what we might expect of the translator. Akkerman ingeniously suggests that members of the Amsterdam Spinoza circle, some of whom probably studied a draft of EI-II in Balling's Dutch translation in 1663-1664, may have added these words to their copy of the ms., as their own interpretation of the axiom, inspired perhaps by Glazemaker's translation of Descartes' *Principles of Philosophy* I, 8. Glazemaker ends that section with these very words, since he follows Picot's French version of the *Principles*, which amplifies the Latin at this point. When Jelles and Rieuwertsz put Balling's early translation of EI-II at Glazemaker's disposal in compiling the NS, Glazemaker did not suspect that these words were not Spinoza's, but his own (ultimately, Picot's). Akkerman does allow that Spinoza may, at some stage, have seen and approved the gloss.

[4] The NS adds: "or in the same man." But this is probably only a double translation, as at 85/17.

[5] NS: "our body."

[6] What Gebhardt adds from the NS, Akkerman (2, 161) regards as a translator's gloss.

P2: *Extension is an attribute of God,* or *God is an extended thing.*

Dem: The demonstration of this proceeds in the same way as that of the preceding Proposition.

P3: *In God there is necessarily an idea, both of his essence and of everything that necessarily follows from his essence.*

Dem.: For God (by P1) can think infinitely many things in infinitely many modes, *or* (what is the same, by IP16) can form the idea of his essence and of all the things which necessarily follow from it. But whatever is in God's power necessarily exists (by IP35); therefore, there is necessarily such an idea, and (by IP15) it is only in God, q.e.d.

Schol.: By God's power ordinary people understand God's free will and his right over all things which are, things which on that account are commonly considered to be contingent. For they say that God has the power of destroying all things and reducing them to nothing. Further, they very often compare God's power with the power of Kings.[7]

But we have refuted this in IP32C1 and C2, and we have shown in IP16 that God acts with the same necessity by which he understands himself, i.e., just as it follows from the necessity of the divine nature (as everyone maintains unanimously) that God understands himself, with the same necessity it also follows that God does infinitely many things in infinitely many modes. And then we have shown in IP34 that God's power is nothing except God's active essence. And so it is as impossible for us to conceive that God does not act as it is to conceive that he does not exist.

Again, if it were agreeable to pursue these matters further, I could also show here that that power which ordinary people fictitiously ascribe to God is not only human (which shows that ordinary people conceive God as a man, or as like a man), but also involves lack of power. But I do not wish to speak so often about the same topic. I only ask the reader to reflect repeatedly on what is said concerning this matter in Part I, from P16 to the end. For no one will be able to perceive rightly the things I maintain unless he takes great care not to confuse God's power with the human power or right of Kings.

P4: *God's idea, from which infinitely many things follow in infinitely many modes, must be unique.*

Dem.: An infinite intellect comprehends nothing except God's attributes and his affections (by IP30). But God is unique (by IP14C1).

---

[7] It is not, of course, only 'ordinary people' who make this comparison, but also philosophers like Descartes (cf. the letter to Mersenne, 15 April 1630).

449

Therefore God's idea, from which infinitely many things follow in infinitely many modes, must be unique, q.e.d.

P5: *The formal being of ideas admits God as a cause only insofar as he is considered as a thinking thing, and not insofar as he is explained by any other attribute. I.e., ideas, both of God's attributes and of singular things, admit not the objects themselves, or the things perceived, as their efficient cause, but God himself, insofar as he is a thinking thing.*

Dem.: This is evident from P3. For there we inferred that God can form the idea of his essence, and of all the things that follow necessarily from it, solely from the fact that God is a thinking thing, and not from the fact that he is the object of his own idea. So the formal being of ideas admits God as its cause insofar[8] as he is a thinking thing.

But another way of demonstrating this is the following. The formal being of ideas is a mode of thinking (as is known through itself), i.e. (by IP25C), a mode that expresses, in a certain way, God's nature insofar as he is a thinking thing. And so (by IP10) it involves the concept of no other attribute of God, and consequently (by IA4) is the effect of no other attribute than thought. And so the formal being of ideas admits God as its cause insofar as he is considered only as a thinking thing, etc., q.e.d.

P6: *The modes of each attribute have God for their cause only insofar as he is considered under the attribute of which they are modes, and not insofar as he is considered under any other attribute.*

Dem.: For each attribute is conceived through itself without any other (by IP10). So the modes of each attribute involve the concept of their own attribute, but not of another one; and so (by IA4) they have God for their cause only insofar as he is considered under the attribute of which they are modes, and not insofar as he is considered under any other, q.e.d.

Cor.: From this it follows that the formal being of things which are not modes of thinking does not follow from the divine nature because [God] has first known the things; rather the objects of ideas follow and are inferred from their attributes[9] in the same way and by the same

---

[8] Various editors have proposed emending this to read: ". . . only insofar. . . ." Gebhardt points out that the text of the OP is supported by the NS, and very probably Spinoza's manuscript did read the way Gebhardt has it. But the emenders are probably true to the spirit of the text, if not its letter. Similarly at ll. 19 and 29.

[9] Spinoza is not very explicit on this point in the *Ethics*, but it seems from other works that we are to assume a distinct idea in thought for every mode of every other attribute, with the result that the attribute of thought appears to be 'more extensive' than the other attributes. See Letter 66 and the Short Treatise (I/119). For comment, see Pollock, 159-163; Joachim 1, 134-138; Curley 3, 147-151; Gueroult 1, 2:45-46, 78-84, 91-92.

necessity as that with which we have shown ideas to follow from the attribute of Thought.

P7: *The order and connection of ideas is the same as the order and connection of things.*

Dem.: This is clear from IA4. For the idea of each thing caused depends on the knowledge of the cause of which it is the effect.

Cor.: From this it follows that God's [NS: actual] power of thinking is equal to his actual power of acting. I.e., whatever follows formally from God's infinite nature follows objectively in God from his idea in the same order and with the same connection.

Schol.: Before we proceed further, we must recall here what we showed [NS: in the First Part], viz. that whatever can be perceived by an infinite intellect as constituting an[10] essence of substance pertains to one substance only, and consequently that the thinking substance and the extended substance are one and the same substance, which is now comprehended under this attribute, now under that. So also a mode of extension and the idea of that mode are one and the same thing, but expressed in two ways. Some of the Hebrews[11] seem to have seen this, as if through a cloud, when they maintained that God, God's intellect, and the things understood by him are one and the same.

For example, a circle existing in nature and the idea of the existing circle, which is also in God, are one and the same thing, which is explained through different attributes. Therefore, whether we conceive nature under the attribute of Extension, or under the attribute of Thought, or under any other attribute, we shall find one and the same order, *or* one and the same connection of causes, i.e., that the same things follow one another.[12]

When I said [NS: before] that God is the cause of the idea, say of a circle, only insofar as he is a thinking thing, and [the cause] of the circle, only insofar as he is an extended thing, this was for no other reason than because the formal being of the idea of the circle can be perceived only through another mode of thinking, as its proximate

---

[10] Most translators (e.g., Elwes, White, Auerbach, Meijer, and Caillois) supply a definite article here. But Appuhn's use of the indefinite article deserves consideration at least. Cf. above at II/45/24-25. The NS use no article at all here.

[11] Wolfson (1, 2:26) cites Maimonides 1, I, 68, and Gueroult (1, 2:85) adds that the doctrine was also held by Christian Aristotelians like Aquinas (1, Ia, 18, 14). But of course these philosophers would have understood the doctrine very differently from the way Spinoza does, as he himself implies.

[12] The NS here adds: "in the same way." But this is probably a translator's gloss, as is what Gebhardt adds from the NS in the next line. The latter addition correctly refers back to P6, but the former is only dubiously correct (cf. 1. 9).

cause, and that mode again through another, and so on, to infinity. Hence, so long as things are considered as modes of thinking, we must explain the order of the whole of nature, *or* the connection of causes, through the attribute of Thought alone. And insofar as they are considered as modes of Extension, the order of the whole of nature must be explained through the attribute of Extension alone. I understand the same concerning the other attributes.

So of things as they are in themselves, God is really the cause insofar as he consists of infinite attributes. For the present, I cannot explain these matters more clearly.[13]

P8: *The ideas of singular things, or of modes, that do not exist must be comprehended in God's infinite idea in the same way as the formal essences of the singular things, or modes, are contained in God's attributes.*

Dem.: This Proposition is evident from the preceding one, but is understood more clearly from the preceding scholium.

Cor.: From this it follows that so long as singular things do not exist, except insofar as they are comprehended in God's attributes, their objective being, *or* ideas, do not exist except insofar as God's infinite idea exists. And when singular things are said to exist, not only insofar as they are comprehended in God's attributes, but insofar also as they are said to have duration, their ideas also involve the existence through which they are said to have duration.

Schol.: If anyone wishes me to explain this further by an example, I will, of course, not be able to give one which adequately explains what I speak of here, since it is unique. Still I shall try as far as possible to illustrate the matter:[14] the circle is of such a nature that the rectangles formed from the segments of all the straight lines intersecting in it are equal to one another.[15] So in a circle there are contained infinitely many rectangles that are equal to one another. Nevertheless, none of them can be said to exist except insofar as the circle exists,

---

[13] Gueroult (1, 2:87) suggests that IIP21S and IIIP2S should be viewed as offering the further explanation hinted at here, since they apply this scholium to the case of the relation between mind and body.

[14] The NS translator renders *illustrare* (here translated by "illustrate"): "explain with an example." Akkerman (2, 87) finds this an unhappy choice given the opening sentence of the scholium, and suggests "clarify." I would take what follows as an example which explains the matter imperfectly, i.e., an analogy. In any case, Gebhardt's assumption that a phrase has been omitted from the Latin text is clearly wrong.

[15] This is theorem 35, Book III, of Euclid's *Elements*, which is more easily stated if we add to Spinoza's diagram some letters he does not use. If AC and FG are any two lines intersecting at a point B in a circle, then the rectangle with base AB and height BC is equal in area to that with base BG and height BF.

452

nor also can the idea of any of these rectangles be said to exist except insofar as it is comprehended in the idea of the circle. Now of these infinitely many [rectangles] let two only, viz. [those formed from the segments of lines][16] D and E, exist. Of course their ideas also exist now, not only insofar as they are only comprehended in the idea of the circle, but also insofar as they involve the existence of those rectangles. By this they are distinguished from the other ideas of the other rectangles.

P9: *The idea of a singular thing which actually exists has God for a cause not insofar as he is infinite,[17] but insofar as he is considered to be affected by another idea of a singular thing which actually exists; and of this [idea] God is also the cause, insofar as he is affected by another third [NS: idea], and so on, to infinity.*

Dem.: The idea of a singular thing which actually exists is a singular mode of thinking, and distinct from the others (by P8C and S), and so (by P6) has God for a cause only insofar as he is a thinking thing. But not (by IP28) insofar as he is a thing thinking absolutely;[18] rather insofar as he is considered to be affected by another [NS: determinate] mode of thinking.[19] And God is also the cause of this mode, insofar as he is affected by another [NS: determinate mode of thinking], and so on, to infinity. But the order and connection of ideas (by P7) is the same as the order and connection of causes.[20] Therefore, the cause of one singular idea is another idea, *or* God, insofar as he is considered to be affected by another idea; and of this also [God is the cause], insofar as he is affected by another, and so on, to infinity, q.e.d.

[16] I think Baensch and Meijer have understood this passage more accurately than Gebhardt, whose appeal to the NS (cf. II/358-359) is indecisive.

[17] Gueroult (1, 2:544-545) takes the phrase "God . . . insofar as he is infinite" to be ambiguous between "the attribute" (as opposed to its infinity of finite modes) and "the infinite mode" or "the infinite chain of singular things" (as opposed to a finite part of the infinite mode, or individual member of the infinite chain). But this seems to rest partly on a doubtful reading of IIP40D, q.v.

[18] Gueroult (1, 2:135) suggests that the qualification "absolute," applied to God's thought (God as the Thinking Thing, or attribute of Thought) implies that it is thought without an object.

[19] Here and in l. 10 the NS translation is more explicit than the OP. No doubt Akkerman is right (2, 165) to say, contrary to Gebhardt, that there is no question here of two drafts. But the translator's gloss is clearly correct and helpful, as a comparison with IP28 will show. Gebhardt, contrary to his usual practice, translates his additions to the text into Latin, relying on the marginalia. But the variance from the wording of P28 seems to confirm that the author of the marginalia is working simply from the Dutch and not consulting a Latin original.

[20] NS: "connection of things." This corresponds more closely to the actual wording of P7.

15   Cor.: Whatever happens in the singular object of any idea, there is knowledge of it in God, only insofar as he has the idea of the same object.

20   Dem.: Whatever happens in the object of any idea, there is an idea of it in God (by P3), not insofar as he is infinite, but insofar as he is considered to be affected by another idea of [NS: an existing] singular thing (by P9); but the order and connection of ideas (by P7) is the same as the order and connection of things; therefore, knowledge of

25   what happens in a singular object will be in God only insofar as he has the idea of the same object, q.e.d.

P10: *The being of substance does not pertain to the essence of man,*[21] *or substance does not constitute the form of man.*

30   Dem.: For the being of substance involves necessary existence (by IP7). Therefore, if the being of substance pertained to the essence of man, then substance being given, man would necessarily be given (by

II/93 | D2), and consequently man would exist necessarily, which (by A1) is absurd, q.e.d.

Schol.: This proposition is also demonstrated from IP5, viz. that

5   there are not two substances of the same nature. Since a number of men can exist,[22] what constitutes the form of man is not the being of substance. Further, this proposition is evident from the other properties of substance, viz. that substance is, by its nature, infinite, im-

10   mutable, indivisible, etc., as anyone can easily see.

Cor.: From this it follows that the essence of man is constituted by certain modifications of God's attributes.

15   Dem.: For the being of substance does not pertain to the essence of man (by P10). Therefore, it is something (by IP15) which is in God, and which can neither be nor be conceived without God, *or* (by IP25C) an affection, *or* mode, which expresses God's nature in a certain and determinate way.

20   Schol.: Everyone, of course, must concede that nothing can either be or be conceived without God. For all confess that God is the only

---

[21] Appuhn remarks that it is tempting to supply an indefinite article here, so as to conform better to the [presumed] requirements of Spinoza's nominalism. He resists the temptation on the grounds that the scholium of this proposition and IP8S both imply that there is a nature common to all men, and that Part IV would be incomprehensible without that assumption. For what it may be worth, the NS confirm this, reading *de mensch* (the use of the definite article is normal in Dutch when nouns are used abstractly or collectively). Cf. Gueroult 1, 2:103n.

[22] The NS add: "at the same time." Probably a translator's gloss, influenced by II/ 51/2, though it has less point here.

cause of all things, both of their essence and of their existence.[23] I.e., God is not only the cause of the coming to be of things, as they say, but also of their being.

But in the meantime many say that anything without which a thing can neither be nor be conceived pertains to the nature of the thing.[24] And so they believe either that the nature of God pertains to the essence of created things, or that created things can be or be conceived without God—or what is more certain, they are not sufficiently consistent.

The cause of this, I believe, was that they did not observe the [proper] order of Philosophizing.[25] For they believed that the divine nature, which they should have contemplated before all else (because it is prior both in knowledge and in nature) is last in the order of knowledge, and that the things that are called objects of the senses are prior to all. That is why, when they contemplated natural things, they thought of nothing less than they did of the divine nature; and when afterwards they directed their minds to contemplating the divine nature, they could think of nothing less than of their first fictions, on which they had built the knowledge of natural things, because these could not assist knowledge of the divine nature. So it is no wonder that they have generally contradicted themselves.

But I pass over this. For my intent here was only to give a reason[26] why I did not say that anything without which a thing can neither be nor be conceived pertains to its nature—viz. because singular things can neither be nor be conceived without God, and nevertheless, God does not pertain to their essence. But I have said that what necessarily constitutes the essence of a thing is that which, if it is given, the thing is posited, and if it is taken away, the thing is taken away, i.e., the essence is what the thing can neither be nor be conceived without,

[23] Cf. Descartes, Fifth Replies (AT VII, 369); Aquinas 1, Ia, 104, 1; and Gueroult 1, 1:333-334.

[24] Descartes is among those aimed at here. Cf. I/183.

[25] NS: "they did not keep to the right path to arrive at wisdom." This is reminiscent of Spinoza's criticism (through Meyer) of Descartes at I/132/31-33. But the immediate target must be the scholastics rather than Descartes, since for him the mind and God are prior to the objects of the senses in the order of knowledge.

[26] NS: "For my intent is not so much to contradict them as to give a reason. . . ." Gebhardt incorporates this in the text (without, however, deleting *tantùm*, "only"). This seems a clear case where the text of the OP is to be preferred. The NS version is liable to suggest that it was, in part, Spinoza's intention to contradict those whose errors he has just exposed. This is uncharacteristic, and no doubt Spinoza intended to avoid that suggestion. This seems to me a case in which it is more plausible to regard the NS as preserving a first draft which has subsequently been altered than as illustrating a translator's gloss (*pace* Akkerman 2, 161).

and vice versa, what can neither be nor be conceived without the thing.

P11: *The first thing that constitutes the actual being of a human Mind is*
15 *nothing but the idea of a singular thing which actually exists.*

Dem.: The essence of man (by P10C) is constituted by certain modes of God's attributes, viz. (by A2) by modes of thinking, of all of which (by A3) the idea is prior in nature, and when it is given, the other
20 modes (to which the idea is prior in nature) must be in the same individual (by A3).[27] And therefore an idea is the first thing that constitutes the being of a human Mind. But not the idea of a thing which does not exist. For then (by P8C) the idea itself could not be said to exist. Therefore, it will be the idea of a thing which actually exists.
25 But not of an infinite thing. For an infinite thing (by IP21 and 22) must always exist necessarily. But (by A1) it is absurd [that this idea should be of a necessarily existing object]. Therefore, the first thing that constitutes the actual being of a human Mind is the idea of a singular thing which actually exists, q.e.d.
30 Cor.: From this it follows that the human Mind is a part of the infinite intellect of God. Therefore, when we say that the human Mind perceives this or that, we are saying nothing but that God, not insofar as he is infinite, but insofar as he is explained through the nature of
II/95 the human Mind, *or* insofar as he constitutes the essence of the human Mind, has this or that idea; and when we say that God has this or that idea, not only insofar as he constitutes the nature of the human Mind, but insofar as he also has the idea of another thing together with the human Mind, then we say that the human Mind perceives
5 the thing only partially, *or* inadequately.

Schol.: Here, no doubt, my readers will come to a halt, and think of many things which will give them pause. For this reason I ask them
10 to continue on with me slowly, step by step, and to make no judgment on these matters until they have read through them all.

P12: *Whatever happens in the object of the idea constituting the human Mind must be perceived by the human Mind, or there will necessarily be an idea of*
15 *that thing in the Mind; i.e., if the object of the idea constituting a human*

---

[27] The NS here reads: "the other modes . . . must constitute one and the same thing with the idea." Akkerman (2, 165) comments: "The translation says that the *idea* and the *modi* necessarily following it form together an indivisible whole (an *individuum*). This is an interesting further specification of the Latin text, and certainly not the other way around, as Gebhardt implies!" Akkerman suggests that the NS variation reflects an explanation Spinoza gave his friends in the Amsterdam Spinoza circle. That they should have requested an explanation of this difficult demonstration "goes to show the high level of discussions" in the circle.

Mind is a body, nothing can happen in that body which is not perceived by the Mind.[28]

Dem.: For whatever happens in the object of any idea, the knowledge of that thing is necessarily in God (by P9C), insofar as he is considered to be affected by the idea of the same object, i.e. (by P11), insofar as he constitutes the mind of some thing. Therefore, whatever happens in the object of the idea constituting the human Mind, the knowledge of it is necessarily in God insofar as he constitutes the nature of the human Mind, i.e. (by P11C), knowledge of this thing will necessarily be in the Mind, *or* the Mind will perceive it, q.e.d.

Schol.: This Proposition is also evident, and more clearly understood from P7S, which you should consult.

P13: *The object of the idea constituting the human Mind is the Body,*[29] *or a certain mode of Extension which actually exists, and nothing else.*

Dem.: For if the object of the human Mind were not the Body, the ideas of the affections of the Body would not be in God (by P9C) insofar as he constituted our Mind, but insofar as he constituted the mind of another thing, i.e. (by P11C), the ideas of the affections of the Body would not be in our Mind; but (by A4) we have ideas of the affections of the body. Therefore, the object of the idea that constitutes the human Mind is the Body, and it (by P11) actually exists.

Next, if the object of the Mind were something else also, in addition to the Body, then since (by IP36) nothing exists from which there does not follow some effect, there would necessarily (by P12) be an idea in our Mind of some effect of it. But (by A5) there is no idea of it. Therefore, the object of our Mind is the existing Body and nothing else, q.e.d.

Cor.: From this it follows that man consists of a Mind and a Body, and that the human Body exists, as we are aware of it.[30]

Schol.: From these [propositions] we understand not only that the

---

[28] What Gebhardt adds here from the NS (which may be translated: "or without there being an idea of it in the mind.") is probably, as Akkerman suggests (2, 161) only a translator's gloss.

[29] The NS have the indefinite article here and throughout the demonstration, but most modern translators agree in supplying a definite article, and the reference to A4 in the demonstration seems to require this.

[30] OP: "& Corpus humanum, prout ipsum sentimus, existere"; NS: "en dat het menschelijk lighaam, gelijk wij het zelfde gewaar worden, wezentlijk is." Gueroult (1, 2:137) renders this in French as "le Corps humain existe pour autant que nous le sentons," "the human body exists insofar as we are aware of it," and rejects "comme" and "tel que" (which would correspond to 'as') on the ground that it is evident that in itself the body is not as it is represented to us by (bodily) sensation. This may be true, but it does not seem to me that Gueroult's rendering is justified by either the Latin or the Dutch.

25

30

human Mind is united to the Body, but also what should be understood by the union of Mind and Body. But no one will be able to understand it adequately, *or* distinctly, unless he first knows adequately the nature of our Body. For the things we have shown so far are completely general and do not pertain more to man than to other Individuals, all of which, though in different degrees, are nevertheless animate.[31] For of each thing there is necessarily an idea in God, of which God is the cause in the same way as he is of the idea of the human Body. And so, whatever we have said of the idea of the human Body must also be said of the idea of any thing.

II/97

5

10

15

However, we also cannot deny that ideas differ among themselves, as the objects themselves do, and that one is more excellent than the other, and contains more reality, just as the object of the one is more excellent than the object of the other and contains more reality. And so to determine what is the difference between the human Mind and the others, and how it surpasses them, it is necessary for us, as we have said, to know the nature of its object, i.e., of the human Body. I cannot explain this here, nor is that necessary for the things I wish to demonstrate. Nevertheless, I say this in general, that in proportion as a Body is more capable than others of doing many things at once, or being acted on in many ways at once, so its Mind is more capable than others of perceiving many things at once. And in proportion as the actions of a body depend more on itself alone, and as other bodies concur with it less in acting, so its mind is more capable of understanding distinctly. And from these [truths] we can know the excellence of one mind over the others, and also see the cause why we have only a completely confused knowledge of our Body, and many other things which I shall deduce from them in the following [propositions]. For this reason I have thought it worthwhile to explain and demonstrate these things more accurately. To do this it is necessary to premise a few things concerning the nature of bodies.

20

A1':[32] All bodies either move or are at rest.

A2': Each body moves now more slowly, now more quickly.

25

L1: *Bodies are distinguished from one another by reason of motion and rest, speed and slowness, and not by reason of substance.*

---

[31] This striking statement is open to very different interpretations. Cf. Wolfson 1, 2:58. Gueroult (1, 2:143-144, and 164-165) restricts its scope by understanding "individual" to apply only to the composite bodies of II/99/26ff.

[32] There are three propositions designated as "Axiom 1" in this part of the *Ethics*. I shall distinguish this one from the others as A1'; and similarly for the "Axiom 2" which follows.

Dem.: I suppose that the first part of this is known through itself. But that bodies are not distinguished by reason of substance is evident both from IP5 and from IP8. But it is more clearly evident from those things which are said in IP15S.

L2: *All bodies agree in certain things.*

Dem.: For all bodies agree in that they involve the concept of one and the same attribute (by D1), and in that they can move now more slowly, now more quickly, and absolutely, that now they move, now they are at rest.

L3: *A body which moves or is at rest must be determined to motion or rest by another body, which has also been determined to motion or rest by another, and that again by another, and so on, to infinity.*

Dem.: Bodies (by D1) are singular things which (by L1) are distinguished from one another by reason of motion and rest; and so (by IP28), each must be determined necessarily to motion or rest by another singular thing, viz. (by P6) by another body, which (by A1′) either moves or is at rest. But this body also (by the same reasoning) could not move or be at rest if it had not been determined by another to motion or rest, and this again (by the same reasoning) by another, and so on, to infinity, q.e.d.

Cor.: From this it follows that a body in motion moves until it is determined by another body to rest; and that a body at rest also remains at rest until it is determined to motion by another.

This is also known through itself. For when I suppose that body A, say, is at rest, and do not attend to any other body in motion, I can say nothing about body A except that it is at rest. If afterwards it happens that body A moves, that of course could not have come about from the fact that it was at rest. For from that nothing else could follow but that body A would be at rest.[33]

If, on the other hand, A is supposed to move, then as often as we attend only to A, we shall be able to affirm nothing concerning it except that it moves. If afterwards it happens that A is at rest, that of

---

[33] Spinoza's version of the principle of inertia here seems to be stated in terms which put him in direct opposition to Descartes' doctrine of continuous creation. In *Principles* I, 21, Descartes derives the need for God's continuous conservation from the fact that (the parts of time being independent of one another) it does not follow from our existing now that we shall also exist at the next moment (*in tempore proxime sequenti*), unless the same cause which first produced us reproduces us. Spinoza does not make it quite explicit that it follows from A's being at rest at one time that it will be at rest at a later time (unless some cause intervenes to initiate motion), since he puts it negatively—viz. *nothing else* follows. But cf. III P4-P8 and Gueroult 1, 2:152, on Spinoza's relation here to Descartes and Hobbes.

course also could not have come about from the motion it had. For from the motion nothing else could follow but that A would move. Therefore, it happens by a thing which was not in A, viz. by an external cause, by which [NS: the Body in motion, A] has been determined to rest.

A1″:[34] All modes by which a body is affected by another body follow both from the nature of the body affected and at the same time from the nature of the affecting body, so that one and the same body may be moved differently according to differences in the bodies moving it. And conversely, different bodies may be moved differently by one and the same body.

A2″: When a body in motion strikes against another which is at rest and cannot give way, then it is reflected, so that it continues to move, and the angle of the line of the reflected motion with the surface of the body at rest which it struck against will be equal to the angle which the line of the incident motion makes with the same surface.[35]

This will be sufficient concerning the simplest bodies, which are distinguished from one another only by motion and rest, speed and slowness. Now let us move up to composite bodies.

Definition: *When a number of bodies, whether of the same or of different size, are so constrained by other bodies that they lie upon one another, or if they so move, whether with the same degree or different degrees of speed, that they communicate their motions to each other in a certain fixed manner, we shall say that those bodies are united with one another and that they all together compose one body or Individual, which is distinguished from the others by this union of bodies.*

A3″: As the parts of an Individual, or composite body, lie upon one another over a larger or smaller surface, so they can be forced to change their position with more or less difficulty; and consequently the more or less will be the difficulty of bringing it about that the Individual changes its shape. And therefore the bodies whose parts lie upon one another over a large surface, I shall call *hard*; those whose parts lie upon one another over a small surface, I shall call *soft*; and finally those whose parts are in motion, I shall call *fluid*.

---

[34] Again I distinguish this "Axiom 1" from the others in this part by designating it A1″. Similarly for the following Axiom.

[35] On the importance of this Cartesian principle for Hobbes and Spinoza, see Gueroult 1, 2:155n.

L4: *If, of a body, or of an Individual, which is composed of a number of bodies, some are removed, and at the same time as many others of the same nature take their place, the [NS: body, or the] Individual will retain its nature, as before, without any change of its form.*

Dem.: For (by L1) bodies are not distinguished in respect to substance; what constitutes the form of the Individual consists [NS: only] in the union of the bodies (by the preceding definition). But this [NS: union] (by hypothesis) is retained even if a continual change of bodies occurs. Therefore, the Individual will retain its nature, as before, both in respect to substance, and in respect to mode, q.e.d.

L5: *If the parts composing an Individual become greater or less, but in such a proportion that they all keep the same ratio of motion and rest to each other as before, then the Individual will likewise retain its nature, as before, without any change of form.*

Dem.: The demonstration of this is the same as that of the preceding Lemma.

L6: *If certain bodies composing an Individual are compelled to alter the motion they have from one direction to another, but so that they can continue their motions and communicate them to each other in the same ratio as before, the Individual will likewise retain its nature, without any change of form.*

Dem.: This is evident through itself. For it is supposed that it retains everything which, in its definition, we said constitutes its form. [NS: See the Definition before L4.][36]

L7: *Furthermore, the Individual so composed retains its nature, whether it, as a whole, moves or is at rest, or whether it moves in this or that direction, so long as each part retains its motion, and communicates it, as before, to the others.*

Dem.: This [NS: also] is evident from the definition preceding L4.

Schol.: By this, then, we see how a composite Individual can be affected in many ways, and still preserve its nature. So far we have conceived an Individual which is composed only of bodies which are distinguished from one another only by motion and rest, speed and slowness, i.e., which is composed of the simplest bodies.[37] But if we should now conceive of another, composed of a number of Individuals of a different nature, we shall find that it can be affected in a great many other ways, and still preserve its nature. For since each part of

---

[36] As Akkerman suggests (2, 161), this addition is probably to be ascribed to the translator.

[37] On this, cf. Joachim 1, 83n, and Gueroult 1, 2:161-162.

5   it is composed of a number of bodies, each part will therefore (by L7) be able, without any change of its nature, to move now more slowly, now more quickly, and consequently communicate its motion more quickly or more slowly to the others.

But if we should further conceive a third kind of Individual, com-
10 posed [NS: of many individuals] of this second kind, we shall find that it can be affected in many other ways, without any change of its form. And if we proceed in this way to infinity, we shall easily conceive that the whole of nature is one Individual, whose parts, i.e., all bodies, vary in infinite ways, without any change of the whole Individual.[38]

If it had been my intention to deal expressly with body,[39] I ought
15 to have explained and demonstrated these things more fully. But I have already said that I intended something else, and brought these things forward only because I can easily deduce from them the things I have decided to demonstrate.

POSTULATES

20 I. The human Body is composed of a great many individuals of different natures, each of which is highly composite.

II. Some of the individuals of which the human Body is composed
25 are fluid, some soft, and others, finally are hard.

III. The individuals composing the human Body, and consequently, the human Body itself, are affected by external bodies in very many ways.

IV. The human Body, to be preserved, requires a great many other
30 bodies, by which it is, as it were, continually regenerated.

V. When a fluid part of the human Body is determined by an ex-
II/103 ternal body so that it frequently thrusts against a soft part [of the Body], it changes its surface and, as it were, impresses on [the soft part] certain traces of the external body striking against [the fluid part].

VI. The human Body can move and dispose external bodies in a
5   great many ways.

P14: *The human Mind is capable of perceiving a great many things, and is the more capable, the more its body can be disposed in a great many ways.*

10 Dem.: For the human Body (by Post. 3 and 6) is affected in a great many ways by external bodies, and is disposed to affect external bod-

---

[38] As various commentators have noted, we have here Spinoza's variation on the classic theme of macrocosm and microcosm. Cf. Wolfson 1, 2:7; Gueroult 1, 2:169; and Maimonides 1, I, Lxxii.

[39] Gebhardt's additions from the NS here are clearly no more than the translator's work. Cf. Akkerman 2, 161.

ies in a great many ways. But the human Mind must perceive everything which happens in the human body (by P12). Therefore, the
human Mind is capable of perceiving a great many things, and is the
more capable [, NS: as the human Body is more capable],[40] q.e.d.

P15: *The idea that constitutes the formal being* [esse] *of the human Mind is
not simple, but composed of a great many ideas.*
    Dem.: The idea that constitutes the formal being of the human
Mind is the idea of a body (by P13), which (by Post. 1) is composed
of a great many highly composite Individuals. But of each Individual
composing the body, there is necessarily (by P8C)[41] an idea in God.
Therefore (by P7), the idea of the human Body is composed of these
many ideas of the parts composing the Body, q.e.d.

P16: *The idea of any mode in which the human Body is affected by external
bodies must involve the nature of the human Body and at the same time the
nature of the external body.*
    Dem.: For all the modes in which a body is affected follow from
the nature of the affected body, and at the same time from the nature
of the affecting body (by A1″ [II/99]). So the idea of them (by IA4)
will necessarily involve the nature of each body. And so the idea of
each mode in which the human Body is affected by an external body
involves the nature of the human Body and of the external body,
q.e.d.
    Cor. 1: From this it follows, first, that the human Mind perceives
the nature of a great many bodies together with the nature of its own
body.
    Cor. 2: It follows, second, that the ideas which we have of external
bodies indicate the condition of our own body more than[42] the nature
of the eternal bodies. I have explained this by many examples in the
Appendix of Part I.

P17: *If the human Body is affected with a mode that involves the nature of
an external body, the human Mind will regard the same external body as*

---

[40] The translator is filling out an abbreviated indication of the conclusion. Cf. II/48/
15 and Akkerman 2, 161.
[41] NS: "P3C." As Gebhardt notes, this must be wrong (there is no P3C and in any
case, the citation is corrected in the errata to the NS). But the reference might well be
to P3.
[42] Robinson (314) objected that Spinoza had gone further than his premises warrant
by saying "more than." Gueroult's discussion is helpful (1, 2:196-197). He notes that in
speaking of the "nature" of external bodies, Spinoza has in mind seventeenth-century
mechanistic accounts of the physiology of perception, according to which a sensation
like that of heat would be caused by the rapid motion of very small particles, a motion
of which the sensation itself gives no indication.

actually existing, or as present to it, until the Body is affected by an affect[43] that excludes the existence or presence of that body.

25

30

II/105

5

10

15

20

25

30

Dem.: This is evident. For so long as the human Body is so affected, the human Mind (by P12) will regard this affection of the body, i.e. (by P16), it will have the idea of a mode that actually exists, an idea that involves the nature of the external body, i.e., an idea that does not exclude, but posits, the existence or presence of the nature of the external body. And so the Mind (by P16C1) will regard the external body as actually existing, or as present, until it is affected, etc., q.e.d.

Cor.: Although the external bodies by which the human body has once been affected neither exist nor are present, the mind will still be able to regard them as if they were present.

Dem.: While external bodies so determine the fluid parts of the human body that they often thrust against the softer parts, they change (by Post. 5) their surfaces with the result (see A2″ after L3) that they are reflected from it in another way than they used to be before, and still later, when the fluid parts, by their spontaneous motion, encounter those new surfaces, they are reflected in the same way as when they were driven against those surfaces by the external bodies. Consequently, while, thus reflected, they continue to move, they will affect the human Body with the same mode, concerning which the Mind (by P12) will think again, i.e. (by P17), the Mind will again regard the external body as present; this will happen as often as the fluid parts of the human body encounter the same surfaces by their spontaneous motion. So although the external bodies by which the human Body has once been affected do not exist, the Mind will still regard them as present, as often as this action of the body is repeated, q.e.d.

Schol.: We see, therefore, how it can happen (as it often does) that we regard as present things that do not exist. This can happen from other causes also, but it is sufficient for me here to have shown one through which I can explain it as if I had shown it through its true cause; still, I do not believe that I wander far from the true [cause] since all those postulates which I have assumed contain hardly anything that is not established by experience which we cannot doubt, after we have shown that the human Body exists as we are aware of it (see P13C).

Furthermore (from P17C and P16C2), we clearly understand what is the difference between the idea of, say, Peter, which constitutes the essence of Peter's mind, and the idea of Peter which is in another man,

---

[43] Probably we should read "affection" here (as at l. 25). The NS have "mode."

say in Paul. For the former directly explains the essence of Peter's body, and does not involve existence, except so long as Peter exists; but the latter indicates the condition of Paul's body more than Peter's nature [NS: see P16C2],[44] and therefore, while that condition of Paul's body lasts, Paul's Mind will still regard Peter as present to itself, even though Peter does not exist.

Next, to retain the customary words, the affections of the human Body whose ideas present external bodies as present to us, we shall call *images* of things, even if they do not reproduce the [NS: external] figures of things. And when the Mind regards bodies in this way, we shall say that it *imagines*.

And here, in order to begin to indicate what error is, I should like you to note that the imaginations of the Mind, considered in themselves contain no error, *or* that the Mind does not err from the fact that it imagines, but only insofar as it is considered to lack an idea that excludes the existence of those things that it imagines to be present to it. For if the Mind, while it imagined nonexistent things as present to it, at the same time knew that those things did not exist, it would, of course, attribute this power of imagining to a virtue of its nature, not to a vice—especially if this faculty of imagining depended only on its own nature, i.e. (by ID7), if the Mind's faculty of imagining were free.

P18: *If the human Body has once been affected by two or more bodies at the same time, then when the Mind subsequently imagines one of them, it will immediately recollect the others also.*

Dem.: The Mind (by P17C) imagines a body because the human Body is affected and disposed as it was affected when certain of its parts were struck by the external body itself. But (by hypothesis) the Body was then so disposed that the Mind imagined two [or more] bodies at once; therefore it will now also imagine two [or more] at once, and when the Mind imagines one, it will immediately recollect the other also, q.e.d.

Schol.: From this we clearly understand what Memory is. For it is nothing other than a certain connection of ideas involving the nature of things which are outside the human Body—a connection that is in the Mind according to the order and connection of the affections of the human Body.

I say, *first*, that the connection is only of those ideas that involve

---

[44] What Gebhardt adds from the NS is, as Akkerman observes (2, 187), not incorrect, but also not necessary, given the reference to P16C2 in l. 31. Gebhardt's "dat deel," however, is a misprint for "dit deel."

5 the nature of things which are outside the human Body, but not of the ideas that explain the nature of the same things. For they are really (by P16) ideas of affections of the human Body which involve both its nature and that of external bodies.

I say, *second*, that this connection happens according to the order
10 and connection of the affections of the human Body in order to distinguish it from the connection of ideas which happens according to the order of the intellect, by which the Mind perceives things through their first causes, and which is the same in all men.

And from this we clearly understand why the Mind, from the thought
15 of one thing, immediately passes to the thought of another, which has no likeness to the first: as, for example, from the thought of the word *pomum* a Roman will immediately pass to the thought of the fruit [viz. an apple], which has no similarity to that articulate sound and nothing in common with it except that the Body of the same man has often
20 been affected by these two [NS: at the same time], i.e., that the man often heard the word *pomum* while he saw the fruit.

And in this way each of us will pass from one thought to another, as each one's association has ordered the images of things in the body. For example, a soldier, having seen traces of a horse in the sand, will immediately pass from the thought of a horse to the thought of a
25 horseman, and from that to the thought of war, etc. But a Farmer will pass from the thought of a horse to the thought of a plow, and then to that of a field. etc. And so each one, according as he has been accustomed to join and connect the images of things in this or that way, will pass from one thought to another.

30 P19: *The human Mind does not know the human Body itself, nor does it know that it exists, except through ideas of affections by which the Body is affected.*

II/108 Dem.: For the human Mind is the idea itself, *or* knowledge of the human Body (by P13), which (by P9) is indeed in God insofar as he is considered to be affected by another idea of a singular thing, or[45]
5 because (by Post. 4) the human Body requires a great many bodies by which it is, as it were, continually regenerated; and [NS: because] the order and connection of ideas is (by P7) the same as the order and connection of causes,[46] this idea will be in God insofar as he is considered to be affected by the ideas of a great many singular things. There-
10 fore, God has the idea of the human Body, *or* knows the human Body, insofar as he is affected by a great many other ideas, and not insofar

---

[45] Gueroult (1, 2:247) comments that this "or" marks neither an identity, nor an alternative or opposition, but is intended to limit and make more precise the preceding clause.
[46] NS: "of things."

as he constitutes the nature of the human Mind, i.e. (by P11C), the human Mind does not know the human Body.[47]

But the ideas of affections of the Body are in God insofar as he constitutes the nature of the human Mind, or the human Mind perceives the same affections (by P12), and consequently (by P16) the human Body itself, as actually existing (by P17).

Therefore to that extent only, the human Mind perceives the human Body itself, q.e.d.

P20: *There is also in God an idea, or knowledge, of the human Mind, which follows in God in the same way and is related to God in the same way as the idea, or knowledge, of the human Body.*

Dem.: Thought is an attribute of God (by P1), and so (by P3) there must necessarily be in God an idea both of [NS: thought] and of all of its affections, and consequently (by P11),[48] of the human Mind also. Next, this idea, or knowledge, of the Mind does not follow in God insofar as he is infinite, but insofar as he is affected by another idea of a singular thing (by P9). But the order and connection of ideas is the same as the order and connection of causes[49] (by P7). Therefore, this idea, or knowledge, of the Mind follows in God and is related to God in the same way as the idea, or knowledge, of the Body, q.e.d.

109 P21: *This idea of the Mind is united to the Mind in the same way as the Mind is united to the Body.*

Dem.: We have shown that the Mind is united to the Body from the fact that the Body is the object of the Mind (see P12 and 13); and so by the same reasoning the idea of the Mind must be united with its own object, i.e., with the Mind itself, in the same way as the Mind is united with the Body, q.e.d.

Schol.: This proposition is understood far more clearly from what is said in P7S; for there we have shown that the idea of the Body and the Body, i.e. (by P13), the Mind and the Body, are one and the same Individual, which is conceived now under the attribute of Thought, now under the attribute of Extension. So the idea of the Mind and the Mind itself are one and the same thing, which is conceived under one and the same attribute, viz. Thought. The idea of the Mind, I say, and the Mind itself follow in God from the same power of thinking and by the same necessity. For the idea of the Mind, i.e., the idea of the idea, is nothing but the form of the idea insofar as this is con-

[47] Consistency with the proposition to be proven and the reference to P11C would both argue for adding "adequately" here.

[48] Perhaps, as Meijer and Gebhardt suggested, we should read "P11C."

[49] NS: "of things." On this alteration, see Gueroult 1, 2:246n.

sidered as a mode of thinking without relation to the object. For as soon as someone knows something, he thereby knows that he knows it, and at the same time knows that he knows that he knows, and so on, to infinity. But more on these matters later.

25   P22: *The human Mind perceives not only the affections of the Body, but also the ideas of these affections.*

    Dem.: The ideas of the ideas of the affections follow in God in the same way and are related to God in the same way as the ideas them-
30 selves of the affections (this is demonstrated in the same way as P20). But the ideas of the affections of the Body are in the human Mind (by
II/110 P12), i.e. (by P11C), in God, insofar as he constitutes the essence of the human Mind. Therefore, the ideas of these ideas will be in God insofar as he has the knowledge, *or* idea, of the human Mind, i.e. (by P21), they will be in the human Mind itself, which for that reason
5 perceives not only the affections of the Body, but also their ideas, q.e.d.

    P23: *The Mind does not know itself, except insofar as it perceives the ideas of the affections of the Body.*
10   Dem.: The idea, *or* knowledge, of the Mind (by P20) follows in God in the same way, and is related to God in the same way as the idea, *or* knowledge, of the body. But since (by P19) the human Mind
15 does not know the human Body itself, i.e. (by P11C), since the knowledge of the human Body is not related to God insofar as he constitutes the nature of the human Mind, the knowledge of the Mind is also not related to God insofar as he constitutes the essence of the human Mind. And so (again by P11C) to that extent the human Mind does not know itself.
20   Next, the ideas of the affections by which the Body is affected involve the nature of the human Body itself (by P16), i.e. (by P13), agree with the nature of the Mind. So knowledge of these ideas will necessarily involve knowledge of the Mind. But (by P22) knowledge of these ideas is in the human Mind itself. Therefore, the human
25 Mind, to that extent only, knows itself, q.e.d.

    P24: *The human Mind does not involve adequate knowledge of the parts composing the human Body.*
30   Dem.: The parts composing the human Body pertain to the essence of the Body itself only insofar as they communicate their motions to one another in a certain fixed manner (see the Definition after L3C),
II/111 and not insofar as they can be considered as Individuals, without relation to the human Body. For (by Post. 1) the parts of the human

Body are highly composite Individuals, whose parts (by L4) can be separated from the human Body and communicate their motions (see A1″ after L3) to other bodies in another manner, while the human Body completely preserves its nature and form. And so the idea, *or* knowledge, of each part will be in God (by P3), insofar as he is considered to be affected by another idea of a singular thing (by P9), a singular thing which is prior, in the order of nature, to the part itself (by P7). The same must also be said of each part of the Individual composing the human Body. And so, the knowledge of each part composing the human Body is in God insofar as he is affected with a great many ideas of things, and not insofar as he has only the idea of the human Body, i.e. (by P13), the idea that constitutes the nature of the human Mind. And so, by (P11C) the human Mind does not involve adequate knowledge of the parts composing the human Body, q.e.d.

P25: *The idea of any affection of the human Body does not involve adequate knowledge of an external body.*

Dem.: We have shown (P16) that the idea of an affection of the human Body involves the nature of an external body insofar as the external body determines the human Body in a certain fixed way. But insofar as the external body is an Individual that is not related to the human Body, the idea, *or* knowledge, of it is in God (by P9) insofar as God is considered to be affected with the idea of another thing which (by P7) is prior in nature to the external body itself. So adequate knowledge of the external body is not in God insofar as he has the idea of an affection of the human Body, *or* the idea of an affection of the human Body does not involve adequate knowledge of the external body, q.e.d.

P26: *The human Mind does not perceive any external body as actually existing, except through the ideas of the affections of its own Body.*

Dem.: If the human Body is not affected by an external body in any way, then (by P7) the idea of the human Body, i.e. (by P13) the human Mind, is also not affected in any way by the idea of the existence of that body, *or* it does not perceive the existence of that external body in any way. But insofar as the human Body is affected by an external body in some way, to that extent [the human Mind] (by P16 and P16C1) perceives the external body, q.e.d.

Cor.: Insofar as the human Mind imagines an external body, it does not have adequate knowledge of it.

Dem.: When the human Mind regards external bodies through ideas of the affections of its own Body, then we say that it imagines (see P17S); and the Mind cannot in any other way (by P26) imagine external bodies as actually existing. And so (by P25), insofar as the Mind imagines external bodies, it does not have adequate knowledge of them, q.e.d.

P27: *The idea of any affection of the human Body does not involve adequate*
25 *knowledge of the human body itself.*

Dem.: Any idea of any affection of the human Body involves the nature of the human Body insofar as the human Body itself is considered to be affected with a certain definite mode (see P16). But insofar
30 as the human Body is an Individual, which can be affected with many
II/113 other modes, the idea of this [affection] etc. (See P25D.)

P28: *The ideas of the affections of the human Body, insofar as they are related*
5 *only to the human Mind, are not clear and distinct, but confused.*

Dem.: For the ideas of the affections of the human Body involve the nature of external bodies as much as that of the human Body (by
10 P16), and must involve the nature not only of the human Body [NS: as a whole], but also of its parts; for the affections are modes (by Post. 3) with which the parts of the human Body, and consequently the whole Body, are affected. But (by P24 and P25) adequate knowledge of external bodies and of the parts composing the human Body is in
15 God, not insofar as he is considered to be affected with the human Mind, but insofar as he is considered to be affected with other ideas.[50] Therefore, these ideas of the affections, insofar as they are related only
20 to the human Mind, are like conclusions without premises, i.e. (as is known through itself), they are confused ideas, q.e.d.

Schol.: In the same way we can demonstrate that the idea that constitutes the nature of the human Mind is not, considered in itself alone,
25 clear and distinct; we can also demonstrate the same of the idea of the human Mind and the ideas of the ideas of the human Body's affections [viz. that are confused],[51] insofar as they are referred to the Mind alone. Anyone can easily see this.

P29: *The idea of the idea of any affection of the human Body does not involve*
30 *adequate knowledge of the human Mind.*

Dem.: For the idea of an affection of the human Body (by P27) does not involve adequate knowledge of the Body itself, *or* does not express

---

[50] What Gebhardt adds here from the NS (which may be translated: "i.e. [by P13], this Knowledge is not in God insofar as he constitutes the nature of the human Mind") Akkerman (2, 151) rejects as the translator's attempt to clarify a difficult passage for himself and his friends.

[51] What Gebhardt here adds from the NS, Gueroult (1, 2:280, n. 16) regards as a deliberate omission from the OP. I see no good reason to regard it as incorrect, but Akkerman is probably right (2, 149) that it is only a translator's clarification.

II/114 its nature adequately, i.e. (by P13), does not agree adequately with the nature of the Mind; and so (by IA6) the idea of this idea does not express the nature of the human mind adequately, *or* does not involve adequate knowledge of it, q.e.d.

5   Cor.: From this it follows that so long as the human Mind perceives things from the common order of nature, it does not have an adequate, but only a confused and mutilated knowledge of itself, of its own Body, and of external bodies. For the Mind does not know itself ex-
10 cept insofar as it perceives ideas of the affections of the body (by P23). But it does not perceive its own Body (by P19) except through the very ideas themselves of the affections [of the body], and it is also through them alone that it perceives external bodies (by P26). And so, insofar as it has these [ideas], then neither of itself (by P29), nor of its
15 own Body (by P27), nor of external bodies (by P25) does it have an adequate knowledge, but only (by P28 and P28S) a mutilated and confused knowledge, q.e.d.

    Schol.: I say expressly that the Mind has, not an adequate, but only
20 a confused [NS: and mutilated] knowledge, of itself, of its own Body, and of external bodies, so long as it perceives things from the common order of nature, i.e., so long as it is determined externally, from for-tuitous encounters with things, to regard this or that, and not so long as it is determined internally, from the fact that it regards a number
25 of things at once, to understand their agreements, differences, and oppositions. For so often as it is disposed internally, in this or another way, then it regards things clearly and distinctly, as I shall show be-low.

P30: *We can have only an entirely inadequate knowledge of the duration of*
30 *our Body.*

    Dem.: Our body's duration depends neither on its essence (by A1),
/115 nor even on God's absolute nature (by IP21). But (by IP28) it is de-termined to exist and produce an effect from such [NS: other] causes as are also determined by others to exist and produce an effect in a certain and determinate manner, and these again by others, and so to infinity. Therefore, the duration of our Body depends on the common order of nature and the constitution of things. But adequate knowl-edge of how things are constituted is in God, insofar as he has the ideas of all of them, and not insofar as he has only the idea of the
5 human Body (by P9C). So the knowledge of the duration of our Body is quite inadequate in God, insofar as he is considered to constitute only the nature of the human Mind, i.e. (by P11C), this knowledge is quite inadequate in our Mind, q.e.d.

15 **P31**: *We can have only an entirely inadequate knowledge of the duration of the singular things which are outside us.*

Dem.: For each singular thing, like the human Body, must be de-
20 termined by another singular thing to exist and produce effects in a certain and determinate way, and this again by another, and so to infinity (by IP28). But since (in P30) we have demonstrated from this common property of singular things that we have only a very inade-quate knowledge of the duration of our Body, we shall have to draw
25 the same conclusion concerning the duration of singular things [out-side us], viz. that we can have only a very inadequate knowledge of their duration, q.e.d.

Cor.: From this it follows that all particular things are contingent
30 and corruptible. For we can have no adequate knowledge of their du-ration (by P31), and that is what we must understand by the contin-
II/116 gency of things and the possibility of their corruption (see IP33S1). For (by IP29) beyond that there is no contingency.

P32: *All ideas, insofar as they are related to God, are true.*
5 Dem.: For all ideas which are in God agree entirely with their objects[52] (by P7C), and so (by IA6) they are all true, q.e.d.

10 **P33**: *There is nothing positive in ideas on account of which they are called false.*

Dem.: If you deny this, conceive (if possible) a positive mode of thinking which constitutes the form of error, *or* falsity. This mode of
15 thinking cannot be in God (by P32). But it also can neither be nor be conceived outside God (by IP15). And so there can be nothing positive in ideas on account of which they are called false, q.e.d.

20 **P34**: *Every idea that in us is absolute,* or *adequate and perfect, is true.*

Dem.: When we say that there is in us an adequate and perfect idea, we are saying nothing but that (by P11C) there is an adequate and perfect idea in God insofar as he constitutes the essence of our
25 Mind, and consequently (by P32) we are saying nothing but that such an idea is true, q.e.d.

P35: *Falsity consists in the privation of knowledge which inadequate, or mu-tilated and confused, ideas involve.*
II/117 Dem.: There is nothing positive in ideas that constitutes the form of falsity (by P33); but falsity cannot consist in an absolute privation[53]

---

[52] What Gebhardt adds here from the NS is almost certainly nothing more than an attempt by the translator to deal with the technical term *ideatum* by a double translation. Cf. Akkerman 2, 88.
[53] What Gebhardt adds here from the NS ("of knowledge"), Parkinson (121n.) rejects

(for it is Minds, not Bodies, which are said to err, or be deceived), nor also in absolute ignorance. For to be ignorant and to err are different. So it consists in the privation of knowledge that inadequate knowledge of things, *or* inadequate and confused ideas, involve, q.e.d.

Schol.: In P17S I explained how error consists in the privation of knowledge. But to explain the matter more fully, I shall give [NS: one or two examples]: men are deceived in that they think themselves free [NS: i.e., they think that, of their own free will, they can either do a thing or forbear doing it],[54] an opinion which consists only in this, that they are conscious of their actions and ignorant of the causes by which they are determined. This, then, is their idea of freedom—that they do not know any cause of their actions. They say, of course, that human actions depend on the will, but these are only words for which they have no idea. For all are ignorant of what the will is, and how it moves the Body; those who boast of something else, who feign seats and dwelling places of the soul, usually provoke either ridicule or disgust.[55]

Similarly, when we look at the sun, we imagine it as about 200 feet away from us, an error that does not consist simply in this imagining, but in the fact that while we imagine it in this way, we are ignorant of its true distance and of the cause of this imagining. For even if we later come to know that it is more than 600 diameters of the earth away from us, we nevertheless imagine it as near. For we imagine the sun so near not because we do not know its true distance, but because an affection of our body involves the essence of the sun insofar as our body is affected by the sun.[56]

P36: *Inadequate and confused ideas follow with the same necessity as adequate, or clear and distinct ideas.*

---

as making the continuation·of the sentence pointless. Akkerman, who ascribes it to the translator (2, 161), also thinks it incorrect.

[54] The phrases added here from the NS are almost certainly translator's glosses (cf. Akkerman 2, 161), but helpful ones, I think.

[55] As many commentators (e.g., Wolfson, Gueroult) have remarked, this last seems aimed at Descartes' doctrine that the pineal gland is the principal seat of the soul (*Passions of the Soul* I, 31-32). Descartes, of course, was not the only previous philosopher to assign a particular location in the body to the soul. Others had favored the heart, as Descartes himself points (*Passions* I, 33). But the tone of Spinoza's criticism in the Preface to EV suggests that this aspect of the Cartesian philosophy did tend to provoke both ridicule and disgust.

[56] This example occurs frequently in Spinoza (cf. II/11, 30, 210, 211). It is quite traditional, going back (as Wolfson pointed out) to Aristotle's *De Anima* 428b2-4. But Spinoza seems to be indebted to Descartes for his estimates of distance; the figure of (100-)200 feet for the imagined distance of the sun is given in *La Dioptrique* (AT VI, 144); that of 600(-700) diameters of the Earth for the true distance is given in the *Principles* III, 5.

II/118   Dem.: All ideas are in God (by IP15); and, insofar as they are related to God, are true (by P32), and (by P7C) adequate. And so there
5   are no inadequate or confused ideas except insofar as they are related
to the singular Mind of someone (see P24 and P28). And so all ideas—
both the adequate and the inadequate—follow with the same necessity
(by P6C), q.e.d.

10   P37: *What is common to all things* (on this see L2, above) *and is equally
in the part and in the whole, does not constitute the essence of any singular
thing.*
Dem.: If you deny this, conceive (if possible) that it does constitute
15   the essence of some singular thing, say the essence of B. Then (by
D2) it can neither be nor be conceived without B. But this is contrary
to the hypothesis. Therefore, it does not pertain to the essence of B,
nor does it constitute the essence of any other singular thing, q.e.d.

20   P38: *Those things which are common to all, and which are equally in the part
and in the whole, can only be conceived adequately.*
Dem.: Let A be something which is common to all bodies, and
which is equally in the part of each body and in the whole. I say that
25   A can only be conceived adequately. For its idea (by P7C) will necessarily be adequate in God, both insofar as he has the idea of the
human Body and insofar as he has ideas of its affections, which (by
P16, P25, and P27) involve in part both the nature of the human Body
30   and that of external bodies. That is (by P12 and P13), this idea will
necessarily be adequate in God insofar as he constitutes the human
II/119   Mind, *or* insofar as he has ideas that are in the human Mind. The
Mind therefore (by P11C) necessarily perceives A adequately, and does
so both insofar as it perceives itself and insofar as it perceives its own
or any external body. Nor can A be conceived in another way, q.e.d.
5   Cor.: From this it follows that there are certain ideas, *or* notions,
common to all men.[57] For (by L2) all bodies agree in certain things,
which (by P38) must be perceived adequately, *or* clearly and distinctly, by all.

10   P39: *If something is common to, and peculiar to, the human Body and certain
external bodies by which the human Body is usually affected, and is equally in
the part and in the whole of each of them, its idea will also be adequate in the
Mind.*

[57] This is the first explicit appearance in the *Ethics* of the doctrine of common notions
(though there has been a suggestion of it in P29S). On its connection with similar
doctrines of other authors (Aristotle, the Stoics, Hobbes, Descartes) see Gueroult 1,
2:332, 354, 358-362, 581-582, and Wolfson 1, 2:117-130.

15   Dem.: Let A be that which is common to, and peculiar to, the human Body and certain external bodies, which is equally in the human Body and in the same external bodies, and finally, which is equally in the part of each external body and in the whole. There will be an
20   adequate idea of A in God (by P7C), both insofar as he has the idea of the human Body, and insofar as he has ideas of the posited external bodies. Let it be posited now that the human Body is affected by an external body through what it has in common with it, i.e., by A; the
25   idea of this affection will involve property A (by P16), and so (by P7C) the idea of this affection, insofar as it involves property A, will be adequate in God insofar as he is affected with the idea of the human Body, i.e. (by P13), insofar as he constitutes the nature of the human Mind. And so (by P11C), this idea is also adequate in the human
30   Mind, q.e.d.

    Cor.: From this it follows that the Mind is the more capable of
II/120   perceiving many things adequately as its Body has many things in common with other bodies.

P40: *Whatever ideas follow in the Mind from ideas that are adequate in the mind are also adequate.*

    Dem.: This is evident. For when we say that an idea in the human Mind follows from ideas that are adequate in it, we are saying nothing but that (by P11C) in the Divine intellect there is an idea of which
0   God is the cause, not insofar as he is infinite,[58] nor insofar as he is affected with the ideas of a great many singular things, but insofar as he constitutes only the essence of the human Mind [NS: and therefore, it must be adequate].[59]

5   Schol. 1:[60] With this I have explained the cause of those notions

[58] NS: "not insofar as he is finite." Gebhardt takes this to indicate the reading of the original manuscript. But "finite" is corrected in the errata. Gueroult (1, 2:544) takes the immediately following phrase—"nor insofar as he is affected with the ideas of a great many singular things"—to be a gloss on this phrase, i.e., to indicate one sense in which God may be said to be infinite. This has some plausibility if we paraphrase "a great many," as Gueroult does, by "un ensemble infini." But there does not seem to be any reason for that paraphrase, and it seems more natural to take Spinoza to be mentioning a separate condition.

[59] No doubt what Gebhardt adds here from the NS is another instance of the translator's making more explicit a conclusion that Spinoza's ms. indicated in a more summary fashion (cf. Akkerman 2, 149).

[60] This scholium is unnumbered both in the OP and NS. Gebhardt inferred from that, and from subsequent references to an unnumbered IIP40S (at 140/10 and 228/2), that originally these scholia were one, that Spinoza subsequently divided that scholium in two, and that the subsequent references are to both scholia. Akkerman (2, 82) takes the second scholium to be a later addition and the subsequent references to be to this first scholium.

475

which are called *common*, and which are the foundations of our reasoning.

But some axioms, *or* notions,[61] result from other causes which it would be helpful to explain by this method of ours. For from these [explanations] it would be established which notions are more useful than the others, and which are of hardly any use; and then, which are common, which are clear and distinct only to those who have no prejudices, and finally, which are ill-founded. Moreover, we would establish what is the origin of those notions they call *Second*,[62] and consequently of the axioms founded on them, and other things I have thought about, from time to time,[63] concerning these matters. But since I have set these aside for another Treatise,[64] and do not wish to give rise to disgust by too long a discussion, I have decided to pass over them here.

But not to omit anything it is necessary to know, I shall briefly add something about the causes from which the terms called *Transcendental* have had their origin—I mean terms like Being, Thing and something. These terms arise from the fact that the human Body, being limited, is capable of forming distinctly only a certain number of images at the same time (I have explained what an image is in P17S). If that number is exceeded, the images will begin to be confused, and if the number of images the Body is capable of forming distinctly in itself at once is greatly exceeded, they will all be completely confused with one another.

Since this is so, it is evident from P17C and P18, that the human Mind will be able to imagine distinctly, at the same time, as many bodies as there can be images formed at the same time in its body. But when the images in the body are completely confused, the Mind

---

[61] So the OP read. The apparent variation in the NS seems to reflect the translator's quandary when he encounters in the same phrase both *axioma* and *notio*, each of which he has previously translated by (*gemene*) *kundigheid* (cf. Akkerman 2, 166). Appuhn emended "notions" to "common notions," an alteration which Akkerman considers unnecessary, but not, it seems, incorrect, appealing to l. 15. Gueroult (1, 2:362, n. 79) regards it as incorrect, appealing to ll. 18-21.

[62] Gueroult (1, 2:364) cites Zabarella, *De Natura Logicae*, as an example of the usual scholastic explanation of this term: "Some terms signify the concept of a thing, like man, animal; but others signify the concept of a concept, like genus, species, word, statement, reasoning, and other things of that kind. The latter are called second notions." Wolfson (1, 2:122) argues that Spinoza is not using "second notions" in its usual sense, but in one derived from Maimonides, where it is equivalent to "conclusion of a demonstrative syllogism." For a rebuttal, see Gueroult 1, 2:587-589.

[63] Or, perhaps: "at one time." Cf. Joachim 2, 12, n. 3.

[64] Of which the present *Treatise on the Emendation of the Intellect* may be regarded as at least a draft.

476

also will imagine all the bodies confusedly, without any distinction, and comprehend them as if under one attribute, viz. under the attribute of Being, Thing, etc. This can also be deduced from the fact that images are not always equally vigorous and from other causes like these, which it is not necessary to explain here. For our purpose it is sufficient to consider only one. For they all reduce to this: these terms signify ideas that are confused in the highest degree.

Those notions they call *Universal*, like Man, Horse, Dog, etc., have arisen from similar causes, viz. because so many images (e.g., of men) are formed at one time in the human Body that they surpass the power of imagining—not entirely, of course, but still to the point where the Mind can imagine neither slight differences of the singular [men] (such as the color and size of each one, etc.) nor their determinate number, and imagines distinctly only what they all agree in, insofar as they affect the body. For the body has been affected most [NS: forcefully] by [what is common], since each singular has affected it [by this property]. And [NS: the mind] expresses this by the word *man*, and predicates it of infinitely many singulars. For as we have said, it cannot imagine a determinate number of singulars.

But it should be noted that these notions are not formed by all [NS: men] in the same way, but vary from one to another, in accordance with what the body has more often been affected by, and what the Mind imagines or recollects more easily. For example, those who have more often regarded men's stature with wonder will understand by the word *man* an animal of erect stature. But those who have been accustomed to consider something else, will form another common image of men—e.g., that man is an animal capable of laughter, or a featherless biped, or a rational animal.

And similarly concerning the others—each will form universal images of things according to the disposition of his body. Hence it is not surprising that so many controversies have arisen among the philosophers, who have wished to explain natural things by mere images of things.

Schol. 2: From what has been said above, it is clear that we perceive many things and form universal notions:

I. from singular things which have been represented to us through the senses in a way that is mutilated, confused, and without order for the intellect (see P29C); for that reason I have been accustomed to call such perceptions knowledge from random experience;

II. from signs, e.g., from the fact that, having heard or read certain words, we recollect things, and form certain ideas of them, which are like them, and through which we imagine the things (P18S). These two ways of regarding things I shall henceforth call knowledge of the first kind, opinion or imagination.

III. Finally, from the fact that we have common notions[65] and adequate ideas of the properties of things (see P38C, P39, P39C, and P40). This I shall call reason and the second kind of knowledge.

[IV.] In addition to these two kinds of knowledge, there is (as I shall show in what follows) another, third kind, which we shall call intuitive knowledge. And this kind of knowing proceeds from an adequate idea of the formal essence of certain attributes of God to the adequate knowledge of the [NS: formal] essence of things.

I shall explain all these with one example. Suppose there are three numbers, and the problem is to find a fourth which is to the third as the second is to the first. Merchants do not hesitate to multiply the second by the third, and divide the product by the first, because they have not yet forgotten what they heard from their teacher without any demonstration, or because they have often found this in the simplest numbers, or from the force of the Demonstration of P7 in Bk. VII of Euclid, viz. from the common property of proportionals. But in the simplest numbers none of this is necessary. Given the numbers 1, 2, and 3, no one fails to see that the fourth proportional number is 6— and we see this much more clearly because we infer the fourth number from the ratio which, in one glance, we see the first number to have the second.[66]

P41: *Knowledge of the first kind is the only cause of falsity, whereas knowledge of the second and of the third kind is necessarily true.*

Dem.: We have said in the preceding scholium that to knowledge of the first kind pertain all those ideas which are inadequate and confused; and so (by P35) this knowledge is the only cause of falsity. Next, we have said that to knowledge of the second and third kinds pertain those which are adequate; and so (by P34) this knowledge is necessarily true.

P42: *Knowledge of the second and third kinds, and not of the first kind, teaches us to distinguish the true from the false.*

---

[65] Gebhardt (II/364) gives the following reading for the NS: "algemene kundigheden/ Notiones universales," "universal notions." *Algemene kundigheden* is what we should expect if *Notiones universales* is correct. But the NS has *gemene kundigheden* (the usual translation for *notiones communes*), though it has *Notiones universales* in the margin.

[66] For the clause beginning "because we infer . . ." the NS have: because we need to think only of the particular ratio of the first two numbers, and not of the universal property of proportional numbers." Akkerman (2, 166) thinks this may be Spinoza's attempt to clarify the Latin text, but may equally well stem from the translator.

Dem.: This Proposition is evident through itself. For he who knows how to distinguish between the true and the false must have an adequate idea of the true and of the false, i.e. (P40S2), must know the true and the false by the second or third kind of knowledge.

P43: *He who has a true idea at the same time knows that he has a true idea, and cannot doubt the truth of the thing.*

Dem.: An idea true in us is that which is adequate in God insofar as he is explained through the nature of the human Mind (by P11C). Let us posit, therefore, that there is in God, insofar as he is explained through the nature of the human Mind, an adequate idea, A. Of this idea there must necessarily also be in God an idea which is related to God in the same way as idea A (by P20, whose demonstration is universal [NS: and can be applied to all ideas]). But idea A is supposed to be related to God insofar as he is explained through the nature of the human Mind; therefore the idea of idea A must also be related to God in the same way, i.e. (by the same P11C), this adequate idea of idea A will be in the Mind itself which has the adequate idea A. And so he who has an adequate idea, *or* (by P34) who knows a thing truly, must at the same time have an adequate idea, *or* true knowledge, of his own knowledge. I.e. (as is manifest through itself), he must at the same time be certain, q.e.d.

Schol.: In P21S I have explained what an idea of an idea is. But it should be noted that the preceding proposition is sufficiently manifest through itself. For no one who has a true idea is unaware that a true idea involves the highest certainty. For to have a true idea means nothing other than knowing a thing perfectly, *or* in the best way. And of course no one can doubt this unless he thinks that an idea is something mute, like a picture on a tablet, and not a mode of thinking, viz. the very [act of] understanding. And I ask, who can know that he understands some thing unless he first understands it? I.e., who can know that he is certain about some thing unless he is first certain about it? What can there be which is clearer and more certain than a true idea, to serve as a standard of truth? As the light makes both itself and the darkness plain, so truth is the standard both of itself and of the false.

By this I think we have replied to these questions: if a true idea is distinguished from a false one, [NS: not insofar as it is said to be a mode of thinking, but] only insofar as it is said to agree with its object, then a true idea has no more reality or perfection than a false one (since they are distinguished only through the extrinsic denomination [NS: and not through the intrinsic denomination])—and so, does the

man who has true ideas [NS: have any more reality or perfection] than
him who has only false ideas? Again, why do men have false ideas?
And finally, how can someone know certainly that he has ideas which
agree with their objects?[67]

To these questions, I say, I think I have already replied. For as far
as the difference between a true and a false idea is concerned, it is
established from P35 that the true is related to the false as being is to
nonbeing. And the causes of falsity I have shown most clearly from
P19 to P35S. From this it is also clear what is the difference between
the man who has true ideas and the man who has only false ideas.
Finally, as to the last, viz. how a man can know that he has an idea
that agrees with its object? I have just shown, more than sufficiently,
that this arises solely from his having an idea that does agree with its
object—*or* that truth is its own standard. Add to this that our Mind,
insofar as it perceives things truly, is part of the infinite intellect of
God (by P11C); hence, it is as necessary that the mind's clear and
distinct ideas are true as that God's ideas are.

P44: *It is of the nature of Reason to regard things as necessary, not as contingent.*

Dem.: It is of the nature of reason to perceive things truly (by P41),
viz. (by IA6) as they are in themselves, i.e. (by IP29), not as contingent but as necessary, q.e.d.

Cor. 1: From this it follows that it depends only on the imagination
that we regard things as contingent, both in respect to the past and in
respect to the future.

Schol.: I shall explain briefly how this happens. We have shown
above (by P17 and P17C) that even though things do not exist, the
Mind still imagines them always as present to itself, unless causes
occur which exclude their present existence. Next, we have shown
(P18) that if the human Body has once been affected by two external
bodies at the same time, then afterwards, when the Mind imagines
one of them, it will immediately recollect the other also, i.e., it will
regard both as present to itself unless causes occur which exclude their
present existence. Moreover, no one doubts but what we also imagine
time, viz. from the fact that we imagine some bodies to move more
slowly, or more quickly, or with the same speed.

Let us suppose, then, a child, who saw Peter for the first time

---

[67] Most of Gebhardt's additions to this scholium from the NS seem to be simply
translator's glosses (cf. Akkerman 2, 149, 161). Where they appeared to me to be genuinely helpful, I have translated them. The phrases he introduces into the text at ll. 26-
27, 35, and 37 represent no more than the translator's attempt to deal with *ideatum*
through a double translation and I have not translated them.

yesterday, in the morning, but saw Paul at noon, and Simon in the evening, and today again saw Peter in the morning. It is clear from P18 that as soon as he sees the morning light, he will immediately imagine the sun taking the same course through the sky as he saw on the preceding day, *or* he will imagine the whole day, and Peter together with the morning, Paul with noon, and Simon with the evening. That is, he will imagine the existence of Paul and of Simon with a relation to future time. On the other hand, if he sees Simon in the evening, he will relate Paul and Peter to the time past, by imagining them together with past time. And he will do this more uniformly, the more often he has seen them in this same order.

But if it should happen at some time that on some other evening he sees James instead of Simon, then on the following morning he will imagine now Simon, now James, together with the evening time, but not both at once. For it is supposed that he has seen one or the other of them in the evening, but not both at once. His imagination, therefore, will vacillate and he will imagine now this one, now that one, with the future evening time, i.e., he will regard neither of them as certainly future, but both of them as contingently future.

And this vacillation of the imagination will be the same if the imagination is of things we regard in the same way with relation to past time or to present time. Consequently we shall imagine things as contingent in relation to present time as well as to past and future time.

Cor 2: It is of the nature of Reason to perceive things under a certain species of eternity.

Dem.: It is of the nature of Reason to regard things as necessary and not as contingent (by P44). And it perceives this necessity of things truly (by P41), i.e. (by IA6), as it is in itself. But (by IP16) this necessity of things is the very necessity of God's eternal nature. Therefore, it is of the nature of Reason to regard things under this species of eternity.

Add to this that the foundations of Reason are notions (by P38) which explain those things that are common to all, and which (by P37) do not explain the essence of any singular thing. On that account, they must be conceived without any relation to time, but under a certain species of eternity, q.e.d.

P45: *Each idea of each body, or of each singular thing which actually exists, necessarily involves an[68] eternal and infinite essence of God.*

---

[68] The idea, it seems, involves God's essence only insofar as that essence is expressed through the attribute under which the idea's object is conceived, not insofar as God's essence is expressed in infinitely many attributes. Cf. Gueroult 1, 1:54.

5   Dem.: The idea of a singular thing which actually exists necessarily involves both the essence of the thing and its existence (by P8C). But singular things (by IP15) cannot be conceived without God—on the
10   contrary, because (by P6) they have God for a cause insofar as he is considered under the attribute of which the things are modes, their ideas must involve the concept of their attribute (by IA4), i.e. (by ID6), must involve an eternal and infinite essence of God, q.e.d.

15   Schol.: By existence here I do not understand duration, i.e., existence insofar as it is conceived abstractly, and as a certain species of quantity. For I am speaking of the very nature of existence, which is attributed to singular things because infinitely many things follow from the eternal necessity of God's nature in infinitely many modes (see
20   IP16). I am speaking, I say, of the very existence of singular things insofar as they are in God. For even if each one is determined by another singular thing to exist in a certain way, still the force by which each one perseveres in existing follows from the eternal necessity of God's nature. Concerning this, see IP24C.

25   P46: *The knowledge of God's eternal and infinite essence which each idea involves is adequate and perfect.*

       Dem.: The demonstration of the preceding Proposition is Univer-
30   sal, and whether the thing is considered as a part or as a whole, its idea, whether of the whole or a part (by P45), will involve God's eternal and infinite essence. So what gives knowledge of an eternal
II/128 and infinite essence of God is common to all, and is equally in the part and in the whole. And so (by P38) this knowledge will be adequate, q.e.d.

       P47: *The human Mind has an adequate knowledge of God's eternal and infinite*
5   *essence.*

       Dem.: The human Mind has ideas (by P22) from which it perceives (by P23) itself, (by P19) its own Body, and (by P16C1 and P17) ex-
10   ternal bodies as actually existing. And so (by P45 and P46) it has an adequate knowledge of God's eternal and infinite essence, q.e.d.

       Schol.: From this we see that God's infinite essence and his eternity are known to all. And since all things are in God and are conceived
15   through God, it follows that we can deduce from this knowledge a great many things which we know adequately, and so can form that third kind of knowledge of which we spoke in P40S2 and of whose excellence and utility we shall speak in Part V.

       But that men do not have so clear a knowledge of God as they do
20   of the common notions comes from the fact that they cannot imagine

God, as they can bodies, and that they have joined the name *God* to the images of things which they are used to seeing. Men can hardly avoid this, because they are continually affected by bodies.

And indeed, most errors consist only in our not rightly applying names to things. For when someone says that the lines which are drawn from the center of a circle to its circumference are unequal, he surely understands (then at least) by a circle something different from what Mathematicians understand. Similarly, when men err in calculating, they have certain numbers in their mind and different ones on the paper. So if you consider what they have in Mind, they really do not err, though they seem to err because we think they have in their mind the numbers which are on the paper. If this were not so, we would not believe that they were erring, just as I did not believe that he was erring whom I recently heard cry out that his courtyard had flown into his neighbor's hen [NS: although his words were absurd], because what he had in mind seemed sufficiently clear to me [viz. that his hen had flown into his neighbor's courtyard].

And most controversies have arisen from this, that men do not rightly explain their own mind, or interpret the mind of the other man badly. For really, when they contradict one another most vehemently, they either have the same thoughts, or they are thinking of different things,[69] so that what they think are errors and absurdities in the other are not.

P48: *In the Mind there is no absolute, or free, will, but the Mind is determined to will this or that by a cause which is also determined by another, and this again by another, and so to infinity.*

Dem.: The Mind is a certain and determinate mode of thinking (by P11), and so (by IP17C2) cannot be a free cause of its own actions, *or* cannot have an absolute faculty of willing and not willing. Rather, it must be determined to willing this or that (by IP28) by a cause which is also determined by another, and this cause again by another, etc., q.e.d.

Schol.: In this same way it is also demonstrated that there is in the Mind no absolute faculty of understanding, desiring, loving, etc. From this it follows that these and similar faculties are either complete fictions or nothing but Metaphysical beings, *or* universals, which we are used to forming from particulars. So intellect and will are to this or that idea, or to this or that volition as 'stone-ness' is to this or that stone, or man to Peter or Paul.

We have explained the cause of men's thinking themselves free in

---

[69] Following Appuhn, whose translation here agrees with that of the NS.

the Appendix of Part I. But before I proceed further, it should be
noted here[70] that by will I understand a faculty of affirming and denying, and not desire. I say that I understand the faculty by which
the Mind affirms or denies something true or something false, and not
the desire by which the Mind wants a thing or avoids it.

But after we have demonstrated that these faculties are universal
notions which are not distinguished from the singulars from which we
form them, we must now investigate whether the volitions themselves
are anything beyond the very ideas of things. We must investigate, I
say, whether there is any other affirmation or negation in the Mind
except that which the idea involves, insofar as it is an idea—on this
see the following Proposition and also D3—so that our thought does
not fall into pictures. For by ideas I understand, not the images that
are formed at the back of the eye (and, if you like, in the middle of
the brain),[71] but concepts of Thought [NS: or the objective Being of
a thing insofar as it consists only in Thought].

P49: *In the Mind there is no volition*, or *affirmation and negation, except
that which the idea involves insofar as it is an idea.*

Dem.: In the Mind (by P48) there is no absolute faculty of willing
and not willing, but only singular volitions, viz. this and that affirmation, and this and that negation. Let us conceive, therefore, some
singular volition, say a mode of thinking by which the Mind affirms
that the three angles of a triangle are equal to two right angles.

This affirmation involves the concept, *or* idea, of the triangle, i.e.,
it cannot be conceived without the idea of the triangle. For to say that
A must involve the concept of B is the same as to say that A cannot
be conceived without B. Further, this affirmation (by A3) also cannot
be without the idea of the triangle. Therefore, this affirmation can
neither be nor be conceived without the idea of the triangle.

Next, this idea of the triangle must involve this same affirmation,
viz. that its three angles equal two right angles. So conversely, this
idea of the triangle also can neither be nor be conceived without this
affirmation.

So (by D2) this affirmation pertains to the essence of the idea of the

---

[70] Subsequently (IIIP9S) Spinoza distinguishes between will and desire in somewhat
different terms; hence Meijer wanted to emend the text so that it would be translated:
". . . it should be noted that by will I here understand. . . ." Gebhardt points out the
text of the OP is confirmed by the NS. But while the text is probably not corrupt, the
emenders are right to emphasize the provisional character of this distinction. Cf. Gueroult 1, 2:492-493, and Appuhn, 3:358-359.

[71] An allusion to Descartes' doctrine of the pineal gland. Cf. the *Passions of the Soul* I,
31-32. Akkerman (2, 149) regards what Gebhardt adds to the text from the NS in the
next line as the work of the translator, but "an intelligent addition" nonetheless.

triangle, and is nothing beyond it. And what we have said concerning this volition (since we have selected it at random), must also be said concerning any volition, viz. that it is nothing apart from the idea, q.e.d.

31   Cor.: The will and the intellect are one and the same.

Dem.: The will and the intellect are nothing apart from the singular volitions and ideas themselves (by P48 and P48S). But the singular volitions and ideas are one and the same (by P49). Therefore the will and the intellect are one and the same, q.e.d.

Schol.: [I.] By this we have removed what is commonly maintained to be the cause of error.[72] Moreover, we have shown above that falsity consists only in the privation that mutilated and confused ideas involve. So a false idea, insofar as it is false, does not involve certainty. When we say that a man rests in false ideas, and does not doubt them, we do not, on that account, say that he is certain, but only that he does not doubt, or that he rests in false ideas because there are no causes to bring it about that his imagination wavers [NS: or to cause him to doubt them]. On this, see P44S.

Therefore, however stubbornly a man may cling to something false [NS: so that we cannot in any way make him doubt it], we shall still never say that he is certain of it. For by certainty we understand something positive (see P43 and P43S), not the privation of doubt. But by the privation of certainty, we understand falsity.

However, to explain the preceding Proposition more fully, there remain certain things I must warn you of. And then I must reply to the objections that can be made against this doctrine of ours. And finally, to remove every uneasiness, I thought it worthwhile to indicate some of the advantages of this doctrine. Some, I say—for the most important ones will be better understood from what we shall say in Part V.

[II.] I begin, therefore, by warning my Readers, first, to distinguish accurately between an idea, *or* concept, of the Mind, and the images of things that we imagine. And then it is necessary to distinguish between ideas and the words by which we signify things. For because many people either completely confuse these three—ideas, images, and words—or do not distinguish them accurately enough, or carefully enough, they have been completely ignorant of this doctrine con-

---

[72] I introduce essentially the division of this scholium suggested by Gueroult (1, 2:505). The "common doctrine" regarding the cause of error is the Cartesian doctrine of the Fourth Meditation, that error occurs because man's will is distinct from, and more extensive than, his intellect. The phrases Gebhardt adds from the NS in these first two paragraphs are probably translator's glosses.

cerning the will. But it is quite necessary to know it, both for the sake of speculation[73] and in order to arrange one's life wisely.

5   Indeed, those who think that ideas consist in images which are formed in us from encounters with [NS: external] bodies, are convinced that those ideas of things [NS: which can make no trace in our brains, or] of which we can form no similar image [NS: in our brain] are not ideas, but only fictions which we feign from a free choice of the will.

10 They look on ideas, therefore, as mute pictures on a panel. and preoccupied with this prejudice, do not see that an idea, insofar as it is an idea, involves an affirmation or negation.[74]

And then, those who confuse words with the idea, or with the very affirmation that the idea involves, think that they can will something contrary to what they are aware of, when they only affirm or deny

15 with words something contrary to what they are aware of.[75] But these prejudices can easily be put aside by anyone who attends to the nature of thought, which does not at all involve the concept of extension. He will then understand clearly that an idea (since it is a mode of thinking) consists neither in the image of anything, nor in words. For the es-

20 sence of words and of images is constituted only by corporeal motions, which do not at all involve the concept of thought.

It should suffice to have issued these few words of warning on this matter, so I pass to objections mentioned above.

[III.A.(i)] The first of these is that they think it clear that the will extends more widely than the intellect, and so is different from the

25 intellect. The reason why they think the will extends more widely than the intellect is that they say they know by experience that they do not require a greater faculty of assenting, *or* affirming, and denying, than we already have, in order to assent to infinitely many other things which we do not perceive—but they do require a greater fac-

---

[73] What Gebhardt adds here from the NS (which might be translated: "and of the sciences") is probably only the translator's attempt to capture the connotations of *speculatio* through a double translation. Cf. Akkerman 2, 89. The variations which appear in the following paragraph, not all of which are mentioned by Gebhardt, are probably translator's glosses.

[74] We have, again, the same comparison as in P43S. Since Descartes generally insisted on drawing a sharp distinction between ideas and images (e.g., at the beginning of the Sixth Meditation, or in his reply to Hobbes' fifth objection), it is curious to see a central tenet of his doctrine of judgment traced to a confusion of ideas with images. On this see Curley 5 and Gueroult 1, 2:509.

[75] Gueroult (1, 2:509) suggests, with some plausibility, that Spinoza has Hobbes in mind here. However, Hobbes rejected Descartes' doctrine of judgment, and criticized it on grounds which might have inspired Spinoza's own criticisms here. In his thirteenth objection to the *Meditations* he distinguishes between the affirmation which is an act of the will—by which he seems to mean an act involving the use of words—and the internal assent which is not.

ulty of understanding. The will, therefore, is distinguished from the intellect because the intellect is finite and the will is infinite.

[III.A.(ii)] Secondly, it can be objected to us that experience seems to teach nothing more clearly than that we can suspend our judgment so as not to assent to things we perceive. This also seems to be confirmed from the fact that no one is said to be deceived insofar as he perceives something, but only insofar as he assents or dissents. E.g., someone who feigns a winged horse does not on that account grant that there is a winged horse, i.e., he is not on that account deceived unless at the same time he grants that there is a winged horse. Therefore, experience seems to teach nothing more clearly than that the will, *or* faculty of assenting, is free, and different from the faculty of understanding.

[III.A.(iii)] Thirdly, it can be objected that one affirmation does not seem to contain more reality than another, i.e., we do not seem to require a greater power to affirm that what is true, is true, than to affirm that something false is true. But [NS: with ideas it is different, for] we perceive that one idea has more reality, *or* perfection, than another. As some objects are more excellent than others, so also some ideas of objects are more perfect than others. This also seems to establish a difference between the will and the intellect.

[III.A.(iv)] Fourth, it can be objected that if man does not act from freedom of the will, what will happen if he is in a state of equilibrium, like Buridan's ass?[76] Will he perish of hunger and of thirst? If I concede that he will, I would seem to conceive an ass, or a statue of a man, not a man.[77] But if I deny that he will, then he will determine himself, and consequently have the faculty of going where he wills and doing what he wills.

Perhaps other things in addition to these can be objected. But because I am not bound to force on you what anyone can dream, I shall only take the trouble to reply to these objections—and that as briefly as I can.

[III.B.(i)] To the first I say that I grant that the will extends more widely than the intellect, if by intellect they understand only clear and distinct ideas. But I deny that the will extends more widely than perceptions, *or* the faculty of conceiving. And indeed, I do not see why the faculty of willing should be called infinite, when the faculty

---

[76] Buridan's ass was supposed to be perishing of both hunger and thirst, and placed at an equal distance from food and drink. But it seems that neither the particular example nor the doctrine it is intended to support are rightly attributed to Buridan. See Wolfson 1, 2:178, and Gueroult 1, 2:513.

[77] I.e., not a rational being, as the more explicit NS translation brings out.

of sensing is not. For just as we can affirm infinitely many things by the same faculty of willing (but one after another, for we cannot affirm infinitely many things at once), so also we can sense, *or* perceive, infinitely many bodies by the same faculty of sensing (viz. one after another [NS: and not at once].[78]

If they say that there are infinitely many things which we cannot perceive, I reply that we cannot reach them by any thought, and consequently, not by any faculty of willing. But, they say, if God willed to bring it about that we should perceive them also, he would have to give us a greater faculty of perceiving, but not a greater faculty of willing than he has given us. This is the same as if they said that, if God should will to bring it about that we understood infinitely many other beings, it would indeed be necessary for him to give us a greater intellect, but not a more universal idea of being, in order for us to embrace[79] the same infinity of beings. For we have shown that the will is a universal being, *or* idea, by which we explain all the singular volitions, i.e., it is what is common to them all.

Therefore, since they believe that this common *or* universal idea of all volitions is a faculty,[80] it is not at all surprising if they say that this faculty extends beyond the limits of the intellect to infinity. For the universal is said equally of one, a great many, or infinitely many individuals.

[III.B(ii)] To the second objection I reply by denying that we have a free power of suspending judgment. For when we say that someone suspends judgment, we are saying nothing but that he sees that he does not perceive the thing adequately. Suspension of judgment, therefore, is really a perception, not [an act of] free will.

To understand this clearly, let us conceive a child imagining a winged horse, and not perceiving anything else. Since this imagination involves the existence of the horse (by P17C), and the child does not perceive anything else that excludes the existence of the horse, he will necessarily regard the horse as present. Nor will he be able to doubt its existence, though he will not be certain of it.

[78] Part of what Gebhardt adds here, the part I have translated, is probably just a translator's elaboration. Part of it is misplaced, representing words which in fact occur in the NS as translating l. 29.

[79] The NS, in a variation not mentioned by Gebhardt, gloss "embrace" as "be able to bring under a universal being."

[80] Gebhardt notes that the NS reads quite differently at this point: "Because they believe that this universal volition of everything, or this universal idea of the will, is a faculty of our mind . . . ." He conjectures that the NS represents the first draft and incorporates the phrase "of our mind" in his text on the basis of that conjecture. Akkerman (2, 149) more plausibly suggests that the divergence comes from the translator's misreading *volitionum* as *volitionem*.

We find this daily in our dreams, and I do not believe there is anyone who thinks that while he is dreaming he has a free power of suspending judgment concerning the things he dreams, and of bringing it about that he does not dream the things he dreams he sees. Nevertheless, it happens that even in dreams we suspend judgment, viz. when we dream that we dream.

Next, I grant that no one is deceived insofar as he perceives, i.e., I grant that the imaginations of the Mind, considered in themselves, involve no error. But I deny that a man affirms nothing insofar as he perceives. For what is perceiving a winged horse other than affirming wings of the horse? For if the Mind perceived nothing else except the winged horse, it would regard it as present to itself, and would not have any cause of doubting its existence, or any faculty of dissenting, unless either the imagination of the winged horse were joined to an idea which excluded the existence of the same horse, or the Mind perceived that its idea of a winged horse was inadequate. And then either it will necessarily deny the horse's existence, or it will necessarily doubt it.

[III.B.(iii)] As for the third objection, I think what has been said will be an answer to it too: viz. that the will is something universal, which is predicated of all ideas, and which signifies only what is common to all ideas, viz. the affirmation, whose adequate essence, therefore, insofar as it is thus conceived abstractly, must be in each idea,[81] and in this way only must be the same in all, but not insofar as it is considered to constitute the idea's essence; for in that regard the singular affirmations differ from one another as much as the ideas themselves do. For example, the affirmation that the idea of a circle involves differs from that which the idea of a triangle involves as much as the idea of the circle differs from the idea of the triangle.

Next, I deny absolutely that we require an equal power of thinking, to affirm that what is true is true, as to affirm that what is false is true. For if you consider the mind,[82] they are related to one another as being to not-being. For there is nothing positive in ideas which constitutes the form of falsity (see P35, P35S, and P47S). So the thing to note here, above all, is how easily we are deceived when we confuse

[81] At this point the NS add an example which is absent from the OP: "as the definition of man must be attributed wholly and equally to each particular man." Gebhardt incorporates the example in the text, but mislocates it, and consequently gives a misleading picture of the variation between the two texts. Cf. Akkerman 2, 81. In l. 4 I follow the punctuation of the OP rather than that of Gebhardt, who follows the NS.

[82] The words Gebhardt incorporates from the NS would make this read: "If you consider only the mind and not the words." Akkerman (2, 149) rejects this as a translator's elaboration.

universals with singulars, and beings of reason and abstractions with real beings.

[III.B. (iv)] Finally, as far as the fourth objection is concerned, I say that I grant entirely that a man placed in such an equilibrium (viz. who perceives nothing but thirst and hunger, and such food and drink as are equally distant from him) will perish of hunger and thirst. If they ask me whether such a man should not be thought an ass, rather than a man, I say that I do not know—just as I also do not know how highly we should esteem one who hangs himself, or children, fools, and madmen, etc.[83]

[IV.] It remains now to indicate how much knowledge of this doctrine is to our advantage in life. We shall see this easily from the following considerations:

[A.] Insofar as it teaches that we act only from God's command, that we share in the divine nature, and that we do this the more, the more perfect our actions are, and the more and more we understand God. This doctrine, then, in addition to giving us complete peace of mind, also teaches us wherein our greatest happiness, *or* blessedness, consists: viz. in the knowledge of God alone, by which we are led to do only those things which love and morality advise. From this we clearly understand how far they stray from the true valuation of virtue, who expect to be honored by God with the greatest rewards for their virtue and best actions, as for the greatest bondage—as if virtue itself, and the service of God, were not happiness itself, and the greatest freedom.

[B.] Insofar as it teaches us how we must bear ourselves concerning matters of fortune, *or* things which are not in our power, i.e., concerning things which do not follow from our nature—that we must expect and bear calmly both good fortune and bad. For all things follow from God's eternal decree with the same necessity as from the essence of a triangle it follows that its three angles are equal to two right angles.

[C.] This doctrine contributes to social life, insofar as it teaches us to hate no one, to disesteem no one, to mock no one, to be angry at no one, to envy no one; and also insofar as it teaches that each of us should be content with his own things, and should be helpful to his neighbor, not from unmanly compassion, partiality, or superstition, but from the guidance of reason, as the time and occasion demand. I shall show this in the Fourth Part.[84]

[83] Cf. Wolfson 1, 2:178-179, on this phrase.
[84] Both the OP and the NS read "Third Part" here. But as Gebhardt remarks this clearly comes from a time when the Third, Fourth, and Fifth Parts formed one part.

[D.] Finally, this doctrine also contributes, to no small extent, to the common society insofar as it teaches how citizens are to be governed and led, not so that they may be slaves, but that they may do freely the things that are best.

And with this I have finished what I had decided to treat in this scholium, and put an end to this our Second Part. In it I think that I have explained the nature and properties of the human Mind in sufficient detail, and as clearly as the difficulty of the subject allows, and that I have set out doctrines from which we can infer many excellent things, which are highly useful and necessary to know, as will be established partly in what follows.

Third Part Of the Ethics
On the Origin and Nature
of the Affects[1]

Preface

Most of those who have written about the Affects, and men's way of living, seem to treat, not of natural things, which follow the common laws of nature, but of things which are outside nature. Indeed they seem to conceive man in nature as a dominion within a dominion. For they believe that man disturbs, rather than follows, the order of nature, that he has absolute power over his actions, and that he is determined only by himself. And they attribute the cause of human impotence, not to the common power of nature, but to I know not what vice of human nature, which they therefore bewail, or laugh at, or disdain, or (as usually happens) curse. And he who knows how to censure more eloquently and cunningly the weakness of the human Mind is held to be Godly.

It is true that there have been some very distinguished men (to whose work and diligence we confess that we owe much), who have written many admirable things about the right way of living, and given men advice full of prudence. But no one, to my knowledge, has determined the nature and powers of the Affects,[2] nor what, on the other hand, the Mind can do to moderate them. I know, of course, that the celebrated Descartes, although he too believed that the Mind has absolute power over its own actions, nevertheless sought to explain

---

[1] Akkerman (2, 69) suggests that the title should read "On the Nature and Origin of the Affects." Cf. the title of Part II and II/186/9.

[2] Akkerman (2, 70), appealing to the NS, suggests reading: "But so far no one, to my knowledge, has determined the true nature and powers of the Affects."

491

human Affects through their first causes, and at the same time to show the way by which the Mind can have absolute dominion over its Affects.[3] But in my opinion, he showed nothing but the cleverness of his understanding, as I shall
5 *show in the proper place.*

For now I wish to return to those who prefer to curse and laugh at the Affects and actions of men, rather than understand them. To them it will doubtless seem strange that I should undertake to treat men's vices and absurd-ities in the Geometric style, and that I should wish to demonstrate in a certain
10 *manner things which are contrary to reason, and which they proclaim to be empty, absurd, and horrible.*

But my reason is this:[4] nothing happens in nature which can be attributed to any defect in it, for nature is always the same, and its virtue and power of acting are everywhere one and the same, i.e., the laws and rules of nature,
15 *according to which all things happen, and change from one form to another, are always and everywhere the same. So the way of understanding the nature of anything, of whatever kind, must also be the same, viz. through the uni-versal laws and rules of nature.*

The Affects, therefore, of hate, anger, envy, etc., considered in themselves,
20 *follow from the same necessity and force of nature as the other singular things. And therefore they acknowledge certain causes, through which they are under-stood, and have certain properties, as worthy of our knowledge as the properties of any other thing, by the mere contemplation of which we are pleased. There-fore, I shall treat the nature and powers of the Affects, and the power of the*
25 *Mind over them, by the same Method by which, in the preceding parts, I treated God and the Mind, and I shall consider human actions and appetites just as if it were a Question of lines, planes, and bodies.*

II/139   DEFINITIONS

D1: I call that cause adequate whose effect can be clearly and dis-tinctly perceived through it. But I call it partial, *or* inadequate, if its
5 effect cannot be understood through it alone.

---

[3] Cf. PA I, 50.

[4] Akkerman (2, 71) notes an allusion here to Micio's monologue on moral education in Terence's *Adelphi* (68ff.). Other allusions to this speech occur at 203/5ff., and 244/18ff. As Appuhn observes (3:370) Spinoza seems to have been much impressed with Micio's contention that a father should accustom his son to do right from inclination rather than from fear (cf. E IVP18). From the frequency of references to Terence's works in general, it appears that Spinoza knew them well. Van den Enden, from whom Spinoza learned his Latin, used student performances of classical plays as a means of instruction, and Spinoza may well have taken part in these. Cf. Meinsma, 185ff. and Akkerman 2, 9. Spinoza's acquaintance with classical authors (not only Terence, but also Ovid, Tacitus, Sallust, Livy, Cicero and Seneca) seems to have greatly influenced his psychology, ethics and political theory.

D2: I say that we act when something happens, in us or outside us, of which we are the adequate cause, i.e. (by D1), when something in us or outside us follows from our nature, which can be clearly and distinctly understood through it alone. On the other hand, I say that we are acted on when something happens in us, or something follows from our nature, of which we are only a partial cause.

D3: By affect I understand affections of the Body by which the Body's power of acting is increased or diminished, aided or restrained, and at the same time, the ideas of these affections.

Therefore, if we can be the adequate cause of any of these affections, I understand by the Affect an action; otherwise, a passion.

POSTULATES

Post. 1: The human Body can be affected in many ways in which its power of acting is increased or diminished, and also in others which render its power of acting neither greater nor less.

This Postulate, or Axiom, rests on Post. 1, L5, and L7 (after IIP13).

Post. 2: The human Body can undergo many changes, and nevertheless retain impressions, *or* traces, of the objects (on this see IIPost. 5), and consequently, the same images of things. (For the definition of images, see IIP17S.)

P1: *Our Mind does certain things [acts] and undergoes other things, viz. insofar as it has adequate ideas, it necessarily does certain things, and insofar as it has inadequate ideas, it necessarily undergoes other things.*

Dem.: In each human Mind some ideas are adequate, but others are mutilated and confused (by IIP40S).[5] But ideas that are adequate in someone's Mind are adequate in God insofar as he constitutes the essence of that Mind [only][6] (by IIP11C). And those that are inadequate in the Mind are also adequate in God (by the same Cor.), not insofar as he contains only the essence of that Mind, but insofar as he also contains in himself, at the same time, the Minds[7] of other things. Next, from any given idea some effect must necessarily follow (IP36), of which effect God is the adequate cause (see D1), not insofar as he is infinite, but insofar as he is considered to be affected by that given idea (see IIP9). But if God, insofar as he is affected by an idea that is

---

[5] See the note at I/120/15.
[6] An addition suggested by Gueroult 1, 2:544. Cf. l.15.
[7] White proposed to read "ideas" here (and at l. 27), pointing out that IIP11C reads that way. But both the OP and the NS support "Minds," and it is not unusual for Spinoza to paraphrase previous statements when he cites them in proofs.

adequate in someone's Mind, is the cause of an effect, that same Mind is the effect's adequate cause (by IIP11C). Therefore, our Mind (by D2), insofar as it has adequate ideas, necessarily does certain things [acts]. This was the first thing to be proven.

25 Next, if something necessarily follows from an idea that is adequate in God, not insofar as he has in himself the Mind of one man only, but insofar as he has in himself the Minds of other things together with the Mind of that man, that man's Mind (by the same IIP11C) is not its adequate cause, but its partial cause. Hence (by D2), insofar as 30 the Mind has inadequate ideas, it necessarily undergoes certain things. This was the second point. Therefore, our Mind, etc., q.e.d.

II/141 Cor.: From this it follows that the Mind is more liable to passions the more it has inadequate ideas, and conversely, is more active the more it has adequate ideas.

5 P2: *The Body cannot determine the Mind to thinking, and the Mind cannot determine the Body to motion, to rest or to anything else (if there is anything else).*

10 Dem.: All modes of thinking have God for a cause, insofar as he is a thinking thing, and not insofar as he is explained by another attribute (by IIP6). So what determines the Mind to thinking is a mode of thinking and not of Extension, i.e. (by IID1), it is not the Body. This was the first point.

15 Next, the motion and rest of the Body must arise from another body, which has also been determined to motion or rest by another; and absolutely, whatever arises in the body must have arisen from God insofar as he is considered to be affected by some mode of Extension, and not insofar as he is considered to be affected by some mode of thinking (also by IIP6), i.e., it cannot arise from the Mind, 20 which (by IIP11) is a mode of thinking. This was the second point. Therefore, the Body cannot determine the Mind, etc., q.e.d.

Schol.: These things are more clearly understood from what is said in IIP7S, viz. that the Mind and the Body are one and the same thing, 25 which is conceived now under the attribute of Thought, now under the attribute of Extension. The result is that the order, *or* connection, of things is one, whether nature is conceived under this attribute or that; hence the order of actions and passions of our Body is, by nature, at one with the order of actions and passions of the Mind. This is also 30 evident from the way in which we have demonstrated IIP12.

But although these things are such that no reason for doubt remains, II/142 still, I hardly believe that men can be induced to consider them fairly unless I confirm them by experience. They are so firmly persuaded that the Body now moves, now is at rest, solely from the Mind's command, and that it does a great many things which depend only on the Mind's will and its art of thinking.

And of course, no one has yet determined what the Body can do, i.e., experience has not yet taught anyone what the Body can do from the laws of nature alone, insofar as nature is only considered to be corporeal, and what the body can do only if it is determined by the Mind. For no one has yet come to know the structure of the Body so accurately that he could explain all its functions[8]—not to mention that many things are observed in the lower Animals that far surpass human ingenuity, and that sleepwalkers do a great many things in their sleep that they would not dare to awake. This shows well enough that the Body itself, simply from the laws of its own nature, can do many things which its Mind wonders at.

Again, no one know how, or by what means, the Mind moves the body, nor how many degrees of motion it can give the body, nor with what speed it can move it. So it follows that when men say that this or that action of the Body arises from the Mind, which has dominion over the Body, they do not know what they are saying, and they do nothing but confess, in fine-sounding words, that they are ignorant of the true cause of that action, and that they do not wonder at it.

But they will say [i] that—whether or not they know by what means the Mind moves the Body—they still know by experience that unless the human Mind were capable of thinking, the Body would be inactive.[9] And then [ii], they know by experience, that it is in the Mind's power alone both to speak and to be silent,[10] and to do many other things which they therefore believe depend on the Mind's decision.

[i] As far as the first [objection] is concerned, I ask them, does not experience also teach that if, on the other hand, the Body is inactive, the Mind is at the same time incapable of thinking? For when the Body is at rest in sleep, the Mind at the same time remains senseless with it, nor does it have the power of thinking, as it does when awake. And then I believe everyone has found by experience that the Mind is not always equally capable of thinking of the same object, but that as the Body is more susceptible to having the image of this or that object aroused in it, so the Mind is more capable of regarding this or that object.

[8] Wolfson (1, 2:190) plausibly suggests PA I, 7-17, as the target of this.

[9] OP: *iners*. The NS glosses this: "without power or incapable." Similarly at l. 27. If "inactive" were interpreted to mean "without motion," then Descartes could not be the intended opponent, since he held the body to be capable of much movement without the aid of the soul (PA, I, 16).

[10] According to Wolfson (1, 2:191) an argument like this may be found in Saadia.

35
II/143

They will say, of course, that it cannot happen that the causes of buildings, of paintings, and of things of this kind, which are made only by human skill, should be able to be deduced from the laws of nature alone, insofar as it is considered to be only corporeal; nor would the human Body be able to build a temple, if it were not determined and guided by the Mind.

5

But I have already shown that they do not know what the Body can do, or what can be deduced from the consideration of its nature alone, and that they know from experience that a great many things happen from the laws of nature alone which they never would have believed could happen without the direction of the Mind—such as the things sleepwalkers do in their sleep, which they wonder at while they are awake.

10

I add here the very structure of the human Body, which, in the ingenuity of its construction, far surpasses anything made by human skill—not to mention that I have shown above, that infinitely many things follow from nature, under whatever attribute it may be considered.

15

[ii] As for the second [objection], human affairs, of course, would be conducted far more happily if it were equally in man's power to be silent and to speak. But experience teaches all too plainly that men have nothing less in their power than their tongue, and can do nothing less than moderate their appetites.

20

That is why most men believe that we do freely only those things we have a weak inclination toward (because the appetite for these things can easily be reduced by the memory of another thing which we frequently recollect), but that we do not at all do freely those things we seek by a strong affect, which cannot be calmed by the memory of another thing. But if they had not found by experience that we do many things we afterwards repent, and that often we see the better and follow the worse (viz. when we are torn by contrary affects), nothing would prevent them from believing that we do all things freely.

25

So the infant believes he freely wants the milk; the angry child that he wants vengeance; and the timid, flight. So the drunk believes it is from a free decision of the Mind that he speaks the things he later, when sober, wishes he had not said. So the madman, the chatterbox, the child, and a great many people of this kind believe they speak from a free decision of the Mind, when really they cannot contain their impulse to speak.

30

So experience itself, no less clearly than reason, teaches that men believe themselves free because they are conscious of their own actions, and ignorant of the causes by which they are determined, that the decisions of the Mind are nothing but the appetites themselves, which therefore vary as the disposition of the Body varies. For each one governs everything from his affect; those who are torn by contrary affects do not know what they want, and those who are not moved by any affect are very easily driven here and there.[11]

All these things, indeed, show clearly that both the decision of the Mind and the appetite and the determination of the Body by nature exist together—or rather are one and the same thing, which we call a decision when it is considered under, and explained through, the attribute of Thought, and which we call a determination when it is considered under the attribute of Extension and deduced from the laws of motion and rest. This will be still more clearly evident from what must presently be said.

For there is something else I wish particularly to note here, that we can do nothing from a decision of the Mind unless we recollect it. E.g., we cannot speak a word unless we recollect it. And it is not in the free power of the Mind to either recollect a thing or forget it.[12] So this only is believed to be in the power of the Mind—that from the Mind's decision alone we can either be silent about or speak about a thing we recollect.

But when we dream that we speak, we believe that we speak from a free decision of the Mind—and yet we do not speak, or, if we do, it is from a spontaneous motion of the Body. And we dream that we conceal certain things from men, and this by the same decision of the Mind by which, while we wake, we are silent about the things we know. We dream, finally, that, from a decision of the Mind, we do certain things we do not dare to do while we wake.

So I should very much like to know whether there are in the Mind two kinds of decisions—those belonging to our fantasies and those that are free? And if we do not want to go that far in our madness, it must be granted that this decision of the Mind which is believed to be free is not distinguished by the imagination itself, *or* the memory, nor is it anything beyond that affirmation which the idea, insofar as it is an idea, necessarily involves (see IIP49). And so these decisions of the Mind arise by the same necessity as the ideas of things that actually exist. Those, therefore, who believe that they either speak or are silent, or do anything from a free decision of the Mind, dream with open eyes.

P3: *The actions of the Mind arise from adequate ideas alone; the passions depend on inadequate ideas alone.*

[11] Cf. Terence, *Andria*, 266, and the note at 138/11.   [12] PA I, 42.

II/145   Dem.: The first thing that constitutes the essence of the Mind is nothing but the idea of an actually existing Body (by IIP11 and P13); this idea (by IIP15) is composed of many others, of which some are adequate (IIP38C), and others inadequate (by IIP29C). Therefore, whatever follows from the nature of the Mind and has the Mind as its proximate cause, through which it must be understood, must necessarily follow from an adequate idea or an inadequate one. But insofar as the Mind has inadequate ideas (by P1), it necessarily is acted on. Therefore, the actions of the Mind follow from adequate ideas alone; hence, the Mind is acted on only because it has inadequate ideas, q.e.d.

    Schol.: We see, then, that the passions are not related to the Mind except insofar as it has something which involves a negation, *or* insofar as it is considered as a part of nature which cannot be perceived clearly and distinctly through itself, without the others. In this way I could show that the passions are related to singular things in the same way as to the Mind,[13] and cannot be perceived in any other way. But my purpose is only to treat of the human Mind.

    P4: *No thing can be destroyed except through an external cause.*

    Dem.: This Proposition is evident through itself. For the definition of any thing affirms, and does not deny, the thing's essence, *or* it posits the thing's essence, and does not take it away. So while we attend only to the thing itself, and not to external causes, we shall not be able to find anything in it which can destroy it, q.e.d.

    P5: *Things*[14] *are of a contrary nature, i.e., cannot be in the same subject, insofar as one can destroy the other.*

    Dem.: For if they could agree with one another, or be in the same subject at once, then there could be something in the same subject which could destroy it, which (by P4) is absurd. Therefore, things etc., q.e.d.

    P6: *Each thing, as far as it can by its own power,*[15] *strives to persevere in its being.*

---

[13] Wolfson (1, II, 192) opposes this to Descartes' statement (PA I, 2) that what is a passion in the soul is generally an action in the body. He also suggests that by "singular things" here Spinoza means "bodies."

[14] Wolfson ((1), II, 192) contends that "thing" here *means* "our body," appealing to P10D. But the statement there is surely better regarded as an instantiation of P5, rather than a paraphrase of it. If P5 were not fully general, then P6 could not have the generality Spinoza wants it to have.

[15] It is unclear whether *quantum in se est* should be regarded as an occurrence of the technical phrase used in the definition of substance (as Elwes and White suggest by translating *insofar as it is in itself*) or merely as an occurrence of an ordinary Latin idiom,

Dem.: For singular things are modes by which God's attributes are expressed in a certain and determinate way (by IP25C), i.e. (by IP34), things that express, in a certain and determinate way, God's power, by which God is and acts. And no thing has anything in itself by which it can be destroyed, *or* which takes its existence away (by P4). On the contrary, it is opposed to everything which can take its existence away (by P5). Therefore, as far as it can, and it lies in itself, it strives to persevere in its being, q.e.d.

P7: *The striving by which each thing strives to persevere in its being is nothing but the actual essence of the thing.*

Dem.: From the given essence of each thing some things necessarily follow (by IP36), and things are able [to produce] nothing but what follows necessarily from their determinate nature (by IP29). So the power of each thing, *or* the striving by which it (either alone or with others) does anything, or strives to do anything—i.e. (by P6), the power, *or* striving, by which it strives to persevere in its being, is nothing but the given, *or* actual, essence of the thing itself, q.e.d.

P8: *The striving by which each thing strives to persevere in its being involves no finite time, but an indefinite time.*

Dem.: For if [the striving by which a thing strives to persevere in its being] involved a limited time, which determined the thing's duration, then it would follow just from that very power by which the thing exists that it could not exist after that limited time, but that it would have to be destroyed. But (by P4) this is absurd. Therefore, the striving by which a thing exists involves no definite time. On the contrary, since (by P4) it will always continue to exist by the same power by which it now exists, unless it is destroyed by an external cause, this striving involves indefinite time, q.e.d.

P9: *Both insofar as the Mind has clear and distinct ideas, and insofar as it has confused ideas, it strives, for an indefinite duration, to persevere in its being and it is conscious of this striving it has.*

Dem.: The essence of the Mind is constituted by adequate and by inadequate ideas (as we have shown in P3). So (by P7) it strives to persevere in its being both insofar as it has inadequate ideas and insofar as it has adequate ideas; and it does this (by P8) for an indefinite duration. But since the Mind (by IIP23) is necessarily conscious of

---

which might be rendered *as far as it lies in itself* or *as far as it lies in its own power*. Caillois (Pléiade, 1433) favors the latter alternative, referring us to Descartes' *Principles of Philosophy* II, 37 and to Spinoza's version of this at I/201. See also Cohen.

itself through ideas of the Body's affections, the Mind (by P7) is conscious of its striving, q.e.d.

Schol.: When this striving is related only to the Mind, it is called
Will; but when it is related to the Mind and Body together, it is called
Appetite. This Appetite, therefore, is nothing but the very essence of
man, from whose nature there necessarily follow those things that
promote his preservation. And so man is determined to do those things.
Between appetite and desire there is no difference, except that desire is generally related to men insofar as they are conscious of their
appetites. So *desire* can be defined as *appetite together with consciousness
of the appetite.*

From all this, then, it is clear that we neither strive for, nor will,
neither want, nor desire anything because we judge it to be good; on
the contrary, we judge something to be good because we strive for it,
will it, want it, and desire it.[16]

P10: *An idea that excludes the existence of our Body cannot be in our Mind,
but is contrary to it.*

Dem.: Whatever can destroy our Body cannot be in it (by P5), and
so the idea of this thing cannot be in God insofar as he has the idea
of our Body (by IIP9C), i.e. (by IIP11 and P13), the idea of this thing
cannot be in our Mind. On the contrary, since (by IIP11 and P13) the
first thing that constitutes the essence of the Mind is the idea of an
actually existing Body, the first and principal [tendency] of the striving[17]
of our Mind (by P7) is to affirm the existence of our Body. And so an
idea that denies the existence of our Body is contrary to our Mind,
etc., q.e.d.

P11: *The idea of any thing that increases or diminishes, aids or restrains, our
Body's power of acting, increases or diminishes, aids or restrains, our Mind's
power of thinking.*

Dem.: This proposition is evident from IIP7, or also from IIP14.

Schol.: We see, then, that the Mind can undergo great changes, and
pass now to a greater, now to a lesser perfection. These passions,
indeed, explain to us the affects of Joy and Sadness. By *Joy*, therefore,

---

[16] Cf. Hobbes, *Leviathan* vi. Descartes, on the other hand, classes desire among the
passions born of the consideration of good and evil. Cf. PA II, 57, 86.

[17] Gebhardt reads: "conatus," which would require a translation like "the first and
principal [sc. thing that constitutes the essence?] of our Mind is the striving to affirm
the existence of our Body." Akkerman (2, 65) argues persuasively for the reading of the
OP and NS: "conatûs," which yields what I have given in the text. Either reading
seems to me to require the English translator to supply some noun for "first and principal" to modify. But "tendency" is only a suggestion.

I shall understand in what follows that *passion by which the Mind passes to a greater perfection*. And by *Sadness*, that *passion by which it passes to a lesser perfection*. The *affect of Joy which is related to the Mind and Body at once* I call *Pleasure* or *Cheerfulness*, and that of *Sadness, Pain* or *Melancholy*.

But it should be noted [NS: here] that Pleasure and Pain are ascribed to a man when one part of him is affected more than the rest, whereas Cheerfulness and Melancholy are ascribed to him when all are equally affected.

Next, I have explained in P9S what Desire is, and apart from these three I do not acknowledge any other primary affect.[18] For I shall show in what follows that the rest arise from these three. But before I proceed further, I should like to explain P10 more fully here, so that it may be more clearly understood how one idea is contrary to another.

In IIP17S we have shown that the idea which constitutes the essence of the Mind involves the existence of the Body so long as the Body itself exists. Next from what we have shown in IIP8C and its scholium, it follows that the present existence of our Mind depends only on this, that the Mind involves the actual existence of the Body. Finally, we have shown that the power of the Mind by which it imagines things and recollects them also depends on this (see IIP17, P18, P18S), that it involves the actual existence of the Body.

From these things it follows that the present existence of the Mind and its power of imagining are taken away as soon as the Mind ceases to affirm the present existence of the Body. But the cause of the Mind's ceasing to affirm this existence of the Body cannot be the Mind itself (by P4), nor also that the Body ceases to exist. For (by IIP6) the cause of the Mind's affirming the Body's existence is not that the Body has begun to exist. So by the same reasoning, it does not cease to affirm the Body's existence because the Body ceases to exist, but (by IIP8)[19] this [sc. ceasing to affirm the Body's existence] arises from another idea which excludes the present existence of our body, and consequently of our Mind, and which is thus contrary to the idea that constitutes our Mind's essence.

[18] Descartes (PA II, 69), by contrast, recognizes six primitive passions. In addition to desire, joy, and sadness: love, hate, and wonder. For a survey of other reductionist programs, see Bidney, 67-75.

[19] It is difficult to see the relevance of IIP8 here, and some have thought this must be a mistake, though there is no agreement on what proposition should have been cited. IIP17, IIP18, and IIP6 have all been suggested. Gebhardt (II/369) defends the text of the OP, on obscure grounds. Bennett suggests (in correspondence) IIP7, which is said (at IIIP2S) to support IIIP2, which in turn supports the conclusion here.

II/150 P12: *The Mind, as far as it can, strives to imagine those things that increase or aid the Body's power of acting.*

5   Dem.: So long as the human Body is affected with a mode that involves the nature of an external body, the human Mind will regard the same body as present (by IIP17) and consequently (by IIP7) so long as the human Mind regards some external body as present, i.e.

10 (by IIP17S), imagines it, the human Body is affected with a mode that involves the nature of that external body. Hence, so long as the Mind imagines those things that increase or aid our body's power of acting, the Body is affected with modes that increase or aid its power of acting

15 (see Post. 1), and consequently (by P11) the Mind's power of thinking is increased or aided. Therefore (by P6 or P9), the Mind, as far as it can, strives to imagine those things, q.e.d.

20 P13: *When the Mind imagines those things that diminish or restrain the Body's power of acting, it strives, as far as it can, to recollect things that exclude their existence.*

    Dem.: So long as the Mind imagines anything of this kind, the

25 power both of Mind and of Body is diminished or restrained (as we have demonstrated in P12); nevertheless, the Mind will continue to imagine this thing until it imagines something else that excludes the thing's present existence (by IIP17), i.e. (as we have just shown), the power both of Mind and of Body is diminished or restrained until the

30 Mind imagines something else that excludes the existence of this thing; so the Mind (by P9), as far as it can, will strive to imagine or recollect that other thing, q.e.d.

II/151   Cor.: From this it follows that the Mind avoids imagining those things that diminish or restrain its or the Body's power.

5   Schol.: From this we understand clearly what Love and Hate are. *Love is* nothing but *Joy with the accompanying idea of an external cause,* and *Hate is* nothing but *Sadness with the accompanying idea of an external cause.* We see, then, that one who loves necessarily strives to have present and preserve the thing he loves; and on the other hand, one

10 who hates strives to remove and destroy the thing he hates. But all of these things will be discussed more fully in what follows.

P14: *If the Mind has once been affected by two affects at once, then afterwards, when it is affected by one of them, it will also be affected by the other.*

15   Dem.: If the human Body has once been affected by two bodies at once, then afterwards, when the Mind imagines one of them, it will immediately recollect the other also (by IIP18). But the imaginations of the Mind indicate the affects of our Body more than the nature of

20 external bodies (by IIP16C2). Therefore, if the Body, and conse-

quently the Mind (see D3) has once been affected by two affects [NS: at once], then afterwards, when it is affected by one of them, it will also be affected by the other, q.e.d.

P15: *Any thing can be the accidental cause of Joy, Sadness, or Desire.*

Dem.: Suppose the Mind is affected by two affects at once, one of which neither increases nor diminishes its power of acting, while the other either increases it or diminishes it (see Post. 1). From P14 it is clear that when the Mind is afterwards affected with the former affect as by its true cause,[20] which (by hypothesis) through itself neither increases nor diminishes its power of thinking, it will immediately be affected with the latter also, which increases or diminishes its power of thinking, i.e. (by P11S), with Joy, or Sadness. And so the former thing will be the cause of Joy or Sadness—not through itself, but accidentally. And in the same way it can easily be shown that that thing can be the accidental cause of Desire, q.e.d.

Cor.: From this alone—that we have regarded a thing with an affect of Joy or Sadness, of which it is not itself the efficient cause, we can love it or hate it.

Dem.: For from this alone it comes about (by P14) that when the Mind afterwards imagines this thing, it is affected with an affect of Joy or Sadness, i.e. (by P11S), that the power both of the Mind and of the Body is increased or diminished. And consequently (by P12), the Mind desires to imagine the thing or (by P13C) avoids it, i.e. (by P13S), it loves it or hates it, q.e.d.

Schol.: From this we understand how it can happen that we love or hate some things without any cause known to us, but only (as they say) from Sympathy or Antipathy. And to this must be related also those objects that affect us with Joy or Sadness only because they have some likeness to objects that usually affect us with these affects, as I shall show in P16. I know, of course, that the Authors who first introduced the words Sympathy and Antipathy intended to signify by them certain qualities of things. Nevertheless, I believe we may be permitted to understand by them also qualities that are known or manifest.

P16: *From the mere fact that we imagine a thing to have some likeness to an object that usually affects the Mind with Joy or Sadness, we love it or hate it, even though that in which the thing is like the object is not the efficient cause of these affects.*

[20] Following Akkerman (2, 162) who proposes to read: "tanquam a sua vera causa" (cf. NS).

503

Dem.: What is like the object, we have (by hypothesis) regarded in the object itself with an affect of Joy or Sadness. And so (by P14), when the Mind is affected by its image, it will immediately be affected also with this or that affect. Consequently the thing we perceive to have this same [quality] will (by P15) be the accidental cause of Joy or Sadness; and so (by P15C) although that in which it is like the object is not the efficient cause of these affects, we shall still love it or hate it, q.e.d.

P17: *If we imagine that a thing which usually affects us with an affect of Sadness is like another which usually affects us with an equally great affect of Joy, we shall hate it and at the same time love it.*

Dem.: For (by hypothesis) this thing is through itself the cause of Sadness, and (by P13S) insofar as we imagine it with this affect, we hate it. And moreover, insofar as it has some likeness to the other thing, which usually affects us with an equally great affect of Joy, we shall love it with an equally great striving of Joy (by P16). And so we shall both hate it and at the same time love it, q.e.d.

Schol.: This *constitution of the Mind which arises from two contrary affects* is called *vacillation of mind*, which is therefore related to the affect as doubt is to the imagination (see IIP44S); nor do vacillation of mind and doubt differ from one another except in degree.

But it should be noted that in the preceding Proposition I have deduced these vacillations of mind from causes which are the cause through themselves of one affect and the accidental cause of the other. I have done this because in this way they could more easily be deduced from what has gone before, not because I deny that vacillations of mind for the most part arise from an object which is the efficient cause of each affect. For the human Body (by IIPost. 1) is composed of a great many individuals of different natures, and so (by IIA1″ [at II/99]), it can be affected in a great many different ways by one and the same body. And on the other hand, because one and the same thing can be affected in many ways, it will also be able to affect one and the same part of the body in many different ways. From this we can easily conceive that one and the same object can be the cause of many and contrary affects.

P18: *Man is affected with the same affect of Joy or Sadness from the image of a past or future thing as from the image of a present thing.*

Dem.: So long as a man is affected by the image of a thing, he will regard the thing as present, even if it does not exist (by IIP17 and P17C); he imagines it as past or future only insofar as its image is joined to the image of a past or future time (see IIP44S). So the image of a thing, considered only in itself, is the same, whether it is related to time past or future, or to the present, i.e. (by IIP16C2), the constitution of the Body, *or* affect, is the same, whether the image is of a thing past or future, or of a present thing. And so, the affect of Joy or Sadness is the same, whether the image is of a thing past or future, or of a present thing, q.e.d.

Schol. 1:[21] I call a thing past or future here, insofar as we have been affected by it, or will be affected by it. E.g., insofar as we have seen it or will see it, insofar as it has refreshed us or will refresh us, has injured us or will injure us. For insofar as we imagine it in this way, we affirm its existence, i.e., the Body is not affected by any affect that excludes the thing's existence. And so (by IIP17) the Body is affected with the image of the thing in the same way as if the thing itself were present. However, because it generally happens that those who have experienced many things vacillate so long as they regard a thing as future or past, and most often doubt the thing's outcome (see IIP44S), the affects that arise from similar images[22] of things are not so constant, but are generally disturbed by the images of other things, until men become more certain of the thing's outcome.

Schol. 2: From what has just been said, we understand what Hope and Fear, Confidence and Despair, Gladness and Remorse are. For *Hope* is nothing but *an inconstant Joy which has arisen from the image of a future or past thing whose outcome we doubt; Fear*, on the other hand, is *an inconstant Sadness, which has also arisen from the image of a doubtful thing*. Next, if the doubt involved in these affects is removed, Hope becomes *Confidence*, and Fear, *Despair*—viz. *a Joy or Sadness which has arisen from the image of a thing we feared or hoped for*. Finally, *Gladness is a Joy which has arisen from the image of a past thing whose outcome we doubted*, while *Remorse is a sadness which is opposite to Gladness.*

P19: *He who imagines that what he loves is destroyed will be saddened; but he who imagines it to be preserved, will rejoice.*

Dem.: Insofar as it can, the Mind strives to imagine those things that increase or aid the Body's power of acting (by P12), i.e. (by P13S), those it loves. But the imagination is aided by what posits the existence of a thing, and on the other hand, is restrained by what excludes

---

[21] In the OP this scholium is not numbered and there are subsequent references (at 177/26 and 195/2) to P18S, without any numbering. Gebhardt inferred from this that originally the two scholia were one, and that the subsequent references were to S1 and S2 collectively. But the NS number both scholia, and some subsequent references are to numbered scholia (e.g., at 177/31 and 210/5). Akkerman (2, 81-2) rejects Gebhardt's theory and takes the unnumbered references both to be to S1. Cf. IIP40S1.

[22] This means, I think, the affects that arise from the process of association described in P16.

25 the existence of a thing (by IIP17). Therefore, the images of things that posit the existence of a thing loved aid the Mind's striving to imagine the thing loved, i.e. (by P11S), affect the Mind with Joy. On the other hand, those which exclude the existence of a thing loved, restrain the same striving of the Mind, i.e. (by P11S), affect the Mind
30 with Sadness. Therefore, he who imagines that what he loves is destroyed will be saddened, etc., q.e.d.

II/156 P20: *He who imagines that what he hates is destroyed will rejoice.*

Dem.: The Mind (by P13) strives to imagine those things that ex-
5 clude the existence of things by which the Body's power of acting is diminished or restrained, i.e. (by P13S), strives to imagine those things that exclude the existence of things it hates. So the image of a thing that excludes the existence of what the Mind hates aids this striving of the Mind, i.e. (by P11S), affects the Mind with Joy. Therefore, he
10 who imagines that what he hates is destroyed will rejoice, q.e.d.

15 P21: *He who imagines what he loves to be affected with Joy or Sadness will also be affected with Joy or Sadness; and each of those affects will be greater or lesser in the lover as they are greater or lesser in the thing loved.*

Dem.: The images of things (as we have demonstrated in P19) which posit the existence of a thing loved aid the striving by which the Mind
20 strives to imagine the thing loved. But Joy posits the existence of the joyous thing, and posits more existence, the greater the affect of Joy is. For (by P11S) it is a transition to a greater perfection. Therefore, the image in the lover of the loved thing's Joy aids his Mind's striving, i.e. (by P11S), affects the lover with Joy, and the more so, the greater
25 this affect was in the thing loved. This was the first thing to be proved.

Next, insofar as a thing is affected with Sadness, it is destroyed, and the more so, the greater the Sadness with which it is affected (by P11S). So (by P19) he who imagines what he loves to be affected with Sadness, will also be affected with Sadness, and the more so, the
30 greater this affect was in the thing loved, q.e.d.

II/157 P22: *If we imagine someone to affect with Joy a thing we love, we shall be affected with Love toward him. If, on the other hand, we imagine him to affect*
5 *the same thing with Sadness, we shall also be affected with Hate toward him.*

Dem.: He who affects a thing we love with Joy or Sadness affects us also with Joy or Sadness, if we imagine that the thing loved is
10 affected by that Joy or Sadness (by P21). But this Joy or Sadness is supposed to be accompanied in us by the idea of an external cause. Therefore (by P13S), if we imagine that someone affects with Joy or Sadness a thing we love, we shall be affected with Love or Hate toward him, q.e.d.

Schol.: P21 explains to us what *Pity* is, which we can define as *Sadness that has arisen from injury to another*. By what name we should call the Joy that arises from another's good I do not know. Next, *Love toward him who has done good to another* we shall call *Favor*, and *Hatred toward him who has done evil to another* we shall call *Indignation*.

Finally, it should be noted that we do not pity only a thing we have loved (as we have shown in P21), but also one toward which we have previously had no affect, provided that we judge it to be like us (as I shall show below). And so also we favor him who has benefited someone like us, and are indignant at him who has injured one like us.

P23: *He who imagines what he hates to be affected with Sadness will rejoice; if, on the other hand, he should imagine it to be affected with Joy, he will be saddened. And both these affects will be the greater or lesser, as its contrary is greater or lesser in what he hates.*

158 Dem.: Insofar as a hateful thing is affected with Sadness, it is destroyed, and the more so, the greater the Sadness by which it is affected (by P11S). Therefore (by P20), he who imagines a thing he hates to be affected with Sadness will on the contrary be affected with Joy, and the more so, the greater the Sadness with which he imagines the hateful thing to have been affected. This was the first point.

Next, Joy posits the existence of the joyous thing (by P11S), and the more so, the greater the Joy is conceived to be. [Therefore] if someone imagines him whom he hates to be affected with Joy, this imagination (by P13) will restrain his striving, i.e. (by P11S), he who hates will be affected with Sadness, etc., q.e.d.

Schol.: This Joy can hardly be enduring and without any conflict of mind. For (as I shall show immediately in P27) insofar as one imagines a thing like oneself to be affected with an affect of Sadness, one must be saddened. And the opposite, if one imagines the same thing to be affected with Joy. But here we attend only to Hate.

P24: *If we imagine someone to affect with Joy a thing we hate, we shall be affected with Hate toward him also. On the other hand, if we imagine him to affect the same thing with Sadness, we shall be affected with Love toward him.*

Dem.: This proposition is demonstrated in the same way as P22.

Schol.: These and similar affects of Hate are related to *Envy* which, therefore, is nothing but *Hate, insofar as it is considered so to dispose a man that he is glad at another's ill fortune and saddened by his good fortune.*

/159 P25: *We strive to affirm, concerning ourselves and what we love, whatever we imagine to affect with Joy ourselves or what we love. On the other hand, we strive to deny whatever we imagine affects with Sadness ourselves or what we love.*

Dem.: Whatever we imagine to affect what we love with Joy or Sadness, affects us with Joy or Sadness (by P21). But the Mind (by P12) strives as far as it can to imagine those things which affect us with Joy, i.e. (by IIP17) and P17C), to regard them as present; and on the other hand (by P13) it strives to exclude the existence of those things which affect us with Sadness. Therefore, we strive to affirm, concerning ourselves and what we love, whatever we imagine to affect with Joy ourselves or what we love, and conversely, q.e.d.

P26: *We strive to affirm, concerning what we hate, whatever we imagine to affect it with Sadness, and on the other hand to deny whatever we imagine to affect it with Joy.*

Dem.: This proposition follows from P23, as P25 follows from P21.

Schol.: From these propositions we see that it easily happens that a man thinks more highly of himself and what he loves than is just, and on the other hand, thinks less highly than is just of what he hates. When this imagination concerns the man himself who thinks more highly of himself than is just, it is called Pride, and is a species of Madness, because the man dreams, with open eyes, that he can do all those things which he achieves only in his imagination, and which he therefore regards as real and triumphs in, so long as he cannot imagine those things which exclude the existence [of these achievements] and determine his power of acting.

Pride, therefore, *is Joy born of the fact that a man thinks more highly of himself than is just.* And the *Joy born of the fact that a man thinks more highly of another than is just* is called *Overestimation*, while *that which stems from thinking less highly of another than is just* is called *Scorn.*[23]

P27: *If we imagine a thing like us, toward which we have had no affect, to be affected with some affect, we are thereby affected with a like affect.*

Dem.: The images of things are affections of the human Body whose ideas represent external bodies as present to us (by IIP17S), i.e. (by IIP16), whose ideas involve the nature of our Body and at the same time the present nature of the external body. So if the nature of the external body is like the nature of our Body, then the idea of the external body we imagine will involve an affection of our Body like the affection of the external body. Consequently, if we imagine someone like us to be affected with some affect, this imagination will ex-

---

[23] Meijer plausibly proposed to emend the text to read: ". . . while *that sadness which stems* . . . is called *scorn.*" In favor of this it may be said that later (at I/195/28-196/7) scorn is so defined that it involves hate, which in turn involves sadness. Against the emendation it may be argued that in virtue of P20 any thought that involves the destruction (or diminution) of a hated object must involve joy. The text may well be correct, but the controversy underlines the complexity this affect must, in Spinoza's psychology, possess.

press an affection of our Body like this affect.[24] And so, from the fact that we imagine a thing like us to be affected with an affect, we are affected with a like affect. But if we hate a thing like us, then (by P23) we shall be affected with an affect contrary to its affect, not like it,[25] q.e.d.

Schol.: This imitation of the affects, when it is related to Sadness is called *Pity* (on which, see P22S); but related to Desire it is called *Emulation*, which, therefore, *is* nothing but *the Desire for a thing which is generated in us from the fact that we imagine others like us to have the same Desire.*

Cor. 1: If we imagine that someone toward whom we have had no affect affects a thing like us with Joy, we shall be affected with Love toward him. On the other hand, if we imagine him to affect it with Sadness, we shall be affected with Hate toward him.

Dem.: This is demonstrated from P27 in the same way P22 is demonstrated from P21.

Cor. 2: We cannot hate a thing we pity from the fact that its suffering affects us with Sadness.

Dem.: For if we could hate it because of that, then (by P23) we would rejoice in its Sadness, which is contrary to the hypothesis.

Cor. 3: As far as we can, we strive to free a thing we pity from its suffering.

Dem.: Whatever affects with Sadness what we pity, affects us also with a like Sadness (by P27). And so (by P13) we shall strive to think of whatever can take away the thing's existence, *or* destroy the thing, i.e. (by P9S), we shall want to destroy it, *or* shall be determined to destroy it. And so we strive to free the thing we pity from its suffering, q.e.d.

Schol.: This will, *or* appetite to do good, born of our pity for the thing on which we wish to confer a benefit, is called *Benevolence*, which *is* therefore nothing but a *Desire born of pity*. As for Love and Hate toward him who has done well or ill to a thing we imagine to be like us, see P22S.

P28: *We strive to further the occurrence of whatever we imagine will lead to Joy, and to avert or destroy what we imagine is contrary to it,* or *will lead to Sadness.*

---

[24] NS: "an affection like this affection of our body." This appears to reflect a mistranslation rather than a textual variation. For a discussion of inaccuracies in Glazemaker's translations, see Akkerman 2, 137-145.

[25] This last sentence is made part of the demonstration in both the OP and the NS. But the demonstration has reached its conclusion in the preceding sentence, and this takes up a different, though related point, which perhaps belongs in a scholium or corollary.

II/162   Dem.: We strive to imagine, as far as we can, what we imagine will lead to Joy (by P12), i.e. (by IIP17), we strive, as far as we can, to

5   regard it as present, *or* as actually existing. But the Mind's striving, *or* power of thinking, is equal to and at one in nature with the Body's striving, *or* power of acting (as clearly follows from IIP7C and P11C). Therefore, we strive absolutely, *or* (what, by P9S, is the same) want and intend that it should exist. This was the first point.

10   Next, if we imagine that what we believe to be the cause of Sadness, i.e. (by P13S), what we hate, is destroyed, we shall rejoice (by P20), and so (by the first part of this [NS: proposition]) we shall strive to destroy it, *or* (by P13) to avert it from ourselves, so that we shall not regard it as present. This was the second point. Therefore, [we strive

15   to further the occurrence of] whatever we imagine will lead to Joy, etc., q.e.d.

P29: *We shall strive to do also whatever we imagine men[a] to look on with Joy, and on the other hand, we shall be averse to doing what we imagine men are averse to.*

20   Dem.: From the fact that we imagine men to love or hate something, we shall love or hate it (by P27), i.e. (by P13S), we shall thereby rejoice in or be saddened by the thing's presence. And so (by P28) we shall strive to do whatever we imagine men to love, or to look on with Joy, etc., q.e.d.

Schol.:[26] *This striving to do something (and also to omit doing something) solely to please men* is called *Ambition*, especially when we strive so ea-

30   gerly to please the people that we do or omit certain things to our own injury, or another's. In other cases, it is usually called *human*

II/163   *kindness.* Next, *the Joy with which we imagine the action of another by which he has striven to please us* I call *Praise.* On the other hand, *the Sadness with which we are averse to his action* I call *Blame.*

5   P30: *If someone has done something which he imagines affects others with Joy, he will be affected with Joy accompanied by the idea of himself as cause, or he will regard himself with Joy. If, on the other hand, he has done something which he imagines affects others with Sadness, he will regard himself with Sadness.*

10   Dem.: He who imagines that he affects others with Joy or Sadness will thereby (by P27) be affected with Joy or Sadness. But since man

---

[a] N.B. Here and in what follows you should understand men toward whom we do not have any affect.

[26] Here and in subsequent scholia the previous practice of italicizing new definitions has not been maintained in the text of the OP. I take the liberty of introducing italics as they seem appropriate.

(by IIP19 and P23) is conscious of himself through the affections by which he is determined to act, then he who has done something which he imagines affects others with Joy will be affected with Joy, together with a consciousness of himself as the cause, *or*, he will regard himself with Joy, and the converse, q.e.d.

Schol.: Since Love (by P13S) is Joy, accompanied by the idea of an external cause, and Hate is Sadness, accompanied also by the idea of an external cause, this Joy and Sadness are species of Love and Hate. But because Love and Hate are related to external objects, we shall signify these affects by other names. *Joy accompanied by the idea of an internal*[27] *cause*, we shall call *love of esteem*, and *the Sadness contrary to it, Shame*—I mean *when the Joy or Sadness arise from the fact that the man believes that he is praised or blamed.* Otherwise, I shall call *Joy accompanied by the idea of an internal cause, Self-esteem*, and *the Sadness contrary to it, Repentance.*

Next, because (by IIP17C) it can happen that the Joy with which someone imagines that he affects others is only imaginary, and (by P25) everyone strives to imagine concerning himself whatever he imagines affects himself with Joy, it can easily happen that one who

64

---

[27] OP: "external," both here and in ll.27-28; NS: "internal," in both places. Van Vloten and Land retained the OP readings, Appuhn and others, the NS. Gebhardt follows the OP in l. 24, the NS in ll. 27-28, a compromise vigorously rejected by Akkerman (2, 69-70, 188-189), who recommends following the NS, as I have done. It seems clear that the OP compositor, influenced by the appearance of "external" three times earlier in this scholium, misread the ms. and failed to see that Spinoza intended to draw a contrast between love and hate in their simplest forms and the four more complex forms enumerated in ll. 24-29. What lends plausibility to the OP reading is the fact that the joy and sadness whose origin is described in P30 are explicitly said to be species of love and hate (at ll. 21-22), from which it follows that they must involve the idea of an external cause. But this does not exclude the possibility of their involving *also* the idea of an internal cause (as Akkerman seems to assume, 189). I take it that this is Spinoza's point: the four more complex forms of love and hate defined in ll. 24-29 arise from the fact that I believe myself (perhaps mistakenly) to have caused joy or sadness to another, *thereby* causing myself joy or sadness. In either case, I am the indirect cause of joy (or sadness) to myself. But the idea of the other as a subject of the joy (or sadness) I (take myself to) have caused is indispensable to this particular form of joy (or sadness). So my affect does involve the idea of something external as its partial and immediate cause, viz. the other's affect. If the other praises (or blames) me for what I have done, my joy (or sadness) is love of esteem (or shame). If not—perhaps because he is not aware that I am the cause of his joy (or sadness), or perhaps because I am mistaken in my belief that I am the cause—then my joy (sadness) is self-esteem (repentance).

Spinoza might have made his point clearer had he written (at ll. 22-23): "But because Love and Hate, considered simply as such, involve only the idea of an external object as cause, we shall use other terms for these more complex affects which also involve the idea of ourselves as a cause of our joy or sadness." Cf. 196/19-199/19. Although the account there is in some ways more refined than that given here (e.g., in the distinction drawn between humility and repentance), taken as a whole it supports the NS version of the text, and not, as Gebhardt thought, his compromise solution.

exults at being esteemed is proud and imagines himself to be pleasing to all, when he is burdensome to all.

P31: *If we imagine that someone loves, desires or hates something we ourselves love, desire, or hate, we shall thereby love, desire or hate it with greater constancy. But if we imagine that he is averse to what we love, or the opposite [NS: that he loves what we hate], then we shall undergo vacillation of mind.*

Dem.: Simply because we imagine that someone loves something, we thereby love the same thing (by P27). But we suppose that we already love it without this [cause of love]; so there is added to the Love a new cause, by which it is further encouraged. As a result, we shall love what we love with greater constancy.

Next, from the fact that we imagine someone to be averse to something, we shall be averse to it (by P27). But if we suppose that at the same time we love it, then at the same time we shall both love and be averse to the same thing, *or* (see P17S) we shall undergo vacillation of mind, q.e.d.

Cor.: From this and from P28 it follows that each of us strives, so far as he can, that everyone should love what he loves, and hate what he hates. Hence that passage of the poet:

> Speremus pariter, pariter metuamus amantes;
> Ferreus est, si quis, quod sinit alter, amat.[28]

Schol.: This striving to bring it about that everyone should approve his love and hate is really Ambition (see P29S). And so we see that each of us, by his nature, wants the others to live according to his temperament; when all alike want this, they are alike an obstacle to one another, and when all wish to be praised, *or* loved, by all, they hate one another.

---

[28] The verses are from Ovid's *Amores* II, xix, 4, 5 (though Spinoza has transposed the lines). There is much room for difference of opinion about their translation. See, for example, Appuhn 3:362. The Spinozistic context virtually requires something like Elwes' version: "As lovers, let us share every hope and fear: iron-hearted were he who should love what the other leaves." The Ovidian context, however, seems to require something more like Lee's free, but spirited version. The poet-lover addresses (in imagination) his mistress' husband:

> Guard your girl, stupid—if only to please me.
> I want to want her more.
> I'm bored by what's allowed, what isn't fascinates me.
> *Love by another man's leave is too cold-blooded.*
> *Lovers need a co-existence of hope and fear—*
> A few disappointments help us to dream.

(Ovid, *Amores*, trans. Guy Lee [London: John Murray, 1968], my italics to emphasize the lines Spinoza quotes.) Differences of literary style apart, the key question is whether *sinit* should be translated "leaves (alone)" or "allows." If it is possible to suppose that Spinoza here understands the lines as Lee does, and if Gebhardt's reading of II/271/21-22 is correct, then the reference there to this corollary would be more intelligible.

II/165 P32: *If we imagine that someone enjoys some thing that only one can possess, we shall strive to bring it about that he does not possess it.*

Dem.: From the mere fact that we imagine someone to enjoy something (by P27 and P27C1), we shall love that thing and desire to enjoy it. But (by hypothesis) we imagine his enjoyment of this thing as an obstacle to our Joy. Therefore (by P28), we shall strive that he not possess it, q.e.d.

Schol.: We see, therefore, that for the most part human nature is so constituted that men pity the unfortunate and envy the fortunate, and (by P32) [envy them] with greater hate the more they love the thing they imagine the other to possess. We see, then, that from the same property of human nature from which it follows that men are compassionate, it also follows that the same men are envious and ambitious.

Finally, if we wish to consult experience, we shall find that it teaches all these things, especially if we attend to the first years of our lives. For we find from experience that children, because their bodies are continually, as it were, in a state of equilibrium, laugh or cry simply because they see others laugh or cry. Moreover, whatever they see others do, they immediately desire to imitate it. And finally, they desire for themselves all those things by which they imagine others are pleased—because, as we have said, the images of things are the very affections of the human Body, *or* modes by which the human Body is affected by external causes, and disposed to do this or that.

P33: *When we love a thing like ourselves, we strive, as far as we can, to bring it about that it loves us in return.*

Dem.: As far as we can, we strive to imagine, above all others, the thing we love (by P12). Therefore, if a thing is like us, we shall strive to affect it with Joy above all others (by P29), *or* we shall strive, as far as we can, to bring it about that the thing we love is affected with Joy, accompanied by the idea of ourselves [as cause], i.e. (by P13S), that it loves us in return, q.e.d.

P34: *The greater the affect with which we imagine a thing we love to be affected toward us, the more we shall exult at being esteemed.*

Dem.: We strive (by P33), as far as we can, that a thing we love should love us in return, i.e. (by P13S), that a thing we love should be affected with Joy, accompanied by the idea of ourselves [as cause]. So the greater the Joy with which we imagine a thing we love to be affected on our account, the more this striving is aided, i.e. (by P11 and P11S), the greater the Joy with which we are affected. But when we rejoice because we have affected another, like us, with Joy, then we regard ourselves with Joy (by P30). Therefore, the greater the

513

affect with which we imagine a thing we love to be affected toward us, the greater the Joy with which we shall regard ourselves, *or* (by P30S) the more we shall exult at being esteemed, q.e.d.

20   **P35:** *If someone imagines that a thing he loves is united with another by as close, or by a closer, bond of Friendship than that with which he himself, alone, possessed the thing, he will be affected with Hate toward the thing he loves, and will envy the other.*

25   Dem.: The greater the love with which someone imagines a thing he loves to be affected toward him, the more he will exalt at being esteemed (by P34), i.e. (by P30S), the more he will rejoice. And so (by P28) he will strive, as far as he can, to imagine the thing he loves

30   to be bound to him as closely as possible. This striving, *or* appetite, is encouraged if he imagines another to desire the same thing he does

II/167   (by P31). But this striving, *or* appetite, is supposed to be restrained by the image of the thing he loves, accompanied by the image of him with whom the thing he loves is united. So (by P11S) he will thereby be affected with Sadness, accompanied by the idea of the thing he

5   loves as a cause, together with the image of the other; i.e. (by P13S), he will be affected with hate toward the thing he loves, and, at the same time, toward the other (by P15C), whom he will envy because of the pleasure the other takes in the thing he loves (by P23), q.e.d.

10   Schol.: This Hatred toward a thing we love, combined with Envy, is called *Jealousy*, which is therefore nothing but *a vacillation of mind born of Love and Hatred together, accompanied by the idea of another who is envied*. Moreover, this hatred toward the thing he loves will be greater in proportion to the Joy with which the Jealous man was usually affected from the Love returned to him by the thing he loves, and also

15   in proportion to the affect with which he was affected toward him with whom he imagines the thing he loves to unite itself. For if he hates him, he will thereby hate the thing he loves (by P24), because he imagines that what he loves affects with Joy what he hates, and also (by P15C) because he is forced to join the image of the thing he

20   loves to the image of him he hates.
This latter reason is found, for the most part, in Love toward a woman. For he who imagines that a woman he loves prostitutes herself to another not only will be saddened, because his own appetite is restrained, but also will be repelled by her, because he is forced to join the image of the thing he loves to the shameful parts and excre-

25   tions of the other. To this, finally, is added the fact that she no longer receives the Jealous man with the same countenance as she used to offer him. From this cause, too, the lover is saddened, as I shall show.

P36: *He who recollects a thing by which he was once pleased desires to possess it in the same circumstances as when he first was pleased by it.*

Dem.: Whatever a man sees together with a thing that pleased him (by P15) will be the accidental cause of Joy. And so (by P28) he will desire to possess it all, together with the thing that pleased him, *or* he will desire to possess the thing with all the same circumstances as when he first was pleased by it, q.e.d.

Cor.: Therefore, if the lover has found that one of those circumstances is lacking, he will be saddened.

Dem.: For insofar as he finds that a circumstance is lacking, he imagines something that excludes the existence of this thing. But since, from love, he desires this thing, *or* circumstance (by P36), then insofar as he imagines it to be lacking, he will be saddened, q.e.d.

Schol.: This Sadness, insofar as it concerns the absence of what we love, is called Longing..

P37: *The Desire that arises from Sadness or Joy, and from Hatred or Love, is greater, the greater the affect is.*

Dem.: Sadness diminishes or restrains a man's power of acting (by P11S), i.e. (by P7), diminishes or restrains the striving by which a man strives to persevere in his being; so it is contrary to this striving (by P5), and all a man affected by Sadness strives for is to remove Sadness. But (by the definition of Sadness) the greater the Sadness, the greater is the part of the man's power of acting to which it is necessarily opposed. Therefore, the greater the Sadness, the greater the power of acting with which the man will strive to remove the Sadness, i.e. (by P9S), the greater the desire, *or* appetite, with which he will strive to remove the Sadness.

Next, since Joy (by the same P11S) increases or aids man's power of acting, it is easily demonstrated in the same way that the man affected with Joy desires nothing but to preserve it, and does so with the greater Desire, as the Joy is greater.

Finally, since Hate and Love are themselves affects of Sadness or of Joy, it follows in the same way that the striving, appetite, or Desire which arises from Hate or Love will be greater as the Hate and Love are greater, q.e.d.

P38: *If someone begins to hate a thing he has loved, so that the Love is completely destroyed, then (from an equal cause) he will have a greater hate for it than if he had never loved it, and this hate will be the greater as the Love before was greater.*

Dem.: For if someone begins to hate a thing he loves, more of his appetites will be restrained than if he had not loved it. For Love is a

515

Joy (by P13S), which the man, as far as he can (by P28), strives to preserve; and (by the same scholium) he does this by regarding the thing he loves as present, and by affecting it, as far as he can, with Joy (by P21). This striving (by P37) is greater as the love is greater, as is the striving to bring it about that the thing he loves loves him in return (see P33). But these strivings are restrained by hatred toward the thing he loves (by P13C and P23); therefore, the lover (by P11S) will be affected with Sadness from this cause also, and the more so as his Love was greater. I.e., apart from the Sadness that was the cause of the Hate, another arises from the fact that he loved the thing. And consequently he will regard the thing he loved with a greater affect of Sadness, i.e. (by P13S), he will have a greater hatred for it than if he had not loved it. And this hate will be the greater as the love was greater, q.e.d.

P39: *He who Hates someone will strive to do evil to him, unless he fears that a greater evil to himself will arise from this; and on the other hand, he who loves someone will strive to benefit him by the same law.*

Dem.: To hate someone (by P13S) is to imagine him as the cause of [NS: one's] Sadness; and so (by P28), he who hates someone will strive to remove or destroy him. But if from that he fears something sadder, *or* (what is the same) a greater evil to himself, and believes that he can avoid this sadness by not doing to the one he hates the evil he was contemplating, he will desire to abstain from doing evil (by the same P28)—and that (by P37) with a greater striving than that by which he was bound to do evil. So this greater striving will prevail, as we maintained.

The second part of this demonstration proceeds in the same way. Therefore, he who hates someone, etc., q.e.d.

Schol.: By good here I understand every kind of Joy, and whatever leads to it, and especially what satisfies any kind of longing, whatever that may be. And by evil [I understand here] every kind of Sadness, and especially what frustrates longing. For we have shown above (in P9S) that we desire nothing because we judge it to be good, but on the contrary, we call it good because we desire it. Consequently, what we are averse to we call evil.

So each one, from his own affect, judges, *or* evaluates, what is good and what is bad, what is better and what is worse, and finally, what is best and what is worst. So the Greedy man judges an abundance of money best, and poverty worst. The Ambitious man desires nothing so much as Esteem and dreads nothing so much as Shame. To the Envious nothing is more agreeable than another's unhappiness, and nothing more burdensome than another's happiness. And so, each one, from his own affect, judges a thing good or bad, useful or useless.

Further, this affect, by which a man is so disposed that he does not will what he wills, and wills what he does not will, is called *Timidity*, which is therefore nothing but *fear insofar as a man is disposed by it to avoid an evil he judges to be future by encountering a lesser evil* (see P28). But if *the evil he is timid toward is Shame*, then the timidity is called *a Sense of shame*. Finally, if *the desire to avoid a future evil is restrained by Timidity regarding another evil, so that he does not know what he would rather do*, then the Fear is called *Consternation*, particularly if each evil he fears is of the greatest.

P40: *He who imagines he is hated by someone, and believes he has given the other no cause for hate, will hate the other in return.*

Dem.: He who imagines someone to be affected with hate will thereby also be affected with hate (by P27), i.e. (by P13S), with Sadness accompanied by the idea of an external cause. But (by hypothesis) he imagines no cause of this Sadness except the one who hates him. So from imagining himself to be hated by someone, he will be affected with Sadness, accompanied by the idea of the one who hates him [as a cause of the sadness] *or* (by the same Scholium) he will hate the other, q.e.d.

Schol. If he imagines he has given just cause for this hatred, he will be affected with Shame (by P30 and P30S). But this rarely happens (by P25). Moreover, this reciprocity of Hatred can also arise from the fact that Hatred is followed by a striving to do evil to him who is hated (by P39). He, therefore, who imagines that someone hates him will imagine the other to be the cause of an evil, *or* Sadness. And so, he will be affected with Sadness, *or* Fear, accompanied by the idea of the one who hates him, as a cause. I.e., he will be affected with hate in return, as above.

Cor. 1: He who imagines one he loves to be affected with hate toward him will be tormented by Love and Hate together. For insofar as he imagines that [the one he loves] hates him, he is determined to hate [that person] in return (by P40). But (by hypothesis) he nevertheless loves him. So he will be tormented by Love and Hate together.

Cor. 2: If someone imagines that someone else, toward whom he has previously had no affect, has, out of hatred, done him some evil, he will immediately strive to return the same evil.

Dem.: He who imagines someone to be affected with Hate toward him, will hate him in return (by P40), and (by P26) will strive to think of everything that can affect [that person] with Sadness, and be eager

517

10 to bring it to him (by P39). But (by hypothesis) the first thing he imagines of this kind is the evil done him. So he will immediately strive to do the same to [that person], q.e.d.

Schol.: *The striving to do evil to him we hate* is called *Anger*; and *the striving to return an evil done us* is called *Vengeance*.

15 P41: *If someone imagines that someone loves him, and does not believe he has given any cause for this,*[b] *he will love [that person] in return.*[29]

20 Dem.: This Proposition is demonstrated in the same way as the preceding one. See also its scholium.

Schol.: But if he believes that he has given just cause for this Love, he will exult at being esteemed (by P30 and P30S). This, indeed,
25 happens rather frequently (by P25) and is the opposite of what we said happens when someone imagines that someone hates him (see P40S).

Next, this *reciprocal Love, and consequent* (by P39) *striving to benefit one who loves us, and strives* (by the same P39) *to benefit us*, is called *Thank-*
30 *fulness, or Gratitude.*

And so it is evident that men are far more ready for Vengeance than for returning benefits.

II/173 Cor.: He who imagines he is loved by one he hates will be torn by Hate and Love together. This is demonstrated in the same way as P40C1.

5 Schol.: But if the Hate has prevailed, he will strive to do evil to the one who loves him. This affect is called *Cruelty*, especially if it is believed that the one who loves has given no ordinary cause for Hatred.

10 P42: *He who has benefited someone—whether moved to do so by Love or by the hope of Esteem—will be saddened if he sees his benefit accepted in an ungrateful spirit.*

15 Dem.: He who loves a thing like himself strives, as far as he can, to be loved by it in return (by P33). So he who has benefited someone from love does this from a longing by which he is bound that he may be loved in return—i.e. (by P34), from the hope of Esteem *or* (by
20 P30S) Joy; so (by P12) he will strive, as far as he can, to imagine this cause of Esteem, *or* to regard it as actually existing. But (by hypothesis) he imagines something else that excludes the existence of this cause. So (by P19) he will be saddened by this.

26 P43: *Hate is increased by being returned, but can be destroyed by Love.*

Dem.: He who imagines one he hates to be affected with Hate

---

[b] This can happen (by P15C and P16).
[29] Cf. Seneca, *Epist. mor.*, ix, 6.

toward him will feel a new Hate (by P40), while the first (by hypothesis) continues. If, on the other hand, he imagines that the one he hates is affected with love toward him, then insofar as he imagines this, he regards himself with Joy (by P30) and will strive to please the one he hates (by P29), i.e. (by P41), he strives not to hate him and not to affect him with Sadness. This striving (by P37) will be greater or lesser in proportion to the affect from which it arises. So if it is greater than that which arises from hate, and by which he strives to affect the thing he hates with Sadness (by P26), then it will prevail over it and efface the Hate from his mind, q.e.d.

P44: *Hate completely conquered by Love passes into Love, and the Love is therefore greater than if Hate had not preceded it.*

Dem.: The proof of this proceeds in the same way as that of P38. For he who begins to love a thing he has hated, *or* used to regard with Sadness, rejoices because he loves, and to this Joy which Love involves (see its definition in P13S) there is also added a Joy arising from this—the striving to remove the Sadness hate involves (as we have shown in P37) is wholly aided by the accompaniment of the idea of the one he hated, [who is regarded] as a cause [of joy].

Schol.: Although this is so, still, no one will strive to hate a thing, or to be affected with Sadness, in order to have this greater Joy, i.e., no one will desire to injure himself in the hope of recovering, or long to be sick in the hope of getting better. For each one will strive always to preserve his being, and to put aside Sadness as far as he can. But if, on the contrary, one could conceive that a man could desire to hate someone, in order afterwards to have the greater love for him, then he would always desire to hate him. For as the Hate was greater, so the Love would be greater, and so he would always desire his Hate to become greater and greater. And by the same cause, a man would strive to become more and more ill, so that afterwards he might have the greater joy from restoring his health; and so he would always strive to become ill, which (by P6) is absurd.

P45: *If someone imagines that someone like himself is affected with Hate toward a thing like himself which he loves, he will hate that [person].*

Dem.: For the thing he loves hates in return the one who hates it (by P40), and so the lover, who imagines that someone hates the thing he loves, thereby imagines the thing he loves to be affected with Hate, i.e. (by P13S), with Sadness. And consequently (by P21), he is saddened, and his Sadness is accompanied by the idea of the one who hates the thing he loves—[this other being regarded] as the cause [of the Sadness]. I.e. (by P13S), he will hate him, q.e.d.

P46: *If someone has been affected with Joy or Sadness by someone of a class,* or *nation, different from his own, and this Joy or Sadness is accompanied by the idea of that person as its cause, under the universal name of the class or nation, he will love or hate, not only that person, but everyone of the same class or nation.*

Dem.: The demonstration of this matter is evident from P16.

P47: *The Joy which arises from our imagining that a thing we hate is destroyed, or affected with some other evil, does not occur without some Sadness of mind.*

Dem.: This is evident from P27. For insofar as we imagine a thing like us to be affected with sadness, we are saddened.

Schol.: This Proposition can also be demonstrated from IIP17C. For as often as we recollect a thing—even though it does not actually exist—we still regard it as present, and the Body is affected in the same way [NS: as if it were present]. So insofar as the memory of the thing is strong, the man is determined to regard it with Sadness. While the image of the thing still remains, this determination is, indeed, restrained by the memory of those things that exclude its existence; but it is not taken away. And so the man rejoices only insofar as this determination is restrained.

So it happens that this Joy, which arises from the misfortune occurring to the thing we hate, is repeated as often as we recollect the thing. For as we have said, when the image of this thing is aroused, because it involves the existence of the thing, it determines the man to regard the thing with the same Sadness as he used to before, when it existed. But because he has joined to the image of this thing other images that exclude its existence, this determination to Sadness is immediately restrained, and the man rejoices anew. This happens as often as the repetition occurs.

This is also the cause of men's rejoicing when they recall some evil now past, and why they enjoy telling of dangers from which they have been freed. For when they imagine a danger, they regard it as future, and are determined to fear it. This determination is restrained anew by the idea of freedom, which they have joined to the idea of the danger, since they have been freed from it. This renders them safe again, and they rejoice again.

P48: *Love or Hate—say, of Peter—is destroyed if the Sadness the Hate involves, or the Joy the Love involves, is attached to the idea of another cause, and each is diminished to the extent that we imagine that Peter was not its only cause.*

Dem.: This is evident simply from the definitions of Love and Hate— see P13S. For this Joy is called Love of Peter, or this Sadness, Hatred of Peter, only because Peter is considered to be the cause of the one affect or the other. If this is taken away—either wholly or in part—the affect toward Peter is also diminished, either wholly or in part, q.e.d.

P49: *Given an equal cause of Love, Love toward a thing will be greater if we imagine the thing to be free than if we imagine it to be necessary. And similarly for Hate.*

Dem.: A thing we imagine to be free must be perceived through itself, without others (by ID7). So if we imagine it to be the cause of Joy or Sadness, we shall thereby love or hate it (by P13S), and shall do so with the greatest Love or Hate that can arise from the given affect (by P48). But if we should imagine as necessary the thing that is the cause of this affect, then (by the same ID7) we shall imagine it to be the cause of the affect, not alone, but with others. And so (by P48) our Love or Hate toward it will be less, q.e.d.

Schol.: From this it follows that because men consider themselves to be free, they have a greater Love or Hate toward one another than toward other things. To this is added the imitation of the affects, on which see P27, 34, 40 and 43.

P50: *Anything whatever can be the accidental cause of Hope or Fear.*

Dem.: This Proposition is demonstrated in the same way as P15. Consult it together with P18S2.[30]

Schol.: Things which are accidental causes of Hope or Fear are called good or bad omens. And insofar as these same omens are causes of Hope or Fear, they are causes of Joy or Sadness[31] (by the definitions of hope and fear—see P18S2); consequently (by P15C), we love them or hate them, and strive (by P28) either to use them as means to the things we hope for, or to remove them as obstacles or causes of Fear.

Furthermore, as follows from P25, we are so constituted by nature that we easily believe the things we hope for, but believe only with difficulty those we fear, and that we regard them more or less highly than is just. This is the source of the Superstitions by which men are everywhere troubled.

For the rest, I do not think it worth the trouble to show here the

---

[30] The OP read simply: "P18S," which Gebhardt takes as a reference to both scholia (cf. my note at 154/24 and Gebhardt's note to 177/26, at II/373-374). Leopold had taken the reference to be to P18S2. Akkerman (2, 81-82) argues that it should be to P18S1. I think Leopold is clearly right here. Granted that P18S2 by itself gives no foundation for P50, nevertheless, the definitions it gives of *hope* and *fear* as species of joy and sadness show how the demonstration of P15 can easily be modified to yield a proof of P50, by substituting the *definiens* for the *definiendum*.

[31] Following Akkerman (2, 190) who reads "causae" for "causa" both in l. 30 and in l. 31.

10 vacillations of mind which stem from Hope and Fear—since it follows simply from the definition of these affects that there is no Hope without Fear, and no Fear without Hope (as we shall explain more fully in its place). Moreover, insofar as we hope for or fear something, we love it or hate it; so whatever we have said of Love and Hate, anyone

15 can easily apply to Hope and Fear.

P51: *Different men can be affected differently by one and the same object; and one and the same man can be affected differently at different times by one and the same object.*

20 Dem.: The human Body (by IIPost. 3) is affected in a great many ways by external bodies. Therefore, two men can be differently affected at the same time, and so (by IIA1″ [II/99]) they can be affected differently by one and the same object.

25 Next (by the same Post.) the human Body can be affected now in this way, now in another. Consequently (by the same Axiom) it can be affected differently at different times by one and the same object, q.e.d.

30 Schol.: We see, then, that it can happen that what the one loves, the other hates, what the one fears, the other does not, and that one and the same man may now love what before he hated, and now dare what before he was too timid for.

Next, because each one judges from his own affect what is good

II/179 and what is bad, what is better and what worse (see P39S) it follows that men can vary[c] as much in judgment as in affect. The result is that when we compare one with another, we distinguish them only by a difference of affects, and call some intrepid, others timid, and

5 others, finally, by another name.

For example, I shall call him *intrepid* who disdains an evil I usually fear. Moreover, if I attend to the fact that his desire to do evil to one he hates, and good to one he loves, is not restrained by timidity regarding an evil by which I am usually restrained, I shall call him

10 *daring.* Someone will seem *timid* to me if he is afraid of an evil I usually disdain. If, moreover, I attend to the fact that his Desire [to do evil to those he hates and good to those he loves] is restrained by timidity regarding an evil which cannot restrain me, I shall call him *cowardly.* In this way will everyone judge.

[c] N.B. This can happen even though the human mind is part of the divine intellect, as we have shown in IIP17S.[32]

[32] So the OP and NS both read. Most editors have had difficulty seeing the relevance of the reference to IIP17S and have suggested as alternatives either IIP11C or IIP13S or perhaps both. Without questioning the relevance of IIP13S (specifically II/97/7-14), I would suggest that there is no pressing need to emend the text, since the discussion of error at II/106/11-18 is equally relevant to explaining how men can vary in judgment.

Finally, because of this inconstancy of man's nature and judgment, and also because he often judges things only from an affect,[33] because the things which he believes will make for Joy or Sadness, and which he therefore strives to promote or prevent (by P28), are often only imaginary—not to mention the other conclusions we have reached in Part II about the uncertainty of things—we easily conceive that a man can often be the cause both of his own Sadness and his own Joy, *or* that he is affected both with Joy and with Sadness, accompanied by the idea of himself as their cause. So we easily understand what Repentance and Self-esteem are: *Repentance is Sadness accompanied by the idea of oneself as cause*, and *Self-esteem is Joy accompanied by the idea of oneself as cause.* Because men believe themselves free, these affects are very violent (see P49).

P52: *If we have previously seen an object together with others, or we imagine it has nothing but what is common to many things, we shall not consider it so long as one which we imagine to have something singular.*

Dem.: As soon as we imagine an object we have seen with others, we shall immediately recollect the others (by IIP18 & P18S), and so from considering one we immediately pass to considering the other. And the reasoning is the same concerning the object we imagine to have nothing but what is common to many things. For imagining that is supposing that we consider nothing in it but what we have seen before with others.

But when we suppose that we imagine in an object something singular, which we have never seen before, we are only saying that when the Mind considers that object, it has nothing in itself which it is led to consider from considering that. And so it is determined to consider only that. Therefore, if we have seen, etc., q.e.d.

Schol.: This affection of the Mind, *or* this *imagination of a singular thing*,[34] *insofar as it is alone in the Mind*, is called *Wonder*. But *if it is aroused by an object we fear*, it is called *Consternation*, because Wonder at an evil keeps a man so suspended in considering it that he cannot think of other things by which he could avoid that evil. But *if what we wonder at is a man's prudence, diligence, or something else of that kind, because we consider him as far surpassing us in this*, then the Wonder is

---

[33] Akkerman suggests reading "naturae" for "natura" in l. 14 (2, 68) and adding "ex eo" after the first ampersand in l. 15 (2, 162), both of which emendations are suggested by the NS and followed here.

[34] The NS make "singular" modify "imagination" rather than "thing," which is not impossible grammatically, perhaps, but nonetheless, clearly wrong in my view. In general, I mention translation errors in the NS only where they do not appear on Akkerman's list (2, 137-145). There are many more of them in Parts III-V than in Parts I-II, which is an important part of Akkerman's evidence for supposing that E I-II were translated by Balling and E III-V by Glazemaker.

called *Veneration*. Otherwise, *if what we wonder at is the man's anger, envy, etc.*, the wonder is called *Dread*.

Next, if we wonder at the prudence, diligence, etc., of a man we love, the Love will thereby (by P12) be greater and this *Love joined to Wonder*, or *Veneration*, we call *Devotion*. In this way we can also conceive Hate, Hope, Confidence, and other Affects to be joined to Wonder, and so we can deduce more Affects than those which are usually indicated by the accepted words. So it is clear that the names of the affects are found more from the ordinary usage [of words] than from an accurate knowledge [of the affects].[35]

To Wonder is opposed *Disdain*, the cause of which, however, is generally this: because we see that someone wonders at, loves or fears something, or something appears at first glance like things we admire, love, fear, etc. (by P15, P15C, and P27), we are determined to wonder at, love, fear, etc., the same thing; but if, from the thing's presence, or from considering it more accurately, we are forced to deny it whatever can be the cause of Wonder, Love, Fear, etc., then the Mind remains determined by the thing's presence to think more of the things that are not in the object than of those that are (though the object's presence usually determines [the Mind] to think chiefly of what is in the object).

Next, as Devotion stems from Wonder at a thing we love, so *Mockery* stems from *Disdain for a thing we hate or fear*, and *Contempt* from *Disdain for folly*, as Veneration stems from Wonder at prudence. Finally, we can conceive Love, Hope, Love of Esteem, and other Affects joined to Disdain, and from that we can deduce in addition other Affects, which we also do not usually distinguish from the others by any single term.

P53: *When the Mind considers itself and its power of acting, it rejoices, and does so the more, the more distinctly it imagines itself and its power of acting.*

Dem.: A man does not know himself except through affections of his Body and their ideas (by IIP19 and P23). So when it happens that the Mind can consider itself, it is thereby supposed to pass to a greater perfection, i.e. (by P11S), to be affected with joy, and with greater joy the more distinctly it can imagine its power of acting, q.e.d.

Cor.: This Joy is more and more encouraged the more the man imagines himself to be praised by others. For the more he imagines himself to be praised by others, the greater the Joy with which he imagines himself to affect others, a Joy accompanied by the idea of

---

[35] The point seems to be simply that accidents of linguistic usage may leave the psychological system-builder without a natural way of referring to certain emotions.

himself (by P29S). And so (by P27) he himself is affected with a greater Joy, accompanied by the idea of himself, q.e.d.

P54: *The Mind strives to imagine only those things that posit its power of acting.*

Dem.: The Mind's striving, *or* power, is its very essence (by P7); but the Mind's essence (as is known through itself) affirms only what the Mind is and can do, not what it is not and cannot do. So it strives to imagine only what affirms, *or* posits, its power of acting, q.e.d.

P55: *When the Mind imagines its own lack of power, it is saddened by it.*

Dem.: The Mind's essence affirms only what the Mind is and can do, *or* it is of the nature of the Mind to imagine only those things that posit its power of acting (by P54). So when we say that the Mind, in considering itself, imagines its lack of power, we are saying nothing but that the Mind's striving to imagine something that posits its power of acting is restrained, *or* (by P11S) that it is saddened, q.e.d.

Cor.: This Sadness is more and more encouraged if we imagine ourselves to be blamed by others. This is demonstrated in the same way as P53C.

Schol.: This *Sadness, accompanied by the idea of our own weakness* is called *Humility.* But *Joy arising from considering ourselves*, is called *Self-love* or *Self-esteem.* And since this is renewed as often as a man considers his virtues, *or* his power of acting, it also happens that everyone is anxious to tell his own deeds, and show off his powers, both of body and of mind—and that men, for this reason, are troublesome to one another.

From this it follows, again, that men are by nature envious (see P24S and P32S), *or* are glad of their equals' weakness and saddened by their equals' virtue. For whenever anyone imagines his own actions, he is affected with Joy (by P53), and with a greater Joy, the more his actions express perfection, and the more distinctly he imagines them, i.e. (by IIP40S1), the more he can distinguish them from others, and consider them as singular things. So everyone will have the greatest gladness from considering himself, when he considers something in himself which he denies concerning others.

But if he relates what he affirms of himself to the universal idea of man or animal, he will not be so greatly gladdened. And on the other hand, if he imagines that his own actions are weaker, compared to others' actions, he will be saddened (by P28), and will strive to put aside this Sadness, either by wrongly interpreting his equals' actions or by magnifying his own as much as he can. It is clear, therefore, that men are naturally inclined to Hate and Envy.

Education itself adds to natural inclination. For parents generally spur their children on to virtue only by the incentive of Honor and Envy.

25   But perhaps this doubt remains—that not infrequently we admire and venerate men's virtues. To remove this scruple, I shall add the following Corollary.

Cor.: No one envies another's virtue unless he is an equal.

30   Dem.: Envy is Hatred itself (see P24S), *or* (by P13S) a Sadness, i.e. (by P11S), an affection by which a man's power of acting, *or* striving, is restrained. But a man (by P9S) neither strives to do, nor desires, anything unless it can follow from his given nature. So no man desires

II/184 that there be predicated of him any power of acting, *or* (what is the same) virtue, which is peculiar to another's nature and alien to his own. Hence, his Desire is restrained, i.e. (by P11S), he cannot be saddened because he considers a virtue in someone unlike himself.

5   Consequently he also cannot envy him. But he can, indeed, envy his equal, who is supposed to be of the same nature as he, q.e.d.

Schol.: So when we said above (in P52S) that we venerate a man

10   because we wonder at his prudence, strength of character, etc., that happens (as is evident from the proposition itself) because we imagine these virtues to be peculiarly in him, and not as common to our nature. Therefore, we shall not envy him these virtues any more than we envy trees their height, or lions their strength.

15   P56: *There are as many species of Joy, Sadness, and Desire, and consequently of each affect composed of these (like vacillation of mind) or derived from them (like Love, Hate, Hope, Fear, etc.), as there are species of objects by which we*

20   *are affected.*[36]

Dem.: Joy and Sadness—and consequently the affects composed of them or derived from them—are passions (by P11S). But we are nec-

25   essarily acted on (by P1) insofar as we have inadequate ideas, and only insofar as we have them (by P3) are we acted on, i.e. (see IIP40S), necessarily we are acted on only insofar as we imagine, *or* (see IIP17 and P17S) insofar as we are affected with an affect that involves both the nature of our Body and the nature of an external body. Therefore,

30   the nature of each passion must necessarily be so explained that the nature of the object by which we are affected is expressed.

For example, the Joy arising from A involves the nature of object

II/185 A, that arising from object B involves the nature of object B, and so these two affects of Joy are by nature different, because they arise from causes of a different nature. So also the affect of Sadness arising

[36] Cf. PA II, 82, 84, 88.

from one object is different in nature from the Sadness stemming from another cause. The same must also be understood of Love, Hate, Hope, Fear, Vacillation of mind, etc.

Therefore, there are as many species of Joy, Sadness, Love, Hate, etc., as there are species of objects by which we are affected.

But Desire is the very essence, *or* nature, of each [man] insofar as it is conceived to be determined, by whatever constitution he has, to do something (see P9S). Therefore, as each [man] is affected by external causes with this or that species of Joy, Sadness, Love, Hate, etc.— i.e., as his nature is constituted in one way or the other, so his Desires vary and the nature of one Desire must differ from the nature of the other as much as the affects from which each arises differ from one another.

Therefore, there are as many species of Desire as there are species of Joy, Sadness, Love, etc., and consequently (through what has already been shown) as there are species of objects by which we are affected, q.e.d.

Schol.: Noteworthy among these species of affects—which (by P56) must be very many—are Gluttony, Drunkenness, Lust, Greed, and Ambition, which are only notions of Love or Desire which explain the nature of each of these affects through the objects to which they are related. For by Gluttony, Drunkenness, Lust, Greed, and Ambition we understand nothing but an immoderate Love or Desire for eating, drinking, sexual union, wealth, and esteem.

Moreover, these affects, insofar as we distinguish them from the others only through the object to which they are related, do not have opposites. For Moderation, which we usually oppose to Gluttony, Sobriety which we usually oppose to Drunkenness, and Chastity, which we usually oppose to Lust, are not affects *or* passions, but indicate the power of the mind, a power that moderates these affects.

I cannot explain the other species of affects here—for there are as many as there are species of objects. But even if I could, it is not necessary. For our purpose, which is to determine the powers of the affects and the power of the Mind over the affects, it is enough to have a general definition of each affect. It is enough, I say, for us to understand the common properties of the affects and of the Mind, so that we can determine what sort of power, and how great a power, the Mind has to moderate and restrain the affects. So though there is a great difference between this or that affect of Love, Hate or Desire— e.g., between the Love of one's children and the Love of one's wife— it is still not necessary for us to know these differences, nor to investigate the nature and origin of the affects further.

P57: *Each affect of each individual differs from the affect of another as much as the essence of the one from the essence of the other.*[37]

Dem.: This Proposition is evident from IIA1″ [II/99]. But nevertheless we shall demonstrate it from the definitions of the three primitive affects.

All the affects are related to Desire, Joy, or Sadness, as the definitions we have given of them show. But Desire is the very nature, *or* essence, of each [individual] (see the definition of Desire in P9S). Therefore the Desire of each individual differs from the Desire of another as much as the nature, *or* essence, of the one differs from the essence of the other.

Next, Joy and Sadness are passions by which each one's power, *or* striving to persevere in his being, is increased or diminished, aided or restrained (by P11 and P11S). But by the striving to persevere in one's being, insofar as it is related to the Mind and Body together, we understand Appetite and Desire (see P9S). So Joy and Sadness are the Desire, *or* Appetite, itself insofar as it is increased or diminished, aided or restrained, by external causes. I.e. (by the same scholium), it is the very nature of each [individual]. And so, the Joy or Sadness of each [individual] also differs from the Joy or Sadness of another as much as the nature, *or* essence, of the one differs from the essence of the other. Consequently, each affect of each individual differs from the affect of another as much, etc., q.e.d.

Schol.: From this it follows that the affects of the animals which are called irrational (for after we know the origin of the Mind, we cannot in any way doubt that the lower animals feel things) differ from men's affects as much as their nature differs from human nature. Both the horse and the man are driven by a Lust to procreate; but the one is driven by an equine Lust, the other by a human Lust. So also the Lusts and Appetites of Insects, fish, and birds must vary. Therefore, though each individual lives content with his own nature, by which he is constituted, and is glad of it, nevertheless that life with' which each one is content, and that gladness, are nothing but the idea, *or* soul, of the individual. And so the gladness of the one differs in nature from the gladness of the other as much as the essence of the one differs from the essence of the other.

Finally, from P57 it follows that there is no small difference between the gladness by which a drunk is led and the gladness a Philosopher possesses. I wished to mention this in passing.

This will be enough concerning the affects that are related to man

---

[37] Bidney (110) notes a similar doctrine in Aristotle (*Nicomachean Ethics* 1176a).

insofar as he is acted on. It remains to add a few words about those that are related to him insofar as he acts.

P58: *Apart from the Joy and Desire that are passions, there are other affects of Joy and Desire that are related to us insofar as we act.*

Dem.: When the Mind conceives itself and its power of acting, it rejoices (by P53). But the Mind necessarily considers itself when it conceives a true, *or* adequate, idea (by IIP43). But the Mind conceives some adequate ideas (by IIP40S2). Therefore, it also rejoices insofar as it conceives adequate ideas, i.e. (by P1), insofar as it acts.

Next, the Mind strives to persevere in its being, both insofar as it has clear and distinct ideas and insofar as it has confused ideas (by P9). But by striving we understand [NS: here] Desire (by P9S). Therefore, Desire also is related to us insofar as we understand, *or* (by P1) insofar as we act, q.e.d.

P59: *Among all the affects that are related to the Mind insofar as it acts, there are none that are not related to Joy or Desire.*

Dem.: All the affects are related to Desire, Joy, or Sadness, as the definitions we have given of them show. But by Sadness we understand the fact that the Mind's power of acting is diminished or restrained[38] (by P11 and P11S). And so insofar as the Mind is saddened, its power of understanding, i.e. (by P1), of acting, is diminished or restrained. Hence no affects of Sadness can be related to the Mind insofar as it acts, but only affects of Joy and Desire, which (by P58) are also so far related to the Mind, q.e.d.

Schol.: *All actions that follow from affects related to the Mind insofar as it understands* I relate to *Strength of character*, which I divide into Tenacity and Nobility. For by *Tenacity* I understand *the Desire by which each one strives, solely from the dictate of reason, to preserve his being.* By *Nobility* I understand *the Desire by which each one strives, solely from the dictate of reason, to aid other men and join them to him in friendship.*

Those actions, therefore, which aim only at the agent's advantage, I relate to Tenacity, and those which aim at another's advantage, I

---

[38] Gebhardt emends the text of the OP, appealing to the NS and P11, but does not make all the changes required by grammar. On his construal we should read "potentiam" for "potentia" and translate: "By Sadness we understand what diminishes or restrains the Mind's power of acting." This is possible, as Akkerman (2, 67-68) points out, citing 168/20-21. But he argues persuasively for retaining the text of the OP, which is what I have translated, and regarding the NS translation as simply mistaken. On his construal, this passage would be more accurate that 168/20-21, since, strictly speaking, sadness is not a thing which diminishes another thing, but the process itself of the diminution of the mind's power.

relate to Nobility. So Moderation, Sobriety, presence of mind in danger, etc., are species of Tenacity whereas Courtesy, Mercy, etc., are species of Nobility.

II/189   And with this I think I have explained and shown through their first causes the main affects and vacillations of mind which arise from the composition of the three primitive affects, viz. Desire, Joy, and
5   Sadness. From what has been said it is clear that we are driven about in many ways by external causes, and that, like waves on the sea, driven by contrary winds, we toss about, not knowing our outcome and fate.

But I said that I have shown only the main [NS: affects], not all the conflicts of mind there can be. For by proceeding in the same way as
10   above, we can easily show that Love is joined to Repentance, Contempt, Shame, etc. Indeed, from what has already been said I believe it is clear to anyone that the various affects can be compounded with one another in so many ways, and that so many variations can arise from this composition that they cannot be defined by any number. But it was sufficient for my purpose to enumerate only the main affects. [To consider] those I have omitted would be more curious
15   than useful.

Nevertheless, this remains to be noted about Love: very often it happens that while we are enjoying a thing we wanted, the Body acquires from this enjoyment a new constitution, by which it is differently determined, and other images of things are aroused in it; and at the same time the Mind begins to imagine other things and desire other things.

20   E.g., when we imagine something that usually pleases us by its taste, we desire to enjoy it—i.e., to consume it. But while we thus enjoy it, the stomach is filled, and the Body constituted differently. So if (while the Body is now differently disposed) the presence of the food or drink encourages the image of it, and consequently also the
25   striving, *or* Desire to consume it, then that new constitution will be opposed to this Desire, *or* striving. Hence, presence of the food or drink we used to want will be hateful. This is what we call *Disgust* and *Weariness*.

As for the external affections of the Body, which are observed in the affects—such as trembling, paleness, sobbing, laughter, etc.—I
30   have neglected them, because they are related to the Body only, without any relation to the Mind. Finally, there are certain things to be noted about the definitions of the affects. I shall therefore repeat them here in order, interposing the observations required on each one.

I. Desire is man's very essence, insofar as it is conceived to be determined, from any given affection of it, to do something.

Exp.: We said above, in P9S, that Desire is appetite together with the consciousness of it. And appetite is the very essence of man, insofar as it is determined to do what promotes his preservation.

But in the same scholium I also warned that I really recognize no difference between human appetite and Desire. For whether a man is conscious of his appetite or not, the appetite still remains one and the same. And so—not to seem to commit a tautology—I did not wish to explain Desire by appetite, but was anxious to so define it that I would comprehend together all the strivings of human nature that we signify by the name of appetite, will, desire, or impulse. For I could have said that Desire is man's very essence, insofar as it is conceived to be determined to do something. But from this definition (by IIP23) it would not follow that the Mind could be conscious of its Desire, *or* appetite. Therefore, in order to involve the cause of this consciousness, it was necessary (by the same proposition) to add: *insofar as it is conceived, from some given affection of it, to be determined* etc. For by an affection of the human essence we understand any constitution of that essence, whether it is innate [NS: or has come from outside], whether it is conceived through the attribute of Thought alone, or through the attribute of Extension alone, or is referred to both at once.

Here, therefore, by the word *Desire* I understand any of a man's strivings, impulses, appetites, and volitions, which vary as the man's constitution varies, and which are not infrequently so opposed to one another that the man is pulled in different directions and knows not where to turn.

91   II. Joy is a man's passage from a lesser to a greater perfection.

III. Sadness is a man's passage from a greater to a lesser perfection.

Exp.: I say a passage. For Joy is not perfection itself. If a man were born with the perfection to which he passes, he would possess it without an affect of Joy.

---

[39] Nearly all of the terms that follow have been previously introduced in scholia. And as Wolfson has pointed out, most of the terms occur in the Latin translation of Descartes' *Passions of the Soul*, published in Amsterdam in 1650. Wolfson (1, 2:209-210) gives a helpful table correlating Spinoza's definitions with the relevant sections of Descartes' work. Spinoza's definitions of his three primitive affects are quite different from the corresponding Cartesian definitions, so that even where the definitions of derived affects seem to agree, this agreement is superficial. His definitions here also differ frequently from those which appear earlier in Part III in the Scholia.

This is clearer from the affect of Sadness, which is the opposite of joy. For no one can deny that Sadness consists in a passage to a lesser perfection, not in the lesser perfection itself, since a man cannot be saddened insofar as he participates in some perfection. Nor can we say that Sadness consists in the privation of a greater perfection. For a privation is nothing, whereas the affect of Sadness is an act, which can therefore be no other act than that of passing to a lesser perfection, i.e., an act by which man's power of acting is diminished or restrained (see P11S).

As for the definitions of Cheerfulness, Pleasure, Melancholy, and Pain, I omit them, because they are chiefly related to the Body, and are only Species of Joy or Sadness.

IV. Wonder is an imagination of a thing in which the Mind remains fixed because this singular imagination has no connection with the others. (See P52 and P52S.)

Exp.: In IIP18S we showed the cause why the Mind, from considering one thing, immediately passes to the thought of another—because the images of these things are connected with one another, and so ordered that one follows the other. This, of course, cannot be conceived when the image of the thing is new. Rather the Mind will be detained in regarding the same thing until it is determined by other causes to think of other things.

So the imagination of a new thing, considered in itself, is of the same nature as the other [imaginations], and for this reason I do not number Wonder among the affects. Nor do I see why I should, since this distraction of the Mind does not arise from any positive cause which distracts the Mind from other things, but only from the fact that there is no cause determining the Mind to pass from regarding one thing to thinking of others.

So as I pointed out in P11S, I recognize only three primitive, *or* primary, affects: Joy, Sadness, and Desire. I have spoken of Wonder only because it has become customary for some[40] to indicate the affects derived from these three by other names when they are related to objects we wonder at. For the same reason I shall also add the definition of Disdain to these.

V. Disdain is an imagination of a thing which touches the Mind so little that the thing's presence moves the Mind to imagining more what is not in it than what is. See P52S.

---

[40] Descartes gives wonder a very prominent (if somewhat anomalous) place among the passions of the soul. Cf. Alquié, 3:999n.

I omit, here, the definitions of Veneration and Contempt because no affects that I know of derive their names from them.

VI. Love is a Joy, accompanied by the idea of an external cause.

Exp.: This definition explains the essence of Love clearly enough. But the definition of those authors[41] who define *Love* as *a will of the lover to join himself to the thing loved* expresses a property of Love, not its essence. And because these Authors did not see clearly enough the essence of Love, they could not have any clear concept of this property. Hence everyone has judged their definition[42] quite obscure.

But it should be noted that when I say it is a property in the lover, that he wills to join himself to the thing loved, I do not understand by will a consent,[43] or a deliberation of the mind, *or* free decision (for we have demonstrated that this is a fiction in IIP48). Nor do I understand a Desire of joining oneself to the thing loved when it is absent or continuing in its presence when it is present.[44] For love can be conceived without either of these Desires. Rather, by will I understand a Satisfaction in the lover on account of the presence of the thing loved, by which the lover's Joy is strengthened or at least encouraged.

VII. Hate is a Sadness, accompanied by the idea of an external cause.

Exp.: The things to be noted here will be perceived easily from what has been said in the explanation of the preceding definition. See also P13S.

VIII. Inclination is a Joy accompanied by the idea of a thing which is the accidental cause of Joy.

IX. Aversion is a Sadness accompanied by the idea of something which is the accidental cause of Sadness. On this see P15S.

X. Devotion is a Love of one whom we wonder at.

Exp.: That Wonder arises from the newness of the thing we have shown in P52. So if it happens that we often imagine what we wonder at, we shall cease to wonder at it. And so we see that the affect of Devotion easily changes into simple Love.

XI. Mockery is a Joy born of the fact that we imagine something we disdain in a thing we hate.

---

[41] Spinoza may have in mind Descartes, PA 79. (Earlier, however, in PA 56, Descartes had given an account of love closer to Spinoza's.) In any case, he need not have only one opponent in mind. The conception of love here objected to goes back as far as Plato's *Symposium* (191-192), and Spinoza himself seems not to have been free of it in the *Short Treatise* (cf. I/62).

[42] NS: "definitions." Akkerman (2, 92) suggests that the NS translator has misread a final "m" as an "s."

[43] Cf. PA II, 80.   [44] Cf. Hobbes, *Leviathan* I, 6.

25 Exp.: Insofar as we disdain a thing we hate, we deny existence to it (see P52S), and so far we rejoice (by P20). But since we suppose that man nevertheless hates what he mocks, it follows that this Joy is not enduring. (See P47S.)

II/194 XII. Hope is an inconstant Joy, born of the idea of a future or past thing whose outcome we to some extent doubt.

XIII. Fear is an inconstant Sadness, born of the idea of a future or

5 past thing whose outcome we to some extent doubt. See P18S2.

Exp.: From these definitions it follows that there is neither Hope without Fear, nor Fear without Hope.[45] For he who is suspended in Hope[46] and doubts a thing's outcome is supposed to imagine some-

10 thing that excludes the existence of the future thing. And so to that extent he is saddened (by P19), and consequently, while he is suspended in Hope, he fears that the thing [he imagines] will happen.

Conversely, he who is in Fear, i.e., who doubts the outcome of a thing he hates, also imagines something that excludes the existence of

15 that thing. And so (by P20) he rejoices, and hence, to that extent has Hope that the thing will not take place.

XIV. Confidence is a Joy born of the idea of a future or past thing, concerning which the cause of doubting has been removed.

XV. Despair is a Sadness born of the idea of a future or past thing

20 concerning which the cause of doubting has been removed.

Exp.: Confidence, therefore, is born of Hope and Despair of Fear, when the cause of doubt concerning the thing's outcome is removed. This happens because man imagines that the past or future thing is

25 there, and regards it as present, or because he imagines other things, excluding the existence of the things that put him in doubt. For though we can never be certain of the outcome of singular things (by IIP31C), it can still happen that we do not doubt their outcome. As we have shown (see IIP49S), it is one thing not to doubt a thing, and another

30 to be certain of it. And so it can happen that we are affected, from the image of a past or future thing, with the same affect of Joy or

II/195 Sadness as from the image of a present thing (as we have demonstrated in P18; see also its [first] scholium).[47]

---

[45] Cf. Seneca, *Epist. mor.*, v, 7: "Just as the same chain binds both the prisoner and his guardian, so these things, though so unlike, march together: fear follows hope." Similarly Descartes, PA 165, 166.

[46] So White, Appuhn et al., render *Spe pendet*. Elwes has "depends on hope," which is supported by the NS. Cf. II/246/15.

[47] The OP and NS have simply: "scholium." Gebhardt emends to "scholia." Cf. the note at 154/24. Akkerman (2, 82) seems clearly right to contend that P18S1 is intended.

XVI. Gladness is a Joy, accompanied by the idea of a past thing that has turned out better than we had hoped.[48]

XVII. Remorse is a Sadness, accompanied by the idea of a past thing that has turned out worse than we had hoped.

XVIII. Pity is a Sadness, accompanied by the idea of an evil that has happened to another whom we imagine to be like us. (See P22S and P27S.)

Exp.: There seems to be no difference between Pity and Compassion, except perhaps that Pity concerns the singular affect, whereas Compassion concerns the habitual disposition of this affect.

XIX. Favor is a Love toward someone who has benefited another.

XX. Indignation is a Hate toward someone who has done evil to another.

Exp.: I know that in their common usage these words mean something else.[49] But my purpose is to explain the nature of things, not the

[48] OP: *"praeter Spem evenit."* In his *corrigenda* (II/393) Gebhardt proposed emending to *praeter Metum.* No argument was offered, but unless the text is emended, we must give *praeter* a different translation here than we do in Def. XVII, where the same Latin phrase occurs (*praeter Spem* = "beyond our hope" in Def. XVI, but = "contrary to our hope" in Def. XVII). Against Gebhardt's emendation is the fact that the text as it stands echoes a line in Terence (*Andria*, 436) and is supported by the NS. If a change must be made, I would prefer to make it in Def. XVII rather than in Def. XVI. But it is not clear that a change is necessary. While Bidney (197) may not be correct to say that the terms "hope" and "fear" are interchangeable, his interpretation of the definitions seems sensible otherwise.

[49] It is clear from this and similar remarks (e.g., at II/80) that Spinoza does not intend to give an analysis of ordinary language. It may, therefore, seem churlish for a commentator to complain when translators are guided, in their choice of terms for the affects, more by Spinoza's definitions than by the ordinary meaning of the terms defined (cf. Bidney, 2-4 and the glossary entry on *remorse*). The translators' practice need not reflect a desire to make Spinoza always speak the truth, no matter what the possible cost in distortion of his meaning.

Still, though Spinoza's definitions are not subject to the constraints analysis of ordinary language would impose, neither are they wholly stipulative. They are intended to have explanatory force, to give us insight into the nature of familiar emotions by indicating their cause. Cf. the theory of definitions in the TdIE, §§ 93-98. (Note that Spinoza's definitions of the affects are developed gradually through the course of his deductive treatment of the affects. They do not precede it, as the axiomatic model would lead us to expect.)

If that is the intent, then the translator does not have a free hand in translating the terms for the affects. For example, Spinoza's definition of *amor* may not be one which an analyst of ordinary language would give, since ordinary usage probably does not entail any theory about the cause of *amor*. It may also be the case that *amor*, as Spinoza defines it, does not have the same extension *amor* as ordinarily used has. The two terms may not pick out exactly the same class of emotions. But there must, at least, be considerable overlap in the extensions of the terms. Spinoza's situation (to borrow an analogy from Hilary Putnam, "Dreaming and 'Depth Grammar,' " in *Analytical Philosophy*, ed. R. J. Butler, 1st series [Oxford: Basil Blackwell, 1966]) is like that of a chemist introducing a new theoretical definition of a term like *acid*. The chemist's definition may

meaning of words. I intend to indicate these things by words whose usual meaning is not entirely opposed to[50] the meaning with which I wish to use them. One warning of this should suffice. As for the cause of these affects, see P27C1 and P22S.

XXI. Overestimation is thinking more highly of someone than is just, out of Love.

XXII. Scorn is thinking less highly of someone than is just, out of Hate.

Exp.: Overestimation, therefore, is an effect, *or* property, of Love, and Scorn an effect of Hate. And so *Overestimation* can also be defined as *love insofar as it so affects a man that he thinks more highly than is just of the thing loved.* On the other hand, Scorn can be defined as *Hate insofar as it so affects a man that he thinks less highly than is just of him he hates.* See P26S.

XXIII. Envy is Hate insofar as it so affects a man that he is saddened by another's happiness and, conversely, glad at his ill fortune.

Exp.: To Envy one commonly opposes Compassion, which can therefore (in spite of the meaning of the word)[51] be defined as follows.

XXIV. Compassion is Love, insofar as it so affects a man that he is glad at another's good fortune, and saddened by his ill fortune.

Exp.: As far as Envy is concerned, see P24S and P32S. These are the affects of Joy and Sadness that are accompanied by the idea of an external thing as cause, either through itself or accidentally. I pass now to the others, which are accompanied by the idea of an internal thing as cause.

XXV. Self-esteem is a Joy born of the fact that a man considers himself and his own power of acting.

XXVI. Humility is a Sadness born of the fact that a man considers his own lack of power, *or* weakness.

Exp.: Self-esteem is opposed to Humility, insofar as we understand by it a Joy born of the fact that we consider our power of acting. But insofar as we also understand by it a Joy, accompanied by the idea of some deed which we believe we have done from a free decision of the Mind, it is opposed to Repentance, which we define as follows.

XXVII. Repentance is a Sadness accompanied by the idea of some

---

lead to some reclassification of chemical substances. But if the term's range of application, as newly defined, were not closely related to its former range of application, there would be no improvement of our understanding, there would only be confusion.

[50] NS: "comes nearest to."

[51] The problem here is partly the etymological connection of *misericordia* with *miser*, 'wretched, unhappy.'

deed we believe ourselves to have done from a free decision of the Mind.

Exp.: We have shown the causes of these affects in P51S, P53, P54, P55, and P55S. On the free decision of the Mind, see IIP35S.

But we ought also to note here that it is no wonder Sadness follows absolutely all those acts which from custom are called *wrong*, and Joy, those which are called *right*. For from what has been said above we easily understand that this depends chiefly on education. Parents—by blaming the former acts, and often scolding their children on account of them, and on the other hand, by recommending and praising the latter acts—have brought it about that emotions of Sadness were joined to the one kind of act, and those of Joy to the other.

Experience itself also confirms this. For not everyone has the same custom and Religion. On the contrary, what among some is holy, among others is unholy; and what among some is honorable, among others is dishonorable. Hence, according as each one has been educated, so he either repents of a deed or exults at being esteemed for it.

XXVIII. Pride is thinking more highly of oneself than is just, out of love of oneself.

Exp.: The difference, therefore, between Pride and Overestimation is that the latter is related to an external object, whereas Pride is related to the man himself, who thinks more highly of himself than is just. Further, as Overestimation is an effect or property of Love, so *Pride* is an effect or property of Self-love. Therefore, it can also be defined as *Love of oneself*, or *Self-esteem, insofar as it so affects a man that he thinks more highly of himself than is just* (see P26S).

198   There is no opposite of this affect. For no one, out of hate, thinks less highly of himself than is just. Indeed, no one thinks less highly of himself than is just, insofar as he imagines that he cannot do this or that. For whatever man imagines he cannot do, he necessarily imagines; and he is so disposed by this imagination that he really cannot do what he imagines he cannot do. For so long as he imagines that he cannot do this or that, he is not determined to do it, and consequently it is impossible for him to do it.

But if we attend to those things that depend only on opinion, we shall be able to conceive it possible that a man thinks less highly of himself than is just. For it can happen that, while someone sad considers his weakness, he imagines himself to be disdained by everyone—even while the others think of nothing less than to disdain him. Moreover, it can happen that a man thinks less highly of himself than

537

is just, if in the present he denies something of himself in relation to a future time of which he is uncertain—e.g., if he denies that he can conceive of anything certain, or that he can desire or do anything but what is wrong or dishonorable. Again, we can say that someone thinks less highly of himself than is just, when we see that, from too great a fear of shame, he does not dare things that others equal to him dare.

So we can oppose this affect—which I shall call Despondency—to Pride. For as Pride is born of Self-esteem, so Despondency is born of Humility. We can therefore define it as follows.

XXIX. Despondency is thinking less highly of oneself than is just, out of Sadness.

Exp.: We are, nevertheless, often accustomed to oppose Humility to Pride. But then we attend more to the effects than to the nature of the two. For we usually call him proud who exults too much at being esteemed (see P30S), who tells of nothing but his own virtues, and the vices of others, who wishes to be given precedence over all others, and finally who proceeds with the gravity and attire usually adopted by others who are placed far above him.

On the other hand, we call him humble who quite often blushes, who confesses his own vices and tells the virtues of others, who yields to all, and finally, who walks with head bowed, and neglects to adorn himself.

These affects—Humility and Despondency—are very rare. For human nature, considered in itself, strains against them, as far as it can (see P13 and P54). So those who are believed to be most despondent and humble are usually most ambitious and envious.

XXX. Love of esteem is a Joy accompanied by the idea of some action of ours which we imagine that others praise.

XXXI. Shame is a Sadness, accompanied by the idea of some action [NS: of ours] which we imagine that others blame.

Exp.: On these, see P30S. But the difference between Shame and a Sense of Shame should be noted here. For Shame is a Sadness that follows a deed one is ashamed of; whereas a Sense of Shame is a Fear of, *or* Timidity regarding, Shame, by which man is restrained from doing something dishonorable. To a Sense of Shame is usually opposed Shamelessness, but the latter is really not an affect, as I shall show in the proper place.[52] But as I have already pointed out, the names of the affects are guided more by usage than by nature.

And with this I have finished what I had set out to explain con-

---

[52] In fact, as Appuhn notes, Spinoza never does return to the topic of shamelessness.

20 cerning the affects of Joy and Sadness. So I proceed to those I relate to Desire.

XXXII. Longing is a Desire, *or* Appetite, to possess something which is encouraged by the memory of that thing, and at the same time restrained by the memory of other things which exclude the existence of the thing wanted.

25 Exp.: When we recollect a thing (as we have often said before), we are thereby disposed to regard it with the same affect as if it were present. But while we are awake, this disposition, *or* striving, is generally restrained by images of things that exclude the existence of what 30 we recollect. So when we remember a thing that affects us with some II/200 kind of Joy, we thereby strive to regard it as present with the same affect of Joy—a striving which, of course, is immediately restrained by the memory of things that exclude its existence.

Longing, therefore, is really a Sadness which is opposed to that Joy which arises from the absence of a thing we hate (see P47S). But because the word *longing* seems to concern Desire, I relate this affect to the affects of Desire.

XXXIII. Emulation is a Desire for a thing which is generated in us because we imagine that others have the same Desire.

Exp.: If someone flees because he sees others flee, or is timid because he sees others timid, or, because he sees that someone else has burned his hand, withdraws his own hand and moves his body as if his hand were burned, we shall say that he imitates the other's affect, but not that he emulates it—not because we know that emulation has one cause and imitation another, but because it has come about by usage that we call emulous only him who imitates what we judge to be honorable, useful, or pleasant.

As for the cause of Emulation, see P27 and P27S. And on why envy is generally joined to this effect, see P32 and P32S.

XXXIV. Thankfulness, *or* Gratitude, is a Desire, *or* eagerness of Love, by which we strive to benefit one who has benefited us from a like affect of love. See P39 and P41S.

XXXV. Benevolence is a Desire to benefit one whom we pity. See P27S.

XXXVI. Anger is a Desire by which we are spurred, from Hate, to do evil to him we hate. See P39.

/201 XXXVII. Vengeance is a Desire by which, from reciprocal Hate, we are roused to do evil to one who, from a like affect, has injured us. See P40C2 and P40C2S.

XXXVIII. Cruelty, *or* Severity, is a Desire by which someone is roused to do evil to one whom we love or pity.[53]

Exp.: To Cruelty is opposed Mercy, which is not a passion, but a power of the mind, by which a man governs anger and vengeance.

XXXIX. Timidity is a Desire to avoid a greater evil, which we fear, by a lesser one. See P39S.

XL. Daring is a Desire by which someone is spurred to do something dangerous which his equals fear to take on themselves.

XLI. Cowardice is ascribed to one whose Desire is restrained by timidity regarding a danger which his equals dare to take on themselves.

Exp.: Cowardice, therefore, is nothing but Fear of some evil, which most people do not usually fear. So I do not relate it to affects of Desire. Nevertheless I wished to explain it here, because insofar as we attend to the Desire, it is really opposed to daring.

XLII. Consternation is attributed to one whose Desire to avoid an evil is restrained by wonder at the evil he fears.

Exp.: Consternation, therefore, is a species of Cowardice. But because Consternation arises from a double Timidity, it can be more conveniently defined as *a Fear that keeps a man senseless or vacillating so that he cannot avert the evil*. I say *senseless* insofar as we understand that

[53] So the text of the OP runs, and it is supported by the NS. Meijer and Baensch proposed emending the text to read: "a Desire by which we are roused to do evil to one whom we love or pity." The idea would be that P41CS implies that cruelty arises when one person hates another, finds his hate returned by love, and suffers a conflict of love and hate in which hate prevails (without, it seems, entirely extinguishing the love). I believe the sequence from Def. XXXVI to Def. XXXVIII makes better sense if we accept the emendation. Anger is the basic form of desire to do evil to someone. Vengeance is anger complicated by the fact that our hate is returned. And cruelty is anger complicated by emotions conflicting with our hate.

Gebhardt retains the OP reading, partly because the only love explicitly mentioned in P41CS is the victim's love for the one who is cruel, but partly because he thinks the emended definition would imply an unfavorable judgment on the activities of jailers and hangmen. This doesn't seem to follow, and the first reason seems insufficient. Akkerman (2, 191), while defending the OP reading of the text, suggests a way of interpreting it that would make it equivalent to the emendation. He notes that "aliquis" and "nos" are both used in the preceding and following definitions (34-40) to refer to the bearer of the affect defined, so "it may not after all be impossible that *aliquis* and *nos* in defin. 38 refer to the same person, the bearer of the affect."

In favor of retaining the text of the OP, Jonathan Bennett suggests (in correspondence) that "the point of D38 *may* be that 'cruel' is a term which nobody uses without giving it a load of moral condemnation, and that emerges—given Spinoza's meta-ethics—simply as the condition that the speaker loves or pities the victim of the so-called 'cruelty.' " He draws attention to the fact that in P41CS Spinoza says that the affect is called cruelty especially when *it is believed* that the victim has given no ordinary cause for hatred. He takes this as indicating that "cruel" involves "a more than usually speaker-relative or subjective element."

Bennett's suggestion is quite plausible, but I still think the emendation has merit.

his Desire to avert the evil is restrained by wonder, and *vacillating* insofar as we conceive that that Desire is restrained by Timidity regarding another evil, which torments him equally, so that he does not know which of the two to avert. On these see P39S and P52S. As for Cowardice and Daring, see P51S.

XLIII. Human kindness, *or* Courtesy, is a Desire to do what pleases men and not do what displeases them.

XLIV. Ambition is an excessive Desire for esteem.

Exp.: Ambition is a Desire by which all the affects are encouraged and strengthened (by P27 and P31); so this affect can hardly be overcome. For as long as a man is bound by any Desire, he must at the same time be bound by this one. As Cicero says,[54] *Every man is led by love of esteem, and the more so, the better he is. Even the philosophers who write books on how esteem is to be disdained put their names to these works.*

XLV. Gluttony is an immoderate Desire for and Love of eating.

XLVI. Drunkenness is an immoderate Desire for and Love of drinking.

XLVII. Greed is an immoderate Desire for and Love of wealth.

XLVIII. Lust is also a Desire for and Love of joining one body to another.

Exp.: Whether this Desire for sexual union is moderate or not, it is usually called Lust.

Moreover, these five affects (as I pointed out in P56S) have no opposites. For Courtesy is a species of Ambition (see P29S), and I have already pointed out also that Moderation, Sobriety, and Chastity indicate the power of the Mind, and not a passion. And even if it can happpen that a greedy, ambitious, or timid man abstains from too much food, drink, and sexual union, still, Greed, Ambition, and Timidity are not opposites of gluttony, drunkenness, or lust.

For the greedy man generally longs to gorge himself on another's food and drink. And the ambitious will not be moderate in anything,[55] provided he can hope he will not be discovered; if he lives among the drunken and the lustful, then because he is ambitious, he will be the more inclined to these vices. Finally, the timid man does what he does not wish to do. For though he may hurl his wealth into the sea to avoid death, he still remains greedy. And if the lustful man is sad because he cannot indulge his inclinations, he does not on that account cease to be lustful.

Absolutely, these affects do not so much concern the acts of eating,

---

[54] *Pro Archia* XI.

[55] Again, both language and thought here are reminiscent of Terence, in this case, the *Adelphi*, 69-71. Cf. the note at 138/11.

drinking, etc., as the Appetite itself and the Love. Therefore, nothing can be opposed to these affects except Nobility and Tenacity, which
15 will be discussed later on.

I pass over in silence the definitions of Jealousy and the other vacillations of mind, both because they arise from the composition of affects we have already defined, and because most of them do not have names. This shows that it is sufficient for practical purposes to know
20 them only in general. Furthermore, from the definitions of the affects which we have explained it is clear that they all arise from Desire, Joy, or Sadness—*or* rather, that they are nothing but these three, each one generally being called by a different name on account of its varying relations and extrinsic denominations. If we wish now to attend
25 to these primitive affects, and to what was said above about the nature of the Mind, we shall be able to define the affects, insofar as they are related only to the Mind,[56] as follows.

General Definition of the Affects

An Affect that is called a Passion of the mind is a confused idea, by
30 which the Mind affirms of its Body, or of some part of it, a greater or lesser force of existing than before, which, when it is given, determines the Mind to think of this rather than that.

II/204 Exp.: I say, first, that an Affect, *or* passion of the mind, is a *confused idea*. For we have shown (P3) that the Mind is acted on only insofar as it has inadequate, *or* confused, ideas.

5 Next, I say *by which the mind affirms of its body or of some part of it a greater or lesser force of existing than before.* For all the ideas that we have of bodies indicate the actual constitution of our own Body (by IIP16C2) more than the nature of the external body. But this [idea], which
10 constitutes the form of the affect, must indicate or express a constitution of the Body (or of some part of it), which the Body (or some part of it) has because its power of acting, *or* force of existing, is increased or diminished, aided or restrained.

But it should be noted that, when I say *a greater or lesser force of existing than before,* I do not understand that the Mind compares its
15 Body's present constitution with a past constitution, but that the idea which constitutes the form of the affect affirms of the body something which really involves more or less of reality than before.

And because the essence of the Mind consists in this (by IIP11 and P13), that it affirms the actual existence of its body, and we under-

---

[56] Previously (II/139) Spinoza has defined an affect as a certain kind of affection of the body together with the idea of that affection.

stand by perfection the very essence of the thing, it follows that the Mind passes to a greater or lesser perfection when it happens that it affirms of its body (or of some part of the body) something which involves more or less reality than before. So when I said above that the Mind's power of Thinking is increased or diminished, I meant nothing but that the Mind has formed of its Body (or of some part of it) an idea which expresses more or less reality than it had affirmed of the Body.

Finally, I added *which determines the Mind to think of this rather than that* in order to express also, in addition to the nature of Joy and Sadness (which the first part of the definition explains), the nature of Desire.

Fourth Part Of the Ethics
On Human Bondage, or the Powers
of the Affects

205

Preface

Man's lack of power to moderate and restrain the affects I call Bondage. For the man who is subject to affects is under the control, not of himself, but of fortune, in whose power he so greatly is that often, though he sees the better for himself, he is still forced to follow the worse.[1] In this Part, I have undertaken to demonstrate the cause of this, and what there is of good and evil in the affects. But before I begin, I choose to say a few words first on perfection and imperfection, good and evil.

If someone has decided to make something, and has finished it, then he will call his thing perfect[2]—and so will anyone who rightly knows, or thinks he knows, the mind and purpose of the Author of the work. For example, if someone sees a work (which I suppose to be not yet completed), and knows that the purpose of the Author of that work is to build a house, he will say that it is imperfect. On the other hand, he will call it perfect as soon as he sees that the work has been carried through to the end which its Author has decided to give it. But if

---

[1] An echo of a well-known line from Ovid, which will be quoted in P17S, and to which we have already had an allusion at II/143/22-23.

[2] In Latin this is a patent tautology. See the Glossary-Index entry on *perfection*.

someone sees a work whose like he has never seen, and does not know
25 the mind of its maker, he will, of course, not be able to know whether
II/206 that work is perfect or imperfect. And this seems to have been the
first meaning of these words.

But after men began to form universal ideas, and devise models of
houses, buildings, towers, etc., and to prefer some models of things
5 to others, it came about that each one called perfect what he saw
agreed with the universal idea he had formed of this kind of thing,
and imperfect, what he saw agreed less with the model he had conceived, even though its maker thought he had entirely finished it.

10 Nor does there seem to be any other reason why men also commonly call perfect or imperfect natural things, which have not been
made by human hand. For they are accustomed to form universal
ideas of natural things as much as they do of artificial ones. They
regard these universal ideas as models of things, and believe that na-
15 ture (which they think does nothing except for the sake of some end)
looks to them, and sets them before itself as models. So when they
see something happen in nature which does not agree with the model
they have conceived of this kind of thing, they believe that Nature
itself has failed or sinned, and left the thing imperfect.

20 We see, therefore, that men are accustomed to call natural things
perfect or imperfect more from prejudice than from true knowledge
of those things. For we have shown in the Appendix of Part I, that
Nature does nothing on account of an end. That eternal and infinite
being we call God, or Nature,[3] acts from the same necessity from
25 which he exists. For we have shown (IP16) that the necessity of nature
from which he acts is the same as that from which he exists. The
reason, therefore, or cause, why God, or Nature, acts, and the reason
why he exists, are one and the same. As he exists for the sake of no
II/207 end, he also acts for the sake of no end. Rather, as he has no principle
or end of existing, so he also has none of acting. What is called a final
cause is nothing but a human appetite insofar as it is considered as a
5 principle, or primary cause, of some thing.

For example, when we say that habitation was the final cause of
this or that house, surely we understand nothing but that a man,
because he imagined the conveniences of domestic life, had an appetite
to build a house. So habitation, insofar as it is considered as a final
10 cause, is nothing more than this singular appetite. It is really an efficient cause, which is considered as a first cause, because men are commonly ignorant of the causes of their appetites. For as I have often

[3] The NS have simply "God" here, and again at ll. 26-27.

said before, they are conscious of their actions and appetites, but not aware of the causes by which they are determined to want something.

As for what they commonly say—that Nature sometimes fails or sins, and produces imperfect things—I number this among the fictions I treated in the Appendix of Part I.

Perfection and imperfection, therefore, are only modes of thinking, i.e., notions we are accustomed to feign because we compare individuals of the same species or genus to one another. This is why I said above (IID6) that by reality and perfection I understand the same thing. For we are accustomed to refer all individuals in Nature to one genus, which is called the most general, i.e., to the notion of being, which pertains absolutely to all individuals in Nature. So insofar as we refer all individuals in Nature to this genus, compare them to one another, and find that some have more being, *or* reality, than others, we say that some are more perfect than others. And insofar as we attribute something to them that involves negation, like a limit, an end, lack of power, etc., we call them imperfect, because they do not affect our Mind as much as those we call perfect, and not because something is lacking in them which is theirs, or because Nature has sinned. For nothing belongs to the nature of anything except what follows from the necessity of the nature of the efficient cause. And whatever follows from the necessity of the nature of the efficient cause happens necessarily.

As far as good and evil are concerned, they also indicate nothing positive in things, considered in themselves, nor are they anything other than modes of thinking, *or* notions we form because we compare things to one another. For one and the same thing can, at the same time, be good, and bad, and also indifferent. For example, Music is good for one who is Melancholy, bad for one who is mourning, and neither good nor bad to one who is deaf.

But though this is so, still we must retain these words. For because we desire to form an idea of man, as a model of human nature which we may look to, it will be useful to us to retain these same words with the meaning I have indicated. In what follows, therefore, I shall understand by good what we know certainly is a means by which we may approach nearer and nearer to the model of human nature that we set before ourselves. By evil, what we certainly know prevents us from becoming like that model. Next, we shall say that men are more perfect or imperfect, insofar as they approach more or less near to this model.

But the main thing to note is that when I say that someone passes from a lesser to a greater perfection, and the opposite, I do not understand that he is changed from one essence, *or* form, to another. For example, a horse is destroyed as much if it is changed into a man as if it is changed into an insect. Rather, we conceive that his power of acting, insofar as it is understood through his nature, is increased or diminished.

II/209   Finally, by perfection in general I shall, as I have said, understand reality, i.e., the essence of each thing insofar as it exists and produces an effect, having no regard to its duration. For no singular thing can
5   be called more perfect for having persevered in existing for a longer time. Indeed, the duration of things cannot be determined from their essence, since the essence of things involves no certain and determinate time of existing. But any thing whatever, whether it is more perfect or less, will always be able to persevere in existing by the same
10   force by which it begins to exist; so they are all equal in this regard.

Definitions

D1: By good I shall understand what we certainly know to be useful to us.

D2: By evil, however, I shall understand what we certainly know
15   prevents us from being masters of some good.
    Exp.: On these definitions, see the preceding preface [208/18-22].

D3: I call singular things contingent insofar as we find nothing, while we attend only to their essence, which necessarily posits their exist-
20   ence or which necessarily excludes it.

D4: I call the same singular things possible, insofar as, while we attend to the causes from which they must be produced, we do not know whether those causes are determined to produce them.
    In IP33S1 I drew no distinction between the possible and the con-
25   tingent, because there was no need there to distinguish them accurately.

D5: By opposite affects I shall understand, in what follows, those
II/210   which pull a man differently, although they are of the same genus—such as gluttony and greed, which are species of love, and are opposite, not by nature, but accidentally.

D6: I have explained in IIIP18S1 and S2 what I shall understand by
5   an affect toward a future thing, a present one, and a past.
    But here it should be noted in addition that just as we can distinctly imagine distance of place only up to a certain limit, so also we can distinctly imagine distance of time only up to a certain limit. I.e., we

usually imagine all those objects which are more than 200 feet away from us,[4] *or* whose distance from the place where we are surpasses what we can distinctly imagine, to be equally far from us; we therefore usually imagine them as if they were in the same plane; in the same way, we imagine to be equally far from the present all those objects whose time of existing we imagine to be separated from the present by an interval longer than that we are used to imagining distinctly; so we relate them, as it were, to one moment of time.

D7: By the end for the sake of which we do something I understand appetite.

D8: By virtue and power I understand the same thing, i.e. (by IIIP7), virtue, insofar as it is related to man, is the very essence, *or* nature, of man, insofar as he has the power of bringing about certain things, which can be understood through the laws of his nature alone.

Axiom

[A1:][5] There is no singular thing in nature than which there is not another more powerful and stronger. Whatever one is given, there is another more powerful by which the first can be destroyed.

211 P1: *Nothing positive which a false idea has is removed by the presence of the true insofar as it is true.*

Dem.: Falsity consists only in the privation of knowledge which inadequate ideas involve (by IIP35), and they do not have anything positive on account of which they are called false (by IIP33). On the contrary, insofar as they are related to God, they are true (by IIP32). So if what a false idea has that is positive were removed by the presence of the true insofar as it is true, then a true idea would be removed by itself, which (by IIIP4) is absurd. Therefore, Nothing positive which a false idea has, etc., q.e.d.

Schol.: This proposition is understood more clearly from IIP16C2. For an imagination is an idea which indicates the present constitution of the human Body more than the nature of an external body—not distinctly, of course, but confusedly. This is how it happens that the Mind is said to err.

For example, when we look at the sun, we imagine it to be about 200 feet away from us. In this we are deceived so long as we are

---

[4] See the note at II/117/30.

[5] It would appear that Spinoza originally had at least three axioms in this Part. See Gebhardt II/377, and below, at II/215/5 and 230/2. Though only one remains, it will simplify subsequent references to give it a number.

ignorant of its true distance; but when its distance is known, the error is removed, not the imagination, i.e., the idea of the sun, which explains its nature only so far as the Body is affected by it. And so, although we come to know the true distance, we shall nevertheless imagine it as near us. For as we said in IIP35S, we do not imagine the sun to be so near because we are ignorant of its true distance, but because the Mind conceives the sun's size insofar as the Body is affected by the sun. Thus, when the rays of the sun, falling on the surface of the water, are reflected to our eyes, we imagine it as if it were in the water, even if we know its true place.

And so it is with the other imaginations by which the Mind is deceived, whether they indicate the natural constitution of the Body, or that its power of acting is increased or diminished: they are not contrary to the true, and do not disappear on its presence.

It happens, of course, when we wrongly fear some evil, that the fear disappears on our hearing news of the truth. But on the other hand, it also happens, when we fear an evil that is certain to come, that the fear vanishes on our hearing false news. So imaginations do not disappear through the presence of the true insofar as it is true, but because there occur others, stronger than them, which exclude the present existence of the things we imagine, as we showed in IIP17.

P2: *We are acted on, insofar as we are a part of Nature, which cannot be conceived through itself, without the others.*

Dem.: We say that we are acted on when something arises in us of which we are only the partial cause (by IIID2), i.e. (by IIID1), something that cannot be deduced from the laws of our nature alone. Therefore, we are acted on insofar as we are a part of Nature, which cannot be conceived through itself without the others, q.e.d.

P3: *The force by which a man perseveres in existing is limited, and infinitely surpassed by the power of external causes.*

Dem.: This is evident from A1. For given a man, there is something else, say A, more powerful. And given A, there is something else again, say B, more powerful than A, and so on, to infinity. Therefore the power of man is limited by the power of another thing and infinitely surpassed by the power of external causes, q.e.d.

P4: *It is impossible that a man should not be a part of Nature, and that he should be able to undergo no changes except those which can be understood through his own nature alone, and of which he is the adequate cause.*

Dem.: [i] The power by which singular things (and consequently, [any] man) preserve their being is the power itself of God, *or* Nature (by IP24C), not insofar as it is infinite, but insofar as it can be explained through the man's actual essence (by IIIP7). The man's power, therefore, insofar as it is explained through his actual essence, is part of God *or* Nature's infinite power, i.e. (by IP34), of its essence. This was the first point.

[ii] Next, if it were possible that a man could undergo no changes except those which can be understood through the man's nature alone, it would follow (by IIIP4 and P6) that he could not perish, but that necessarily he would always exist. And this would have to follow from a cause whose power would be either finite or infinite, viz. either from the power of the man alone, who would be able to avert from himself other changes which could arise from external causes, or from the infinite power of Nature, by which all singular things would be directed so that the man could undergo no other changes except those which assist his preservation.

But the first is absurd (by P3, whose demonstration is universal and can be applied to all singular things).

Therefore, if it were possible for a man to undergo no changes except those which could be understood through the man's nature alone, so that (as we have already shown) he would necessarily always exist, this would have to follow from God's infinite power; and consequently (by IP16) the order of the whole of Nature, insofar as it is conceived under the attributes of Extension and Thought, would have to be deduced from the necessity of the divine nature, insofar as it is considered to be affected with the idea of some man. And so (by IP21) it would follow that the man would be infinite. But this (by part [i] of this demonstration) is absurd.

Therefore, it is impossible that a man should undergo no other changes except those of which he himself is the adequate cause, q.e.d.

Cor.: From this it follows that man is necessarily always subject to passions, that he follows and obeys the common order of Nature, and accommodates himself to it as much as the nature of things requires.

214 P5: *The force and growth of any passion, and its perseverance in existing, are not defined by the power by which we strive to persevere in existing, but by the power of an external cause compared with our own.*

Dem.: The essence of a passion cannot be explained through our essence alone (by IIID1 and D2), i.e. (by IIIP7), the power of a passion cannot be defined by the power by which we strive to persevere in our being; but (as has been shown in IIP16) it must necessarily be defined by the power of an external cause compared with our own, q.e.d.

P6: *The force of any passion, or affect, can surpass the other actions, or power, of a man, so that the affect stubbornly clings to the man.*

Dem.: The force and growth of any passion, and its perseverance in existing, are defined by the power of an external cause compared with our own (by P5). And so (by P3) it can surpass the power of a man, etc., q.e.d.

P7: *An affect cannot be restrained or taken away except by an affect opposite to, and stronger than, the affect to be restrained.*

Dem.: An affect, insofar as it is related to the Mind, is an idea by which the Mind affirms of its body a greater or lesser force of existing than before (by the general Definition of the Affects [II/203/29-33]). When, therefore, the Mind is troubled by some affect, the Body is at the same time affected with an affection by which its power of acting is increased or diminished.

Next, this affection of the Body (by P5) receives from its cause its force for persevering in its being, which therefore, can neither be restrained nor removed, except by a corporeal cause (by IIP6) which affects the Body with an affection opposite to it (by IIIP5), and stronger than it (by A1).[6]

And so (by IIP12), the Mind will be affected with the idea of an affection stronger than, and opposite to, the first affection, i.e. (by the general Definition of the Affects), the Mind will be affected with an affect stronger than, and opposite to, the first affect, which will exclude or take away the existence of the first affect.

Therefore, an affect can neither be taken away nor restrained except through an opposite and stronger affect, q.e.d.

Cor.: An affect, insofar as it is related to the Mind, can neither be restrained nor taken away except by the idea of an opposite affection of the Body stronger than the affection through which it is acted on. For an affect through which we are acted on can neither be restrained nor taken away except by an affect stronger than it and contrary to it (by P7), i.e. (by the general Definition of the Affects), except by an idea of an affection of the Body stronger than and contrary to the affection through which we are acted on.

P8: *The knowledge of good and evil is nothing but an affect of Joy or Sadness, insofar as we are conscious of it.*

Dem.: We call good, or evil, what is useful to, or harmful to, preserving our being (by D1 and D2), i.e. (by IIIP7), what increases or diminishes, aids or restrains, our power of acting. Therefore (by the Definitions of Joy and Sadness in IIIP11S), insofar as we perceive that

---

[6] The OP does have: "by A1." This is corrected in the errata to: "by the Axiom."

a thing affects us with Joy or Sadness, we call it good or evil. And so knowledge of good and evil is nothing but an idea of Joy or Sadness which follows necessarily from the affect of Joy or Sadness itself (by IIP22).

But this idea is united to the affect in the same way as the Mind is united to the Body (by IIP21), i.e. (as I have shown in IIP21S), this idea is not really distinguished from the affect itself, *or* (by the general Definition of the Affects) from the idea of the Body's affection; it is only conceptually distinguished from it. Therefore, this knowledge of good and evil is nothing but the affect itself, insofar as we are conscious of it, q.e.d.

P9: *An affect whose cause we imagine to be with us in the present is stronger than if we did not imagine it to be with us.*

Dem.: An imagination is an idea by which the Mind considers a thing as present (see its definition in IIP17S), which nevertheless indicates the constitution of the human Body more than the nature of the external thing (by IIP16C2). An affect, therefore (by the general Definition of the Affects), is an imagination, insofar as [the affect] indicates the constitution of the body. But an imagination (by IIP17) is more intense so long as we imagine nothing that excludes the present existence of the external thing. Hence, an affect whose cause we imagine to be with us in the present is more intense, *or* stronger, than if we did not imagine it to be with us, q.e.d.

Schol.: I said above (in IIIP18) that when we imagine a future or past thing, we are affected with the same affect as if we were imagining something present; but I expressly warned then that this is true insofar as we attend to the thing's image only. For it is of the same nature whether we have imagined the thing[7] as present or not. But I did not deny that it is made weaker when we consider as present to us other things, which exclude the present existence of the future thing. I neglected to point this out then, because I had decided to treat the powers of the affects in this Part.

Cor.: Other things equal, the image of a future or past thing (i.e., of a thing we consider in relation to a future or past time, the present being excluded) is weaker than the image of a present thing; and consequently, an affect toward a future or past thing is milder, other things equal, than an affect toward a present thing.

P10: *We are affected more intensely toward a future thing which we imagine will quickly be present, than if we imagined the time when it will exist to be further from the present. We are also affected more intensely by the memory of*

---

[7] Reading "rem ut praesentem," as suggested by Akkerman (2, 178).

a thing we imagine to be not long past, than if we imagined it to be long past.

10   Dem.: Insofar as we imagine that a thing will quickly be present, or is not long past, we thereby imagine something that excludes the presence of the thing less than if we imagined that the time when it will exist were further from the present, or that it were far in the past (as is known through itself). And so (by P9), to that extent we will be

15   affected more intensely toward it, q.e.d.

    Schol.: From what we noted at D6, it follows that we are still affected equally mildly toward objects separated from the present by an interval of time longer than that we can determine by imagining, even

20   though we may understand that they are separated from one another by a long interval of time.

P11: *An affect toward a thing we imagine as necessary is more intense, other things equal, than one toward a thing we imagine as possible or contingent,*

25   *or not necessary.*

    Dem.: Insofar as we imagine a thing to be necessary, we affirm its existence. On the other hand, we deny its existence insofar as we

30   imagine it not to be necessary (by IP33S1), and therefore (by P9), an

II/218 affect toward a necessary thing is more intense, other things equal, than toward one not necessary, q.e.d.

P12: *An affect toward a thing which we know does not exist in the present,*

5   *and which we imagine as possible, is more intense, other things equal, than one toward a contingent thing.*

    Dem.: Insofar as we imagine a thing as contingent, we are not affected by any image of another thing that posits the thing's existence

10   (by D3); but on the other hand (according to the hypothesis), we imagine certain things that exclude its present existence. But insofar as we imagine a thing in the future to be possible, we imagine certain things that posit its existence (by D4), i.e. (by IIIP18), which encourage Hope or Fear. And so an affect toward a possible thing is more violent

15   [, other things equal, than one toward a contingent thing], q.e.d.

    Cor.: An affect toward a thing which we know does not exist in the present, and which we imagine as contingent, is much milder than if we imagined the thing as with us in the present.

20   Dem.: An affect toward a thing which we imagine to exist in the present is more intense than if we imagined it as future (by P9C), and [an affect toward a thing we imagine to exist in the future is] much more violent if we imagine the future time to be not far from the

25   present (by P10).[8] Therefore, an affect toward a thing which we imag-

---

[8] Accepting Akkerman's defense and interpretation of the OP text (2, 90-91).

ine will exist at a time far from the present is much milder than if we imagined it as present. And nevertheless (by P12), it is more intense than if we imagined that thing as contingent. And so an affect toward a contingent thing will be much milder than if we imagined the thing to be with us in the present, q.e.d.

19 P13: *An affect toward a contingent thing which we know does not exist in the present is milder, other things equal, than an affect toward a past thing.*

Dem.: Insofar as we imagine a thing as contingent, we are not affected by any image of another thing that posits the thing's existence (by D3). But on the other hand (according to the hypothesis), we imagine certain things that exclude its present existence. Now insofar as we imagine a thing in relation to past time, we are supposed to imagine something that brings it back to our memory, *or* that arouses the image of the thing (see IIP18 and P18S), and therefore brings it about that we consider it as if it were present (by IIP17C). And so (by P9) an affect toward a contingent thing which we know does not exist in the present will be milder, other things equal, than an affect toward a past thing, q.e.d.

P14: *No affect can be restrained by the true knowledge of good and evil insofar as it is true, but only insofar as it is considered as an affect.*[9]

Dem.: An affect is an idea by which the Mind affirms of its Body a greater or lesser force of existing than before (by the general Definition of the Affects). So (by P1), it has nothing positive which could be removed by the presence of the true. Consequently the true knowledge of good and evil, insofar as it is true, cannot restrain any affect.

But insofar as it is an affect (see P8), it can restrain the affect, if it is stronger than it (by P7), q.e.d.

20 P15: *A Desire which arises from a true knowledge of good and evil can be extinguished or restrained by many other Desires which arise from affects by which we are tormented.*

Dem.: From a true knowledge of good and evil, insofar as this is an affect (by P8), there necessarily arises a Desire (by Def. Aff. I), which is the greater as the affect from which it arises is greater (by IIIP37). But because this Desire arises (by hypothesis) from the fact that we understand something truly, it follows in us insofar as we act (by IIIP3).[10] And so it must be understood through our essence alone (by IIID2), and consequently (by IIIP7), its force and growth can be defined only by human power alone.

[9] Cf. Descartes, PA I, 47-79.

[10] Some editors (e.g., Van Vloten and Land, Baensch, Appuhn, Caillois, and Akkerman) have thought that the reference here should be to IIIP1.

Next, Desires which arise from affects by which we are torn are
15 also greater as these affects are more violent. And so their force and
growth (by P5) must be defined by the power of external causes, which,
if it were compared with ours, would indefinitely surpass our power
20 (by P3). Hence, Desires which arise from such affects can be more
violent than that which arises from a true knowledge of good and evil,
and can therefore (by P7) restrain or extinguish it, q.e.d.

P16: *A Desire which arises from a true knowledge of good and evil, insofar as*
25 *this knowledge concerns the future, can be quite easily restrained or extin-*
guished by a Desire for the pleasures of the moment.

Dem.: An affect toward a thing we imagine as future is milder than
one toward a present thing (by P9C). But a Desire which arises from
30 a true knowledge of good and evil, even if this knowledge concerns
things which are good now, can be restrained or extinguished by some
II/221 rash Desire (by P15, whose demonstration is universal). Therefore, a
Desire which arises from the same knowledge, insofar as this concerns
a future thing, can be quite easily restrained or extinguished, etc.,
q.e.d.

5 P17: *A Desire which arises from a true knowledge of good and evil, insofar as*
this concerns contingent things, can be restrained much more easily still by a
Desire for things which are present.

10 Dem.: This Proposition is demonstrated in the same way as the
preceding one, from P12C.

Schol.: With this I believe I have shown the cause why men are
moved more by opinion than by true reason, and why the true knowl-
15 edge of good and evil arouses disturbances of the mind, and often
yields to lust of every kind. Hence that verse of the Poet:

> . . . video meliora, proboque,
> deteriora sequor . . .[11]

Ecclesiastes also seems to have had the same thing in mind when he
said: "He who increases knowledge increases sorrow."[12]

I do not say these things in order to infer that it is better to be
20 ignorant than to know, or that there is no difference between the fool
and the man who understands[13] when it comes to moderating the af-

---

[11] Ovid, *Metamorphoses* VII, 20-21: "I see and approve the better, but follow the worse."
(Medea is torn between reason's demand that she obey her father and her passion for
Jason.) These lines are often quoted, or alluded to, in seventeenth-century discussions
of freedom of the will. Cf. Descartes, Letter to Mesland, 9 Feb. 1645; Hobbes, "Of
Liberty and Necessity," *EW* IV, p. 269; Locke, *Essay*, II, xxi. 35.
[12] *Eccles.* 1:18.
[13] An allusion to Terence's *Eunuch*, 232, as Leopold pointed out.

fects. My reason, rather, is that it is necessary to come to know both our nature's power and its lack of power, so that we can determine what reason can do in moderating the affects, and what it cannot do. I said that in this part I would treat only of man's lack of power. For I have decided to treat Reason's power over the affects separately.

P18: *A Desire that arises from Joy is stronger, other things equal, than one that arises from Sadness.*

Dem.: Desire is the very essence of man (by Def. Aff. I), i.e. (by IIIP7), a striving by which a man strives to persevere in his being. So a Desire that arises from Joy is aided or increased by the affect of Joy itself (by the Def. of Joy in IIIP11S), whereas one that arises from Sadness is diminished or restrained by the affect of Sadness (by the same Schol.). And so the force of a Desire that arises from Joy must be defined both by human power and the power of the external cause, whereas the force of a Desire that arises from Sadness must be defined by human power alone. The former, therefore, is stronger than the latter, q.e.d.

Schol.: With these few words I have explained the causes of man's lack of power and inconstancy, and why men do not observe the precepts of reason. Now it remains for me to show what reason prescribes to us, which affects agree with the rules of human reason, and which, on the other hand, are contrary to those rules. But before I begin to demonstrate these things in our cumbersome Geometric order,[14] I should like first to show briefly here the dictates of reason themselves, so that everyone may more easily perceive what I think.

Since reason demands nothing contrary to nature, it demands that everyone love himself, seek his own advantage, what is really useful to him, want what will really lead man to a greater perfection, and absolutely, that everyone should strive to preserve his own being as far as he can. This, indeed, is as necessarily true as that the whole is greater than its part (see IIIP4).

Further, since virtue (by D8) is nothing but acting from the laws of one's own nature, and no one strives to preserve his being (by IIIP7) except from the laws of his own nature, it follows:

(i) that the foundation of virtue is this very striving to preserve one's

[14] "Cumbersome" renders "prolixus," which might be translated "full" (White) or "detailed" (Elwes). But the same term is used in a similar context in the Prolegomenon to *Descartes' Principles* (I/141/14), and I take it that Spinoza feels somewhat defensive about his preferred manner of writing, recognizing that it makes great demands on the reader's patience and perseverance, and will inevitably encounter resistance. This is no doubt the reason for the summations at the end of Parts Three and Four.

own being, and that happiness consists in man's being able to preserve his being;

(ii) that we ought to want virtue for its own sake, and that there is not anything preferable to it, or more useful to us, for the sake of which we ought to want it; and finally

(iii) that those who kill themselves are weak-minded and completely conquered by external causes contrary to their nature.

Again, from IIPost. 4 [II/102/29-31] it follows that we can never bring it about that we require nothing outside ourselves to preserve our being, nor that we live without having dealings with things outside us. Moreover, if we consider our Mind, our intellect would of course be more imperfect if the Mind were alone and did not understand anything except itself. There are, therefore, many things outside us which are useful to us, and on that account to be sought.

Of these, we can think of none more excellent than those that agree entirely with our nature. For if, for example, two individuals of entirely the same nature are joined to one another, they compose an individual twice as powerful as each one. To man, then, there is nothing more useful than man. Man, I say, can wish for nothing more helpful to the preservation of his being than that all should so agree in all things that the Minds and Bodies of all would compose, as it were, one Mind and one Body; that all should strive together, as far as they can, to preserve their being; and that all, together, should seek for themselves the common advantage of all.

From this it follows that men who are governed by reason—i.e., men who, from the guidance of reason, seek their own advantage—want nothing for themselves that they do not desire for other men. Hence, they are just, honest, and honorable.

These are those dictates of reason which I promised to present briefly here before I began to demonstrate them in a more cumbersome order. I have done this to win, if possible, the attention of those who believe that this principle—that everyone is bound to seek his own advantage—is the foundation, not of virtue and morality, but of immorality. After I have shown briefly that the contrary is true, I shall proceed to demonstrate this in the same way I have followed up to this point.

P19: *From the laws of his own nature, everyone necessarily wants, or is repelled by, what he judges to be good or evil.*

Dem.: Knowledge of good and evil (by P8) is itself an affect of Joy or Sadness, insofar as we are conscious of it. And therefore (by IIIP28), everyone necessarily wants what he judges to be good, and conversely, is repelled by what he judges to be evil. But this appetite is nothing but the very essence, *or* nature, of man (by the Definition of Appetite; see IIIP9S and Def. Aff. I). Therefore, everyone, from the laws of his own nature, necessarily, wants or is repelled by, etc., q.e.d.

P20: *The more each one strives, and is able, to seek his own advantage, i.e., to preserve his being, the more he is endowed with virtue; conversely, insofar as each one neglects his own advantage, i.e., neglects to preserve his being, he lacks power.*

Dem.: Virtue is human power itself, which is defined by man's essence alone (by D8), i.e. (by IIIP7), solely by the striving by which man strives to persevere in his being. So the more each one strives, and is able, to preserve his being, the more he is endowed with virtue. And consequently (by IIIP4 and P6), insofar as someone neglects to preserve his being, he lacks power, q.e.d.

Schol.: No one, therefore, unless he is defeated by causes external, and contrary, to his nature, neglects to seek his own advantage, *or* to preserve his being. No one, I say, avoids food or kills himself from the necessity of his own nature.[15] Those who do such things are compelled by external causes, which can happen in many ways. Someone may kill himself because he is compelled by another, who twists his right hand (which happened to hold a sword) and forces him to direct the sword against his heart; or because he is forced by the command of a Tyrant (as Seneca was) to open his veins, i.e., he desires to avoid a greater evil by [submitting to] a lesser; or finally because hidden external causes so dispose his imagination, and so affect his Body, that it takes on another nature, contrary to the former, a nature of which there cannot be an idea in the Mind (by IIIP10). But that a man should, from the necessity of his own nature, strive not to exist, or to be changed into another form, is as impossible as that something should come from nothing. Anyone who gives this a little thought will see it.

P21: *No one can desire to be blessed, to act well and to live well, unless at the same time he desires to be, to act, and to live, i.e., to actually exist.*

Dem.: The Demonstration of this Proposition, *or* rather the thing itself, is evident through itself, and also from the definition of Desire. For the Desire (by Def. Aff. I) to live blessedly, *or* well, to act, etc.,

---

[15] Spinoza's moral thought shows the influence of the Stoics in many ways. But as Appuhn notes, his treatment of suicide marks an important point of difference from the Stoics. It is true that Spinoza does not condemn suicide, but neither does he regard it as an act which could ever be virtuous, much less paradigmatically free. So Caillois is wrong to argue that even on this point Spinoza is a Stoic (Pléiade, 1439). For an excellent discussion of the various Stoic positions see Rist, 233-255.

is the very essence of man, i.e. (by IIIP7), the striving by which each one strives to preserve his being. Therefore, no one can desire, etc., q.e.d.

P22: *No virtue can be conceived prior to this [virtue] (viz. the striving to preserve oneself).*

Dem.: The striving to preserve itself is the very essence of a thing (by IIIP7). Therefore, if some virtue could be conceived prior to this [virtue], viz. to this striving, the very essence of the thing would be conceived prior to itself (by D8), which is absurd (as is known through itself). Therefore, no virtue, etc., q.e.d.

Cor.: The striving to preserve oneself is the first and only foundation of virtue. For no other principle can be conceived prior to this one (by P22) and no virtue can be conceived without it (by P21).

P23: *A man cannot absolutely be said to act from virtue insofar as he is determined to do something because he has inadequate ideas, but only insofar as he is determined because he understands.*

Dem.: Insofar as a man is determined to act from the fact that he has inadequate ideas, he is acted on (by IIIP1), i.e. (by IIID1 and D2), he does something which cannot be perceived through his essence alone, i.e. (by D8), which does not follow from his virtue. But insofar as he is determined to do something from the fact that he understands, he acts (by IIIP1), i.e. (by IIID2), does something which is perceived through his essence alone, *or* (by D8) which follows adequately from his virtue, q.e.d.

P24: *Acting absolutely from virtue is nothing else in us but acting, living, and preserving our being (these three signify the same thing) by the guidance of reason, from the foundation of seeking one's own advantage.*

Dem.: Acting absolutely from virtue is nothing but acting from the laws of our own nature (by D8). But we act only insofar as we understand (by IIIP3). Therefore, acting from virtue is nothing else in us but acting, living, and preserving one's being by the guidance of reason, and doing this (by P22C) from the foundation of seeking one's own advantage, q.e.d.

P25: *No one strives to preserve his being for the sake of anything else.*

Dem.: The striving by which each thing strives to persevere in its being is defined by the thing's essence alone (by IIIP7). If this [essence] alone is given, then it follows necessarily that each one strives to preserve his being—but this does not follow necessarily from the essence of any other thing (by IIIP6).

This Proposition, moreover, is evident from P22C. For if a man strove to preserve his being for the sake of something else, then that thing would be the first foundation of virtue (as is known through itself). But (by P22C) this is absurd. Therefore, no one strives, etc., q.e.d.

P26: *What we strive for from reason is nothing but understanding; nor does the Mind, insofar as it uses reason, judge anything else useful to itself except what leads to understanding.*

Dem.: The striving to preserve itself is nothing but the essence of the thing itself (by IIIP7), which, insofar as it exists as it does, is conceived to have a force for persevering in existing (by IIIP6) and for doing those things that necessarily follow from its given nature (see the Definition of Appetite in IIIP9S). But the essence of reason is nothing but our Mind, insofar as it understands clearly and distinctly (see the Definition of this in IIP40S2). Therefore (by IIP40) whatever we strive for from reason is nothing but understanding.

Next, since this striving of the Mind, by which the Mind, insofar as it reasons, strives to preserve its being, is nothing but understanding (by the first part of this demonstration), this striving for understanding (by P22C) is the first and only foundation of virtue, nor do we strive to understand things for the sake of some end (by P25). On the contrary, the Mind, insofar as it reasons, cannot conceive anything to be good for itself except what leads to understanding (by D1), q.e.d.

P27: *We know nothing to be certainly good or evil, except what really leads to understanding or what can prevent us from understanding.*

Dem.: Insofar as the Mind reasons, it wants nothing other than to understand, nor does it judge anything else to be useful to itself except what leads to understanding (by P26). But the Mind (by IIP41, P43, and P43S) has certainty of things only insofar as it has adequate ideas, *or* (what is the same thing, by IIP40S)[16] insofar as it reasons. Therefore, we know nothing to be certainly good except what really leads to understanding, and conversely, know nothing to be certainly evil except what can prevent us from understanding, q.e.d.

P28: *Knowledge of God is the Mind's greatest good; its greatest virtue is to know God.*

Dem.: The greatest thing the Mind can understand is God, i.e. (by ID6), a Being absolutely infinite, without which (by IP15) it can nei-

---

[16] Gebhardt takes the reference to indicate an earlier state of the ms., when the present two scholia to IIP40 were one. Akkerman (2, 82) takes IIP40S2 to be a later addition, and this reference to be to P40S1, which originally required no distinguishing number. But P40S2 (specifically ll. 11-14) seems more relevant than anything in P40S1. Appuhn, Baensch, Caillois, and Leopold all assume that reference.

ther be nor be conceived. And so (by P26 and P27), the Mind's greatest advantage, *or* (by D1) good, is knowledge of God.

15   Next, only insofar as the Mind understands (by IIIP1 and P3), does it act, and can it be said absolutely to act from virtue (by P23). The absolute virtue of the Mind, then, is understanding. But the greatest thing the Mind can understand is God (as we have already demon-
20   strated). Therefore, the greatest virtue of the Mind is to understand, *or* know, God, q.e.d.

P29: *Any singular thing whose nature is entirely different from ours can*
25   *neither aid nor restrain our power of acting, and absolutely, no thing can be either good or evil for us, unless it has something in common with us.*

Dem.: The power of each singular thing, and consequently (by IIP10C), man's power,[17] by which he exists and produces an effect, is
30   not determined except by another singular thing (by IP28), whose nature must be understood (by IIP6) through the same attribute through
II/229   which human nature is conceived. Our power of acting, therefore, however it is conceived, can be determined, and hence aided or restrained, by the power of another singular thing which has something in common with us, and not by the power of a thing whose nature is
5   completely different from ours.

And because we call good or evil what is the cause of Joy or Sadness (by P8), i.e. (by IIIP11S), what increases or diminishes, aids or restrains, our power of acting, a thing whose nature is completely dif-
10   ferent from ours can be neither good nor evil for us, q.e.d.

P30: *No thing can be evil through what it has in common with our nature; but insofar as it is evil for us, it is contrary to us.*
15   Dem.: We call evil what is the cause of Sadness (by P8), i.e. (by the Definition of Sadness, see IIIP11S), what diminishes or restrains our power of acting. So if a thing were evil for us through what it has
20   in common with us, then the thing could diminish or restrain what it has in common with us. But (by IIIP4) this is absurd. Therefore, no thing can be evil for us through what it has in common with us. On the contrary, insofar as it is evil, i.e. (as we have already shown),
25   insofar as it can diminish or restrain our power of acting, it is contrary to us (by IIIP5), q.e.d.

P31: *Insofar as a thing agrees with our nature, it is necessarily good.*
30   Dem.: Insofar as a thing agrees with our nature, it cannot be evil (by P30). So it must either be good or indifferent. If the latter is

---

[17] NS: "the mind's power." Given the content of IIP10C, this is probably just a mistake.

30 posited, viz. that it is neither good nor evil, then (by A3)[18] nothing will follow from its nature that aids the preservation of our nature, i.e. (by hypothesis), that aids the preservation of the nature of the thing itself. But this is absurd (by IIIP6). Hence, insofar as it agrees with our nature, it must be good, q.e.d.

Cor.: From this it follows that the more a thing agrees with our nature, the more useful, *or* better, it is for us, and conversely, the more a thing is useful to us, the more it agrees with our nature.

For insofar as it does not agree with our nature, it will necessarily be different from it or contrary to it. If it is different from it, then (by P29) it can be neither good nor evil. And if it is contrary, then it will also be contrary to that which agrees with our nature, i.e. (by P31), contrary to the good, *or* evil. Nothing, therefore, can be good except insofar as it agrees with our nature. So the more a thing agrees with our nature, the more useful it is, and conversely, q.e.d.

P32: *Insofar as men are subject to passions, they cannot be said to agree in nature.*

Dem.: Things that are said to agree in nature are understood to agree in power (by IIIP7), but not in lack of power, *or* negation, and consequently (see IIIP3S) not in passion either. So insofar as men are subject to passions, they cannot be said to agree in nature, q.e.d.

Schol.: This matter is also evident through itself. If someone says that black and white agree only in this, that neither is red, he affirms absolutely that black and white agree in nothing. Similarly, if someone says that a stone and a man agree only in this, that each is finite, lacks
31 power, does not exist from the necessity of its nature, or, finally, is indefinitely surpassed by the power of external causes, he affirms completely that a stone and a man do not agree in anything. For things that agree only in a negation, *or* in what they do not have, really agree in nothing.

P33: *Men can disagree in nature insofar as they are torn by affects which are passions; and to that extent also one and the same man is changeable and inconstant.*

[18] So the OP read. The errata of the OP, followed by the NS, "correct" to "the axiom of this part." Other emendations have been proposed: IA3(?), IVD1 (plausible), IVD2,3(?). Gebhardt is probably right to think that originally this part had at least three axioms of which two were later dropped. Akkerman, who points out additional evidence in favor of this theory (2, 192, alluding to the marginalia corresponding to 210/24), conjectures a reconstruction of the missing axiom: "From the nature of a singular thing which is neither good nor evil, nothing can follow which aids the preservation of our nature." If this is correct, one can understand Spinoza's thinking it sufficiently obvious, given his definitions of good and evil, that it would not need to appear as a separate assumption.

10   Dem.: The nature, *or* essence, of the affects cannot be explained through our essence, *or* nature, alone (by IIID1 and D2), but must be defined by the power, i.e. (by IIIP7), by the nature of external causes compared with our own. That is why there are as many species of

15   each affect as there are species of objects by which we are affected (see IIIP56); that is why men are affected differently by one and the same object (see IIIP51), and to that extent, disagree in nature. And finally, that is also why one and the same man (again, by IIIP51) is affected differently toward the same object, and to that extent is

20   changeable, etc., q.e.d.

P34: *Insofar as men are torn by affects which are passions, they can be contrary to one another.*

25   Dem.: A man—Peter, say—can be a cause of Paul's being saddened, because he has something like a thing Paul hates (by IIIP16), or because Peter alone possesses something which Paul also loves (see IIIP32 and P32S), or on account of other causes (for the main causes, see

30   IIIP55S). And so it will happen, as a result (by Def. Aff. VII), that Paul hates Peter. Hence, it will easily happen (by IIIP40 and P40S)

II/232 that Peter hates Paul in return, and so (by IIIP39) that they strive to harm one another; i.e. (by P30), that they are contrary to one another. But an affect of Sadness is always a passion (by IIIP59). Therefore,

5   men, insofar as they are torn by affects which are passions, can be contrary to one another, q.e.d.

        Schol.: I have said that Paul hates Peter because he imagines that Peter possesses what Paul himself also loves. At first glance it seems

10   to follow from this that these two are injurious to one another because they love the same thing, and hence, because they agree in nature. If this were true, then P30 and P31 would be false.

        But if we are willing to examine the matter fairly, we shall see that all these propositions are completely consistent. For these two are not

15   troublesome to one another insofar as they agree in nature, i.e., insofar as each loves the same thing, but insofar as they disagree with one another. For insofar as each loves the same thing, each one's love is thereby encouraged (by IIIP31). I.e. (by Def. Aff. VI), each one's Joy is thereby encouraged. So it is far from true that they are troublesome to one another insofar as they love the same thing and agree in nature.

20   Instead, as I have said, the cause of [their enmity] is nothing but the fact that (as we suppose) they disagree in nature. For we suppose that Peter has the idea of a thing he loves which is already possessed, whereas Paul has the idea of a thing he loves which is lost. That is why the one is affected with Joy and the other with Sadness, and to that extent they are contrary to one another.

25   In this way we can easily show that the other causes of hate depend only on the fact that men disagree in nature, not on that in which they agree.

30   P35: *Only insofar as men live according to the guidance of reason, must they always agree in nature.*

Dem.: Insofar as men are torn by affects which are passions, they can be different in nature (by P33), and contrary to one another (by
II/233   P34). But insofar as men live according to the guidance of reason, they are said only to act (by IIIP3). Hence, whatever follows from human nature, insofar as it is defined by reason, must be understood through
5   human nature alone (by IIID2), as through its proximate cause. But because each one, from the laws of his own nature, wants what he judges to be good, and strives to avert what he judges to be evil (by P19), and moreover, because what we judge to be good or evil when we follow the dictate of reason must be good or evil (by IIP41), it
10   follows that insofar as men live according to the guidance of reason, they must do only those things that are good for human nature, and hence, for each man, i.e. (by P31C), those things that agree with the nature of each man. Hence, insofar as men live according to the guid-
15   ance of reason, they must always agree among themselves, q.e.d.

Cor. 1: There is no singular thing in Nature that is more useful to man than a man who lives according to the guidance of reason.

For what is most useful to man is what most agrees with his nature
20   (by P31C), i.e. (as is known through itself), man. But a man acts entirely from the laws of his own nature when he lives according to the guidance of reason (by IIID2), and only to that extent must he always agree with the nature of the other man (by P35). Therefore, among singular things there is nothing more useful to man than a man, etc., q.e.d.

25   Cor. 2.: When each man most seeks his own advantage for himself, then men are most useful to one another.

For the more each one seeks his own advantage, and strives to preserve himself, the more he is endowed with virtue (by P20), *or* what
30   is the same (by D8), the greater is his power of acting according to the laws of his own nature, i.e. (by IIIP3), of living from the guidance of reason. But men most agree in nature, when they live according to the guidance of reason (by P35). Therefore (by P35C1), men will be most useful to one another, when each one most seeks his own advantage, q.e.d.

234   Schol.: What we have just shown is also confirmed by daily experience, which provides so much and such clear evidence that this saying is in almost everyone's mouth: man is a God to man.

563

Still, it rarely happens that men live according to the guidance of reason. Instead, their lives are so constituted that they are usually envious and burdensome to one another. They can hardly, however, live a solitary life; hence, that definition which makes man a social animal[19] has been quite pleasing to most. And surely we do derive, from the society of our fellow men, many more advantages than disadvantages.

So let the Satirists laugh as much as they like at human affairs, let the Theologians curse them, let Melancholics praise as much as they can a life that is uncultivated and wild, let them disdain men and admire the lower animals. Men still find from experience that by helping one another they can provide themselves much more easily with the things they require, and that only by joining forces can they avoid the dangers that threaten on all sides—not to mention that it is much preferable and more worthy of our knowledge to consider the deeds of men, rather than those of the lower animals. But I shall treat this topic more fully elsewhere.

P36: *The greatest good of those who seek virtue is common to all, and can be enjoyed by all equally.*

Dem.: To act from virtue is to act according to the guidance of reason (by P24), and whatever we strive for from reason is understanding (by P26). Hence (by P28), the greatest good of those who seek virtue is to know God, i.e. (by IIP47 and P47S), a good that is common to all men, and can be possessed equally by all men insofar as they are of the same nature, q.e.d.

Schol.: But suppose someone should ask: what if the greatest good of those who seek virtue were not common to all? Would it not follow from that, as above (see P34), that men who live according to the guidance of reason, i.e. (by P35), men, insofar as they agree in nature, would be contrary to one another?

To this the answer is that it is not by accident that man's greatest good is common to all; rather, it arises from the very nature of reason, because it is deduced from the very essence of man, insofar as [that essence] is defined by reason, and because man could neither be nor be conceived if he did not have the power to enjoy this greatest good. For it pertains to the essence of the human Mind (by IIP47) to have an adequate knowledge of God's eternal and infinite essence.

P37: *The good which everyone who seeks virtue wants for himself, he also*

---

[19] Ultimately this goes back to Aristotle's *Politics*, 1253a3. But the formula is also Stoic. Cf. Seneca, *De clementia*, I, iii, 2.

desires for other men; and this Desire is greater as his knowledge of God is greater.

Dem.: Insofar as men live according to the guidance of reason, they are most useful to man (by P35C1); hence (by P19), according to the guidance of reason, we necessarily strive to bring it about that men live according to the guidance of reason. Now, the good which everyone who lives according to the dictate of reason (i.e., by P24, who seeks virtue) wants for himself is understanding (by P26). Therefore, the good which everyone who seeks virtue wants for himself, he also desires for other men.

Next, Desire, insofar as it is related to the Mind, is the very essence of the Mind (by Def. Aff. I). Now the essence of the Mind consists in knowledge (by IIP11), which involves knowledge of God (by IIP47). Without this [knowledge the Mind] can neither be nor be conceived (by IP15). Hence, as the Mind's essence involves a greater knowledge of God, so will the Desire also be greater by which one who seeks virtue desires for another the good he wants for himself, q.e.d.

Alternative dem.: The good which man wants for himself and loves, he will love more constantly if he sees that others love it (by IIIP31). So (by IIIP31C), he will strive to have the others love the same thing. And because this good is common to all (by P36), and all can enjoy it, he will therefore (by the same reason) strive that all may enjoy it. And this striving will be the greater, the more he enjoys this good (by IIIP37), q.e.d.

Schol. 1: He who strives, only because of an affect, that others should love what he loves, and live according to his temperament, acts only from impulse and is hateful—especially to those to whom other things are pleasing, and who also, therefore, strive eagerly, from the same impulse, to have other men live according to their own temperament. And since the greatest good men seek from an affect is often such that only one can possess it fully, those who love are not of one mind in their love—while they rejoice to sing the praises of the thing they love, they fear to be believed. But he who strives from reason to guide others acts not by impulse, but kindly, generously, and with the greatest steadfastness of mind.

Again, whatever we desire and do of which we are the cause insofar as we have the idea of God, *or* insofar as we know God, I relate to Religion. The Desire to do good generated in us by our living according to the guidance of reason, I call Morality. The Desire by which a man who lives according to the guidance of reason is bound to join others to himself in friendship, I call Being Honorable, and I call that honorable which men who live according to the guidance of reason

565

25 praise; on the other hand, what is contrary to the formation of friendship, I call dishonorable.

In addition to this, I have also shown what the foundations of the state are.[20]

Furthermore, from what has been said above, one can easily perceive the difference between true virtue and lack of power; true virtue is nothing but living according to the guidance of reason, and so lack of power consists only in this, that a man allows himself to be guided
30 by things outside him, and to be determined by them to do what the common constitution of external things demands, not what his own nature, considered in itself, demands.

These are the things I promised, in P18S, to demonstrate. From them it is clear that the law against killing animals is based more on
35 empty superstition and unmanly compassion than sound reason. The
II/237 rational principle of seeking our own advantage teaches us the necessity of joining with men, but not with the lower animals, or with things whose nature is different from human nature. We have the same right against them that they have against us. Indeed, because
5 the right of each one is defined by his virtue, *or* power, men have a far greater right against the lower animals than they have against men. Not that I deny that the lower animals have sensations. But I do deny that we are therefore not permitted to consider our own advantage, use them at our pleasure, and treat them as is most convenient for us.
10 For they do not agree in nature with us, and their affects are different in nature from human affects (see IIIP57S).

It remains now for me to explain what is just and what unjust, what sin is, and finally, what merit is. These matters will be taken up in the following scholium.

15 Schol. 2: In the Appendix of Part I, I promised to explain what praise and blame, merit and sin, and justice and injustice are. As far as praise and blame are concerned, I have explained them in IIIP29S. This will be the place to speak of the others. But first a few words must be said about man's natural state and his civil state.

20 Everyone exists by the highest right of nature, and consequently everyone, by the highest right of nature, does those things that follow from the necessity of his own nature. So everyone, by the highest right of nature, judges what is good and what is evil, considers his

---

[20] Meijer thought that this remark should be placed at the end of the Scholium and put in the future tense, a plausible suggestion, since Scholium 2 is the first substantial account of Spinoza's political philosophy. But the *foundations* of that philosophy in human nature have already been laid in the various propositions cited in Scholium 2. So Gebhardt is probably right to retain the text of the OP.

own advantage according to his own temperament (see P19 and P20), avenges himself (see IIIP40C2), and strives to preserve what he loves and destroy what he hates (see IIIP28).

If men lived according to the guidance of reason, everyone would possess this right of his (by P35C1) without any injury to anyone else. But because they are subject to the affects (by P4C), which far surpass man's power, *or* virtue (by P6), they are often drawn in different directions (by P33) and are contrary to one another (by P34), while they require one another's aid (by P35S).

In order, therefore, that men may be able to live harmoniously and be of assistance to one another, it is necessary for them to give up their natural right and to make one another confident that they will do nothing which could harm others. How it can happen that men who are necessarily subject to affects (by P4C), inconstant and changeable (by P33) should be able to make one another confident and have trust in one another, is clear from P7 and IIIP39. No affect can be restrained except by an affect stronger than and contrary to the affect to be restrained, and everyone refrains from doing harm out of timidity regarding a greater harm.

By this law, therefore, Society can be maintained,[21] provided it appropriates to itself the right everyone has of avenging himself, and of judging concerning good and evil. In this way Society has the power to prescribe a common rule of life, to make laws, and to maintain them—not by reason, which cannot restrain the affects (by P17S), but by threats. This Society, maintained by laws and the power it has of preserving itself, is called a State, and those who are defended by its law, Citizens.

From this we easily understand that there is nothing in the state of nature which, by the agreement of all, is good or evil; for everyone who is in the state of nature considers only his own advantage, and decides what is good and what is evil from his own temperament, and only insofar as he takes account of his own advantage. He is not bound by any law to submit to anyone except himself. So in the state of nature no sin can be conceived.

But in the Civil state, of course, it is decided by common agreement what is good or what is evil. And everyone is bound to submit to the State. Sin, therefore, is nothing but disobedience, which for that rea-

---

[21] Here I translate Gebhardt's text (*firmari*), which is that of the OP. But I think there is more plausibility than he would admit in Tönnies' suggestion that we should read *formari*, 'formed' or 'established.' Tönnies appealed to a parallel passage in the *Theological-Political Treatise* (III/193/20). But for *vindicet* (l. 10) I accept Akkerman's reinstatement of the OP: *vendicet*. Cf. Akkerman 2, 85 and the NS.

son can be punished only by the law of the State. On the other hand, obedience is considered a merit in a Citizen, because on that account he is judged worthy of enjoying the advantages of the State.

30 Again, in the state of nature there is no one who by common consent is Master of anything, nor is there anything in Nature which can be said to be this man's and not that man's. Instead, all things belong to all. So in the state of nature, there cannot be conceived any will to give to each his own, or to take away from someone what is his. I.e., in the state of nature nothing is done which can be called just or unjust.

35 But in the civil state, of course, where it is decided by common II/239 consent what belongs to this man, and what to that [, things are done which can be called just or unjust].

From this it is clear that just and unjust, sin and merit, are extrinsic notions, not attributes that explain the nature of the Mind. But enough of this.

5 P38: *Whatever so disposes the human Body that it can be affected in a great many ways, or renders it capable of affecting external Bodies in a great many ways, is useful to man; the more it renders the Body capable of being affected in a great many ways, or of affecting other bodies, the more useful it is; on* 10 *the other hand, what renders the Body less capable of these things is harmful.*

Dem.: The more the Body is rendered capable of these things, the more the Mind is rendered capable of perceiving (by IIP14). And so what disposes the Body in this way, and renders it capable of these 15 things, is necessarily good, *or* useful (by P26 and P27), and the more useful the more capable of these things it renders the Body. On the other hand (by the converse of IIP14, and by P26 and P27), it is harmful if it renders the body less capable of these things, q.e.d.

20 P39: *Those things are good which bring about the preservation of the proportion of motion and rest the human Body's parts have to one another; on the other hand, those things are evil which bring it about that the parts of the human Body have a different proportion of motion and rest to one another.*

25 Dem.: To be preserved, the human Body requires a great many other bodies (by IIPost. 4). But what constitutes the form of the human Body consists in this, that its Parts communicate their motions to one another in a certain fixed proportion (by the Definition [at II/ 99-100]). Therefore, things which bring it about that the Parts of the II/240 human Body preserve the same proportion of motion and rest to one another, preserve the human Body's form. Hence, they bring it about that the human Body can be affected in many ways, and that it can

affect external bodies in many ways (by IIPost. 3 and Post. 6). So they are good (by P38).

Next, things which bring it about that the human Body's parts acquire a different proportion of motion and rest to one another bring it about (by the same Definition [at II/99-100]) that the human Body takes on another form, i.e. (as is known through itself, and as I pointed out at the end of the preface of this Part), that the human Body is destroyed, and hence rendered completely incapable of being affected in many ways. So (by P38), they are evil, q.e.d.

Schol.: In Part V I shall explain how much these things can be harmful to or beneficial to the Mind. But here it should be noted that I understand the Body to die when its parts are so disposed that they acquire a different proportion of motion and rest to one another. For I dare not deny that—even though the circulation of the blood is maintained, as well as the other [signs] on account of which the Body is thought to be alive—the human Body can nevertheless be changed into another nature entirely different from its own. For no reason compels me to maintain that the Body does not die unless it is changed into a corpse.

And, indeed, experience seems to urge a different conclusion. Sometimes a man undergoes such changes that I should hardly have said he was the same man. I have heard stories, for example, of a Spanish Poet[22] who suffered an illness; though he recovered, he was left so oblivious to his past life that he did not believe the tales and tragedies he had written were his own. He could surely have been taken for a grown-up infant[23] if he had also forgotten his native language.

If this seems incredible, what shall we say of infants? A man of advanced years believes their nature to be so different from his own that he could not be persuaded that he was ever an infant, if he did

[22] Gebhardt (1, 170) suggests that this was probably Góngora, whose works Spinoza possessed, and who lost his memory a year before his death. Why does Spinoza think that cases like this (and the one described in the following paragraph) might provide the superstitious with material for raising new questions (cf. ll. 31-33)? Perhaps because they encourage speculation about the possibility of transmigration of souls, or perhaps because they encourage the postulation of an immaterial spiritual substance to provide a principle of personal identity unaffected by radical changes in the constitution of the body. That Spinoza was concerned at an early stage about the latter of these issues, at least, seems clear from the long note to the Preface to Part II of the KV (I/51/16-52/41). For discussion of the controversy about personal identity as it was pursued by other figures in the period, see Curley 11.

[23] Part of the point is that *infans* is connected etymologically with *fari*, 'to speak,' so that an infant is literally someone incapable of speech.

not make this conjecture concerning himself from [NS: the example of] others. But rather than provide the superstitious with material for raising new questions, I prefer to leave this discussion unfinished.

II/241 P40: *Things which are of assistance to the common Society of men, or which bring it about that men live harmoniously, are useful; those, on the other hand, are evil which bring discord to the State.*

5 Dem.: For things which bring it about that men live harmoniously, at the same time bring it about that they live according to the guidance of reason (by P35). And so (by P26 and P27) they are good.

And on the other hand (by the same reasoning), those are evil which arouse discord, q.e.d.

10 P41: *Joy is not directly evil, but good; Sadness, on the other hand, is directly evil.*

Dem.: Joy (by IIIP11 and P11S) is an affect by which the body's
15 power of acting is increased or aided. Sadness, on the other hand, is an affect by which the body's power of acting is diminished or restrained. And so (by P38) joy is directly good, etc., q.e.d.

20 P42: *Cheerfulness cannot be excessive, but is always good; Melancholy, on the other hand, is always evil.*

Dem.: Cheerfulness (see its Def. in IIIP11S) is a Joy which, insofar as it is related to the Body, consists in this, that all parts of the Body are equally affected. I.e. (by IIIP11), the Body's power of acting is
25 increased or aided, so that all of its parts maintain the same proportion of motion and rest to one another. And so (by P39), Cheerfulness is always good, and cannot be excessive.

II/242 But Melancholy (see its Def., also in IIIP11S) is a Sadness, which, insofar as it is related to the Body, consists in this, that the Body's power of acting is absolutely diminished or restrained. And so (by P38) it is always evil, q.e.d.

5 P43: *Pleasure can be excessive and evil, whereas Pain can be good insofar as the Pleasure, or Joy, is evil.*

10 Dem.: Pleasure is a Joy which, insofar as it is related to the Body, consists in this, that one (or several) of its parts are affected more than the others (see its Def. in IIIP11S). The power of this affect can be so great that it surpasses the other actions of the Body (by P6), remains
15 stubbornly fixed in the Body, and so prevents the Body from being capable of being affected in a great many other ways. Hence (by P38), it can be evil.

Pain, on the other hand, which is a Sadness, cannot be good, considered in itself alone (by P41). But because its force and growth are defined by the power of an external cause compared with our power (by P5), we can conceive infinite degrees and modes of the powers of this effect (by P3). And so we can conceive it to be such that it can restrain Pleasure, so that it is not excessive, and thereby prevent the body from being rendered less capable (by the first part of this Proposition). To that extent, therefore, it will be good, q.e.d.

P44: *Love and Desire can be excessive.*

Dem.: Love is Joy, accompanied by the idea of an external cause (by Def. Aff. VI). Pleasure, therefore (by IIIP11S), accompanied by the idea of an external cause, is Love. And so, Love (by P43) can be excessive.

Again, Desire is greater as the affect from which it arises is greater (by IIIP37). Hence, as an affect (by P6) can surpass the rest of man's actions, so also the Desire which arises from that affect can surpass the rest of his Desires. It can therefore be excessive in the same way we have shown Pleasure can be (in P43), q.e.d.

Schol.: Cheerfulness, which I have said is good, is more easily conceived than observed. For the affects by which we are daily torn are generally related to a part of the Body which is affected more than the others. Generally, then, the affects are excessive, and occupy the Mind in the consideration of only one object so much that it cannot think of others. And though men are liable to a great many affects, so that one rarely finds them to be always agitated by one and the same affect, still there are those in whom one affect is stubbornly fixed. For we sometimes see that men are so affected by one object that, although it is not present, they still believe they have it with them.

When this happens to a man who is not asleep, we say that he is mad or insane. Nor are they thought to be less mad who burn with Love, and dream, both night and day, only of a lover or a courtesan. For they usually provoke laughter. But when a greedy man thinks of nothing else but profit, or money, and an ambitious man of esteem, they are not thought to be mad, because they are usually troublesome and are considered worthy of Hate. But Greed, Ambition, and Lust really are species of madness, even though they are not numbered among the diseases.

P45: *Hate can never be good.*

Dem.: We strive to destroy the man we hate (by IIIP39), i.e. (by P37), we strive for something that is evil. Therefore, etc., q.e.d.

Schol.: Note that here and in what follows I understand by Hate only Hate toward men.

Cor. 1: Envy, Mockery, Disdain, Anger, Vengeance, and the rest

571

of the affects which are related to Hate or arise from it, are evil. This too is evident from P37 and IIIP39.

Cor. 2: Whatever we want because we have been affected with hate is dishonorable; and [if we live] in a State, it is unjust. This too is evident from IIIP39, and from the Definitions of dishonorable and unjust (see P37S).

Schol.: I recognize a great difference between Mockery (which, in Cor. 1, I said was evil) and laughter. For laughter and joking are pure Joy. And so, provided they are not excessive, they are good through themselves (by P41). Nothing forbids our pleasure except a savage and sad superstition. For why is it more proper to relieve our hunger and thirst than to rid ourselves of melancholy?

My account of the matter,[24] the view I have arrived at, is this: no deity, nor anyone else, unless he is envious, takes pleasure in my lack of power and my misfortune; nor does he ascribe to virtue our tears, sighs, fear, and other things of that kind, which are signs of a weak mind. On the contrary, the greater the Joy with which we are affected, the greater the perfection to which we pass, i.e., the more we must participate in the divine nature. To use things, therefore, and take pleasure in them as far as possible—not, of course, to the point where we are disgusted with them, for there is no pleasure in that— this is the part of a wise man.

It is the part of a wise man, I say, to refresh and restore himself in moderation with pleasant food and drink, with scents, with the beauty of green plants, with decoration, music, sports, the theater, and other things of this kind, which anyone can use without injury to another. For the human Body is composed of a great many parts of different natures, which constantly require new and varied nourishment, so that the whole Body may be equally capable of all the things which can follow from its nature, and hence, so that the Mind also may be equally capable of understanding many things.

This plan of living, then, agrees best both with our principles and with common practice. So, if any other way of living [is to be commended], this one is best, and to be commended in every way. Nor is it necessary for me to treat these matters more clearly or more fully.

P46: *He who lives according to the guidance of reason strives, as far as he can, to repay the other's Hate, Anger, and Disdain toward him, with Love, or Nobility.*

Dem.: All affects of Hate are evil (by P45C1). So he who lives

---

[24] It is fitting that this defense of laughter, the theater, and amusement in general, contains one of many allusions in the *Ethics* to Terence, in this case, to the *Adelphi*, 68.

according to the guidance of reason will strive, as far as he can, to bring it about that he is not troubled with affects of Hate (by P19), and consequently (by P37), will strive that the other also should not undergo those affects. Now Hate is increased by being returned, and on the other hand, can be destroyed by Love (by IIIP43), so that the Hate passes into Love (by IIIP44). Therefore, one who lives according to the guidance of reason will strive to repay the other's Hate, etc., with Love, i.e., with Nobility (see its Def. in IIIP59S), q.e.d.

Schol.: He who wishes to avenge wrongs by hating in return surely lives miserably. On the other hand, one who is eager to overcome Hate by Love, strives joyously and confidently, resists many men as easily as one, and requires the least help from fortune. Those whom he conquers yield joyously, not from a lack of strength, but from an increase in their powers. All these things follow so clearly simply from the definitions of Love and of intellect, that there is no need to demonstrate them separately.

P47: *Affects of Hope and Fear cannot be good of themselves.*

Dem.: There are no affects of Hope or Fear without Sadness. For Fear is a Sadness (by Def. Aff. XIII), and there is no Hope without Fear (see the explanation following Def. Aff. XII and XIII). Therefore (by P41) these affects cannot be good of themselves, but only insofar as they can restrain an excess of Joy (by P43), q.e.d.

Schol.: We may add to this that these affects show a defect of knowledge and a lack of power in the Mind. For this reason also Confidence and Despair, Gladness and Remorse are signs of a mind lacking in power. For though Confidence and Gladness are affects of Joy, they still presuppose that a Sadness has preceded them, viz. Hope and Fear. Therefore, the more we strive to live according to the guidance of reason, the more we strive to depend less on Hope, to free ourselves from Fear, to conquer fortune as much as we can, and to direct our actions by the certain counsel of reason.

P48: *Affects of Overestimation and Scorn are always evil.*

Dem.: These affects are contrary to reason (by Def. Aff. XXI and XXII). So (by P26 and P27) they are evil, q.e.d.

P49: *Overestimation easily makes the man who is overestimated proud.*

Dem.: If we see that someone, out of love, thinks more highly of us than is just, we shall easily exult at being esteemed (by IIIP41S), *or* be affected with Joy (by Def. Aff. XXX), and we shall easily believe the good we hear predicated of us (by IIIP25). And so, out of love of ourselves, we shall think more highly of ourselves than is just, i.e. (by Def. Aff. XXVIII), we shall easily become proud, q.e.d.

573

II/247 P50: *Pity, in a man who lives according to the guidance of reason, is evil of itself, and useless.*[25]

5   Dem.: For pity (by Def. Aff. XVIII) is a Sadness, and therefore (by P41), of itself, evil.

Moreover, the good which follows from it, viz. that we strive to free the man we pity from his suffering (by IIIP27C3), we desire to do from the dictate of reason alone (by P37), and we can only do from
10   the dictate of reason alone something which we know certainly to be good (by P27).

Hence, Pity is both evil of itself, and, in a man who lives according to the dictate of reason, useless, q.e.d.

Cor.: From this it follows that man who lives according to the dic-
15   tate of reason, strives, as far as he can, not to be touched by pity.

Schol.: He who rightly knows that all things follow from the necessity of the divine nature, and happen according to the eternal laws and rules of nature, will surely find nothing worthy of Hate, Mockery[26]
20   or Disdain, nor anyone whom he will pity. Instead he will strive, as far as human virtue allows, to act well, as they say,[27] and rejoice.

To this we may add that he who is easily touched by the affect of Pity, and moved by another's suffering or tears, often does something he later repents—both because, from an affect, we do nothing which we certainly know to be good, and because we are easily deceived by
25   false tears.

Here I am speaking expressly of a man who lives according to the guidance of reason. For one who is moved to aid others neither by reason nor by pity is rightly called inhuman. For (by IIIP27) he seems to be unlike a man.[28]

II/248 P51: *Favor is not contrary to reason, but can agree with it and arise from it.*

5   Dem.: For Favor is a Love toward him who has benefited another

---

[25] Appuhn (3:371) notes the affinity between Spinoza's moral conclusions and those of Nietzsche. This appears also in his evaluations of humility and repentance (P53, P54) and in his sketch of the free man's life (P67-P73). Though the differences of temperament and style are, of course, tremendous, the affinity is, I think, rooted in an anticipation of the idea of a will to power (cf. IIIP11, P12).

[26] The OP have *risu*, 'laughter,' which is confirmed by the NS. But after P45C2S, this is very surprising. Gebhardt retains *risu* without comment, but Appuhn and Elwes both translate as if we had *irrisione*, and I follow their example.

[27] Van der Tak suggests a number of possible sources for this motto, among them: Franciscus de le Boe (a professor at the University of Leiden), the Dutch poet Jacob Cats, and ultimately, *Psalms* 64:11 (63:11 in the Vulgate).

[28] What Gebhardt adds here from the NS (which might be translated: "or to have stripped himself of all humanity") is probably only a translator's elaboration of the text, rather than an indication of something that has been omitted in the OP. Cf. Akkerman 2, 89.

(by Def. Aff. XIX), and so can be related to the Mind insofar as it is said to act (by IIIP59), i.e. (by IIIP3), insofar as it understands. Therefore, it agrees with reason, etc., q.e.d.

Alternate dem.: He who lives according to the guidance of reason, desires for the other, too, the good he wants for himself (by P37). So because he sees someone benefiting another, his own striving to do good is aided, i.e. (by IIIP11S), he will rejoice. And this Joy (by hypothesis) will be accompanied by the idea of him who has benefited another. He will, therefore (by Def. Aff. XIX), favor him, q.e.d.

Schol.: Indignation, as we define it (see Def. Aff. XX), is necessarily evil (by P45). But it should be noted that when the supreme power, bound by its desire to preserve peace, punishes a citizen who has wronged another, I do not say that it is indignant toward the citizen. For it punishes him, not because it has been aroused by Hate to destroy him, but because it is moved by duty.

P52: *Self-esteem can arise from reason, and only that self-esteem which does arise from reason is the greatest there can be.*

Dem.: Self-esteem is a Joy born of the fact that man considers himself and his power of acting (by Def. Aff. XXV). But man's true power of acting, *or* virtue, is reason itself (by IIIP3), which man considers clearly and distinctly (by IIP40 and P43). Therefore, self-esteem arises from reason.

Next, while a man considers himself, he perceives nothing clearly and distinctly, *or* adequately, except those things which follow from his power of acting (by IIID2), i.e. (by IIIP3), which follow from his power of understanding. And so the greatest self-esteem there can be arises only from this reflection, q.e.d.

Schol.: Self-esteem is really the highest thing we can hope for. For (as we have shown in P25) no one strives to preserve his being for the sake of any end. And because this self-esteem is more and more encouraged and strengthened by praise (by IIIP53C), and on the other hand, more and more upset by blame (by IIIP55C), we are guided most by love of esteem and can hardly bear a life in disgrace.

P53: *Humility is not a virtue,* or *does not arise from reason.*

Dem.: Humility is a Sadness which arises from the fact that a man considers his own lack of power (by Def. Aff. XXVI). Moreover, insofar as a man knows himself by true reason, it is supposed that he understands his own essence, i.e. (by IIIP7), his own power. So if a man, in considering himself, perceives some lack of power of his, this is not because he understands himself, but because his power of acting is restrained (as we have shown in IIIP55). But if we suppose that the man conceives his lack of power because he understands something more powerful than himself, by the knowledge of which he determines his power of acting, then we conceive nothing but that the man understands himself distinctly *or* (by P26) that his power of acting is aided. So Humility, *or* the Sadness which arises from the fact that a man reflects on his own lack of power, does not arise from a true reflection, *or* reason, and is a passion, not a virtue, q.e.d.

P54: *Repentance is not a virtue,* or *does not arise from reason; instead, he who repents what he has done is twice wretched,* or *lacking in power.*

Dem.: The first part of this is demonstrated as P53 was. The second is evident simply from the Definition of this affect (see Def. Aff. XXVII). For first he suffers himself to be conquered by an evil Desire, and then by Sadness.

Schol.: Because men rarely live from the dictate of reason, these two affects, Humility and Repentance, and in addition, Hope and Fear, bring more advantage than disadvantage. So since men must sin, they ought rather to sin in that direction.[29] If weak-minded men were all equally proud, ashamed of nothing, and afraid of nothing, how could they be united or restrained by any bonds?

The mob is terrifying, if unafraid. So it is no wonder that the Prophets, who considered the common advantage, not that of the few, commended Humility, Repentance, and Reverence so greatly. Really, those who are subject to these affects can be guided far more easily than others, so that in the end they may live from the guidance of reason, i.e., may be free and enjoy the life of the blessed.

P55: *Either very great Pride or very great Despondency is very great ignorance of oneself.*

Dem.: This is evident from Defs. Aff. XXVIII and XXIX.

P56: *Either very great Pride or very great Despondency indicates very great weakness of mind.*

Dem.: The first foundation of virtue is preserving one's being (by P22C) and doing this from the guidance of reason (by P24). Therefore, he who is ignorant of himself is ignorant of the foundation of all the virtues, and consequently, of all the virtues. Next, acting from virtue is nothing but acting from the guidance of reason (by P24), and he who acts from the guidance of reason must know that he acts from

---

[29] Here begins a whole sequence of classical allusions: in ll. 12-13 to Terence's *Adelphi*, 174; in ll. 14-16, to the *Adelphi*, 84; and in l. 16 to Tacitus, *Annales*, I, 29. Cf. Leopold and Akkerman, 2, 27. The comment about the mob will be discussed more critically in the *Political Treatise* VII, 27, but Spinoza's experience of the assassination of the de Witts no doubt confirmed it.

30

II/250

5

10

15

20

25

II/251

5

the guidance of reason (by IIP43). Therefore, he who is ignorant of himself, and consequently (as we have just now shown) of all the virtues, does not act from virtue at all, i.e. (as is evident from D8), is extremely weak-minded. And so (by P55) either very great pride or very great despondency indicate very great weakness of mind, q.e.d.

Cor.: From this it follows very clearly that the proud and the despondent are highly liable to affects.

Schol.: Nevertheless, despondency can be corrected more easily than pride, since pride is an affect of Joy, whereas despondency is an affect of Sadness. And so (by P18), pride is stronger than despondency.

P57: *The proud man loves the presence of parasites, or flatterers, but hates the presence of the noble.*

Dem.: Pride is a Joy born of the fact that man thinks more highly of himself than is just (see Defs. Aff. XXVIII and VI). The proud man will strive as far as he can to encourage this opinion (see IIIP13S). And so the proud will love the presence of parasites or flatterers (I have omitted the definitions of these because they are too well known),[30] and will flee the presence of the noble, who think of them as is appropriate, q.e.d.

Schol.: It would take too long to enumerate all the evils of Pride here, since the proud are subject to all the affects (though they are least subject to affects of Love and Compassion).

But we ought not to pass over in silence here the fact that he also is called proud who thinks less highly of others than is just. So in this sense Pride should be defined as a Joy born of a man's false opinion that he is above others. And the Despondency contrary to this Pride would need to be defined as a Sadness born of a man's false opinion that he is below others.

But this being posited, we easily conceive that the proud man must be envious (see IIIP55S) and hate those most who are most praised for their virtues, that his Hatred of them is not easily conquered by Love or benefits (see IIIP41S), and that he takes pleasure only in the presence of those who humor his weakness of mind and make a madman of a fool.

Although Despondency is contrary to Pride, the despondent man is still very near the proud one. For since his Sadness arises from the fact that he judges his own lack of power from the power, *or* virtue, of others, his Sadness will be relieved, i.e., he will rejoice, if his imag-

---

[30] As Appuhn notes, the parasite or flatterer was a stock figure in Latin comedy, like the braggart soldier. Cf. Terence's *Eunuch*, which is alluded to at ll.14-15 in the scholium.

20 ination is occupied in considering the vices of others. Hence the proverb: *misery loves company*.

On the other hand, the more he believes himself to be below others,
the more he will be saddened. That is why no one is more prone to
Envy than the despondent man is, and why they strive especially to
25 observe men's deeds, more for the sake of finding fault than to improve
them, and why, finally, they praise only Despondency, and exult over
it—but in such a way that they still seem despondent.

These things follow from this affect as necessarily as it follows from
the nature of a triangle that its three angles are equal to two right
30 angles. I have already said that I call these, and like affects, evil insofar
as I attend only to human advantage. But the laws of nature concern
the common order of nature, of which man is a part. I wished to
remind my readers of this here, in passing, in case anyone thought
my purpose was only to tell about men's vices and their absurd deeds,
35 and not to demonstrate the nature and properties of things. For as I
II/253 said in the Preface of Part III, I consider men's affects and properties
just like other natural things. And of course human affects, if they do
not indicate man's power, at least indicate the power and skill of nature, no less than many other things we wonder at and take pleasure
5 in contemplating. But I continue to note, concerning the affects, those
things that bring advantage to men, and those that bring them harm.

P58: *Love of esteem is not contrary to reason, but can arise from it.*

10 Dem.: This is evident from Def. Aff. XXX, and from the Definition of what is Honorable (see P37S1).

Schol.: The love of esteem which is called empty is a self-esteem
that is encouraged only by the opinion of the multitude. When that
15 ceases, the self-esteem ceases, i.e. (by P52S), the highest good that
each one loves. That is why he who exults at being esteemed by the
multitude is made anxious daily, strives, sacrifices, and schemes, in
order to preserve his reputation. For the multitude is fickle and inconstant; unless one's reputation is guarded,[31] it is quickly destroyed. Indeed, because everyone desires to secure the applause of the multi-
20 tude, each one willingly puts down the reputation of the other. And
since the struggle is over a good thought to be the highest, this gives
rise to a monstrous lust of each to crush the other in any way possible.
The one who at last emerges as victor exults more in having harmed

---

[31] OP: *conservetur*, 'preserved.' But as Leopold pointed out, the NS have: *waargenomen*,
which suggests that they read: *observetur*. Gebhardt rejects the emendation without offering a satisfactory reason. Cf. Akkerman 2, 94.

the other than in having benefited himself. This love of esteem, *or* self-esteem, then, is really empty, because it is nothing.

The things which must be noted about Shame are easily inferred from what we said about Compassion and Repentance. I add only this, that like Pity, Shame, though not a virtue, is still good insofar as it indicates, in the man who blushes with Shame, a desire to live honorably. In the same way pain is said to be good insofar as it indicates that the injured part is not yet decayed. So though a man who is ashamed of some deed is really sad, he is still more perfect than one who is shameless, who has no desire to live honorably.

These are the things I undertook to note concerning the affects of Joy and Sadness. As far as desires are concerned, they, of course, are good or evil insofar as they arise from good or evil affects. But all of them, really, insofar as they are generated in us from affects which are passions, are blind (as may easily be inferred from what we said in P44S), and would be of no use if men could easily be led to live according to the dictate of reason alone. I shall now show this concisely.

P59: *To every action to which we are determined from an affect which is a passion, we can be determined by reason, without that affect.*

Dem.: Acting from reason is nothing but doing those things which follow from the necessity of our nature, considered in itself alone (by IIIP3 and D2). But Sadness is evil insofar as it decreases or restrains this power of acting (by P41). Therefore, from this affect we cannot be determined to any action which we could not do if we were led by reason.

Furthermore, Joy is bad [only][32] insofar as it prevents man from being capable of acting (by P41 and P43), and so to that extent also, we cannot be determined to any action which we could not do if we were guided by reason.

Finally, insofar as Joy is good, it agrees with reason (for it consists in this, that a man's power of acting is increased or aided), and is not a passion except insofar as the man's power of acting is not increased to the point where he conceives himself and his actions adequately. So if a man affected with Joy were led to such a great perfection that

---

[32] The OP has *tantum*, 'only,' here, a reading which is supported by the NS. Meijer proposed to suppress it. Baensch and Appuhn followed him in this, and in the related suggestion that the reference should be to P43 and P44, rather than P41 and P43. Gebhardt accepts the suppression of *tantum*, but then produces a convincing argument for retaining the reference to P41. This seems an illogical compromise, and I see no difficulty in following the OP. Cf. Akkerman 2, 182.

30   he conceived himself and his actions adequately, he would be capable—indeed more capable—of the same actions to which he is now determined from affects which are passions.

II/255   But all affects are related to Joy, Sadness, or Desire (see the explanation of Def. Aff. IV), and Desire (by Def. Aff. I) is nothing but the striving to act itself. Therefore, to every action to which we are determined from an affect which is a passion, we can be led by reason alone, without the affect, q.e.d.

5   Alternate dem.: Any action is called evil insofar as it arises from the fact that we have been affected with Hate or with some evil affect (see P45C1). But no action, considered in itself, is good or evil (as we have shown in the Preface of this Part); instead, one and the same action is

10   now good, now evil. Therefore, to the same action which is now evil, *or* which arises from some evil affect, we can (by P19) be led by reason, q.e.d.

    Schol.: These things are more clearly explained by an example. The

15   act of beating, insofar as it is considered physically, and insofar as we attend only to the fact that the man raises his arm, closes his fist, and moves his whole arm forcefully up and down, is a virtue, which is conceived from the structure of the human Body. Therefore, if a man moved by Anger or Hate is determined to close his fist or move his

20   arm, that (as we have shown in Part II) happens because one and the same action can be joined to any images of things whatever. And so we can be determined to one and the same action both from those images of things which we conceive confusedly and [from those images of things?] we conceive clearly and distinctly.

    It is evident, therefore, that every Desire that arises from an affect

25   which is a passion would be of no use if men could be guided by reason. Let us see now why we call a Desire blind which arises from an affect which is a passion.

P60: *A Desire arising from either a Joy or a Sadness related to one, or several,*

30   *but not to all parts of the Body, has no regard for the advantage of the whole man.*

II/256   Dem.: Suppose, for example, that part A of the Body is so strengthened by the force of some external cause that it prevails over the others (by P6). This part will not, on that account, strive to lose its powers

5   so that the other parts of the body may fulfill their function. For [if it did], it would have to have a force, *or* power, of losing its own powers, which (by IIIP6) is absurd. Therefore, that part will strive, and consequently (by IIIP7 and P12), the Mind also will strive, to preserve

that state. And so the Desire that arises from such an affect of Joy does not have regard to the whole.

If, on the other hand, it is supposed that part A is restrained so that the others prevail, it is demonstrated in the same way that the Desire which arises from Sadness also does not have regard to the whole, q.e.d.

Schol.: Therefore, since Joy is generally (by P44S) related to one part of the body, for the most part we desire to preserve our being without regard to our health as a whole. To this we may add that the Desires by which we are most bound (by P9C) have regard only to the present and not to the future.

P61: *A Desire that arises from reason cannot be excessive.*

Dem.: Desire, considered absolutely, is the very essence of man (by Def. Aff. I), insofar as it is conceived to be determined in any way to doing something. And so a Desire that arises from reason, i.e. (by IIIP3), that is generated in us insofar as we act is the very essence, *or* nature, of man, insofar as it is conceived to be determined to doing those things that are conceived adequately through man's essence alone (by IIID2). So if this desire could be excessive, then human nature, considered in itself alone, could exceed itself, *or* could do more than it can. This is a manifest contradiction. Therefore, this Desire cannot be excessive, q.e.d.

57 P62: *Insofar as the Mind conceives things from the dictate of reason, it is affected equally, whether the idea is of a future or past thing, or of a present one.*

Dem.: Whatever the Mind conceives under the guidance of reason, it conceives under the same species of eternity, *or* necessity (by IIP44C2) and is affected with the same certainty (by IIP43 and P43S). So whether the idea is of a future or a past thing, or of a present one, the Mind conceives the thing with the same necessity and is affected with the same certainty. And whether the idea is of a future or a past thing or of a present one, it will nevertheless be equally true (by IIP41), i.e. (by IID4), it will nevertheless always have the same properties of an adequate idea. And so, insofar as the Mind conceives things from the dictate of reason, it is affected in the same way, whether the idea is of a future or a past thing, or of a present one, q.e.d.

Schol.: If we could have adequate knowledge of the duration of things, and determine by reason their times of existing, we would regard future things with the same affect as present ones, and the Mind would want the good it conceived as future just as it wants the good it conceives as present. Hence, it would necessarily neglect a lesser present good for a greater future one, and what would be good in the present, but the cause of some future ill, it would not want at all, as we shall soon demonstrate.

But we can have only a quite inadequate knowledge of the duration of things (by IIP31), and we determine their times of existing only by the imagination (by IIP44S), which is not equally affected by the image of a present thing and the image of a future one. That is why the true knowledge we have of good and evil is only abstract, *or* universal, and the judgment we make concerning the order of things and the connection of causes, so that we may be able to determine what in the present is good or evil for us, is imaginary, rather than real. And so it is no wonder if the Desire that arises from a knowledge of good and evil, insofar as this looks to the future, can be rather easily restrained by a Desire for the pleasures of the moment. On this, see P16.

P63: *He who is guided by Fear, and does good to avoid evil, is not guided by reason.*

Dem.: The only affects that are related to the Mind insofar as it acts, i.e. (by IIIP3), that are related to reason, are affects of Joy and Desire (by IIIP59). And so (by Def. Aff. XIII) one who is guided by Fear, and does good from timidity regarding an evil, is not guided by reason, q.e.d.

Schol.: The superstitious know how to reproach people for their vices better than they know how to teach them virtues, and they strive, not to guide men by reason, but to restrain them by Fear, so that they flee the evil rather than love virtues. Such people aim only to make others as wretched as they themselves are, so it is no wonder that they are generally burdensome and hateful to men.

Cor.: By a Desire arising from reason, we directly follow the good, and indirectly flee the evil.

Dem.: For a Desire that arises from reason can arise solely from an affect of Joy which is not a passion (by IIIP59), i.e., from a Joy which cannot be excessive (by P61). But it cannot arise from Sadness, and therefore this Desire (by P8) arises from knowledge of the good, not knowledge of the evil. And so from the guidance of reason we want the good directly, and to that extent only, we flee the evil, q.e.d.

Schol.: This Corollary may be illustrated by the example of the sick and the healthy. The sick man, from timidity regarding death, eats what he is repelled by, whereas the healthy man enjoys his food, and in this way enjoys life better than if he feared death, and directly desired to avoid it. Similarly, a judge who condemns a guilty man to death—not from Hate or Anger, etc., but only from a Love of the general welfare—is guided only by reason.

P64: *Knowledge of evil is an inadequate knowledge.*

Dem.: Knowledge of evil (by P8) is Sadness itself, insofar as we are conscious of it. But Sadness is a passage to a lesser perfection (by Def. Aff. III), which therefore cannot be understood through man's essence itself (by IIIP6 and P7). Hence (by IIID2), it is a passion, which (by IIIP3) depends on inadequate ideas. Therefore (by IIP29), knowledge of this, viz. knowledge of evil, is inadequate, q.e.d.

Cor.: From this it follows that if the human Mind had only adequate ideas, it would form no notion of evil.

P65: *From the guidance of reason, we shall follow the greater of two goods or the lesser of two evils.*

Dem.: A good that prevents us from enjoying a greater good is really an evil. For good and evil (as we have shown in the Preface of this Part) are said of things insofar as we compare them to one another. By the same reasoning, a lesser evil is really a good, so (by P63C)[33] from the guidance of reason we want, *or* follow, only the greater good and the lesser evil, q.e.d.

Cor.: From the guidance of reason, we shall follow a lesser evil as a greater good, and pass over a lesser good which is the cause of a greater evil. For the evil which is here called lesser is really good, and the good which is here called lesser, on the other hand, is evil. So (by P63C) we want the [lesser evil] and pass over the [greater good], q.e.d.

P66: *From the guidance of reason we want a greater future good in preference to a lesser present one, and a lesser present evil in preference to a greater future one.*

Dem.: If the Mind could have an adequate knowledge of a future thing, it would be affected toward it with the same affect as it is toward a present one (by P62). So insofar as we attend to reason itself, as in this Proposition we suppose ourselves to do, the thing will be the same, whether the greater good or evil is supposed to be future or present. And therefore (by P65), we want the greater future good in preference to the lesser present one, etc., q.e.d.

Cor.: From the guidance of reason, we shall want a lesser present evil which is the cause of a greater future good, and pass over a lesser present good which is the cause of a greater future evil. This Corollary stands to P66 as P65C does to P65.

[33] Here and below (II/260/1) the OP has "by the Corollary of the preceding Proposition." But clearly P63C is intended. So P64 and its corollary appear to be later additions.

20   Schol.: If these things are compared with those we have shown in this Part up to P18, concerning the powers of the affects, we shall easily see what the difference is between a man who is led only by an affect, *or* by opinion, and one who is led by reason. For the former,

25   whether he will or no, does those things he is most ignorant of, whereas the latter complies with no one's wishes but his own, and does only those things he knows to be the most important in life, and therefore desires very greatly. Hence, I call the former a slave, but the latter, a free man.

    I wish now to note a few more things concerning the free man's temperament and manner of living.

II/261   P67: *A free man thinks of nothing less than of death, and his wisdom is a meditation on life, not on death.*[34]

5   Dem.: A free man, i.e., one who lives according to the dictate of reason alone, is not led by Fear (by P63), but desires the good directly (by P63C), i.e. (by P24), acts, lives, and preserves his being from the foundation of seeking his own advantage. And so he thinks of nothing

10   less than of death. Instead his wisdom is a meditation on life, q.e.d.

    P68: *If men were born free, they would form no concept of good and evil so long as they remained free.*

15   Dem.: I call him free who is led by reason alone. Therefore, he who is born free, and remains free, has only adequate ideas, and so has no concept of evil (by P64C). And since good and evil are correlates, he also has no concept of good, q.e.d.

20   Schol.: It is evident from P4 that the hypothesis of this proposition is false, and cannot be conceived unless we attend only to human nature, *or* rather to God, not insofar as he is infinite, but insofar only as he is the cause of man's existence.

25   This, and the other things I have now demonstrated seem to have been indicated by Moses in that story[35] of the first man. For in it the

---

[34] Appuhn contrasts this with Plato's dictum in the *Phaedo*, 67e: "The true philosophers practice dying, and death is less terrible to them than to any other men." But it seems more likely that Spinoza has in mind Seneca, who contended that to relieve oneself of the fear of death one must meditate regularly on its inevitability. Cf. his *Epistulae morales* IV, 5, 9. Russell, in his well-known essay, "A Free Man's Worship," seems closer to Seneca than to Spinoza. Cf. Russell, 112-115.

[35] OP: *historiâ*, NS: *historie*. Both the Latin and the Dutch terms can mean either 'history' or 'story.' But Spinoza's tone here seems slightly skeptical and ironic, particularly if we keep in mind what has been said about divine teleology in the Appendix to Part I (II/79) and what is said about allegorical interpretations of Scripture in the *Theological-Political Treatise*. Spinoza's version of the fall points up certain problems in the story (Gen. 2:15-3:24), e.g., that God expected Adam to be restrained by the fear of death before he ate of the tree, and similarly, that Eve saw that the tree was good for food before she was supposed to know good and evil. Some commentators, however, seem to take this scholium at face value. Cf. Bidney, 76, 150-151.

only power of God conceived is that by which he created man, i.e., the power by which he consulted only man's advantage. And so we are told that God prohibited a free man from eating of the tree of knowledge of good and evil, and that as soon as he ate of it, he immediately feared death, rather than desiring to live; and then, that, the man having found a wife who agreed completely with his nature, he knew that there could be nothing in nature more useful to him than she was; but that after he believed the lower animals to be like himself, he immediately began to imitate their affects (see IIIP27) and to lose his freedom; and that afterwards this freedom was recovered by the Patriarchs, guided by the Spirit of Christ, i.e., by the idea of God, on which alone it depends that man should be free, and desire for other men the good he desires for himself (as we have demonstrated above, by P37).

P69: *The virtue of a free man is seen to be as great in avoiding dangers as in overcoming them.*

Dem.: The affects can be neither restrained nor removed except by an affect contrary to and stronger than the affect to be restrained (by P7). But blind Daring and Fear are affects which can be conceived to be equally great (by P3 and P5). Therefore, an equally great virtue of the mind, *or* strength of character (for the definition of this, see IIIP59S) is required to restrain Daring as to restrain Fear, i.e. (by Defs. Aff. XL and XLI), a free man avoids dangers by the same virtue of the mind by which he tries to overcome them, q.e.d.

Cor.: In a free man, a timely flight is considered to show as much Tenacity as fighting; or a free man chooses flight with the same Tenacity, *or* presence of mind, as he chooses a contest.

Schol.: I have explained in IIIP59S what Tenacity is, or what I understand by it. And by danger I understand whatever can be the cause of some evil, such as Sadness, Hate, Discord, etc.

P70: *A free man who lives among the ignorant strives, as far as he can, to avoid their favors.*

Dem.: Everyone judges according to his own temperament what is good (see IIIP39). Someone who is ignorant, therefore, and who has conferred a favor on someone else, will value it according to his own temperament, and will be saddened if he sees it valued less by him to whom it was given (by IIIP42). But a free man strives to join other men to him in friendship (by P37), not to repay men with benefits that are equivalent in their eyes, but to lead himself and the others by the free judgment of reason, and to do only those things that he himself knows to be most excellent. Therefore, a free man will strive, as far as he can, to avoid the favors of the ignorant, so as not to be hated by them, and at the same time to yield only to reason, not to their appetite, q.e.d.

Schol.: I say *as far as he can*. For though men may be ignorant, they are still men, who in situations of need can bring human aid. And there is no better aid than that. So it often happens that it is necessary to accept favors from them, and hence to return thanks to them according to their temperament [i.e., in a way they will appreciate].

To this we may add that we must be careful in declining favors, so that we do not seem to disdain them, or out of Greed to be afraid of repayment. For in that way, in the very act of avoiding their Hate, we would incur it. So in declining favors we must take account both of what is useful and of what is honorable.

P71: *Only free men are very thankful to one another.*

Dem.: Only free men are very useful to one another, are joined to one another by the greatest necessity of friendship (by P35 and P35C1), and strive to benefit one another with equal eagerness for love (by P37). So (by Def. Aff. XXXIV) only free men are very thankful to one another, q.e.d.

Schol.: The thankfulness which men are led by blind Desire to display toward one another is for the most part a business transaction *or* an entrapment, rather than thankfulness.

Again, ingratitude is not an affect. Nevertheless, ingratitude is dishonorable because it generally indicates that the man is affected with too much Hate, Anger, Pride, or Greed, etc. For one who, out of foolishness, does not know how to reckon one gift against another, is not ungrateful; much less one who is not moved by the gifts of a courtesan to assist her lust,[36] nor by those of a thief to conceal his thefts, nor by those of anyone else like that. On the contrary, he shows firmness of mind who does not allow any gifts to corrupt him, to his or to the general ruin.

P72: *A free man always acts honestly, not deceptively.*

Dem.: If a free man, insofar as he is free, did anything by deception, he would do it from the dictate of reason (for so far only do we call him free). And so it would be a virtue to act deceptively (by P24), and hence (by the same Prop.), everyone would be better advised to act deceptively to preserve his being. I.e. (as is known through itself), men would be better advised to agree only in words, and be contrary to one another in fact. But this is absurd (by P31C). Therefore, a free man etc., q.e.d.

---

[36] What Gebhardt adds here from the NS represents only the translator's attempt to deal with a difficult term through a double translation. Cf. Akkerman 2, 133.

Schol.: Suppose someone now asks: what if a man could save himself from the present danger of death by treachery? would not the principle of preserving his own being recommend, without qualification, that he be treacherous?

The reply to this is the same. If reason should recommend that, it would recommend it to all men.[37] And so reason would recommend, without qualification, that men make agreements, join forces, and have common rights only by deception—i.e., that really they have no common rights. This is absurd.

P73: *A man who is guided by reason is more free in a state, where he lives according to a common decision, than in solitude, where he obeys only himself.*

Dem.: A man who is guided by reason is not led to obey by Fear (by P63), but insofar as he strives to preserve his being from the dictate of reason, i.e. (by P66S), insofar as he strives to live freely, desires to maintain the principle of common life and common advantage (by P37). Consequently (as we have shown in P37S2), he desires to live according to the common decision of the state. Therefore, a man who is guided by reason desires, in order to live more freely, to keep the common laws of the state, q.e.d.

Schol.: These and similar things which we have shown concerning the true freedom of man are related to Strength of Character, i.e. (by IIIP59S), to Tenacity and Nobility. I do not consider it worthwhile to demonstrate separately here all the properties of Strength of Character, much less that a man strong in character hates no one, is angry with no one, envies no one, is indignant with no one, scorns no one, and is not at all proud. For these and all things which relate to true life and Religion are easily proven from P37 and P46, viz. that Hate is to be conquered by returning Love, and that everyone who is led by reason desires for others also the good he wants for himself.

To this we may add what we have noted in P50S and in other places: a man strong in character considers this most of all, that all things follow from the necessity of the divine nature, and hence, that whatever he thinks is troublesome and evil, and moreover, whatever seems immoral, dreadful, unjust, and dishonorable, arises from the fact that he conceives the things themselves in a way that is disordered, mutilated, and confused. For this reason, he strives most of all to conceive things as they are in themselves, and to remove the obstacles to true knowledge, like Hate, Anger, Envy, Mockery, Pride, and the rest of the things we have noted in the preceding pages.

---

[37] The Kantian rigor of this passage seems difficult to reconcile with the spirit of other passages (e.g., II/268/10-18).

And so, as we have said [II/47/21], he strives, as far as he can, to act well and rejoice. In the following Part I shall demonstrate how far human virtue can go in the attainment of these things, and what it is capable of.

II/266

APPENDIX

The things I have taught in this Part concerning the right way of living have not been so arranged that they could be seen at a glance. Instead, I have demonstrated them at one place or another, as I could more easily deduce one from another. So I have undertaken to collect them here and bring them under main headings.

I. All our strivings, *or* Desires, follow from the necessity of our nature in such a way that they can be understood either through it alone, as through their proximate cause, or insofar as we are a part of nature, which cannot be conceived adequately through itself without other individuals.

II. The Desires which follow from our nature in such a way that they can be understood through it alone are those that are related to the Mind insofar as it is conceived to consist of adequate ideas. The remaining Desires are not related to the Mind except insofar as it conceives things inadequately, and their force and growth must be defined not by human power, but by the power of things that are outside us. The former, therefore, are rightly called actions, while the latter are rightly called passions. For the former always indicate our power, whereas the latter indicate our lack of power and mutilated knowledge.

III. Our actions—i.e., those Desires that are defined by man's power, *or* reason—are always good; but the other [Desires] can be both good and evil.

II/267

IV. In life, therefore, it is especially useful to perfect, as far as we can, our intellect, *or* reason. In this one thing consists man's highest happiness, *or* blessedness. Indeed, blessedness is nothing but that satisfaction of mind that stems from the intuitive knowledge of God. But perfecting the intellect is nothing but understanding God, his attributes, and his actions, which follow from the necessity of his nature. So the ultimate end of the man who is led by reason, i.e., his highest Desire, by which he strives to moderate all the others, is that by which he is led to conceive adequately both himself and all things that can fall under his understanding.

V. No life, then, is rational without understanding, and things are good only insofar as they aid man to enjoy the life of the Mind, which is defined by understanding. On the other hand, those that prevent man from being able to perfect his reason and enjoy the rational life, those only we say are evil.

VI. But because all those things of which man is the efficient cause must be good, nothing evil can happen to a man except by external causes, viz. insofar as he is a part of the whole of nature, whose laws human nature is compelled to obey, and to which it is forced to accommodate itself in ways nearly infinite.

268   VII. It is impossible for man not to be a part of nature and not to follow the common order of nature. But if he lives among such individuals as agree with his nature, his power of acting will thereby be aided and encouraged. On the other hand, if he is among such as do not agree at all with his nature, he will hardly be able to accommodate himself to them without greatly changing himself.

VIII. It is permissible for us to avert, in the way that seems safest, whatever there is in nature that we judge to be evil, *or* able to prevent us from being able to exist and enjoy a rational life. On the other hand, we may take for our own use, and use in any way, whatever there is that we judge to be good, *or* useful for preserving our being and enjoying a rational life. And absolutely, it is permissible for everyone to do, by the highest right of nature, what he judges will contribute to his advantage.

IX. Nothing can agree more with the nature of any thing than other individuals of the same species. And so (by VII) nothing is more useful to man in preserving his being and enjoying a rational life than a man who is guided by reason. Again, because, among singular things, we know nothing more excellent than a man who is guided by reason,

269   we can show best how much our skill and understanding are worth by educating men so that at last they live according to the command of their own reason.

X. Insofar as men are moved against one another by Envy or some [NS: other] affect of Hate, they are contrary to one another, and consequently are the more to be feared, as they can do more than other individuals in nature.

XI. Minds, however, are conquered not by arms, but by Love and Nobility.

XII. It is especially useful to men to form associations, to bind themselves by those bonds most apt to make one people of them, and absolutely, to do those things which serve to strengthen friendships.

XIII. But skill and alertness are required for this. For men vary— there being few who live according to the rule of reason—and yet generally they are envious, and more inclined to vengeance than to

589

20 Compassion. So it requires a singular power of mind to bear with each one according to his understanding, and to restrain oneself from imitating their affects.

But those who know how to find fault with men, to castigate vices rather than teach virtues, and to break men's minds rather than
25 strengthen them—they are burdensome both to themselves and to others. That is why many, from too great an impatience of mind, and a false
II/270 zeal for religion, have preferred to live among the lower animals rather than among men. They are like boys or young men who cannot bear calmly the scolding of their parents, and take refuge in the army.[38] They choose the inconveniences of war and the discipline of an ab-
5 solute commander in preference to the conveniences of home and the admonitions of a father; and while they take vengeance on their parents, they allow all sorts of burdens to be placed on them.

XIV. Though men, therefore, generally direct everything according
10 to their own lust, nevertheless, more advantages than disadvantages follow from their forming a common society. So it is better to bear men's wrongs calmly, and apply one's zeal to those things that help to bring men together in harmony and friendship.

15 XV. The things that beget harmony are those which are related to justice, fairness, and being honorable. For men find it difficult to bear, not only what *is* unjust and unfair, but also what is *thought* dishonor-
20 able, *or* that someone rejects the accepted practices of the state. But especially necessary to bring people together in love, are the things which concern Religion and Morality. On this, see P37S1 and S2, P46S, and P73S.

25 XVI. Harmony is also commonly born of Fear, but then it is without trust. Add to this that Fear arises from weakness of mind, and
II/271 therefore does not pertain to the exercise of reason. Nor does Pity, though it seems to present the appearance of Morality.

5 XVII. Men are also won over by generosity, especially those who do not have the means of acquiring the things they require to sustain life. But to bring aid to everyone in need far surpasses the powers and advantage of a private person. For his riches are quite unequal to the
10 task. Moreover the capacity of one man[39] is too limited for him to be

[38] The situation is that of Clinia, in Terence's *Heautontimorumenos*.

[39] The OP read: "Unius praeterea viri facultas ingenii limitatior est," and though the errata called for the deletion of *ingenii*, some modern editors (e.g., Land) have reinstated it. Elwes' translation of that text is reasonable: "Again, an individual man's resources of character are too limited. . . ." Gebhardt thinks Spinoza probably first wrote: "Unius viri ingenium limitatius est," "the character of one man is too limited . . . ," and then replaced *ingenium* by *facultas*. In any case, it seems likely that by capacity here we should understand something more than financial resources.

able to unite all men to him in friendship. So the case of the poor falls upon society as a whole, and concerns only the general advantage.

XVIII. In accepting favors and returning thanks an altogether different care must be taken. See P70S, and P71S.

XIX. A purely sensual love,[40] moreover, i.e., a lust to procreate that arises from external appearance, and absolutely, all love that has a cause other than freedom of mind, easily passes into hate—unless (which is worse) it is a species of madness. And then it is encouraged more by discord than by harmony. See IIIP31C.[41]

XX. As for marriage, it certainly agrees with reason, if the Desire for physical union is not generated only by external appearance but also by a Love of begetting children and educating them wisely, and moreover, if the Love of each, of both the man and the woman, is caused not by external appearance only, but mainly by freedom of mind.

XXI. Flattery also gives rise to harmony, but by the foul crime of bondage, or by treachery. No one is more taken in by flattery than the proud, who wish to be first and are not.

XXII. In Despondency, there is a false appearance of morality and religion. And though Despondency is the opposite of Pride, still the despondent man is very near the proud. See P57S.

XXIII. Shame, moreover, contributes to harmony only in those things that cannot be hidden. Again, because Shame itself is a species of Sadness, it does not belong to the exercise of reason.

XXIV. The other affects of Sadness toward men are directly opposed to justice, fairness, being honorable, morality, and religion. And though Indignation seems to present an appearance of fairness, never-

[40] More literally: "love of a courtesan." But I agree with Matheron (2, 444) that *meretricius* is not meant to refer strictly to prostitution. See also the Glossary-Index entry: *courtesan*. Matheron's discussion of Spinoza's attitude toward sexuality is very helpful.

[41] The OP read: "atque tum magis discordiâ, quam concordiâ fovetur. Vid. Coroll., Prop. 31, p. 3." This is what I have translated, but the text is in doubt. Van Vloten and Land make *discordia* and *concordia* nominatives: "and then discord is encouraged more than harmony is." The question, I take it, is whether Spinoza is saying that a purely sensual love which is a species of madness encourages, or is encouraged by, discord. In favor of the proposed emendation is the fact that throughout these sections of the appendix Spinoza seems concerned more with the causes of harmony and discord than with their effects. In favor of retaining the text is the fact that it makes nice sense of the reference to IIIP31C—or at least it does if the lines quoted there are taken in their original context. (Ovid's poet-lover goes on to say that he loves nothing which never injures him and that his mistress exploits this weakness of his by pretending to deceive him, thereby reviving (*refovere*) his passion.) Strangely, Gebhardt defends the text by appealing to the NS (though Spinoza's ms. would not have contained accent marks anyway) and then emends the reference from IIIP31C to IIIP31CS on the ground that only in the scholium does Spinoza discuss the transition from love to hate. Cf. Akkerman 2, 92.

theless, when each one is allowed to pass judgment on another's deeds, and to enforce either his own or another's right, we live without a law.

XXV. Courtesy, i.e., the Desire to please men which is determined by reason, is related to Morality (as we said in P37S1). But if it arises from an affect, it is Ambition, *or* a Desire by which men generally arouse discord and seditions, from a false appearance of morality. For one who desires to aid others by advice or by action, so that they may enjoy the highest good together, will aim chiefly at arousing their Love for him, but not at leading them into admiration so that his teaching will be called after his name.[42] Nor will he give any cause for Envy. Again, in common conversations he will beware of relating men's vices, and will take care to speak only sparingly of a man's lack of power, but generously of the man's virtue, *or* power, and how it can be perfected, so that men, moved not by Fear or aversion, but only by an affect of Joy, may strive to live as far as they can according to the rule of reason.

XXVI. Apart from men we know no singular thing in nature whose Mind we can enjoy, and which we can join to ourselves in friendship, or some kind of association. And so whatever there is in nature apart from men, the principle of seeking our own advantage does not demand that we preserve it. Instead, it teaches us to preserve or destroy it according to its use, or to adapt it to our use in any way whatever.

XXVII. The principal advantage which we derive from things outside us—apart from the experience and knowledge we acquire from observing them and changing them from one form into another—lies in the preservation of our body. That is why those things are most useful to us which can feed and maintain it, so that all its parts can perform their function properly. For the more the Body is capable of affecting, and being affected by, external bodies in a great many ways, the more the Mind is capable of thinking (see P38 and P39).

But there seem to be very few things of this kind in nature. So to nourish the body in the way required, it is necessary to use many different kinds of food. Indeed, the human Body is composed of a great many parts of different natures, which require continuous and varied food so that the whole Body may be equally capable of doing

---

[42] This passage (an allusion, incidentally, to Terence's *Eunuch*, 263) is appealed to by the editors of the OP to explain Spinoza's request that he not be identified as the author on the title page. Cf. also II/202/16-18. There is no serious attempt at concealment, of course, since the editors make it plain that B.D.S. was also the author of *Descartes' Principles of Philosophy* and the *Metaphysical Thoughts*, which were published under Spinoza's name. Cf. also IP19S.

everything which can follow from its nature, and consequently, so that the Mind may also be equally capable of conceiving many things.

XXVIII. But to achieve these things the powers of each man would hardly be sufficient if men did not help one another. And indeed, money has provided a convenient instrument for acquiring all these aids. That is why its image usually occupies the Mind of the multitude more than anything else. For they can imagine hardly any species of Joy without the accompanying idea of money as its cause.

XXIX. But this is a vice only in those who seek money neither from need nor on account of necessities, but because they have learned the art of making money and pride themselves on it very much. As for the body, they feed it according to custom, but sparingly, because they believe they lose as much of their goods as they devote to the preservation of their Body. Those, however, who know the true use of money, and set bounds to their wealth according to need, live contentedly with little.

XXX. Since those things are good which assist the parts of the Body to perform their function, and Joy consists in the fact that man's power, insofar as he consists of Mind and Body, is aided or increased, all things that bring Joy are good. Nevertheless, since things do not act in order to affect us with Joy, and their power of acting is not regulated by our advantage, and finally, since Joy is generally related particularly to one part of the body, most affects of Joy are excessive (unless reason and alertness are present). Hence, the Desires generated by them are also excessive. To this we may add that when we follow our affects, we value most the pleasures of the moment,[43] and cannot appraise future things with an equal affect of mind. See P44S and P60S.

XXXI. Superstition, on the other hand, seems to maintain that the good is what brings Sadness, and the evil, what brings Joy. But as we have already said (see P45S), no one, unless he is envious, takes pleasure in my lack of power and misfortune. For as we are affected with a greater Joy, we pass to a greater perfection, and consequently participate more in the divine nature. Nor can Joy which is governed by the true principle of our advantage ever be evil. On the other hand, he who is led by Fear, and does the good only to avoid the evil, is not governed by reason.

XXXII. But human power is very limited and infinitely surpassed by the power of external causes. So we do not have an absolute power

---

[43] Echoing 220/26, 31, 258/2, and ultimately, perhaps, Terence's *Heautontimorumenos*, 962. Cf. Leopold 62.

to adapt things outside us to our use. Nevertheless, we shall bear calmly those things which happen to us contrary to what the principle of our advantage demands, if we are conscious that we have done our duty, that the power we have could not have extended itself to the point where we could have avoided those things, and that we are a part of the whole of nature, whose order we follow. If we understand this clearly and distinctly, that part of us which is defined by understanding, i.e., the better part of us, will be entirely satisfied with this, and will strive to persevere in that satisfaction. For insofar as we understand, we can want nothing except what is necessary, nor absolutely be satisfied with anything except what is true. Hence, insofar as we understand these things rightly, the striving of the better part of us agrees with the order of the whole of nature.

II/277

Fifth Part of the Ethics
On the Power of the Intellect,
or *on Human Freedom*

Preface

I pass, finally, to the remaining Part of the Ethics,[1] *which concerns the means, or way, leading to Freedom. Here, then, I shall treat of the power of reason, showing what it can do against the affects, and what Freedom of Mind, or blessedness, is. From this we shall see how much more the wise man can do than the ignorant. But it does not pertain to this investigation to show how the intellect must be perfected, or in what way the Body must be cared for, so that it can perform its function properly. The former is the concern of Logic, and the latter of Medicine.*[2]

[1] "Ad alteram Ethices Partem." Perhaps this *should* mean "to the second Part of the Ethics," and Gueroult (1, 1:14n) constructs an interesting hypothesis about the first stage of the composition of the *Ethics* on the assumption that it does. On this theory, the present Parts I and II formed an Introduction, the present Parts III and IV were Part I and the present Part V was Part II. But this seems contrary to other indications of early stages of the text (cf. the note at II/136/18). It also seems unlikely that if Spinoza had written the present Parts I and II as an introduction he would have written them *ordine geometrico.* But the Correspondence makes it clear that early in the 1660s Spinoza was working on geometric versions of the material in Part I. Most translators (including those of the NS) have preferred to translate *alteram* in a way which would not suggest Gueroult's hypothesis. The use of *alter* in TdIE 33-34 makes it clear that it is not always used to refer to one of two.
[2] Cf. the *Treatise on the Intellect,* §§ 14-16.

Here, then, as I have said, I shall treat only of the power of the Mind, or of reason, and shall show, above all, how great its dominion over the affects is, and what kind of dominion it has for restraining and moderating them. For we have already demonstrated above that it does not have an absolute dominion over them. Nevertheless, the Stoics thought that they depend entirely on our will, and that we can command them absolutely. But experience cries out against this, and has forced them, in spite of their principles, to confess that much practice and application are required to restrain and moderate them. If I remember rightly, someone tried to show this by the example of two dogs, one a house dog, the other a hunting dog. For by practice he was finally able to bring it about that the house dog was accustomed to hunt, and the hunting dog to refrain from chasing hares.

Descartes was rather inclined to this opinion. For he maintained that the Soul, or Mind, was especially united to a certain part of the brain, called the pineal gland, by whose aid the Mind is aware of all the motions aroused in the body and of external objects, and which the Mind can move in various ways simply by willing. He contended that this gland was suspended in the middle of the brain in such a way that it could be moved by the least motion of the animal spirits. He maintained further that this gland is suspended in the middle of the brain in as many varying ways as there are varying ways that the animal spirits strike against it, and moreover, that as many varying traces are impressed upon it as there are varying external objects which drive the animal spirits against it. That is why, if the Soul's will afterwards moves the gland so that it is suspended as it once was by the motion of the animal spirits, the gland will drive and determine the animal spirits in the same way as when they were driven back before by a similar placement of the gland.

Furthermore, he maintained that each will of the Mind is united by nature to a certain fixed motion of this gland. For example, if someone has a will to look at a distant object, this will brings it about that the pupil is dilated. But if he thinks only of the pupil which is to be dilated, nothing will be accomplished by having a will for this, because nature has not joined the motion of the gland which serves to drive the animal spirits against the Optic nerve in a way suitable for dilating or contracting the pupil with the will to dilate or contract it. Instead, it has joined that motion with the will to look at distant or near objects.

Finally, he maintained that even though each motion of this gland seems to have been connected by nature from the beginning of our life with a particular one of our thoughts, they can still be joined by habit to others. He tries to prove this in The Passions of the Soul I, 50.

From these claims, he infers that there is no Soul so weak that it cannot—when it is well directed—acquire an absolute power over its Passions. For as he defines them, these are

. . . perceptions, or feelings, or emotions of the soul, which are particularly related to the soul, and which [NB] are produced, preserved, and strengthened by some motion of the spirits (see *The Passions of the Soul I, 27*).[3]

10 *But since to any will we can join any motion of the gland (and consequently any motion of the spirits), and since the determination of the will depends only on our power, we shall acquire an absolute dominion over our Passions, if we determine our will by firm and certain judgments according to which we will*
15 *to direct the actions of our life, and if we join to these judgments the motions of the passions we will to have.*[4]

Such is the opinion of that most distinguished Man—as far as I can gather it from his words. I would hardly have believed it had been propounded by so great a Man, had it not been so subtle. Indeed, I cannot wonder enough that
20 *a Philosopher of his caliber—one who had firmly decided to deduce nothing except from principles known through themselves, and to affirm nothing which he did not perceive clearly and distinctly, one who had so often censured the Scholastics for wishing to explain obscure things by occult qualities—that such a Philosopher should assume a Hypothesis more occult than any occult quality.*[5]

25 *What, I ask, does he understand by the union of Mind and Body? What clear and distinct concept does he have of a thought so closely united to some little portion of quantity? Indeed, I wish he had explained this union by its*
II/280 *proximate cause. But he had conceived the Mind to be so distinct from the Body that he could not assign any singular cause, either of this union or of the Mind itself. Instead, it was necessary for him to have recourse to the cause of the whole Universe, i.e., to God.*

Again, I should like very much to know how many degrees of motion the
5 *Mind can give to that pineal gland, and how great a force is required to hold it in suspense. For I do not know whether this gland is driven about more slowly by the Mind than by the animal spirits, or more quickly; nor do I know whether the motions of the Passions which we have joined closely to firm judgments can be separated from them again by corporeal causes. If so, it would*
10 *follow that although the Mind had firmly resolved to face dangers, and had joined the motions of daring to this decision, nevertheless, once the danger had been seen, the gland might be so suspended that the Mind could think only of flight. And of course, since there is no common measure between the will and motion, there is also no comparison between the power, or forces, of the Mind*

---

[3] Spinoza quotes from the Latin translation of Descartes' *Passions of the Soul* which was first published in Amsterdam in 1650. From subsequent explanations (in §§ 28, 29) it seems clear that Descartes regards *perceptiones* (Fr. *perceptions*), *sensus* (*sentiments*) and *commotiones animae* (*émotions de l'âme*) as alternative designations of one and the same kind of thoughts, rather than different kinds of passion. The "NB" is Spinoza's comment.
[4] Cf. PA 44-50.
[5] Cf. Descartes' Letter to Elisabeth, 28 June 1643.

15 *and those of the Body. Consequently, the forces of the Body cannot in any way be determined by those of the Mind.*

To this we may add that this gland is not found to be so placed in the middle of the brain that it can be driven about so easily and in so many ways, and that not all the nerves extend to the cavities of the brain.[6]

20 *Finally, I pass over all those things he claimed about the will and its freedom, since I have already shown, more than adequately, that they are false.*

Therefore, because the power of the Mind is defined only by understanding, as I have shown above, we shall determine, by the Mind's knowledge alone, the remedies for the affects.[7] *I believe everyone in fact knows them by experi-*
25 *ence, though they neither observe them accurately, nor see them distinctly. From that we shall deduce all those things which concern the Mind's blessedness.*

II/281

AXIOMS

A1: If two contrary actions are aroused in the same subject, a change will have to occur, either in both of them, or in one only, until they cease to be contrary.

A2: The power of an effect is defined by the power of its cause, insofar as its essence is explained or defined by the essence of its cause.
This axiom is evident from IIIP7.

P1: *In just the same way as thoughts and ideas of things are ordered and connected in the Mind, so the affections of the body, or images of things are ordered and connected in the body.*

Dem.: The order and connection of ideas is the same as the order and connection of things (by IIP7), and vice versa, the order and connection of things is the same as the order and connection of ideas (by IIP6C and P7). So just as the order and connection of ideas happens in the Mind according to the order and connection of affections of the Body (by IIP18), so vice versa (by IIIP2), the order and connection of affections of the Body happens as thoughts and ideas of things are ordered and connected in the Mind, q.e.d.

P2: *If we separate emotions, or affects,*[8] *from the thought of an external cause, and join them to other thoughts, then the Love, or Hate, toward the external cause is destroyed, as are the vacillations of mind arising from these affects.*

282 Dem.: For what constitutes the form of Love, or Hate, is Joy, or Sadness, accompanied by the idea of an external cause (by Defs. Aff.

---

[6] Cf. PA 31-32.
[7] On this Stoic theme, see Wolfson 1, 2:263.
[8] Reading "commotiones, seu affectus," with Akkerman 2, 93.

597

VI, VII). So if this is taken away, the form of Love or Hate is taken away at the same time. Hence, these affects, and those arising from them, are destroyed, q.e.d.

P3: *An affect which is a passion ceases to be a passion as soon as we form a clear and distinct idea of it.*

Dem.: An affect which is a passion is a confused idea (by Gen. Def. Aff.). Therefore, if we should form a clear and distinct idea of the affect itself, this idea will only be distinguished by reason from the affect itself, insofar as it is related only to the Mind (by IIP21 and P21S). Therefore (by IIIP3), the affect will cease to be a passion, q.e.d.

Cor.: The more an affect is known to us, then, the more it is in our power, and the less the Mind is acted on by it.

P4: *There is no affection of the Body of which we cannot form a clear and distinct concept.*

Dem.: Those things that are common to all can only be conceived adequately (by IIP38), and so (by IIP12 and L2 [II/98]) there is no affection of the Body of which we cannot form some clear and distinct concept, q.e.d.

Cor.: From this it follows that there is no affect of which we cannot form some clear and distinct concept. For an affect is an idea of an affection of the Body (by Gen. Def. Aff.), which therefore (by P4) must involve some clear and distinct concept.

Schol.: There is nothing from which some effect does not follow (by IP36), and we understand clearly and distinctly whatever follows from an idea which is adequate in us (by IIP40); hence, each of us has—in part, at least, if not absolutely—the power to understand himself and his affects, and consequently, the power to bring it about that he is less acted on by them.

We must, therefore, take special care to know each affect clearly and distinctly (as far as this is possible), so that in this way the Mind may be determined from an affect to thinking those things which it perceives clearly and distinctly, and with which it is fully satisfied, and so that the affect itself may be separated from the thought of an external cause and joined to true thoughts. The result will be not only that Love, Hate, etc., are destroyed (by P2), but also that the appetites, *or* Desires, which usually arise from such an affect, cannot be excessive (by IVP61).

For it must particularly be noted that the appetite by which a man is said to act, and that by which he is said to be acted on, are one and the same. For example, we have shown that human nature is so con-

598

stituted that each of us wants the others to live according to his temperament (see IIIP31S).[9] And indeed, in a man who is not led by reason this appetite is the passion called Ambition, which does not differ much from Pride. On the other hand, in a man who lives according to the dictate of reason it is the action, *or* virtue, called Morality (see IVP37S1 and P37 Alternate dem.).

In this way, all the appetites, *or* Desires, are passions only insofar as they arise from inadequate ideas, and are counted as virtues when they are aroused or generated by adequate ideas. For all the Desires by which we are determined to do something can arise as much from adequate ideas as from inadequate ones (by IVP59). And—to return to the point from which I have digressed—we can devise no other remedy for the affects which depends on our power and is more excellent than this, which consists in a true knowledge of them. For the Mind has no other power than that of thinking and forming adequate ideas, as we have shown (by IIIP3) above.

P5: *The greatest affect of all, other things equal, is one toward a thing we imagine simply, and neither as necessary, nor as possible, nor as contingent.*

Dem.: An affect toward a thing we imagine to be free is greater than that toward a thing we imagine to be necessary (by IIIP49), and consequently is still greater than that toward a thing we imagine as possible or contingent (by IVP11). But imagining a thing as free can be nothing but simply imagining it while we are ignorant of the causes by which it has been determined to act (by what we have shown in IIP35S). Therefore, an affect toward a thing we imagine simply is, other things equal, greater than that toward a thing we imagine as necessary, possible, or contingent. Hence, it is the greatest of all, q.e.d.

P6: *Insofar as the Mind understands all things as necessary, it has a greater power over the affects, or is less acted on by them.*

Dem.: The Mind understands all things to be necessary (by IP29), and to be determined by an infinite connection of causes to exist and produce effects (by IP28). And so (by P5) to that extent [the mind] brings it about that it is less acted on by the affects springing from these things, and (by IIIP48) is less affected toward them, q.e.d.

Schol.: The more this knowledge that things are necessary is concerned with singular things, which we imagine more distinctly and vividly, the greater is this power of the Mind over the affects, as

[9] I give the citation as it is given in the OP and NS. Gebhardt prints a conjecture of Schmidt's (IIIP31C), though he rejects that conjecture in his notes. Cf. Akkerman 2, 83.

experience itself also testifies. For we see that Sadness over some good which has perished is lessened as soon as the man who has lost it realizes that this good could not, in any way, have been kept. Similarly, we see that no one pities infants because of their inability to speak, to walk, or to reason, or because they live so many years, as it were, unconscious of themselves. But if most people were born grown up, and only one or two were born infants, then everyone would pity the infants, because they would regard infancy itself, not as a natural and necessary thing, but as a vice of nature, *or* a sin. We could point out many other things along this line.

P7: *Affects that arise from, or are aroused by, reason are, if we take account of time, more powerful than those that are related to singular things which we regard as absent.*

Dem.: We regard a thing as absent, not because of the affect by which we imagine it, but because the Body is affected by another affect which excludes the thing's existence (by IIP17). So an affect which is related to a thing we regard as absent is not of such a nature that it surpasses men's other actions and power (see IVP6); on the contrary, its nature is such that it can, in some measure, be restrained by those affections which exclude the existence of its external cause (by IVP9). But an affect that arises from reason is necessarily related to the common properties of things (see the Def. of reason in IIP40S2), which we always regard as present (for there can be nothing which excludes their present existence) and which we always imagine in the same way (by IIP38).[10] So such an affect will always remain the same, and hence (by A1), the affects that are contrary to it, and that are not encouraged by their external causes, will have to accommodate themselves to it more and more, until they are no longer contrary to it. To that extent, an affect arising from reason is more powerful, q.e.d.

P8: *The more an affect arises from a number of causes concurring together, the greater it is.*

Dem.: A number of causes together can do more than if they were fewer (by IIIP7). And so (by IVP5), the more an affect is aroused by a number of causes together, the stronger it is, q.e.d.

Schol.: This proposition is also evident from A2.

P9: *If an affect is related to more and different causes which the Mind considers together with the affect itself, it is less harmful, we are less acted on by it, and*

---

[10] It is surprising to see "imagine" used in connection with knowledge which is necessarily adequate.

we are affected less toward each cause, than is the case with another, equally great affect, which is related only to one cause, or to fewer causes.

Dem.: An affect is only evil, *or* harmful, insofar as it prevents the Mind from being able to think (by IVP26 and P27). And so that affect which determines the Mind to consider many objects together is less harmful than another, equally great affect which engages the Mind solely in considering one, or a few objects, so that it cannot think of others. This was the first point.

Next, because the Mind's essence, i.e., power (by IIIP7), consists only in thought (by IIP11), the Mind is less acted on by an affect which determines it to consider many things together than by an equally great affect which keeps the Mind engaged solely in considering one or a few objects. This was the second point.

Finally (by IIIP48), insofar as this affect is related to many external causes, it is also less toward each one, q.e.d.

P10: *So long as we are not torn by affects contrary to our nature, we have the power of ordering and connecting the affections of the Body according to the order of the intellect.*

Dem.: Affects which are contrary to our nature, i.e. (by IVP30), which are evil, are evil insofar as they prevent the Mind from understanding (by IVP27). Therefore, so long as we are not torn by affects contrary to our nature, the power of the Mind by which it strives to understand things (by IVP26) is not hindered. So long, then, the Mind has the power of forming clear and distinct ideas, and of deducing some from others (see IIP40S2 and P47S). And hence, so long do we have (by P1) the power of ordering and connecting the affections of the Body according to the order of the intellect, q.e.d.

Schol.: By this power of rightly ordering and connecting the affections of the Body, we can bring it about that we are not easily affected with evil affects. For (by P7) a greater force is required for restraining Affects ordered and connected according to the order of the intellect than for restraining those which are uncertain and random. The best thing, then, that we can do, so long as we do not have perfect knowledge of our affects, is to conceive a correct principle of living, *or* sure maxims of life, to commit them to memory, and to apply them constantly to the particular cases frequently encountered in life. In this way our imagination will be extensively affected by them, and we shall always have them ready.

For example, we have laid it down as a maxim of life (see IVP46 and P46S) that Hate is to be conquered by Love, *or* Nobility, not by repaying it with Hate in return. But in order that we may always

II/288 have this rule of reason ready when it is needed, we ought to think about and meditate frequently on the common wrongs of men, and how they may be warded off best by Nobility. For if we join the image of a wrong to the imagination of this maxim, it will always be

5 ready for us (by IIP18) when a wrong is done to us. If we have ready also the principle of our own true advantage, and also of the good which follows from mutual friendship and common society, and keep in mind, moreover, that the highest satisfaction of mind stems from the right principle of living (by IVP52), and that men, like other things,

10 act from the necessity of nature, then the wrong, *or* the Hate usually arising from it, will occupy a very small part of the imagination, and will easily be overcome.

Or if the Anger which usually arises from the greatest wrongs is not so easily overcome, it will still be overcome, though not without some vacillation. And it will be overcome in far less time than if we

15 had not considered these things beforehand in this way (as is evident from P6, P7, and P8).

To put aside Fear, we must think in the same way of Tenacity: i.e., we must recount and frequently imagine the common dangers of life, and how they can be best avoided and overcome by presence of mind and strength of character.

20 But it should be noted that in ordering our thoughts and images, we must always (by IVP63C and IIIP59) attend to those things which are good in each thing so that in this way we are always determined to acting from an affect of Joy. For example, if someone sees that he pursues esteem too much, he should think of its correct use, the end

25 for which it ought be pursued, and the means by which it can be acquired, not of its misuse and emptiness, and men's inconstancy, or other things of this kind, which only someone sick of mind thinks of. For those who are most ambitious are most upset by such thoughts when they despair of attaining the honor they strive for; while they spew forth their Anger, they wish to seem wise. So it is certain that

30 they most desire esteem who cry out most against its misuse, and the emptiness of the world.

Nor is this peculiar to the ambitious—it is common to everyone whose luck is bad and whose mind is weak. For the poor man, when he is also greedy, will not stop talking about the misuse of money and the vices of the rich. In doing this he only distresses himself, and

35 shows others that he cannot bear calmly either his own poverty, or
II/289 the wealth of others.

So also, one who has been badly received by a lover thinks of nothing but the inconstancy and deceptiveness of women, and their other, often sung vices. All of these he immediately forgets as soon as his lover receives him again.[11]

One, therefore, who is anxious to moderate his affects and appetites from the love of Freedom alone will strive, as far as he can, to come to know the virtues and their causes, and to fill his mind with the gladness which arises from the true knowledge of them, but not at all to consider men's vices, or to disparage men, or to enjoy a false appearance of freedom. And he who will observe these [rules] carefully—for they are not difficult—and practice them, will soon be able to direct most of his actions according to the command of reason.

P11: *As an image is related to more things, the more frequent it is,* or *the more often it flourishes, and the more it engages the Mind.*

Dem.: For as an image, *or* affect, is related to more things, there are more causes by which it can be aroused and encouraged, all of which the Mind (by Hypothesis) considers together with the affect. And so the affect is the more frequent, *or* flourishes more often, and (by P8) engages the Mind more, q.e.d.

P12: *The images of things are more easily joined to images related to things we understand clearly and distinctly than to other images.*

Dem.: Things we understand clearly and distinctly are either common properties of things or deduced from them (see the Def. of reason in IIP40S2), and consequently (by P11) are aroused in us more often. And so it can more easily happen that we consider other things together with them rather than with [things we do not understand clearly and distinctly]. Hence (by IIP18), [images of things] are more easily joined with [things we understand clearly and distinctly] than with others, q.e.d.

P13: *The more an image is joined with other images, the more often it flourishes.*

Dem.: For the more an image is joined with other images, the more causes there are (by IIP18) by which it can be aroused, q.e.d.

P14: *The Mind can bring it about that all the Body's affections,* or *images of things, are related to the idea of God.*

Dem.: There is no affection of the Body of which the Mind cannot form some clear and distinct concept (by P4). And so it can bring it about (by IP15) that they are related to the idea of God, q.e.d.

P15: *He who understands himself and his affects clearly and distinctly loves God, and does so the more, the more he understands himself and his affects.*

[11] A reminiscence of Terence's *Eunuch*, 56ff., as pointed out by Akkerman 2, 7-8.

603

20   Dem.: He who understands himself and his affects clearly and distinctly rejoices (by IIIP53), and this Joy is accompanied by the idea of God (by P14). Hence (by Def. Aff. VI), he loves God, and (by the same reasoning) does so the more, the more he understands himself and his affects, q.e.d.

25   P16: *This Love toward God must engage the Mind most.*

         Dem.: For this Love is joined to all the affections of the Body (by

II/291   P14), which all encourage it (by P15). And so (by P11), it must engage the Mind most, q.e.d.

5   P17: *God is without passions, and is not affected with any affect of Joy or Sadness.*

         Dem.: All ideas, insofar as they are related to God, are true (by

10   IIP32), i.e. (by IID4), adequate. And so (by Gen. Def. Aff.), God is without passions.

         Next, God can pass neither to a greater nor a lesser perfection, (by IP20C2); hence (by Defs. Aff. II, III) he is not affected with any affect of Joy or Sadness, q.e.d.

15   Cor.: Strictly speaking, God loves no one, and hates no one. For God (by P17) is not affected with any affect of Joy or Sadness. Consequently (by Defs. Aff. VI, VII), he also loves no one and hates no one.

20   P18: *No one can hate God.*

         Dem.: The idea of God which is in us is adequate and perfect (by IIP46, P47). So insofar as we consider God, we act (by IIIP3). Con-

25   sequently (by IIIP59), there can be no Sadness accompanied by the idea of God, i.e. (by Def. Aff. VII), no one can hate God, q.e.d.

         Cor.: Love toward God cannot be turned into hate.

30   Schol.: But, it can be objected, while we understand God to be the

II/292   cause of all things, we thereby consider God to be the cause of Sadness. To this I reply that insofar as we understand the causes of Sadness, it ceases (by P3) to be a passion, i.e. (by IIIP59), to that extent it ceases to be Sadness. And so, insofar as we understand God to be

5   the cause of Sadness, we rejoice.

     P19: *He who loves God cannot strive that God should love him in return.*

10   Dem.: If a man were to strive for this, he would desire (by P17C) that God, whom he loves, not be God. Consequently (by IIIP19), he would desire to be saddened, which is absurd (by IIIP28). Therefore, he who loves God, etc., q.e.d.

P20: *This Love toward God cannot be tainted by an affect of Envy or Jealousy: instead, the more men we imagine to be joined to God by the same bond of Love, the more it is encouraged.*

Dem.: This Love toward God is the highest good which we can want from the dictate of reason (by IVP28), and is common to all men (by IVP36); we desire that all should enjoy it (by IVP37). And so (by Def. Aff. XXIII), it cannot be stained by an affect of Envy, nor (by P18 and the Def. of Jealousy, see IIIP35S) by an affect of Jealousy. On the contrary (by IIIP31), the more men we imagine to enjoy it, the more it must be encouraged, q.e.d.

Schol.: Similarly we can show that there is no affect which is directly contrary to this Love and by which it can be destroyed. So we can conclude that this Love is the most constant of all the affects, and insofar as it is related to the Body, cannot be destroyed, unless it is destroyed with the Body itself. What the nature of this Love is insofar as it is related only to the Mind, we shall see later.

And with this, I have covered all the remedies for the affects, *or* all that the Mind, considered only in itself, can do against the affects. From this it is clear that the power of the Mind over the affects consists:

I. In the knowledge itself of the affects (see P4S);

II. In the fact that it separates the affects from the thought of an external cause, which we imagine confusedly (see P2 and P4S);

III. In the time by which the affections related to things we understand surpass those related to things we conceive confusedly, *or* in a mutilated way (see P7);

IV. In the multiplicity of causes by which affections related to common properties or to God are encouraged (see P9 and P11);

V. Finally,[12] in the order by which the Mind can order its affects and connect them to one another (see P10, and in addition, P12, P13, and P14).

But to understand better this power of the Mind over the affects, the most important thing to note is that we call affects great when we compare the affect of one man with that of another, and see that the same affect troubles one more than the other, or when we compare the affects of one and the same man with each other, and find that he is affected, *or* moved, more by one affect than by another. For (by IVP5) the force of each affect is defined by the power of the external cause compared with our own. But the power of the Mind is defined

---

[12] As Wolfson (1, 2:266) notes, this list is incomplete, omitting any reference to P6.

by knowledge alone, whereas lack of power, *or* passion, is judged solely by the privation of knowledge, i.e., by that through which ideas are called inadequate.

From this it follows that that Mind is most acted on, of which inadequate ideas constitute the greatest part, so that it is distinguished more by what it undergoes than by what it does. On the other hand, that Mind acts most, of which adequate ideas constitute the greatest part, so that though it may have as many inadequate ideas as the other, it is still distinguished more by those which are attributed to human virtue than by those which betray man's lack of power.

Next, it should be noted that sickness of the mind and misfortunes take their origin especially from too much Love toward a thing which is liable to many variations and which we can never fully possess. For no one is disturbed or anxious concerning anything unless he loves it, nor do wrongs, suspicions, and enmities arise except from Love for a thing which no one can really fully possess.

From what we have said, we easily conceive what clear and distinct knowledge—and especially that third kind of knowledge (see IIP47S), whose foundation is the knowledge of God itself—can accomplish against the affects. Insofar as the affects are passions, if clear and distinct knowledge does not absolutely remove them (see P3 and P4S), at least it brings it about that they constitute the smallest part of the Mind (see P14). And then it begets a Love toward a thing immutable and eternal (see P15), which we really fully possess (see IIP45), and which therefore cannot be tainted by any of the vices which are in ordinary Love, but can always be greater and greater (by P15), and occupy the greatest part of the Mind (by P16), and affect it extensively.

With this I have completed everything which concerns this present life. Anyone who attends to what we have said in this Scholium, and at the same time, to the definitions of the Mind and its affects, and finally to IIIP1 and P3, will easily be able to see what I said at the beginning of this Scholium, viz. that in these few words I have covered all the remedies for the affects. So it is time now to pass to those things which pertain to the Mind's duration without relation to the body.[13]

---

[13] Meijer (followed by Appuhn) emended this to read: "without relation to the body's existence," thereby bringing it closer to the formula of P40S. Gebhardt retains the text of the OP, because it is supported by the NS. But whether we emend or not, the text is troublesome, partly because it is difficult to see how Spinoza can, consistently with his general account of the relation of mind and body, conceive of the mind's having any kind of existence apart from the body, partly because here he ascribes duration to the mind, whereas he will soon argue that it (or the part of it which exists without the body) is eternal. The whole section which this scholium introduces (Props. 21-40) is

25   P21: *The Mind can neither imagine anything, nor recollect past things, except while the Body endures.*

30   Dem.: The Mind neither expresses the actual existence of its Body, nor conceives the Body's affections as actual, except while the Body endures (by IIP8C); consequently (by IIP26), it conceives no body as actually existing except while its body endures. Therefore, it can neither imagine anything (see the Def. of Imagination in IIP17S) nor

II/295   recollect past things (see the Def. of Memory in IIP18S) except while the body endures, q.e.d.

P22: *Nevertheless, in God there is necessarily an idea that expresses the essence*
5   *of this or that human Body, under a species of eternity.*

Dem.: God is the cause, not only of the existence of this or that human Body, but also of its essence (by IP25), which therefore must be conceived through the very essence of God (by IA4), by a certain
10   eternal necessity (by IP16), and this concept must be in God (by IIP3), q.e.d.

P23: *The human Mind cannot be absolutely destroyed with the Body, but*
15   *something of it remains which is eternal.*

Dem.: In God there is necessarily a concept, *or* idea, which expresses the essence of the human Body (by P22), an idea, therefore, which is necessarily something that pertains to the essence of the hu-
20   man Mind (by IIP13). But we do not attribute to the human Mind any duration that can be defined by time, except insofar as it expresses the actual existence of the Body, which is explained by duration, and can be defined by time, i.e. (by IIP8C), we do not attribute duration to it except while the Body endures. However, since what is con-
25   ceived, with a certain eternal necessity, through God's essence itself (by P22) is nevertheless something, this something that pertains to the essence of the Mind will necessarily be eternal, q.e.d.

Schol.: There is, as we have said, this idea, which expresses the
30   essence of the body under a species of eternity, a certain mode of thinking, which pertains to the essence of the Mind, and which is

II/296   necessarily eternal. And though it is impossible that we should recollect that we existed before the Body—since there cannot be any traces of this in the body, and eternity can neither be defined by time nor have any relation to time—still, we feel and know by experience that

---

generally regarded as more than usually obscure. Among the older commentators, see Pollock, 260–288; Joachim 1, 292–306. Three interesting recent struggles with this topic are Harris 3, Kneale, and Donagan 3.

5   we are eternal.[14] For the Mind feels those things that it conceives in understanding no less than those it has in the memory. For the eyes of the mind, by which it sees and observes things, are the demonstrations themselves.

     Therefore, though we do not recollect that we existed before the body, we nevertheless feel that our mind, insofar as it involves the essence of the body under a species of eternity, is eternal, and that

10   this existence it has cannot be defined by time *or* explained through duration. Our mind, therefore, can be said to endure, and its existence can be defined by a certain time, only insofar as it involves the actual existence of the body, and to that extent only does it have the power of determining the existence of things by time, and of conceiving them

15   under duration.

     P24: *The more we understand singular things, the more we understand God.*[15]

20   Dem.: This is evident from IP25C.

     P25: *The greatest striving of the Mind, and its greatest virtue is understanding things by the third kind of knowledge.*

25   Dem.: The third kind of knowledge proceeds from an adequate idea of certain attributes of God to an adequate knowledge of the essence of things (see its Def. in IIP40S2), and the more we understand things in this way, the more we understand God (by P24). Therefore (by IVP28), the greatest virtue of the Mind, i.e. (by IVD8), the Mind's

30   power, *or* nature, *or* (by IIIP7) its greatest striving, is to understand things by the third kind of knowledge, q.e.d.

II/297   P26: *The more the Mind is capable of understanding things by the third kind of knowledge, the more it desires to understand them by this kind of knowledge.*

5   Dem.: This is evident. For insofar as we conceive the Mind to be capable of understanding things by this kind of knowledge, we conceive it as determined to understand things by the same kind of knowl-

---

[14] This sentence illustrates well the kind of difficulty characteristic of this part of the *Ethics*. On the face of it, Spinoza implies that we (who are here identified with parts of our minds; cf. IIP13C) not only will exist *after* the body, but did exist *before* it (though he denies the Platonic doctrine that we can come to recollect our preexistence). But in the same breath he asserts that we are eternal (cf. IIA1 and ID8) and that the eternal has no relation to time.

[15] Gebhardt here adds a phrase from the NS which might very literally be translated: "or the more we have God's intellect." He takes this to be the key to understanding this "much debated and obscure proposition." However, as Parkinson pointed out (179, n. 2), it is more natural to take the Dutch as an idiomatic paraphrase of 'the more we understand God.' Cf. also Akkerman 2, 100. Even if Gebhardt were right to conjecture a missing phrase in the Latin text, it is hard to see how it would help us understand this proposition.

edge. Consequently (by Def. Aff. I), the more the Mind is capable of
this, the more it desires it, q.e.d.

P27: *The greatest satisfaction of Mind there can be arises from this third kind
of knowledge.*

Dem.: The greatest virtue of the Mind is to know God (by IVP28),
or to understand things by the third kind of knowledge (by P25). Indeed, this virtue is the greater, the more the Mind knows things by
this kind of knowledge (by P24). So he who knows things by this kind
of knowledge passes to the greatest human perfection, and consequently (by Def. Aff. II), is affected with the greatest Joy, accompanied (by IIP43) by the idea of himself and his virtue. Therefore (by
Def. Aff. XXV), the greatest satisfaction there can be arises from this
kind of knowledge, q.e.d.

P28: *The Striving, or Desire, to know things by the third kind of knowledge
cannot arise from the first kind of knowledge, but can indeed arise from the
second.*

Dem.: This Proposition is evident through itself. For whatever we
understand clearly and distinctly, we understand either through itself,
or through something else which is conceived through itself; i.e., the
ideas which are clear and distinct in us, *or* which are related to the
third kind of knowledge (see IIP40S2), cannot follow from mutilated
and confused ideas, which (by IIP40S2) are related to the first kind of
knowledge; but they can follow from adequate ideas, *or* (by IIP40S2)
from the second and third kind of knowledge. Therefore (by Def. Aff.
I), the Desire to know things by the third kind of knowledge cannot
arise from the first kind of knowledge, but can from the second, q.e.d.

P29: *Whatever the Mind understands under a species of eternity, it understands not from the fact that it conceives the Body's present actual existence,
but from the fact that it conceives the Body's essence under a species of eternity.*

Dem.: Insofar as the Mind conceives the present existence of its
Body, it conceives duration, which can be determined by time, and
to that extent it has only the power of conceiving things in relation to
time (by P21 and IIP26). But eternity cannot be explained by duration
(by ID8 and its explanation). Therefore, to that extent the Mind does
not have the power of conceiving things under a species of eternity.

But because it is of the nature of reason to conceive things under a
species of eternity (by IIP44C2), and it also pertains to the nature of
the Mind to conceive the Body's essence under a species of eternity
(by P23), and beyond these two, nothing else pertains to the Mind's

essence (by IIP13), this power of conceiving things under a species of eternity pertains to the Mind only insofar as it conceives the Body's essence under a species of eternity, q.e.d.

30   Schol.: We conceive things as actual in two ways: either insofar as we conceive them to exist in relation to a certain time and place, or insofar as we conceive them to be contained in God and to follow

II/299 from the necessity of the divine nature. But the things we conceive in this second way as true, *or* real, we conceive under a species of eternity, and to that extent they involve the eternal and infinite essence of God (as we have shown in IIP45 and P45S).

5   P30: *Insofar as our Mind knows itself and the Body under a species of eternity, it necessarily has knowledge of God, and knows that it is in God and is conceived through God.*

10   Dem.: Eternity is the very essence of God insofar as this involves necessary existence (by ID8). To conceive things under a species of eternity, therefore, is to conceive things insofar as they are conceived through God's essence, as real beings, *or* insofar as through God's essence they involve existence. Hence, insofar as our Mind conceives

15 itself and the Body under a species of eternity, it necessarily has knowledge of God, and knows, etc., q.e.d.

    P31: *The third kind of knowledge depends on the Mind, as on a formal cause, insofar as the Mind itself is eternal.*

20   Dem.: The Mind conceives nothing under a species of eternity except insofar as it conceives its Body's essence under a species of eternity (by P29), i.e., (by P21 and P23), except insofar as it is eternal. So (by P30) insofar as it is eternal, it has knowledge of God, knowl-

25 edge which is necessarily adequate (by IIP46). And therefore, the Mind, insofar as it is eternal, is capable of knowing all those things which can follow from this given knowledge of God (by IIP40), i.e., of knowing things by the third kind of knowledge (see the Def. of this in IIP40S2);

30 therefore, the Mind, insofar as it is eternal, is the adequate, *or* formal, cause of the third kind of knowledge (by IIID1), q.e.d.

II/300 Schol.: Therefore, the more each of us is able to achieve in this kind of knowledge, the more he is conscious of himself and of God, i.e., the more perfect and blessed he is. This will be even clearer from what follows.

5   But here it should be noted that although we are already certain that the Mind is eternal, insofar as it conceives things under a species of eternity, nevertheless, for an easier explanation and better understanding of the things we wish to show, we shall consider it as if it were now beginning to be, and were now beginning to understand

things under a species of eternity, as we have done up to this point. We may do this without danger of error, provided we are careful to draw our conclusions only from evident premises.

P32: *Whatever we understand by the third kind of knowledge we take pleasure in, and our pleasure is accompanied by the idea of God as a cause.*

Dem.: From this kind of knowledge there arises the greatest satisfaction of Mind there can be (by P27), i.e. (by Def. Aff. XXV), Joy; this Joy is accompanied by the idea of oneself, and consequently (by P30) it is also accompanied by the idea of God, as its cause, q.e.d.

Cor.: From the third kind of knowledge, there necessarily arises an intellectual Love of God. For from this kind of knowledge there arises (by P32) Joy, accompanied by the idea of God as its cause, i.e. (by Def. Aff. VI), Love of God, not insofar as we imagine him as present (by P29), but insofar as we understand God to be eternal. And this is what I call intellectual love of God.

P33: *The intellectual Love of God, which arises from the third kind of knowledge, is eternal.*

Dem.: For the third kind of knowledge (by P31 and by IA3) is eternal. And so (by IA3), the Love that arises from it must also be eternal, q.e.d.

Schol.: Although this Love toward God has had no beginning (by P33), it still has all the perfections of Love, just as if it had come to be (as we have feigned in P32C). There is no difference here, except that the Mind has had eternally the same perfections which, in our fiction, now come to it, and that it is accompanied by the idea of God as an eternal cause. If Joy, then, consists in the passage to a greater perfection, blessedness must surely consist in the fact that the Mind is endowed with perfection itself.

P34: *Only while the Body endures is the Mind subject to affects which are related to the passions.*

Dem.: An imagination is an idea by which the Mind considers a thing as present (see its Def. in IIP17S), which nevertheless indicates the present constitution of the human Body more than the nature of the external thing (by IIP16C2). An imagination, then, is an affect (by the gen. Def. Aff.), insofar as it indicates the present constitution of the Body. So (by P21) only while the body endures is the Mind subject to affects which are related to passions, q.e.d.

Cor.: From this it follows that no Love except intellectual Love is eternal.

Schol.: If we attend to the common opinion of men, we shall see

II/302 that they are indeed conscious of the eternity of their Mind, but that they confuse it with duration, and attribute it to the imagination, *or* memory, which they believe remains after death.

P35: *God loves himself with an infinite intellectual Love.*

5 Dem.: God is absolutely infinite (by ID6), i.e. (by IID6), the nature of God enjoys infinite perfection, accompanied (by IIP3) by the idea of himself, i.e. (by IP11 and D1), by the idea of his cause. And this 10 is what we said (P32C) intellectual Love is.

P36: *The Mind's intellectual Love of God is the very Love of God by which God loves himself, not insofar as he is infinite, but insofar as he can be explained* 15 *by the human Mind's essence, considered under a species of eternity; i.e., the Mind's intellectual Love of God is part of the infinite Love by which God loves himself.*

Dem.: This Love the Mind has must be related to its actions (by P32C and IIIP3); it is, then, an action by which the Mind contem- 20 plates itself, with the accompanying idea of God as its cause (by P32 and P32C), i.e. (by IP25C and IIP11C), an action by which God, insofar as he can be explained through the human Mind, contemplates himself, with the accompanying idea of himself [as the cause];[16] so (by P35), this Love the Mind has is part of the infinite love by which God 25 loves himself, q.e.d.

Cor.: From this it follows that insofar as God loves himself, he loves men, and consequently that God's love of men and the Mind's intellectual Love of God are one and the same.

II/303 Schol.: From this we clearly understand wherein our salvation, *or* blessedness, *or* Freedom, consists, viz. in a constant and eternal Love of God, *or* in God's Love for men. And this Love, *or* blessedness, is 5 called Glory in the Sacred Scriptures[17]—not without reason. For whether this Love is related to God or to the Mind, it can rightly be called satisfaction of mind, which is really not distinguished from Glory (by Defs. Aff. XXV and XXX). For insofar as it is related to God (by P35), it is Joy (if I may still be permitted to use this term),[18] accom- 10 panied by the idea of himself [as its cause].[19] And similarly insofar as it is related to the Mind (by P27).

Again, because the essence of our Mind consists only in knowledge, of which God is the beginning and foundation (by IP15 and IIP47S),

---

[16] Adopting a suggestion of Meijer, which Gebhardt rejects for no clear reason.
[17] Wolfson (1, 2:311-317) considers a number of scriptural passages Spinoza may have had in mind, among them Psalms 16:9 and 73:24. See also the Glossary-Index on *esteem*.
[18] Cf. P17 and P33S.
[19] Cf. II/302/24.

it is clear to us how our Mind, with respect both to essence and existence, follows from the divine nature, and continually depends on God.

I thought this worth the trouble of noting here, in order to show by this example how much the knowledge of singular things I have called intuitive, *or* knowledge of the third kind (see IIP40S2), can accomplish, and how much more powerful it is than the universal knowledge I have called knowledge of the second kind. For although I have shown generally in Part I that all things (and consequently the human Mind also) depend on God both for their essence and their existence, nevertheless, that demonstration, though legitimate and put beyond all chance of doubt, still does not affect our Mind as much as when this is inferred from the very essence of any singular thing which we say depends on God.

P37: *There is nothing in nature which is contrary to this intellectual, Love, or which can take it away.*

Dem.: This intellectual Love follows necessarily from the nature of the Mind insofar as it is considered as an eternal truth, through God's nature (by P33 and P29). So if there were something contrary to this Love, it would be contrary to the true; consequently, what could remove this Love would bring it about that what is true would be false. This (as is known through itself) is absurd. Therefore, there is nothing in nature, etc., q.e.d.

Schol.: IVA1 concerns singular things insofar as they are considered in relation to a certain time and place. I believe no one doubts this.

P38: *The more the Mind understands things by the second and third kind of knowledge, the less it is acted on by affects which are evil, and the less it fears death.*

Dem.: The Mind's essence consists in knowledge (by IIP11); therefore, the more the Mind knows things by the second and third kind of knowledge, the greater the part of it that remains (by P23 and P29), and consequently (by P37), the greater the part of it that is not touched by affects which are contrary to our nature, i.e., which (by IVP30) are evil. Therefore, the more the Mind understands things by the second and third kind of knowledge, the greater the part of it that remains unharmed, and hence, the less it is acted on by affects, etc., q.e.d.

Schol.: From this we understand what I touched on in IVP39S, and what I promised to explain in this Part, viz. that death is less harmful to us, the greater the Mind's clear and distinct knowledge, and hence, the more the Mind loves God.

Next, because (by P27) the highest satisfaction there can be arises from the third kind of knowledge, it follows from this that the human Mind can be of such a nature that the part of the Mind which we have shown perishes with the body (see P21) is of no moment in relation to what remains. But I shall soon treat this more fully.

30

P39: *He who has a Body capable of a great many things has a Mind whose greatest part is eternal.*

II/305   Dem.: He who has a Body capable of doing a great many things is least troubled by evil affects (by IVP38), i.e. (by IVP30), by affects 5   contrary to our nature. So (by P10) he has a power of ordering and connecting the affections of his Body according to the order of the intellect, and consequently (by P14), of bringing it about that all the affections of the Body are related to the idea of God. The result (by P15) is that it is affected with a Love of God, which (by P16) must 10   occupy, *or* constitute the greatest part of the Mind. Therefore (by P33), he has a Mind whose greatest part is eternal, q.e.d.

Schol.: Because human Bodies are capable of a great many things, 15   there is no doubt but what they can be of such a nature that they are related to Minds which have a great knowledge of themselves and of God, and of which the greatest, *or* chief, part is eternal. So they hardly fear death.

But for a clearer understanding of these things, we must note here that we live in continuous change, and that as we change for the better 20   or worse, we are called happy or unhappy. For he who has passed from being an infant or child to being a corpse is called unhappy. On the other hand, if we pass the whole length of our life with a sound Mind in a sound Body, that is considered happiness. And really, he who, like an infant or child, has a Body capable of very few things, and very heavily dependent on external causes, has a Mind which 25   considered solely in itself is conscious of almost nothing of itself, or of God, or of things. On the other hand, he who has a Body capable of a great many things, has a Mind which considered only in itself is very much conscious of itself, and of God, and of things.

In this life, then, we strive especially that the infant's Body may change (as much as its nature allows and assists) into another, capable 30   of a great many things and related to a Mind very much conscious of itself, of God, and of things. We strive, that is, that whatever is related to its memory or imagination is of hardly any moment in relation to the intellect (as I have already said in P38S).

II/306   P40: *The more perfection each thing has, the more it acts and the less it is acted on; and conversely, the more it acts, the more perfect it is.*

Dem.: The more each thing is perfect, the more reality it has (by IID6), and consequently (by IIIP3 and P3S), the more it acts and the less it is acted on. This Demonstration indeed proceeds in the same way in reverse, from which it follows that the more a thing acts, the more perfect it is, q.e.d.

Cor.: From this it follows that the part of the Mind that remains, however great it is, is more perfect than the rest.

For the eternal part of the Mind (by P23 and P29) is the intellect, through which alone we are said to act (by IIIP3). But what we have shown to perish is the imagination (by P21), through which alone we are said to be acted on (by IIIP3 and the gen. Def. Aff.). So (by P40), the intellect, however extensive it is, is more perfect than the imagination, q.e.d.

Schol.: These are the things I have decided to show concerning the Mind, insofar as it is considered without relation to the Body's existence. From them—and at the same time from IP21 and other things—it is clear that our Mind, insofar as it understands, is an eternal mode of thinking, which is determined by another eternal mode of thinking, and this again by another, and so on, to infinity; so that together, they all constitute God's eternal and infinite intellect.

P41: *Even if we did not know that our Mind is eternal, we would still regard as of the first importance Morality, Religion, and absolutely all the things we have shown (in Part IV) to be related to Tenacity and Nobility.*

Dem.: The first and only foundation of virtue, *or* of the method of living rightly (by IVP22C and P24) is the seeking of our own advantage. But to determine what reason prescribes as useful, we took no account of the eternity of the Mind, which we only came to know in the Fifth Part. Therefore, though we did not know then that the Mind is eternal, we still regarded as of the first importance the things we showed to be related to Tenacity and Nobility. And so, even if we also did not know this now, we would still regard as of the first importance the same rules of reason, q.e.d.

Schol.: The usual conviction of the multitude[20] seems to be different. For most people apparently believe that they are free to the extent that they are permitted to yield to their lust, and that they give up their right to the extent that they are bound to live according to the rule of the divine law. Morality, then, and Religion, and absolutely

[20] This, of course, is not only the creed of the multitude, but a belief often encouraged by Scripture, as Spinoza well knows. These concluding portions of the *Ethics* can be read as a secular sermon against (a very natural reading of) the Sermon on the Mount. Cf. Matt. 5-7. For an interpretation more favorable to the Judaeo-Christian tradition, see Wolfson 1, 2:326-329.

everything related to Strength of Character, they believe to be burdens, which they hope to put down after death, when they also hope
to receive a reward for their bondage, that is, for their Morality and
Religion. They are induced to live according to the rule of the divine
15   law (as far as their weakness and lack of character allows) not only by
this hope, but also, and especially, by the fear that they may be punished horribly after death. If men did not have this Hope and Fear,
but believed instead that minds die with the body, and that the
wretched, exhausted with the burden of Morality, cannot look forward to a life to come, they would return to their natural disposition,
and would prefer to govern all their actions according to lust, and to
20   obey fortune rather than themselves.

These opinions seem no less absurd to me than if someone, because
he does not believe he can nourish his body with good food to eternity, should prefer to fill himself with poisons and other deadly things,
or because he sees that the Mind is not eternal, *or* immortal, should
prefer to be mindless, and to live without reason. These [common
25   beliefs] are so absurd they are hardly worth mentioning.

P42: *Blessedness is not the reward of virtue, but virtue itself; nor do we enjoy
it because we restrain our lusts; on the contrary, because we enjoy it, we are
able to restrain them.*

30   Dem.: Blessedness consists in Love of God (by P36 and P36S), a
Love which arises from the third kind of knowledge (by P32C). So
II/308   this Love (by IIIP59 and P3) must be related to the Mind insofar as it
acts. Therefore (by IVD8), it is virtue itself. This was the first point.

Next, the more the Mind enjoys this divine Love, *or* blessedness,
5   the more it understands (by P32), i.e. (by P3C), the greater the power
it has over the affects, and (by P38) the less it is acted on by evil
affects. So because the Mind enjoys this divine Love *or* blessedness,
it has the power of restraining lusts. And because human power to
10   restrain the affects consists only in the intellect, no one enjoys blessedness because he has restrained the affects. Instead, the power to restrain lusts arises from blessedness itself, q.e.d.

Schol.: With this I have finished all the things I wished to show
15   concerning the Mind's power over the affects and its Freedom. From
what has been shown, it is clear how much the Wise man is capable
of, and how much more powerful he is than one who is ignorant and
is driven only by lust. For not only is the ignorant man troubled in
many ways by external causes, and unable ever to possess true peace
of mind, but he also lives as if he knew neither himself, nor God, nor
20   things; and as soon as he ceases to be acted on, he ceases to be. On

the other hand, the wise man, insofar as he is considered as such, is hardly troubled in spirit, but being, by a certain eternal necessity, conscious of himself, and of God, and of things, he never ceases to be, but always possesses true peace of mind.

If the way I have shown to lead to these things now seems very hard, still, it can be found. And of course, what is found so rarely must be hard. For if salvation were at hand, and could be found without great effort, how could nearly everyone neglect it? But all things excellent are as difficult as they are rare.

Glossary-Index

I BEGAN to compile this index at a very early stage of my work, mainly as an aid to translation. Anxious to achieve as much consistency as I could in the treatment of technical terms, I wanted a record of what English term(s) I had used for a given Latin term. As I accumulated data about Spinoza's usage, I found that I was apt to change my mind about English terms to use, and not, in the beginning, having Professor Giancotti Boscherini's *Lexicon* available, I also needed a record of the occurrences of key Latin terms, so that I could go back to make the necessary changes. Looking ahead to the time when I would begin translating works that were written in Dutch, or that have survived only in a Dutch translation, I also decided to keep a record of the terms used by Spinoza's contemporary translators in the Dutch versions of works for which we possess a Latin original.

This was a laborious task and it has contributed much to delaying the appearance of the translation. But gradually I became convinced that the information I had originally compiled for my own use should be shared with my readers. Desirable as it might be to establish a one-to-one correspondence between the terms of the text and the terms of the translation, it cannot be done consistently without loss. Often it is hard enough just to find a term or phrase that will do for the context at hand, not to mention *all* the contexts. And often it seems best to blur in the translation distinctions in the text that seem to be merely verbal. And then there is the problem that arises when a family of words in the language of the text—a noun, related verb, related adjective, etc.—cannot easily be rendered by a family of words in the language of the translation. These are among the eternal problems of the translator, and all of them, it seemed, might be lessened if I made the language of the text the basis for the index and explained systematically how it was correlated with the language of the translation.[1] One bonus of this procedure is that it should make it easier for students to use aids like the term index in Wolfson's commentary.

So the first section of the Glossary-Index lists key terms used in the translation and indicates the Latin or Dutch terms they represent. (If only a Latin term is given, that means that the third section contains no Dutch correlate of the English. Similarly, if only a Dutch term is given, the second section contains no Latin correlate of the English.) Here I take the opportunity to comment on the reasons for adopting some possibly contentious translations, note alternatives, and offer explanations of terms where this seems necessary and has not already been done in the notes to the text. Hence the title "Glossary-Index."

---

[1] This was suggested to me partly by the Glossary in McKeon 1.

But I must stress again that it is not my intention to produce a translation and commentary. No doubt many terms that get no explanation deserve some. No doubt many that get some, deserve more. The idea is simply to centralize and organize information which otherwise might appear in notes scattered throughout the text, but which would be no more appropriate in one place than another. In many cases the reader will have to work out his own theory of Spinoza's meaning from the data supplied in the Index. The terms most apt to attract a Glossary entry are those which have caused me the most trouble as a translator, not necessarily those which would cause a commentator the most trouble. Much of the information one might want to give here is readily accessible in Wolfson's commentary, and rather than multiply references to that work, I will limit myself to this general recommendation: Wolfson's work contains a great deal of fascinating lore about the medieval and classical ancestry of Spinoza's language, but it should be used critically and with caution.

The second section indexes key terms used in Spinoza's Latin works, indicates the terms used for them by Spinoza's contemporary Dutch translators (recording patterns of usage where I have noticed them) and also indicates the English terms used in this translation. Terms here are grouped in families (generally in the order: noun; verb; adjective; adverb). There is much to be said for providing separate entries for related words, as Professor Giancotti Boscherini does in her *Lexicon*. But that work was compiled for the specialist, who is presumed to have a good command of Latin and Dutch. Since I compiled my index to meet somewhat different needs, I have constructed it on different principles. References are to the volume and page numbers of the Gebhardt edition, which are given in the margins of this edition.

The third section indexes key terms used in those works which either were written in Dutch or have survived only in Dutch,[2] and generally relates these Dutch terms to the Latin terms they are presumed to translate. Usually this relation has been established by examining the contemporary Dutch translations of Spinoza's Latin works. In the case of letters written in Dutch and translated into Latin for the *Opera posthuma*, the Latin terms are those used in the OP. Sometimes the correlation is a matter of judgment or conjecture. Where serious doubt exists about the correlation, a question mark or a com-

---

[2] In this volume, that means, in practice, the *Short Treatise* and Letters 18, 19, 20, 22, 23, 24, and 27. A Dutch term occurring in a predominantly Latin context (e.g., in additions made in Balling's translation of *Descartes' Principles*, or in interpolations into the *Ethics* from the NS) will be indexed here only if an occurrence of its Latin correlate is not already noted for the Gebhardt page.

ment in the first section indicates that fact. If the Dutch term has been translated by an English term used for its Latin analogue, then no English term will appear, and the reader who is working from Dutch to English must consult the second section to see what the possible English terms are. Where the Dutch term has no Latin analogue in section II or where it is translated differently than its Latin analogue, then the English will be given in section III.

The indexes of the second and third sections do not profess to offer an exhaustive list of occurrences of the given term. For example, if a term has both a technical and a nontechnical use, I may index only one or two occurrences of the nontechnical use in order to illustrate it, but will leave many occurrences unnoted. And even with technical uses, quite apart from the inevitable inadvertencies, I have often deliberately been quite selective in the occurrences noted, omitting some which I judged of little importance for fixing the meaning of the term or displaying its use. No doubt this introduces an element of subjectivity, but those who wish a more objective approach and a more exhaustive coverage have the *Lexicon Spinozanum* available to them. What I offer here is, for the serious student, no substitute for the *Lexicon*. But it may in some cases usefully supplement that work even for the serious student, since I have sometimes indexed terms or noted occurrences that do not appear in the *Lexicon*.

Contexts where a more or less official definition of a term is given, or where the use of that term attracts comment in a note (either by Spinoza or by myself), are italicized numbers in the indexes. Where a term is defined in more than one place I have italicized each entry only where the definitions seemed, on the face of it, to differ.

Many of the terms Spinoza uses in Parts III and IV of the *Ethics* were also used by the Latin translator of Descartes' *Passions of the Soul* (PA). The correlations with Descartes' French terms are also given in the Latin-Dutch-English section, since they often help to establish the connotations of the terms. These terms are inevitably the most difficult to translate,[3] and are the ones most likely to attract comment in the Glossary.

The irregularity of seventeenth-century Dutch spelling presents a problem. Often the same word will be spelled differently in different passages—and sometimes even in the same passage. For the purposes of the Index, I have thought it best to settle on one spelling, and to give preference to the way the word would be spelled in modern Dutch.

Again, some Latin terms (*idea, a priori, ideatum, attributum, proprium*)

---

[3] For my policy regarding these terms, see the note at II/295/20.

are not always translated into Dutch in the *Short Treatise*; sometimes the Latin itself is simply carried over. For simplicity these terms will be treated in the Index as if they had been translated into Dutch.

This section concludes with an index of proper names and Biblical references.

English–Latin–Dutch

ABILITY, NATIVE
ingenium

A PRIORI/A POSTERIORI
van voren/van achteren

I have left this pair of terms untranslated. It should be noted that in the seventeenth century the medieval usage deriving from Ockham was still current. An *a priori* proof proceeds from cause to effect; an *a posteriori* one from effect to cause. Cf. Alquié 1, II, 582n. The equivalent terms in earlier writers like Aquinas are *propter quid* and *quia*. Cf. *Summa theologiae* Ia, 2, 2.

ABSOLUTE
absolutus

Generally I have simply anglicized the Latin. But the sense seems usually to be *unconditional* or *without exception*. Cf. Gueroult 1, 2:309.

ABSTRACT
abstractus
aftreksel, abstractlijk

ACCIDENT
accidens
toeval

In early correspondence (IV/13) Spinoza was content to define the term *accidens* in the way he would later define the term *modus*. There are traces of this usage in his exposition of Descartes, but it is rejected firmly in the *Metaphysical Thoughts* (I/236, 237). See Gueroult 1, 1:65, n. 193.

Generally *per accidens* occurs only as part of the phrase *causa per accidens*. See *cause through itself.*

Generally *toeval* represents *accidens*, but in KV App. I it apparently represents *modificatio*.

ACT
actus, opus
doening, daad, werk

I mark the distinction between *actus* and *actio* by using *act* for the former and *action* for the latter. In scholastic Latin *actus* was regularly used in contrast with *potentia* to render Aristotle's *energeia* and *dunamis* (Aquinas 1, IV, 131). So an affect like madness which is, by definition, a passion, may still be an *actus* insofar as it involves the actualization of a capacity (cf. II/191). Nevertheless, *actus* also seems to be used in a nontechnical sense in which it denotes whatever anyone does (cf. II/197).

ACTED ON, TO BE
See passio

ACTION
actio, opus, facinus
doening, daad, werking, werk, aktie

See *act*. In its technical sense an *actio* is an affect of which we can be the adequate cause (E III D 3), but it seems to be used sometimes in a nontechnical sense even after the formal definition has been introduced. Cf. II/117, 142, 254. In their nontechnical senses *actus* and *actio* seem equivalent.

624

ACTIVITY
operatio

ACTUALITY
actualitas
dadelijkheid

ADEQUATE
See adaequare

ADMIRATION
admiratio

ADVANTAGE
utilitas
nut, voordeel

AFFECT
affectus

Elwes and Shirley use *emotion* for *affectus*; White simply anglicizes it, as I have, and as many commentators do. *Emotion* has the disadvantage of suggesting a passive state, whereas an *affectus* may well be active (II/139) in spite of the apparent equation with *pathema animi* at II/203 (cf. Rice 1, 105). It also has the disadvantages of suggesting an exclusively psychological state (whereas an *affectus* is a state both of the mind and of the body) and of not being broad enough. (It seems unnatural to call *desire* an emotion.)

The disadvantage of *affect* is that it has a technical meaning in psychology (the felt component of a stimulus or motive to action) which does not fit the Spinozistic context. But this usage is specialized enough that it should not confuse most readers.

On balance I prefer to preserve the etymological connection with *affectio* and *afficere*.

Wolfson says that Spinoza sometimes uses *affectus* in the sense of *affectio* (Wolfson 1, II, 194) but the text he cites (II/104/21) is probably corrupt.

See also emotion; passion.

AFFECTION
affectio
aandoening, toevoeging?

In classical and medieval Latin both *affectio* and *affectus* were used indifferently for *emotion* or *passion* (Wolfson 1, 2:193). Descartes, however, uses *affectio* as a synonym for quality or mode (Gilson 1, 9) and Spinoza generally follows him in this. The definition at II/190 is more characteristic than that at I/240. Wolfson observes that Spinoza sometimes uses *affectio* in the sense of *affectus* and Gebhardt (II/390) goes so far as to say that he uses them as synonyms, citing II/104/21, 25 and II/183/32. Perhaps. But since *affectus* is usually used for a specific kind of *affectio*, the more general term might well be used correctly in those contexts without the terms being synonymous. So, for example, the occurrence of *aandoening* at I/48/28 might equally well be rendered by *affect*. See also Hubbeling 1, 59.

AFFIRMATION
affirmatio
bevestiging

AGREEMENT
convenientia

AIDS
auxilia

ALL, THE
de Al

AMBITION
ambitio

ANALYSIS
analysis

ANGEL
angelus

ANGER
ira
gramschap, toorn

ANIMAL, LOWER
brutum

ANIMATE
animatus

This is the adjectival form of *anima* so *besouled* (Joachim) is also to be considered, but no translation can resolve the question of what Spinoza means by using this term in the famous passage in which he says that all individuals are, in varying degrees, *animata* (II/96/27-28). The commentators (Wolfson 1, 2:56-64; Gueroult 1, 2:143-144) are helpful. In view of the conceptual connection between *life* and *soul* (see *mind*, cf. also *Summa theologiae* Ia, 75, 1) and Spinoza's definition of *life* (at I/260), it seems likely that Spinoza would attribute life to all things. Cf. II/187/14 But it seems a reasonable inference from E V P39S that he would not attribute consciousness to all things.

Apparently *animatus* occurs only in the famous passage.

ANTIPATHY
antipathia

ANXIETY
benauwdheid

APPEARANCE
species
vertoning

APPEARANCE, EXTERNAL
forma

APPETITE
appetitus
lust

ART
ars

TO ASCRIBE FICTITIOUSLY
affingere

ASSENT
assensus
   See toestemmen

ASSOCIATION
consuetudo

ATOM
atomus

ATTRIBUTE, 'ATTRIBUTE'
attributum
eigenschap (KV)

The central definition of this key term (at II/45) is very ambiguous. For contrasting interpretations see Wolfson 1, ch. 5, and Haserot 1. See also Gueroult 1, t. I, app. 3 & 4, Wolf 1, and Curley 3, 4-18.

Eigenschap is the term normally used in the KV where the context makes it clear that it must be translated *attribute*. But *eigenschap* is also used for properties which are generally (but in Spinoza's view, incorrectly) regarded as attributes. I mark these nonstandard uses of *eigenschap* by putting *attribute* in single quotes. Cf. I/27/11-29 and 44/22-35.

See also mode.

AUTOMATON
automaton

AVERSION
aversio
afkeer

The Scholastics opposed *aversio* to *cupiditas*, as flight from evil to pursuit of good. There is an echo of this usage in Hobbes (*Leviathan*, I, 6), but Descartes rejects it on the ground that there is no pursuit of good which is not at the same time an avoidance of evil (PA II, 87). Hence, desire is a passion that has no contrary. Spinoza follows Descartes in regarding desire as a passion that has no contrary, but makes a place for aversion as a species of sadness. Cf. Bidney 1, 182-189.

The contrast between *afkeer* and *haat* in the KV is different from that between *aversio* and *odium* in E.

TO AVOID
   See aversio

AWARE
   See sensatio
   See gevoel, gewaarwording

AXIOM
axioma

An axiom is a proposition suitable for use as a first principle in demonstrations. For this, truth is required, but not necessarily self-evidence (pace Joachim 2, 202n) or indemonstrability. In Letter 3 Oldenburg asks whether Spinoza regards the axioms he has sent as indemonstrable principles, known by the light of nature and requiring no proof. Spinoza treats this (in Letter 4) as an inquiry as to whether his axioms are common notions. He grants that they are not (IV/13/28), but resists the suggestion that they are not true and endeavors to derive them from his definitions of substance and accident. (See also II/139/25 where Spinoza uses *axioma* for a postulate derivable from previous postulates.)

On this reading Meyer's statements about definitions, axioms and postulates (I/127) must be regarded as expressing his own view, not Spinoza's. Evidence for this is Meyer's neglect of the distinction between real and nominal definitions.

BAD
malus, *see also* mali
kwaad

While I generally prefer to translate *malus* by evil (q.v.), sometimes I use *bad*.

BEAST
bestia, *see also* brutum
beest

BEAUTY
pulchritudo

TO BE
esse

The phrase *esse in se* is central to Spinoza's philosophy, since it is used in the definition of his most important metaphysical concept, *substantia*. I would distinguish between a metaphysical use of the phrase (illustrated in II/45-47 and helpfully glossed at II/34), in which it connotes independent existence (cf. Curley 3, 14-18, and

Gueroult 1, I, 58, 61-63), and an epistemological use (illustrated at II/125), in which it connotes the reality with which true ideas are supposed to conform.

BEGET
procreare

BEING
esse, entitas, ens
zijn, wezen (*see* wezenheid)

BELIEF; TRUE BELIEF; 'BELIEF'
fides?, vera fides?, opinio?
geloof, ware geloof, geloof

Generally the second of KV's three kinds of knowledge is designated indifferently as *geloof* (probably = *fides*) or *ware geloof* (probably = *vera fides*). But the example (at I/55/3) and definitions (at I/55/23 and I/59/23) Spinoza gives always suggest a belief that is not merely true, but based on demonstrative reasoning. Wolf notes precedents for this in Crescas and Maimonides. Particularly interesting is a passage from the *Guide for the Perplexed*, I, 50. At I/77/4 we will have a transition to the terminology of the *Ethics* when *ware geloof* is equated with *reden*.

Sometimes *geloof* is used where we would expect *waan*. I mark what appear to be nonstandard uses of *geloof* by putting *belief* in single quotes. See the note at I/54/10.

BLAME
vituperium
laster, beschuldigen

BLESSEDNESS
beatitudo
zaligheid, gelukzaligheid

Sometimes *beatitudo* and its cognates clearly have the religious connotations suggested by *blessedness*, but it can equally mean *happiness*. If Balling was the translator of the KV, as some have suggested, then it seems likely that *gelukzaligheid* represents *beatitudo* rather than *felicitas*.

BODY
corpus
lichaam

BONDAGE
servitus
On the theological background of *servitus* see Wolfson 1, II, 184. It is unfortunate that the same term occurs both with negative connotations (when it is rendered by *bondage*) and with positive connotations (when it is rendered by *service*). Cf. II/136/6.

BRAIN
cerebrum

BRAVERY
dapperheid

BULK
moles, *see also* magnitudo
Wolf uses *mass*, but at this stage the term does not have the theoretical implications it acquired in Newtonian physics. Boyle's English uses *bulk*, which I take to be equivalent to *size*.

BURDENSOME
molestus

BURIDAN'S ASS
asinus Buridani

CALX
calx

CAPABLE
aptus

CAUSE
causa
oorzaak
It should be understood that Spinoza's tendency to identify *causa* and *ratio* (e.g., in E I P11D2) does not sound so strange in Latin as it does in English, since *reason* is a standard dictionary entry for *causa* and *causa* does occur in Spinoza (e.g., at II/74/30) in a nontechnical use most naturally rendered by *reason*.
Spinoza distinguishes many different kinds of cause. See Gueroult 1, I, 60n, 243-257, and 330 for a good account of

the relation between Spinoza's terminology and that of the Scholastics.

CAUSE, ACCIDENTAL
causa per accidens
oorzaak door een toeval
See cause through itself.

CAUSE OF ITSELF
causa sui
oorzaak van zich
Wolf 2, 172, contends that Spinoza understands this expression in a purely negative way, as implying that the thing which is *causa sui* "really has no cause at all." But his evidence seems insufficient. Wolfson 1, 1:127, comes close to the same view (on equally inadequate evidence), but later avoids the trap (1:129). Spinoza's adherence to the principle of sufficient reason, like Descartes', is exceptionless. Cf. E IP11D2 with AT VII, 164-165. Also relevant are AT VII, 109-111, and the note at TdIE § 97.

CAUSE, REMOTE
causa remota
Gueroult (1, I, 225n) cites a passage in Heereboord in which a remote cause is defined as one which produces its effect by the mediation of causes of the same kind. This is thought to be a reason for saying that a remote cause is not united in any way with its effect.

CAUSE THROUGH ITSELF
causa per se
oorzaak door zich zelfs
Spinoza regularly contrasts *causa per se* and *causa per accidens*. This traditional contrast goes back to Aristotle (*Physics* II, 5) and has been variously rendered into English (e.g., essential/incidental cause, direct/indirect cause). Wolfson 1, 1:307 glosses it with references to Burgersdijk and Heereboord, where it appears that an essential cause is one that produces something like itself (e.g., an animal of the same kind). But

Gueroult 1, 1:253, n. 36 is sharply critical of Wolfson's interpretation.

Whether or not Wolfson is correct about the passage there under dispute (E I P16C2), his account will not fit most of Spinoza's uses of the contrast. Aquinas' editors (Aquinas 1, XIV, 197) gloss two senses of *causa per accidens*: 1) an agent in respect to an effect that does not correspond to its power of purpose, or with respect to a side effect of its direct action; 2) an agent whose proper effect opens the way to another effect's happening, especially as removing an obstacle to that effect. Examples occur at *Summa theologiae* Ia, 49, 1 and Ia, 104, 4 respectively.

Spinoza's normal use of *causa per accidens* is in psychological contexts, where it seems most closely related to the first of these senses. An accidental cause is one that has its effect not because of its own nature but because of its coincidental association with something whose nature it is to produce that effect.

CENSURE
carpere

CERTAINTY
certitudo

The Latin *certus* can mean both *definite* and *sure* (or *beyond doubt*) and the English *certain* conveniently has the same ambiguity, so I have felt no need to use two words for one. *Pace* Caillois (Pléiade, 1420), Spinoza does sometimes use *certus* to mean *sure*, as a survey of the index entries will show. But in conjunction with *determinatus*, the sense does always seem to be *definite*. See, however, Gueroult 1, 1:75-76.

Spinoza's use of *certus* at II/11/29 is puzzling, but presumably reflects a tendency to vacillate between a purely psychological conception of certainty (= absence of doubt) and a normative conception (= absence of legitimate doubt). Both senses seem to be at work in TdIE § 26.

CHANCE
casus
geval

CHANGE
mutatio, variatio
verandering

CHANGEABLE THINGS, SINGULAR
mutabiles, res singulares

If the fixed and eternal things are, as I would guess, the attributes and infinite modes, then presumably the singular changeable things are the finite modes.

CHARACTER
hoedanigheid

CHARITY
aalmoes

CHASTITY
castitas

CHEERFULNESS
hilaritas
vrolijkheid

CHEMISTRY
Chymia

CHILD
puer, liberi

CHIMAERA
chimaera

CHOICE
electio

CHRISTIANS
christiani
christenen

CHRIST
Christus

CIRCUMSTANCE
circumstantia
omstandigheid

CITIZEN
civis

CIVIL
civilis

CLASS
classis

CLEAR AND DISTINCT
clarus et distinctus
klaar en onderscheiden(lijk)

CLEVERNESS
ingenium

COLD
frigus

COLOR
color

COMMAND
imperium, nutus
gebod

COMMEND
commendare

COMMON
communis

COMMON GOOD
gemeen best

COMMON NOTION
notio communis

This term sometimes occurs merely as a synonym for *axioma* (cf. Wolfson 1, 2:118-199). But it seems to connote, more strongly than axiom does, a proposition known to all. See *axiom*. Note that in Descartes (*Principles* I, 50) a common notion is a truth which *can* be known very clearly and distinctly, but which *may* not be, because of prejudice.

A notion may also be called common because it involves properties common to all things (cf. E II P38C and TTP VII [III/102]).

COMMUNITY
civitas
gemeenschap

In most of its occurrences in the KV, *gemeenschap* seems adequately rendered by *something in common*. But not, I think, in II, xxiv. Wolf has *fellowship*.

COMPARISON
comparatio

COMPASSION
misericordia

barmhartigheid
See pity.

COMPELLED
coactus

COMPOSITION
compositio

CONCEPT
conceptus
begrip, bevatting, concept

CONCURRENCE, GOD'S
concursus Dei
medewerking, Gods; samenlopen

CONDUCT
mos

CONFIDENCE
securitas
verzekerheid

CONFIRM, 'CONFIRM'
confirmare, comprobare

The two Latin terms occur frequently in the Boyle-Spinoza correspondence. *Confirmare* seems invariably to mean what its English cognate generally means in philosophical English: *to make (more) probable*. But *confirm*, in ordinary English, can also mean *to make certain*. When translated by *comprobare* (as it sometimes is by the Latin translator of Boyle's *Essays*) it leans heavily toward the stronger interpretation. Some of the disagreement between Boyle and Spinoza over the values of experiments may stem from a misunderstanding of *comprobare* (e.g., at IV/29/12ff.).

Wolf dealt with the ambiguity of *comprobare* by vacillating between *confirm* and *prove*. I have tried to give readers a better feel for the Latin by using *confirm* consistently for *comprobare* and putting it in scare-quotes when I think it means *prove*.

This policy has the disadvantage that readers encountering *confirm* may wonder which Latin term it represents. But a glance at the Index should resolve these doubts, since *confirmare* and *comprobare* never seem both to occur on the same page.

CONFUSION
confusio
verwarring

CONNECTION
concatenatio, connexio, nexus

CONSCIENCE
conscientie, medegeweten

CONSCIOUSNESS
conscientia
bewust(heid), medegeweten

CONSENT
consensus

CONSTANCY
constantia
bestandigheid

CONSTERNATION
consternatio
vervaardheid

The equation of E's *consternatio* with KV's *vervaardheid* is purely conjectural.

CONSTITUTION
constitutio

CONTEMPT
dedignatio

Elwes, White: *scorn*. Etymology favors *disdain*, but I have used that for *contemptus*. In Descartes *dedignatio* is a species of *contemptus* which occurs when we consider the object of our disesteem as a free cause. This would suggest *contempt*, which seems to have the proper moralistic flavor. At II/192 Spinoza declines to define *dedignatio*, but at II/181 he says that it arises from our disdain for foolishness. See also *disdain* and *scorn*.

CONTINGENCY
contingentia
gebeurlijkheid

CONTINUOUS
continuus

CONTRADICTION
implicantia, conradictio

Implicantia and *contradictio* are synonymous as Ep. XII illustrates (*pace* Wolf). *Implicare* is a trap, since it is equivalent to *implicare contradictionem* (cf. TdIE 19-20).

CONTRARY
contrarius

CONVENIENCES
commoda

CONVERSION
bekering

CORPOREAL
See corpus

CORRUPTION
corruptio
See vergaan

COURTESAN
meretrix

The *meretrix* is a standard figure in Latin comedies, where she is often portrayed quite sympathetically. Given Spinoza's familiarity with the works of Terence, we should bear these associations in mind in those passages in which Spinoza discusses sexual relationships.

COURTESY
modestia

COWARDICE
pusillanimitas
flauwmoedigheid

CREATION
creatio, procreare
schepping, herschepping

CRUELTY
crudelitas

CRYSTAL
crystallus

CUSTOM
consuetudo, mos

DARING
audacitas

DEATH
mors
dood

DECEPTION
deceptio, dolus malus

DECISION, DECREE
decretum
besluit

DEDUCE
deducere

DEED
factum

Sometimes the temptation to render *factum* by *fact* (with the suggestion of a correspondence theory of truth) is strong (I/246). But though I believe Spinoza usually thinks of truth in terms of correspondence, to introduce that technical term would be anachronistic. So far as I have been able to discover that usage has no classical or medieval precedent. The usual classical meaning always seems appropriate in Spinoza. Hobbes' use of *fact* is interesting. The etymological connection with the past participle of *facere* (to do) is dominant, but the seeds of the modern usage are clearly discernible. Cf. *Leviathan*, chapters 5, 9, 26, and 27.

DEFECT
vitium

DEFINITION
definitio
bepaling, beschrijving, definitie

Dunin-Borkowski 1, 4:487, alleged that Spinoza's theory of definition derived from the Port Royal *Logic*, but as Gueroult (1, 1:25n) observes, this seems excessive. For a comparison and contrast of the two theories, see Curley 3, 108-113.

It is crucial in understanding the role of definition in Spinoza's axiomatic method to determine whether he regarded his definitions as real or nominal. Each alternative can be supported and Gueroult (1, I, 21) contends that they are both real and nominal, a conclusion I find difficult to understand. But perhaps Bennett's useful discussion (in Bennett 2, 17-18) articulates in a clearer way the intuition Gueroult sought to express. It is important to be aware of Spinoza's discussions of definition in the KV, TdIE, and Letters 9 and 10. Gueroult's emphasis on the influence of Hobbes and the constructive character of Spinoza's definitions seems right.

DEGREE
gradus

DELIBERATION
deliberatio

DEMONSTRATION
demonstratio
See Descartes' letter to Morin, 13 July 1638 (A II, 72).

DENOMINATION
denominatio
afnoeming, benaming

DEPENDENCE
dependentia
dependentie, *see also* afhangen

DESCRIPTION
descriptio

DESIRE
cupiditas
begeerte

DESPAIR
desperatio
wanhoop

DESPONDENCY
abjectio

Elwes and Shirley use *self-abasement*, which has the advantage of preserving the connection with Descartes' *bassesse* (= *humilité vicieuse*, PA 159), but wrongly suggests that the person himself is the cause of his condition. The emphasis on sadness favors White's choice of despondency, but fails to capture the element of misjudgment of one's capacities. No term seems entirely satisfactory.

632

DESTRUCTION
destructio
verderf, vernietiging

DETERMINATION
determinatio
bepaling

Gueroult (1, 1:338n) observes that *determinari* can have two distinct senses. In an expression like *determinatum ad existendum* it means *to be caused to exist*; in *determinata existentia* it can mean *finite* or *limited existence*. And since whatever is finite is also caused to exist by something else, both senses may come into play in a context like E IP28. In other contexts, the sense of *determinatus* may be *assignable* (cf. Gueroult 1, 1:75).

Determinatio is also a technical term in Cartesian physics. In such contexts it will sometimes occur in conjunction with a phrase like *versus certam aliquam partem* (= in some definite direction). Whether that phrase occurs explicitly or not, I think it should always be understood. I take *determinatio* in these contexts to be equivalent to *tendency*. For different views, see Sabra 1, 116-121, and Westfall 1, 91.

DEVIL
diabolus, princeps scelestorum spirituum
    duivel

DEVOTION
devotio

DICTATE (OF REASON, INTELLECT)
dictamen (rationis, intellectus)

DIFFERENCE
diversitas, differentia
verscheidenheid

Donagan (1, 164) thinks *diversus* is used technically, as a synonymn for *realiter distinctus*, but some of the contexts disconfirm this (e.g., II/178/17, II/132/24, II/99/13, II/79/9) and the NS renders *distinctus* and *diversus* by different terms. I take it that *diversus* is a more general term, appropriate when

the things differentiated are really distinct (as in E IP10S), but also where they are not.

DIRECTION
determinatio, pars
    See determination

DISCORD
discordia

DISDAIN
contemptus
versmading, verachting
    Elwes, White, Shirley: *contempt*. Etymology makes *contempt* a natural choice (analogously, *disdain* for *dedignatio*). But *contempt* seems to have changed its meaning since the seventeenth century. (Cf. Hobbes' *Leviathan* vi: "Those things which we neither desire nor hate we said to contemn.") Spinoza's definition reflects Cartesian usage. When first introduced at PA54, *contemptus* represents *mépris*, is opposed to *estime*, and is defined as an inclination to consider the baseness or smallness of what is *mépris*. So something closer to *disesteem* seems preferable. See also *contempt* and *scorn*.

Versmading represents *contemptus* in the NS and possibly in the KV also. The definitions seem sufficiently close to let one term translate both. But in the KV *versmading* is opposed to *achting*, whereas in E, *contemptus* is opposed to *admiratio*.

Verachting is sometimes used in the NS for *despectus*. But in the KV it seems to be used interchangeably with *versmading*. I assume that there it too represents *contemptus*.

Wolf treats *versmading* and *verachting* as interchangeable in the KV, but thinks they represent *despectus* rather than *contemptus*. Possibly they do, or possibly the variation corresponds to a merely verbal distinction in the Latin. The Latin translation of Descartes' PA which Spinoza used would have encouraged some confusion about the relation of these terms. The translator uses *contemptus* for *mépris* in 2:54, and *despectus* for *dédain*, which is a species of *mépris*, in 2:55. But later (at 3:149) he uses *despectus* for *mépris*.

DISGRACE
probrum

DISHONORABLE
turpis
    Elwes, White, Shirley: *base*. I have preferred *dishonorable*, as less ambiguous.

DISOBEDIENT
ongehoorsam

DISGUST
fastidium

DISPOSITION, NATURAL
ingenium

DISTINCTION
distinctio
onderscheid

DISTINCTION, REAL
distinctio realis
onderscheid, dadelijk
    The definitions Spinoza gives of a real distinction seem to follow the Cartesian usage of the Second Replies (AT VII, 162) and the *Principles* (AT VIII-1, 28), but it is difficult to see how Spinoza could allow that any two things might be really distinct in the Cartesian sense. For Descartes a real distinction can occur only between two or more substances, but for Spinoza there is really only one substance. Of course, each of the attributes satisfies the definition of substance, and each is really distinct from every other, but there is no possibility of any attribute existing without the others.

DISTURBANCE OF THE MIND
commotio animi
    See emotion

DIVERSITY
diversitas
    See difference

DIVINITY
    See divinus
goddelijkheid

DIVISION
divisio
    See deel

DO
    See actio

DOCTRINE
doctrina, dogma

DOMINION
imperium

DOUBT
dubitatio
twijfel

DREAD
horror

DREAM
somnium
droom

DRUNKENNESS
ebrietas

DURATION
duratio
during

DUTY
officium, pietas
plicht

EASILY
facile

EDUCATION
educatio

EFFECT
effectus
gewrocht, uitwerking, uitwerksel

ELASTICITY
elastica proprietas

ELEMENT
elementum

EMENDATION
emendatio

EMINENTLY
eminenter
uitstekendlijk

EMPIRICISTS
empirici

EMPTINESS
vanitas

EMOTION
commotio animi
ontroering, ontsteltenis, beweging van de ziel, des gemoeds
Sometimes *commotio animi* seems to be used in a very neutral and general way, as equivalent to *affectus*. Cf. E VP2 and Descartes' PA 27 (quoted at II/279) where it translates the French *émotion*. In those contexts I have used *emotion*. But other contexts (e.g., II/7/22) seem to require something less general and more negative. There I have used *disturbance of the mind*. Perhaps the more negative term would have been preferable in KV II, vi.

EMULATION
aemulatio
volgijver

END
finis
eind

ENJOYMENT
fruitio
genieting
See also joy. Cf. Pléiade, 1391.

ENVY
invidia
nijd, wangunst?

ENMITY
inimicitia

EQUAL
See aequitas
gelijk

ERROR
error
doling (usu.), waan (occ.?)

ESSENCE
essentia
wezenheid
The conception of essence which Spinoza criticizes in E IIP10CS is exemplified in Descartes' *Principles* I, 53.
Joachim (2, 212n) notes Spinoza's apparent identification (through *sive*) of *essentia* and *definitio* at II/34/19, but argues that this does not exclude all difference between the alternatives, and that Spinoza "sharply distinguishes" *essentia* and *definitio* at II/34/29. Nevertheless, it seems fair to identify essence with what a good definition states.

ESTEEM, LOVE OF ESTEEM
gloria
achting, eer
Few terms in Spinoza's moral psychology are as troublesome as *gloria*. Classically it can mean *fame, renown, praise, honor*, etc., or *the desire for and tendency to claim fame, renown, etc.* Spinoza defines it as a species of joy felt when we believe ourselves to be praised, but seems also to use it for the state of being praised or well thought of. In the latter contexts I have used *esteem*, reserving *praise* for *laus*. In the former, *love of esteem*. (Elwes uses *honor*, which seems possible in the nonpsychological contexts, though I have rejected it as too ambiguous. White has *self-exaltation*, which is plausible in the psychological contexts, but has the disadvantage of suggesting that the person's satisfaction with himself results from self-praise, not praise by others.)
One difficulty is to find a suitable verb for *gloriari*. The classical meanings (*brag, pride o.s.*, etc.), generally seem inappropriate. In most contexts I have settled on *to exult at being esteemed*. If it were not so cumbersome I would use *exultation at being esteemed* for *gloria* in psychological contexts.
Although the *miles gloriosus* (braggart

soldier) is a stock figure of fun in classical comedy, a concern for reputation is also an important element in the conception of the hero in tragedies like those of Corneille. Neither Descartes nor Spinoza gives it an entirely negative evaluation. Cf. Alquié 1, 3:1097, with helpful annotation, and II/253. *See also* honor.

I have also used *esteem* for *achting* in KV. Although *achting* represents *existimatio* in the NS version of E, and perhaps represents *existimatio* in KV also, I assume that *achting* in KV expresses a different concept than *existimatio* in E, the concept expressed by *gloria* in its nonpsychological sense. *Existimatio* in E implies a misjudgment of the things's worth. *Achting* in KV (like *existimatio* in PA III, 149) does not. Hence I use *esteem* for *achting, overestimation* for *existimatio,* and *love of esteem* for *eer* (*gloria* in its psychological sense).

ETERNITY
aeternitas, *see also* aeternitatis, aeterno, aeternum
eeuwigheid

The major question here is whether to translate *species* in the famous phrase *sub specie aeternitatis* by *species* (= kind, sort) or by *aspect* (= point of view). Gueroult 1, 2:609-615, sets out the issues very nicely. He favors *aspect*. The main weakness in his argument, it seems to me, is the assumption that there is only one species of necessity or eternity. Cf. II/74/5ff. I note that Spinoza's contemporary Dutch translators consistently render *species* by *gedaante* in this phrase.

ETERNAL THINGS, FIXED AND
aeternae, res (fixae et)

These are generally identified either with the infinite modes, or with the attributes and infinite modes. Cf. Pollock 1, 140-144; Curley 3, 66-73; Wolfson 1, 1:251; Delbos 1, 103; Harris 1, passim.

ETHICS
ethica
zedenkunst

EVIL
malus, pravus
kwaad

Malus can be translated by either *bad* or *evil*. At one stage I preferred *bad* wherever possible, since *evil* has connotations which seem inappropriate to Spinoza's philosophy. I now think it best to retain the term and to regard Spinoza's definition as deflationary. Like Nietzsche's, Spinoza's philosophy is, in some sense, beyond good and evil.

TO BE EXCESSIVE
excessum habere

EXISTENCE
existentia, esse
wezenlijkheid, bestaan, existeren

EXPERIENCE
experientia
bevinding, ervarenheid, ervaring, ondervinding

EXPERIENCE, RANDOM
experientia vaga

Elwes: *mere experience*; White: *vague experience*. I once proposed *vagrant experience* (Curley 2), which has the advantage of preserving etymological connections and the connotations of the Baconian passage from which the phrase originates (*Novum Organum* I, 100). But *random* also conveys the appropriate disorderliness and requires less explanation. The suggestion goes back at least to Joachim (2, 135) but was particularly urged on me by Bennett.

EXPERIMENT
explicatio

EXPRESS
exprimere
uitdrukken

EXTENSION
extensio
uitgebreidheid

FACULTY
facultas

FAIRNESS
aequitas

FALL
lapsus
afvall

FALSITY
falsitas
valsheid

FANTASY
phantasia

FATE
fatum

FAULT
See carpere

FAVOR
favor
gunst

FEAR
metus (usu.), timor (occ.)
vrees
    Elwes: *fear*; White: *fear, apprehension.*
Descartes (PA 36) had made a distinction between *crainte* (Kemp Smith: *anxious apprehension*), which anyone would feel at the sight of something strange and frightful, and *peur* (fear?), which one *might* subsequently feel, depending on the body's temperament or the soul's strength (though one might also feel *hardiesse, boldness*). Unfortunately, Descartes' translator blurred this distinction by using *timor* for *crainte* and *metus* for both *crainte* and *peur* (see Voss 1). Spinoza's *metus* apparently corresponds to Descartes' *crainte* and his *timor* to Descartes' *peur.* Generally I use *fear* for the more fundamental emotion and *timidity* for the disposition to respond to fear in a particular way. See II/170. But it is not clear that Spinoza maintains a sharp distinction here.

FEELING
affectus, sensatio
gevoel

FEIGN
  See fictio
dichten
  See fiction

FELLOWMAN, FELLOW
proximus
evenmens, evennaast, naast

FICTION
fictio, commentum
versiering
    I use *to feign* and *fiction* for *fingere* and *fictio*, but it is important to realize that the English terms have connotations which may be misleading. A feigned or fictitious idea is not necessarily a false one, as the references in the TdIE illustrate. *To hypothesize* and *hypothesis* are closer to the meaning and might have been used, if *hypothesis* were not wanted to represent *hypothesis.*
    It is unclear what distinction Spinoza intends to make between *fingere* and *putare* in contexts like II/21/11. I have used *allow* there for *putare*, but find it difficult to see a difference between 'allowing' and what Spinoza usually calls fiction.
    I am skeptical of de Deugd's contention (1, 92-93) that *fictio* and related terms have significant aesthetic connotations.

FIGURE
figura
gedaante

FINITE
finitus
eindig, eindelijk

FIRE
ignis

FIXED
fixus

FLATTERY
adulatio

FLUID
liquor

FLUIDITY
fluiditas

FOLLY
stultitia

FORBEARANCE
verdraagzaamheid

FORCE
vis

Where it has seemed possible I have rendered *vis* by *force*, but where this would sound very unnatural I have used *power*, which see.

On the ambiguity of *force* (*vis*) in Cartesian physics see Westfall 1, ch. 2, and Appendix B.

FORGETFULNESS
vergetenheid

FORM
forma
vorm, gestalt, gedaante

Sometimes *forma* and the Dutch terms which translate it seem equivalent to *nature* or *essence* (e.g., at II/208/26). Cf. Gueroult 1, 2:306n. 6. Sometimes they seem equivalent to *quality* (e.g., at I/79/27). Sometimes *external appearance* is clearly indicated.

FORMAL CHARACTER, FORMALLY
formalitas, formaliter

Formaliter is usually opposed to *objective* (q.v.), rarely to *materialiter* (cf. IV/49/28).

FORTUNE
fortuna

FOUNDATION
fundamentum

FREEDOM
libertas, *see also* causa libera, homo
  liber
vrijheid

FRIENDSHIP
amicitia
vriendschap

FRIGHT
schrik

FUNCTION
functio, officium

FUTURE
futurus
toekomend

GENERATION
generatio
voortbrenging, genereren

GENEROSITY
largitio

GENIUS
ingenium

GENUS
genus
geslacht

GEOMETRIC STYLE
mos geometricus

See Meyer's preface to *Descartes "Principles,"* my preface to the *Ethics*, and the glossary entries on *axiom, definition*, and *known through itself*.

GLADNESS
gaudium

Elwes, *joy*. In *Principles* IV, 190, Descartes had used *gaudium* for that species of purely intellectual joy, entirely independent of the state of the body, which the Stoics had allowed that their wise man might experience. This distinction is not observed in the PA where *laetitia* is the usual term for *joie*, even when it is intellectual (PA 147). *Gaudium* is also used there for *joie*, without any apparent distinction being intended. (See Voss 1.) Classically a distinction is made between *gaudium* as *inward joy* and *laetitia* as *joy which shows itself externally* (LS). None of this seems to correspond to Spinoza's usage. In St. Thomas (*De Veritate* 26, 5) *gaudium* is listed with *tristitia, spes* and *timor* as one of the four principal passions of the soul (cf. *Summa theologiae* Ia, IIae, 25, 2-3.

GLUTTONY
luxuria

GOAL
institutum

GOD
Deus
God
   See also cognitio Dei; divinus; ens perfectissimum; essentia Dei; existentia Dei; idea Dei; intellectus Dei; substantia increata.

GODLESS
goddeloos

GODLY
godzalig

GOOD
bonus
goed
   See also cognitio boni et mali, boni, bonum.

GOOD PLEASURE, GOD'S
beneplacitum (Dei)
   This translation is sanctioned both by Lewis and Short and by Deferrari and Barry. But in Spinoza's use *beneplacitum* is associated with the extreme Cartesian view of God's will as completely indifferent.

GRACE
genade

GRASP
captus

GREED
avaritia
gierigheid, gulzigheid

GROUP
collegium
   The group at IV/12 and 37 is the nascent Royal Society. The group at IV/39 is Spinoza's circle of friends.

HABIT, HABITUAL DISPOSITION
habitus

HAPPINESS
felicitas
geluk

HARDNESS
durities

HARMONY
concordia, harmonia

HATE
odium
haat

HEAT
color

HEALTH
valetudo

HEAVY
   See pondus

HEBREW
Hebraeus

HELL
inferi
hel

HERETIC
haereticus

HETEROGENEOUS
heterogeneus

HISTORY
historia

HOLY
sacer

HONESTY
fides

HONOR
honor
eer
   Generally the Latin *honor* is translated in NS by *eer*. But in KV *eer* sometimes seems to represent *gloria* and I have translated it accordingly. Appuhn 1, I, 410, sees a distinction between *eer* in KV and *gloria* in E on the ground that *gloria* can arise from a knowledge of our own perfection and hence need not be contrary to reason (II/253). I do not find either the definitions or the evaluations of *eer* (in II, xii, though not in II, v) and *gloria* to be sufficiently different to warrant a distinction.

Spinoza never defines *honor*, but in the early sections of the TdIE seems to use *honor* and *gloria* interchangeably. See also *esteem*.

HONORABLE, BEING
honestas

Classically the person who has *honestas* may either be honored or be worthy of honor. Spinoza's definition suggests that the latter meaning is primary for him. (That definition also makes *honestas* difficult to distinguish from *generositas*.) Elwes and White use *honor*, but I have preferred to reserve that for its Latin double. None of the classical meanings of *honestas* seems quite appropriate to Spinoza's usage, since his definition makes it a particular kind of desire.

HOPE
spes
hoop

HUMAN
See homo; mens humana; corpus humanum

HUMANITY
humanitas

HUMAN KINDNESS
humanitas

HUMILITY
humilitas
nederigheid

I have used *humility* both for *humilitas* in E and for *nederigheid* in KV. The definitions of these terms are not the same but it would be very misleading to translate otherwise. In KV *nederigheid* involves an accurate judgment of one's imperfection and presumably is (like *edelmoedigheid*) dispassionate. In E *humilitas* seems to be neutral as regards the accuracy of the judgment involved and is certainly not dispassionate. This should be borne in mind in estimating the apparent change in Spinoza's evaluation of *nederigheid/humilitas*.

See also self-depreciation and the note to I/68/25.

HYPOTHESIS
hypothesis

IDEA
idea
denkbeeld, idee, idea

Descartes' use of the term *idea* to mean *the form of any thought by the immediate perception of which I am conscious of the thought itself* (AT VII, 160) caused much misunderstanding among his contemporaries. See particularly the First and Third Replies. Descartes explained to Hobbes (AT VII, 181) that he used the term *idea* because it was commonly used by the philosophers to signify the forms of the perceptions of the divine mind (cf. *Summa theologiae* I, 44, 3). The point was that man, like God, might conceive of something without having an image of it.

Spinoza follows Descartes in sharply distinguishing ideas from images (e.g., at II/131/30ff.) and is aware of the medieval usage (cf. I/42/28ff.). But he differs from Descartes in regarding ideas as the bearers of truth & falsity. For discussion see Curley 5.

In E & TdIE the Latin *idea* is usually translated by *denkbeeld*. In KV *idea* is usually carried over into the Dutch without being translated. Notable exceptions are the Second Dialogue of KV, I, and II, xxvi, 8-9.

IGNORANCE
ignorantia
See also asylum ignorantiae.

IMAGINATION
imaginatio
inbeelding, verbeelding

IMITATION (OF AFFECTS)
imitatio (affectuum)

IMMANENT CAUSE
causa immanens
inblijvende oorzaak

IMMEDIATELY
immediatus
onmiddelijk, immediate

IMMENSITY
immensitas

IMMORTALITY
immortalitas
onsterfelijkheid

IMMUTABILITY
immutabilitas
onveranderlijkheid

IMPETUS
impetus

IMPOSSIBLE
impossibilis

IMPRESSION
impressio

IMPULSE
impetus, impulsus

INBORN
innatus, nativus

INCLINATION
propensio
neiging

INCONSTANCY
inconstantia

INDEFINITE
indefinitus

INDIFFERENCE
  See indifferens
onverschillendheid

INDIGNATION
indignatio
evelneming

INDIVIDUAL
individuum
ondeelbar

INFANT
infans

INFINITY
infinitas, *see also* intellectus infinitus
oneindigheid
  To be considered here is Kline 1.

INFLAMMABLE
inflammabilis

INFLUENCE
invloeging

INGENUITY
ars

INGRATITUDE
ingratitudo
ondankbarheid

INHERE IN
inhaerere

INJURY
damnum

INNATE
innatus

INTELLECT
intellectus, *see also* dictamen intellectus
verstand

INTENTION
animus
intentie

INTERACT
commercium habere

INTEREST
commoditas

INTREPID
intrepidus

INTUITION
intuitus, *see also* scientia intuitiva; cognitio intuitiva
  Intuitus was used by the medievals
  to designate an immediate (noninferen-
  tial), intellectual awareness, such as we
  might have of first principles (see
  McKeon 1, 2:466). It is used in a similar sense by Descartes (AT X, 368),
  though primarily in a work which Spinoza may not have had access to (the
  Regulae ad directionem ingeni, first published in Glazemaker's Dutch translation in 1684).
  Intuitus (and its related forms) also
  has a classical nontechnical use in
  which it may simply mean a look or
  consideration. Sometimes it is used in
  this sense by Spinoza (e.g., at II/5).
  Descartes sometimes uses *intueri* as a

verb of sense perception (e.g., at AT VII, 19; but cf. AT VII, 36), as does Spinoza (II/117, 278).

We should be cautious about assuming that *intuitus* must mean in Spinoza what it means in his predecessors. Spinoza's discussions of his three kinds of knowledge are very brief and arguably his conceptions of them changed somewhat from KV to E. See Curley 2.

JEALOUSY
zelotypia
belgzucht

JOKING
jocus

JOY
laetitia
blijdschap
Elwes, Shirley: *pleasure*; White: *joy*. Wolfson 1, 2:206 defends the rendering of *laetitia* by *pleasure* on the ground that *laetitia* was one of a number of terms used for the Greek *hēdonē* in Latin translations of Aristotle. Nevertheless, I believe that *joy* is more suggestive of the overall sense of well-being that I believe Spinoza has in mind. I also think it preferable to reserve *pleasure* for *titillatio*. See pleasure and sadness

JUDGE
judex
rechter

JUDGMENT
judicium
oordeel

JUSTICE
justitia
rechtvaardigheid

KILLING
doodslaan

KIND
genus
geslacht

KNAVERY
scelus
schelmstuk

KNOWLEDGE
cognitio, scientia, notitia
kennis, wetenschap
Cognitio is Spinoza's most common and general term for *knowledge*, but sometimes *scientia* is used in an equivalent way. When it is not, it is generally approximately equivalent to our *science*, except that Spinoza would be more apt than we are to number mathematics and metaphysics among the sciences. He apparently does not distinguish *cognitio* from *scientia* in the way Descartes does (AT III, 65; VII, 141). When *cognitio* occurs with *Dei*, the genitive is almost invariably objective; when *scientia* occurs with *Dei*, the genitive is invariably subjective.

It is important to remember that *cognitio* does not imply the truth of the proposition 'known.' The first kind of *cognitio* may involve false ideas (E IIP41).

KNOWN THROUGH ITSELF
notum per se
bekend(gekend) door zich
Traditionally this Scholastic phrase has been rendered in English by *self-evident*. The tradition has this much in its favor: in Scholastic usage being known *per se* was connected with what a twentieth-century philosopher is apt to call analyticity, so that a *per se nota* proposition might plausibly be identified with one which would be known as soon as the terms were understood (cf. Aquinas 2, I, 10, where this connection is considered a possible ground for regarding *per se nota* propositions as indemonstrable). Similarly English usage of *self-evident* is colored by Locke's assumption that "universal and ready assent on hearing and understanding the terms" is characteristic of self-evident propositions (Locke 1, I, ii, 18).

But Aquinas distinguishes between what is *per se nota* in itself and what is *per se nota* to us (Aquinas 2, I, ii, or 1, Ia, 2, 1). What is *per se nota* in itself but not to us will not be self-evident in Locke's sense. So even in Aquinas the traditional rendering can be misleading.

The same is true both in Descartes and in Spinoza. Descartes, for example, thinks the proposition that God exists is *per se nota* only to those who are free of prejudices (AT VII, 162, 163, 164, 167). In Spinoza the principle of inertia provides an analogous example. Most people, prejudiced by random experience, will instinctively reject it as false. Though it would be legitimate to take a *per se nota* proposition as an axiom, it is not always necessary to do so, since some are demonstrable. Cf. II/98-99 and I/201-203. See Curley 2, 52-54, Gueroult 1, 1:355n; Rivaud 1.

LANGUAGE
lingua

LARGE
  See magnitudo

LAUGHTER
risus
lachen

LAW
lex, jus
wet

LETTER
litera

LIFE
vita
leven

LIGHT, NATURAL; OF NATURE
lumen naturale
  The natural light (of reason) is to be contrasted with the supernatural light (of revelation), not with experience. Cf. Descartes, *Principles* I, 30; Locke, *Essay* I, iii, 13.

LIKE
similis
gelijk

LIKENESS
exemplar

LIME
calx

LIMIT
finis, limes
eind

LOGIC
logica
logica

LONGING
desiderium
beklag
  White and Elwes sometimes use *regret* for *desiderium* which in turn represented Descartes' *regret* in the PA (III, 209). Wolf used *grief* for *beklag*, which is generally thought to represent *desiderium* in KV. I have preferred *longing* in the hope of conveying the mixture of sadness and desire which is involved. At II/168 *desiderium* is defined as a species of sadness (as *beklag* is at I/76 and as *regret* was). But at II/199 *desiderium* is defined as a species of desire. Spinoza's explanation of this (II/200) seems to display an uncharacteristic concern for ordinary usage. The emphasis on memory at II/199 suggests *nostalgia* as a possible alternative. In some contexts (e.g., I/248, II/170) *desiderium* seems to be used in an extrasystematic sense in which it would be a synonym for *cupiditas*. Not to prejudge that, however, and to preserve the verbal distinction, I have abstained from *desire*.

LOVE
amor
liefde
  To the various references in Wolfson 1 (see particularly 2:275-283, 302-308) may be added Descartes' letter to Chanut of 1 February 1647.

643

LUCK
fortuna

LUST
libido
begeerlijkheid
Libido is troublesome. LS give the following classical meanings: *pleasure, desire, eagerness, longing, fancy, inclination, unlawful or inordinate desire, passion, caprice, wilfullness, wantonness, sensual desire, lust.* Spinoza's definitions at II/185, 202 suggest *lust* as most appropriate for E, insofar as *libido* clearly refers to an immoderate sexual desire in those passages. (II/185 specifies an immoderate desire, II/202 doesn't, *pace* White, but the contexts at II/202-203 and II/243/25 seem to settle the matter.) I take it that both the sexual and the negative connotations are implied in current English usage of *lust.*

However, *libido* in E is not always a specifically sexual desire, and sometimes is both the desire for sexual union (the term I prefer for *coitus* since it seems to me that Spinoza's language need not be construed as referring exclusively to genital intercourse, cf. Matheron 2, 443) and the joy one derives from satisfying that desire. Since *lust* in the sense of *pleasure* or *delight* is now obsolete in English, something is lost by using *lust* for *libido.*

In TdIE *libido* seems generally to refer more to the state desired than to the desire. It is also not clear that the state desired necessarily involves sexual gratification. So there I have normally used *sensual pleasure* (as Elwes did). It seems clear that in TdIE *libido* does not always imply a negative evaluation (cf. §§ 6-7 with § 11).

MADNESS
delirium, insanus

MALICE
malitia

MAN
homo, *see also* mens humana, corpus humanum
mens

MANIFESTATION
vertoning

TO MATCH
adaequare

MANLY
mannelijk

MARRIAGE
matrimonium

MATERIAL
materia
stof

MATHEMATICS
mathematica

MATRICIDE
moedermoord

MATTER
materia
stof

MAXIM
dogma

MEANING
sensus, significatio
mening

MEANS
medium

MEASURE
analogia, mensura

MECHANICS
mechanica

MEDICINE
medicina

MEDITATION
meditatio

MELANCHOLY
melancholia

MEMORY
memoria
geheugenis
   Spinoza distinguishes *memoria* from

reminiscentia in TdIE § 83. The distinction goes back to Aristotle's short treatise on the subject in the *Parva naturalia* (449b-453b), though it is not clear that Spinoza's distinction is equivalent to Aristotle's. For further discussion see Wolfson 1, 2:88-90, and Gueroult 1, 2:230-231.

MERCY
clementia

MERIT
meritum

METAPHYSICS
metaphysica

METHOD
methodus, *see also* mos; ordo

MICROSCOPE
microscopium

MIND
mens (usu.), animus (occ.)
geest, gemoed, ziel
Animus, like *anima*, derives from the Greek *anemos* (*wind*). But whereas classically *anima* is often used in the sense of *wind*, *air* or *breath*, *animus* is not. LS give a line from Nonius Marcellus which expresses a key classical distinction: *animus est, quo sapimus, anima qua vivimus*, i.e., *animus* designates the intellect, reason, or principle of thought, *anima* the principle of life. When Descartes, then, identifies *mens, animus, intellectus*, and *ratio* (Second Meditation, AT VII, 29) his usage is classical.
Descartes also identifies *mens* and *anima rationalis* (Fifth Replies, AT VII, 355-356). And since he rejects Aristotelian talk of nutritive and sensitive souls as a symptom of intellectual confusion, he is willing simply to identify *mens* and *anima* (though with the reservation expressed in the Second Replies, AT VII, 161).
As Gueroult notes (Gueroult 1, 2:10), Spinoza's usage of *mens, animus* and *anima* is generally Cartesian, i.e., he uses all three terms pretty much in-

differently for the mind, conceived intellectualistically. A good passage to illustrate this is II/29/19ff. Nevertheless Spinoza does tend to use *anima* more frequently in his earlier works and *mens* more frequently in his later works (see Giancotti Boscherini 1, and Akkerman, 173-176). This may be because *anima* is more suggestive of traditional religious views, which Spinoza increasingly wishes to dissociate himself from.
I have generally used *mind* for *mens* and *animus*, and *soul* for *anima*. But sometimes *animus* used in a nontechnical sense which requires translation by *spirit* (e.g., at II/173/12) or in the idiom *aequo animo* (calmly).

MIRACLE
miraculum
mirakel
Often connections are at the surface in the Latin which are concealed in the English. In this case, it is helpful in some contexts (e.g., II/81) to recall that *miraculum* is related etymologically to *admirari, to wonder at*.

MIXTURE
mixtura

MOB
vulgus
See people

MOCKERY
irrisio
bespotting

MODERATE
moderari

MODE
modus
wijz
Modus is a technical term in Descartes (though with Scholastic precedent) for relatively specific (hence, accidental, potentially transient) properties of things, as opposed to *attributum*, which designates highly general

(hence, essential, enduring) properties of things. Cf. *The Principles of Philosophy* I, 53-58. In Spinoza, however, particular things (which in Cartesian usage would normally be finite substances) are modes (E IP25SC). There is an important transition to the Spinozistic usage in the Synopsis to Descartes' *Meditations*, where Descartes argues that only "body taken generally" is a substance and hence that particular bodies are not substances.

Note also that *modus* has a nontechnical sense in which it might be rendered by *way* or *manner*. Often it is unclear whether the technical or the nontechnical sense is intended, e.g., at E IP16.

MODEL
exemplar
Exemplar is a term of considerable importance for Spinoza's ethical theory. Cf. Eisenberg 2, 148.

MODERATION
temperantia
Spinoza seems to be thinking primarily of moderation in eating. Cf. II/185 and II/202.

MODIFICATION
modificatio
A synonym for *modus*.

MOMENT
momentum

MONEY
nummi, pecunia

MORALITY
pietas
I have generally followed Appuhn (3:367) who argues that Spinoza's definition and usage require something broader than *piété* with its religious connotations. White, Elwes, and Shirley all have *piety*. This might be defensible if you think Spinoza is engaging here in a persuasive redefinition. But in fact the classical meaning of *pietas* is quite broad, encompassing dutifulness toward your native country and your relatives, and kindness in general.

MOTION
motus
beweging, roering
Hayes 1, v, takes Spinoza's consistent use of *movere* in the passive in his exposition of Descartes to reflect the Cartesian doctrine that bodies are always moved, because they have no force of themselves whereby they can move themselves. "For Descartes God is the principal cause of motion." Hence he consistently translates the Latin passives by English passives.

I take these regular occurrences of the passive of *movere*, both in Descartes and in Spinoza, to have no philosophical significance, but to represent a conventional use of the passive in a middle sense. Spinoza uses the active only when *movere* is transitive. What Westfall 1, 61, observes regarding the causal interaction of finite bodies applies here also: "Descartes might not have admitted that one body can ever act, in the true sense of the word, on another. God is the only causal agent in the universe. . . . In practice, Descartes made no effort to maintain this ultimate metaphysical point of view, and he spoke of one body acting on another when it strikes it."

I take it that the passage cited to show that Descartes conceives of matter as wholly inert (viz. AT VII, 26) does not show this, since it reflects a prephilosophic conception of body Descartes is in the process of disowning. For example, by the end of the Second Meditation he will reject the notion that bodies are perceptible by the senses. His physics seems content to assume that bodies have a *viz se movendi*. Cf. *Principles* III, 57-59 (and Spinoza I/209/12, 215/2).

MULTITUDE
vulgus
See people

MULTIPLICITY
multitudo

MUTILATED
mutilatus

NAME
nomen

NATION
natio

NATURE
natura, *see also* ordo Naturae, origo
   Naturae
natuur
   Kline 1 distinguishes three senses: 1)
= universe or cosmos, 2) = kind, and
3) = essence. He contends that sense
(1) is distinguished from the others by
capitalization, but his data show that
there is much inconsistency in the capitalization. Nevertheless, there are at
least two senses which usually can be
distinguished fairly easily: one in
which *natura* = the whole of nature
(in which it is frequently capitalized),
and one in which *natura* = essence (in
which case it is normally not capitalized). I have divided my index entries
in two to reflect this division. No doubt
in some of the occurrences indexed under my second heading *natura* is being
used not as a synonym for *essentia*, but
more generally, to refer to nonessential
characteristics as well. A clear example
is at II/104/14-15. But to try systematically to distinguish the more general
from the more specific usage would introduce too many conjectures. See also
Gueroult 1, 1:269n

NATURA NATURANS/NATURA NATURATA
natura naturans/natura naturata
natuurende Natuur/genatuurde Natuur
   Elwes: *nature viewed as active/nature
viewed as passive*. I have preferred to
leave the Latin untranslated, since any
translation would involve more interpretation than I care to engage in.
Spinoza's predecessors used these
terms to mark various contrasts. Gueroult 1, 1:564-568, gives the best avail-

able survey. But I think it is questionable whether Spinoza intended to use
these terms in any of the senses in
which they were used by his predecessors.

NATURAL
naturalis

NECESSITY
necessitas, *see also* existentia necessaria
noodzakelijkheid
   I still think the account in Curley 3,
83-117, is correct.

NEED
usus

NEGATION
negatio
ontkenning, negatie

NITER
nitrum

NOBILITY
generositas
   Elwes uses *high-mindedness*, White
generosity. The definition at II/188
makes the latter plausible, with its emphasis on a concern for the welfare of
others. The former suggests more accurately the connection with Descartes' *générosité* (PA 54, 153-156, 161,
164), which has a central role in his
aristocratic ethic. Nowadays, however,
high-mindedness has acquired negative
connotations which are inappropriate.
Wolfson 1, 2:219, 220, properly emphasizes the ancestry of this concept in
Aristotle's discussion of the great-
souled man (*Nicomachean Ethics* 1123a-
33ff.). Descartes' *générosité* has volun-
taristic connotations (PA III, 153)
which distinguish the concept from
Spinoza's *generositas*.

NON-BEING
non ens

NOTHING
nihil, tò nihil
niet
   Sometimes (e.g., at I/162, 268) Spinoza will use the Greek definite article

τò to indicate that special use of *nihil* in which it is treated as if it were an expression referring to a thing which does not exist, has no properties, and yet might be the material out of which things are created. One of Spinoza's criticisms of the traditional doctrine of creation *ex nihilo* is that it involves imagining that the negation of all reality is something real.

At I/83 the expressions in italics are in Latin in an otherwise Dutch context.

NOTION
notio
kundigheid

NUMBER
numerus

OBEDIENCE
obedientia, *see also* obtemperare

OBJECT
objectum, ideatum resideata
voorwerp

OBJECTIVELY
See objectum
In general Spinoza seems to follow the Cartesian (ultimately, Scholastic) usage which contrasts formal reality with objective reality. All ideas have the same formal reality insofar as they are modes of a thinking thing. They differ in their objective reality insofar as they represent things which differ in their formal reality. Substances have more formal reality than modes, so ideas of substances would have more objective reality than ideas of modes. Cf. the Third Meditation (AT VII, 40, 41) and the First Replies (AT VII, 102-3). Cf. also Joachim (2, 56n) for an argument that Spinoza's usage may differ significantly from Descartes'.

ODOROUS
See odor

OMNIPOTENCE
omnipotentia
almachtigheid

OMEN
omen

OMNIPRESENCE
ubiquitas
overaltegenwoordigheid

OMNISCIENCE
omniscientia
alwetendheid

ONE
See unitas

OPINION
opinio, *see also* imaginatio, cognitio
   primi generis
waan, opinie, mening
Waan is the usual term for the first kind of knowledge in KV (though sometime *geloof* occurs—*see* belief). Probably it represents *opinio*, which occasionally designates the first kind of knowledge in E. Always there is a connotation of inferiority and liability to error.

Opinie is troublesome. Sometimes it clearly designates the first kind of knowledge (e.g., at I/99/17). Sometimes it is used to designate that species of the first kind of knowledge which is elsewhere designated by *experientia vaga* (e.g., at I/57/12 = I/559/26). Sometimes it is used in conjunction with *waan* as if these terms designated two different cognitive states (e.g., at I/68/5). The first two occurrences may be accounted for by supposing that the Latin had *opinio* in both cases. (The fluctuation between *waan* and *opinie* for *opinio* would then be regarded as the work of a translator.) The third occurrence is more difficult. Wolf solves it by using *imaginatio* for *waan*, Appuhn and Francès by using *erreur* for *waan*. Since *error* captures the normal meaning of *waan* in ordinary Dutch, I have preferred their solution.

OPPOSITE
contrarius

ORDER
ordo
orde

ORDINARY
See people

ORIGIN
origo, primordium
See Gueroult 1, 1:169, 170.

OVERESTIMATION
existimatio
achting
  Existimatio is used in PA III, 149 for *estime*, where nothing is implied about the correctness of the judgment of the thing's worth. Apparently it is used in a similar sense in KV II, 8. But in E it implies *overestimation*, the term White uses. Elwes uses *partiality* which has the advantage of suggesting the cause of overestimation. It would be desirable to have a term which captured the implication of the definition at II/160, that *existimatio* is a species of joy. But I can think of nothing suitable.

PAIN
dolor
pijn

PARABLE
parabola
parabel

PARADOXES
paradoxa

PARASITE
parasitus

PART
pars
deel

PARTIALITY
partialitas

PARTICIPATE
participare

PARTICLE
particula
  See deel

PARTICULAR
particularis, specialis
bijzonder
  Both Caillois (Pléiade, 1429) and Gueroult (1, 2:294) see a distinction between *particularis* and *singularis* which escapes me. I should have thought that E IIP31C indicated that Spinoza was using these terms interchangeably. Cf. E IIP48S.

PASSAGE
transitio

PASSION, 'PASSION'
passio
lijding, passie, tocht
  I have not used "affect" to translate any of the psychological terms of the KV, partly because it is not clear to me that at the time of writing that work, Spinoza has clearly distinguished between active and passive emotions. From the standpoint of the *Ethics* many of the occurrences of the various Dutch terms rendered by *passion* seem 'nonstandard' insofar as they embrace affects of which we might be the adequate cause (cf. E IIID2). Cf. I/56, n. 2, and I/65, n. 6. Rather than introduce "affect" into the *Short Treatise*, I have marked what I regard as nonstandard uses by single quotes. The term *passie*, which is used interchangeably with *lijding*, and which one would naturally assume to render *passio*, sometimes seems to require the same treatment, as does *tocht*. But it is often difficult to be sure whether a use should be marked as nonstandard. It should be observed that even in the *Ethics* Spinoza is not perfectly consistent about distinguishing between *affectus* and *passio*. Cf. II/204/2. See also Wolfson 1, 2:193. *Passio* is also awkward because there is no verb in English related to *passion* as *passio* is to *pati*. Some remedy this defect by pressing

649

suffer into service. I have preferred *to be acted on.*

PAST
praeteritus

PATIENCE
geduld

PEACE
tranquillitas

PEOPLE, ORDINARY, THE PEOPLE
vulgus
volk
  Classically *vulgus* can mean variously *the people, the multitude, the public,* or *a mass, a crowd,* etc. But it can also imply contempt, and Lewis and Short suggest such terms as *the vulgar, the mob, the rabble.* Spinoza does regularly use *vulgus* for people whose intelligence and opinions he has little respect for, but the contemptuous terms Lewis and Short suggest sound unduly priggish to my ear. Sometimes Spinoza contrasts *vulgus* with the philosophers (I/246) and the sense seems something like that of the modern philosopher's *man-in-the-street.* Sometimes he will speak of a *vulgus* of philosophers (I/ 168), presumably meaning those philosophers whose opinions are quite conventional. Sometimes, particularly when he is echoing classical political commentary, *the mob* does seem right. For more on this, cf. Pléiade, 1443.

PERCEPTION
perceptio
gewaarwording

PERFECTION
perfectio
volmaaktheid
  As White observed, it is important in understanding Spinoza's analysis of perfection (see particularly the Preface to Part IV), to realize that *perfectus* is simply the past participle of *perficere,* to complete or finish, itself a derivative of *facere,* to make or do.
  That Spinoza is quite self-conscious

about using the term in a nonevaluative, metaphysical sense, is well indicated by his note at I/165/3-9.

PERIPATETICS
peripatetici

PERSEVERANCE
perseverantia
  See volharden

PERSONALITY
personalitas

PHENOMENA
phaenomena

PHILOSOPHY
philosophia
wijsbegeerte, filosoof
  Note that the occurrences of *philosophia* in the TdIE appear to be as a title for a projected systematic treatise.

PHYSICS
Physica

PINEAL GLAND
glandula pinealis

PIOUS
probus, *see also* pietas
vroom

PITY
commiseratio
  White: *commiseration.* The use of *commiseratio* in this sense is not classical (LS), but *commiseratio* is used (indifferently with *misericordia*) for *pitié,* in PA (cf. 62, 185, 186 and see Voss 1). This perhaps accounts for Spinoza's difficulty in seeing a distinction between them at II/195.

PLACE
locus

PLAN
institutum

PLEASURE
titillatio, deliciae, libido, *see also* jucundus, libido
vermaak
  Elwes: *stimulation*; White: *pleasurable excitement.* Normally *titillatio* refers to

a tickling sensation. But Spinoza regularly opposes it to *dolor*. Similarly, *titillatio* in the PA represents *chatouillement* which normally refers to a tickling sensation, but is opposed by Descartes to *douleur*. Alquié 1, 3:1024 n. 2 glosses *chatouillement* as *plaisir* and ascribes to Descartes the theory that pleasure is caused by moderate stimulation of the nerves, pain by excessive stimulation. Cf. also AT VII, 76

POSITION
situs

POSITIVE
positivus
positief, stellig

TO POSSESS
possidere, (esse) compos
Cf. Pléiade, 1391, 1447.

POSSIBILITY
possibilitas
mogelijkheid

POSTULATE
postulatum

POWER
potentia, potestas, vis, virtus
macht, kracht
    Some French scholars see an important distinction between *potestas* (which they render *pouvoir*, suggesting a mere capacity) and *potentia* (which they render *puissance*, suggesting a power "en acte"—cf. Pléiade, 1421, 345, Appuhn 3:31, 59, 60). Gueroult, who appears to accept this distinction (1, I, 387-389, 2:43, 44, 49, 50) comments that Spinoza introduces the distinction in order to reduce it immediately to nothing. It is unclear that a systematic examination of Spinoza's usage would confirm even a prima facie distinction between *potentia* and *potestas*. The main symptoms of one seem to be that *power* in the phrase *power of acting* always represents *potentia*, whereas in the phrase *in one's power* it always represents *potestas*. And *potestas* is the term

used to refer to the political power held by an established government. But sometimes Spinoza uses the terms interchangeably, as he sometimes does *vis* and *potentia*. Cf. I/275, 280; II/54, 87, 210.

PRACTICE
mos, praxis, usus

PRAISE
laus
lof

PRAYER
prex
gebed

PREDESTINATION
predestinatie

PREDETERMINATION; PREDETERMINE
praedeterminare
voorbeschikking; voorbepalen

PREDICATE
praedicatum

PREJUDICE
praejudicium

PREORDINATION
praeordinatio

PRESENCE
praesentia

PRESENTATION
repraesentamen

PRESERVATION
conservatio
behoudenis, onderhouden, voortgang

PRESSURE
impulsio

PRIDE
superbia
verwaandheid, verhovaardiging, hovaardigheid
    Pride (Elwes,White) seems inevitable as a translation of *superbia* and its Dutch equivalents. But since these terms seem always to have a negative connotation in Spinoza, since Spinoza rejects the claim of *humilitas* to be a virtue, and since *acquiescentia in se ipso*

651

has very positive connotations, *arrogance* and *haughtiness* deserve serious consideration as translations of *superbia*.

PRINCIPLE
principium (usu.) ratio (occ.)
beginsel, grondregel, regel

PRIVATE
privatus

PRIVATION
privatio
beroving
See Gueroult 1, 2:311n

PROBABILITY
verisimilitudo

PROBLEM
quaestio
kwestie
I adopt this translation from Joachim (2, 120), who observes that a *quaestio* is a special problem in any branch of knowledge. He refers us to Descartes' *Regulae* XII (AT X, 428-30)

PROCREATE
procreare

PRODUCE AN EFFECT
operari (aliquid)
Appuhn (1, 3:343) notes that Spinoza uses *agere* for the activities of a free thing and *operari* for what a compelled thing does (e.g., in E ID7). It seems desirable to reproduce this distinction in the translation in some way and the English represents an attempt to do that. (The most natural suggestion, *operate*, is awkward in contexts where *operari* takes a direct object.)

PROHIBITION
verbod

PROPERTY
proprietas
eigenschap
Though *eigenschap* generally represents *attributum* in the KV, sometimes it seems to represent *proprietas*, e.g., in II, xxvii.

PROPORTION
analogia

PROPOSITION
propositio, pronuntiatum

PROPRIUM, PL. PROPRIA
proprium
eigen
I have often left *proprium* untranslated in its occurrences as a noun, since *property* is wanted for *proprietas* and I do not want to prejudge the question whether *proprium* is used in its common technical sense, a property which all and only members of a species always have, though it does not pertain to the essence of the species (e.g., having a capacity for laughter in men, cf. Gilson 1, 246-247). Eisenberg 1, 31-32, thinks it clear that in the TdIE Spinoza makes no distinction between *proprietas* and *proprium*. I find it not so clear. Certainly he sometimes makes the distinction in other works and his contemporary Dutch translators seem to have thought there was a distinction worth marking. And I find that the contract between *proprium* and *essential property* is wanted in both TdIE contexts. Spinoza does use *proprium* and *proprietas* interchangeably there but I think that is because he uses *proprietas* where *proprium* would have been more accurate.

PROVABLE
probabilis

PROVIDENCE
providentia
voorzienigheid

PRUDENCE
prudentia
voorzichtigheid

PUNISHMENT
poena, supplicium
straf

PURIFY; PURE
expurgare; purus, castus
In connection with *mens* and *intellec-*

652

tus, purus means, roughly, free of ideas arising from external sources. Cf. II/ 34/3 the note to II/5/7, and the secondary sources cited there.

PURPOSE
finis, institutum
eind

QUALITY
qualitas
hoedanigheid

QUANTITY
quantitas

RAREFACTION
rarefactio

REALITY
realitas

REASON
ratio (usu.), causa (rar.), *see also* dictamen rationis
reden

REBIRTH
wedergeboorte

RECOLLECTION
reminiscentia

See memory. I have assumed that *recordari* corresponds to *reminiscentia* rather than to *memoria*.

RECONSTITUTION
redintegratio

REFUGE FOR IGNORANCE
asylum ignorantiae
toevlucht der onwetenheid

REGARD
contemplari

RELATION
relatio, respectus
betrekking

RELIGION
religio
godsdienst

REMEDIES
remedia

REMORSE
conscientiae morsus
knaging van 't geweten

The translation of *conscientiae morsus* is quite controversial. See Bidney 1, 4, 195-204. Some translators have been guided by the usual meaning of the term (White: *remorse*). Others have been influenced by Spinoza's definition (Elwes: *disappointment*). Nietzsche (*The Geneology of Morals* II, xv) saw Spinoza's definition at II/195 as deflationary (in the manner of Bierce's *Devil's Dictionary*), as expressing the view that if good and evil are fictions, there is nothing more to the sting of conscience than a disappointed expectation. I agree that to render *conscientiae morsus* by disappointment would be a mistake, but am influenced mainly by the considerations in the note at II/ 195/20. See also *repentance*.

REPENTANCE
poenitentia
berouw

As Spinoza sometimes defines *poenitentia* (e.g., at II/163), *lack of self-esteem* seems appropriate. Elsewhere (e.g., at II/197) *repentance* is clearly required. For the sake of consistency I have stuck to the latter term. Perhaps we have another deflationary definition in the first occurrence (cf. *remorse*). But the variation is puzzling. In the KV Spinoza draws a distinction between *knaging* (= *conscientiae morsus*?) and *berouw* (= *poenitentia*) which follows Descartes' distinction between *remords de conscience* and *repentir* (PA 177, 191), but which does not, so far as I can see, correspond to any distinction in English.

REPORT
auditus
hooren zeggen

In Curley 2, 30ff., I argued that *report* was preferable to the more literal *hearing* or *hearsay* in that it does not suggest a limitation to things heard rather than read, and that it does suggest a belief based on authority alone. Interesting in this connection is Descartes' gloss on a passage in the First Meditation in his *Conversation with Burman*, and the commentary in Cottingham, 3, 53-54. See also the exchange between Ariew and Cottingham in *Studia Cartesiana* 1 (1979): 185-188.

REPUBLIC
res publica

REPUTATION
fama

RESPECT
respectus

REST
quies, *see also* motus et quies
rust, stilte
  The Cartesian doctrine (AT XI, 40) is that rest is not merely the privation of motion, but a quality which must be atributed to a portion of matter while it remains in the same place. Spinoza apparently accepts this doctrine.

RESTRAIN
coercere

REVELATION
revelatio
openbaring
  Reveal also translates *manifestare*.

REVERENCE
reverentia

REWARD
praemium, pretium
beloning, loon

RIDICULE
boerterij
  Perhaps, as Voss suggests, *boerterij* in KV II, 11, represents the PA's *jocus* (= *raillerie*). But Spinoza seems to make no distinction between *boerterij* and *bespotting* (cf. Pléiade, 1383), whereas Descartes does make a distinction between *mocquerie* and *raillerie* (cf. *Passions of the Soul* III, 178-181), the latter being a characteristic of the *honnête homme*. If *boerterij* in the KV is the same affect as *jocus* in E, then Spinoza has reversed his negative evaluation of *boerterij*. More likely they are not equivalent.

RIGHT
jus, rectus
recht

RULE
regula
regel

RULER
regeerder

SADNESS
tristitia
droefheid
  Elwes, Shirley: *pain*; White: *sorrow*. I reject *pain* because II/149/4ff. seems to dictate *pain* as a translation of *dolor* and something less tied to a specific sensory stimulation for *tristitia*. These choices are also influenced by PA 94. *Sorrow* seems a reasonable alternative.

SALT
sal

SALVATION
salus
heil
  Classically, *salus* means *health, welfare, safety*. But (except in the phrase *salus publica*) Spinoza seems always to use it in the sense it acquired in the Christian tradition.

SANCTUARY OF IGNORANCE
asylum ignorantiae

SATISFACTION
acquiescentia
vergenoeging
  When *acquiescentia* occurs alone, *satisfaction* generally seems satisfactory. When it occurs in the phrase *acquiescentia in se ipso*, *self-esteem* (q.v.) seems better.

SCHOLASTICS
scholastici

654

SCIENCE
scientia
wetenschap, kennis
  See also knowledge

SCORN
despectus
  Elwes: *disparagement*; White: *contempt*.
Contempt is a possible classical meaning, but its use earlier for *dedignatio* excludes its use here. *Disparagement*
seems too mild, both for classical
usage and Spinoza's definition. If there
were a noun for the verb *to despise*, that
would be the natural choice. But *scorn*
may suggest the element of hatred involved in this species of disdain.

SCRIPTURE
scriptura
schriftuur

SEDITION
seditio

SEEDS
semina

SEEK
  See appetitus

SELF-DEPRECIATION
strafbare nederigheid
  As Wolf suggested, *strafbare nederigheid* very probably represents *abjectio*, for
which I have used *despondency* in E, a
debatable choice defended elsewhere.
In the KV the emphasis is on the intellectual aspect rather than on the af-
fective. *Abjectio* was the term used by
the Latin translator of Descartes for
bassesse (= *humilité vicieuse*, PA 159).
Wolf has *culpable humility*, which is a
good literal translation of the Dutch.
But if the Dutch is itself a translation
we need not be bound by it. It has the
disadvantage of suggesting that *strafbare nederigheid* is a species of *nederigheid*, which it can't be, and of suggesting that Spinoza thinks that blame
may sometimes be legitimate, which is
doubtful (cf. II/81/32, I/75/14).

SELF-ESTEEM
acquiescentia in se ipso
  The Latin represents Descartes' *satisfaction de soi-même* at PA 190, so
White's *self-satisfaction* was quite reasonable. But it has acquired negative
connotations which are inappropriate.
Elwes' *self-approval* seems an acceptable
alternative.

SELF-ESTEEM, LEGITIMATE
edelmoedigheid
  Edelmoedigheid probably represents
generositas in KV II, 8, but its definition
is so different from that of *generositas* in
E that the two terms should not be
rendered by the same English term.
Nevertheless both *edelmoedigheid* as defined in KV and *generositas* as defined
in E would be traits of Aristotle's
"great-souled man." See *nobility*.

SELF-LOVE
philautia

SENSATION, SENSE, SENSE PERCEPTION
sensatio
gevoel, zin

SENSE, COMMON
sensus communis
  In Aristotle (*De Anima*, 426b8-
427a16), a faculty by which the soul
discriminates between the perceptions
of the different senses. In Descartes,
sometimes the term is used in an Aristotelian sense (*Dioptrique* AT VI, 109;
Regulae AT X, 414), sometimes it is
identified with the power of imagination (*Meditations* AT VII, 32).

SENSELESS
  See stupor

SENSUAL PLEASURE
libido, *see also* meretrix
zinnelijkheid
  For comment *see* lust.

SEPARATE
amovere

SERVANT
  See servitas
dienaar

SEVERITY
saevitia

SHAME; SENSE OF SHAME, SHAMELESS-
  NESS
pudor; verecundia; impudentia
beschaamdheid, schaamte;
  onbeschaamdheid
  Spinoza distinguishes between the
sadness we feel at being blamed by
others for something we have done
(*pudor*) and a fear of being blamed
which would prevent us from doing
something shameful (*verecundia*). Elwes
and White used *shame* and *modesty* to
reflect this distinction, but *modesty* has
connotations I preferred to avoid.
  See also disgraceful.
  So far as I can see, Spinoza intends
no distinction between *beschaamdheid*
and *schaamte* in the KV.

SHAPE
figura
gedaante

SICKNESS OF MIND
aegritudo animi

SIGN
  See significatio

SIMILARITY
similaritas
gelijkheid

SIMPLICITY
simplicitas
eenvoudigheid

SIN
peccatum
zonde

SINGULAR
singularis
bijzonder

SIZE
magnitudo, *see also* moles

SKEPTIC
scepticus
twijfelaar

SKILL
ars

SLEEP
somnus

SMELL
odor

SOBRIETY
sobrietas

SOCIETY
societas

SOCINIANS
Sociniani

SOFT
mollis

SOLIDIFICATION
consistentia

SOLIDITY
firmitudo

SOMETHING
Iet

SON OF GOD
filius Dei

SORROW
verdriet

SOUL
anima
ziel
  See also mind and animate. Since *ziel*
is the term which always represents *anima* and usually represents *mens* as well,
in contemporary Dutch translations of
Spinoza's works, there is no way of
knowing what Latin term *ziel* represents in the KV. But Giancotti Boscherini's results incline me to translate
as if it represents *anima*.

SOUND
sanus

SPACE
spatium

SPECIES
species
gedaante

SPEED
celeritas
snelheid (PP), gezwindheid (E)

SPIRIT
animus
See also mind.

SPIRIT OF NITER
spiritus nitri

SPIRITS, ANIMAL
spiritus animales
geesten, dierlijke

SPIRITUAL
spiritualis

STANDARD
norma

STATE
status, civitas
stand

When *state* represents *status*, *condition* would be a plausible alternative. When it represents *civitas*, it refers to a political entity.

STEAL
stelen

STOICS
stoici

STORY
historia

STRENGTH OF CHARACTER
fortitudo
moed?

Elwes: *strength of character*; White: *fortitude*. Either is possible from a classical point of view, but Elwes' seems preferable from the standpoint of generality since *animositas* (= *tenacity?*) and *generositas* (= *nobility?*) are both species of *fortitudo*. Cf. Wolfson 1, 2:218-220. One can only conjecture that *moed* represents *fortitudo* in the *Short Treatise*, but the emphasis there on manliness fits well with that conjecture.

STRIVING
conatus
poging, trachten

Elwes, White: *endeavor*. The term *conatus* is often left untranslated in the secondary literature. There is much to be said for this, since any translation will be contentious and potentially misleading. *Endeavor* is one classical meaning of *conatus*, along with *effort*, *exertion*, *struggle*, *attempt*, etc. (LS). I prefer *striving* only for stylistic reasons. The real question is whether *conatus* should not be rendered by *tendency*, also a classical meaning of *conatus*. In favor of *tendency* is the fact that *conatus* is a central concept in Spinozistic-Cartesian physics, where the *conatus ad motum* refers to the tendency of things to 'obey' the principle of inertia (cf. I/ 206, 229 and in Descartes, *Principles of Philosophy* III, 56) with no implication of there being any psychic state present. Against *tendency* is the fact that Spinoza deliberately uses a term which he is aware will suggest the presence of a psychic state (cf. I/229). In any case I think the *conatus* by which *each* thing 'strives' to persevere in its being is best regarded as a metaphysical generalization of physical principle of inertia. For a discussion of its historical antecedents see Wolfson 1, II, 195-204. For a discussion of the concept's relations to other concepts in the seventeenth-century physics and a critique of some recent interpretations see Rice 1. *See also* animate.

STRONG
See fortitudo

STRUCTURE
fabrica

SUBJECT
subjectum
onderwerp, subject (Ep.)

In the KV *subjectum* sometimes occurs untranslated (but only in footnotes).

SUBSTANCE
substantia
zelfstandigheid

Spinoza's central definition of *substantia*, because of its formal similarity to scholastic definitions, is apt to suggest that the relation of modes to substance is the inherence of predicates in a subject. Both Gueroult (1, 1:44-64) and Curley (3, 4-28), however, argue that the formal similarity is radically misleading.

SUPERNATURAL
supernaturalis

SUPERSTITION
superstitio

SURPRISE
verrassing

SUSPICION
suspicio

SYMPATHY
sympathia

SYNTHESIS
synthesis

TABLET
tabula

TASTE
sapor

TELESCOPE
telescopium

TEMPORARY
tijdelijk

TEMPERAMENT
ingenium

TENACITY
animositas
kloekmoedigheid

Elwes and Shirley have *courage*, which is certainly one classical meaning of *animositas* (the English cognate, however, comes from Ecclesiastical Latin). But Spinoza regards presence of mind in danger, along with moderation and sobriety, as species of *animositas*. White has *strength of mind*, which

has appropriate generality, but which I reject because I have used *strength of character* for *fortitudo*. *Self-control* is possible, but *tenacity* seems to suggest better the element of striving for self-preservation. See Wolfson 1, II, 218-220. The decision to use *tenacity* for *kloekmoedigheid* and *stoutheid* in KV is based on the fact that *kloekmoedigheid* is the term most often used for *animositas* in the NS version of E and that *stoutheid* seems to be used equivalently to *kloekmoedigheid* in KV. See also *strength of character*.

TERM
terminus, vocabulum

TEXTURE
textura

THANKFULNESS
gratia
dankbarheid

THEOLOGY
theologia
theologie, *see also* godgeleerde

THIEF
dief

THING
res
zaak

THOUGHT
cogitatio
denking

It is sometimes said that *thought* is a misleading translation of *cogitatio*, since the latter term was traditionally used to cover a wider range of activities of consciousness than the former. See Anscombe and Geach 1, xlvii. Against this it is argued that Latin usage was never as wide as that found in Descartes and that Descartes was consciously extending existing usage. See Kenny 1, 68-69. Spinoza seems to regard Cartesian usage as needing explanation. See I/145.

Note that *think* sometimes translates

sentire and *gevoelen* (though *thought* never translates *sensatio* or *gevoeling*).

TIME
tempus

TIMIDITY
timor

    Elwes: *timidity*; White: *fear. See also* fear.

TO BE TORN
conflictari

TOTALITY
verzameling

TRACE
vestigium

TRANSFORMATION
transformatio

TRANSGRESSION
delictum

TRANSMISSION
tradux

TREACHERY
perfidia

TREMBLING
tremor

TO BE TROUBLED
conflictari

TROUBLESOME
molestus

TRUST
fides

TRUTH
veritas
waarheid

UGLINESS
deformitas

UNCONDITIONALLY
    See absolutus

UNDERGO
    See passio

UNHOLY
profanus

UNION
    See unitas
    See eenheid

UNIQUE
    See unitas
    See eenheid

UNITY
unitas
eenheid

UNIVERSAL
universalis, notio universalis
algemeen

UNIVERSAL BEING
alwezen

UNIVERSE
universum
heelal

UNMANLY
    See mulier

UNJUST
    See injuria

USAGE
usus

USEFUL
    See utilitas
    See nut

VACILLATION OF MIND
fluctuatio animi
wankelmoedigheid

    Elwes has *vacillation of soul*, but the decision to use *mind* for *animus* excludes that. See *mind*. The definition given in E of *fluctuatio animi* is different from that given in KV of *wankelmoedigheid*, but not enough different to warrant the use of different English terms.

VACUUM
vacuum
ijdel

VARIATION
variatio

659

VENERATION
veneratio

In Descartes *vénération* is a species of *estime* of an object considered as a free cause. Though Spinoza declines to define it at II/192, at II/180 he makes it a species of wonder at someone who far surpasses us in prudence, diligence or some other virtue.

VENGEANCE
vindicta

VERACITY, GOD'S
veracitas Dei

VERBAL
See verbum

VICE
vitium

VIRTUE
virtus
deugd

VISIBLE
visibilis

VISION OF GOD
visio Dei

VOLATILE
volatilis

VOLITION
See voluntas
See wil

WANT
See appetitus

I have generally used this as the verb corresponding to *appetite*.

WAY
modus, mos

WEALTH
divitiae
rijkdom

WEARINESS
taedium

WEIGHT
pondus

WELFARE, GENERAL
salus publica

WELL-BEING
welstand

The ambiguity noted in connection with *salus* and *heil* (see *salvation*) also seems to characterize *welstand*. In some contexts *well-being* or *welfare* seems clearly indicated (e.g., at I/104-105). In others *salvation* is a serious alternative (e.g., at I/80, 88, 89). I have opted for *well-being*, but with misgivings. See also the note at I/11.

WELL-WISHING
benevolentia

WHOLE
universus
geheel

WILL
voluntas
wil

Generally the distinction between particular acts of volition and the general faculty of will is marked in Latin by the *volitio/voluntas* pair and in Dutch by *willing/wil*. For an exception, see I/82/9.

WISDOM
sapientia
wijsheid

WOMAN
mulier

WONDER
admiratio
verwondering

White: *astonishment*. But this seems too strong. Occasionally *admiratio* is used in the sense of its English cognate (e.g., at II/273). *See also* surprise.

WONDER, FOOLISH
stupor
Cf. Gueroult 1, 1:396n.

WORD
verbum, nomen, vocabulum
woord

WORLD
mundus
wereld

WORSHIP OF GOD
cultus Dei
Gods dienst

WRONG
injuria

WRONG
pravus

Latin–Dutch–English

ABJECTIO; ABJECTUS
[PA 159: bassesse]
neerslachigheid (E), strafbare nederigheid (KV); nederig, neerslachtig
despondency (E), self-depreciation (KV); despondent, II/*198*, 199, 250, 251, 252, 272

ABSOLUTUS; ABSOLUTE
volstrekt (usu.), volkomen (occ.); volstrektelijk, volkomenlijk, ganselijk (rar.)
absolute; absolutely, unconditionally, I/148, 151, 161, 163, 182, 183, 217, 219, 224, 238, 247, 249, 253, 254, 255, 266, 267, II/11, 18, 38, 39, 45, 46, 49, 54, 61, 62, 65, 66, 67, 69, 70, 72, *92*, 116, 117, 129, 162, 225, 226, 230, 233, 256, 277, 279, 283, 295, IV/8, 13, 43, 47, 66, 127, 147

ABSTRACTUS; ABSTRACTE
aftrekkig; abstractlijk (Ep.)
abstract, abstractly, I/132, II/11, 28, 29, 34, 35, 36, 59, 135, 257, IV/9, 56, 58, 61, 91

ACCIDENS; ACCIDENTALIS
toeval; toevallig
accident; accidental; I/150, 154, 165, 203, 236, 237, 249, 255, 269, II/13, 235, IV/11, *13*, 14

ACCIDENS, PER
bij (door) toeval
accidental(ly), II/210. *See also* causa per accidens.

ACCIDENS REALE
zakelijk toeval
real accident, I/249, 281, IV/65

ACQUIESCENTIA; ACQUIESCERE
gerustheid; in gerust wezen
satisfaction, peace; to be satisfied, II/193, 267, 276, 283, 288, 297, 300, 304, 308

ACQUIESCENTIA IN SE IPSO
[PA 190: satisfaction de soi-même]
gerustheid op (in) zich zelf (E), edelmoedigheid (KV?)
self-esteem, II/*163*, 179, 183, *196*, 197, 198, 248, 249, 253

ACTIO; AGERE; AGENS
doening, werking, bedrijf (rar.), werk (KV); werken, doen; doender
action; to act (usu.), to do (occ.), to be active (rar.); agent, I/175, 182, 183 221, 243, 259, 273, II/24, 25, 26, 46, 61, 78, 79, 84, 85, 87, 97, 105, 117, 135, 136, 137, 138, *139*, 140, 141, 142, 143, 144, 145, 163, 183, 187, 188, 206, 207, 214, 222, 226, 246, 254, 255, 266, 281, 283, 289, 291, 302, 306

ACTUALITAS; ACTUALIS; ACTU
dadelijkheid (usu.), werkelijkheid (CM); dadelijk; werkelijk, in der daad, dadelijk
actuality; actual; actually, I/185, 190, 191, 230, 239, 244, 252, II/20, 22, 50, 62, 71, 72, 75, 89, 91, 92, 94, 96, 104, 108, 128, 144, 162, 176, 204, 225, 294, 295, 296, *298* IV/59

AFFECTUS CONTRARIUS
strijdige hartstocht
opposite affect, II/*209, 210*, 214, 215, 304, 305

AFFECTUS PRIMARIUS, PRIMITIVUS
voorname, eerste en oorspronkelijke hartstocht
primary, primitive affect, II/149, 186, 189, 192, 203

AFFIRMATIO; AFFIRMARE; AFFIRMATIVUS
bevestiging; bevestigen; bevestiglijk
affirmation; to affirm; affirmative, I/132, 234, 277, 278, II/15, 20, 33, 34, 35, 49, 129, 130, 132, 133, IV/130

AFFINGERE
verdichten
to ascribe fictitiously, I/227, II/20, 21, 49

AMBITIO; AMBITIOSUS
roemzucht; roemzuchtig
ambition; ambitious, II/*162*, 164, 165, 170, 185, *202*, 203, 243, 273, 283, 288

AMICITIA; INIMICITIA; AMICUS
vriendschap; vijandschap; vriend
friendship; enmity; friend, II/166, 188, 236, 263, 269, 270, 271, 273, 288, 294, IV/5, 7, 69

AMOR; AMARE, AMASIA
[PA 56, 79-85: amour]
liefde; beminnen (usu.), liefhebben (occ.), lieven (occ.); vrister
love; to love; lover, I/235, 247, 264, II/7, 40, 71, 85, 136, 151, 152, 153, 155, 156, 157, 158, 159, 160, 162, 163, 164, 165, 166, 169, 171, 172, 173, 174, 175, 176, 177, 178, 184, 185, 186, 189, *192*, 193, 222, 242, 243, 245, 252, 269, 271, 272, 281, 283, 287, 289, 294

AMOR DEI (SUBJ. GEN.)
Gods liefde
God's love, I/264, II/291, 292, 302, 303

AMOR DEI (OBJ. GEN.), ERGA DEUM
Gods liefde, liefde tot God

love of, toward God, I/158, II/7, 290, 291, 292, *300*, 301, 302, 303, 304, 307, 308

ANALOGIA
evenredenheid, gelijkvormigheid
proportion, measure, I/162, 263, IV/8

ANALYSIS
ontbinding
analysis, I/129, IV/48, 49

ANGELUS
engel
angel, I/161, 179, 188, 262, 267, 275

ANIMA; ANIMATUS
ziel; bezielt
soul; animate, I/132, 144, 146, *150*, 188, 260, 275, 276, 277, 278, II/11, 15, 22, 23, 25, 28, 29, 31, 32, 96, 117, 187, 278, 279, IV/6, 77

ANIMA SIVE MENS
ziel of geest, II/278

ANIMA ALTRIX
voedende ziel
nutritive soul, I/259

ANIMA INTELLECTIVA
verstandelijke ziel
intellective soul, I/259

ANIMA SENSITIVA
gevoelige ziel
sensitive soul, I/259

ANIMA VEGETATIVA
groeijige ziel
vegetative soul, I/259

ANIMOSITAS
[PA 171: courage]
kloekmoedigheid (usu.), stoutmoedigheid (rar.), stoutheid (KV)
tenacity, II/*188*, 203, 262, 265, 288, 306, 307

ANIMUS
gemoed
mind (usu.), spirit (occ.), intention (occ.), disposition (rar.), I/141, 159, 249, 273, II/5, 6, 7, 18, 29, 30, 74, 93, 102, 135, 136, 142, 158, 173, 174, 183, 201, 222, 244, 246, 250,

251, 252, 264, 269, 270, 276, 288,
289, 307, 308, IV/39, 73, 151, 159

ANTIPATHIA
afkeerlijkheid, antipatie
antipathy, I/197, II/152

A POSTERIORI
van achteren, afteren
a posteriori, I/159, 250, II/54

APPETITUS; APPETERE
begeerte (CM, EI), lust (EIII-V); begeren (usu.), betrachten (occ.)
appetite; to want (usu.), to seek (occ.),
I/278, II/78, 80, 138, 143, 144, 147,
148, 161, 166, 167, 168, 169, 186,
187, *190*, 199, 203, 207, 210, 223,
263, 283, 289, IV/128, 129

A PRIORI
van voren
a priori, I/250, II/54

APTUS
bekwaam
capable, II/10, 11, 97, 103, 142, 297,
304, 305

ARS
kunst
art, skill, ingenuity, II/6, 9, 81, 142,
143, 269, 274, 277

ASINUS (BURIDANI)
de Buridansche ezel
Buridan's ass, I/277, 278, II/133, 135

ASSENSUS; ASSENTIRI
toestemming; toestemmen
assent; to assent, I/146, 173, 174, 175,
239, II/23, 24, 25, 132, 133

ASYLUM IGNORANTIAE
toevlucht, schuilplaats, der onwetenheid
refuge for, sanctuary of, ignorance,
II/81, IV/12

ATOMUS
ondelig
atom, I/*181*, 190, 191

ATTRIBUTUM; TRIBUERE
toeeigening (usu.), eigenschap (KV),
sometimes untrans., toevoeging
(rar.); toeeigenen

attribute; to attribute, I/145, 150, 158,
160, 161, 163, 185, 237, 238, 239,
240, 244, 248, 250, 253, 254, 255,
257, 258, 259, 261, 266, 269, 273,
274, 275, 280, II/29, *45*, 46, 47, *48*,
49, 51, 52, 55, 56, 60, 62, 64, 65,
67, 68, 69, 71, 72, 82, 86, 88, 89,
90, 91, 93, 94, 98, 108, 109, 121,
127, 141, 143, 144, 190, 213, 228,
239, 267, IV/5, *7*, 11, 13, 14, 36,
41, 44, 45, *46*, 47, 127, 133, 148

ATTRIBUTUM DEI
toeeigening van God, sometimes
untranslated
attribute of God, I/158, 238, 239, 244,
248, 253, 255, 257, 259, 274, 275,
II/29, 64, 65, 66, 86, 88, 89, 90, 91,
122, 146, 267, IV/36, 124

AUDACIA; AUDAX
[PA 171: hardiesse]
stoutheid; stout
daring; daring, II/*179*, *201*, 262, 280

AUDITUS
gehoor (TdIE, Ep), horen zeggen (KV)
report, hearing (nontech.), II/10, 12,
28, IV/77

AUTOMATON
zelfsbewegsel, zelfsbeweegbar
automaton, II/18, 32

AUXILIA (INTELLECTUS, IMAGINATIONIS)
hulpmiddelen (van het verstand, van
d'inbeelding)
aids (of the intellect, of the imagination), II/15, 37, IV/57, 58

AVARITIA; AVARUS
gierigheid, gulzigheid; gierigaard
greed; greedy (man), II/7, 79, 170,
185, *202*, 203, 210, 243, 288

AVERSIO; AVERSARI
[PA 80: aversion]
afkeer; afkeer hebben
aversion; to be averse to, avoid, be repelled by, II/162, 163, *193*, 223, 258

AXIOMA
kundigheid (TdIE, and usu. E), gemene Kennis (PP), geloofspreuk (rar.
E), gemene kundigheid (Ep.)

axiom, I/127, *151*, 201, II/12, 28, 34, 50, 120, 139, IV/10, 11, 13, 40, 43, 72

BEATITUDO; BEATUS
zaligheid (usu. in E), gelukzaligheid (PP, EII); zalig (usu.), gelukzalig (CM)
blessedness; blessed, I/158, 159, 264, 271, II/84, 135, 225, 250, 267, 277, 280, 300, 301, 303, 307, 308, IV/127, 131

BENEFICIUM; BENEFACERE
weldaad; weldoen
benefit, favor; to do good to, benefit, II/157, 161, 169, 172, 173, 179, 236, 248, 252, 262, 263, 271

BENEPLACITUM (DEI)
(God's) welbehagen
(God's) good pleasure, I/201, II/76, 77

BENEVOLENTIA
[PA 81: bienveillance]
goedwilligheid
benevolence, II/161, *200*

BONI, SUB RATIONE
in opzicht van 't goede, onder schijn van goed
for the sake of the good, for what seems good, I/278, II/76

BONUM, SUMMUM
het opperste goed
the greatest good, II/5, 8, 228, 234, 235, 236, 253, 273, 292

BONUS
goed
good (usu.), good fortune (rar.), I/235, 247, 248, 249, 264, 278, 279, II/5, 6, 7, 8, 76, 78, 81, 82, 83, 148, *170*, 179, 205, 208, *209*, *215*, 223, 224, 227, 228, 229, 230, 233, 237, 238, 239, 240, 241, 242, 253, 254, 255, 257, 259, 260, 261, 262, 266, 267, 268, 275, 276, 288, IV/130

BRUTUM (= ANIMALE IRRATIONALE)
stomme beest
lower animal, I/160, 247, 259, 260, II/26, 142, 187, 234, 236, 237, 262, 270

CALOR; CALIDUS
hitte; warm
heat; warm, II/81, IV/25, 28, 67, 68

CALX
kalk
lime, calx, IV/25, 65, 68

CAPTUS; CAPERE
verstand (PP, CM), bevatting (E, TdIE); verstaan
grasp, power of understanding; grasp, I/132, 190, 191, 243, 244, 254, II/6, 9, 33, 79, IV/129, 130

CARPERE
overhalen en uitmaken, berispen
to censure, find fault, II/137, 197, 252, 269

CASTITAS; CASTUS
kuisheid; zuiver en oprecht
chastity; pure, II/185, 203, IV/28

CASUS
geval
chance, II/81

CAUSA
oorzaak (usu.), reden (occ.)
cause (usu.), reason (occ.), ground (occ.), I/150, 154, 155, 156, 157, 158, 159, 161, 164, 165, 169, 170, 172, 173, 176, 179, 180, 196, 197, 201, 220, 221, 222, 226, 227, 229, 236, 237, 238, 240, 241, 243, 250, 262, 277, 280, II/10, 11, 15, 20, 22, 24, 25, 26, 27, 28, 32, 34, 36, 46, 47, 48, 49, 50, 51, 52, 53, 63, 64, 67, 68, 69, 70, 73, 74, 75, 77, 78, 80, 85, 88, 89, 90, 92, 93, 96, 120, 122, 125, 129, 131, 137, 138, 142, 154, 163, 166, 167, 190, 191, 192, 209, 210, 213, 215, 261, 280, 281, 284, 286, 289, 290, 291, 292, 293, 295, 300, 301, 302, IV/9, 11, 14, 20, 32, 53, 61, 62, 65, 68, 77, 91, 93, 128, 130

CAUSA ADAEQUATA
evenmatige oorzaak
adequate cause, II/*139*, 140, 212, 213, 299

209, 210, 211, 212, 213, 214, 215, 216, 219, 221, 222, 223, 224, II/97, 99, 100, 101, 142

CEREBRUM
hersenen (usu.), brein (occ.)
brain, I/149, 160, II/21, 31, 82, 83, 130, 132, 278, 280

CERTITUDO; CERTUS
zekerheid; zeker
certainty; certain, I/128, 129, 141, 142, 143, 144, 145, 146, 147, 148, 149, 151, 152, 153, 155, 166, 172, 174, 201, 207, 209, 234, 244, 247, 267, II/5, 6, 8, 11, 12, 13, 15, 18, 23, 28, 29, 30, 32, 38, 39, 46, 50, 52, 54, 57, 58, 68, 70, 72, 78, 84, 96, 124, 131, 134, 155, 194, 228, 246, 257, 278, 279, 287, 300, IV/40, 132

CHIMAERA
verdichtzel (CM, Ep.), 't gedrocht (TdIE), untranslated (KV)
chimaera, I/82, 233, 240, 241, 242, II/20, IV/45

CHRISTIANI
christenen
Christians, IV/39

CHRISTUS
Christus
Christ, II/262

CHYMIA; CHEMICUS
stoffscheiding; stoffscheider, stoffscheidig
chemistry; chemist, chemical, IV/48, 49, 50, 51

CIRCUMSTANTIA
omstandigheid
circumstance, I/221, II/36, 167, 168

CIVITAS; CIVIS; CIVILIS
staat (usu.), burgerschap (rar.); burger; burgerlijk
state (usu.), community; citizen; civil, II/9, 136, 236, 237, 238, 241, 244, 248, 264, 265, 270

CLARUS ET DISTINCTUS; CLARE ET DISTINCTE

klaar en onderscheiden(lijk); klaar en onderscheid
clear and distinct; clearly and distinctly, I/132, 142, 144, 145, 146, 153, 157, 168, 171, 172, 173, 179, 190, 192, 196, 200, 233, 238, 243, 247, 260, 261, II/24, 25, 26, 28, 29, 30, 34, 36, 38, 39, 50, 113, 114, 117, 119, 120, 125, 127, 139, 227, 248, 249, 255, 276, 279, 282, 283, 287, 289, 290, 294, 297, 298, 304, IV/13, 59, 130

CLASSIS
schok (CM), stand (E), bende (Ep)
class, I/234, 235, II/175, IV/57

CLEMENTIA
goedertierenheid
mercy, II/188, 201

COACTUS
gedwongen
compelled, II/46, 61, 72, 224

COERCERE
intomen, bedwingen
to restrain, II/277, 285, 287, 307, 308

COGITATIO; COGITARE
denking (usu.), gedacht (rar.); denken
thought; to think, I/132, 143, 144, 145, 146, 147, 148, 149, 152, 153, 154, 155, 156, 157, 160, 173, 175, 225, 229, 233, 234, 235, 244, 245, 246, 250, 257, 269, 270, 277, 279, 280, II/6, 7, 9, 22, 23, 26, 28, 30, 38, 45, 65, 66, 72, 85, 86, 87, 88, 89, 90, 92, 93, 94, 107, 108, 109, 129, 130, 132, 135, 141, 144, 148, 162, 188, 203, 204, 207, 208, 274, 278, 279, 280, 281, 283, 286, 288, 295, 306, IV/5, 6, 10, 13, 40, 45, 57, 78, 132

COGNITIO; COGNOSCERE
kennis; kennen
knowledge; to know, I/127, 132, 133, 144, 148, 151, 158, 162, 226, 227, 229, 244, 262, 263, 266, 275, II/8, 11, 13, 19, 26, 29, 30, 34, 36, 37, 38, 46, 50, 57, 74, 84, 89, 92, 93, 95, 97, 107, 108, 110, 116, 117,

288, 289, 292, 293, 301, 307, IV/7, 14

COMMUNIS NATURAE ORDO
gemene ordening (loop) de natuur
common order of nature, II/114, 115, 213, 252, 268

COMPARATIO; COMPARARE
vergelijking; vergelijken, stellen, verkrijgen
comparison; to compare, constitute, acquire, I/162, 234, 244, 245, 262, II/7, 165, 179, 183, 204, 207, 208, 214, 220, 231, 234, 242, 271, 274, 280, 283, 293, IV/128

COMPOSITIO; COMPONERE; COMPOSITUS
zamenzetting; te zamen zetten (maken); te zamen gezet
composition; to compose; composite, I/227, 258, II/24, 25, 26, 32, 99, 100, 101, 102, 103, 111, 189, 203, IV/50, 56, 67, 68

COMPROBARE
bewijzen, bevestigen
to confirm, 'confirm,' IV/21, 29, 30

CONATUS, CONAMEN (II/153); CONARI
poging; pogen (usu.), trachten (occ.), betrachten (rar.)
striving; to strive, I/206, 229, 248, II/8, 79, 146, 147, 148, 150, 153, 155, 156, 158, 161, 162, 164, 165, 166, 167, 168, 169, 170, 171, 172, 174, 182, 183, 186, 188, 189, 190, 199, 200, 214, 221, 222, 223, 224, 225, 226, 227, 248, 255, 266, 276, 292, 296, 297

CONCATENATIO; CONCATENARE
samenschakeling; samenschakelen
connection; to connect, II/23, 30, 34, 35, 77, 107, 141, 281, 287, 293, 305, IV/77

CONCEPTUS; CONCIPERE; INCONCEPTIBILIS
bevatting, begrip; bevatten, begrijpen; onbevattelijk
concept; to conceive; inconceivable, I/132, 145, 148, 150, 151, 155, 157, 162, 192, 240, 244, 245, 251, 257, 258, 264, 269, II/11, 20, 21, 23, 24,

25, 26, 27, 28, 29, 33, 34, 35, 45, 46, 47, 50, 52, 55, 56, *84*, 85, 86, 89, 98, 109, 126, 127, 128, 130, 131, 133, 212, 216, 257, 261, 265, 274, 279, 282, 293, 294, 295, 296, 298, 299, IV/7, 10, 13, 43, 44, 45, 46, 55, 132

CONCORDIA; CONCORDITER
eendracht; eendrachtiglijk
harmony; harmoniously, II/237, 241, 270, 271, 272

CONCURSUS DEI; CONCURRERE
medewerking, Gods; samenlopen
God's concurrence; to concur, I/181, 200, 201, 202, 243, 247, 262, 263, 273, 274, 275, 280

CONDENSATIO
verdikking
condensation, I/186

CONFIRMARE
bevestigen
to confirm, IV/17, 24, 31, 50, 66

CONDENSATIO
condensation, I/186

CONFLICTARI
bestrijden werden
to be torn, troubled, II/143, 144, 173, 178, 214, 220, 231, 287, 293, 305

CONFUSIO; CONFUNDERE; CONFUSUS; CONFUSE
verwarring; verwarren (usu.), vermengen (rar.); verward; verwardelijk
confusion; to confuse; confused; confusedly, I/144, 145, 164, 175, 182, 234, 245, II/11, 20, 21, 24, 25, 26, 28, 29, 30, 39, 49, 72, 78, 81, 82, 83, 97, 113, 114, 117, 121, 122, 123, 140, 147, 203, 204, 211, 265, 293, 298, IV/8, 9, 61, 77

CONNEXIO
samenknoping
connection, I/273, 274, II/36, 89, 90, 92, 108, 191, 281

CONSCIENTIA; CONSCIUS; INSCIUS, SUI
meewustigheid, medeweting, geweten,

medegeweten; meewustig, bewust,
kundig; onkundig van zich zelf
consciousness; conscious, aware of; unconscious of oneself, I/149, II/18,
21, 78, 117, 143, 147, 148, 163,
190, 207, 215, 216, 223, 259, 276,
285, 300, 301, 305, 308

CONSCIENTIAE MORSUS
[PA 177: remords de conscience]
knaging van 't geweten
remorse, II/155, 195, 246

CONSENSUS
toestemming, stemming
consent, II/192, 238

CONSERVATIO; CONSERVARE
behoudenis, behoudening; onderhouden, behouden, bewaren
preservation; to preserve, I/145, 157,
161, 163, 165, 166, 169, 170, 172,
188, 191, 200, 242, 243, 247, 248,
252, 255, 262, 263, 264, 267, 269,
270, 274, II/7, 102, 147, 151, 155,
168, 174, 188, 190, 213, 215, 222,
223, 224, 225, 226, 227, 238, 239,
240, 241, 251, 253, 256, 261, 264,
265, 268, 273, 274, IV/129

CONSISTENTIA; CONSISTERE; CONSISTENS
bestandigheid; bestandig worden; bestandig
coming to rest, solidification; to come
to rest, solidify; solid, IV/17, 18,
28, 29, 31, 65

CONSTANTIA
standvastigheid, bestandigheid
constancy, I/179, 243

CONSTERNATIO
verslagenheid (usu.), verbaasdheid
(rar.)
consternation, II/171, 180, 201

CONSTITUTIO; CONSTITUERE
gesteltheid (usu.), gesteltenis (occ.);
stellen
constitution, condition; to constitute,
II/45, 51, 52, 104, 106, 115, 153,
189, 190, 204, 211

CONSUETUDO
gewoonte, gemeenschap

custom, association, II/107, 197, 269,
273, 274

CONTEMPLARI
aanschouwen
regard (usu.), contemplate (rar.),
II/104, 105, 106, 112, 114, 291

CONTEMPTUS; CONTEMNERE
[PA 54: mépris]
versmading; versmaden, verachten
disdain; to disdain, II/136, 179, 180,
181, 192, 198, 244, 245, 247

CONTINGENTIA; CONTINGENS
gebeurlijkheid; gebeurlijk
contingency; contingent, I/155, *242*,
247, 261, 262, II/70, 71, *74*, 87,
115, 125, 126, 209, 217, 218, 219,
221, 284, IV/130

CONTINUUS; CONTINUO
gedurig; geduriglijk
continuous; continually, I/127, 130,
148, 170, 172, 179, 203, 204, 205,
206, 220, 221, 222, 228, 234, 250,
251, 252, 254, 255, 270, 276, II/58,
100, 165, 244, 274, 287, 303, 305,
IV/130, 149

CONTRADICTIO; CONTRADICTORIUM
tegenzeglijkheid; tegenstelling
contradiction; contradictory, I/162,
227, 233, II/19, 20, 48, 53, 56, 74,
256, IV/53

CONTRARIUS
strijdig, tegendelig
opposite, contrary, I/185, 204, 207,
208, 211, 216, 221, 222, 281, II/81,
143, *145*, 149, 153, 154, 185, 206,
212, 215, 222, 224, 229, 230, 231,
232, 269, 281, 287, 292

CONVENIENTIA; CONVENIRE
overeenkoming (usu.), overeenkomst;
overeenkomen
agreement; to agree, I/154, 162, 185,
235, 245, 246, II/12, 16, 17, 22, 47,
63, 82, *85*, 98, 110, 114, 116, 119,
124, 146, 206, 222, 223, 229, 230,
232, 268, 276, IV/50, 66

CORPUS; CORPOREUS
lichaam; lichamelijk

body; corporeal, I/132, *150*, 151, 152,
153, 167, 176, 177, 181, 182, 184,
185, 186, 187, 188, 189, 196, 198,
202, 203, 206, 207, 209, 210, 211,
212, 213, 214, 215, 216, 217, 218,
219, 220, 221, 222, 223, 224, 225,
260, *275*, 276, 281, II/11, 21, 22,
28, 31, 32, 33, 45, 53, 55, *57*, 58,
59, *84*, 86, 95, 96, 97, 98, 99, 100,
101, 102, 103, 104, 105, 109, 110,
111, 112, 113, 114, 119, 120, 121,
141, 142, 143, 144, 150, 162, 165,
189, 191, 215, 223, 278, 279, 280,
281, 282, 287, 293, 294, 295, IV/10,
29, 55, 60, 74, 77, 131

CORPUS HUMANUM
het menselijke lichaam
the human body, II/96, 97, 102, 103,
104, 105, 106, 107, 108, 110, 111,
112, 113, 114, 115, 119, 120, 121,
139, 141, 142, 143, 144, 148, 239,
240, 241, 244, 274, 295, 296, 298,
299, 300, 301, 304, 305, 306

CORPUSCULUM
lichaamtje
particle, I/220, 221, IV/68

CORRUPTIO; CORRUMPI; CORRUPTUS;
CORRUPTIBILIS
verderving, verdervenis; vergaan; be-
dorven; verderfelijk, vergankelijk
corruption; to be corrupted; corrupt;
corruptible, I/255, 276, II/31, 60,
82, 83, 115

CREATIO; CREATOR; CREATURA; CREARE;
CREATUS; CREABILIS
schepping; schepper; schepsel; scheppen; geschapen; schepbar
creation; creator; creature; to create;
created; creatable, I/143, 146, 161,
162, 163, 165, 166, 168, *170*, 172,
177, 179, 191, 201, 237, 238, 239,
240, 241, 242, 243, 248, 249, 250,
251, 252, 254, 255, 256, 263, 264,
267, *268*, 269, 270, 271, 272, 273,
274, 275, 276, 280, II/23, 27, 35,
50, 57, 62, 75, 76, 80, 82, 83, 93,
120, 261, IV/11, 14, 36, 129

CREATIO CONTINUA
gedurige schepping
continuous creation, I/170, 254, 273,
IV/129, 130

CRUDELITAS
wreedheid
cruelty, II/*173, 201*

CRYSTALLUS; CRYSTALLISARE
kristal; kristallig maken
crystal; to crystallize, IV/17, 23, 49

CULTUS DEI
Gods dienst
worship of God, II/79, 81

CUPIDITAS; CUPERE
[PA: désir]
begeerte; begeren
desire; to desire, I/132, 145, 166, 173,
256, 267, II/6, 8, 12, 71, 72, 79, 80,
85, 129, 130, *148*, 149, 151, 152,
160, 161, 164, 165, 167, 168, 169,
170, 183, 184, 185, 186, 187, 188,
189, 190, 192, 193, 199, 200, 201,
202, 203, 204, 220, 221, 225, 235,
242, 253, 254, 255, 256, 257, 258,
260, 261, 263, 265, 266, 267, 271,
275, 283, 297, IV/149, 150, 151

DAMNUM; DAMNUM INFERRE
schade; schade aandoen
injury; to injure, II/157, 162, 174, 201,
232, 234, 237, 238, 244

DECEPTIO; DECEPTOR
bedrog; bedrieger
deception; deceiver, I/145, 147, 148,
171, 172, II/28, 30

DECRETUM
besluit
decision, II/142, 143, *144*, 192, 197,
264, 265, 280

DECRETUM DEI
Gods besluit
God's decree, I/177, 179, 240, 241,
243, 263, 264, 265, 266, 267, 276,
II/62, 75, 136, IV/127, 128, 130

DEDIGNATIO
[PA 163; dédain]

verontwaardiging
contempt, II/*181*, 189, 192

DEDUCERE
afleiden (usu.), deduceren (rar.), uit-
trekken
deduce, I/153, 172, 227, 229, II/16,
23, 24, 36, 78, 97, 102, 128, 143,
153, 180, 212, 213, 235, 266, 279,
280, 287, 289, IV/91, 149

DEFINITIO; DEFINIRE; DEFINITUS
bepaling (usu.), beschrijving (KV), definitie (Ep.); bepalen (usu.), beschrijven (KV); bepaald
definition; to define, limit; definite,
I/127, 130, 158, 160, 163, 171, 203,
233, 235, 236, 239, II/34, 35, 36,
37, 38, 46, 50, 51, 60, 74, *92*, 145,
186, 190, 280, IV/8, 10, 13, 39, 40,
42, 43, 44, 47, 53, 54

DEFORMITAS
lelijkheid
ugliness, II/78, 81, 82, 83

DELIBERATIO
berading
deliberation, II/192

DELICIAE; DELECTARE; DELECTARI
(+ABL.)
geneugten; aangenaam aan . . . zijn,
vermaken, verheugen; vermak hebben (scheppen) in, z. verheugen over
pleasures; to please; to take pleasure
in, be pleased by, II/9, 82, 83, 138,
163, 165, 167, 168, 189, 244, 252,
253, 300

DELICTUM
kwaad
transgression, IV/131

DELIRIUM; DELIRARE; DELIRANS
spoorloosheid (usu.), suffing (occ.);
spoorloos zijn; spoorloos
madness; to be mad; mad, II/23, 24,
143, 159, 243, 271, IV/77

DEMONSTRATIO; DEMONSTRARE
betoging, bewijs; betogen, bewijzen
demonstration, to demonstrate, I/127,
128, 129, 130, 131, 141, 142, 202,
203, II/11, 17, 20, 23, 35, 138, 222,

296, 303, IV/8, 25, 29, 34, 39, 40,
44, 72, 77, 126, 133

DENOMINATIO
afnoeming, benaming
denomination, I/240

DENOMINATIO EXTRINSECA
uitwendige, uitterlijke afnoeming
extrinsic denomination, I/246, 250,
II/26, 36, 124, 203, IV/29

DENOMINATIO INTRINSECA
innerlijke afnoeming
intrinsic denomination, II/85, 124, 216

DEPENDENTIA; DEPENDERE; DEPENDENS
afhangelijkheid; afhangen; afhangig,
dependent
dependence; to depend; dependent,
I/142, 144, 153, 154, 197, 241, 242,
253, 266, 274, II/27, 46, 70, IV/36,
131

DESCRIPTIO
beschrijving
description, I/233, 236, IV/43

DESIDERIUM; DESIDERARE
[PA: regret (usu.), désir (occ.)]
verlangen, begeerte; begeren
longing; to long for, desire, I/248,
II/*168*, 170, 173, *199*, 200, 248

DESPECTUS; DESPICERE
[PA 55: dédain; 149, 150: mépris]
verachting, ongeachtheid; versmaden
scorn; to scorn, II/*160*, *195*, 196, 246,
265

DESPERATIO; DESPERARE
[PA 160: désespoir]
wanhoop; wanhopen
despair; to despair, II/155, *193*, 246,
288

DESTRUCTIO; DESTRUERE
verderf, vernietiging; vernietigen
destruction; to destroy, I/275, 276,
278, II/87, 145, 146, 147, 148, 151,
155, 156, 161, 162, 170, 175, 176,
208, 210, 273, 281, 282, 283, 292,
295

DETERMINATIO; DETERMINARE; DETERMINATUS
bepaling (E, KV, Ep.), afpaling (PP: *bepaling* regularly corrected to *afpaling* in errata); bepalen; bepaald
determination (usu.), direction (usu. in PP); to determine; determined, determinate, I/132, 164, 171, 173, 174, 196, 204, 207, 208, 211, 212, 213, 214, 215, 216, 234, 242, 244, 261, 273, 274, 277, 278, 279, 280, 281, II/10, 26, 28, 30, 31, 34, 37, 38, 39, 46, 58, 61, 65, 66, 68, 69, 70, 72, 74, 77, 84, 85, *92*, 93, 98, 99, 105, 111, 114, 115, 121, 129, 141, 143, 144, 146, 147, 163, 176, 180, 181, 185, 192, 203, 209, 225, 236, 249, 254, 273, 279, 283, 284, 288, 306, IV/9, 42, 47, 53, 55, 56, 57, 59, 60, 77, 129, 148

DEUS
God
God, I/145, 146, 147, 148, 149, *150*, 155, 158, 159, 160, 165, 166, 167, 168, 169, 170, 171, 178, 179, 188, 191, 200, 201, 237, 241, 243, 246, 247, 248, 249, 250, 251, 253, 254, 256, 257, 258, 259, 263, 266, 267, 270, 271, 272, 273, 274, 276, II/20, 26, 34, *45*, 49, 52, 53, 54, 56, 57, 58, 60, 61, 62, 63, 64, 65, 66, 67, 68, 69, 70, 71, 73, 74, 75, 76, 77, 78, 80, 83, 84, 86, 87, 89, 90, 92, 93, 94, 127, 128, 135, 136, 140, 141, 206, 213, 228, 235, 267, 270, 271, 272, 273, 274, 276, 291, 292, 293, 295, 296, 299, 300, 302, 306, 308, IV/7, 8, 10, 11, 14, 36, 127, 128, 130, 131

DEUS DECEPTOR
bedrieger God
deceiving God, I/147, 172, II/26, 30

DEUS SEU (SIVE) NATURA
God of natuur
God *or* Nature, II/206, 213

DEVOTIO
[PA 83: dévotion]
verloving, overgeving
devotion, II/180, *193*

DIABOLUS
duivel
devil, IV/129

DICTAMEN INTELLECTUS
gezeg van de verstand
dictate of the intellect, I/278

DICTAMEN RATIONIS
voorspelling, voorschrift van de reden
dictate of reason, II/188, 222, 223, 233, 235, 247, 250, 254, 257, 261, 264, 265, 283, 292

DIFFERENTIA
onderscheid, verscheidenheid
difference, I/203, IV/48

DISCORDIA
tweedracht
discord, II/241, 262, 271, 273

DISTINCTIO; DISTINGUERE; DISTINCTUS; DISTINCTE
onderscheid(ing); onderscheiden; onderscheiden; onderscheidelijk
distinction; to distinguish; distinct; distinctly, I/145, 237, 244, 257, 259, 266, II/17, 21, 28, 96, 97, 99, 100, 120, 121, 123, 181, 210, 211, 249, 285, IV/55

DISTINCTIO MODALIS
wijzige onderscheid
modal distinction, I/248, *257*, 258, II/59

DISTINCTIO RATIONIS
onderscheid van reden
distinction of reason, I/248, *258*, 259, 280, II/282

DISTINCTIO REALIS
zakelijke onderscheid
real distinction, I/146, *151*, 248, *257*, 258, II/33, 52, 59, IV/55

DISTINCTIO VERBIS
onderscheid door woorden
verbal distinction, I/248

DIVERSITAS; DIVERSUS
verscheidenheid; verscheiden
difference, diversity; different, I/245, II/12, 47, 48, 52, 74, 79, 90, 99,

117, 132, 175, 178, 230, IV/11, 41, 54

DIVINUS
goddelijk
divine, I/201, 239, 251, II/49, 53, 56, 57, 60, 61, 63, 64, 68, 81, 89, 93, 135, 137, 307, IV/132, 133

DIVISIO; DIVIDERE; DIVISIBILIS; DIVISIBILITAS
deeling; delen; deelbaar; deelbaarheid
division; to divide; divisible, divisibility, I/176, *181*, 184, 190, 191, 192, 194, 199, 200, 201, 228, 229, 230, 235, *236*, 237, 244, 249, 251, 257, 267, 274, 275, II/24, 55, 57, 58, 59, 60, IV/29, 53, 55, 56, 58, 61

DIVITIAE
rijkdom
wealth, II/5, 6, 7, 185, 202, 275, 289

DOCTRINA
lering
doctrine, instruction, II/9, 80, 131, 132, 135, 136

DOGMA
leerstuk
doctrine, maxim, I/129, 131, II/287, 288, IV/132

DOLOR
[PA 94: douleur]
treurigheid, pijn (KV)
pain (usu.), sorrow (rar.), I/142, 179, II/*149*, 191, 221, 242, 253

DOLUS MALUS
bedrog
deception, II/264

DUBITATIO; DUBITARE; DUBIUS; INDUBIE
twijfel, twijfeling; twijfelen, twijfelachtig; ontwijfelijk
doubt; to doubt; doubtful; without doubt, I/129, 141, 142, 143, 144, 145, 146, 147, 148, 149, 151, 160, 166, 173, 247, 248, II/10, 17, 19, 29, *30*, 32, 50, 54, 105, 123, 124, 131, 134, 153, 154, 155, 194, IV/39, 40, 67

DURATIO; DURARE
during; duren
duration; to have duration, to endure, to last, I/202, 234, *244*, 250, 251, 252, 269, 270, 271, 272, 273, 274, II/31, 39, 46, 65, 66, 67, *85*, 91, 114, 115, 127, 147, 209, 257, 294, 295, 296, 298, 301, 302, IV/53, 54, 55, 56, 57, 58, 60

DURITIES; DURUS
hardheid; hard
hardness; hard, I/184, 186, 187, 189, 225, II/82, 100, 102

EBRIETAS; EBRIUS
dronkenschap; dronke mensch
drunkenness; drunk, II/143, 185, 187, 202

EDUCATIO; EDUCARE
opvoeding; opvoeden
education; to educate, II/9, 183, 197, 203, 269, 272

EFFECTUS
gewrocht, uitwerksel (KV), uitwerking (KV)
effect, I/150, II/23, 32, 63, 70, 77, 80, 89, 96, 140, 196, 197, 198, 283, 283, IV/22, 77

ELASTICA PROPRIETAS
voortpassende eigenschap
elasticity, IV/6

ELECTIO
verkiezing
choice, I/256, 264

ELEMENTUM
beginsel
element, IV/74

ELEMENTA, PRIMA
eerste beginselen
first elements, II/28, *29*

EMENDATIO; EMENDARE
verbetering; verbeteren (usu.), zuiveren
emendation; to emend, II/5, 9, 25, 26, IV/36

EMINENTER
uitstekendlijk

675

EXISTENTIA NECESSARIA
noodzakelijke wezenlijkheid
necessary existence, I/155, 157, 158,
164, 165, 166, 168, 169, 170, 233,
236, 240, 242, 243, 256, II/25, 46,
51, 53, 61, 66, 67, 85, 93, 206, 217,
231, 299, IV/60, 62

EXISTERE PER SE
door zich wezenlijk zijn
exist through itself, I/177, 258, 273

EXISTIMATIO; EXISTIMARE
[PA 149: estime]
achting; achten
overestimation; to overesteem, II/160,
195, 196, 197, 246

EXPERIENTIA; EXPERIRI
ervarenheid, ondervinding, bevinding;
bevinden, ondervinden
experience; to know (find) by experience, test, I/182, 262, 279, II/5, 12,
13, 14, 23, 30, 79, 105, 132, 141,
142, 143, 165, 197, 234, 240, 273,
277, 285, 296, IV/26, 32, 47, 77

EXPERIENTIA QUOTIDIANA
dagelijks ervarenheid
daily experience, I/175, II/234, IV/66

EXPERIENTIA VAGA
losse ervarenheid (TdIE), zwervende
of losse ondervinding (E)
random experience, II/10, 28, 122, 287

EXPERIMENTUM; EXPERIRI
ondervinding; ondervinden
experiment; to experiment, II/10, 37,
IV/16, 21, 24, 25, 29, 32, 34, 37,
49, 50, 66, 67, 68, 70, 71, 74, 75,
131, 132, 158

EXPLICATIO; EXPLICARE
verklaring; verklaren
explanation; to explain, I/127, 233,
234, II/19, 34, 35, 46, 56, 64, 83,
88, 90, 94, 95, 123, 141, 213, 239,
IV/17, 19, 21, 26, 28, 33, 42, 43,
50, 51, 53, 57, 64, 65

EXPRIMERE
uitdrukken
to express, I/149, 241, 263, 270, II/10,
33, 35, 39, 45, 50, 52, 56, 60, 64,

67, 68, 71, 72, 77, 84, 85, 86, 88,
93, 114, 146, 183, 294, 295, IV/132

EXPURGARE
zuiveren
to purify, II/9

EXTENSIO; EXTENSUS
uitstrekking (usu.), uitgestrektheid
(occ.), uitgebreidheid (KV); uitges-
trekt
extension; extended, I/132, 150, 168,
181, 184, 185, 187, 188, 191, 192,
237, 250, 257, 258, II/33, 56, 86,
90, 96, 109, 144, 190, IV/5, 6, 7,
13, 14

FABRICA (CORPORIS HUMANI)
gebou [E], maakskel [CM] (van 't menselijke lichaam)
structure (of the human body), I/276
II/81, 142, 143

FACILE
lichtelijk
easily, I/161, 162, II/12, 54, 178

FACINUS
daad, werk
action, IV/147

FACTUM
daad
deed, I/246, II/183, 197, 234, 252,
253, 272

FACULTAS
vermogen (usu.), macht (occ.), be-
kwaamheid (rar.)
faculty, I/132, 145, 171, 174, 176,
II/129, 130, 132, 133, 134, 271

FALSITAS; FALSUS
valsheid; vals
falsity; false, I/145, 171, 173, 196, 228,
235, 246, 247, II/19, 23, 25, 26, 27,
28, 29, 32, 33, 40, 63, 116, 117,
122, 123, 124, 131, 135, 211, 272,
273,
IV/40, 43

FAMA
gerucht
reputation
II/253

157, 159, 160, 163, 237, II/14, 32, 34, 38, 89, IV/14, 49

FORTITUDO; FORTIS; FORTIS ESSE
vroomheid (usu.), kloekmoedigheid, moed (KV?); vroom; kraftig zijn
strength of character; strong, strong in character; to have force, I/212, 213, 214, 215, 218, 219, II/184, *188*, 210, 212, 214, 215, 216, 262, 265, 288, 307, IV/76

FORTUNA; FORTUITUS
geval; gevallig
fortune, luck; fortuitous, II/32, 34, 114, 136, 205, 245, 246, 288, 307, IV/76, 158

FRIGUS; FRIGIDUS
koude; koud
cold; cold, II/81, IV/23, 28, 158

FUNCTIO
doening, ambt en bediening
function, I/277, II/142

FUNDAMENTUM
grondvest
foundation, I/127, 128, 131, 132, 141, 142, 143, 144, 153, 154, 159, 236, II/33, 38, 54, 78, 80, 120, 126, 222, 223, 225, 226, 227, 236, 251, 294, 306, IV/149, 151

FUTURUS
toekomend (usu.), aanstaande
future, I/252, 266, 273, II/125, 126, 154, 170, 194, 198, 210, 216, 217, 218, 220, 256, 257, 275, IV/77

GAUDIUM; GAUDERE
[PA 61: joie]
vreugd; vermaak scheppen in, zich ver-heugen over
gladness; to be glad at, of, enjoy, II/155, 158, 165, 187, *195*, 246, 289, 302

GENERATIO; GENERARE
voortteling, voortbrenging, gelijklijktel-ing; voorttelen, genereren (KV)
generation; to generate, I/162, 170, 226, 255, 268, 275, 276, II/60, IV/14

GENEROSITAS; GENEROSUS
[PA 153-156, 161: générosité]
edelmoedigheid; edelmoedig
nobility; noble, II/*188*, 203, 245, 251, 265, 269, 287, 288, 306, 307

GENUS
geslacht
genus, kind, I/234, II/31, 37, 45, 46, 50, 60, 70, 207, 210, IV/7, 8, 13, 42

GENERA, SUMMA
opperste geslachten
chief kinds, I/250, IV/28

GENUS GENERALISSIMUM
algemeenst geslacht
most general genus, II/207

GLANDULA PINEALIS
pijnappelklier
pineal gland, II/278, 279, 280

GLORIA; GLORIARI; GLORIOSUS
[PA 204: gloire]
roem, roemzucht, heerlijkheid (rar.); roemen; roemrijk
esteem, love of esteem, glory (rar.); to exult at being esteemed (usu.), to pride o.s. (occ.); one who exults at being esteemed, II/7, 8, *163*, 164, 166, 170, 172, 173, 181, 185, 197, *199*, 202, 243, 246, 249, 252, 253, 288, *303*

GRADUS
trap
degree, I/154, 156, 164, 175, 182, 185, 261, II/83, 96, 100, 121, 142, 280, IV/131, 149

GRATIA (SEU GRATITUDO); CONGRATU-LARI; GRATUS
[PA 193: reconnaissance]
dankbewijs (of dankbaarheid), dank; dank te bewijzen; dankbaar
thankfulness (or gratitude); to return thanks; thankful, II/172, *200*, 263, 264, 271

HABITUS
hebbelijkheid, gewoonte en gebruik
habitual disposition, habit, II/195, 279

IDEA IDEAE
het denkbeeld van het (een) denkbeeld
the idea of the (an) idea, II/15, 109,
110, 113, 114, 123

IDEA SIMPLEX, SIMPLICISSIMA
enkel (eenvoudig), zeer enkel denkbeeld
simple, most simple idea, I/142, 146,
II/26, 27, 32, 103

IDEATUM
a) gedenkbeelde, b) gedenkbeelde of
gedachte zaak, c) gedachte zaak, d)
de zaak daar af het een denkbeeld is,
e) voorwerp (m: objectum), f) [voor-
werp (m: objectum) of] gedachte
zaak, g) ideatum
object, I/16(g), 234(a), 235(a), 246(a),
247(a), II/14(a), 16(b), 47(c), 71(d),
85(a), 88(e), 116(f), 124(f)

IGNIS
vuur
fire, IV/20, 21, 27, 49

IGNORANTIA; IGNORARE; IGNARUS
onwetenheid; onkundig van . . . zijn,
niet weten; onkundig
ignorance; to be ignorant of; ignorant,
II/49, 74, 78, 79, 81, 117, 132, 142,
143, 207, 262, 263, 277, 284, 308

IMAGINATIO; IMAGO; IMAGINARI; IMAGI-
NARIA
inbeelding (E, TdIE, Ep.), verbeelding
(PP, Ep.); beeld; zich inbeelden (E,
TdIE, Ep.), zich verbeelden (PP,
CM, Ep.); inbeeldig
imagination; image, appearance (rar.);
to imagine; imaginary, I/145, 149,
153, 156, 157, 160, 173, 191, 192,
233, *234*, 241, II/11, 21, 22, 28, 31,
32, 33, 39, 59, 81, 82, 83, *106*, 107,
112, 117, 120, 121, 122, 125, 126,
128, 130, 131, 132, 133, 134, 142,
144, 149, 150, 151, 153, 154, 155,
156, 163, 165, 180, 184, 191, 198,
210, 211, 212, 216, 217, 218, 255,
257, 281, 284, *285*, 288, 289, 290,
294, 301, 302, 305, 306, IV/33, 53,
56, 57, 58, 76, 77, 78, 128, 131

IMITATIO (AFFECTUUM); IMITARI
navolging (van hartstochten); navolgen
imitation (of affects); to imitate, II/160,
165, 177, 200, 262, 269

IMMEDIATUS; IMMEDIATE
onmiddelijk (usu.), immediatelijk; immediate
immediate; immediately, I/149, 181,
183, 184, 196, 234, II/67, *70*, 80

IMMENSITAS
onmetelijkheid
immensity, I/253, 254, 255

IMMORTALITAS; IMMORTALIS
onsterfelijkheid; onsterfelijk
immortality; immortal, I/275, 276,
277, II/128, 307

IMMUTABILITAS; IMMUTABILIS
onveranderlijkheid; onveranderlijk
immutability; immutable, I/178, 243,
252, 255, 256, 257, 266, 267, 276,
II/22, 65, 66, 75, 93, 294, IV/127

IMPERFECTIO
See perfectio

IMPERIUM; IMPERARE
heerschappij (usu.), gebied (occ.); ge-
bieden
dominion (usu.), command (occ.); to
command, II/137, 138, 142, 269,
270, 277, 279

IMPETUS
stoot, drift
impetus, impulse, I/207, II/190, IV/19

IMPIETAS
See pietas

IMPLICANTIA; (CONTRADICTIONEM) IMPLI-
CARE
tegenzeglijkheid (usu.), strijdigheid, in-
gewikkeldheid (Ep.); tegenzeglijkheid
(strijdigheid) inwikkeln (insluiten),
strijdig (tegenzeglijk) zijn
contradiction; to involve (imply) a contradiction, I/162, 174, 193, 227, 228,
240, 242, 251, 275, II/19, 20, 56,
IV/53

INJURIA; INJUSTUS
ongelijk; ongerechtig
(a) wrong; unjust, II/79, 237, 238, 244,
245, 248, 265, 270, 288, 294

INNATUS
ingeboren
innate, inborn, II/13, 14, 15, 16, 38,
79, 190

INSANUS; INSANIRE
onzinnig; buiten wetten zijn
madman; to be insane, II/243, 252

INSTITUTUM
ooggemerk, gewoonte
goal, purpose, plan, II/5, 6, 7, 145,
189, 245

INTELLECTUS; INTELLECTIO; INTELLIGEN-
TIA; INTELLIGERE; INTELLECTUALIS; IN-
TELLIGIBILIS
verstand; verstaning; verstand, verstaning, kennis; verstaan; verstandelijk;
verstandelijk
intellect; intellection; understanding; to
understand; intellectual; intelligible,
I/132, 133, 141, 142, 145, 146, 149,
162, 167, 168, 172, 173, 174, 175,
176, 177, 186, 190, 191, 192, 193,
194, 195, 196, 253, 259, 267, 274,
277, II/8, 9, 10, 14, 15, 20, 22, 23,
24, 25, 26, 27, 28, 29, 31, 32, 33,
34, 35, 36, 37, 38, 39, 40, 45, 59,
62, 63, 71, 72, 73, 81, 82, 83, 97,
107, 122, 124, 129, 131, 132, 133,
134, 162, 188, 220, 223, 225, 227,
249, 267, 276, 277, 280, 283, 284,
287, 290, 296, 297, 298, 300, 304,
305, 306, 308, IV/8, 9, 36, 40, 43,
46, 51, 53, 56, 57, 70, 77, 126, 127,
129, 130, 132, 146, 162

INTELLECTUS ACTU
het dadelijke (in daad) verstand
the actual intellect, II/71, 72, 75

INTELLECTUS (INTELLIGENTIA, INTELLEC-
TIO) DEI (DIVINA)
Gods (het goddelijke) verstand (verstaning)
God's (the divine) intellect (understanding, intellection), I/167, 168,
171, 177, 238, 257, 260, 261, 262,

263, 264, II/27, 62, 63, 71, 73, 75,
90, 94, 120, 306, IV/129, 130, 131,
132

INTELLECTUS INFINITUS
oneindig verstand
infinite intellect, I/264, II/60, 71, 83,
88, 90, 94, 125, 306, IV/45

INTELLECTUS PRACTICUS
oefenig verstand
practical intellect, I/279

INTELLECTUS PURUS
zuiver verstand
pure intellect, I/173, II/33, IV/131

INTREPIDUS
onversaagd
intrepid, II/179

INTUITUS; INTUERI; INTUITIVUS; INTUITIVI
aanschou, opzicht; aanschouwen;
zienig; inzieniglijk
intuition, glance; to look at, consider;
intuitive; intuitively, I/190, II/5, 11,
12, 117, 122, 206, 208, 211, 278,
303

INVIDIA; INVIDERE; INVIDUS
[PA 182: envie]
nijd, wangunst (KV?); benijden; nijdig
envy; to envy; envious, II/7, 136, 138,
158, 165, 166, 167, 170, 180, 183,
196, 199, 200, 234, 244, 252, 265,
269, 273, 275, 292, IV/42

IRA; IRASCI
[PA 199: colère]
gramschap, toorn; toornig op . . . zijn
anger; to be angry at, I/264, II/136,
138, 172, 200, 201, 244, 245, 264,
265, 288

IRRISIO; IRRIDERE
[PA 178: moquerie]
bespotting; bespotten
mockery; to mock, II/136, 181, 193,
244, 247?, 265

JOCUS
jok of boerterij
joking, II/244

LIMES; LIMITARE
paal; bepalen
limit; to limit, I/132, 146, 173, 174,
178, II/66, 134, 210, 212

LINGUA
taal
language, I/246

LITERA
letter
letter, IV/132

LOCUS
plaats
place, I/182, 192, 193, 194, 195, 196,
197, 198, II/298, 304, IV/11

LOGICA
redekunst
logic, I/130, 233, II/277

LUMEN NATURALE (NATURAE), LUX NATU-
RAE; LUMEN NATURALIS INTELLECTUS
natuurlijk licht, het licht der natuur;
licht van het natuurlijke verstand
natural light, light of the natural intellect, I/156, 265, 275, 276, IV/10,
126

LUXURIA
overdaad, brasserij
gluttony, II/185, 202, 203, 210

MAGNITUDO; MAGNUS
grootheid; groot
size; large, I/184, 186, 189, 212, 216,
IV/49, 59

MALI, SUB RATIONE
als 't kwaad
as bad, I/278

MALITIA
boosheid
malice, I/171

MALUS
kwaad
bad (freq.), evil (freq.), ill-fortune
(occ.), misfortune (occ.), I/235, 247,
248, 249, 262, 264, 278, 279, II/5,
7, 8, 78, 81, 82, 83, 158, 169, 170,
171, 172, 179, 195, 196, 205, 208,
209, 215, 220, 221, 223, 227, 228,
229, 230, 233, 237, 238, 239, 241,

252, 254, 255, 257, 258, 259, 261,
265, 266, 267, 268, 270, 275, 276,
286, 304, 305, IV/129, 130

MATERIA
stof
matter (usu.), material (occ.), I/162,
180, 181, 184, 185, 187, 189, 191,
192, 193, 194, 195, 196, 199, 200,
228, 229, 230, 238, 244, 257, 259,
261, 262, 268, 269, 270, 274, II/59,
60, 83, 102, IV/21, 22, 28, 59, 60,
74

MATERIALITER
stoffelijk
materially, IV/49

MATERIA PRIMA
eerste stof
prime matter, I/280, IV/74

MATERIA SUBTILIS, SUBTILISSIMA
(zeer) fijne stof
(very) fine matter, IV/18, 26, 49, 65,
66, 67

MATHEMATICA, MATHESIS; MATHEMA-
TICI; MATHEMATICE
wiskunde; wiskundigen, wiskundig
mathematics; mathematicians; mathematically, I/127, 128, 129, 141, 142,
143, 149, 184, 227, 266, II/12, 79,
83, 128, IV/25, 59, 75, 133

MATRIMONIUM
huwelijk
marriage, II/271

MECHANICA; MECHANICUS
werkdaad; werkdadig (Ep.), tuigwerk-
lijk (CM)
mechanics; mechanical, I/259, II/9, 81,
IV/12, 25, 50, 67, 158

MEDICINA
geneeskunde
medicine, II/9, 277

MEDITATIO
overdenking
meditation, II/17

MEDIUM
middel
means, II/8, 9, 78, 208

MODIFICATIO
wijziging
modification, I/228, II/49, 50, 66, 67,
   69, 93, IV/*13*

MODUS
wijze
mode, way, I/154, 165, 185, 192, 201,
   211, 233, 236, 237, 238, 239, 249,
   257, 258, 269, 275, 276, II/9, *45*,
   49, 50, 56, 57, 60, 68, 69, 70, 71,
   72, 77, 84, 86, 88, 89, 90, 93, 99,
   101, 102, 103, 104, 108, 109, 113,
   146, 306, IV/*13*, 47, 53, 54, 55, 56,
   57, 58

MODUS (MODIFICATIO) INFINITUS
oneindige wijze (wijziging)
infinite mode (modification), (pl.) infinitely many modes, II/60, 66, 87

MODI NON EXISTENTES
wijzen die niet wezentlijk zijn
modes that do not exist, I/239, II/50,
   90, 91, IV/54

MODUS COGITANDI
wijze van denken
mode of thinking, I/145, 155, 156,
   173, 175, 233, 234, 235, 236, 244,
   245, 246, 262, 269, II/72, 85, 86,
   88, 89, 90, 92, 109, 124, 129, 130,
   132, 141, 207, 208, 295, 306, IV/57

MOLES
grootheid
bulk, I/212, 213, IV/29

MOLESTUS
lastig, tot een last verstrekken
troublesome, burdensome, II/164, 183,
   243, 265, 269

MOLLIS
zacht
soft, II/82, 100, 102, 103, 105

MOMENTUM
ogenblik
moment, I/263, IV/58

MORS; MORTALIS; MORTUUS
dood; sterfelijk
death; mortal; dead, II/203, 240, 261,
   264, 302, 304, 305, 307, IV/131

MOS
zede (en gewoonte)
custom, practice, conduct, way, I/*255*,
   260, II/9, 270

MOS GEOMETRICUS
meetkundige wijze
geometric style, I/129, 130, II/138,
   IV/8, 10, 63, 70

MOTUS; MOVERI
beweging, roering (KV); bewegen
motion; to move, I/150, 176, *181*, 182,
   183, 184, 191, 192, 193, 194, 195,
   196, 197, 198, 199, 200, 201, 202,
   203, 204, 205, 206, 207, 208, 209,
   210, 211, 212, 213, 214, 215, 216,
   217, 218, 219, 220, 221, 222, 223,
   224, 225, 228, 229, 237, 248, 274,
   II/22, 27, 28, 34, 39, 97, 98, 99,
   100, 101, 102, 103, 132, 278, 279,
   280, IV/7, 12, 18, 19, 20, 25, 29,
   30, 32, 50, 60, 74

MOTUS ET QUIES
beweging en rust (usu. E, rar. PP), en
   stilte (usu. PP, rar. E)
motion and rest, I/132, 184, 200, 201,
   207, 209, 210, 216, II/73, 97, 98,
   99, 101, 102, 141, 144, 239, 240,
   241, IV/28, 49

MULIER; MULIEBRIS
vrouw; vrouwelijk
woman; unmanly, II/136, 167, 289

MULTITUDO
veelheid
multiplicity, I/246, IV/59

MUNDUS
wereld
world, I/191, 200, 226, 228, 251, 252,
   262, 267, 269, 270, 271, 272, II/288

MUTABILES, RES SINGULARES
bijzondere veranderlijke dinge
singular changeable things, II/36, 37

MUTATIO; MUTARI; MUTABILIS
verandering; veranderen; veranderlijk
change; to change; changeable, I/211,
   212, 213, 216, 217, 219, 220, 243,
   255, 256, 257, II/29, 36, 37, 65, 75,

word, name, I/127, 149, 235, 242, 274, II/11, 22, 28, 33, 63, 83, 128, 175, 180, 203, IV/46

NORMA
(regel en) rechtsnoer
standard, II/15, 16, 17, 18, 26, 79, 129

NOTIO
kundigheid (usu.), kennis (rar.), stelling (II/120?)
notion, I/132, 244, 245, II/81, 82, 83, 120, 121, 185, 207, IV/28, 33, 57

NOTIO COMMUNIS
gemene kundigheid (usu.), kennis (PP)
common notion, I/127, II/50, 119, 120, 122, 126, 128, IV/13

NOTIO SIMPLEX
eenvoudige kennis
simple notion, I/146

NOTIO SECUNDA
tweede kundigheid
second notion, II/120

NOTIO UNIVERSALIS
algemene kundigheid
universal notion, II/121, 122, 130

NOTUM (COGNITUM) PER SE
door zich bekend, door zich blijkt, uit zich bekend
known through itself, I/146, 152, 174, 182, II/17, 26, 65, 71, 72, 97, 98, 182, 279

NUMERUS
getal
number, I/190, 234, 270, 271, II/39, 50, 57, IV/53, 57, 58, 59, 60, 61

NUMMI
geld
money, II/8, 9, 243, 274, 275

NUTUS
wenk
command, II/135, 142

NON ENS
non ens
non-being, IV/83

OBEDIENTIA
gehoorzaamheid
obedience, II/238

OBJECTUM; OBJECTIVUS; OBJECTIVE
voorwerp; voorwerpig; voorwerpiglijk
object; objective; objectively, I/150, 153, 154, 155, 156, 160, 234, 238, 261, II/7, 14, 16, 23, 26, 27, 28, 32, 34, 35, 36, 38, 39, 63, 71, 82, 85, 88, 89, 91, 92, 95, 96, 97, 109, 116, 124, 139, 243, IV/42

OBTEMPERARE
gehoorzamen, onderdanig zijn
to obey, II/264, 265, 267

ODIUM; ODIO HABERE
[PA 56, 79, 80, 84, 85: haine]
haat; haten
hate; to hate, I/264, II/7, 136, 138, 151, 152, 153, 156, 157, 158, 159, 160, 161, 163, 164, 166, 169, 170, 171, 172, 173, 174, 175, 176, 177, 178, 183, 184, *193*, 195, 196, 198, 200, 201, 231, 243, 244, 245, 247, 248, 252, 255, 259, 265, 269, 271, 281, 283, 287, 288, 291, IV/36

ODOR; ODORUS
reuk; sterkruikend
smell; odorous, IV/25, 26, 50, 68, 74

OFFICIUM
plicht
duty, function, II/274, 276, 277

OMEN
voorteken, voorspook
omen, II/177, IV/76, 77

OMNIPOTENTIA; OMNIPOTENS
almogenheid, almachtigheid; almachtig
omnipotence, I/263, 266, 267, 270, 275, II/62

OMNISCIENTIA; OMNISCIUS
alwetendheid; alwetend
omniscience; omniscient, I/261, 263, II/20

OPUS; OPERATIO; OPERARI (ALIQUID); OPERATOR
werk; werking; werken; werker
act, action, work; activity, actuality (rar.), procedure; act, do something,

produce an effect; workman, I/149, 238, 243, 256, 259, 265, 268, 269, 273, 274, 277, II/5, 9, 11, 12, 14, 46, 68, 69, 70, 72, 73, 76, 115, 133, 209, IV/127, 130, 131

OPINIO
waan (usu.), gevoelen (occ.), opinie (occ. perhaps in KV, though not usual even there), mening
opinion, II/76, 117, 122, 198, 221, 252, 253, 260, 278, 301, IV/40, 64, 76, 130, 131

ORDO; ORDINARE
orde (usu. in PP, CM, TdIE), ordening (usu. in E); schikken
order; to order, I/129, 130, 228, 229, 239, 245, 261, 267, II/8, 9, 10, 15, 17, 18, 19, 23, 26, 28, 30, 34, 36, 37, 43, 73, 75, 78, 81, 82, 83, 93, 122, 191, 281, 287, 288, 293, 305, 306, IV/72, 77

ORDO ET CONNEXIO (CONCATENATIO) IDEARUM
ordening en samenknoping (samemschakeling) der denkbeelden
order and connection of ideas, II/89, 92, 107, 108, 281

ORDO (ET CONNEXIO, CONCATENATIO) RERUM
ordening (en samenknoping) der dingen
order (and connection) of things, II/89, 92, 107, 108, 141, 257, 281

ORDO MATHEMATICUS, GEOMETRICUS
wiskundige, meetkundige orde
mathematical, geometrical order, I/128, 130, 141, II/*222*

ORDO NATURAE, COMMUNIS
de gemene ordening (loop) der natuur
the common order of nature, II/114, 115, 213, 252, 268

ORDO NATURAE, (TOTUS); ORDO TOTIUS (UNIVERSAE) NATURAE
de (hele) orde der natuur; de ordening van de gehele (algemene) natuur
the (whole) order of Nature; the order of the whole of Nature, I/241, 243,

266, 267, II/16, 21, 25, 28, 53, 73, 75, 82, 85, 90, 111, 137, 213, 276, IV/*54, 55*

ORDO (SERIES) CAUSARUM
orde (rij) der oorzaaken
order (series) of causes, I/241, 243, II/36, 74

ORDO SIVE CONNEXIO CAUSARUM
ordening of samenknoping der oorzaaken
order *or* connection of causes, II/90, 92, 98

ORIGO OMNIUM RERUM, NATURAE
oorsprong aller dingen, der natuur
origin of all things, of Nature, II/17, 29, 30

PARABOLA
parabel
parable, IV/132

PARADOXA
wonderspreuken
paradoxes, II/18

PARASITUS
vleier
parasite, II/251

PARS
deel, zijde
part, direction, I/144, 176, 177, 179, 190, 207, 208, 211, 244, 250, 251, 258, 267, II/24, 28, 33, 55, 57, 58, 59, 60, 94, 95, 100, 110, 111, 113, 118, 127, 213, 222, 276, 302, IV/16, 18, 20, 21, 22, 23, 26, 27, 30, 33, 49, 50, 53, 55, 56, 58, 59, 61, 77

PARS MATERIAE
deel van de stof
part of matter, I/182, 184, 228, 229, 230, 257, IV/14

PARS MENTIS
deel van de ziel
part of the mind, II/293, 304, 305, 306

PARS NATURAE
deel van de natuur
part of nature, I/267, II/145, 212, 252, 266, 267, 268, 276

690

PARTIALITAS
eenzijdigheid
partiality, II/136

PARTICIPARE
deelachtig zijn
to participate, I/253, II/244, 275,
IV/77, 78

PARTICULARIS; PARTICULARITER
bijzonder; bijzonderlijk
particular; particularly, I/200, 274,
II/10, 20, 29, 36, 68, 115, 129, IV/9

PARTICULA
deeltje
particle, I/220, 221, 222, 225, 228,
229, 230, IV/17, 18, 19, 20, 21, 23,
24, 26, 27, 28, 29, 30, 31, 32, 49,
50, 65, 68, 74

PASSIO (= PATHEMA [RAR.]); PATI;
PATIBILIS
lijding (usu.), tocht (rar.), hartstocht
(rar.); lijden (usu.), lijding onderwer-
pen (rar.); lijdelijk
passion; to be acted on, undergo, admit; susceptible of being acted on,
I/162, 256, 270, II/12, 31, 32, 57,
58, 60, 85, 97, 139, 140, 141, 144,
145, 148, 149, 164, 184, 185, 187,
201, 203, 204, 212, 213, 214, 215,
230, 231, 236, 240, 249, 254, 255,
266, 279, 282, 283, 284, 286, 291,
292, 293, 294, 301, 304, 305, 306,
308, IV/39, 40, 55, 59, 60

PECCATUM; PECCARE
zonde; zondigen
sin; to sin, I/256, 262, 265, II/78, 79,
81, 83, 206, 207, 208, 237, 238,
239, 250, 285

PECUNIA
geld
money, II/274, 288

PERCEPTIO; PERCIPERE; PERCEPTIBILIS
begrijping (usu.), bevatting (oft.), begrip (occ.), gewaarwording (rar.),
bemerking (rar.); begrijpen, bevatten, gewaarworden, bemerken, verstaan (rar.); bevattelijk

perception; to perceive; perceptible,
I/142, 144, 146, 149, 150, 153, 154,
166, 169, 171, 173, 174, 175, 181,
186, 191, 233, 241, 242, 243, II/10,
11, 12, 18, 19, 23, 24, 25, 26, 27,
28, 36, 38, 39, 45, 67, 72, 77, 84,
86, 94, 95, 97, 104, 107, 108, 109,
110, 112, 114, 119, 122, 125, 126,
132, 133, 134, 139, 145, 249, 279,
IV/56

PERFECTIO; PERFICERE; PERFECTUS; IM-
PERFECTIO; IMPERFECTUS
volmaaktheid; volmaken; volmaakt; on-
volmaaktheid; onvolmaakt
perfection; to perfect; imperfection;
imperfect, I/150, 153, 154, 155, 156,
157, 163, 164, 165, 166, 168, 169,
171, 174, 175, 176, 237, 238, 249,
253, 254, 261, 266, II/8, 9, 10, 12,
13, 18, 39, 54, 58, 61, 62, 74, 75,
76, 80, 83, 85, 86, 116, 148, 149,
150, 151, 191, 204, 205, 206, 207,
208, 209, 222, 223, 244, 254, 277,
291, 297, 300, 301, 302, 306,
IV/131

PERFECTIO OBJECTIVA
voorwerpige volmaaktheid
objective perfection, I/150, 153, 154

PERIPATETICI
Peripatetischen
Peripatetics, I/259, 280, IV/61

PERSEVERANTIA; PERSEVERARE
volharding; volharden
perseverance; to persevere, I/157, 201,
209, 244, 248, II/67, 127, 146, 147,
186, 193, 209, 212, 214, 276

PERSONALITAS
persoonlijkheid
personality, I/264, Letter 12a

PERFIDIA; PERFIDUS
meinedigheid; meinedig
treachery; treacherous, II/264

PHAENOMENA
verschijnselen
phenomena, I/196, 226, 227, 228,
II/22, IV/16, 17, 21, 26, 49, 50, 64,
66, 67, 70

183, 184, 187, 188, 191, 196, 204, 208, 211, 214, 215, 228, 229, 233, 241, 242, 248, 249, 254, 268, 280

POTENTIA COGITANDI
macht, vermogen van te denken
power of thinking, II/109, 135, 148, 150, 152, 162, 188, *204*

POTENTIA DEI (DIVINA)
Gods (goddelijke) macht, vermogen, mogendheid, kracht
God's (divine) power, I/166, 167, 177, 188, 238, 243, 255, 260, 264, 266, 267, 271, 272, 273, 274, 275, 276, 280, II/57, 62, 63, 76, 87, 89, 146, 213, 261, IV/127

POTENTIA EXTRAORDINARIA
buitengewone macht
extraordinary power, I/267

POTENTIA ORDINARIA
gewone macht
ordinary power, I/267

POTENTIA ORDINATA
geordende macht
ordained power, I/267

POTESTAS
macht (usu.), vermogen (occ.), mogendheid (rar.), mogelijkheid (rar.)
power, I/146, 155, 161, 162, 163, 164, 173, 174, 175, 265, 275, 276, 278, 279, 280, II/13, 14, 134, 136, 142, 143, 144, 205, 210, 235, 238, 276, 279, 282, 283, 287, 298, 305

POTESTAS DEI
Gods macht
God's power, II/61, 77, 87

POTESTAS, SUMMA
opperste macht
supreme power, II/248

PRAEDETERMINARE
voorbepalen
to predetermine, II/77

PRAEDICATUM; PRAEDICARE
gezeg; toeschrijven, zeggen, toeëigenen, verkondigen
predicate; to predicate, II/24, 121, 135, 184, 246

PRAEJUDICIUM
vooroordeel
prejudice, I/141, 159, 180, 188, 192, 193, 202, 248, II/17, 18, 54, 77, 79, 80, 120, 132, 206, IV/36, 130, 131, 159

PRAEMIUM
vergelding (E), beloning (KV), loon (Ep.)
reward, II/136, 307

PRAEORDINATIO DEI
Gods voorschikking
God's preordination, I/178, 179

PRAESENTIA; PRAESENS
tegenwoordigheid; tegenwoordig(lijk)
presence; present, I/251, 252, 254, 255, II/37, 79, 104, 105, 106, 125, 126, 134, 149, 150, 151, 154, 162, 169, 170, 181, 188, 189, 194, 195, 198, 204, 210, 211, 212, 216, 217, 218, 219, 220, 221, 243, 251, 256, 257, 260, 264, 275, 285, 288, 294, 298, 300, IV/77

PRAETERITUS
voorgaand, verleden
past, II/125, 126, 154, 155, 194, 195, 210, 216, 217, 219, 240, 257, 294

PRAVUS
kwaad
wrong, evil, II/197, 198, 250

PRAXIS
oefening
practice, II/245

PRETIUM
vergelding en loon
reward, II/301

PREX
gebed
prayer, IV/130

PRIMORDIUM RERUM
oorsprong der dingen
origin of things, IV/51

PRINCIPIUM
beginsel
principle, I/141, 142, 143, 149, 153, 172, 174, 226, 227, II/26, 49, 207,

279, 303, IV/10, 40, 50, 66, 70, 75,
126

PRIVATIO; PRIVARE
beroving (PP, Ep., KV), derving (E);
beroven
privation; to deprive, I/171, 173, 175,
176, 261, II/116, *117*, 131, 191, 293,
IV/*128*

PRIVATUS
bijzonder
private, II/271

PROBABILIS
bewijsbar
provable, IV/*25*

PROBRUM
schand
disgrace, II/249

PROBUS
vroom
pious, IV/127

PROCREARE
scheppen, voortbrengen, voortschep-
pen, telen, voorttelen
to create, produce, procreate, beget,
I/172, 177, 202, 243, 244, 254, 262,
274, 276, II/187, 272

PROFANUS
onheilig
unholy, II/197

PRONUNTIATUM
uitspraak
proposition, IV/40

.PROPENSIO
toegenegenheid
inclination, II/*193*

PROPHETA
profeet
prophet, I/266, II/250, IV/132, 133

PROPOSITIO
voorstelling
proposition, I/129, 130, 131, 144,
IV/43, 44, 47

PROPRIETAS
eigenschap
property, I/150, 161, 163, 168, 176,

183, 190, 227, 245, II/10, 11, 33,
35, 36, 38, 40, 60, 77, 79, 85, 119,
122, 136, 138, 165, 192, 196, 197,
257, 265, IV/65

PROPRIETAS COMMUNIS
gemene eigenschap
common property, II/115, 186, 285,
289, 293

PROPRIUM
eigen
proprium, peculiar, proper, II/10, 34,
119, 184, 288

PROVIDENTIA
voorzienigheid
providence, I/261

PROXIMUS
naast
fellowman, IV/133

PRUDENTIA; PRUDENS
voorzightigheid, wijsheid; voorzichtig,
voorbedachtelijk
prudence; prudent, intentionally,
I/233, 277, II/137, 180, IV/38, 76

PUDOR
[PA 205: honte]
schaamte (E), beschaamdheid (KV)
shame, II/163, 170, 171, 189, 198,
199, 253, 254, 272

PUER
jong, kind
child, II/134, 135, 143, 165, 270, 305

PULCHRITUDO; PULCHER
schoonheid; schoon
beauty; beautiful, I/*165*, II/78, 81, 82

PURUS
zuiver
pure, II/31, 33, 34, IV/131

PUSILLANIMITAS; PUSILLANIMIS
[PA 174: lâcheté]
kleinmoedigheid; kleinmoedig
cowardice; cowardly, II/179, 201

QUAESTIO
geschil
problem (usu.), question, I/127, 133,
250, II/21, 30, 35, IV/10, 50, 61

QUALITAS
hoedanigheid
quality, I/150, 163, II/7, IV/12, 48,
49, 64, 74

QUALITAS SENSILIS
gevoelige hoedanigheid
sensible quality, I/184, 186, 187, 189

QUALITAS TACTILIS
raakbare hoedanigheid
tangible quality, IV/25

QUALITAS OCCULTA
verborge hoedanigheid
occult quality, II/152, 279, IV/12

QUALITAS NOTA VEL MANIFESTA
bekende of openbare hoedanigheid
known or manifest quality, II/152

QUANTITAS
hoegrootheid
quantity, I/142, 193, 200, 201, 203,
208, 209, 234, 254, 274, II/39, 57,
58, 59, 279, IV/56, 57, 65

QUIES; QUIESCERE
rust; rusten
rest; to be at rest, I/182, 184, 194,
225, IV/17, 19, 20

RAREFACTIO
verdunning
rarefaction, I/186

RATIO; RATIOCINARI; RATIONCINATIO, RA-
TIOCINIUM; RATIONALIS
reden; redeneren; redenering; redelijk
reason, principle, reasoning, way,
method, relation, nature; to reason;
reasoning; rational, I/146, 154, 195,
201, 265, II/15, 16, 17, 32, 39, 59,
77, 122, 125, 126, 138, 143, 206,
221, 227, 237, 248, 249, 250, 253,
254, 255, 256, 257, 258, 159, 263,
264, 265, 266, 267, 268, 271, 272,
273, 276, 277, 283, 285, 289, 306,
IV/29, 50, 66, 67, 132

RATIONIS, CONSILIUM
berading der reden
counsel of reason, II/246.

RATIONIS, DICTAMEN
See dictamen rationis

RATIONIS, (EX) DUCTU
uit (door, naar) 't beleid der reden
according to the guidance of reason,
I/236, II/83, 136, 223, 226, 232,
233, 234, 235, 236, 237, 241, 245,
246, 247, 250, 251, 259, 260

RATIONIS, EX IMPERIO
naar 't gebied der reden
according to the command of reason,
II/269, 289

RATIONIS, PRAECEPTUM
onderwijzing der reden
precept of reason, II/222

RATIONIS, PRAESCRIPTUM
voorschrift van de reden
rule of reason, II/222, 269, 273, 288,
307

REALITAS; REALIS; REALITER
zakelijkheid; zakelijk, wezenlijk, dadelijk (KV); zakelijk
reality; real; really, I/154, 155, 165,
242, 245, 249, 268, II/14, 16, 36,
51, 52, 54, 60, *85*, 86, 97, 124, 133,
204, 207, 257, 299, IV/45

REALITAS OBJECTIVA
voorwerpelijke zakelijkheid
objective reality, I/*150*, 153, 154, 155,
156, 157

RECTUS
recht (usu.), goed en oprecht (occ.)
right, I/173, II/9, 34, 137, 197, 266,
287, 288

REDINTEGRATIO; REDINTEGRARE
herstelling; herstellen
reconstitution; to reconstitute, IV/16,
17, 19, 49, 65, 66, 74

REGULA
regel
rule, I/142, 144, 205, 206, 234, II/9,
15, 16, 18, 33, 38, 222

RELATIO
betrekking
relation, I/252, II/36, 203, 298

RELIGIO; RELIGIOSUS
godsdienst, godsdienstig

SCHOLASTICI; SCHOLAE; SCHOLASTICUS
Schoolsgezinden; Scholen
scholastics; the schools; scholastic,
II/67, 279, IV/48, 51

SCIENTIA; SCIRE; SCIENTIFICUS
wetenschap (usu.), kennis (occ.); weten; bekendmakend
science (usu.), knowledge (occ.); to
know; scientific, I/127, 132, 133,
141, 142, 143, 144, 153, 233, 261,
262, 263, 274, II/6, 8, 9, 10, 12, 14,
15, 18, 32, 75, 109, 221, IV/39

SCIENTIA DEI
Gods wetenschap
God's knowledge, I/261, 262, 274

SCIENTIA INTUITIVA
zienige kennis
intuitive knowledge, II/122

SCRIPTURA, SACRA (SACRAE LITTERAE,
SACRI CODICES)
(Heilige) Schrift, schriftuur
(Sacred) Scripture, I/256, 264,
265, II/303, IV/126, 132, 133

SECURITAS; SECURUM REDDERE; SECURE
[PA 166: sécurité]
gerustheid, verzekerheid (KV); verzek-
eren; met veiligheid
confidence; to make confident; confidently, II/155, 180, 194, 238, 245,
246

SEDITIO
beroerte
sedition, II/273

SEMINA
zaden
seeds, I/226, 227

SENSATIO; SENSUS; SENTIRE
gevoeling, voeling; zin, gevoeling, gevoel (KV); voelen, gevoelen, gewaarworden
sensation, awareness; sense, sense perception, feeling, meaning; to sense,
feel, be aware of, think, I/142, 145,
149, 156, 157, 171, 173, 179, 180,
184, 186, 191, 192, 193, 194, 195,
196, 234, 239, 277, II/11, 15, 18,
23, 24, 29, 30, 31, 32, 37, 68, 82,

83, 86, 93, 96, 105, 122, 132, 133,
159, 160, 187, 195, 197, 208, 222,
237, 252, 278, 279, 296, IV/8, 20,
27, 28, 29, 33, 56, 67, 68, 70, 77,
78, 132

SENSUS COMMUNIS
gemene zin
common sense, II/31

SERVITUS; SERVUS; SERVIRE
dienstbaarkeid, dienst; slaaf; dienen
bondage, service; slave; to serve, be a
slave, II/136, 205, 260, 272, 307,
IV/127

SIGNIFICATIO; SIGNUM; SIGNIFICARE
betekening, betekenis; teken; beteken
meaning; sign; to mean, signify, I/246,
264, 281, II/10, 15, 122, 195, 196,
206

SIMILITUDO; SIMILIS
gelijkheid; gelijk
similarity; like, II/107, 157, 158, 160,
161, 165, 175

SIMPLICITAS; SIMPLEX; SIMPLICITER
eenvoudigheid; eenvoudig, enkel; enke-
lijk
simplicity; simple; simply, I/142, 177,
201, 203, 226, 227, 229, 248, 255,
263, II/14, 24, 25, 26, 27, 32, 50,
70, 99, 101, 103, 122, 193, 284

SIMPLICISSIMA CORPORA
eenvoudigste lichamen
simplest bodies, II/99, 101

SIMPLICITAS DEI
Gods eenvoudigheid
God's simplicity, I/177, 255, 257, 258,
259, 263, 267

SINGULARIS; SINGULARITER
bijzonder(lijk)
singular; peculiarly, singly, separately,
I/263, 265, II/12, 31, 32, 34, 36, 37,
69, 70, 85, 86, 90, 91, 92, 94, 98,
115, 118, 121, 122, 127, 130, 131,
135, 138, 146, 179, 180, 183, 184,
191, 195, 207, 209, 210, 233, 273,
280, 285, 296, 303, 304, IV/131

45, 47, 48, 49, *50*, 51, 52, 53, 54,
55, *56*, 57, 59, 60, 64, 71, 72, 90,
92, 93, 97, IV/8, 11, *13*, 14, 41, 44,
45, 46, 53, 54, 56, 57, 58, 65

SUBSTANTIA (ABSOLUTE) INFINITA
(volstrekt) oneindige zelfstandigheid
(absolutely) infinite substance, I/154,
163, II/8, 45, 46, 49, 55, IV/41

SUBSTANTIA COGITANS
denkende zelfstandheid
thinking substance, I/132, 162, 163,
167, 275, II/90

SUBSTANTIA CORPOREA, EXTENSA
lichamelijke, uitgestrekte zelfstandigheid
corporeal, extended substance, I/167,
179, 180, 181, 189, 275, II/57, 58,
59, 60, 90, IV/55, 56, 60

SUBSTANTIA CREATA
geschape zelfstandigheid
created substance, I/269, 275, 276,
II/50

SUBSTANTIA FINITA
eindige zelfstandigheid
finite substance, I/163, II/55, 56

SUBSTANTIA INCREATA
ongeschape zelfstandigheid
uncreated substance, I/237

SUPERBIA; SUPERBIRE; SUPERBUS
[PA 157: orgueuil]
verwaandheid, hovaardigheid; ver-
waand (en hovaardig) worden; ver-
waand
pride; to become proud; proud, II/159,
164, *197*, 198, 246, 250, 251, 252,
264, 265, 272, 283

SUPERNATURALIS
bovennatuurlijk
supernatural, II/81

SUPERSTITIO; SUPERSTITIOSUS
waangeloof (usu. E, Ep.) waangelovig-
heid (occ. E), overgelovigheid (PP,
CM); waangelovig
superstition; superstitious, I/165, 261,
II/79, 136, 178, 236, 240, 244, 258,
275, IV/39, 130, 131

SUPPLICIUM
straf
punishment, II/307

SUSPICIO
achterdenking, vermoeden
suspicion, II/294, IV/40

SYMPATHIA
toegenegenheid
sympathy, I/197, II/152

SYNTHESIS
zamenzetting
synthesis, I/129

TABULA
schilderij
tablet, II/124

TABULA RASA
zuiver tafereel
blank tablet, I/279

TAEDIUM
zatheid
weariness, II/189

TELESCOPIUM
verrekijker
telescope, IV/159

TEMPERANTIA; SIBI TEMPERARE
matigheid; zich matigen
moderation; to be moderate, II/185,
188, 202, 203

TEMPUS
tijd
time, I/157, 161, 182, 185, 193, 194,
195, 196, 197, 234, 243, *244*, 269,
271, 273, 275, II/46, 125, 126, 147,
154, 178, 208, 209, 210, 216, 217,
218, 219, 220, 221, 256, 257, 293,
295, 296, 298, 304, IV/11, 57, 58,
60, 78

TERMINUS; TERMINARE
uiterste, bewoording, kunstwoord,
paal; bepalen
term, technical term, limit; to limit,
I/127, 234, 270, II/10, 45, 57, 67,
207

TERMINUS TRANSCENDENTALIS
overklimmend uiterste (CM), bewoording (E)

252, 255, 263, 265, 267, 268, 269, 271, 273, 276, 288, 306, IV/73, 130

Vacuum; vacuista
ijdel; beweerders van het ijdel
vacuum; those who affirm a vacuum,
I/*181*, 188, 197, II/59, IV/32, 34,
49, *65*, 70, 74

Valetudo
gezondheid
health, II/9, 81, 256

Vanitas; vanus
ijdelheid; ijdel
emptiness; empty, II/5, 138, 236, 253, 288

Variatio
verandering
variation, change, I/185, 191, 211,
212, 219, 220, 255, II/189, 294, 305,
IV/67

Veneratio; venerari
[PA 162: vénération]
eerbiedigheid; eren
veneration; to venerate, II/*180*, 181,
183, 192

Verbum; verbalis
woord; woordelijk
word; verbal, I/156, 157, 246, 248,
251, II/29, 31, 33, 35, 122, 131,
132, 195, 264, IV/36, 77, 148

Verecundia
beschaamtheid, schaamachtigheid
a sense of shame, II/*170*, 199

Verisimilitudo; verisimilis, vero similis
waarschijnlijkheid; waarschijnlijk
probability; probable, I/128, IV/13

Veracitas Dei
Gods waarachtigheid
God's veracity, I/171, 267

Veritas, verum; verus; vere
waarheid; waar; waarlijk
truth; true; truly, I/127, 128, 129, 133,
141, 144, 145, 150, *151*, 171, 174,
175, 192, 235, 236, *246*, 247, 251,
265, II/8, 13, 14, 15, 16, 17, 18, 19,
22, 23, 24, 25, *26*, 27, 28, 29, 30,

32, 37, 38, 47, 48, 50, 51, 63, 71,
105, 116, 117, 118, 122, 123, 124,
129, 135, 211, 212, 219, 220, 221,
249, 257, 276, 291, 299, 303, 304,
IV/39, 40, 42, 43, 44, 45, 47, 51,
73, 76, 146

Veritas aeterna
ewige waarheid
eternal truth, I/158, 250, II/20, 25, 36,
46, 50, 63, 64, 65, 303, IV/43, 47

Vestigium
spoor, merkteken, voetstap
trace, II/103, 106, 139, 140, 278, 296,
IV/77

Vindicta; (sese) vindicare
[PA 88: vengeance]
wraak; (z.) wreken, z. verdedigen
vengeance; to avenge (o.s.), appropriate, II/143, *172*, *201*, 237, 238, 244,
245, 269

Virtus
deugd, kracht
virtue (usu.), power (occ.), I/161, 271,
272, II/54, 86, 106, 136, 138, 183,
184, *210*, 222, 223, 224, 225, 226,
228, 234, 235, 236, 237, 247, 248,
249, 250, 251, 252, 253, 255, 262,
273, 283, 289, 293, 296, 297, 306,
307, IV/49, 70

Vis
kracht, macht, vermogen
force, power, I/157, 161, 163, 165,
166, 169, 182, 183, 185, 202, 203,
204, 208, *209*, 210, 211, 214, 215,
216, 220, 221, 222, 223, 224, 225,
230, 237, 240, 241, 242, 243, 248,
251, 256, 258, 260, II/10, 14, 16,
23, 27, 31, 37, 38, 54, 61, 121, 127,
137, 183, 203, 204, 209, 212, 214,
215, 220, 222, 227, 234, 242, 256,
264, 266, 271, 280, 287, 293, IV/29,
31, 35, 36, 53, 61, 62

Visibilis
zienlijk, zichtbaar
visible, IV/28, 29, 50, 66

VISIO DEI
aanschouwing Gods
vision of God, I/264

VITA; VIVERE
leven; leven
life; to live, I/175, 259, 260, II/5, 6, 7,
9, 11, 18, 132, 137, 164, 187, 207,
225, 226, 234, 236, 237, 238, 240,
245, 249, 253, 260, 261, 265, 267,
268, 275, 279, 287, 288, 305, 306,
307, 308, IV/127

VITIUM
gebrek
vice, defect, II/106, 137, 138, 198,
269, 273, 285, 289, 294

VITUPERIUM; VITUPERARE
[PA 157, 206; blâme]
laster; lasteren
blame; to blame, II/78, 81, *163*, 182,
237, 249

VOCABULUM
woord, naam
word, term, I/246, II/180, 181, IV/40

VOLATILIS
vluchtig
volatile, IV/16, 21, 22, 64

VOLUNTAS; VOLITIO; VELLE
wil; willing; willen

will; volition; to will, I/132, 146, 149,
153, 171, 173, 174, 175, 176, 244,
256, 263, 273, 274, 277, 278, 279,
280, 281, II/15, 63, 71, 72, 73, 74,
78, 117, 129, 130, 131, 133, 134,
135, 147, 148, 161, 190, 192, 277,
278, 279, 280, IV/9, 129, 130, 132

VOLUNTAS DEI
Gods wil
God's will, I/176, 177, 179, 238, 243,
257, 260, 261, 263, 264, II/62, 63,
71, 73, 75, 81, IV/128

VULGUS; VULGARIUS; VULGO
't gemeen volk, 't gemeen, de menigte;
gemeen; gemenelijk
ordinary people, the people, the mob,
the multitude; ordinary, common;
ordinarily, I/127, 168, 246, 254,
261, II/6, 7, 9, 33, 81, 83, 87, 162, ,
180, 250, 253, 274, 307, IV/28, 29,
48

ZELOTYPIA; ZELOTYPUS
[PA 167: jalousie]
ijverzucht of jaloersheid, naivering,
belgzucht (KV); ijverzuchtig
jealousy; jealous, II/*167*, 203, 292

Dutch–Latin–English

AALMOES
eleemosyna
charity, IV/140, 149, 150, 156

AANDOENING
affectio, I/48

ABSTRACTLIJK
abstractè, IV/92

ACHTING
[existimatio?]
esteem, I/*68*

AFHANGEN; AFHANGIG
dependere; dependens, I/17, 26, 28,
29, 30, 32, 33, 34, 36, 39, 41, 47,
64, 74, 85, 87, IV/149

AFKEER, AFKEERLIJKHEID; AFKEER HEB-
BEN, AFKEERIG ZIJN
aversio; aversari, I/65, *66*, 67

AFNOEMING
denominatio, I/4

702

AFTREKSEL; AFTREKKEN; AFTREKKIG
[abstractio]; [abstrahere]; abstractus,
abstractè, I/17

AFVAL
lapsus
fall, IV/115

AKTIE
actio, IV/108

DE AL
the All, I/19

ALGEMEEN
universalis, I/17, 32, 40, 42, 43, 47,
48, 49, 51, 56, 61, 81, 82, 83

**ALMACHTIGHEID, ALMOGENHEID;
ALMACHTIG**
omnipotentia; omnipotens, I/18, 19,
20, 22, 28, 29, 44

ALWETENDHEID; ALWETEND
omniscientia; omnisciens, I/22, 23, 29,
44, 45

ALWEZEN
universal being, I/24

ANTIPATIE
antipathia, IV/90

**BARMHARTIGHEID; BARMHARTIG;
OMBARMHARTIG**
misericordia; misericors; immisericors,
I/44, 45, IV/147

BEEST
bestia, IV/109

BEGEERLIJKHEID
libido? concupiscentia?
lust, I/28, 29, 30

BEGEERTE; BEGEREN
cupiditas, appetitus, desiderium; cupere, appetere, desiderare, I/38, 56,
58, 67, 77, 80, 84, 85, 86, 118,
IV/136, 137

BEGINSEL
principium (usu.), elementum (rar.),
I/21, 26, 109

BEGRIP, BEGRIJPING; BEGRIJPEN
conceptus, perceptio; concipere, perci-

pere, comprehendere, continere,
I/16, 26, 30, 54, 57, 61, 64, 70, 81,
96

BEHOUDENIS, BEHOUDING; BEHOUDEN
conservatio, I/40, 52, 58, 72, 82, 90,
118

BEKERING
conversion, I/107

BEKLAG
desiderium, I/76

BELGZUCHT
zelotypia, I/72

BELONING
reward, I/87, 104

BENAMING
denominatio, I/84, 89

BENAMING, UITWENDIGE
denominatio, extrinseca, I/27

BENAUWDHEID
anxiety, I/92

BEPALING; PAAL; BEPALEN; BEPAALD
determinatio (KV), definitio (elsewhere); terminus; determinare, definire, terminare; determinatus, I/16,
19, 20, 26, 28, 37, 51, 53, 82, 92,
107, 114, IV/88, 89

BEROVING
privatio, IV/91, 99, 100, 101, 102,
103, 104, 107, 109, 136

BEROUW; BEROUW HEBBEN
poenitentia; poenitere, I/29, 73

BESCHAAMTHEID (= SCHAAMTE IN KV)
verecundia (E), pudor (KV), I/74, 75

BESCHRIJVING; BESCHRIJVEN
descriptio (CM), definitio (KV); definire (KV), I/3, 4, 15, 22, 32, 39, 44,
45, 46, 47, 49, 50, 53, 56, 69, 71,
75, 78, 119, 120

BESCHULDIGEN
accusare
to blame, IV/147

DEPENDENT; DEPENDENTIE
dependens; dependentia, IV/105, 106,
107, 111, 143

DETERMINATIE; DETERMINEREN
determinatio; determinare, IV/83, 84,
148

DEUGD
virtus, I/11, 108, IV/93, 94, 112, 137,
138, 141, 142, 151, 152, 156

DICHTEN
fingere, IV/93, 118, 119

DIEF
fur
thief, IV/150, 151

DIENAAR; DIENEN
servus; servire
servant; to serve, I/87, IV/94, 95

DOENING, DAAD
actio, actus, functio, facinus, opus, actio, I/*110*, 111, IV/83, 84, 100, 101,
103, 108, 109, 111, 112, 143, 147

DOLING; DOLEN
error; errare, I/54, 55, 58, 61, 78, 79,
80, IV/99, 103, 104, 105, 106, 114,
115, 116, 140, 147, 154

DOOD
mors, I/52, 70, IV/122

DOODSLAAN
occidere
killing, IV/140, 149, 150, 156. *See also*
moedermord

DROEFHEID; Z. BEDROEVEN
tristitia; contristari, I/66, 68, 71, 73,
75, 76, 77, 88, 93, 94, 95, 96, 120

DROOM; DROMEN
somnium; somniare, I/79

DUIVEL
diabolus, I/88, 107, 108

DURING
duratio, I/33, 82, 102, 103, 104, 107,
112

EDELMOEDIGHEID; EDELMOEDIG
generositas (E, probably KV also); generosus

legitimate self-esteem (KV), I/68, *69*,
IV/92

EENHEID; VERENIGING; ENIG, EEN, EEN
ENIG
unitas; unio; unicus, I/18, 23, 27, 28,
29, 30, 31, 33, 44, 52, 57, 59, 61,
62, 63, 81, 96, 97, 99, 100, 101,
102, 108

EENHEID, GODS
unitas Dei, I/23, 44

[VER]ENIGING MET GOD
union with God, I/34, 93, 100, 101,
102, 103, 105, 106, 108, 110, 111,
121

[VER]ENIGING VAN ZIEL EN LICHAAM
unio animae et corporis, I/81, 91, 93,
96, 97, 98, 101, 102, 103, 117

EENVOUDIGHEID; EENVOUDIG
simplicitas; simplex, I/22, 24, 44

EER
gloria (KV?), honor (E, TdIE), I/63,
74, 75, 77, 111

EEUWIGHEID, EEUWIG
aeternitas; aeternus, I/15, 27, 37, 44,
45, 52, 62, 64, 103, 105, 108, 109,
111, 112, IV/84

[VAN] EEUWIGHEID
ab aeterno, I/15, 33, 37, 38, 48, 101,
105

[VOOR] EEUWIG, IN EEUWIGHEID
in aeternum, I/15, 39, 48

EIGEN, EIGENHEID
proprium, I/4, *18*, 27, *35*, 40, 45

EIGENSCHAP
proprietas (usu.), attributum (usu. in
KV), I/3, *4*, 15, 17, *18*, 19, 21, 22,
23, 24, 27, 28, 29, 32, 33, 34, 35,
39, 40, 44, 45, 46, 47, 48, 51, 53,
90, 91, 92, 96, 97, 98, 114, 115,
116, 117, 118, 119, 120, IV/94

EIND
finis, I/60, 61, 69, 88, 105, 111, IV/94,
115, 118

EINDIG, EINDELIJK
finitus, I/16, 18, 25, 26, 82, 117

GEVOEL; GEVOELEN
sensus; sentire, I/29, *52*, 55, 74, 79, 81, 83, 94, 98, 120, 121, IV/160

GEWAARWORDING; GEWAARWORDEN
perceptio; percipere, sentire, I/52, 56, 60, 64, 74, 79, 81, 83, 84, 85, 89, 90, 91, 93, 94, 95, 96, 101, 102, 105, 111

GEWROCHT
effectus, I/31, 33, 107, *110*, 111, 112

GIERIGHEID; GIERIGAARD
avaritia; avarus, I/76, 111

GOD
Deus, I/3, 4, 8, 9, 10, 15, 16, 18, *19*, 20, 21, 22, 23, 24, 26, 27, 30, 31, 32, 33, 34, 35, 36, 37, 38, 39, 40, 42, 43, 44, 45, 46, 47, 48, 51, 53, 60, 61, 63, 64, 65, 68, 70, 74, 77, 78, 79, 82, 87, 88, 90, 97, 100, 101, 103, 104, 105, 106, 107, 108, 109, 110, 111, 112, 116, 117, 121, IV/88, 90, 91, 92, 93, 94, 138, 139, 147, 148, 149, 150, 151

GOD, NATUUR, WEZENHEID VAN
natura, essentia Dei, I/15, 32, 106, 111

GODDELIJKHEID; GODDELIJK
[divinitas]; divinus, I/19, 40, 107, 108

GODDELOOS
improbus, impius
godless, IV/92, 94, 109, 110, 138, 139, *148*

GODGELEERDE
theologi, I/109

GODSDIENST
religio, cultus Dei, I/58, *88*

GODZALIG
pius
godly, IV/109, 110

GOED; GOEDHEID
bonus, I/5, 19, 21, 22, 37, 38, 43, 49, 50, 55, 56, 57, 58, 60, 61, 62, 63, 65, 66, 68, 69, 70, 71, 72, 73, 74, 76, 77, 78, 80, 84, 85, 89, 94, 95, 96, 99, 100, IV/88, 142, 150

GOED, HET OPPERSTE
summum bonum, I/44, 45, 88, 109

GOED, IN OPZICHT VAN HET, ONDER SCHIJN VAN, GEDAANTE VAN
sub ratione boni, sub specie boni, I/58, 84

GOED, KENNIS VAN . . . EN KWAAD
cognitio boni et mali, I/60, 77

GRAMSCHAP
ira, I/74

GRONDREGEL
principle, I/16, 53

GUNST; BEGUNSTIGEN
favor; favere, I/76, 77

GULZIGHEID
avaritia, IV/92

HAAT; HATEN
odium; odio habere, I/29, 58, *65*, *66*, 67, 77, 87, 92, 94, 95, 108, IV/150

HEELAL
universus, I/4

HEIL; HEILIG
salus?; salutaris?, I/*37*, 67, 69, 70, 86, 88, 109, 110, 112

HEL
inferi, I/*88*

HERSCHEPPING, GEDURIGE
creatio continua, IV/88, 139

HOEDANIGHEID
qualitas
quality (usu.), character, I/62, 79, 112

HOOP; VERHOPEN
spes; sperare, I/70, *71*, 72

HOREN ZEGGEN
auditus, I/54, 55, 57, 58, 61, 99

HOVAARDIGHEID
superbia, IV/92

IDEE, IDEA
idea, I/17, 42, 43, 49, 51, 52, 60, 74, 78, 79, 81, 82, 83, 84, 91, 96, 97, 98, 101, 102, 103, 116, 117, 118, 119, 120, 121

(rar.); pati; patibilis, I/24, 26, 55, 56, 61, 79, 83, 92, 110, 111

LOF; PRIJZEN
laus; laudare, I/74, 75

LOGICA; LOGICI
logic; logicians, I/46

LOON
praemium, IV/93

LUST
appetitus, libido, I/58, 85, 86

MACHT; MACHTIG
potentia, potestas, vis; potens, I/16, 19, 62, 63, 64, 68, 69, 80, 89, 92, 95, 99, 100, 112, IV/86, 87

MACHT, GODS
potentia (potestas) Dei, I/19, 21, 38

MANNELIJK
manly, I/71

MEDEGEWETEN
conscientia
conscience, I/54

MEDEWERKING, GODS
concursus Dei, IV/83, 88

MENING; MENEN
opinio, sententia, mens; opinari, velle, intelligere, animus esse
opinion, meaning; think, mean, intend, I/19, 27, 43, IV/88, 95, 145, 146, 149, 150, 160, 161

MENS
homo, I/26, 40, 42, 43, 46, 49, 51, 53, 54, 73, 82, 98, 105, 106, 117, 120, IV/89, 151

MENS, VOLMAAKT
[homo perfectus], I/60, 61, 67, 72, 76, 80, 87, IV/148

MIRAKEL
miraculum, I/107

MOED
fortitudo?, I/70, 71, 73

MOEDERMOORD
matricidium
matricide, IV/147

MOGELIJKHEID; MOGELIJK
possibilitas, potestas; possibilis
possibility, power; possible, I/17, 19, 91, 99

NAAST
proximus, I/87, 111, 112

NATUUR
natura [= tota Natura], I/4, 22, 23, 24, 25?, 26, 27, 28, 38, 40, 46, 49, 64, 90, 96, 97, 98, 101, 104, 105, 116, 117

NATUUR, GENATUURDE
natura naturata, I/5, 47, 48

NATUUR, NATURENDE
natura naturans, I/5, 47

NATUUR, SCHIFTING VAN DE
nature, division of, I/46, 47, 116?

NATUUR, SCHIK EN LOOP VAN DE
order and course of Nature, I/86

NATUUR
natura [= essentia, constitutio], I/15, 17, 20, 25, 42, 53, 91

NATUUR, BIJZONDERE
natura singularis, IV/141, 142, 149

NEDERIGHEID
humilitas, I/68, 69

NEDERIGHEID, STRAFBARE
abjectio
self-depreciation, I/68, 69, 70

NEGATIE
negatio, IV/103

NEIGING
inclination, I/65, 76, 80, 84, 85

NIET
nihil, I/19, 21, 28, 83, 91, 107

NIJD, NIJDIGHEID
invidia, I/66, 74, 88, 108

NOODZAKELIJKHEID; NOODZAKELIJK
necessitas; necessarius, I/4, 17, 24, 34, 36, 37, 38, 41, 42, 62, 64, 68, 70, 71, 72, 74, 76, 81, 90, 97, 98, 100, 105, 107, 111, 115, 117, 118

Oorzaak, naaste
causa proxima, I/36

Oorzaak, natuurlijke
natural cause, I/35

Oorzaak, noodzakelijke
necessary cause, I/4

Oorzaak, overgaande
causa transiens, I/30, 35

Oorzaak, uitvloeiende, of darstel-
lende
emanative or productive cause, I/35

Oorzaak, uitwendige, uitterlijke
causa externa, I/17, 18, 42, 81, 110,
111, 112

Oorzaak, van zich (zijn zelfs)
causa sui, I/18, 36, 46, 47, 48, 86,
114, 115

Oorzaak, verder, laatste
causa remota, I/31, 36

Oorzaak, voorgaande
predisposing cause, I/36

Oorzaak, voorname
causa principalis, I/35, 77

Oorzaak, vrije
causa libera, I/35, 38, 39, 63, 110

Oorzaak, werkende
causa efficiens, I/35

Openbaring
revelatio, IV/92, 93, 96, 118, 119, 120
121

Opinie
opinio, I/57, 58, 66, 68, 72

Orde der Natuur
ordo Naturae, I/64

Orde en gevolg van oorzaaken
orde et series causorum, I/72

Overaltegenwoordigheid, Gods; ov-
eral
ubiquitas (Dei); ubique, I/44

Parabel
parabola, IV/93, 118

Passie
passio, I/58, 59, 60, 61, 65, 66, 77, 88,
89, 94, 95, 99, IV/114

Pijn, pijnlijkheid; pijnlijk
dolor, I/96, 120

Plicht
officium, I/109

Poging; pogen
conatus; conari, I/40, IV/82, 83, 84

Positief
positivus, IV/156

Predestinatie
predestination, I/4, 35, 36, 40

Profeet
propheta, IV/92, 93, 118, 119, 120

Recht; rechtvaardigheid; rechtvaar-
dig
jus; justitia, justus, I/38, 42, 78, 87,
IV/137, 140, 149, 150

Rechter
judex, I/87, IV/112, 138, 139

Reden; redeneren; redenering; rede-
lijk
ratio; ratiocinari; ratiocinium; rationalis, I/28, 29, 30, 55, 58, 59, 63, 65,
66, 67, 73, 74, 77, 99, 121, IV/114

Regeerder
ruler, I/27

Regel
regula, I/42, 54, 55, 59, 78, 99, 100,
104

Rijkdom
divitiae, I/63

Roering
motus, I/35

Rust; rusten
quies
rest, peace; to be at rest, content, I/26,
29, 64, 65, 91, 97, 98, 102, 108,
109, 121

Samenlopen
concurrere, comitari
to concur (with), to accompany,
IV/83, 98, 107, 108, 109

VERWARRING; VERWARREN; VERWARD;
VERWARDELIJK
confusio; confundere; confusus; confuse, I/30, 31, 42, 43, IV/148

VERWONDERING; VERWONDEREN
admiratio, stupor; admirari, I/56, 57,
61, 62, 67

VERZAMELING, DE GEHELE . . . DER
DINGEN
the totality of things, I/4

VERZEKERDHEID
securitas, I/70, *71*, 72

VOLGIJVER
aemulatio, I/70, *71*, 73

VOLHARDEN
perseverare, IV/82

VOLK, HET GEMEEN
plebs (Ep.), vulgus (elsewhere), popu-
lus (Ep.)
the (ordinary) people, IV/92, 119, 120

VOLMAAKTHEID; VOLMAAKT
perfectio; perfectus, I/3, 17, 18, 19,
20, 21, 22, 23, 24, 26, 28, 29, 36,
37, 38, 39, 42, 43, 44, 49, 51, 60,
64, 65, 67, 69, 70, 87, 96, 108, 111,
115, 116, IV/89, 90, 91, 94, 97, 98,
99, 100, 101, 102, 103, 104, 105,
106, 107, 108, 109, 110, 111, 112,
115, 116, 117, 136, 137, 138, 139,
140, 148, 150, 152, 156. *See also*
mens, volmaakt

VOLMAAKST, 'T ALDERVOLMAAKST; TEN
HOOGSTEN, OPPERSTEN VOLMAAKT
perfectissimum; summe perfectum,
I/19, 28, 42, 88

VOLMAAKTHEID, UITSTEKENDE
perfectio eminens
eminent perfection, I/33

VOORBEPALEN
predetermine, I/37, 38

VOORBESCHIKKING; VOORBESCHIKKER
predetermination; predeterminer, I/4,
27

VOORDEEL
utile, I/72, 74, 78, 109

VOORTBRENGING; VOORTBRENGEN
generatio; producere, procreare, I/3,
19, 20, 21, 22, 23, 90

VOORTGANG
conservatio, IV/139

VOORWERP; VOORWERPIG; VOORWERPIG-
LIJK
objectum; objectivus; objective, I/16,
61, 62, 63, 64, 79, 93, 94, 95, 97,
116, 117, 118, 119, 120

VOORZICHTIGHEID
prudentia, IV/144

VOORZIENIGHEID, VOORZORG; VOOR-
ZORGER
providentia
providence; provider, I/4, 40, 42, 43,
IV/87, 88

VORM; VORMELIJKHEID; VORMELIJK
forma; formalitas; formaliter, I/15, 16,
19, 20, 21, 22, 23, 117, 118

VREES; VRESEN
metus, timor; timere, I/58, 70, *71*, 72,
88

VRIENDSCHAP
amicitia, IV/86, 87

VRIJHEID; VRIJ; VRIJWILLIG
libertas; liberus; libere, I/35, 37, 39,
62, 75, 77, 80, 81, 82, 83, 85, 86,
104, 109, 110, 111, 112, IV/116,
117, 143, 152, 154

VROLIJKHEID; VROLIJK
hilaritas
cheerfulness; merry, I/92, 121

VROOM
probus
pious, IV/92, 94, 110, 136, 138, 139,
140, *148*, 151

WAAN, WAANBEGRIP; WANEN
opinio (usu.), error (occ.?); opinari,
I/44, *54*, 55, 56, 57, 58, 59, 60, 66,
68, *69*, 74, 75, 80, 89, 96, *99*

WAARHEID; WAAR; WAARLIJK
veritas; verus; vere, I/11, 17, 24, 30,
59, 63, 70, 73, *78*, 79, 84, 112,
IV/86, 87

WAARSCHIJNLIJK
probable, I/45

WANGUNST; WANGUNSTIG
invidia (?), I/20, 21

WANHOOP
desperatio, I/70, *71*, 72, 88, IV/92

WANKELMOEDIGHEID
fluctuatio animi, I/70, *71*, 72, 73

WEDERGEBOORTE
rebirth, I/102

WELLUST
libido, I/63, 109, 111, IV/136, 137,
138, 139, 149

WELSTAND
salus?
well-being, I/*11*, 40, 80, 86, 88, 89,
100, 104, 105

WERELD
mundus, I/73, 109, IV/151

WERKING, WERK; WERKEN; WERKER
actio, operatio, facinus, opus, effectus
(rar.); agere, operari; agens?, I/26,
35, 36, 49, 50, 61, 65, 66, 74, 75,
87, 94, 107, 110, IV/82, 100, 106,
107, 108, 110, 137, 138, 139, 140,
141, 148, 149, 150, 151

WET
lex, IV/92, 93, 141

WET, MENSELIJK
lex humana, I/89, 104, 105

WET, VAN DE NATUUR, GODDELIJK
lex Naturae, divina, I/88, 104, 105,
IV/149

WETENSCHAP, WETEN; WETEN
scientia; scire, I/43, 54, 59, 78

WETENSCHAP, GODS
scientia Dei, I/43

WEZENHEID; WEZEN; ESSENTIEËLIJK
essentia; ens; essentiâ, I/4, 15, 17, 19,
23, 28, 31, 32, 40, 43, 46, 49, 51,
64, 79, 80, 90, 96, 97, 107, 110,
111, 116, IV/89, 90, 100, 110, 112,
137, 138, 139, 147, 149, 152

WEZEN, DADELIJK
ens reale, I/24, 49, 60, 81, 82, 83

WEZEN VAN REDEN
ens rationis, I/5, 24, 49, 60, 61, 81,
82, 83

WEZENHEID, BIJZONDERE
essentia particularis, I/24

WEZENHEID, DADELIJK
essentia actualis, I/64

WEZENHEID, VOORWERPIGE
essentia objectiva, I/18

WEZENLIJKHEID; WEZENLIJK ZIJN; WEZEN-
LIJK
existentia; existere; realis?, I/17, 18,
22, 24, 41, 42, 51, 52, 96, 97, 116,
119, IV/100, 140

WEZENLIJKHEID, GODS
existentia Dei, I/15, 16, 17, 18

WEZENLIJK ZIJN, DOOR ZICH
existere per se, I/20

WIJSBEGEERTE; WIJSGEER
philosophia; philosophus, I/11

WIJSHEID, WIJS
sapientia; sapiens, I/44, 45

WIJZ(ING)
modus, methodus, I/24, 25, 26, 29,
45, 46, 47, 48, 51, 52, 53, 62, 64,
81, 105, 106, 117, 118, 119, 120

WIL; WILLING, TE WILLEN; WILLEN
voluntas; volitio; velle, I/42, 56, *80*,
81, 82, 83, 84, 85, IV/82, 83, 90,
103, 104, 105, 106, 111, 113, 114,
116, 124, 143

WIL, GODS
voluntas Dei, I/19, 37, 38, 39, IV/83,
88, 90, 98, 99, 100, 118, 119, 138,
139, 140, 141, 142, 143

WOORD
verbum, I/30, 79, 83, 106, 107

ZAAK; ZAKELIJK
res; reale, I/16, 18, 24, 27, 30, 31, 40,
41, 43, 45, 46, 49, 50, 55, 59, 64,
81, 82, 96, 97, 103, 104, 107, 110,
IV/150

Index of Proper Names

THIS INDEX covers only references (direct and indirect) to Spinoza's predecessors and contemporaries, made by Spinoza, his correspondents, or the editor, in the text, notes, and prefaces. It excludes editorial references in the Glossary-Index and to subsequent philosophers and commentators in the notes and prefaces. References in the text are indexed by the Gebhardt page numbers. Editorial references are prefixed by "(ed.)" and are indexed by the pagination of this edition.

Aquinas, Thomas, I/18
   (ed.) 29n, 67n, 82n, 87n, 88n,
  89n, 91n, 306n, 320n, 321n, 333-
  336nn, 342n, 344n, 437n, 451n
Archimedes, I/205
Aristotle, I/42, 56n, 235, 259, 278
   (ed.) 8n, 42n, 126n, 272n, 325n,
  344n, 421n, 473n, 474n, 528n, 564n
Averroes, (ed.) 87n

Bacon, Francis, IV/6, 8, 9, 25, 67
   (ed.) 11n, 12n, 16n, 167n, 169n
Balling, Pieter, IV/41
   (ed.) x, 50, 224, 239n, 254n, 351,
  405, 406, 409n, 413n, 414n, 430n,
  440n, 442n, 443n, 448n, 523n
Blyenbergh, Willem van, IV/79, 86,
  96, 126, 134, 145, 153, 160
   (ed.) 349-352
Boe, Franciscus de le, (ed.) 574n
Borelli, Giovanni, IV/39, 40, 44
   (ed.) 191n
Bouwmeester, Johannes, IV/162
   (ed.) 5, 351
Boyle, Robert, IV/6, 15, 37, 48, 50,
  51, 64, 66, 69-71, 73-75, 158, 159
   (ed.) 159-161, 164n, 173n, 174n,
  178n, 179n, 180n, 181n, 182n,
  183n, 184n, 185n, 186n, 187n,
  198n, 199n, 200n, 213n, 214n,
  216n, 265n
Bruno, Giordano, (ed.) 73n
Burgersdijk, Franco, (ed.) 80n, 82n,
  223, 318n, 319n
Buridan, John, II/133
   (ed.) 487n

Cajetan, (ed.) 302n
Calvin, Jean, (ed.) 82n, 84n, 85n
Casearius, IV/39, 42, 63
   (ed.) 190n, 193n, 207n
Cats, Jacob, (ed.) 574n
Cicero, II/202
   (ed.) 443n, 541n
Clavius, Christopher, IV/40
   (ed.) 191n
Crescas, Chasdai, IV/61
   (ed.) 102n, 205n

Descartes, René, I/ 47, 128-133, 141-
  147, 151, 154-156, 158-163, 167,
  171, 174, 181-184, 190-192, 195,
  201, 202, 208, 211, 212, 218, 219,
  225, 226, 240, 257, II/137, 278-280,
  IV/6, 8, 9, 18, 24, 25, 34, 49, 50,
  63, 66, 67, 72, 75, 81, 83, 116, 124,
  129-133, 135, 143, 154, 155, 159
   (ed.) xx, 5-6, 16n, 26n, 28n, 29n,
  31n, 48, 63n, 65n, 67n, 71n, 82n,
  87n, 99n, 102n, 105n, 107n, 110n,
  111n, 115n, 124n, 125n, 159, 161,
  175n, 185n, 196n, 204n, 216n, 221-
  224, 232-234nn, 236n, 238-241nn,
  243n, 248n, 250n, 253n, 254n,
  256n, 258n, 260-266nn, 268n, 273n,
  275-277nn, 280-285nn, 287-291nn,
  295-298nn, 300n, 303n, 307n, 310-
  313nn, 315n, 316n, 320n, 321n,
  324n, 335n, 341n, 342n, 345n,
  422n, 423n, 437n, 438n, 440n,
  447n, 449n, 459n, 460n, 473n,
  474n, 484-486nn, 492n, 495n, 499-
  501nn, 526n, 531-533nn, 553-555nn,
  596n

Index of Biblical and Talmudic References

Reference List

Akkerman, Hubbeling, and Westerbrink (AHW). Spinoza. *Briefwisseling*. Translated and edited by F. Akkerman, H. G. Hubbeling and A. G. Westerbrink. Amsterdam: Wereldbibliotheek, 1977.

Akkerman, Hubbeling, Mignini, Petry and van Suchtelen (AHMPS). Spinoza. *Korte Geschriften*. Amsterdam: Wereldbibliotheek, 1982. Contains translations of *Descartes' "Principles,"* the *Metaphysical Thoughts*, the *Treatise on the Emendation of the Intellect*, and new editions of the *Short Treatise, Algebraic Calculations on the Rainbow*, and *Calculation of Chances*.

Akkerman 1. F. Akkerman. *Spinoza's tekort aan woorden*. Mededelingen vanwege het Spinozahuis XXXVI. Leiden: Brill, 1977.

Ackkerman 2. *Studies in the Posthumous Works of Spinoza, on style, earliest translation and reception, and modern edition of some texts*. Thesis defended at the University of Groningen in 1980. Published by Krips Repro Meppel.

Alquié. F. Aliquié, ed. *Oeuvres philosophiques de Descartes*. 3 vols. Paris: Garnier, 1963-1973.

Appuhn. *Oeuvres de Spinoza*. Translated and edited by C. Appuhn. 4 vols. I: *Court traité, Traité de la réforme de l'entendement, Principes de la philosophie de Descartes, Pensées métaphysiques*; II: *Traité théologico-politique*; III: *Ethique*; IV: *Traité politique, Lettres*. Paris: Garnier, 1964.

Anscombe and Geach. *Descartes, Philosophical Writings*. Translated by E. Anscombe and P. Geach. London: Nelson, 1969.

Aquinas 1. St. Thomas Aquinas. *Summa theologiae*. 60 vols. Blackfriars edition. London: Eyre & Spottiswoode, 1964-1966.

Aquinas 2. *Summa contra gentiles*. 4 vols. Paris: P. Lethielleux, 1961.

Avenarius. R. Avenarius. *Uber die beiden ersten Phasen des spinozistischen Pantheismus*. Leipzig, 1868.

Bacon. Francis Bacon. *Opera*. Edited by J. Spedding, R. L. Ellis, and D. D. Heath. 15 vols. Boston 1857-1876.

Barnes. J. Barnes. *The Presocratic Philosophers*. 2 vols. London: Routledge and Kegan Paul, 1979.

Bayle. P. Bayle. *Historical and Critical Dictionary*. Selected and translated by R. Popkin. Indianapolis: Bobbs-Merrill, 1965.

Bennett 1. J. Bennett. "A Note on Descartes and Spinoza." *Philosophical Review* 74 (1965):379-380.

Bennett 2. *A Study of Spinoza's "Ethics."* Indianapolis: Hackett, 1984.

Bidney. D. Bidney. *The Psychology and Ethics of Spinoza*. New Haven: Yale University Press, 1940.

Boehm. R. Boehm. " 'Dieses war die Ethic und zwar Niederlandisch, wie sie Spinoza anfangs verferttiget,'—Spinozas 'Korte Verhandeling,' eine Übersetzung aus einem lateinischen Urtext?" *Studia Philosophica Gandensia* 5 (1967):175-206.

Bouillier. F. Bouillier. *Histoire de la philosophie cartésienne*. 2 vols. 1868. Reprint. Geneva: Slatkine, 1970.

Boyle 1. Robert Boyle. *New Experiments, touching the spring of the air and its effects (made, for the most part in a new pneumatical engine)*. Oxford, 1660.

Boyle 2. *Certain Physiological Essays, written at distant times, and on several occasions*. London, 1661.

L

Boyle 3. *Tentamina quaedam physiologica, diversis temporibus et occasionibus conscripta.* London, 1661. A Latin translation of Boyle 2.

Boyle 4. *The Sceptical Chemist.* London, 1661.

Boyle 5. *Chymista scepticus.* London, 1662. A Latin translation of Boyle 4.

Burgersdijk. F. Burgersdijk, *Institutionum metaphysicarum libri duo.* Edited by A. Heereboord. London, 1653.

Calvin. J. Calvin. *Institutes of the Christian Religion.* Edited and translated by J. T. McNeill and F. L. Battles. Philadelphia: Westminster Press, 1967.

Cassirer. E. Cassirer. *Das Erkenntnisproblem in der Philosophie und Wissenschaft der neueren Zeit.* 2 vols. Berlin: B. Cassirer, 1911.

Chronicon Spinozanum. 5 vols. The Hague: Spinoza Society, 1921-1927.

Cohen. I. B. Cohen. " 'Quantum in se est': Newton's Concept of Inertia in Relation to Descartes and Lucretius." *Notes and Records of the Royal Society of London* 19 (1964):131-155.

Conant. J. B. Conant. *Robert Boyle's Experiments in Pneumatics.* Cambridge, Mass.: Harvard University Press, 1958.

Cottingham. J. Cottingham. *Descartes' Conversation with Burman.* Oxford: Clarendon Press, 1976.

Crommelin. C. A. Crommelin. *Spinoza's natuurwetenschappelijk denken.* Mededelingen vanwege het Spinozahuis VI. Leiden: Brill, 1939.

Curley 1. E. M. Curley. "Notes on the Immortality of the Soul in Spinoza's *Short Treatise.*" *Giornale,* 327-336.

Curley 2. "Experience in Spinoza's Theory of Knowledge." In Grene, 25-59.

Curley 3. *Spinoza's Metaphysics.* Cambridge, Mass.: Harvard University Press, 1969.

Curley 4. "Spinoza's Moral Philosophy." In Grene, 354-376.

Curley 5. "Descartes, Spinoza and the Ethics of Belief." In Mandelbaum and Freeman, 159-189.

Curley 6. "Recent Work on 17th Century Continental Philosophy." *American Philosophical Quarterly* 11 (1974):235-255.

Curley 7. "Spinoza as an Expositor of Descartes." In Hessing, 133-142.

Curley 8. *Descartes Against the Skeptics.* Cambridge, Mass.: Harvard University Press, 1978.

Curley 9. "Spinoza on Truth." In Tucker.

Curley 10. "Descartes on the Creation of the Eternal Truths." *Philosophical Review* 569-597 (October 1984).

Curley 11. "Leibniz on Locke on Personal Identity." In *Leibniz: Critical and Interpretive Essays.* Edited by M. Hooker. Minneapolis: University of Minnesota Press, 1982.

DeFerrari and Barry. R. Deferrari and M. Barry. *A Lexicon of St. Thomas Aquinas.* 5 vols. Washington, D.C.: Catholic University of America Press, 1948.

Delbos. V. Delbos. *Le spinozisme.* Paris: Vrin, 1964.

de Deugd. C. de Deugd. *The Significance of Spinoza's First Kind of Knowledge.* Assen: Van Gorcum, 1966.

de Dijn. H. de Dijn. Review of Curley (3). *Tijdschrift voor filosofie* 32 (1970):335-338.

Dibon. P. Dibon. "Notes bibliographiques sur les cartésiens hollandais." In Dijksterhuis, 261-300.

Dijksterhuis. E. J. Dijksterhuis et al. *Descartes et le cartésianisme hollandais.* Paris: PUF, 1950.

Dilthey. W. Dilthey. "Die Autonomie des Denkens, der konstruktive Rationalismus und der pantheistische Monismus nach ihrem Zusammenhang im 17. Jahrhundert." *Archiv für Geschichte der Philosophie* 7 (1894):28-91.

Diogenes Laertius. Diogenes Laertius. *The Lives of the Philosophers.* Translated by R. D. Hicks. 2 vols. London: W. Heineman, 1925.

Donagan 1. A. Donagan. "Essence and the Distinction of Attributes in Spinoza's Metaphysics." In Grene, 164-181.

Donagan 2. "A Note on Spinoza, *Ethics*, I, 10." *Philosophical Review* 75 (1966):380-382.

Donagan 3. "Spinoza's Proof of Immortality." In Grene, 241-258.

Dunin-Borkowski. S. von Dunin-Borkowski. *Spinoza.* 4 vols. Munster: Aschendorff, 1933.

Eisenberg 1. B. de Spinoza. *Treatise on the Improvement of the Understanding.* Translated, with a preface, notes and index by Paul D. Eisenberg. *Philosophy Research Archives*, 5 July 1977.

Eisenberg 2. "Is Spinoza an Ethical Naturalist?" In Hessing, 145-164.

Eisenberg 3. "How to Understand *De Intellectus Emendatione.*" *Journal of the History of Philosophy* 9 (1971):171-191.

Ellis. B. Ellis. "The Origin and Nature of Newton's Laws of Motion." In *Beyond the Edge of Certainty*, edited by R. Colodny. Englewood Cliffs, N.J.: Prentice-Hall, 1965.

Feuer. L.S. Feuer. *Spinoza and the Rise of Liberalism.* Boston: Beacon Press, 1958.

Fischer. K. Fischer. *Geschichte der neueren Philosophie.* 5th ed. Heidelberg: Carl Winter, 1909.

Freudenthal 1. J. Freudenthal. *Die Lebensgeschichte Spinoza's in Quellenschriften, Urkunden und nichtamtlichen Nachrichten.* Leipzig, 1899.

Freudenthal 2. "Spinozastudien." In *Zeitschrift für Philosophie und philosophische Kritik* 108:238-282; 109:1-25.

Freudental 3. "Spinoza und die Scholastik." In *Philosophische Aufsätze E. Zeller gewidmet.* Leipzig, 1887.

Freudenthal 4. Critique of Fischer. *Zeitschrift für Philosophie.*

Freudenthal 5. *Spinoza: Leben und Lehre.* Heidelberg: Carl Winter, 1927.

Garber and Cohen. D. Garber and L. Cohen. "A Point of Order: Analysis, Synthesis and Descartes's *Principles.*" *Archiv für Geschichte der Philosophie* 64 (1982).

Gebhardt 1. C. Gebhardt. "Rembrandt und Spinoza." *Chronicon Spinozanum*, 4:160-183.

Gebhardt 2. "Spinoza und der Platonismus." *Chronicon Spinozanum*, 1:178-234.

Gebhardt 3. *Spinozas Abhandlung über die Verbesserung des Verstandes.* Heidelberg, 1905.

Giancotti Boscherini 1. E. Giancotti Boscherini and G. Crapulli. *Ricerche lessicali su opere di Descartes e Spinoza.* Roma: Ateneo, 1969.

Giancotti Boscherini 2. *Lexicon spinozanum.* 2 vols. The Hague: M. Nijhoff, 1970.

Gilson 1. E. Gilson. *Index Scolastico-Cartésien.* New York: Burt Franklin, n.d.

Gilson 2. "Spinoza interprète de Descartes." In *Chronicon Spinozanum*, 3:68-87.

Giornale. Giornale critico della filosofia italiana 56, nos. 3-4 (1977). A special tercentennial number devoted to Spinoza, with articles by van der Bend, Caillois, Corsano, Curley, de Dijn, Floistad, Giancotti Boscherini, Guzzo, Hubbeling, Iljenkov and Naumenko, McShea, Matheron, Misrahi, Motroshilova, Mugnier-Pollet, Préposiet, Saccaro Battisti, Semerari, Sokolov, de Vries, and Zac.

Gouhier. H. Gouhier. *La pensée métaphysique de Descartes*. Paris: Vrin, 1962.

Grene. M. Grene, ed. *Spinoza, a collection of critical essays*. Garden City, N.Y.: Doubleday/Anchor, 1973.

Gueroult 1. M. Gueroult. *Spinoza*. 2 vols. to date. I: *Dieu*; II: *L'âme*. Paris: Aubier, 1968-1974. For a fragment of the uncompleted third volume, see *Revue* 2, 285-302.

Gueroult 2. *Etudes sur Descartes, Spinoza, Malebranche et Leibniz*. Hildesheim: Georg Olms, 1970.

Gueroult 3. *Descartes selon l'ordre des raisons*. 2 vols. Paris: Aubier, 1953.

Hall 1. M. B. Hall. *Robert Boyle on Natural Philosophy, an essay with selections from his writings*. Bloomington: Indiana University Press, 1966.

Hall 2. *Robert Boyle and 17th Century Chemistry*. Cambridge: Cambridge University Press, 1958.

Hall 3. A. R. and M. B. Hall. "Philosophy and Natural Philosophy: Boyle and Spinoza." In *Melanges Alexandre Koyré*, II: *L'aventure de l'esprit*, 241-246. Paris: Hermann, 1964.

Harris 1. E. Harris. *Salvation From Despair*. The Hague: M. Nijhoff, 1973.

Harris 2. "Finite and Infinite in Spinoza's System." In Hessing, 197-211.

Harris 3. "Spinoza's Theory of Immortality." In Mandelbaum and Freeman, 245-262.

Haserot. F. S. Haserot. "Spinoza's Definition of Attribute." *Philosophical Review* 62 (1953):499-513. Reprinted in Kashap, 28-42.

Hayes. B. Spinoza. *Earlier Philosophical Writings*, *The Cartesian Principles* and *Metaphysical Thoughts*. Translated by F. Hayes, introduction by D. Bidney. Indianapolis: Bobbs-Merrill, 1963.

Heereboord 1. A. Heereboord. *Disputationes ex philosophia selectae*. Leiden, 1650.

Heereboord 2. *Meletemata philosophica*. Amsterdam, 1680.

Herivel. J. Herivel. *The Background to Newton's Principia*. Oxford: Clarendon Press, 1965.

Hessing. S. Hessing, ed. *Speculum spinozanum*. London: Routledge and Kegan Paul, 1977.

Hobbes. T. Hobbes. *Works*. Edited by W. Molesworth. London, 1839-1845. EW = English Works (11 vols.); LW = Latin Works (5 vols.).

Hubbeling. H. Hubbeling. "The Development of Spinoza's Axiomatic Method." In *Revue* 1, 53-68.

Jansonius. H. Jansonius. *Nieuw Groot Nederlands-Engels Woordenboek*. Leiden: Nederlandsche Uitgeversmaatschappij, 1972, 3 vols.

Joachim 1. H. H. Joachim. *A Study of the Ethics of Spinoza*. Oxford: Clarendon Press, 1901.

Joachim 2. *Spinoza's Tractatus de Intellectus Emendatione*. Oxford: Clarendon Press, 1940.

Kashap. S. P. Kashap, ed. *Studies in Spinoza*. Berkeley: University of California Press, 1972.

Kenny. A. Kenny. *Descartes*. New York: Random House, 1968.

Kline. G. Kline. "On the Infinity of Spinoza's Attributes." In Hessing, 333-352.

Kneale. M. Kneale. "Eternity and Sempiternity." In Grene, 227-240.

Koyré 1. A. Koyré. *From the Closed World to the Infinite Universe*. Baltimore: Johns Hopkins Press, 1957.

Koyré 2. *Traité de la réforme de l'entendement*. Text, translation and notes. 3rd ed. Paris: Vrin, 1964.

Koyré 3. *Newtonian Studies*. London: Chapman and Hall, 1965.

Lachièze-Rey. P. Lachièze-Rey. *Les origines cartésiennes du Dieu de Spinoza*. Paris: Vrin, 1950.

Leibniz. G. W. von Leibinz. *Philosophische Schriften*. Edited by C. I. Gerhardt. 7 vols. Berlin, 1875-1890.

Leopold. J. H. Leopold. *Ad Spinozae opera posthuma*. The Hague: M. Nijhoff, 1902.

Lewkowitz. J. Lewkowitz. *Spinoza's Cogitata Metaphysica und Ihr Verhaltnis zu Descartes und zur Scholastik*. Breslau, 1902.

Lewis and Short. C. T. Lewis and C. Short. *A Latin Dictionary*. Oxford: Clarendon Press, 1969.

Locke. J. Locke. *An Essay Concerning Human Understanding*. Edited by P. Nidditch. Oxford: Clarendon Press, 1975.

Lovejoy. A. Lovejoy. *The Great Chain of Being*. New York: Harper, 1960.

Luther. M. Luther. *On the Bondage of the Will*. Translated by J. L. Packer and O. R. Johnston. London: James Clark, 1957.

McKeon. R. McKeon. *Selections from Medieval Philosophers*. 2 vols. New York: Scribner, 1930.

Maimonides 1. Moses ben Maimon. *The Guide of the Perplexed*. Translated with introduction and notes by Shlomo Pines, introductory essay by Leo Strauss. Chicago: University of Chicago Press, 1963.

Maimonides 2. *Le livre de connaissance*. Translated by V. Nikiprowetzky and A. Zaoui. Paris: PUF, 1961.

Mandelbaum and Freeman. M. Mandelbaum and E. Freeman. *Spinoza, Essays in Interpretation*. La Salle, Ill.: Open Court, 1975. A reprint of the special number of *The Monist* dedicated to Spinoza in 1971, to which have been added four new essays and a bibliography supplementing the work of Oko and Wetlesen, up to the end of 1972.

Mark. T. Mark. *"Ordine Geometrico Demonstrata*: Spinoza's Use of the Axiomatic Method." *Review of Metaphysics* 29 (1975):263-286.

Matheron 1. A. Matheron. *Individu et communauté chez Spinoza*. Paris: Les éditions de Minuit, 1969.

Matheron 2. "Spinoza et la sexualité." *Giornale*, 436-457.

Mattern. R. Mattern. "Spinoza and Ethical Subjectivism." *Canadian Journal of Philosophy*, Supplementary Volume IV: *New Essays on Rationalism and Empiricism*, edited by C. Jarrett, J. King-Farlow, and F. J. Pelletier (1978):59-82.

McKeon. R. McKeon. *Selections from Medieval Philosophers*. 2 vols. New York: Scribners, 1930.

Meinsma. K. O. Meinsma. *Spinoza en zijn kring*. The Hague, 1896. A classic, but even readers who have Dutch should now prefer the recent French translation by S. Roosenburg and J.-P. Osier (*Spinoza et son cercle*, Paris, J. Vrin, 1983), with extensive updating by H. Méchoulan, P.-F. Moreau, and others.

Mignini 1. F. Mignini. Critical edition of the KV in Akkerman, Hubbeling, Mignini, Petry, and van Suchtelen.

Mignini 2. "Per la datazione e l'interpretazione del *Tractatus de Intellectus Emendatione* di B. Spinoza." *La Cultura* 17 (1979):87-160.

Mignini 3. "Un documento trascurato della revisione spinoziana del Breve Trattato." *La Cultura* 18 (1980):223-273.

Niermeyer. J. F. Niermeyer, *Mediae latinitatis lexicon minus*, Leiden: Brill, 1976.

Offenberg. A. K. Offenberg. *Brief van Spinoza aan Lodewijk Meijer, 26 juli 1663*.

Text, Dutch translation, and commentary (in Dutch). Amsterdam: Universiteitsbibliotheek, 1975.

Oko. A. S. Oko. *The Spinoza Bibliography*. Boston: Hall, 1964. A thorough bibliography up to 1942.

Oldenburg. *The Correspondence of Henry Oldenburg*. Edited by A. R. and M. B. Hall. 11 vols. Madison: University of Wisconsin Press, 1965-1977.

Parkinson. G.H.R. Parkinson. *Spinoza's Theory of Knowledge*. Oxford: Clarendon Press, 1954.

Pléiade. *Oeuvres complètes de Spinoza*. Translated and edited by R. Caillois, M. Francès, and R. Misrahi. Paris: Gallimard, 1954.

Pollock. F. Pollock. *Spinoza, his life and philosophy*. 2nd ed. London: C. K. Paul, 1899.

Revah 1. I. S. Revah. *Spinoza et le Dr. Juan de Prado*. Paris, La Haye: Mouton, 1959.

Revah 2. "Aux origines de la rupture spinozienne." *Revue des études juives* 3 (1964):

Revue 1. *Revue internationale de philosophie* 31 (1977), nos. 119, 120, devoted to Spinoza. Articles by Akkerman, Abraham, Di Vona, Hubbeling, Matson, Rice, Röd, Rotenstreich, Préposiet, Parkinson, Sokolov, Giancotti Boscherini, Méchoulan, Misrahi.

Revue 2. *Revue philosophique de la France et de l'Etranger* 167 (1977), nos. 2 and 3, devoted to Spinoza. Articles by Misrahi, Hessing, Matheron, Zac, Offenberg, Gueroult, Violette.

Rice. L. Rice. "Emotion, Appetition and Conatus in Spinoza." *Revue* 1, 101-116.

Rist. J. M. Rist. *Stoic Philosophy*. Cambridge: Cambridge University Press, 1969.

Rivaud. A. Rivaud. "Les *Per se Nota* dans l'Ethique." In *Chronicon Spinozanum*, 2:138-154.

Robinson. L. Robinson. *Kommentar zu Spinozas Ethik*. Leipzig: Felix Meiner, 1928.

Roth. C. Roth. "The Role of Spanish in the Marrano Diaspora." In *Studies in Books and Booklore*. Boston: Gregg Inter. Pub., 1972.

Russell. B. Russell. *Why I Am Not a Christian*. New York: Simon and Schuster, 1957.

Sabra. A. I. Sabra. *Theories of Light From Descartes to Newton*. London: Oldbourne, 1967.

Scotus. Duns Scotus. *Quaestiones in quattuor libros sententiarum*. In *Opera omnia*, vols. 8-21, edited by L. Wadding. Paris: Vives, 1891-1894.

Sigwart 1. B. Spinoza. *Kurzer Tractat*. Translated and edited by C. Sigwart. Freiburg, 1870.

Sigwart 2. C. Sigwart. *Spinoza's neuentdeckter Tractat in seiner Bedeutung für das Verstandnis des Spinozismus*. Gotha, 1866.

Suarez. F. Suarez. *Disputationes metaphysicae*. 2 vols. Hildesheim: Georg Olms, 1965.

Taylor. A. E. Taylor. "Some Incoherencies in Spinozism." *Mind* 46 (1937):137-158, 281-301.

Thijssen-Schoute 1. C. L.Thijssen-Schoute. *Lodewijk Meijer en diens verhouding tot Descartes en Spinoza*. Mededelingen vanwege het Spinozahuis XI. Leiden: Brill, 1954.

Thijssen-Schoute 2. *Nederlands Cartesianisme*. Amsterdam: North Holland, 1954.

Thijssen-Schoute 3. "Le Cartésianisme aux pays-bas." In Dijksterhuis (1), 183-260.

Tucker. G. Tucker, ed. *Spinoza Rediscovered*. New York: Jewish Theological Seminary of America, 1985. Papers read at the tercentennial conference held in 1977.

Van der Tak. W.G. van der Tak. "Bene agere et laetari." In *Chronicon Spinozanum*, 1:263-264.

Vernière. P. Vernière. *Spinoza et la pensée française avant la Révolution*. 2 vols. Paris: PUF, 1954.

Voss. S. Voss. "How Spinoza Enumerated the Affects." *Archiv für Geschichte der Philosophie* 63 (1981):167-179.

Walker. D. P. Walker. *The Decline of Hell*. Chicago: University of Chicago Press, 1964.

Westfall. R. S. Westfall. *Force in Newton's Physics, the science of dynamics in the Seventeenth Century*. New York: American Elsevier, 1971.

Wetlesen. J. Wetlesen. *A Spinoza Bibliography 1940-1970*. Oslo: Universitetsvorlaget, 1971. Supplements Oko.

Wolf 1. A. Wolf. "Spinoza's Conception of the Attributes of Substance." *Proceedings of the Aristotelian Society* 27 (1927):177-192. Reprinted in Kashap, 16-27.

Wolf 2. *Spinoza's Short Treatise on God, Man and his Well-Being*. New York: Russell and Russell, 1963.

Wolf 3. *The Correspondence of Spinoza*. New York: Dial Press, n.d.

Wolf 4. "An Addition to the Correspondence of Spinoza." *Philosophy* 10 (1935):200-204.

Wolfson 1. M. A. Wolfson. *The Philosophy of Spinoza*. 2 vols. Cambridge, Mass.: Harvard University Press, 1934.

Wolfson 2. *Religious Philosophy*. Cambridge, Mass.: Harvard University Press, 1961.

Wolfson 3. *Crescas' Critique of Aristotle*. Cambridge, Mass.: Harvard University Press, 1929.

Zac. S. Zac. *L'Idée de vie dans la philosophie de Spinoza*. Paris: PUF, 1963.

Edwin Curley is Professor of Philosophy at the University of Illinois at Chicago. He is the author of *Spinoza's Metaphysics: An Essay in Interpretation* and *Descartes Against the Skeptics* (Harvard, 1969 and 1978). His translation of volume II of *The Collected Works of Spinoza* is in preparation.

Library of Congress Cataloging in Publication Data
Spinoza, Benedictus de, 1632-1677.
The collected works of Spinoza.
Includes bibliographies and index.
1. Philosophy—Collected works.
I. Curley, E. M. (Edwin M.), 1937-   . II. Title.
B3958 1984   199'.492   84-11716
ISBN 0-691-07222-1 (v. 1 : alk. paper)